TALLINN MANUAL
INTERNATIONAL
TO CYBER OPERATIONS

MW01027521

Tallinn Manual 2.0 expands on the highly influential first edition by extending its coverage of the international law governing cyber warfare to peacetime legal regimes. The product of a four-year follow-on project by a new group of 19 renowned international law experts, it addresses such topics as sovereignty, State responsibility, human rights, and the law of air, space, and the sea. *Tallinn Manual 2.0* identifies 154 'black letter' rules governing cyber operations and provides extensive commentary on each rule. Although *Tallinn Manual 2.0* represents the views of the experts in their personal capacity, the project benefited from the unofficial input of many States and over 50 peer reviewers.

The Director of the Project, MICHAEL N. SCHMITT, is Chairman of the Stockton Center for the Study of International Law at the United States Naval War College and Professor of Public International Law at the University of Exeter. He is also Senior Fellow at the NATO Cooperative Cyber Defence Centre of Excellence.

TALLINN MANUAL 2.0 ON THE INTERNATIONAL LAW APPLICABLE TO CYBER OPERATIONS

Prepared by the International Groups of Experts at the Invitation of the NATO Cooperative Cyber Defence Centre of Excellence

General Editor

MICHAEL N. SCHMITT

Managing Editor

LIIS VIHUL

CAMBRIDGE UNIVERSITY PRESS

CAMBRIDGE
UNIVERSITY PRESS

University Printing House, Cambridge CB2 8BS, United Kingdom

One Liberty Plaza, 20th Floor, New York, NY 10006, USA

477 Williamstown Road, Port Melbourne, VIC 3207, Australia

4843/24, 2nd Floor, Ansari Road, Daryaganj, Delhi – 110002, India

79 Anson Road, #06–04/06, Singapore 079906

Cambridge University Press is part of the University of Cambridge.

It furthers the University's mission by disseminating knowledge in the pursuit of education, learning, and research at the highest international levels of excellence.

www.cambridge.org
Information on this title: www.cambridge.org/9781107177222
10.1017/9781316822524

© Cambridge University Press 2017

This publication is in copyright. Subject to statutory exception and to the provisions of relevant collective licensing agreements, no reproduction of any part may take place without the written permission of Cambridge University Press.

First published 2017
Reprinted 2017

Printed in the United Kingdom by TJ International Ltd, Padstow, Cornwall

A catalogue record for this publication is available from the British Library.

Library of Congress Cataloging-in-Publication Data
Names: Schmitt, Michael N., editor. | NATO Cooperative Cyber Defence Centre of Excellence
Title: Tallinn manual 2.0 on the international law applicable to cyber operations / Prepared by the International Groups of Experts at the Invitation of the NATO Cooperative Cyber Defence Centre of Excellence / General Editor Michael N. Schmitt.
Description: New York, NY : Cambridge University Press, 2016.
Identifiers: LCCN 2016044621| ISBN 9781107177222 (Hardback : alk. paper) | ISBN 9781316630372 (pbk. : alk. paper)
Subjects: LCSH: Information warfare (International law) | Cyberspace operations (Military science)
Classification: LCC KZ6718 .T34 2016 | DDC 341.6/3–dc23 LC record available at https://lccn.loc.gov/2016044621

ISBN 978-1-107-17722-2 Hardback
ISBN 978-1-316-63037-2 Paperback

Cambridge University Press has no responsibility for the persistence or accuracy of URLs for external or third-party Internet Web sites referred to in this publication and does not guarantee that any content on such Web sites is, or will remain, accurate or appropriate.

CONTENTS

TALLINN MANUAL 2.0 INTERNATIONAL GROUP OF EXPERTS AND OTHER PARTICIPANTS[1]

International Group of Experts

Director and General Editor

Professor Michael N. Schmitt*
United States Naval War College
University of Exeter

Managing Editor

Liis Vihul*
NATO Cooperative Cyber Defence Centre of Excellence

Legal Experts

Professor Dapo Akande
University of Oxford

Colonel (retired, United States Air Force) Gary D. Brown*
Marine Corps University

Professor (Brigadier General) Paul Ducheine
University of Amsterdam
Netherlands Defence Academy

Professor Terry D. Gill*
University of Amsterdam
Netherlands Defence Academy

Professor Wolff Heintschel von Heinegg*
Europa-Universität Viadrina

---

[1] Affiliations during participation in the project.
* Individuals who contributed draft text for consideration by the International Group of Experts are marked with an asterisk.

Dr Gleider I Hernández*
Durham University School of Law

Deborah Housen-Couriel*
University of Haifa Faculty of Law
Tel Aviv University Interdisciplinary Cyber Research Center

Professor Zhixiong Huang
Wuhan University Institute of International Law

Professor Eric Talbot Jensen*
Brigham Young University Law School

Professor Kriangsak Kittichaisaree
Member of the International Law Commission of the United Nations

Associate Professor Andrey L. Kozik
International Law and Arbitration Association (BILA Association)
KIMEP University

Professor Claus Kreß
University of Cologne

Professor Tim McCormack
University of Melbourne
University of Tasmania

Professor Kazuhiro Nakatani
University of Tokyo

Gabor Rona*
Visiting Professor of Law, Cardozo School of Law
Formerly International Legal Director, Human Rights First

Phillip Spector*
Formerly Senior Adviser to the Legal Adviser, United States Department of State

Professor Sean Watts*
Creighton University School of Law

Technical Expert

Bernhards Blumbergs
NATO Cooperative Cyber Defence Centre of Excellence

Non-Voting Observer

Steven Hill
North Atlantic Treaty Organization

Other Participants

Contributors

Air Commodore (Retired) William H. Boothby*
Formerly Deputy Director of Legal Services, Royal Air Force (UK)

Professor Michel Bourbonnière*
Royal Military College of Canada

Dr Robert Heinsch*
Leiden University

Professor Stephan Hobe*
University of Cologne

Colonel Darren Huskisson*
United States Air Force

Professor Jann K. Kleffner*
Swedish Defence University

Professor James Kraska*
United States Naval War College

Dr Rob McLaughlin*
Australian National University

Lieutenant Colonel Jan Stinissen
Army Legal Service, the Netherlands

Legal Peer Reviewers

Squadron Leader Thomas Allan
Royal Air Force (UK)

Dr Louise Arimatsu
London School of Economics

Evelyn Mary Aswad
University of Oklahoma College of Law

Wing Commander Duncan Blake
Royal Australian Air Force

Professor Gabriella Blum
Harvard Law School

Dr Tare Brisibe
Formerly Chair, Legal Subcommittee of the United Nations Committee on the Peaceful
  Uses of Outer Space

Dr Russell Buchan
University of Sheffield

Major-General Blaise Cathcart
Canadian Armed Forces

Colonel Gary P. Corn
United States Army

Professor Ashley Deeks
University of Virginia Law School

Eileen Denza
Formerly Legal Counsellor, Foreign and Commonwealth Office
Visiting Professor, University College London

Professor Alison Duxbury
University of Melbourne

Dr Dieter Fleck
Formerly Director, International Agreements and Policy, German Ministry of Defence

Daniel B. Garrie
Journal of Law & Cyber Warfare
Law & Forensics LLC

Professor Robin Geiß
University of Glasgow

Lieutenant Commander David Goddard
Royal Navy (UK)

Jason A. Greene
United States Naval Postgraduate School

Professor Juan Pablo González Jansana
Faculty of Law, Universidad Diego Portales

Dr Douglas Guilfoyle
Faculty of Law, Monash University

Dr Heather A. Harrison Dinniss
Swedish Defence University

Dr Sarah Heathcote
Australian National University

Group Captain Ian Henderson
Royal Australian Air Force
University of Adelaide

Professor Duncan B. Hollis
Temple University School of Law

Colonel Rob Holman
Canadian Armed Forces

Dr Jiefang Huang
International Civil Aviation Organization

Lieutenant Colonel Robert Jarman
United States Air Force

Professor David Kaye
University of California, Irvine

Major Israel D. King
United States Air Force

Lieutenant Colonel Matthew King
United States Air Force

Commander Jude Klena
United States Navy

Professor Dino Kritsiotis
University of Nottingham

Associate Professor David Letts
Australian National University

Dr Catherine Lotrionte
Georgetown University

Dr Kubo Mačák
University of Exeter

Dr Marko Milanovic
University of Nottingham

Naz K. Modirzadeh
Harvard Law School Program on International Law and Armed Conflict

Lieutenant Colonel Sarah Mountin
United States Strategic Command

Dr Alexander Orakhelashvili
University of Birmingham

Dr Bruce 'Ossie' Oswald
Asia Pacific Centre for Military Law, University of Melbourne

Commander Ian Park
Royal Navy (UK)
University of Oxford

Professor Ki Gab Park
Korea University School of Law

Professor Nohyoung Park
Korea University School of Law

Professor Bimal N. Patel
Gujarat National Law University
Member, 21st Law Commission of India

Major General Jeff Rockwell
United States Air Force

Professor Marco Roscini
University of Westminster

Professor Scott J. Shackelford
Indiana University
Harvard University

David A. Simon
Sidley Austin LLP

Dr Dale Stephens
University of Adelaide

Professor Christian J. Tams
University of Glasgow
Matrix Chambers (London)

Major Susan Trepczynski
United States Air Force

Professor Nicholas Tsagourias
University of Sheffield

Dr Antonios Tzanakopoulos
University of Oxford

Professor Ian Walden
Centre for Commercial Law Studies, Queen Mary University of London

Commander (Retired, United States Navy) Paul Walker
American University

Dr Chanaka Wickremasinghe
Foreign and Commonwealth Office of the United Kingdom

Colonel Philip T. Wold
United States Air Force

Em. Professor Rüdiger Wolfrum
Max Planck Institute for Comparative Public and International Law

Dr Marten Zwanenburg
Ministry of Foreign Affairs, the Netherlands

Technical Peer Reviewers

Jeffrey Carr
Taia Global, Inc.

Ragnar Rattas
NATO Cooperative Cyber Defence Centre of Excellence

Legal Research

Harvard Law School

Molly Doggett
Jiawei He
Ariane Moss

University of Amsterdam

Nicolò Bussolati

United States Army

Lieutenant Allyson Hauptman

University of Tartu

Carel Kivimaa
Liis Semjonov
Aleksander Tsuiman

Cardozo School of Law

Barry Dynkin

Fletcher School of Diplomacy

Mark Duarte

NATO Cooperative Cyber Defence Centre of Excellence

Nicolas Jupillat

Emory University School of Law

Kiana Arakawa
Ryan Light
Tariq Mohideen
Christopher Pitts
Daniel Rubin

TALLINN MANUAL 1.0 INTERNATIONAL GROUP OF EXPERTS AND OTHER PARTICIPANTS[2]

International Group of Experts

Director

Professor Michael N. Schmitt
United States Naval War College

Editorial Committee

Air Commodore (Retired) William H. Boothby
Formerly Deputy Director of Legal Services, Royal Air Force (UK)

Bruno Demeyere
Catholic University of Leuven

Professor Wolff Heintschel von Heinegg
Europa-Universität Viadrina

Professor James Bret Michael
United States Naval Postgraduate School

Professor Thomas Wingfield
George C. Marshall European Center for Security Studies

Legal Group Facilitators

Professor Eric Talbot Jensen
Brigham Young University Law School

Professor Sean Watts
Creighton University Law School

[2] Affiliations during participation in the project.

Legal Experts

Dr Louise Arimatsu
Chatham House

Captain (Navy) Geneviève Bernatchez
Office of the Judge Advocate General, Canadian Forces

Colonel Penny Cumming
Australian Defence Force

Professor Robin Geiß
University of Potsdam

Professor Terry D. Gill
University of Amsterdam, Netherlands Defence Academy, and Utrecht University

Professor Derek Jinks
University of Texas School of Law

Professor Jann Kleffner
Swedish National Defence College

Dr Nils Melzer
Geneva Centre for Security Policy

Brigadier General (Retired, Canadian Forces) Kenneth Watkin
United States Naval War College

Technical Experts

Dr Kenneth Geers
NATO Cooperative Cyber Defence Centre of Excellence

Dr Rain Ottis
NATO Cooperative Cyber Defence Centre of Excellence

Observers

Colonel Gary D. Brown, United States Air Force
United States Cyber Command

Dr Cordula Droege
International Committee of the Red Cross

Dr Jean-François Quéguiner
International Committee of the Red Cross

Ulf Häußler
Headquarters, Supreme Allied Commander Transformation, NATO

Other Participants

Peer Reviewers

Professor Geoffrey Corn
South Texas College of Law

Professor Ashley Deeks
University of Virginia

Dr Heather A. Harrison Dinniss
Swedish National Defence College

Commander Clive Dow
Royal Navy (UK)

Professor Charles Garraway
Human Rights Centre, University of Essex

Group Captain Ian Henderson
Royal Australian Air Force

Dr Gleider Hernandez
Durham University

Professor Chris Jenks
Southern Methodist University School of Law

Dr Noam Lubell
University of Essex

Sasha Radin
University of Melbourne Law School

Commander Paul Walker
United States Navy

Colonel David Wallace, United States Army
United States Military Academy

Dr Katharina Ziolkowski
NATO Cooperative Cyber Defence Centre of Excellence

Project Coordinator

Dr Eneken Tikk
NATO Cooperative Cyber Defence Centre of Excellence

Project Manager

Liis Vihul
NATO Cooperative Cyber Defence Centre of Excellence

Rapporteurs

Jean Callaghan
George C. Marshall European Center for Security Studies

Dr James Sweeney
Durham University

Legal Research

Creighton University Law School

Jennifer Arbaugh
Nicole Bohe
Christopher Jackman
Christine Schaad

Emory University Law School

Anand Shah

Chatham House

Hemi Mistry

FOREWORD

TOOMAS HENDRIK ILVES

President of the Republic of Estonia

In 2007, several Estonian private and public e-services fell victim to an onslaught of malicious cyber operations. These coordinated attacks focused the international community's attention on the severe risks posed by the increasing reliance of States and their populations on cyberspace. In retrospect, these were fairly mild and simple DDoS attacks, far less damaging than what has followed. Yet it was the first time one could apply the Clausewitzean dictum: War is the continuation of policy by other means.

The attacks also sped up the establishment of the NATO Cooperative Cyber Defence Centre of Excellence (NATO CCD COE) in Tallinn. Estonia is honoured to host and contribute to this world-class think tank and training institution that is a valued partner for NATO, Allies, and the international community. Among the NATO CCD COE's first activities was to commission a major study on cyber warfare conducted by an international group of legal experts. The experts examined how international law governs the use of cyber force by States and the employment of cyber operations during an armed conflict. The resulting Tallinn Manual has become a guidebook for governments around the world as they assess the application of international law in such situations.

Upon publication of the Tallinn Manual in 2013, the NATO CCD COE launched a follow-on research effort to expand the Manual to encompass the international law governing cyber activities occurring in peacetime. The outcome is by far one of the most comprehensive analyses of international law applicable to cyber operations. The publication you are holding covers topics ranging from space law and jurisdiction to international human rights law, as well as an analysis of conflict law from the first Tallinn Manual.

The fact that international law is often dismissed as window-dressing on realpolitik is misleading. Such an approach understates the importance of international agreements in maintaining peace and security. For liberal democracies that respect the rule of law, international law undoubtedly shapes and bounds governments' activities. At a time when the actions of unscrupulous States and violent extremist groups continue to threaten peace and security internationally, it is even more important that such actions are countered with a strong commitment to existing international law and the values that it represents.

On the diplomatic level, governments should continue to interact in order to foster a better understanding of how international law regulates their cyber conduct. That said, these initiatives have proven to be slow and laborious, sometimes hobbled by narrow national interest and perspectives. The creation of the second Tallinn Manual has been unconstrained by politics and the book will serve as a road-map for governments as they seek greater clarity regarding their rights and obligations in cyberspace. The book will also be useful to the international community while struggling with the complexity of identifying extant cyber norms and promulgating new ones.

I am glad that the journey of the international group of experts began in my nation's capital and the understanding of international law matures under Tallinn's name. I congratulate the NATO CCD COE, the experts, and the many others scattered around the world who contributed to this trailblazing endeavour.

FOREWORD

Minister of Foreign Affairs of the Kingdom of the Netherlands

We find ourselves in an exciting age. Information technology has stirred innovation in an unprecedented fashion. The Internet has connected people in ways and numbers that were previously unimaginable. Knowledge and information have become public property as never before. This has proven especially true for the Netherlands, the European leader in responding to technological trends and effectively applying information and communication technologies and related skills.

All new technologies present new opportunities and challenges. As was the case, for instance, with gunpowder and the aeroplane, the same holds true with respect to digital technologies. For the Netherlands, and many other countries, our reliance on digital technology is both a boon and a bane. It fosters innovation, but increasingly also represents a point of vulnerability that can be exploited by malicious actors. In the face of this threat, we must develop capabilities to defend ourselves in a manner that preserves the international legal order. At the same time, it is the responsibility of the international community to ensure that peace, security, and stability are maintained, and that such capabilities are only used in accordance with international law.

In the past, *inter arma enim silent leges* – 'In times of war, the law falls silent' – was an oft-heard claim. More recently, some have argued that the law falls silent in the face of the challenges of the digital age. Neither assertion is correct. States have developed a body of law that regulates armed conflict, commonly known as international humanitarian law. They have also recognised that existing international law applies to the digital domain.

It is not always immediately evident how rules that were developed before a new technology existed should be applied to that technology. Yet, it is important to reach common understandings on such applications in order to promote an open, secure, stable, accessible, and peaceful ICT environment. This is something that States should debate among themselves. Academic experts have an important role to play in informing the debate.

In 2013, that role was clearly illustrated with the publication of the Tallinn Manual on the International Law Applicable to Cyber Warfare. The manual has made a valuable and significant contribution to promoting and informing the debate among States regarding the application of international law in the cyber domain.

The scope of the 2013 manual was limited to international law on the use of force and international humanitarian law. In practice, many questions concerning the application of international law fall outside of its scope. Fortunately, situations of armed conflict are the exception rather than the rule. Most cyber activities take place in times of peace.

The invitation that the NATO Cooperative Cyber Defence Centre of Excellence extended to the experts led by Professor Schmitt to update the manual and explore the application of peacetime international law was therefore a welcome initiative. It offered a unique opportunity for exchanges and engagement between academic experts and national legal advisors.

I am proud that the Netherlands was able to facilitate these exchanges by organising a series of consultation meetings between the authors of the new manual, Tallinn Manual 2.0, and States of diverse regional backgrounds. This 'Hague Process' offered the authors of the updated manual an opportunity to gain insight into State practices, and provided States with a forum for dialogue. My intention is for the Hague Process to continue, even after the publication of the new manual.

The Netherlands has long attached great importance to promoting the development of the international legal order. In fact, our constitution explicitly cites doing so as one of the government's tasks. The international legal order provides a measure of stability, predictability, and accountability in States' international relations and is of paramount importance in preventing conflict. I believe that the application of international law to State conduct in the digital domain can serve as a bedrock for peace and security, as it does in all other domains, because technological advances have no bearing on the underlying legal principles. By facilitating the Hague Process, I am convinced that The Hague is fulfilling its role as international city of peace, justice, and security.

I have no doubt that this Tallinn Manual 2.0, like the original version, will become an important resource for national legal advisors. This is in no small part due to the high quality of the experts involved and the rigorous drafting process employed.

I am also confident that the manual will continue to play an important role in the continuing dialogue regarding how international law applies to cyber activities. Its ultimate and most important role lies in helping States reach common understandings. After all, only by safeguarding the international order can we ensure security in an open and innovative digital domain. This must be our objective, and it is one that the Netherlands remains committed to achieving.

SHORT FORM CITATIONS

Treaties

1884 Cable Convention: Convention for the Protection of Submarine Telegraph Cables, 14 March 1884, USTS 380.

ACHR: American Convention on Human Rights, 22 November 1969, 1144 UNTS 123.

Additional Protocol I: Protocol Additional to the Geneva Conventions of 12 August 1949, and Relating to the Protection of Victims of International Armed Conflicts, 8 June 1977, 1125 UNTS 3.

Additional Protocol II: Protocol Additional to the Geneva Conventions of 12 August 1949, and Relating to the Protection of Victims of Non-International Armed Conflicts, 8 June 1977, 1125 UNTS 609.

Additional Protocol III: Protocol Additional to the Geneva Conventions of 12 August 1949, and Relating to the Adoption of an Additional Distinctive Emblem, 8 December 2005, 2404 UNTS 261.

African Charter: African Charter on Human and Peoples' Rights, 27 June 1981, 21 ILM 58, OAU Doc. CAB/LEG/67/3 rev. 5.

Amended Mines Protocol: Protocol [to the Convention on Prohibitions or Restrictions on the Use of Certain Conventional Weapons Which May Be Deemed to Be Excessively Injurious or to Have Indiscriminate Effects] on Prohibitions or Restrictions on the Use of Mines, Booby-Traps and Other Devices, as amended on 3 May 1996, 2048 UNTS 133.

Arab Convention on Combating Information Technology Offences: Arab Convention on Combating Information Technology Offences, 15 February 2012.

CEDAW: Convention on the Elimination of All Forms of Discrimination Against Women, 18 December 1979, 1249 UNTS 13.

CERD: International Convention on the Elimination of All Forms of Racial Discrimination, 21 December 1965, 660 UNTS 195.

Chicago Convention: Convention on Civil Aviation, 7 December 1944, 15 UNTS 295.

Convention on Cybercrime: Convention on Cybercrime, 23 November 2001, ETS No. 185.

Convention on Jurisdictional Immunities: Convention on Jurisdictional Immunities of States and their Property, 2 December 2004, UN Doc. A/59/38 (not yet in force).

Conventional Weapons Convention: Convention on Prohibitions or Restrictions on the Use of Certain Conventional Weapons Which May Be Deemed to Be Excessively Injurious or to Have Indiscriminate Effects, 10 April 1981, 1342 UNTS 137.

CRC: Convention on the Rights of the Child, 20 November 1989, 1577 UNTS 3.

CRC Optional Protocol: Optional Protocol to the Convention on the Rights of the Child on the Involvement of Children in Armed Conflict, 25 May 2000, 2173 UNTS 222.

CRPD: Convention on the Rights of Persons with Disabilities, 30 March 2007, 2515 UNTS 3.

Cultural Property Convention: Hague Convention for the Protection of Cultural Property in the Event of Armed Conflict with Regulations for the Execution of the Convention, 14 May 1954, 249 UNTS 240.

ECHR: European Convention for the Protection of Human Rights and Fundamental Freedoms, 4 November 1950, 213 UNTS 222.

Environmental Modification Convention: Convention on the Prohibition of Military or Any Other Hostile Use of Environmental Modification Techniques ('ENMOD'), 10 December 1976, 1108 UNTS 151.

Geneva Convention I: Convention (I) for the Amelioration of the Condition of the Wounded and Sick in Armed Forces in the Field, 12 August 1949, 75 UNTS 31.

Geneva Convention II: Convention (II) for the Amelioration of the Condition of Wounded, Sick and Shipwrecked Members of Armed Forces at Sea, 12 August 1949, 75 UNTS 85.

Geneva Convention III: Convention (III) Relative to the Treatment of Prisoners of War, 12 August 1949, 75 UNTS 135.

Geneva Convention IV: Convention (IV) Relative to the Protection of Civilian Persons in Time of War, 12 August 1949, 75 UNTS 287.

Genocide Convention: The Convention on the Prevention of the Crime of Genocide, 9 December 1948, 78 UNTS 277.

Hague Convention IV: Convention (IV) Respecting the Laws and Customs of War on Land, 18 October 1907, 36 Stat. 2277.

Hague Convention V: Convention (V) Respecting the Rights and Duties of Neutral Powers and Persons in Case of War on Land, 18 October 1907, 36 Stat. 2310.

Hague Convention VIII: Convention (VIII) Relative to the Laying of Automatic Submarine Contact Mines, 18 October 1907, 32 Stat. 2332.

Hague Convention XIII: Convention (XIII) Concerning the Rights and Duties of Neutral Powers in Naval War, 18 October 1907, 36 Stat. 2415.

Hague Regulations: Convention (IV) Respecting the Laws and Customs of War on Land and its annex: Regulations concerning the Laws and Customs of War on Land, 18 October 1907, 36 Stat. 2277.

ICCPR: International Covenant on Civil and Political Rights, 16 December 1966, 999 UNTS 171.

ICESCR: International Covenant on Economic, Social and Cultural Rights, 16 December 1966, 993 UNTS 3.

ICTR Statute: Statute of the International Criminal Tribunal for Rwanda, SC Res. 955 annex, UN Doc. S/RES/955 (8 November 1994).

ICTY Statute: Statute of the International Criminal Tribunal for the Former Yugoslavia, SC Res. 827 annex, UN Doc. S/RES/827 (25 May 1993).

ITU 1988 International Telecommunication Regulations: International Telecommunication Regulations, WATTC-88, Melbourne, 9 December 1988.

ITU 2012 International Telecommunication Regulations: International Telecommunication Regulations, WCIT-2012, Dubai, 14 December 2012.

ITU Constitution: Constitution of the International Telecommunication Union, 22 December 1992, 1825 UNTS 331.

ITU Radio Regulations: International Telecommunication Union Radio Regulations, WRC-15, Geneva, 2015.

Law of the Sea Convention: United Nations Convention on the Law of the Sea, 10 December 1982, 1833 UNTS 3.

Liability Convention: Convention on International Liability for Damage Caused by Space Objects, 29 November 1971, 961 UNTS 187.

Mines Protocol: Protocol [to the Convention on Prohibitions or Restrictions on the Use of Certain Conventional Weapons Which May Be Deemed to Be Excessively Injurious or to Have Indiscriminate Effects] on Prohibitions or Restrictions on the Use of Mines, Booby-Traps and Other Devices, 10 October 1980, 1342 UNTS 168.

Montreal Convention of 1971: Convention for the Suppression of Unlawful Acts Against the Safety of Civil Aviation, 23 September 1971, 24 UST 564.

Moon Agreement: Agreement Governing Activities of States on the Moon and Other Celestial Bodies, 5 December 1979, 1363 UNTS 3.

Optional Protocol to the United Nations Safety Convention: Optional Protocol to the Convention on the Safety of United Nations and Associated Personnel, 8 December 2005, 2689 UNTS 59.

Outer Space Treaty: Treaty on Principles Governing the Activities of States in the Exploration and Use of Outer Space, including the Moon and Other Celestial Bodies, 27 January 1967, 610 UNTS 205.

Registration Convention: Convention on Registration of Objects Launched into Outer Space, 12 November 1974, 1023 UNTS 15.

Rome Statute: Statute of the International Criminal Court, 17 July 1998, 2187 UNTS 90.

Second Cultural Property Protocol: Second Protocol to the Hague Convention of 1954 for the Protection of Cultural Property in the Event of Armed Conflict, 26 March 1999, 2253 UNTS 212.

Sierra Leone Statute: Agreement between the UN and the Government of Sierra Leone on the Establishment of a Special Court for Sierra Leone, annex, 16 January 2002, 2178 UNTS 138.

St Petersburg Declaration: Declaration Renouncing the Use, in Time of War, of Explosive Projectiles Under 400 Grammes Weight, 29 November/11 December 1868, 18 Martens Nouveau Recueil (ser. 1) 474.

United Nations Safety Convention: Convention on the Safety of United Nations and Associated Personnel, 9 December 1994, 2051 UNTS 363.

Vienna Convention on Consular Relations: Vienna Convention on Consular Relations, 24 April 1963, 596 UNTS 261.

Vienna Convention on Diplomatic Relations: Vienna Convention on Diplomatic Relations, 18 April 1961, 500 UNTS 95.

Vienna Convention on the Law of Treaties: Vienna Convention on the Law of Treaties, 23 May 1969, 1155 UNTS 331.

Case law

***Aerial Incident* judgment:** *Aerial Incident of 10 August 1999 (Pak. v. India)* judgment on jurisdiction, 2000 ICJ 12 (22 June).

***Ahmadou Sadio Diallo* judgment:** *Case Concerning Ahmadou Sadio Diallo (Guinea v. Dem. Rep. Congo)*, judgment, 2010 ICJ 639 (30 November).

***Air Services* arbitral award:** *Air Services Agreement of 27 March 1946 (US v. Fra.)*, 18 RIAA 416 (1979).

***Akayesu* judgment:** *Prosecutor v. Akayesu,* Case No. ICTR-96-4-T, Trial Chamber judgment (Int'l Crim. Trib. for Rwanda, 2 September 1998).

***Al-Skeini* judgment:** *Al-Skeini v. United Kingdom*, App. No. 55721/07, ECtHR (7 July 2011).

***Archer Daniels* arbitral award:** *Archer Daniels Midland Company v. Mexico*, award, ICSID Case No. ARB(AF)/04/05 (21 November 2007).

***Armed Activities* judgment:** *Armed Activities on the Territory of the Congo (Dem. Rep. Congo v. Uganda)*, judgment, 2005 ICJ 168 (19 December).

***Arrest Warrant* judgment:** *Arrest Warrant of 11 April 2000 (Dem. Rep. Congo v. Belg.)*, judgment, 2002 ICJ 3 (14 February).

***Barcelona Traction* judgment:** *Case Concerning the Barcelona Traction, Light and Power Company Limited (Second Phase) (Spain v. Belg.)*, judgment, 1970 ICJ 3 (5 February).

***Certain Questions of Mutual Assistance* judgment:** *Certain Questions of Mutual Assistance in Criminal Matters (Djib. v. Fr.)*, judgment, 2008 ICJ 177 (4 June).

***CMS v. Argentina* arbitral award:** *CMS Gas Transmission Co. v. Argentina*, award, ICSID Case No. ARB/01/8 (12 May 2005).

***Corfu Channel* judgment:** *Corfu Channel Case (UK v. Alb.)*, 1949 ICJ 4 (9 April).

***Delalić* judgment:** *Prosecutor v. Delalić/Mucić*, Case No. IT-96-21-T, Trial Chamber judgment (Int'l Crim. Trib. for the Former Yugoslavia 16 November 1998).

***Enron v. Argentina* award:** *Enron Co. v. Argentina*, award, ICSID Case No. ARB/01/3 (22 May 2007).

Factory at Chorzow **judgment:** *Factory at Chorzow (Ger. v. Pol.),* merits, 1928 PCIJ (ser. A) No. 17 (13 September).

Furundžija **judgment:** *Prosecutor* v. *Anto Furundžija,* Case No. IT-95-17-T, Trial Chamber judgment (Int'l Crim. Trib. for the Former Yugoslavia 10 December 1998).

Gabčíkovo-Nagymaros **judgment:** *Gabčíkovo-Nagymaros Project (Hung. v. Slovk.),* 1997 ICJ 7 (25 September).

Galić **Appeals Chamber judgment:** *Prosecutor* v. *Galić,* Case No. IT-98-29-A, Appeals Chamber judgment (Int'l Crim. Trib. for the Former Yugoslavia 30 November 2006).

Galić **Trial Chamber judgment:** *Prosecutor* v. *Stanislav Galić,* Case No. IT-98-29-T, Trial Chamber judgment (Int'l Crim. Trib. for the Former Yugoslavia 5 December 2003).

Genocide **judgment:** *Application of the Convention on the Prevention and Punishment of the Crime of Genocide (Bosn. and Herz.* v. *Serb. and Montenegro),* 2007 ICJ 108 (26 February).

Hadžihasanović **judgment:** *Prosecutor* v. *Hadžihasanović,* Case No. IT-01-47-T, Trial Chamber judgment (Int'l Crim. Trib. for the Former Yugoslavia 15 March 2006).

Haradinaj **judgment:** *Prosecutor* v. *Haradinaj,* Case No. IT-04-84-T, Trial Chamber judgment (Int'l Crim. Trib. for the Former Yugoslavia 3 April 2008).

Immunity of a Special Rapporteur **advisory opinion:** *Difference Relating to Immunity from Legal Process of a Special Rapporteur of the Commission on Human Rights,* Advisory Opinion, 1999 ICJ 62 (29 April).

Island of Palmas **arbitral award:** *Island of Palmas (Neth.* v. *US)* 2 RIAA 829 (Perm. Ct. Arb. 1928).

Kayishema **judgment:** *Prosecutor* v. *Kayishema and Ruzindana,* Case No. ICTR 95-1-T, Trial Chamber judgment (Int'l Crim. Trib. for Rwanda 21 May 1999).

Kosovo **advisory opinion:** *Accordance with International Law of the Unilateral Declaration of Independence in Respect of Kosovo,* advisory opinion, 2010 ICJ 403 (22 July).

Krstić **judgment:** *Prosecutor* v. *Krstić,* Case No. IT-98-33-T, Trial Chamber judgment (Int'l Crim. Trib. for the Former Yugoslavia 2 August 2001).

LG&E Energy Corp. **v.** *Argentina* **decision on liability:** *LG&E Energy Corp.* v. *Argentina,* ICSID Case No. ARB/02/1, decision on liability (3 October 2006).

Limaj **judgment:** *Prosecutor* v. *Limaj,* Case No. IT-03-66-T, Trial Chamber judgment (Int'l Crim. Trib. for the Former Yugoslavia 30 November 2005).

Lotus **judgment:** *The Case of the SS 'Lotus' (Fr.* v. *Turk.),* 1927 PCIJ (ser. A) No. 10 (7 September).

Lubanga **judgment:** *Prosecutor* v. *Lubanga,* Case No. ICC-01/04-01/06, Trial Chamber judgment (Int'l Crim. Ct. 14 March 2012).

Martić **judgment:** *Prosecutor* v. *Martić,* Case No. IT-95-11-T, Trial Chamber judgment (Int'l Crim. Trib. for the Former Yugoslavia 12 June 2007).

Milošević **decision on motion:** *Prosecutor* v. *Milošević,* Case No. IT-02-54-T, decision on motion for judgment of acquittal (Int'l Crim. Trib. for the Former Yugoslavia 16 June 2004).

Mrkšić **judgment:** *Prosecutor* v. *Mrkšić*, Case No. IT-95-13/1-T, Trial Chamber judgment (Int'l Crim. Trib. for the Former Yugoslavia 27 September 2007).

Namibia **advisory opinion:** *Legal Consequences for States of the Continued Presence of South Africa in Namibia (South West Africa) notwithstanding Security Council Resolution 276 (1970)*, Advisory Opinion, 1971 ICJ 16 (21 June).

Naulilaa **arbitral award:** *Responsibility of Germany for Damage Caused in the Portuguese Colonies in the South of Africa (Naulilaa Arbitration) (Port. v. Ger.)*, 2 RIAA 1011 (1928) (unofficially translated).

Nicaragua **judgment:** *Military and Paramilitary Activities in and against Nicaragua (Nicar. v. US)*, 1986 ICJ 14 (27 June).

Nuclear Weapons **advisory opinion:** *Legality of the Threat or Use of Nuclear Weapons*, Advisory Opinion, 1996 ICJ 226 (8 July).

Nuremburg Tribunal **judgment:** *Judgment of the International Military Tribunal Sitting at Nuremberg, Germany* (30 September 1946), in 22 The Trial of German Major War Criminals: Proceedings of the International Military Tribunal Sitting at Nuremberg, Germany (1950).

Oil Platforms **judgment:** *Oil Platforms (Iran v. US)*, 2003 ICJ 161 (6 November).

Phosphates in Morocco **preliminary objections:** *Phosphates in Morocco (It. v. Fr.)*, Preliminary Objections, 1938 PCIJ (ser. A/B), No. 74, at 10 (14 June).

Rainbow Warrior **arbitral award:** *Rainbow Warrior (NZ v. Fr.)*, 20 RIAA 217 (Arb. Trib. 1990).

Russian Indemnity **arbitral award:** *Russian Indemnity (Russ. v. Turk.)* 11 RIAA 421 (1912).

Sempra **v. *Argentina* arbitral award:** *Sempra Energy Int'l v. Argentine Republic*, award, ICSID Case No. ARB/02/16 (28 September 2007).

Tadić, **Appeals Chamber judgment:** *Prosecutor* v. *Tadić*, Case No. IT-94-1-A, Appeals Chamber judgment (Intl'l Crim. Trib. for the Former Yugoslavia 15 July 1999).

Tadić, **decision on the defence motion for interlocutory appeal:** *Prosecutor* v. *Tadić*, Case No. IT-94-1-I, decision on the defence motion for interlocutory appeal on jurisdiction (Int'l Crim. Trib. for the Former Yugoslavia 2 October 1995).

Tadić, **Trial Chamber judgment:** *Prosecutor* v. *Tadić*, Case No. IT-94-1-T, Trial Chamber judgment (Int'l Crim. Trib. for the Former Yugoslavia 7 May 1997).

Tehran Hostages **judgment:** *United States Diplomatic and Consular Staff in Tehran (US v. Iran)*, 1980 ICJ 3 (24 May).

Trail Smelter **arbitral award:** *Trail Smelter Arbitration (US v. Can.)*, Arbitral Tribunal, 3 UN Rep. Int'l Arb. Awards 1905 (1941).

Wall **advisory opinion:** *Legal Consequences of the Construction of a Wall in the Occupied Palestinian Territory*, Advisory Opinion, 2004 ICJ 136 (9 July).

Wimbledon **judgment:** *Wimbledon judgment (United Kingdom v. Germany)*, 1923 PCIJ (ser. A) No. 1 (17 August).

Other sources

AMW Manual: Harvard Program on Humanitarian Policy and Conflict Research, Manual on International Law Applicable to Air and Missile Warfare, with Commentary (2010).

Articles on State Responsibility: International Law Commission, Responsibility of States for Internationally Wrongful Acts, GA Res. 56/83 annex, UN Doc. A/RES/56/83 (12 December 2001).

Articles on the Responsibility of International Organizations: International Law Commission, Draft Articles on the Responsibility of International Organizations, with Commentaries, UN Doc. A/66/10 (2011).

Articles on Transboundary Harm: International Law Commission, Draft Articles on Prevention of Transboundary Harm from Hazardous Activities, with commentaries, in Report of the International Law Commission to the General Assembly, 53 UN GAOR Supp. (No. 10), at 370–436, UN Doc. A/56/10 (2001).

ASEAN Human Rights Declaration: ASEAN Human Rights Declaration, 18 November 2012.

Bothe, et al., New Rules: Michael Bothe et al., New Rules for Victims of Armed Conflicts: Commentary on the Two 1977 Protocols Additional to the Geneva Conventions of 1949 (1982).

Canadian Manual: Canada, Office of the Judge Advocate General, Law of Armed Conflict at the Operational and Tactical Levels, B-GJ-005-104/FP- 021 (2001).

Capstone Doctrine: United Nations Department of Peacekeeping Operations & United Nations Department of Field Support, United Nations Peacekeeping Operations: Principles and Guidelines (2008).

Crawford, State Responsibility: James Crawford, State Responsibility: The General Part (2013).

Declaration on Friendly Relations: Declaration on Principles of International Law concerning Friendly Relations and Cooperation among States in accordance with the Charter of the United Nations, GA Res. 2625 (XXV), UN GAOR, 25th Sess., Supp. No. 28, at 121, UN Doc. A/8082 (28 September 1970).

Declaration on Inadmissibility of Intervention and Interference: Declaration on the Inadmissibility of Intervention and Interference in the Internal Affairs of States, GA Res. 36/103 annex, UN Doc. A/RES/36/103 (9 December 1981).

Declaration on the Use of Outer Space: Declaration of Legal Principles Governing the Activities of States in the Exploration and Use of Outer Space, GA Res. 1962 (XVIII), UN Doc. A/RES/1962(XVIII) (13 December 1963).

Definition of Aggression: Definition of Aggression, GA Res. 3314 (XXIX) (14 December 1974).

Denza, Diplomatic Law: Eileen Denza, Diplomatic Law: Commentary on the Vienna Convention on Diplomatic Relations (4th edn, 2016).

Dinstein, Conduct of Hostilities: Yoram Dinstein, The Conduct of Hostilities under the Law of International Armed Conflict (3rd edn, 2016).

Dinstein, War, Aggression and Self-Defence: Yoram Dinstein, War, Aggression and Self-Defence (5th edn, 2011).

DoD Manual: US Department of Defense, Office of the General Counsel, Law of War Manual (June 2015).

General Comment No. 3: Human Rights Committee, General Comment No. 3: 'Implementation at the National Level', UN Doc. HRI/GEN/R/Rev.1 (29 July 1994).

General Comment No. 16: Human Rights Committee, General Comment No. 16: 'Right to Privacy', UN Doc. HRI/GEN/1/Rev.9 (8 April 1988).

General Comment No. 18: Human Rights Committee, General Comment No. 18: 'Non-discrimination' (37th Sess., 1989), UN Doc. HRI/GEN/1/Rev.1 (29 July 1994).

General Comment No. 27: Human Rights Committee, General Comment No. 27: 'Freedom of Movement', UN Doc. CCPR/C/21/Rev.1/Add.9 (2 November 1999).

General Comment No. 29: Human Rights Committee, General Comment No. 29: 'States of Emergency' (Article 4), UN Doc. CCPR/C21.Rev.1/Add.11 (31 August 2001).

General Comment No. 31: Human Rights Committee, General Comment No. 31: 'The Nature of the General Legal Obligations Imposed on States Parties to the Covenant', UN Doc. CCPR/C/21/Rev.1/Add.13 (29 March 2004).

General Comment No. 34: Human Rights Committee, General Comment No. 34: 'Article 19: Freedoms of Opinion and Expression', UN Doc. CCPR/C/GC/34 (12 September 2011).

German Manual: The Federal Ministry of Defence of the Federal Republic of Germany, Humanitarian Law in Armed Conflicts Manual (ZDv 15/2) (1992).

Government Response to AIV/CAVV Report: Government of the Netherlands, Government Response to AIV/CAVV Report on Cyber Warfare (n.d).

Hague Air Warfare Rules: Rules Concerning the Control of Wireless Telegraphy in Time of War and Air Warfare (Drafted by a Commission of Jurists, The Hague, December 1922–February 1923), reprinted in Documents on the Laws of War 139 (Adam Roberts and Richard Guelff eds., 3rd edn, 2000).

ICRC Additional Protocols 1987 Commentary: International Committee of the Red Cross, Commentary on the Additional Protocols of 8 June 1977 to the Geneva Conventions of 12 August 1949 (Yves Sandoz et al. eds., 1987).

ICRC Challenges Report: ICRC, International Humanitarian Law and the Challenges of Contemporary Armed Conflicts, 32nd International Conference of the Red Cross and Red Crescent (8–10 December 2015).

ICRC Customary IHL Study: International Committee of the Red Cross, Customary International Humanitarian Law (Jean-Marie Henckaerts and Louise Doswald-Beck eds., 2005).

ICRC Geneva Convention I 1952 Commentary: Commentary: Geneva Convention for the Amelioration of the Condition of the Wounded and Sick in Armed Forces in the Field (Jean Pictet ed., 1952).

ICRC Geneva Convention I 2016 Commentary: Commentary: Geneva Convention for the Amelioration of the Condition of the Wounded and Sick in Armed Forces in the Field (2016).

ICRC Geneva Convention II 1960 Commentary: Commentary: Geneva Convention for Amelioration of the Condition of Wounded, Sick and Shipwrecked Members of Armed Forces at Sea (Jean Pictet ed., 1960).

ICRC Geneva Convention III 1960 Commentary: Commentary: Geneva Convention Relative to the Treatment of Prisoners of War of August 12, 1949 (Jean Pictet ed., 1960).

ICRC Geneva Convention IV 1958 Commentary: Commentary: Geneva Convention Relative to the Protection of Civilian Persons in Time of War (Jean Pictet ed., 1958).

ICRC Interpretive Guidance: International Committee of the Red Cross, Interpretive Guidance on the Notion of Direct Participation in Hostilities under International Humanitarian Law (Nils Melzer ed., 2009).

Mann 1964: F. A. Mann, The Doctrine of Jurisdiction in International Law (1964).

Mann 1984: F. A. Mann, The Doctrine of International Jurisdiction Revisited After Twenty Years (1984).

NATO 2016 Warsaw Summit Communiqué: Warsaw Summit Communiqué Issued by the Heads of State and Government participating in the meeting of the North Atlantic Council in Warsaw 8–9 July 2016, Press Release 2016 (100) (9 July 2016).

NIA Glossary: Committee on National Security Systems (CNSS) Glossary Working Group, National Information Assurance (IA) Glossary, CNSS Instruction No. 4009 (26 April 2010).

NIAC Manual: Michael N. Schmitt, Charles H. B. Garraway and Yoram Dinstein, The Manual on the Law of Non-International Armed Conflict, with Commentary (2006).

Oppenheim's International Law: Lassa Oppenheim, Oppenheim's International Law (Robert Jennings & Arthur Watts eds., 9th edn, 1992).

Report of the Special Rapporteur on the Promotion and Protection of Human Rights and Fundamental Freedoms while Countering Terrorism: Report of the Special Rapporteur on the Promotion and Protection of Human Rights and Fundamental Freedoms while Countering Terrorism, UN Doc. A/69/397 (23 September 2014).

Resolution on International Cooperation in Outer Space: International Co-operation in the Peaceful Uses of Outer Space, GA Res. 1721 (XVI), UN GAOR 16th Sess. (20 December 1961).

Restatement (Third): American Law Institute Restatement (Third) of the Foreign Relations Law of the United States (1986).

Rome Statute Elements of the Crimes: International Criminal Court, Elements of Crimes, UN Doc. ICC-ASP/1/3 (9 September 2002).

SAN REMO MANUAL: INTERNATIONAL INSTITUTE OF HUMANITARIAN LAW, SAN REMO MANUAL ON INTERNATIONAL LAW APPLICABLE TO ARMED CONFLICTS AT SEA (Louise Doswald-Beck ed., 1995).

SHAW'S INTERNATIONAL LAW: MALCOLM N. SHAW, INTERNATIONAL LAW (7th edn, 2014).

THE CHARTER OF UNITED NATIONS: A COMMENTARY: THE CHARTER OF UNITED NATIONS: A COMMENTARY (Bruno Simma, *et al.* eds., 3rd edn, 2013).

THE LAW OF STATE IMMUNITY: HAZEL FOX QC & PHILIPPA WEBB, THE LAW OF STATE IMMUNITY (3rd edn, 2013).

The Right to Privacy in the Digital Age: Report of the Office of the United Nations High Commissioner for Human Rights, The Right to Privacy in the Digital Age, UN Doc. A/HRC/27/37 (30 June 2014).

UDHR: Universal Declaration of Human Rights, GA Res. 217A (III), UN Doc. A/810 (10 December 1948).

UK Additional Protocol Ratification Statement: UK Statement made upon Ratification of Additional Protocols I and II, reprinted in Documents on the Law of War 510 (Adam Roberts and Richard Guelff eds., 3rd edn, 2000).

UK MANUAL: UK MINISTRY OF DEFENCE, THE JOINT SERVICE MANUAL OF THE LAW OF ARMED CONFLICT, JSP 383 (2004).

UN GGE 2013 Report: Group of Governmental Experts on Developments in the Field of Information and Telecommunications in the Context of International Security, UN Doc. A/68/98* (24 June 2013).

UN GGE 2015 Report: Group of Governmental Experts on Developments in the Field of Information and Telecommunications in the Context of International Security, UN Doc. A/70/174 (22 July 2015).

US 1997 Comments: Comments, United States, regarding Draft Articles on State Responsibility by ILC, 30 December 2007, Digest of the United States Practice in International Law 1991–1999, www.state.gov/documents/organization/65781.pdf.

US 2001 Comments: US Comments on the International Law Commission's Draft Articles on the Responsibility of States for Internationally Wrongful Acts, 1 March 2001, Digest of United States Practice in International Law 2001, www.state.gov/documents/organization/28993.pdf.

TABLE OF CONCORDANCE

Rule number in the first edition	Rule number in the current edition
Rule 1 – Sovereignty	On this issue, new Rules 1–4
Rule 2 – Jurisdiction	On this issue, new Rules 8–13
Rule 3 – Jurisdiction of flag States and States of registration	On this issue, new Rules 8–13
Rule 4 – Sovereign immunity and inviolability	Rule 5
Rule 5 – Control of cyber infrastructure	On this issue, new Rules 6–7
Rule 6 – Legal responsibility of States	On this issue, new Rules 14–30
Rule 7 – Cyber operations launched from governmental cyber infrastructure	N/A
Rule 8 – Cyber operations routed through a State	N/A
Rule 9 – Countermeasures	On this issue, new Rules 20–25
Rule 10 – Prohibition of threat or use of force	Rule 68
Rule 11 – Definition of use of force	Rule 69
Rule 12 – Definition of threat of force	Rule 70
Rule 13 – Self-defence against armed attack	Rule 71
Rule 14 – Necessity and proportionality	Rule 72
Rule 15 – Imminence and immediacy	Rule 73
Rule 16 – Collective self-defence	Rule 74
Rule 17 – Reporting measures of self-defence	Rule 75
Rule 18 – United Nations Security Council	Rule 76
Rule 19 – Regional organisations	Rule 77
Rule 20 – Applicability of the law of armed conflict	Rule 80
Rule 21 – Geographical limitations	Rule 81
Rule 22 – Characterisation as international armed conflict	Rule 82

(cont.)

Rule number in the first edition	Rule number in the current edition
Rule 23 – Characterisation as non-international armed conflict	Rule 83
Rule 24 – Criminal responsibility of commanders and superiors	Rule 85
Rule 25 – Participation generally	Rule 86
Rule 26 – Members of the armed forces	Rule 87
Rule 27 – *Levée en masse*	Rule 88
Rule 28 – Mercenaries	Rule 90
Rule 29 – Civilians	Rule 91
Rule 30 – Definition of cyber attack	Rule 92
Rule 31 – Distinction	Rule 93
Rule 32 – Prohibition on attacking civilians	Rule 94
Rule 33 – Doubt as to status of persons	Rule 95
Rule 34 – Persons as lawful objects of attack	Rule 96
Rule 35 – Civilian direct participants in hostilities	Rule 97
Rule 36 – Terror attacks	Rule 98
Rule 37 – Prohibition on attacking civilian objects	Rule 99
Rule 38 – Civilian objects and military objectives	Rule 100
Rule 39 – Objects used for civilian and military purposes	Rule 101
Rule 40 – Doubt as to status of objects	Rule 102
Rule 41 – Definitions of means and methods of warfare	Rule 103
Rule 42 – Superfluous injury or unnecessary suffering	Rule 104
Rule 43 – Indiscriminate means or methods	Rule 105
Rule 44 – Cyber booby traps	Rule 106
Rule 45 – Starvation	Rule 107
Rule 46 – Belligerent reprisals	Rule 108
Rule 47 – Reprisals under Additional Protocol I	Rule 109
Rule 48 – Weapons review	Rule 110
Rule 49 – Indiscriminate attacks	Rule 111
Rule 50 – Clearly separated and distinct military objectives	Rule 112
Rule 51 – Proportionality	Rule 113

(cont.)

Rule number in the first edition	Rule number in the current edition
Rule 52 – Constant care	Rule 114
Rule 53 – Verification of targets	Rule 115
Rule 54 – Choice of means or methods	Rule 116
Rule 55 – Precautions as to proportionality	Rule 117
Rule 56 – Choice of targets	Rule 118
Rule 57 – Cancellation or suspension of attack	Rule 119
Rule 58 – Warnings	Rule 120
Rule 59 – Precautions against the effects of cyber attacks	Rule 121
Rule 60 – Perfidy	Rule 122
Rule 61 – Ruses	Rule 123
Rule 62 – Improper use of the protective indicators	Rule 124
Rule 63 – Improper use of United Nations emblem	Rule 125
Rule 64 – Improper use of enemy indicators	Rule 126
Rule 65 – Improper use of neutral indicators	Rule 127
Rule 66 – Cyber espionage	Rule 89 – Spies
Rule 67 – Maintenance and enforcement of blockade	Rule 128
Rule 68 – Effect of blockade on neutral activities	Rule 129
Rule 69 – Zones	Rule 130
Rule 70 – Medical and religious personnel, medical units and transports	Rule 131
Rule 71 – Medical computers, computer networks, and data	Rule 132
Rule 72 – Identification	Rule 133
Rule 73 – Loss of protection and warnings	Rule 134
Rule 74 – United Nations personnel, installations, materiel, units, and vehicles	Rule 79
Rule 75 – Protection of detained persons	Rule 135
Rule 76 – Correspondence of detained persons	Rule 136
Rule 77 – Compelled participation in military activities	Rule 137
Rule 78 – Protection of children	Rule 138

(cont.)

Rule number in the first edition	Rule number in the current edition
Rule 79 – Protection of journalists	Rule 139
Rule 80 – Duty of care during attacks on dams, dykes, and nuclear electrical generating stations	Rule 140
Rule 81 – Protections of objects indispensable to survival	Rule 141
Rule 82 – Respect and protection of cultural property	Rule 142
Rule 83 – Protection of the natural environment	Rule 143
Rule 84 – Protection of diplomatic archives and communications	On this issue, new Rules 39–42
Rule 85 – Collective punishment	Rule 144
Rule 86 – Humanitarian assistance	Rule 145
Rule 87 – Respect for protected persons in occupied territory	Rule 146
Rule 88 – Public order and safety in occupied territory	Rule 147
Rule 89 – Security of the Occupying Power	Rule 148
Rule 90 – Confiscation and requisition of property	Rule 149
Rule 91 – Protection of neutral cyber infrastructure	Rule 150
Rule 92 – Cyber operations in neutral territory	Rule 151
Rule 93 – Neutral obligations	Rule 152
Rule 94 – Response by parties to the conflict to violations	Rule 153
Rule 95 – Neutrality and Security Council actions	Rule 154

Introduction

In 2009, the NATO Cooperative Cyber Defence Centre of Excellence (NATO CCD COE), a renowned research and training institution based in Tallinn, Estonia, invited an independent group of experts to produce a manual on the international law governing cyber warfare. In doing so, it followed in the footsteps of earlier efforts, such as those resulting in the 1880 *Oxford Manual*, the International Institute of Humanitarian Law's 1994 *San Remo Manual on International Law Applicable to Armed Conflicts at Sea*, and the Harvard Program on Humanitarian Policy and Conflict Research's 2009 *Manual on International Law Applicable to Air and Missile Warfare*. The project brought together distinguished international law practitioners and scholars, the so-called 'International Group of Experts' or 'Experts', in an effort to examine how extant legal norms apply to this new form of warfare. In 2013, the effort resulted in the publication of the *Tallinn Manual on the International Law Applicable to Cyber Warfare*. That product has served as an invaluable resource for government legal advisors and scholars since its publication.

The *Tallinn Manual*'s focus was on cyber operations involving the use of force and those that occur in the context of armed conflict. Although such cyber operations will typically be more worrisome from a national security perspective than those that occur in peacetime, States have to deal with cyber issues that lie below the use of force threshold on a daily basis. Therefore, in 2013, the NATO CCD COE launched a follow-on initiative to expand the Manual's scope to include the public international law governing cyber operations during peacetime. To do so, it convened a new International Group of Experts consisting of scholars and practitioners with expertise in the legal regimes implicated by peacetime cyber activities.

Following the format of the original *Tallinn Manual*, these Experts adopted additional rules that have been added to the original ones to produce this *Tallinn Manual 2.0 on the International Law Applicable to Cyber Operations*. Accordingly, *Tallinn Manual 2.0* supersedes the first

1

Tallinn Manual. Several modifications to the original *Tallinn Manual* rules, including complete renumbering, and commentary have been made and one new rule has been added. A Table of Concordance is included to facilitate cross-referencing between the *Tallinn Manual* and *Tallinn Manual 2.0* rules.

As was the case with the original *Tallinn Manual, Tallinn Manual 2.0*'s primary audience consists of State legal advisers charged with providing international law advice to governmental decision makers, both civilian and military. However, it is hoped that *Tallinn Manual 2.0* also will prove valuable in academic and other endeavours.

Authority of the Manual

It is essential to understand that *Tallinn Manual 2.0* is not an official document, but rather the product of two separate endeavours undertaken by groups of independent experts acting solely in their personal capacity. The Manual does not represent the views of the NATO CCD COE, its sponsoring nations, or NATO. Nor does it reflect the position of any other organisation or State represented by observers or of any of the States involved in the 'Hague Process', which is described below. Finally, participation as members of the International Group of Experts or as peer reviewers by individuals who hold governmental positions in their respective countries must not be interpreted as indicating that the Manual echoes the viewpoints of those countries.

Ultimately, *Tallinn Manual 2.0* must be understood only as an expression of the opinions of the two International Groups of Experts as to the state of the law. Modifications to the original *Tallinn Manual* text, and the new rule on individual criminal responsibility, were approved by members of the first International Group of Experts. Therefore, the original rules and commentary, as modified for inclusion in *Tallinn Manual 2.0*, represent the views of that International Group of Experts and not those of the Experts convened for the *Tallinn Manual 2.0* project. Analogously, the rules and commentary concerning the peacetime international law governing cyber operations represent only the understandings of the second International Group of Experts. They were not vetted by the original group. Of particular note is the fact that the first nine rules of the original *Tallinn Manual* have been superseded by rules and commentary drafted and approved by the second International Group of Experts.

This Manual is meant to be a reflection of the law as it existed at the point of the Manual's adoption by the two International Groups of

Experts in June 2016. It is not a 'best practices' guide, does not represent 'progressive development of the law', and is policy and politics-neutral. In other words, *Tallinn Manual 2.0* is intended as an objective restatement of the *lex lata*. Therefore, the Experts involved in both projects assiduously avoided including statements reflecting *lex ferenda*.

Scope

The rules and commentary drawn from the original *Tallinn Manual* address two subjects – the *jus ad bellum*, which regulates the use of force by States, and the *jus in bello*, the law that governs how States may conduct their military operations during an armed conflict and provides protection for various specified persons, objects, and activities. The remainder of *Tallinn Manual 2.0* examines key aspects of the public international law governing 'cyber operations' during peacetime. It is not comprehensive in this regard. For instance, the Manual does not deal with international criminal law, trade law, or intellectual property. Nor does the Manual deal with either private international law or domestic law. Rather, the topics selected for inclusion include public international law regimes that the second International Group of Experts deemed most likely to be encountered by State legal advisors *vis-à-vis* cyber activities.

Rules and commentary

There are very few treaties that directly deal with cyber operations and those that have been adopted are of limited scope. Similarly, because State cyber practice is mostly classified and publicly available expressions of *opinio juris* are sparse, it is difficult to definitively identify any cyber-specific customary international law. This lack of cyber-specific international law does not mean, however, that cyber operations exist in a normative void. Both International Groups of Experts were unanimous in their estimation that existing international law applies to cyber operations, an assessment now shared by most States and acknowledged by, *inter alia*, NATO and two United Nations Groups of Governmental Experts on Information Security in 2013 and 2015. Accordingly, the task of the International Groups of Experts was to determine how such law applies in the cyber context, and to identify any cyber-unique aspects thereof.

The rules were adopted employing the principle of consensus within the International Groups of Experts. All of the Experts agreed that, as formulated, they reflect customary international law (unless they expressly reference a treaty) as applied in the cyber context. To the extent the rules accurately articulate customary international law, they are binding on all States, subject to the possible existence of an exception for persistent objectors.

At times, the text of a rule closely resembles that of an existing treaty norm. In such cases, the respective International Group of Experts concluded that the treaty text represents a reliable and accurate restatement of customary international law. Users of this Manual are cautioned that States may be subject to additional rules of international law set forth in treaties to which they are Parties.

Although the observers participated in all discussions, the unanimity that was required for adoption of a rule was limited to the International Group of Experts. Accordingly, no conclusions may be drawn as to the position of any entity represented by an observer as to the validity of any particular rule.

The commentary accompanying each rule is intended to identify the rule's legal basis, explain its normative content, address practical implications in the cyber context, and set forth differing positions as to scope or interpretation. Of particular note is the fact that both International Groups of Experts diligently sought to capture all reasonable positions for inclusion in the commentary. When a clear majority and minority position was apparent in their deliberations, such positions are reflected in the commentary. The commentary also highlights issues upon which the Experts were evenly split and singles out various positions held by only a few of them. Finally, the International Groups of Experts attempted to capture the views of various States on particular issues with which none of the Experts agreed. As neither treaty application nor State practice is well developed in this field, the groups considered it of the utmost importance to articulate all competing views fully and fairly for consideration by *Tallinn Manual 2.0*'s users.

Terminology posed a particular obstacle during the drafting of *Tallinn Manual 2.0*. Many commonly used words and phrases also have specific military or legal meanings. For instance, the word 'attack' refers in common usage to a cyber operation against a particular object or entity, and in the military sense it usually indicates a military operation targeting a particular person or object. However, attack in the *jus ad bellum* sense, qualified by the word 'armed', refers to a cyber operation that justifies a response in self-defence (Rule 71), whereas the term as used in the *jus in bello* indicates a particular type of military operation that involves the use of violence, whether in offence or defence (Rule 92). Users of this Manual therefore are cautioned that it employs most terminology in its international law sense, subject to particular meanings of commonly used terms set forth in the Glossary. With respect to Glossary terms, the definitions are meant solely to describe how the terms are used for the purposes of the Manual. They do not necessarily represent consensus definitions in the field of information technology.

Drafting process

Members of both International Groups of Experts were carefully selected to include legal practitioners, academics, and technical experts. Additionally, several organisations were invited to provide observers to the process. The observers participated fully in the discussions and drafting of the Manual, but their consent was not necessary to achieve the unanimity required for adoption of a rule. Despite the invaluable active participation of the observers in the process, it must be emphasised that *Tallinn Manual 2.0* is not intended to reflect the legal positions or doctrine of any of these organisations.

In light of the divergent scope of the *Tallinn Manual* and *Tallinn Manual 2.0* processes, their drafting approaches differed. In the former, all members of the International Group of Experts were tasked with researching and preparing proposed rules and the draft commentary that might accompany them. Their drafts were then split among teams of experts led by group facilitators that refined the drafts for consideration at plenary sessions of the International Group of Experts. In all, eight plenary meetings of three days each were held in Tallinn between 2010 and 2012. Upon completion of the plenary sessions, an editorial committee drawn from among the International Group of Experts worked on the Manual to ensure the accuracy, thoroughness, and clarity of the commentary. The resulting draft was then divided among peer reviewers with deep expertise in the various subjects addressed by the Manual. The editorial committee considered their comments and revised the Manual as appropriate. In July 2012, the International Group of Experts convened for the last time in Tallinn to consider the final draft, make any last changes, and approve the rules and commentary.

Whereas all members of the *Tallinn Manual* International Group of Experts possessed expertise in its subject matter, *Tallinn Manual 2.0's* wide array of topics necessitated a different process. That process began with experts in the respective subjects that were to be included in the Manual preparing initial drafts of rules and commentary. Many of these drafters were also members of the International Group of Experts. The initial drafts were refined by the editors and then submitted to a rigorous peer review process. The revised drafts were subsequently considered and revised by the International Group of Experts in three one week-long sessions held between 2015 and 2016. Further peer review and editing followed. In April 2016 the last plenary meeting was held and all of the draft chapters were vetted for a final time and adopted by the International Group of Experts.

In addition to the formal meetings, workshops were held by the NATO CCD COE on various subjects addressed in *Tallinn Manual 2.0*. In 2014, a workshop was conducted in collaboration with the University of Tartu to discuss cross-cutting issues such as the law of State responsibility. The NATO CCD COE also co-hosted two workshops in collaboration with Syracuse University Law School in 2015 – one on cyber espionage and another on international human rights law in cyberspace.

During the first *Tallinn Manual* process, States maintained a distance from the work of the International Group of Experts. However, with respect to *Tallinn Manual 2.0*, the Netherlands Ministry of Foreign Affairs hosted the so-called 'Hague Process', whereby it convened States to unofficially comment on the working drafts of the Manual in a Chatham House environment. Three two-day sessions in The Hague were attended by delegations from over 50 States and international organisations. Some States also provided unofficial written comments that in many cases resulted in additional refinement of the text of the Manual. This 'Hague Process' proved invaluable to the initiative, as the International Group of Experts was uniformly of the opinion that international law is made and authoritatively interpreted by States. It must be emphasised, however, that the views expressed in this Manual are solely those of the International Group of Experts and do not necessarily reflect those of States that participated in the Hague Process.

Supporters of the projects

Both projects were generously sponsored by the NATO CCD COE, which hosted all sessions of the International Groups of Experts, as well as meetings of the drafting and editorial teams. The Centre engaged its highly professional staff in managing the complex logistical challenges associated with convening the meetings. The International Group of Experts is especially grateful for the freedom afforded them in preparing this Manual. At no time did the NATO CCD COE or anyone associated with the organisation attempt to influence the groups' conclusions.

Support for various workshops that buttressed the process was kindly provided by the University of Tartu, Syracuse University Law School, Cardozo School of Law, and the *Journal of Law and Cyber Warfare*. Creighton University Law School, Emory University Law School, and the University of Tartu made available gifted and dedicated law students to conduct research for the project. Of particular note is Harvard Law School's Program on International Law and Armed Conflict, which funded a team of law students to substantively review all of the drafts and assist in their editing.

The Netherlands Ministry of Foreign Affairs generously convened States in the Hague Process and has agreed to further support dissemination of the *Tallinn Manual 2.0* following its publication. This contribution by the Dutch Government helped ensure the Manual is grounded in State understandings of the law and that it addresses the practical challenges States face on a daily basis.

The International Groups of Experts is deeply appreciative of all the support received by these entities, without which the publication of *Tallinn Manual 2.0* would not have been possible.

Finally, as Project Director, I also want to commend the dedication displayed by the individual members of the International Groups of Experts. All of them contributed selflessly to the successful completion of their respective Manuals. Moreover, the work of peer reviewers proved invaluable and on behalf of the International Group of Experts, I thank them for their contributions. Finally, any success of the *Tallinn Manual* and *Tallinn Manual 2.0* initiatives is in great part the direct result of the diligence and commitment, as well as the legal acumen, displayed by our Project Manager and Managing Editor, Ms. Liis Vihul. Her contribution to the process is inestimable.

Professor Michael N. Schmitt
Project Director

PART I

General international law and cyberspace

1

Sovereignty

Rule 1 – Sovereignty (general principle)

The principle of State sovereignty applies in cyberspace.

1.   Sovereignty is a foundational principle of international law. Its Latin origin – *sui juris, esse suae potestatis, superanus* or *summa potestas* – indicates that sovereignty refers to the supreme authority of the prince or king or, applied to modern international law, the State.[3] This Rule recognises that various aspects of cyberspace and State cyber operations are not beyond the reach of the principle of sovereignty.[4] In particular, States enjoy sovereignty over any cyber infrastructure located on their territory and activities associated with that cyber infrastructure. Although territoriality lies at the heart of the principle of sovereignty, in certain circumstances, States may also exercise sovereign prerogatives such as jurisdiction over cyber infrastructure and activities abroad, as well as over certain persons engaged in those activities (Rules 10–11). Finally, the territorial nature of sovereignty also places restrictions on other States' cyber operations directed at cyber infrastructure located in sovereign territory (see further discussion in Rule 4).

2.   A well-accepted definition of 'sovereignty' was set forth in the *Island of Palmas* arbitral award of 1928. It provides that: 'Sovereignty in the relations between States signifies independence. Independence in regard to a portion of the globe is the right to exercise therein, to the exclusion of any other State, the functions of a State.'[5]

3.   A number of principles and rules of conventional and customary international law derive from the general principle of sovereignty. Examples include those relating to jurisdiction (Chapter 3), including

---

[3] Sovereignty has also been described as 'the supreme authority of every state within its territory'. OPPENHEIM'S INTERNATIONAL LAW, at 564.

[4] UN GGE 2013 Report, para. 20; UN GGE 2015 Report, paras. 27, 28(b).

[5] *Island of Palmas* arbitral award, at 838.

the obligation to respect certain immunities of other States (Rule 5), and the principle of due diligence (Rule 6). In addition, the International Court of Justice has held that the 'principle of respect for State sovereignty . . . is . . . closely linked with the principles of the prohibition of the use of force and non-intervention',[6] binding norms that are set forth in Rules 66–68.

4.   For the purposes of this Manual, the physical, logical, and social layers of cyberspace are encompassed in the principle of sovereignty. The physical layer comprises the physical network components (i.e., hardware and other infrastructure, such as cables, routers, servers, and computers). The logical layer consists of the connections that exist between network devices. It includes applications, data, and protocols that allow the exchange of data across the physical layer. The social layer encompasses individuals and groups engaged in cyber activities.

5.   Cyberspace has been described variously as a 'global domain'[7] or 'fifth domain'[8] that lacks physicality and is virtual in nature. It also is sometimes suggested that it should be assimilated to the high seas, international airspace, or outer space in the sense of constituting a 'global common' (a *res communis omnium*).[9] While such characterisations may be useful in other than legal contexts, the International Group of Experts did not adopt them on the ground that they disregard the territorial features of cyberspace and cyber operations that implicate the principle of sovereignty. Cyber activities occur on territory and involve objects, or are conducted by persons or entities, over which States may exercise their sovereign prerogatives. In particular, the Experts noted that although cyber activities may cross multiple borders, or occur in international waters, international airspace, or outer space, all are conducted by individuals or entities subject to the jurisdiction of one or more States.

6.   The fact that cyber infrastructure located in a given State's territory is linked to cyberspace cannot be interpreted as a waiver of its

---

[6] *Nicaragua* judgment, para. 212.
[7] Joint Chiefs of Staff, Joint Publication 1-02, US Department of Defense Dictionary of Military and Associated Terms, at 57 (8 November 2010, as amended through 15 January 2016).
[8] The Netherlands Ministry of Defence, Defence Cyber Strategy, at 4 (2012) (describing cyberspace as the fifth domain for military operations in addition to air, sea, land, and space). *See also* NATO 2016 Warsaw Summit Communiqué, para. 70; (US) Joint Publication 3-12 *(R)* (2013), at I-2; US DoD Strategy for Operating in Cyberspace (2011), at 5.
[9] *See, e.g.*, US Department of Defense, The Strategy for Homeland Defense and Civil Support (2005), at 12.

sovereignty. Indeed, States have the right, pursuant to the principle of sovereignty, to disconnect from the Internet, in whole or in part, any cyber infrastructure located on their territory, subject to any treaty or customary international law restrictions, notably in the area of international human rights law (Chapter 6).

7. The International Group of Experts agreed that no State may claim sovereignty over cyberspace *per se*. This is so because much of cyber infrastructure comprising cyberspace is located in the sovereign territories of States.

8. Sovereignty has an internal and an external element. These interrelated elements are discussed in Rules 2 and 3, respectively.

9. With regard to cyber infrastructure aboard sovereign immune platforms, see Rule 5.

10. The Experts agreed that international organisations do not enjoy sovereignty. On international organisations, see also Section 4 of Chapter 4.

Rule 2 – Internal sovereignty

A State enjoys sovereign authority with regard to the cyber infrastructure, persons, and cyber activities located within its territory, subject to its international legal obligations.

1. This Rule relates to 'internal sovereignty'. In principle, a State is free to adopt any measure it considers necessary or appropriate with regard to cyber infrastructure, persons engaged in cyber activities, or cyber activities themselves within its territory, unless prevented from doing so by a rule of international law binding on the State, such as those resident in international human rights law (Rule 35).

2. A State's sovereignty over cyber infrastructure and activities within its territory has two international legal consequences. First, the cyber infrastructure and activities are subject to domestic legal and regulatory control by the State. In particular, the State may promulgate and enforce domestic laws and regulations regarding them. Second, the State's sovereignty over its territory affords it the right under international law to protect cyber infrastructure and safeguard cyber activity that is located in, or takes place on, its territory.

3. With respect to a State's internal sovereignty, it is irrelevant as a matter of international law whether the cyber infrastructure in question is public or private in character, or whether the cyber activities concerned

are engaged in by the State's organs or by private individuals or entities. A State's sovereign prerogatives also exist irrespective of the purpose of the cyber infrastructure or, as a general matter, the nationality of its owner. For example, a State enjoys sovereignty over a private ISP's server located on its territory even if the ISP is domiciled abroad.

4. The physical layer of cyberspace (see also discussion in Rule 1) within a State's territory is self-evidently subject to that State's sovereignty. Of particular note with respect to the physical layer is a coastal State's sovereignty over the seabed of its territorial sea. Such sovereignty affords that State control over the placement of any submarine communication cables thereon. This is a critical right in light of the fact that submarine communication cables currently carry the bulk of international communications. As to the status and protection of such cables, see Rule 54.

5. The International Group of Experts noted that unlike physical cyber infrastructure, like the landline cables over which 'wired' telecommunications are transmitted, electromagnetic frequencies do not easily fit with a notion of sovereignty that is confined to State borders. The international community has taken measures to govern the use of the electromagnetic spectrum when the frequencies used for cyber communications transcend State borders, so as to enable its shared and optimal use and the unhampered transmission of communications. On this issue, see Rule 63.

6. In addition to authority over the physical layer, the principle of sovereignty affords States the right to control aspects of the logical layer of cyberspace within their territories. For instance, a State may promulgate legislation that requires certain e-services to employ particular cryptographic protocols, such as the Transport Layer Security protocol, to guarantee secure communications between web servers and browsers. Similarly, a State may legislatively require electronic signatures to meet particular technical requirements, such as reliance on certificate-based encryption or that the certificates include certain information, such as their cryptographic fingerprint, owner, or expiration date.

7. As to the social layer of cyberspace, a State may regulate the cyber activities of those on its territory, including both natural and legal persons. For example, a State may criminalise the posting of material such as child pornography or that which incites violence online. It must be cautioned that State censorship of, or restrictions on, online communications and activities are subject to applicable international human rights law (Chapter 6).

8.   In that a State enjoys internal sovereignty, it may, *inter alia,* restrict, in part or in whole, access to cyberspace by those within its territory, in particular to certain online content. For example, a number of States, sometimes in cooperation with private social media companies, have blocked access to terrorist content on social media and other websites. Of course, the right of a State to limit access must take account of any applicable international law norms. For instance, Rules 35 and 37 recognise that freedom of expression is a right under customary international human rights law and that limitations thereon, as in the case of blocking access to the Internet in situations of widespread civil unrest fuelled by social media, must be, *inter alia,* non-discriminatory and authorised by law. Similarly, a State that suspends an international telecommunication service must notify other States of the suspension (Rule 62). The Experts noted that a State's domestic legislation, such as a domestic law on civil liberties, may, however, impose further limitations on the exercise of said sovereign right.[10]

9.   Customary or treaty law may restrict the exercise of sovereign rights by the territorial State. For example, States may not exercise jurisdiction or authority within their territory over another State's non-commercial governmental activities, particular organs of other States (e.g., heads of State, heads of government, and foreign ministers) (Rule 12), diplomatic and consular personnel (Rule 44), or State ships and aircraft that enjoy sovereign immunity and inviolability (Rule 5). The International Group of Experts agreed that these limitations on internal sovereignty equally apply in the cyber context.

10.   Internal sovereignty also includes the authority of a State to independently decide on its political, social, cultural, economic, and legal order.[11] Accordingly, the principle of sovereignty underlies the prohibition of unlawful intervention into a State's *domaine réservé* (Rule 66).

11.   A few of the Experts were of the view that States are also entitled to exercise sovereign rights, including jurisdiction, over government data and that of their nationals stored or transmitted outside their territory, subject to specific restrictions imposed by international law.[12] For these

---

[10]   *See, e.g.,* the Constitution of Greece, revised by the parliamentary resolution of 27 May 2008 of the 8th Revisionary Parliament, Hellenic Parliament, Art. 5A(2); Constitutional Council of France, Case No. 2009-580 DC (10 June 2009); Judgment, 12790 of the Supreme Court of Costa Rica, File 09-013141-0007-CO (30 July 2010).

[11]   *See, e.g., Nicaragua* judgment, para. 263.

[12]   With regard to governmental data located in the territory of another State and associated rights, if any, *see Questions Relating to the Seizure and Detention of Certain Documents*

Experts, a State's sovereignty over data that is stored or in transit abroad can exist independently of its sovereignty over cyber infrastructure located in its territory and the persons and activities therein. The majority, by contrast, took the position that States do not enjoy such sovereignty over data located abroad unless international law specifically so provides, as in the case of data stored aboard certain objects like warships. They acknowledged, however, that a State may, in certain circumstances, exercise prescriptive jurisdiction over data located outside its territory (Rule 10).

12.   Sovereignty not only affords rights, but imposes legal obligations,[13] such as that requiring the exercise of due diligence to terminate harmful cyber activities emanating from a State's territory (Chapter 2).

Rule 3 – External sovereignty

A State is free to conduct cyber activities in its international relations, subject to any contrary rule of international law binding on it.

1.   External sovereignty derives from the sovereign equality of States.[14] As recognised in Article 2(1) of the UN Charter, States are juridically equal. Each State is obliged to respect the personality, territorial integrity, and political independence of other States and must comply faithfully with its international obligations.[15] In a community of sovereign equal States, there is no legal supremacy of one State over another.

2.   External sovereignty means that a State is independent in its external relations from other States and is free to engage in cyber activities beyond its territory subject only to international law. Such sovereignty encompasses the freedom to formulate foreign policy,[16] including to enter into international agreements.[17] Therefore, with

---

and Data (Timor-Leste v. Austl.), provisional measure, 2014 ICJ 147, paras. 24–25, 27 (3 March); Questions Relating to the Seizure and Detention of Certain Documents and Data (Timor-Leste v. Austl.), order, 2015 ICJ Gen. List No. 156, at 3 (11 June).

[13] See, e.g., Corfu Channel judgment, holding that: 'Sovereignty confers rights upon States and imposes obligations on them.' Corfu Channel judgment, at 43 (separate opinion of Judge Alvarez).

[14] The applicability in the cyber context of the principle of sovereign equality was also affirmed by the UN Group of Governmental Experts in 2015. UN GGE 2015 Report, paras. 26, 28(b).

[15] See Report to the San Francisco Conference, 9 UNCIO (1945); Declaration on Friendly Relations, pmbl. See also Nicaragua judgment, para. 202.

[16] Nicaragua judgment, para. 205.   [17] Wimbledon judgment, at 25.

respect to cyber activities, States are free to decide whether to opt into specific cyber treaty regimes or issue expressions of *opinio juris* regarding the customary law nature of any particular State cyber practice. In particular, a State is not obliged to agree to particular treaty rules governing the cyber activities of its organs or nationals or conduct taking place in its sovereign territory.

3. This Rule expressly recognises that a State's engagement in cyber operations by virtue of its external sovereignty is without prejudice to binding treaty or customary international law norms to the contrary.[18] Of particular note in this regard are the prohibitions of violating another State's sovereignty (Rule 4), intervention (Rule 66), and the use of force (Rule 68).

4. External sovereignty is the source of State immunity (Rule 12).

Rule 4 – Violation of sovereignty

A State must not conduct cyber operations that violate the sovereignty of another State.

1. As noted in Rules 2 and 3, States enjoy internal and external sovereignty, respectively. Cyber operations that prevent or disregard another State's exercise of its sovereign prerogatives constitute a violation of such sovereignty and are prohibited by international law. Of course, in certain situations international law permits or envisages exceptions to the obligation to respect another State's sovereignty. The paradigmatic examples are when an action that would otherwise violate the latter's sovereignty is authorised by the Security Council (Rule 76) or is engaged in pursuant to the exercise of the right of self-defence (Rule 71).

2. This Rule applies in the relations between States, that is, to actions undertaken by, or attributable to, States. The International Group of Experts agreed that it does not extend to the actions of non-State actors unless such actions are attributable to a State (Rules 15 and 17).[19] In other words, only States shoulder an obligation to respect the sovereignty of other States as a matter of international law and therefore only States can breach that obligation. For instance,

---

[18] *Wimbledon* judgment, at 25; *Lotus* judgment, at 18.
[19] This statement is without prejudice to international law with respect to *de facto* States.

consider a case in which a corporation is the target of a malicious cyber operation by a State. The corporation does not violate the sovereignty of that State if it hacks back. Similarly, cyber operations conducted by a terrorist group whose conduct is not attributable to a State do not constitute a violation of the victim State's sovereignty. In these examples, it must be cautioned that the fact that the non-State actors are not bound to respect the target State's sovereignty does not mean that their actions are lawful. On the contrary, such operations are likely to violate the domestic law of States having jurisdiction over, *inter alia*, the persons or activities involved.

3.   The Experts acknowledged a view that some non-State actors (in particular, organised armed groups) can violate a State's sovereignty; none of the Experts shared it.[20]

4.   The fact that, in the view of the Experts, non-State actors do not violate the sovereignty of a State when they conduct harmful cyber operations against or into it does not necessarily prevent the target State from responding to the cyber operation pursuant to international law. In appropriate cases, a State may respond based on the plea of necessity (Rule 26) or in self-defence, at least by the majority view with respect to the latter (Rule 71). The International Group of Experts agreed that countermeasures (Rule 20) may also be available against another State on the basis that it has failed to comply with its due diligence obligation with respect to the actions of non-State actors operating from its territory (Chapter 2).

5.   As discussed in Rule 2, the principle of sovereignty encompasses cyber infrastructure located in a State's territory irrespective of whether it is government or private cyber infrastructure. For instance, if one State conducts cyber operations that cause damage to the cyber infrastructure of a private company located in another State, such as privately owned critical infrastructure, the former's actions amount to a violation of the second State's sovereignty. This is so even though there is no effect on any government cyber infrastructure, assets, or activities.

6.   Based on its internal sovereignty, a State may control access to its territory and to the superjacent national airspace.[21] A State's territory includes the land territory, internal waters, territorial sea (including its

---

[20] In a related legal context, see *Kosovo* advisory opinion, para. 80 (stating that 'the scope of the principle of territorial integrity is confined to the sphere of relations between States'.).

[21] *See* Law of the Sea Convention, Art. 2; Chicago Convention, Arts. 1–3.

bed and subsoil), and archipelagic waters (where applicable). The Experts agreed that a violation of sovereignty occurs whenever one State physically crosses into the territory or national airspace of another State without either its consent or another justification in international law (see Rule 19 on circumstances precluding wrongfulness). As an example, the non-consensual exercise of enforcement jurisdiction in another State's territory (Rule 11) is a violation of that State's sovereignty.[22] In the cyber context, therefore, it is a violation of territorial sovereignty for an organ of a State, or others whose conduct may be attributed to the State, to conduct cyber operations while physically present on another State's territory against that State or entities or persons located there. For example, if an agent of one State uses a USB flash drive to introduce malware into cyber infrastructure located in another State, a violation of sovereignty has taken place.

7.   In this regard, the Experts were divided over the unique case of cyber espionage (Rule 32) by one State that is conducted while physically present on the territory of another State. The majority took the position that the activity violates this Rule. For example, if organs of one State are present in another State's territory and conduct cyber espionage against it without its consent or other legal justification, the latter's sovereignty has been violated. Although these Experts acknowledged that there is widespread State practice of engaging in non-consensual espionage while present on another State's territory, they pointed out that States have not defended such actions on the basis of international law.

8.   A few of the Experts were of the view that the extensive State practice of conducting espionage on the target State's territory has created an exception to the generally accepted premise that non-consensual activities attributable to a State while physically present on another's territory violate sovereignty. They emphasised, however, that this exception is narrow and limited solely to acts of espionage. Moreover, while it includes exfiltration of data and surveillance operations, it does not encompass any cyber espionage operation that damages cyber infrastructure or deletes or alters data.

9.   The International Group of Experts agreed, however, that the mere interception of wireless signals from outside the target State's territory does not constitute a violation of that State's sovereignty because

---

[22] *See, e.g.,* SC Res. 138, para. 1, UN Doc. S/RES/138 (23 June 1960).

the cyber operation does not manifest in cyber infrastructure on the target State's territory (but see discussion in Rule 35 on privacy).[23]

10.   The precise legal character of remote cyber operations that manifest on a State's territory is somewhat unsettled in international law. The International Group of Experts assessed their lawfulness on two different bases: (1) the degree of infringement upon the target State's territorial integrity; and (2) whether there has been an interference with or usurpation of inherently governmental functions. The first is based on the premise that a State controls access to its sovereign territory, as described above, and the second on the sovereign right of a State to exercise within its territory, 'to the exclusion of any other State, the functions of a State'.[24]

11.   As to the first base, the Experts analysed it on three distinct levels: (1) physical damage; (2) loss of functionality; and (3) infringement upon territorial integrity falling below the threshold of loss of functionality. First, most of the Experts agreed that cyber operations constitute a violation of sovereignty in the event they result in physical damage or injury, as in the case of malware that causes the malfunctioning of the cooling elements of equipment, thereby leading to overheating that results in components melting down. To the extent that non-consensual physical presence on another State's territory to conduct cyber operations amounts to a violation of sovereignty, the Experts concurred that the causation of physical consequences by remote means on that territory likewise constitutes a violation of sovereignty. Both conclusions are consistent with the object and purpose of the principle of sovereignty, which clearly protects territorial integrity against physical violation. The Experts noted that such operations may also constitute prohibited intervention (Rule 66), an unlawful use of force (Rule 68), or an armed attack (Rule 71).

12.   A few Experts, however, took the position that physical damage or injury is but one of the relevant factors, as distinct from the determinative factor, in assessing whether a cyber operation constitutes a violation of sovereignty. In the view of these Experts, there may be situations involving physical damage (or loss of functionality, see below) or injury that do not constitute a violation of sovereignty standing alone.

13.   Second, the Experts agreed that, in addition to physical damage, the remote causation of loss of functionality of cyber infrastructure located in another State sometimes constitutes a violation of

---

[23] See, e.g., Weber and Saravia v. Germany, 2006-XI ECtHR App. No. 54934/00, admissibility decision, para. 88 (2006).

[24] Island of Palmas arbitral award, at 838.

sovereignty, although no consensus could be achieved as to the precise threshold at which this is so due to the lack of expressions of *opinio juris* in this regard. There was full agreement that a cyber operation necessitating repair or replacement of physical components of cyber infrastructure amounts to a violation because such consequences are akin to physical damage or injury. As an example, and assuming attribution to a State, the Shamoon virus that required repair or replacement of thousands of Saudi Arabia's oil company Saudi Aramco's hard drives in 2012 qualified as a violation of that State's sovereignty. The Experts further agreed that the loss of functionality of equipment or other physical items that rely on the targeted infrastructure in order to operate constitutes a loss of functionality. Some of the Experts suggested that a cyber operation that necessitates reinstallation (albeit not mere rebooting) of the operating system or other data upon which the targeted cyber infrastructure relies in order to perform its intended purpose qualifies as an operation resulting in loss of functionality.[25] The International Group of Experts cautioned that State practice based on a sense of legal obligation is needed to fully clarify this issue.

14.   Third, no consensus could be achieved as to whether, and if so, when, a cyber operation that results in neither physical damage nor the loss of functionality amounts to a violation of sovereignty. The Experts who were willing to characterise as violations of sovereignty cyber operations falling below the threshold of loss of functionality proffered a number of possibilities. These included, but were not limited to, a cyber operation causing cyber infrastructure or programs to operate differently; altering or deleting data stored in cyber infrastructure without causing physical or functional consequences, as described above; emplacing malware into a system; installing backdoors; and causing a temporary, but significant, loss of functionality, as in the case of a major DDoS operation. With respect to all of the aforementioned examples, the argument of the proponents was that the proposed interpretation is consistent with the object and purpose of the principle of sovereignty that affords States the full control over access to and activities on their territory.

15.   The second basis upon which the Experts determined a violation of sovereignty occurs is when one State's cyber operation interferes with or usurps the inherently governmental functions of another State. This is because the target State enjoys the exclusive right to perform them, or to

---

[25] On the notion of loss of functionality, *see also* Rule 92.

decide upon their performance. It matters not whether physical damage, injury, or loss of functionality has resulted or whether the operation qualifies in accordance with the various differing positions outlined above for operations that do not result in a loss of functionality.

16.   Although the International Group of Experts could not define 'inherently governmental functions' definitively, it agreed that a cyber operation that interferes with data or services that are necessary for the exercise of inherently governmental functions is prohibited as a violation of sovereignty (and in some cases the prohibition of intervention, Rule 66). Examples include changing or deleting data such that it interferes with the delivery of social services, the conduct of elections, the collection of taxes, the effective conduct of diplomacy, and the performance of key national defence activities. The Experts further agreed that it is irrelevant whether the inherently governmental function is performed by the State itself or has been privatised.

17.   The Experts cautioned that under this test, the function in question must be inherently governmental.[26] For example, official communications among a State's leadership are inherently governmental, but when a State posts information on terrorist organisations on a website, the activity, while governmental, is not inherently so because other entities, such as non-governmental organisations, also engage in it. Thus, interference with the former would violate the sovereignty of the target State, whereas interfering with the latter would not. Similarly, a cyber operation that is designed to empty a governmental employee's bank account does not interfere with an inherently governmental function, but one that disrupts the government's ability to pay employee salaries does.

18.   With respect to usurpation, the International Group of Experts concurred that a State may not conduct inherently governmental functions exclusively reserved to another State on the latter's territory. An example on point is the exercise of law enforcement functions within another State's borders in the absence of either an allocation of authority under international law or consent (Rule 11). To illustrate, if one State conducts a law enforcement operation against a botnet in order to obtain evidence for criminal prosecution by taking over its command and control servers located in another State without that State's consent, the former has violated the latter's sovereignty because the operation usurps

---

[26] In assessing the inherently governmental nature of cyber activities, the International Group of Experts pointed out that the notion of *acta jure imperii*, used in the context of State immunity, could prove helpful.

an inherently governmental function exclusively reserved to the territorial State under international law. It must be cautioned that this conclusion bears solely on the international law nature of the activity. Its consequences in the domestic legal sphere depend on the domestic laws of the States concerned.

19. Although the International Group of Experts agreed that a violation of sovereignty generally requires that the cyber operation in question occur or otherwise manifest on cyber infrastructure in the sovereign territory of the affected State, it was divided over whether a cyber operation purportedly violating sovereignty through interference with or usurpation of an inherently governmental function need do so. The majority of the Experts adopted the position that in this particular case sovereignty is violated irrespective of where the cyber operation occurs or manifests. For them the determinative factor is whether the activities interfered with qualify as inherently governmental functions. For example, Estonia has announced the establishment of so-called 'digital embassies' that allow the State to back up critical governmental data in other States (see also discussion in Rule 39). Interference with such data in a way that affects the performance by Estonia of its inherently governmental functions would, by the majority view, amount to a violation of this Rule. They acknowledged that the cyber operation in question might also violate the sovereignty of the State where the infrastructure is located on the basis that it occurs on the sovereign territory of the latter.

20. A few of the Experts, by contrast, were of the view that such operations must occur or manifest on a State's territory or sovereign platform (Rule 5) to constitute a violation. They reasoned that otherwise, the sovereignty, which is by definition exclusive, of at least two States would be implicated by the act, that of the State exercising the inherently governmental function and that of the State where the cyber infrastructure is located.

21. An interesting case is a cyber operation by a State to preclude access, in whole or in part, by another State to the Internet or to otherwise impede (e.g., by filtering or performing traffic shaping to limit bandwidth) said access. In some cases, doing so would be possible without any incursion into the target State's infrastructure. The International Group of Experts was of the view that such an operation will only violate the sovereignty of the target State to the extent it usurps or interferes with inherently governmental functions, for example, online services that are necessary for the delivery of social services. However, the Experts noted that the operation may violate other rules of international law, such as the prohibition of intervention (Rule 66).

22.   Usurpation of an inherently governmental function differs from intervention in that the former deals with inherently governmental functions, whereas the latter involves the *domaine réservé*, concepts that overlap to a degree but that are not identical. Moreover, intervention requires an element of coercion. For instance, in the aforementioned case of extraterritorial law enforcement, the coercive element is absent since the State in which the activity occurs is not compelled to act in an involuntary manner or involuntarily refrain from acting in a particular way.

23.   The International Group of Experts was of the view that a State's cyber operations may constitute a violation of another State's sovereignty, whatever the basis for that violation, irrespective of whether the operations are launched from the acting State's territory, the target State's territory, the territory of a third State, the high seas, international airspace, or outer space. Any damage caused to cyber infrastructure aboard a sovereign platform is similarly a violation of the target State's sovereignty no matter where the platform is located (Rule 5).

24.   The International Group of Experts agreed that if a State's cyber operation that is designed to result in consequences breaching the sovereignty of another State fails, for instance due to effective defensive measures or because the operation was flawed, the latter's sovereignty has not been breached. The Experts concurred that in order for sovereignty to be violated by a cyber operation, the requisite consequences must manifest.

25.   The Experts agreed that a cyber operation by or attributable to a State that is not intended to result in consequences that violate the sovereignty of another State, but that nevertheless generates them, is a violation of sovereignty. For instance, if a State conducts cyber espionage (Rule 32) against a network located in another State, and the operation was not intended to result in consequences that violate sovereignty, but such consequences nevertheless eventuate, the latter State's sovereignty has been violated. Similarly, if a State conducts a cyber operation against another State, but that operation unexpectedly bleeds over into third States and causes harm at the level necessary to qualify as a violation of sovereignty, this Rule has been breached *vis-à-vis* those States despite the unintentional and unforeseeable nature of the harm. The Experts concurred that intent is not a constitutive element of a breach of sovereignty.

26.   It merits noting that cyber operations often affect States other than the State on whose territory the targeted cyber infrastructure is located. For instance, consider the case of cloud computing. Operations

against the cloud infrastructure would generally not violate the sovereignty of other States that are affected by the operations unless the consequences that manifest in those States are of the requisite nature, as discussed in this Rule. Similarly, while a State's cyber operation against the SWIFT international banking payment system could cause financial disarray and loss globally, it is likely only the sovereignty of the State where the servers are located that is potentially implicated (except with respect to certain inherently governmental functions as discussed above). Finally, an operation against cyber infrastructure located on the high seas or international airspace that does not enjoy sovereign immunity or inviolability (Rule 5), such as a privately owned aircraft that provides Internet access, does not generally constitute a violation of sovereignty because it is not located in the territory of a State. The Experts emphasised, however, that the conclusion that such cyber operations do not usually constitute violations of sovereignty is without prejudice to their potentially breaching other norms of international law, such as those resident in international trade law or the law governing international civil aviation (see also Chapter 9).

27. International law does not directly address peacetime espionage as such. As a general matter, mere characterisation of a cyber operation as espionage or not has no legal significance with respect to violation of sovereignty. Nor does the fact that the cyber operation comprises intelligence gathering or counterintelligence. Rather, one must look to the underlying acts to determine whether the operation in question violates international law. For instance, as discussed in Rule 32, if espionage is carried out by means of cyber operations that are of a nature to breach this Rule, said operations qualify as a violation of sovereignty. The same is true with regard to active defence measures. To the extent that an active defence measure would violate the sovereignty of the State into which it is conducted, it must be justified on one of the grounds precluding wrongfulness (Rule 19).

28. The International Group of Experts acknowledged that States appear to be increasingly concerned about cyber operations that result in severe economic loss or that affect critical infrastructure. Consider a case in which a State discovers malware that monitors transactions in its national stock market. The cyber operation is publicly revealed, thereby causing confidence in the stock market to plummet, resulting in severe financial losses. Or consider the case of other States conducting cyber operations to monitor activities in a State's critical infrastructure. The target State is concerned that the information acquired could be used to facilitate disruptive or destructive cyber operations. Although there is no

State practice establishing the necessary uniformity, duration, frequency, or significance to justify a conclusion that such operations, severe as they may be, qualify as violations of the principle of sovereignty according to the *lex lata*, statements by governments seem to indicate that a consequence-based approach is increasingly favoured by States.[27] Nevertheless, the International Group of Experts agreed that this approach was not *lex lata*.

29.   With regard to propaganda, the International Group of Experts agreed that its transmission into other States is generally not a violation of sovereignty.[28] However, the transmission of propaganda, depending on its nature, might violate other rules of international law. For instance, propaganda designed to incite civil unrest in another State would likely violate the prohibition of intervention (Rule 66). Similarly, propaganda by a vessel in transit through the territorial sea renders the passage non-innocent (Rule 48).

30.   The Experts noted that cyber crime as such does not violate sovereignty unless it is engaged in by, or attributable to, a State (Rules 15–18) and meets the other criteria for violation of this Rule. As an example, theft of Bitcoins by an organised crime group acting on its own accord would not violate the sovereignty of any State. By contrast, if a State instructs (Rule 17) an organised crime group to carry out a large-scale DDoS

---

[27] *See, e.g.,* International Code of Conduct for Information Security (Letter dated 9 January 2015 from the Permanent Representative of China, Kazakhstan, Kyrgyzstan, the Russian Federation, Tajikistan and Uzbekistan to the UN addressed to the Secretary-General), UN Doc. A/69/723 (13 January 2015), stating that each State pledges:

(3) Not to use information and communications technologies and information and communications networks to interfere in the internal affairs of other States or with the aim of undermining their political, economic and social stability;

(6) To reaffirm the rights and responsibilities of all States, in accordance with the relevant norms and rules, regarding legal protection of their information space and critical information infrastructure against damage resulting from threats, interference, attack and sabotage.

See also Leon E. Panetta, Sec'y of Def., Defending the Nation from Cyber Attack, Remarks to the Business Executives for National Security (11 October 2012).

[28] Numerous instruments stipulate that States in which other States' broadcasts, especially satellite broadcasts, are available should have some degree of control over the information that is being transmitted into their territories. *See, e.g.,* ITU Radio Regulations, Art. 23.13; United Nations Educational, Scientific and Cultural Organization, Declaration of Guiding Principles on the Use of Satellite Broadcasting for the Free Flow of Information, the Spread of Education and Greater Cultural Exchange, Arts. II(1), VI(2), IX, X (15 November 1972); Principles Governing the Use by States of Artificial Earth Satellites for International Direct Television Broadcasting, paras. 13–14, GA Res. 37/92, UN Doc. A/RES/37/92 (10 December 1982). However, the Experts agreed that this premise has not crystallised into a customary international law requirement.

operation against another State's governmental mail servers that cripples that State's official email communications over an extended period of time, this Rule has been breached because the act is attributable to a State and interferes with an inherently governmental function.

31.   A State may consent to (Rule 19) another State's cyber operations that would otherwise violate its sovereignty. Consider a case in which non-State actors are engaged in harmful cyber activities on a State's territory against that State. The State in question does not have the technical ability to put an end to those activities and therefore requests the assistance of another State. The assisting State's ensuing cyber operations on the other State's territory would not violate the latter's sovereignty as long as the operations remain within the scope of its consent.

32.   To illustrate, NATO has established a mechanism by which Allies can request the assistance of a NATO 'Rapid Reaction Team' of cyber defence experts in dealing with cyber incidents. Depending on the precise nature and scope of the request, it could serve as the basis of consent to the cyber operations the team conducts in that capacity. Consent may also be set forth in a standing treaty. For example, if a basing agreement authorises a sending State's military forces to conduct cyber operations from the receiving State's territory, the receiving State may not claim a violation of its sovereignty when said operations are conducted.

Rule 5 – Sovereign immunity and inviolability

Any interference by a State with cyber infrastructure aboard a platform, wherever located, that enjoys sovereign immunity constitutes a violation of sovereignty.

1.   International law clearly accords sovereign immunity to certain objects used for non-commercial governmental purposes, regardless of their location. It is generally accepted that warships and 'ships owned or operated by a State and used only for government non-commercial service' enjoy immunity from the jurisdiction of any State other than the flag State.[29] Further, State aircraft enjoy sovereign immunity.[30] Persons or objects, including those involved in cyber activities, on such vessels or aircraft are immune from another State's exercise of enforcement

---

[29] Law of the Sea Convention, Arts. 95–96.
[30] UK MANUAL, para. 12.6.1; AMW MANUAL, commentary accompanying Rule 1(cc).

jurisdiction (Rules 9 and 11) while aboard those platforms in light of the inviolability (see below) of the platforms.

2.   In order to enjoy sovereign immunity and inviolability, the cyber infrastructure aboard the platform in question must be devoted exclusively to government purposes. For example, government institutions that operate as market participants *vis-à-vis* the Internet cannot claim that the cyber infrastructure involved enjoys sovereign immunity, because that infrastructure does not serve exclusively governmental purposes.

3.   Sovereign immunity entails inviolability; any interference with an object enjoying sovereign immunity constitutes a violation of international law.[31] Interference includes, but is not limited to, activities that damage the object or significantly impair its operation. For instance, a denial of service attack against a State's military unmanned aerial vehicle would constitute a violation of its sovereign immunity. Similarly, taking control of the object would violate sovereign immunity.

4.   Despite enjoying sovereign immunity, sovereign platforms and structures must comply with the rules and principles of international law, such as the obligation to respect the sovereignty of other States. As an example, non-consensual entry of a military aircraft into the national airspace of another State to conduct cyber operations can, despite the aircraft's sovereign status, trigger the State's right to take necessary measures against the intruding aircraft, including, in certain circumstances, the use of force (see also discussion in Rule 55). The same would be true of a warship that conducts cyber activities in a State's territorial sea in violation of the innocent passage regime (Rule 48). In both cases, the platforms retain their sovereign immunity, but that immunity does not prevent the other States from taking those actions that are lawful, appropriate, and necessary in the circumstances to safeguard their legally recognised interests.

5.   With respect to the immunity from jurisdiction of governmental cyber infrastructure used for non-commercial purposes, see Rule 12.

6.   In times of international armed conflict, the principles of sovereign immunity and inviolability cease to apply in relations between the

---

[31] *See, e.g., Owners of the Jessie, the Thomas F. Bayard, and the Pescawha (UK v. US),* 6 RIAA 57 (1926) (Anglo American Claims Commission 1921); *Player Larga (Owners of Cargo Lately Laden on Board) Appellants* v. *I Congreso del Partido (Owners) Respondents; Marble Islands (Owners of Cargo Lately Laden on Board) Appellants* v. *same Respondents, I Congreso del Partido* [1983] 1 AC 244 (HL).

parties to the conflict (subject to any specific rule of international law to the contrary, such as Article 45 of the Vienna Convention on Diplomatic Relations). Objects enjoying sovereign immunity and inviolability may be destroyed if they qualify as military objectives (Rule 100), or may be seized as booty of war by the respective enemy armed forces.[32] It should be noted that governmental cyber infrastructure of neutral States may qualify as a military objective in certain limited circumstances (Rule 150).

7. Locations and objects that do not fall within the scope of this Rule may nevertheless enjoy special protection affording inviolability by virtue of bilateral or multilateral agreements, such as status of forces agreements. Additionally, under diplomatic and consular law, special protections exist for certain cyber infrastructure (Rule 39), as well as electronic archives, documents, and correspondence (Rule 41).

---

[32] AMW MANUAL, Rule 136(a) and accompanying commentary.

2

Due diligence

Rule 6 – Due diligence (general principle)

A State must exercise due diligence in not allowing its territory, or territory or cyber infrastructure under its governmental control, to be used for cyber operations that affect the rights of, and produce serious adverse consequences for, other States.

1.   This Rule is based on the general international law principle that States must exercise due diligence in ensuring territory and objects over which they enjoy sovereignty are not used to harm other States.[33] For the purposes of this Manual, the principle shall be referred to as the 'due diligence principle', as that is the term most commonly used with respect to the obligation of States to control activities on their territory.[34] Properly understood, due diligence is the standard of conduct expected of States when complying with this principle. It is a principle that is reflected in the rules, and interpretation thereof, of numerous specialised regimes of international law.[35]

---

[33] *United States* v. *Arjona*, 120, US 479, 483 (1887); *Lotus* judgment, at 88 (Moore, J., dissenting); *Island of Palmas* arbitral award, at 839; *Corfu Channel* judgment, at 22; UN Secretary-General, *Survey of International Law in Relation to the Work of Codification of the International Law Commission*, para. 57, UN Doc. A/CN.4/1/Rev.1 (1 February 1949); Permanent Mission of the Federal Republic of Germany to the United Nations, General appreciation of the issues of information security, at 4, Note No. 516/2012; Developments in the Field of Information and Telecommunications in the Context of International Security, Report of the Secretary General, at 9, UN Doc. A/68/156 Add. 1 (9 September 2013) (Ger.). *See also Tehran Hostages* judgment, paras. 67–68; *Nicaragua* judgment, para. 157.

[34] For the purposes of this Manual, the due diligence principle encompasses the notion *sic utere tuo ut alienum non laedas* ('Use your own property so as not to injure that of another').

[35] Fields of law cited by the International Law Association include the law of neutrality, international human rights law, international investment law, the *jus ad bellum* with respect to self-defence against non-State actors based in other States (Rule 71), and international environmental law. *See generally* International Law Association, Study

2. A dictum in the International Court of Justice's *Corfu Channel* judgment, which observes that 'it is every State's obligation not to allow knowingly its territory to be used for acts contrary to the rights of other States', sets forth the generally recognised contemporary definition of the due diligence principle.[36] An obligation deriving from the notion of sovereignty, it requires a State 'to protect within [its] territory the rights of other States'.[37]

3. The International Group of Experts acknowledged a view, which no member held, that a general due diligence principle, and therefore its application in the context of cyber operations, has not achieved *lex lata* status. Advocates of this position point to the United Nations Groups of Governmental Experts' (UN GGE) exhortation that States 'should' engage in due diligence, as distinct from a statement that they 'must' engage as a matter of law.[38] However, the Experts agreed that the GGEs' comments do not definitively refute the existence of such a principle. Indeed, the due diligence principle derives from the principle of sovereignty (Rule 1), and the UN GGEs have themselves acknowledged that principles of international law that 'flow' from that of sovereignty are binding in the cyber context.[39]

4. The Experts further observed that the due diligence principle has long been reflected in jurisprudence; it is a general principle that has been particularised in specialised regimes of international law. Since new technologies are subject to pre-existing international law absent a legal exclusion therefrom,[40] they concluded that the due diligence principle applies in the cyber context.

5. The due diligence principle is sometimes also referred to as the 'obligation of vigilance',[41] the 'obligation of prevention', or the 'duty of

---

Group on Due Diligence in International Law: First Report, 7 March 2014. In international environmental law, the due diligence principle is known as the 'no harm principle'. *See also Alabama Claims Arbitration (United States/Great Britain)* 29 RIAA 125, 129 (1872) (describing the requirement of due diligence in various contexts); Declaration of the United Nations Conference on the Human Environment, prin. 21, UN Doc. A/CONF.48/14 (1972); Rio Declaration on Environment and Development, prin. 2, UN Doc. A/CONF.151/26/Rev.1 (Vol. I), Annex I (12 August 1992); *Nuclear Weapons* advisory opinion, para. 29.

[36] *Corfu Channel* judgment, at 22.   [37] *Island of Palmas* arbitral award, at 839.

[38] UN GGE 2013 Report, para. 23; UN GGE 2015 Report, paras. 13(c), 28(e).

[39] UN GGE 2013 Report, para. 20; UN GGE 2015 Report, para. 27.

[40] In this regard, they recalled the approach adopted by the International Court of Justice in the *Nuclear Weapons* advisory opinion, para. 39.

[41] *See, e.g., Corfu Channel* judgment, at 44 (separate opinion of Judge Alvarez).

prevention'. The International Group of Experts adopted the term 'due diligence' in light of its prevalent use, but concurred that it can be regarded as synonymous with the term 'obligation of vigilance'. However, the International Group of Experts rejected the use of the term 'obligation of prevention' because the Experts agreed that the due diligence principle does not encompass an obligation to take material preventive steps to ensure that the State's territory is not used in violation of this Rule (a point discussed in Rule 7).

6.   In this regard, the International Group of Experts observed that international law contains certain primary rules, the very aim of which is the prevention of a particular occurrence. The paradigmatic example is the duty to prevent genocide.[42] These obligations are not inferred from the general principle of due diligence, but rather represent separate primary obligations. By contrast, there is no such distinct primary obligation with respect to harmful cyber operations as such. Accordingly, the Rule applies the general principle of due diligence in the cyber context.

7.   This Rule assumes the involvement of at least three parties: (1) the target State of the cyber operation; (2) the territorial State that is the subject of the Rule; and (3) a third party that is the author of the cyber operation. It applies to any third party cyber operation, irrespective of whether it is carried out by a private person, corporation, non-State group, or State.

8.   The obligation of due diligence applies throughout the sovereign territory of the territorial State. It encompasses any cyber infrastructure used for, as well as people carrying out, cyber operations in that territory. Note that the party launching the cyber operation in question may be operating remotely from a third State. As an example, consider a hacker group located in State A that carries out a destructive cyber operation against State B using cyber infrastructure located in State C. If State C knows of said usage and fails to take feasible measures to put an end to the operation, it is in violation of the due diligence principle (see detailed discussion on the knowledge requirement below and on 'feasibility' in Rule 7).

9.   The International Group of Experts agreed that the Rule also extends extraterritorially in two cases. First, a State may be in control of territory abroad without exercising sovereignty over it, as in the case of

---

[42] Genocide Convention, Art. I; *Genocide* judgment, para. 430.

annexation of territory or military occupation.[43] When this is the case, the State has a due diligence obligation *vis-à-vis* cyber infrastructure and activities thereon.

10.   Second, a State must exercise due diligence over government cyber infrastructure that it controls located abroad. The term 'governmental control' is used to indicate that it is the government, as distinct from a private entity, that controls the use of the infrastructure in question. Examples of situations in which the due diligence obligation attaches with respect to government cyber infrastructure located abroad include a national mission network on a military installation in a foreign country, cyber infrastructure aboard sovereign platforms on the high seas or in international airspace, and cyber infrastructure in diplomatic premises.

11.   The Experts cautioned that the notion of control is not necessarily synonymous with that of jurisdiction. For instance, a State may enjoy prescriptive jurisdiction (Rule 10) over the activities of its companies abroad, but lack the ability to control the cyber infrastructure they operate. The key to attachment of the due diligence obligation extraterritorially is that the State is in actual control of the cyber infrastructure in question because it operates said infrastructure or that infrastructure is on territory, premises, or objects it factually controls.

12.   Attachment of the due diligence obligation extraterritorially clearly occurs when a State exercises exclusive control over particular cyber infrastructure or activities. In cases of concurrent control by more than one State, both States bear the obligation of due diligence.[44] An example would be a cyber operations facility run jointly by two States.

13.   The International Group of Experts discussed the issue of whether a State through which data only transits, for instance through a fibre optic cable, shoulders the due diligence obligation. The Experts differentiated this situation from that in which specific cyber infrastructure is set up on a State's territory for malicious purposes, such as that comprising a botnet. They agreed that, as a strict matter of law, the 'transit State' shoulders the due diligence obligation and must act pursuant to Rule 7 when it (1) possesses knowledge (on actual and constructive knowledge, see below) of an offending operation that reaches the requisite threshold of harm and (2) can take feasible measures to effectively terminate it.

---

[43] Articles on Transboundary Harm, Art. 1, para. 12 of commentary.
[44] *See, e.g.,* Articles on Transboundary Harm, Art. 1, para. 11 of commentary.

14.   However, the Experts, taking into account the present state of cyber communications, acknowledged that it is usually unlikely that such 'transit States' would know of, and be able to identify, malicious traffic transiting their cyber infrastructure. The malware signature may be unknown and will not be detected by antivirus software or the malware may use encryption. Additionally, most Internet traffic passes over privately owned cyber infrastructure of Internet service providers (ISP). Even if malware is detected, national law determines whether the ISP has a legal duty to report it to the State's authorities. Nevertheless, the Experts agreed that the legal principle set forth in the previous paragraph correctly reflects the legal obligation borne by transit States. The issue is one of knowledge, not the applicability of the due diligence principle.

15.   With regard to the requisite material harm that must be sustained by the target State for application of this Rule, the International Group of Experts agreed that the Rule embraces all cyber operations that are 'contrary to the rights' (a term drawn from dictum in *Corfu Channel*[45]) of the affected State under international law and have 'serious adverse consequences' (see below). These requirements are cumulative. The term 'contrary to the rights' refers to those cyber operations by a State that breach an international legal obligation owed to the target State. It does not encompass an act that violates only domestic law, as in the case of cross-border criminal activity, although such activity may implicate agreements regarding cooperative law enforcement (Rule 13).

16.   To illustrate, consider a case in which State A launches malware that is controlled by, and reports back to, command and control infrastructure in State B. State B is aware of the operation. The malware manipulates the functioning of a gas pipeline control system in State C, thereby causing an explosion. Since State A has acted unlawfully with respect to State C (see Rule 68 on the use of force), State B must take measures to terminate the operation if it has the capability to do so.

17.   The International Group of Experts agreed that if an operation by a State is not unlawful *vis-à-vis* the target State, it would be incongruent to impose a requirement on the territorial State to put an end to the operation. Therefore, the Experts concluded that the due diligence obligation only applies when the cyber operation in question amounts to an internationally wrongful act (but see discussion of non-State actor

---

[45]   *Corfu Channel* judgment, at 22.

cyber operations below). For instance, if State A monitors State B's governmental databases in an act of cyber espionage by employing cyber infrastructure in State C, State C shoulders no due diligence obligation to terminate State's A's operations because espionage *per se* is not unlawful under international law (Rule 32).

18.   The Experts further agreed that the due diligence obligation only applies to a State when the cyber operation that is being mounted from or through its territory would be unlawful under international law if it had been conducted by the territorial State itself. In cases where the conduct breaches an obligation owed by the acting State to the target State, but not any obligation owed to the target State by the territorial State, imposition of a due diligence obligation on the territorial State would effectively amount to requiring it to enforce legal obligations with respect to which it is not bound. This situation only arises in the case of bi- or multilateral treaty obligations since customary international law binds all States.

19.   Consider a bilateral international agreement that obligates States A and B to refrain from conducting espionage against each other. State A employs cyber infrastructure in State C to engage in espionage against State B in a manner that would not otherwise violate international law. State C is under no obligation to terminate the operation on the basis of this Rule because it is not a Party to the bilateral agreement and espionage *per se* does not violate international law (Rule 32).

20.   As a general matter, States, rather than individuals or private entities, violate international law.[46] Recall, in particular, that the International Group of Experts agreed that only cyber operations conducted by or attributable to States violate a State's sovereignty (Rule 4) or the prohibition of the use of force (Rule 68).

21.   However, the Experts concurred that the due diligence principle extends to cyber operations conducted by non-State actors that, while not violating international law *per se*, nevertheless result in serious adverse consequences and, as discussed below, affect a right of the target State. The Experts noted that in various areas of international law, due diligence obligations have clearly crystallised in light of the growing danger non-State actors pose to States. This has occurred, for instance, in international environmental law based on the likelihood of cross-border environmental damage caused by the activities of private

---

[46] In the regime of international criminal law, which includes war crimes, individuals may also be held liable for violation of international law (Rule 84).

companies.[47] The International Group of Experts identified no convincing rationale for excluding non-State actor cyber operations having serious adverse extraterritorial consequences from the ambit of the State's due diligence obligation. They took particular note of the fact that cyber operations are especially suited to causing harm in other States.

22.   The Experts cautioned that not all harmful non-State cyber operations from one State's territory that cause 'serious adverse consequences' in another's are encompassed in this Rule. As with the cyber operations of States (see above), the due diligence obligation only attaches when a non-State actor engages in conduct that affects a right of the target State, that is, the conduct would, if conducted by the territorial State, breach an obligation that State owes the target State.

23.   For example, if non-State actors launch cyber operations against a State that would, if conducted by a State, constitute prohibited intervention (Rule 66), the territorial State shoulders a due diligence obligation *vis-à-vis* those operations. The same logic would apply to an operation that would violate sovereignty (Rule 4) if conducted by a State. Contrast this situation with, for example, one in which a non-State actor transmits truthful information into another State that has serious adverse consequences for that State's economy. Had a State transmitted the information, it would have breached no obligation owed the target State. Therefore, there is no due diligence obligation in this case.

24.   Or, consider a case in which a private company that is in possession of a State's highly classified documents publishes them online in another State. Even though their publication causes serious adverse consequences for the State whose documents have been released, the State where they have been posted is not obliged to ensure removal of the documents from the Internet because no international law right of the target State is affected. To hold otherwise would create an incongruent situation in which a State would be in breach of its due diligence obligation when non-State actors engage in particular cyber operations from its territory, but not if it had engaged in the same conduct itself.

25.   The precise threshold of harm at which the due diligence principle applies is unsettled in international law.[48] All of the Experts

---

[47] *See, e.g., Trail Smelter* arbitral award, at 1963.

[48] As acknowledged in the *Trail Smelter* arbitration, 'the real difficulty often arises rather when it comes to determine what, *pro subjecta materie*, is deemed to constitute an injurious act.' *Trail Smelter* arbitral award, at 1963.

agreed that the due diligence requirement arises when the situation involves a cyber operation that results in 'serious adverse consequences', although they could identify no bright line threshold for the identification of such consequences. They adopted this standard by analogy from application of the due diligence principle in the context of international environmental law.[49] Some of them supported a lower threshold of application for the Rule, for instance, by proposing the term 'significant' or 'substantial' in lieu of 'serious'.

26.   The International Group of Experts agreed that merely affecting the interests of the target State, as in the case of causing inconvenience, minor disruption, or negligible expense, is not the type of harm envisaged; thus, not every use of a State's territory that produces negative effects for a target State implicates the due diligence principle. Take the case of defacement of an official website of a State's Ministry of Sports that provides information on its national teams by hackers in another State. The cyber operation has not caused sufficient harm to render the territorial State in violation of this Rule should it not engage in measures to put an end to the activity.

27.   Similarly, the due diligence principle is not implicated when a non-State actor, such as a media outlet or a blogger, merely publishes information unfavourable to another State, even if the information is transmitted into that State. This is both because no right of the target State under international law is affected (i.e., had the territorial State engaged in the same action, it would have breached no obligation owed the target State) and because the requisite threshold of harm has not been reached. By contrast, if a website providing critical government services, as with one used for payment of taxes, voting, or providing disaster relief guidance, is defaced in a manner that renders it unusable, the State from which the operations are mounted has a due diligence obligation to terminate the offending operations subject to Rule 7.

28.   The International Group of Experts agreed that there is no requirement that the cyber operation in question result in physical

---

[49] In the context of international environmental law, international case law provides that 'under the principles of international law . . . no State has the right to use or permit the use of its territory in such a manner as to cause injury by fumes in or to the territory of another or the properties or persons therein, when the case is of serious consequence . . .'. *Trail Smelter* arbitral award, at 1965. In that field of law, the damage sustained by the affected State must meet a certain threshold, that, in addition to 'serious', has also been characterised as 'significant' or 'substantial'. Articles on Transboundary Harm, Art. 2, paras. 4, 6 of commentary.

damage to objects or injuries to individuals. In the context of the principle of due diligence, serious adverse consequences could involve, for instance, interference with the operation of critical infrastructure or a major impact on the economy. Consider cyber operations targeting one State that are carried out primarily by hackers based in another that cause the severe disruption of online banking, media, governmental functions, and business. The harm sustained is sufficiently serious to bring the due diligence principle into operation even though no physical damage or injuries resulted.

29.   A particularly troublesome situation with respect to determining whether harm caused constitutes 'serious adverse consequences' is one involving botnets. As an illustration, take the case of a hacker group in one State that uses a botnet located in many other States to conduct operations against another particular State. The operation causes serious adverse consequences for the target State. However, the use of bots located on the territory of any single State does not alone generate serious adverse consequences. This raises the question of whether the individual territorial States concerned are in violation of the principle of due diligence if they fail to take action to terminate such use.

30.   The International Group of Experts was split on the matter. A minority of them followed the approach taken with regard to aggregating cyber incidents for the purpose of the law of self-defence (Rule 71). In that context, a minority of the Experts concluded that the individual operations may be treated as a composite armed attack if conducted by the same originator or by originators acting in concert. By analogy, a minority of Experts suggested that the operations from the States in which the botnet is dispersed can be aggregated such that the requisite severity threshold is reached and every State involved shoulders a due diligence obligation. This approach places emphasis on the target State's perspective; it treats the due diligence principle as one designed to protect the rights of other States. Note that by this approach each State will be assessed individually regarding whether it has exercised the requisite degree of due diligence to terminate the operation of the bots located on its territory.

31.   The majority of the International Group of Experts, however, suggested that aggregation is inappropriate. For them, the due diligence principle derives from the sovereign prerogatives of the territorial State. In the view of these Experts, it would create an imbalance between the right to control territory and the duty to ensure it is not used to harm other States to impose a due diligence obligation in such situations. For

them, it would be incongruent to assert that the sovereignty of the territorial State must yield to the target State's rights in cases in which its connection to the harm might be slight. Moreover, they suggested that interpreting the due diligence principle in the minority's fashion would mean that States could be held responsible for an internationally wrongful act based primarily upon the omissions of other States (i.e., those of the other States from which the botnet is operated).

32.   The International Group of Experts took the position that so long as the harm suffered by a State meets the threshold set forth in this Rule, it is irrelevant where that harm manifests. Consider a case in which State A stores government data that is required for the performance of inherently governmental functions (Rule 4) on servers in State B. A non-State group operating in State C conducts cyber operations against the servers, thereby corrupting State A's data. State C's due diligence obligation attaches *vis-à-vis* State A because its territory is being used to harm another State.

33.   The seriousness of the particular consequences can be mitigated to a greater or lesser degree by the underlying circumstances. This is so because the due diligence obligation is by nature flexible. It is always partly dependent upon the relevant circumstances. In particular, the activities of the State claiming a breach of its rights are relevant.

34.   For instance, assume a State conducts an extremely harmful cyber operation against a private entity in another State; the operation constitutes a violation of the latter State's sovereignty. The target State does not respond with countermeasures (Rule 20) because it lacks the capacity to do so, fears escalation, or the situation is unfolding too rapidly for the State's organs to act decisively. Faced with the State's inaction, the private entity hacks back against the first State in order to make it terminate its harmful cyber operations. Because non-State actors are not entitled to take countermeasures (Rule 24), there is no underlying international law basis for the private entity's operations. This being so, the first State now claims that the second State is in breach of its due diligence obligation to ensure its territory is not used for purposes that cause serious adverse consequences for other States, that is, the cyber operations conducted by the private entity. Accordingly, the first State begins to take what it now claims are countermeasures in the form of further harmful cyber operations against the second State, purportedly to force it to terminate the private entity's defensive operations in accordance with its due diligence obligation.

35.   Assuming for the sake of analysis that the territorial State had a due diligence obligation to take action with respect to the private entity's actions, its failure to do so could itself be characterised as a countermeasure in response to the first State's initial wrongful cyber operations. The first State's further operations would constitute, therefore, an internationally wrongful act. Moreover, the International Group of Experts agreed that the fact that the first State initiated the exchange in a manner that constituted an internationally wrongful act precludes it from claiming a right to take countermeasures. This is because any serious adverse consequences it is suffering are essentially of its own making. The Experts concurred that States may not benefit from their unlawful conduct, nor may they take actions to the detriment of other States in response to activities that would not have occurred but for such conduct.

36.   The application of the due diligence principle does not depend on whether the targeted cyber infrastructure is governmental or private in nature. As an example, if an oil company based in one State launches a destructive cyber operation against a private competitor based in another State, the State in which the former is based is in violation of this Rule if it knows of the operation, fails to take feasible measures to stop it, and the consequences reach the requisite severity threshold.

37.   Knowledge is a constitutive element in the application of this Rule. Obviously, the Rule applies if the territorial State has actual knowledge of the fact that its territory is being used for hostile cyber operations against other States.[50] A State will be regarded as having actual knowledge if, for example, State organs such as intelligence agencies have detected a cyber operation originating from its territory or if it has received credible information that a harmful cyber operation is underway from its territory.

38.   The Experts acknowledged that it may be extremely difficult for the target State to demonstrate that the territorial State knew its territory was being used in said manner and nevertheless disregarded that knowledge. Although this practical difficulty may provide uncooperative territorial States plausible deniability, it does not render the legal obligation moot.[51]

[50] *See, e.g.,* IAN BROWNLIE, BROWNLIE'S PRINCIPLES OF PUBLIC INTERNATIONAL LAW 543 (James Crawford ed., 8th edn, 2012); *Corfu Channel* judgment, at 71 (dissenting opinion of Judge Krylov); *Corfu Channel* judgment, at 44–5 (separate opinion of Judge Alvarez).
[51] Recall that in the *Corfu Channel* judgment, Albania denied that it had had knowledge of the minefield laid in its territorial waters. The International Court of Justice nevertheless

39.   The International Group of Experts agreed that knowledge encompasses constructive knowledge for the purposes of this Rule.[52] As a general matter, if the factual circumstances are such that a State in the normal course of events would have become aware of said use, it is appropriate to constructively attribute knowledge to the State. Accordingly, a State breaches its due diligence obligation if it is in fact unaware of the cyber operations in question, but objectively should have known that its territory was being used for the operation.

40.   An array of factors may influence a determination that the territorial State should have known of the cyber operations in question. For instance, when a State's governmental cyber infrastructure is being exploited by another State or non-State actor for an operation, the 'should have known' standard is more likely to be met than in the case of the use of private infrastructure.[53] Similarly, ascribing constructive knowledge is more appropriate when malware and vulnerabilities that are publicly known, such as the Heartbleed vulnerability discovered in 2014, are employed, and when involving cyber operations that are generally always detected, such as DDoS attacks that significantly increase bandwidth usage compared to normal usage.

41.   That said, the difficulty of discovering certain hostile uses of a State's governmental cyber infrastructure may make it unreasonable to assert constructive knowledge. As an example, a third party in the territorial State who is conducting a cyber operation against a target State may employ complex, previously unknown malware when exploiting the territorial State's governmental cyber infrastructure. If it is unreasonable to expect the territorial State to have known of the operation in the attendant circumstances and to have been able to terminate it, this Rule will not have been breached.

42.   The International Group of Experts agreed, however, that a constructive knowledge standard does not levy, in itself, any obligation

---

concluded that in the circumstances Albania 'must have known' of the mining and that thereby the knowledge requirement was satisfied. *Corfu Channel* judgment, at 20.

[52]   In support of the constructive knowledge standard, see *Corfu Channel* judgment, at 44 (separate opinion of Judge Alvarez); *Genocide* judgment, para. 432. The International Group of Experts acknowledged that in international law generally, the constructive knowledge standard is somewhat controversial.

[53]   *See, e.g.*, Judge Alvarez's separate opinion in the *Corfu Channel* judgment, in which he argued that 'every State is considered . . . as having a *duty* to have known . . . of prejudicial acts committed in parts of its territory where local authorities are installed . . .'. *Corfu Channel* judgment, at 44 (separate opinion of Judge Alvarez) (emphasis in original).

to take preventive measures (Rule 7). In particular, this Rule is not to be interpreted as including a requirement of monitoring or taking other steps designed to alert authorities to misuse of cyber infrastructure located on the State's territory. Rather, States must act as a reasonable State would in same or similar circumstances. If the factual circumstances are such that a similarly situated and equipped State in the normal course of events would have discovered the use of the cyber infrastructure in question, it is appropriate to conclude that the knowledge criterion is satisfied.

43.   Failure to exercise due diligence must be distinguished from 'aiding or assisting' (Rule 18) another State's cyber operations. For instance, a State that makes its cyber infrastructure available for another State's use with a view to facilitating the commission of an internationally wrongful act by the latter is aiding or assisting. One that merely fails to act when another State operates from its territory, by contrast, is responsible for breach of its due diligence obligation. The distinction between aiding or assisting and a breach of this Rule is that the former involves commission, whereas the latter is based on an omission.[54]

44.   One must also be careful to distinguish application of the due diligence principle from the international wrongfulness of the particular cyber operation that has been mounted from, or employed cyber infrastructure on, the State's territory. For instance, if State A launches a destructive cyber operation against State B using command and control cyber infrastructure located in State C, State C may be in violation of this Rule, whereas State A has potentially violated State B's sovereignty (Rule 4).

45.   If the third party's cyber operation is attributable to the territorial State under the law of State responsibility (Rules 17–18), this Rule is not implicated. As an example, if hackers in one State are operating under the effective control of that State (Rule 17) and direct their destructive cyber operations against another State, the hackers' cyber operations are attributable to the territorial State. Although the territorial State will have committed the internationally wrongful act of (at least) an attributable violation of the second State's sovereignty, it is not in breach of its due diligence obligation.

46.   In situations involving international armed conflict, application of this Rule is without prejudice to the obligation of neutral States *vis-à-*

---

[54] *Genocide* judgment, para. 432.

vis the activities of belligerents on neutral territory or involving cyber infrastructure located there (Rule 152).

Rule 7 – Compliance with the due diligence principle

The principle of due diligence requires a State to take all measures that are feasible in the circumstances to put an end to cyber operations that affect a right of, and produce serious adverse consequences for, other States.

1.   The International Group of Experts agreed that once the territorial State acquires knowledge (Rule 6) of the fact that its territory is being used in a manner that causes serious adverse consequences for another State with respect to a right under international law, the former must take all reasonably available measures to stop that cyber operation. However, as will be explained, the precise scope of action required by the due diligence principle is unsettled.

2.   The due diligence principle is a legal obligation that is violated by omission. In this regard, omission not only encompasses inaction, but also the taking of ineffective or insufficient measures when other more appropriate measures are feasible, that is, reasonably available and practicable. For instance, a State that stands idle as cyber infrastructure on its territory is being used by a terrorist group to undertake a cyber operation against another State is in violation of this Rule, as is a State that, upon credible notification by another State that such activity is being carried out, fails to exhaust feasible measures to terminate it.

3.   The majority of the International Group of Experts was of the view that this Rule also applies to specific cyber operations that have not yet been launched, but with respect to which material steps to execute the operation are being taken and a reasonable State would conclude it will be carried out.[55] Consider a case in which an intelligence agency has infiltrated a closed online forum used by a terrorist group that is based on its territory. The agency discovers that the group has installed destructive malware in another State's stock exchange cyber infrastructure that it is about to activate. In this situation, the territorial State must act to stop the cyber operation because it is highly likely that it will eventuate. The key in such situations is that the State has reliable knowledge that its

---

[55] *Genocide* judgment, para. 431.

territory is going to be used for a cyber operation against another State and a material step has been taken to effectuate it.

4.   By contrast, the minority opined that the obligation accrues only at the point that the harmful operation is actually underway. These Experts were concerned that to hold otherwise would impose an unreasonable burden on territorial States. They were also concerned that cyber activities on a State's territory might be misinterpreted as material steps and, if the territorial State fails to take action to terminate them, it could be subject to, for instance, countermeasures (Rule 20). They argued that such a situation would be destabilising.

5.   The International Group of Experts discussed a situation in which a territorial State has gained knowledge of an internationally wrongful cyber operation at the requisite level of severity being conducted from its territory against another State, but the target State is unaware of the operation. This scenario raises, in particular, sensitive issues pertaining to intelligence sharing. The International Group of Experts acknowledged that territorial States may be hesitant to inform target States of the specifics of the operation because doing so might reveal their cyber and intelligence capabilities.

6.   The Experts agreed that the territorial State must act to terminate the wrongful operation, but that it is at that State's discretion to choose the means to comply with this Rule. If, for instance, it can stop the harmful cyber operation by arresting the actors and compelling them to uninstall the malware, infiltrate the terrorist group's computers and terminate the operation itself, or anonymously or via a third party inform the target State of the particular cyber operation, thereby allowing that State to take remedial action, it has fulfilled its obligation under this Rule. The Experts noted that the fact that the territorial State's domestic legislation may set limits on intelligence sharing with other States does not excuse its inaction in stopping harmful cyber operations emanating from its territory.

7.   The International Group of Experts carefully considered whether the due diligence principle imposes a requirement to take preventive measures, such as hardening one's cyber infrastructure, to reduce general, as distinct from particularised, risks of future cyber operations falling within the purview of this Rule. It rejected the premise of a requirement to take purely preventive measures of a general nature. The Experts drew support from the *Genocide* judgment, according to which 'a State's obligation to prevent, and the corresponding duty to act, arise at the instant that the state learns of . . . the existence of a serious risk that the act [of

genocide] will be committed'.[56] The International Court of Justice did not assert that a general duty to prevent genocide exists, but instead took the position that the duty to prevent genocide exists *vis-à-vis* each specific instance of an act of genocide. In other words, the term 'prevent' in this context means 'stop'.

8.   The Experts suggested that given the difficulty of mounting comprehensive and effective defences against all possible cyber threats, it would be unreasonable to assert that an obligation of prevention exists in the cyber context. Such a requirement would impose an undue burden on States, one for which there is no current basis in either the extant law or current State practice. They noted that States have not indicated that they believe such a legal obligation exists with respect to cyber operations, either by taking preventive measures on this basis or by condemning the failure of other States to adopt such measures. The Experts further noted that the obligations of States under international human rights law could run counter to such a duty, depending on how it was fulfilled (see, *inter alia*, discussion on privacy in Rule 35).

9.   Finally, since knowledge is a requirement under this Rule, it would be, in the view of the International Group of Experts, contradictory to expand the Rule to hypothetical future cyber operations. A State cannot know (whether actually or constructively) of a cyber operation that has yet to be decided upon by the actor. Extending this Rule to a general duty of prevention would accordingly render the knowledge requirement – which all the Experts agreed was necessary for the breach of the obligation – moot.

10.   In light of their rejection of an obligation to take preventive measures, the Experts concurred that a State is not required to monitor cyber activities on its territory. That said, should a State elect to monitor cyber activities on its territory, the fact that it is doing so may bear on whether it has knowledge of any cyber operations directed at another State from its territory.

11.   The International Group of Experts acknowledged the contrary view, which none of them held, that the due diligence obligation extends to situations in which the relevant harmful acts are merely possible. By it, States must take reasonable measures to prevent them from emanating from their territory.[57] This view is based in part on the existence of an obligation to take preventive measures in the context of transboundary

---

[56]   *Genocide* judgment, para. 431.
[57]   *Corfu Channel* judgment, at 44 (separate opinion of Judge Alvarez).

environmental harm.[58] Moreover, in light of the nature of cyber activities, preventive measures are arguably prudent. For instance, the speed of cyber operations often makes an act of mitigation less effective than the successful prevention thereof.

12.   According to this position, a State must take feasible preventive measures that are proportionate to the risk of potential harm. They have to take account of technological and scientific developments, as well as the unique circumstances of each case.[59] Examples include introducing information security policies, setting up CERTs, and adopting appropriate domestic legislation requiring companies to report cyber incidents in order to be able to generate accurate threat assessments.

13.   Although the Experts rejected the argument that the due diligence obligation requires preventive measures, they noted that if such an approach were to be adopted, it would be unclear when the obligation would be breached. One possibility is that a breach takes place when a target State is placed at the risk of harm by virtue of the territorial State not having taken appropriate measures to prevent harmful cyber operations being mounted from or through its territory. Another is that although the due diligence principle requires States to take appropriate preventive measures, they cannot be held responsible for having failed to do so unless and until the target State actually suffers the requisite harm.[60]

14.   The International Group of Experts was divided over situations in which a State foresees with reasonable certainty that cyber infrastructure on its territory, having previously been so used, will again be employed for harmful cyber operations directed at another State, but fails to act. For instance, if particular cyber infrastructure has been repeatedly exploited for the purposes of conducting harmful cyber operations against other States, it may be reasonable to conclude that it will be so used again. Similarly, if a particular group has repeatedly mounted such operations, it may be highly likely that the group will do so in the future. The question is whether the due diligence obligation has been breached by the State's inaction in taking measures to preclude the anticipated cyber operations.

15.   A majority of the International Group of Experts took the position that imposing an obligation to act in such situations is consistent

---

[58] Articles on Transboundary Harm, Art. 3.
[59] SHAW'S INTERNATIONAL LAW, at 624–625.
[60] Articles on State Responsibility, Art. 14(3).

with the object and purpose of this Rule. Since the cyber operations in question are not speculative, and a reasonable State would conclude they will in fact be launched if it fails to act, they may be analogised to on-going operations. The minority was of the view that a requirement to take remedial measures is effectively a requirement of prevention (see discussion above) and therefore does not attach.

16.   With respect to the scope of the measures required by this Rule, the Experts agreed that the territorial State must use all feasible, that is, reasonably available, means within its sovereign prerogatives that a reasonably acting State in the same or similar circumstances would employ (i.e., undertake so-called 'best efforts'). The feasibility of particular measures is always contextual. Developed States will often be more capable of stopping harmful cyber operations that emanate from their territory than developing States. Feasibility depends, *inter alia*, on the technical wherewithal of the State concerned, the intellectual and financial resources at its disposal, the State's institutional capacity to take measures, and the extent of its control over cyber infrastructure located on its territory.[61] To illustrate, if a territorial State is informed by the target State that severe cyber operations are originating from certain IP addresses that have been allocated to the territorial State, it is reasonable for the territorial State to take measures to block those IP addresses since nearly all States have the ability to take such steps.

17.   By contrast, a State may lack the ability to respond effectively to highly complex and dynamic cyber operations involving cyber infrastructure on its territory. If this is the case, it will not be in breach of its due diligence obligation, as remedial measures are not feasible. Note, however, that if the State lacks the required capability to stop the on-going harmful cyber operations itself, a reasonably feasible measure might be to hire a private company to perform that task.

18.   In considering feasibility, it is essential to apply the Rule in a measured fashion. Consider the case of a terrorist group that is conducting harmful cyber operations from a State's territory against another State. The latter is unaware of the operations. It may be more prudent to monitor the activities to gain further intelligence than to immediately terminate them. Indeed, the benefits for the target State of delayed action may outweigh those of immediate action because the group's actions can

---

[61] *See, e.g., Genocide* judgment, paras. 430–431; *Tehran Hostages* judgment, paras. 63–68; *Armed Activities* judgment, para. 301.

be more effectively and definitively foiled once the territorial State can leverage the intelligence acquired during the period of delay.

19.   This Rule applies if the relevant remedial cyber operations can be undertaken by State organs or by individuals under State control. The International Group of Experts also agreed that if a remedial action can only be performed by a private entity, such as a private Internet service provider, the State is obliged to use all means at its disposal to require that entity to take the actions necessary to terminate the offending activity.

20.   It may be that the private entity or individual in control of cyber infrastructure being used by a State or non-State actor to conduct harmful cyber operations abroad refuses to cooperate fully with the territorial State in putting an end to the operations. The Experts took the position that such a lack of cooperation does not preclude the wrongfulness of the territorial State's due diligence breach. Rather, the State must exhaust all feasible means to secure the cooperation of the person or entity involved, so long as such measures are consistent with international law. It is only if a State has done so and is still unable to secure the cooperation necessary to terminate the harmful operations that it will not be in breach of the principle.

21.   The International Group of Experts carefully considered the issue of whether a State must establish the legal conditions to be able to comply with its due diligence obligation, or at least remove any legal obstacles to said ability. It concluded that no such obligation exists as such, although many States have done so and international agreements sometimes require States Parties to adopt legislative measures that enable them to address cyber operations that constitute crimes.[62] Nor is there any obligation under the due diligence principle for the State to prosecute those engaging in the underlying cyber operations; rather, the obligation is limited to taking feasible measures to terminate the operations.

22.   Additionally, the Experts agreed that domestic legal limitations do not justify a State's failure to comply with its due diligence obligation. For instance, if a State's domestic legal system requires a court order to take the necessary measures to terminate the harmful cyber operation, an inability to obtain such an order does not preclude the wrongfulness of the State's failure to terminate the harmful operation

---

[62] *See, e.g.*, Convention on Cybercrime, Art. 14.

unless such inability is based on compliance with international law (as in the case of international human rights law, Chapter 6).

23. That said, the Experts concurred that, as a practical matter, States should take steps to ensure measures they might have to take to respond to such operations are available under their domestic law. As an example, a State could pass legislation empowering it to require Internet service providers to take down botnet command and control servers in the event such servers are set up on its territory. Such legislation would permit the State to react promptly and effectively to comply with this Rule.

24. The requirement to terminate cyber operations encompassed by this Rule is complicated by the nature of harmful cyber operations, especially time and space compression and the fact that they are often specific to a particular vulnerability or system. If a State has diligently exhausted all feasible measures to stop harmful cyber activities from its territory, but its attempts prove futile and the target State nevertheless suffers harm, the territorial State will not have violated this Rule. In that the due diligence principle is an obligation of conduct, not of result, it does not demand that the territorial State always be successful in bringing to an end harmful uses of its territory; it only requires that the State act diligently in its efforts to do so. However, if the lack of success is the result of the State's failure to exhaust reasonably available measures to terminate harmful cyber operations, it is in breach of this Rule.[63] For example, the territorial State may not act rapidly enough to preclude the harm that is being caused by the cyber operations from its territory. If it could have reacted more quickly in the attendant circumstances, it is in breach.

25. There may be circumstances in which it is not reasonable for a State to act to preclude harm to another State from cyber operations originating from its territory. For example, the territorial State may know that a harmful cyber operation is being prepared and will be launched from its territory against the target State. However, because it has not identified the attack's exact signature and timing, the only effective option may be to isolate the network that will be used to launch the attack. Doing so will result in an unreasonable 'self-denial' of service to the territorial State. Or consider the case of a large botnet on the State's territory that is being used to conduct a DDoS operation against cyber infrastructure in another State. In order to terminate the operation,

---

[63] Articles on State Responsibility, Art. 12, paras. 11–12 of commentary; *Genocide* judgment, para. 430.

it would be necessary to shut down a number of essential networks on the State's territory. In such situations, the nature, scale, and scope of the (potential) harm to both States must be assessed to determine whether a remedial measure is required. The test in such circumstances is that of reasonableness.

26.   It may sometimes happen that the territorial State is unable to terminate the use of its territory, but other able States are willing to assist. This raises the question of whether the territorial State bears an obligation to request assistance from other States in such cases. The International Group of Experts answered this question in the negative. The due diligence principle derives from the principle of sovereignty. It only creates obligations that fall within the ambit of the territorial State's sovereign prerogatives. In other words, a State need only engage in actions that are incident to its own exercise of sovereignty. Thus, whereas a State may seek external assistance, it is not legally obligated to do so. In particular, the Experts took note of some practice in CERT-to-CERT and other forms of cooperation, but were unable to point to *opinio juris* accompanying such practice.

27.   The International Group of Experts considered the situation in which use of a State's territory is underway, but the operation fails. Consider the case of a State that knows hackers on its territory are sharing instructions for a DDoS operation directed against another State in an online forum. The State does nothing to thwart the operation. However, the DDoS operation fails because only a few people participate in it. The Experts concluded that the territorial State has not committed an internationally wrongful act by breaching its due diligence obligation because the intended target State suffered no actual harm.

28.   If a State is unwilling to terminate harmful cyber operations encompassed by the due diligence principle as opposed to unable to do so, the injured State may be entitled to resort to countermeasures (Rule 20) based on the territorial State's failure to comply with this Rule. See Rule 23 as to how the proportionality of the countermeasure is assessed in such situations.

29.   With regard to use of cyber infrastructure or the conduct of cyber operations from the territory of a neutral State during an international armed conflict, see Rule 153.

3

Jurisdiction

Rule 8 – Jurisdiction (general principle)

Subject to limitations set forth in international law, a State may exercise territorial and extraterritorial jurisdiction over cyber activities.

1. Jurisdiction refers to the competence of States to regulate persons, objects, and conduct under their national law, within the limits imposed by international law.[64] It grants States authority over the full scope of civil, administrative, and criminal matters. Such jurisdiction may be territorial (Rule 9) or extraterritorial (Rules 10–11) in nature. The Rules in this Chapter are limited to public international law as it relates to the exercise of jurisdiction involving domestic public law, especially criminal law. No effort has been made to examine private international law issues regarding civil jurisdiction. See also the discussion of jurisdiction with respect to space objects (Rule 59), aircraft (Rules 5 and 55), and vessels (Rule 5, chapeau to Chapter 8, and Rule 50).

2. The International Group of Experts agreed that, in principle, cyber activities and the individuals who engage in them are subject to the same jurisdictional prerogatives and limitations as any other form of activity.

3. States possess three types of jurisdictional competence: (1) prescriptive (legislative) jurisdiction, which concerns the authority of a State to enact laws and regulations relating to a particular matter or conduct; (2) enforcement (executive) jurisdiction, which deals with the authority of a State to apply and enforce its laws and regulations through executive

---

[64] *See, e.g.*, The Draft Convention on Research in International Law of the Harvard Law School, 29 Am. J. Int'l L. 435, 466 (Supp. 1935); Restatement (Third), Part IV; Mann 1964, at 1; Mann 1984, at 19; Oppenheim's International Law, at 456; Shaw's International Law, at 469.

or administrative action, such as law enforcement; and (3) judicial (adjudicatory) jurisdiction, which refers to the competence of a State's national courts to regulate disputes that come before them.[65] The extent to which a State possesses the three forms of competence differs, as discussed below.

4.   Jurisdiction is closely related to the principle of State sovereignty (Rule 1). Since sovereignty is predominantly territorial under international law, the most common basis for the exercise of jurisdiction is territoriality. Under international law, a State enjoys full territorial jurisdiction (prescriptive, enforcement, and judicial) over persons and objects located on its territory, as well as conduct occurring there (Rule 9).

5.   The scope of extraterritorial jurisdictional competence over cyber activities and the persons who engage in them, as distinct from jurisdiction based on territoriality, depends, *inter alia*, upon the type of jurisdiction being exercised, that is, whether the jurisdiction in question is prescriptive, enforcement, or judicial in nature.

6.   Prescriptive jurisdiction over persons engaged in cyber activities abroad, cyber infrastructure located abroad, or cyber-related conduct taking place or having effects beyond a State's territory, must be grounded upon one of the generally recognised bases for extraterritorial jurisdiction. These bases are discussed in Rule 10.

7.   The existence of multiple bases of prescriptive jurisdiction can lead to two or more States having concurrent jurisdiction over the same cyber activity. Consider the case of nationals of one State located in another State who are carrying out cyber operations. The first State enjoys extraterritorial prescriptive jurisdiction on the basis of nationality (Rule 10), whereas the second does so on the basis of territoriality (Rule 9). The fact that both States have criminalised the conduct in question is appropriate under international law. The same result would attend a situation in which nationals of multiple States constitute a hacker cell that operates from a single State. That State enjoys prescriptive jurisdiction on the basis of territoriality, whereas all of the States of which the hackers are nationals do so based on nationality.

8.   Extraterritorial enforcement jurisdiction is more limited than extraterritorial prescriptive jurisdiction, for States generally do not

---

[65] *See, e.g.,* Restatement (Third), Sec. 401; OPPENHEIM'S INTERNATIONAL LAW, at 456–458.

possess enforcement authority outside their territory. Rather, such jurisdiction is an exclusive attribute of sovereignty and, as such, may only be exercised extraterritorially with the consent of the State in which the jurisdiction is to be exercised or pursuant to a specific allocation of authority under international law (Rule 11).

9.   As a general matter, the substantive scope of judicial jurisdiction over persons engaged in cyber activities and related cyber infrastructure is co-existent with that of prescriptive jurisdiction. In other words, a State enjoys judicial competence over any person, object, or conduct regarding which it may prescribe laws or regulations, subject to any immunity from judicial process (in this regard, see, for instance, the discussion in Rule 44 on the immunities diplomatic agents and consular officers enjoy).

10.   However, with the exception of the exercise of judicial competence by an occupying power during military occupation under the law of armed conflict (Rule 147), the actual exercise of judicial jurisdiction over persons engaged in cyber activities may only physically take place on the territory of another State with the consent of that State. As an example, States may conduct overseas courts-martial of their military personnel for cyber-related criminal activity on the territory of another State if so provided for in a status of forces agreement.

11.   As to the exercise of judicial jurisdiction from a State's own territory over natural or legal persons abroad, courts may sometimes act even though the person concerned is *in absentia*. This is particularly important in the cyber context in light of the high likelihood of criminal activity being mounted from abroad. However, such cases are rare and without prejudice to applicable international human rights law. In this regard, it must be noted that in many States, judicial proceedings *in absentia* are neither permissible nor feasible due to domestic human rights requirements and procedural safeguards. Moreover, as a practical matter, the effective exercise of judicial jurisdiction over individuals involved in cyber activities usually depends on the presence of the parties before the court or other adjudicatory body.

12.   With respect to the exercise of judicial jurisdiction over cyber-related crimes under international, as distinct from domestic, law, the issue of whether suspected perpetrators must be physically present in the State's territory before criminal proceedings may be initiated against them remains unsettled. For a discussion of crimes under

international law, see Rule 10 on extraterritorial prescriptive jurisdiction, as well as Rule 84 on individual criminal responsibility for war crimes.

13. International agreements between States may distribute enforcement or judicial jurisdiction authority. This is so, for instance, with status of forces agreements, which may allocate exclusive, primary, or concurrent judicial jurisdiction with respect to cyber-related acts that violate the law of both the sending and receiving States.[66] Beyond such agreements, there is no formal hierarchy of judicial jurisdictional claims under international law.

14. In practice, however, the State where an offence occurs is normally accorded primary jurisdiction. In some cases, it will usually be a matter of which State has the closest connection to, or is most seriously affected by, the cyber-related conduct. In addition, other considerations, such as the location of the suspected perpetrator and the existence or lack of an extradition treaty can influence which State will be most likely to exercise judicial jurisdiction. Treaties may address this situation. For instance, Article 22(5) of the Convention on Cybercrime provides that: 'When more than one Party claims jurisdiction over an alleged offence established in accordance with this Convention, the Parties involved shall, where appropriate, consult with a view to determining the most appropriate jurisdiction for prosecution.'

15. The International Group of Experts acknowledged that cyber activities pose a number of challenges to the rational and equitable exercise of jurisdiction. This is due, *inter alia*, to their pervasiveness, the fact that they can originate from anywhere on the globe, the relative speed and ease of crossing a State's borders in cyberspace, and the possibility of generating effects in multiple States. These factors could lead any number of States to attempt to assert different types of jurisdiction over particular cyber activities, thereby generating confusion and friction between States. To illustrate, a criminal who is a national of State A, but located in State B, may conduct a cyber operation against a web server in State C in order to steal the bank information of individuals located in State D. In this case, all four States may invoke one or more types of jurisdiction. Hence, with regard to cyber activities, international cooperation in law enforcement is especially important (Rule 13).

---

[66] THE HANDBOOK OF THE LAW OF VISITING FORCES 110 (Dieter Fleck, ed. 2001).

Rule 9 – Territorial jurisdiction

A State may exercise territorial jurisdiction over:

(a) cyber infrastructure and persons engaged in cyber activities on its territory;
(b) cyber activities originating in, or completed on, its territory; or
(c) cyber activities having a substantial effect in its territory.

1.   The primary basis for the exercise of jurisdiction is, as stated in Rule 8, territorial. Territorial jurisdiction is a fundamental attribute of the principle of sovereignty (Rule 1). Accordingly, *lit.* (a) confirms that, within the scope provided under international law, every State is entitled to exercise all three forms of jurisdictional competence (prescriptive, enforcement, judicial; see Rule 8) over persons and objects located on its territory. Indeed, States do so on a regular basis. Thus, territorial jurisdiction applies to persons, natural and legal, involved in cyber activities that are present within a State's territory and to cyber infrastructure[67] and data that are located on that territory.

2.   The International Group of Experts agreed with regard to transnational cyber operations that if cyber infrastructure in an intermediary State constitutes an integral facet of an operation, that State will enjoy jurisdiction based on the territorial principle. For instance, if individuals in State A deploy a botnet by taking control of cyber infrastructure in State B in order to conduct a DDoS operation against systems in State C, all three States will possess jurisdictional competence. The Experts agreed that the use of such compromised cyber infrastructure was not of *de minimis* character and therefore would be encompassed within *lit.* (a).

3.   However, the International Group of Experts was split with respect to whether a State may exercise jurisdiction on the basis of the territorial principle when there is only minimal connection with cyber infrastructure on that State's territory. In the cyber context, this situation is most likely to occur when data simply transits a State's cyber infrastructure. In this regard, the Experts noted that, given the nature of the Internet, data will often traverse the territory of many States *en route* to its intended destination.

4.   Consider the case of a cyber operation that is initiated in State A. The data transits a router in State B that is monitored by State B in order to exact effects in State C. Some of the Experts held the view that

---

[67] UN GGE 2013 Report, para. 20; UN GGE 2015 Report, paras. 27, 28(a).

although the operation was launched from State A (see *lit.* (b)), the connection between the operation and the infrastructure on State B's territory is *de minimis*, as are the relevant interests of State B. Therefore, State B does not enjoy, for instance, criminal jurisdiction over the activity, particularly in light of the jurisdictional interests of the States where the operation originated and concluded. Other Experts suggested that although State B should yield to the jurisdiction of the other States, it is not precluded as a matter of law from exercising criminal jurisdiction to prohibit malicious data transiting its territory. In that the operation involved cyber infrastructure located on its territory, its interest *vis-à-vis* it is not *de minimis*. Note that territoriality is not the sole basis for the exercise of jurisdiction. In the case of mere transit States, for example, the transit State may have jurisdiction over the matter on the basis of the nationality of the actor (Rule 10).

5.   *Lit.* (b) reflects the fact that a State is also entitled to exercise territorial jurisdiction over cyber activities that are initiated or completed on its territory.[68] 'Subjective' territorial jurisdiction will apply to any cyber activity originating in a State's territory, notwithstanding whether it has an extraterritorial effect. The exercise of 'objective' territorial jurisdiction in relation to a cyber activity that originates outside a State's territory, but is completed within it, is appropriate if the act concerned is directed against persons or objects located there, or is otherwise intended to culminate in the State.[69]

6.   As an illustration, take the case of a terrorist group located in one State's territory directing cyber operations against the electrical distribution grid of another State, thereby causing a widespread blackout. The operations are subject to the full jurisdiction (prescriptive, enforcement, and judicial) of the State where they commenced on the basis of the subjective territorial principle because they originated on that State's territory. In that the operations manifested on cyber infrastructure located in the other State's territory, they are equally subject to its jurisdiction on the basis of objective territoriality. Or suppose operatives of a State A's intelligence agency undertake cyber operations from State B that are designed to obtain restricted data relating to the production of

---

[68] *Lotus* judgment, at 23.
[69] *See, e.g.,* MANN 1964, at 45–47 (explaining the requirement that for an act originating abroad to be subject to jurisdiction it must have a substantial connection with or impact upon the State purporting to exercise jurisdiction); Restatement (Third), Sec. 402(1)(a); OPPENHEIM'S INTERNATIONAL LAW, at 458–461.

military equipment by a private corporation of State C. The operation involves using a rootkit attack to gain privileged access to the corporation's files stored on servers in C's territory. State B has jurisdiction based on subjective territoriality, whereas State C enjoys jurisdiction on the basis of objective territoriality.

7.   In some cases, multiple States may be entitled to exercise objective territorial jurisdiction, as when malware is directed at networks in more than one State with the intention of culminating in each of them.

8.   Laws and regulations promulgated pursuant to the prescriptive authority of a State may encompass cyber operations intended to be completed on that State's territory, but that prove unsuccessful. For instance, in the terrorism example above, if the electrical distribution grid's intrusion prevention system effectively foils the cyber operation, that fact may have no bearing on whether the target State enjoys jurisdiction to prescribe the laws in question.

9.   The use of digital networks and other factors can render it unclear where or when a specific offence started or ended. Cyber technologies enable offenders to structure offences to avoid strict jurisdictional templates or conceal points of origin or destination. Establishing jurisdiction therefore can prove difficult. As a result, jurisdictional rules have moved towards models in which any substantial connection between the offence and the territory of a State may serve as the basis for jurisdiction.[70]

10.   This 'effects doctrine' is reflected in *lit.* (c). It deals with acts, including cyber operations, that do not originate, conclude, or materially take place in the State in question, but have effects therein.

11.   Unqualified application of the effects doctrine in order to assert jurisdiction has been the frequent cause of friction between States, the classic example being when a State purports to exercise jurisdiction over economic or financial activity conducted by foreign nationals outside its territory, but that has an impact on its economy. Furthermore, the International Group of Experts acknowledged a view, which none of them held, that jurisdiction over a crime requires that a constituent element of that crime occurs within the territory or has some other territorial nexus.[71] Nevertheless, the effects doctrine is increasingly accepted, albeit subject to a number of conditions to guard against over-

---

[70] In Canada, see *Libman* v. *The Queen* [1985], 2 SCR 178; in the UK, see *R.* v. *Smith (Wallace Duncan)* [2004] QB 1418. Much of this trend, at least in common law countries, traces back to the dissent of Diplock LJ in *Treacy* v. *DPP* [1971] AC 573 at 561–562.

[71] *Libman* v. *The Queen*, [1985], 2 SCR 178 (Can.), para. 74.

breadth.[72] The Experts agreed that it may now reasonably be said to reflect customary international law.

12.   The effects doctrine is of particular import in the cyber context because cyber means lend themselves to causing effects in States where the operations in question neither originate nor culminate, as with a cyber operation from one State against a bank in another that has significant impact on depositors in a third. Moreover, a single cyber operation can generate effects in many countries. In such cases, the threshold for the uncontested exercise of jurisdiction is somewhat higher than in those captured in *lit.* (a) and (b). The Experts agreed that these situations must be addressed on a case-by-case basis.

13.   While the conditions imposed on the effects doctrine are not fully settled in international law and the doctrine itself remains some-what controversial, the International Group of Experts agreed that if a State exercises effects-based jurisdiction with respect to cyber-related activities and the persons who engage in them, it must do so in a reasonable fashion and with due regard for the interests of other States. Generally recognised conditions include: that the State which enacts effects-based legislation has a clear and internationally acceptable interest in doing so; that the effects which it purports to regulate must be sufficiently direct and intended or foreseeable; that those effects must be substantial enough to warrant extending the State's law to foreign nationals outside its territory; and that the exercise of effects-based jurisdiction does not unduly infringe upon the interests of other States, or upon foreign nationals, without a significant connection to the State that purports to exercise such jurisdiction.[73]

14.   The International Group of Experts agreed that the more attenu-ated the causal relationship between the cyber operations and the effects they cause in a State, the less compelling the case for applying the effects doctrine. Ultimately, application of the effects doctrine must be reason-able because the State concerned is under a duty to respect other affected States' sovereignty and their relationship to their own nationals. In addition, considerations of comity may come in to play.

---

[72]   *See, e.g.,* OPPENHEIM'S INTERNATIONAL LAW, at 472–475; SHAW'S INTERNATIONAL LAW, at 499–505; Restatement (Third), Sec. 402(1)(c) ('[C]onduct outside its territory that has or is intended to have substantial effect within its territory'). This is made subject to the reasonableness criteria set out in Sec. 403 and accompanying commentary.

[73]   *See, e.g.,* Michael Akehurst, *Jurisdiction in International Law,* 46 BRIT. Y. B. INT'L. L. 145, 198–201 (1972–1973).

15.   The Experts agreed that, within the scope of the aforementioned conditions and considerations, a State may enact legislation that regulates or criminalises cyber operations taking place abroad and have a substantial effect upon its territory, its financial and economic activity and stability, and legal order. It may also enact such legislation with respect to cyber activities, including those in which said effects are reached by virtue of the aggregation of related cyber operations, each of which alone might not be sufficient to cross the threshold. Consequently, enacting legislation on the basis of the effects doctrine would be permissible, for instance, to protect the intellectual property of a State's key industries against the substantial effects of cyber operations conducted outside its territory, so long as the legitimate interests of other States are not unduly infringed upon. To the extent the State regulates these cyber activities based on a clear interest that is generally accepted by the international community, the Experts suggested that there is no reason, in principle, why such effects-based jurisdiction may not be exercised.

16.   As an illustration of the effects doctrine, consider the case of hacktivists who conduct cyber operations against cloud computing infrastructure in which a corporation stores its data, thereby rendering corporate operations unable to continue. The State where the corporation operates enjoys jurisdiction irrespective of the location of the hackers or the infrastructure concerned. By contrast, if the same operation results in the loss of value of the corporation's stock, thereby affecting stockholders in third States, the International Group of Experts agreed that the relationship between the action and the loss in stock value for nationals of third States would generally be too attenuated to justify the assertion of jurisdiction by those States, and that the other considerations set forth above likewise augured against such exercise of jurisdiction.

17.   It is not permissible for a State to extend its legislation to foreign nationals located outside its territory for cyber activity that does not have a substantial effect upon that State. Hence, a website located abroad and operated by foreign nationals that does not specifically target persons or objects in a particular State is not subject to that State's jurisdiction unless there are substantial and foreseeable consequences within that State.

18.   The Experts cautioned that the effects doctrine must be distinguished from the protective principle, which is a basis for the extraterritorial exercise of jurisdiction (Rule 10), and from subjective and objective territoriality. It is also without prejudice to any applicable treaty law on the subject.

19.   A State that enacts legislation criminalising cyber activity conducted abroad by foreign nationals that is legal in their respective States could infringe upon the legitimate interests and sovereignty of the latter States. For example, a State may generally not promulgate laws to govern foreign NGO online campaigns on websites located in their parent States that merely criticise the first State's leadership, reflect negatively on elements of its foreign or domestic policy, or encourage its respect for human rights. In this case, exercising jurisdiction would infringe upon the NGO's parent State's legal order. But a State could, for example, rely upon the effects doctrine to prohibit online activity occurring beyond its borders that is resulting in violence against the government, even if such activity is not criminalised where it takes place. The Experts agreed that such situations must be assessed on a case-by-case basis.

20.   The exercise of any form of jurisdiction on the basis of territoriality is subject to certain limitations set forth in the international law on jurisdictional competence.[74] A number of these are universally recognised. They include sovereign (Rules 5 and 12) and diplomatic and consular immunity and inviolability (Rules 39, 41–42, and 44), and the rights associated with the exercise of innocent (Rule 48), transit (Rule 52), or archipelagic sea lanes passage (Rule 53) by foreign vessels and aircraft.

Rule 10 – Extraterritorial prescriptive jurisdiction

A State may exercise extraterritorial prescriptive jurisdiction with regard to cyber activities:

(a) **conducted by its nationals;**
(b) **committed on board vessels and aircraft possessing its nationality;**
(c) **conducted by foreign nationals and designed to seriously undermine essential State interests;**
(d) **conducted by foreign nationals against its nationals, with certain limitations; or**
(e) **that constitute crimes under international law subject to the universality principle.**

---

[74] *See, e.g.,* Oppenheim's International Law, at 458; Shaw's International Law, at 478.

1.   Whereas Rule 9 dealt with the authority of a State to exercise jurisdiction with respect to cyber infrastructure, cyber activities, and persons who engage in such cyber activities within its territory, this Rule addresses the scope of a State's prescriptive jurisdiction regarding them outside its territory.

2.   The exercise of extraterritorial prescriptive jurisdiction over persons engaged in cyber operations, cyber infrastructure, and cyber activities must be reasonable and conducted with due regard to the interests of other States.[75] The Experts based this conclusion on the fact that there must be a reasonable balance between a State's competence to regulate cyber activities affecting it on the one hand, and the interests of other States in having their sovereignty and the interests of their nationals respected on the other. They likewise looked to the interest of the international community in a functioning allocation of jurisdictional competence over cyber activities. Consequently, the extension of jurisdiction to persons and activities that do not have a substantial connection with the State purporting to exercise such jurisdiction, or that unnecessarily infringes upon another State's sovereignty or upon foreign nationals not located on the first State's territory, can not only lead to international tension, but in some cases constitute an internationally wrongful act (Rule 4).

3.   For example, it would likely be deemed unreasonable for one State to criminalise online criticism of its national leadership or of the State's human rights record by non-nationals abroad on the basis of the protective principle (see *lit.* (c)). Similarly, the International Group of Experts agreed that legislation that places restrictions on the posting of photographs of a State's nationals on social media by non-nationals abroad generally could not be justified on the basis of the passive personality principle (see *lit.* (d)) because doing so would both be unreasonable and unduly interfere with other States' interests with respect to their domestic policy on freedom of expression (Rule 35).

4.   *Lit.* (a) of this Rule sets forth prescriptive jurisdiction over persons engaged in cyber activities based on nationality. A State may exercise prescriptive jurisdiction by extending the reach of its domestic law to encompass the conduct of its nationals abroad.[76] While most States that

---

[75] *See, e.g.,* MANN 1964, at 45–47; MANN 1984, at 20–21; OPPENHEIM'S INTERNATIONAL LAW, at 467–468, 475–476; Restatement (Third), Sec. 403.

[76] *See* OPPENHEIM'S INTERNATIONAL LAW, at 462–466; SHAW'S INTERNATIONAL LAW, at 479–482; MANN 1964, at 88; Restatement (Third), Sec. 402(2).

exercise such jurisdiction over extraterritorial activities of their nationals tend to do so, in light of the interests of other States, only with respect to serious violations of its law or to specific categories of offences, international law does not prohibit a State from extending its jurisdiction over any offence committed abroad, including those involving cyber activities, by natural or legal persons having the nationality of the State. Some States extend the scope of nationality based jurisdiction to foreign nationals who are permanently resident in the State.

5.   Nationality is based on the relationship between a natural or a legal person, such as a corporation, and a State. It is governed primarily by domestic law, but is subject to certain limitations and conditions imposed by international law, like the prohibition of arbitrarily imposing legal nationality on corporations engaging in cyber activities. With respect to natural persons, nationality is usually conferred on the basis of place of birth (*jus soli*); nationality of one or both of an individual's parents (*jus sanguinis*); marriage; adoption; naturalisation; ethnic or linguistic connections to the State; descent from the State's nationals; or, arguably, permanent residency. As to legal persons, nationality is grounded primarily on the location of corporate headquarters or the place where their primary economic and legal operations occur (*siège social*).[77] States frequently refuse to recognise other States' extension of nationality to legal or natural persons who have no meaningful connection to those States.

6.   A State may exercise prescriptive jurisdiction over a wide range of cyber activities that are conducted or carried out by its nationals abroad. For example, a State can make cyber theft of intellectual property or cyber operations that involve the transfer of sensitive technological information by persons or corporations possessing its nationality a criminal offence under its domestic law. Similarly, it may prescribe laws and regulations regarding electronic financial transactions conducted entirely abroad by its natural or legal nationals in breach of sanctions or embargoes that it or a supranational authority has imposed. Of particular note is a State's prescriptive jurisdictional authority to criminalise cyber activities by nationals abroad that incite violence against the parent State or a foreign government. In the latter case, the foreign State could also exercise prescriptive jurisdiction on the basis of the protective principle, discussed in *lit.* (c).

---

[77] *Barcelona Traction* judgment, para. 70.

7. Particular mention must be made of the armed forces because they regularly operate abroad and may include individuals who are nationals of other States. The armed forces of a State are *ipso facto* considered to 'belong' to that State irrespective of the nationality of its individual members. Accordingly, a State may exercise criminal prescriptive jurisdiction over members of its armed forces for cyber activities in which they engage irrespective of their nationality.

8. It should be noted that a few Experts distinguished between prescriptive jurisdiction over the cyber activities of nationals and jurisdiction over data created during those activities. They were of the view that the jurisdiction of the State over data often cannot be equated to its jurisdiction over the cyber activities of its nationals. All Experts agreed, however, that the State where the data is located will possess full jurisdiction over the data.

9. With regard to *lit.* (b), the nationality of vessels and aircraft is based upon the State of registration. The State of registration, sometimes referred to as the 'flag State', is entitled to exercise its jurisdiction over persons engaged in cyber activities, and the cyber activities that take place, on board the vessel or aircraft. In addition, other States may exercise prescriptive jurisdiction over those on board who bear their nationality.[78] For instance, it is appropriate for a flag State to criminalise narcotics smuggling or arms trafficking from its vessels or aircraft. The prohibition would include, as an example, using a mobile Internet network to coordinate logistics of the criminal activity from aboard such platforms. Note that *lit.* (b) does not apply to spacecraft and activities in outer space. With respect to that subject, see Rule 59.

10. *Lit.* (c) deals with national security based jurisdiction, otherwise known as the protective principle. States have the right to subject cyber-related activities engaged in by foreign nationals abroad to their prescriptive jurisdiction based upon the protective principle when such acts compromise their national security, financial solvency and stability, or other vital national interests.[79] Although the precise parameters of

[78] *See* OPPENHEIM'S INTERNATIONAL LAW, at 479–484; SHAW'S INTERNATIONAL LAW, at 443–445; Restatement (Third), Sec. 402 commentary (h), Sec. 502(2) and commentary (d). *See also* Law of the Sea Convention, Art. 92(1); Chicago Convention, Art. 17.

[79] *See, e.g.,* OPPENHEIM'S INTERNATIONAL LAW, at 466–467; MANN 1964, at 93–94; SHAW'S INTERNATIONAL LAW, at 484–485; Restatement (Third), Sec. 402(3) commentary (f).

such jurisdiction are unsettled, there is general consensus that only acts involving vital State interests are included.

11.   Acts that are generally accepted as falling within this category include: attempts upon the life or physical safety of key State officials; acts that are directed at forcibly overthrowing a State's government or seriously interfering with key State functions or national security, such as terrorism; and acts that are aimed at seriously compromising a State's financial solvency and stability, such as counterfeiting its currency or seriously compromising its banking system. Since cyber activities can facilitate each of these activities, they are in principle subject to protective principle jurisdiction. For example, a State could promulgate legislation to protect against serious compromise of its military command, control, and communications systems abroad that encompasses foreign nationals acting beyond its territory; prohibit the use of the Internet to incite violence on its territory; and prohibit social media or online virtual worlds from being used to recruit its citizens for acts of terrorism. Note that these offences may also fall under other bases for jurisdiction.

12.   There is a degree of overlap between jurisdiction based on this principle and jurisdiction based on the 'effects doctrine' (Rule 9), but the two are distinct. The protective principle is limited to a fairly narrow range of offences and does not necessarily require an effect to be triggered upon the State's territory. Effects-based jurisdiction requires such an effect and is not limited to a particular category of offences. However, the two bases for jurisdiction can be seen as complementary and some cyber activities would satisfy the requirements for both. For instance, some States maintain financial assets abroad. Prescriptive jurisdiction over criminal cyber operations against those assets is appropriate because their theft, distortion, or exfiltration could compromise the State's legal order. The exercise of jurisdiction in such a case is based on the effects doctrine. At the same time, if such operations were serious enough to compromise the financial solvency of the State, it would be permissible to exercise prescriptive jurisdiction on the basis of the protective principle.

13.   *Lit.* (d) reflects the passive personality (also referred to as the passive nationality) principle. Passive personality jurisdiction involves the extension of a State's criminal legislation to foreign State nationals who commit criminal acts against the first State's nationals abroad, such as hijacking an aircraft bearing its nationals or the commission of a terrorist act against them. Such offences are increasingly likely to be facilitated by cyber operations. While this form of jurisdiction was

previously considered somewhat controversial, it has become a generally accepted basis for the exercise of extraterritorial prescriptive jurisdiction in relation to specific types of offences and subject to a number of considerations. These include due regard for the sovereignty of other States, the relationship between those States and their nationals, and due process. To the extent the exercise of such jurisdiction is reasonable in that it does not unduly infringe upon another State's sovereignty or legal order, or subject foreign nationals to criminal prosecution for acts that they could not reasonably be expected to know constituted criminal conduct, it has become generally accepted.

14.   Criminalising online recruitment abroad of foreign nationals by organisations that conduct terrorist acts against nationals of that State, for instance, would arguably be reasonable, even if the transaction takes place wholly outside its territory and the attacks would also take place outside the territory of that State. In such a case, the legislating State has a reasonable and internationally recognised interest in preventing terrorist attacks against its citizens and the measure is tailored to protecting that interest. However, the passive personality principle would not provide a basis on which a State could subject to its criminal jurisdiction a foreign national abroad who offered medical services online to nationals of that State who were also abroad. The act falls outside the limited range of acts in respect of which the passive personality principle has been recognised. Additionally, extension of criminal jurisdiction would be unreasonable given the degree of interference with the sovereign prerogatives of the territorial State in determining how medical services in its territory are provided. Moreover, the service provider might have no reasonable basis for knowing that the conduct is criminal in the State of nationality.

15.   *Lit.* (e) restates the principle of universal jurisdiction. Under the principle, a State may (and in some cases has a treaty obligation to) extend its prescriptive jurisdiction over certain universally recognised crimes under international law irrespective of the nationality of the perpetrator, the location of the offence, or the nationality of the victims.[80] Such crimes can be facilitated by cyber-related activities. Many States nevertheless impose a condition under their domestic law that some kind of link exist between the crime and their territory or nationals for the exercise of jurisdiction pursuant to this principle.

---

[80] *See* OPPENHEIM'S INTERNATIONAL LAW, at 469–470; SHAW'S INTERNATIONAL LAW, at 485–489; Restatement (Third), Sec. 404; THE LAW OF STATE IMMUNITY, at 80–81.

16.   The International Group of Experts agreed that crimes recognised under both customary and conventional international law as subject to the universality principle include piracy, slave trade, genocide, crimes against humanity, war crimes, and torture.[81] It is necessary to distinguish these crimes under international law from those covered by multilateral conventions providing for multiple bases of jurisdiction. Examples include aerial hijacking, violation of the safety of civil aviation and maritime safety, assaults upon internationally protected persons, terrorist hostage taking, terrorist financing, and terrorist bombings. The conventions often include a requirement to either prosecute or extradite the suspected perpetrators (*aut dedere aut judicare*).

17.   The International Group of Experts acknowledged a view, which none of the Experts shared, that, as a matter of the *lex lata*, no crimes are subject to universal jurisdiction under customary international law, with the possible exception of piracy. Proponents of this view suggest that there is a relative paucity of State practice and *opinio juris* with respect to the exercise of jurisdiction on this basis.

18.   To the extent a cyber activity amounts to a material aspect of a crime under international law, the activity falls within the ambit of universal jurisdiction. For instance, conducting cyber attacks in order to incite terror among the civilian population in the context of an armed conflict (Rule 98) or a network intrusion to acquire the names of individuals registered as a certain race in a State census in order to engage in genocide would fall within the ambit of universal jurisdiction.

Rule 11 – Extraterritorial enforcement jurisdiction

A State may only exercise extraterritorial enforcement jurisdiction in relation to persons, objects, and cyber activities on the basis of:

(a) a specific allocation of authority under international law; or
(b) valid consent by a foreign government to exercise jurisdiction on its territory.

1.   In light of the principle of sovereignty (Rule 1), enforcement jurisdiction over cyber infrastructure, cyber activities, and persons who engage in such cyber activities is generally limited to the territory of the

---

[81]   With respect to universal jurisdiction over the crime of aggression, the International Group of Experts considered the law to be unsettled.

State that is exercising the jurisdiction and to vessels and aircraft registered in that State. Accordingly, the exercise of enforcement jurisdiction on another State's territory constitutes a violation of that State's sovereignty (Rule 4) except when international law provides a specific allocation of authority to exercise enforcement jurisdiction extraterritorially or when the State in which it is to be exercised consents.[82]

2. With respect to enforcement jurisdiction over activities and objects in outer space, see Rule 59.

3. As noted in *lit.* (a), a State may engage in extraterritorial enforcement jurisdiction in relation to particular cyber-related activities or purposes specifically provided for under treaties or customary international law. Allocation of extraterritorial enforcement authority under treaty and customary international law must be explicit, that is, it may not be implied on the basis of other rules of general international law.

4. There are numerous grants of such authority in international law. For instance, coastal States may exercise enforcement jurisdiction for particular purposes under the law of the sea in certain maritime areas, such as the exclusive economic zone (EEZ), contiguous zone, and continental shelf (Rules 45–53). International conventions and customary international law also permit the exercise of enforcement jurisdiction on vessels, aircraft, and spacecraft by the State of nationality in international waters, international airspace, and outer space, respectively. Although there is no cyber-specific international law allocating enforcement authority in these cases, the International Group of Experts agreed that enforcement jurisdiction on the aforementioned bases extends to cyber operations conducted from these platforms.

5. States enjoy extraterritorial enforcement jurisdiction in relation to the crime of piracy on the high seas, in the exclusive economic zone, and places outside the jurisdiction of any State (Rule 46). This is so irrespective of the State that has flagged the vessel or the nationality of the pirate. Thus, for example, it would be lawful for a State to exercise its enforcement jurisdiction in the exclusive economic zone of another State by using an access control list to block Internet traffic to and from a vessel engaged in piracy.

---

[82] *Lotus* judgment, at 18. Ian Brownlie, Principles of Public International Law 478–479 (8th edn, 2012); Michael Akehurst, *Jurisdiction in International Law*, 46 Brit. Y. B. Int'l. L. 145, 145–151 (1972–1973).

6. During a belligerent occupation (Rules 147–149), the occupying power may exercise certain forms of enforcement jurisdiction, including over cyber activities conducted in occupied territory.

7. Pursuant to *lit.* (b), a State may also exercise enforcement jurisdiction in another State's territory, as well as on board its flag vessels, aircraft, and spacecraft, on the basis of the latter's valid consent (Rule 19). The consent may be granted on an *ad hoc* basis or by means of a treaty. For instance, the International Group of Experts agreed that a State's law enforcement authorities may not hack into servers in another State to extract evidence or introduce so-called white worms to disinfect bots there that are being used for criminal purposes without the territorial State's agreement (unless doing so is permissible under *lit.* (a)).

8. The Experts noted that it sometimes may be impossible or difficult to reliably identify the State in which the digital evidence or other data subject to extraterritorial enforcement jurisdiction resides. They agreed that international law does not address this situation with clarity. Therefore, no consensus could be achieved as to whether a State may exercise extraterritorial enforcement jurisdiction in such cases by taking law enforcement measures regarding that evidence or data.

9. Consent to enforcement jurisdiction is sometimes granted by means of a treaty. This is commonly the case with a status of forces agreement, by which a sending State is granted exclusive, primary, or concurrent enforcement and judicial jurisdiction over its armed forces stationed in the receiving State, including members thereof conducting cyber operations.[83] A treaty can also provide that individuals other than State officials may consent to certain exercises of extraterritorial enforcement jurisdiction. The Convention on Cybercrime, for example, permits States Parties to 'access or receive, through a computer system in its territory, stored computer data located in another Party, if the Party obtains the lawful and voluntary consent of the person who has the lawful authority to disclose the data to the Party through that computer system'.[84] In this case, States that are Parties to the Convention have consented in advance to the acquisition of the computer data by the process set forth therein. Thus, *lit.* (b) is satisfied.

---

[83] TERRY D. GILL & DIETER FLECK, THE HANDBOOK ON THE LAW OF MILITARY OPERATIONS 94 (2010).

[84] Convention on Cybercrime, Art. 32(b). *See also* Arab Convention on Information Technology Offences, Art. 40(2).

10. Consent, whether granted *ad hoc* or pursuant to a treaty, is subject to any conditions imposed by the consenting State.[85] For instance, the Parties to the aforementioned Convention on Cybercrime have made consent conditional on the approval of the person with lawful authority to disclose the data.[86] Consent may, in the absence of an agreement to the contrary, be modified or withdrawn at any time and for any reason by the consenting State.

11. The United Nations Security Council may authorise the exercise of enforcement powers extraterritorially to implement sanctions imposed under Article 41 of the UN Charter (Rule 76). As an example, the Security Council could authorise a cyber embargo of a particular State, thereby cutting it off from most access to the Internet. To illustrate, such measures, unless related to combating piracy or other criminal activity, are not an exercise of extraterritorial State jurisdiction, but rather steps aimed at maintaining or restoring international peace and security under the UN Charter.

12. The International Group of Experts acknowledged that determining whether enforcement jurisdiction is territorial or extraterritorial can be complex in the cyber context. In particular, the Experts discussed whether accessing electronic data that is publicly available, such as that on the Internet, amounts to an exercise of extraterritorial enforcement jurisdiction if the data is hosted on servers located abroad. In the view of the Experts, a State is in these situations exercising territorial, as opposed to extraterritorial, enforcement jurisdiction based on the fact that the data is publicly available in their State.[87] Their conclusion in this regard is without prejudice to international human rights law (Chapter 6).

13. The Experts further considered the case of data that can be accessed on the Internet, but that is not publicly available, such as the content of closed online forums, chat channels, or private Internet hosting services that are not indexed in public search engines or are hidden in the so-called 'dark web'. In their view, the same logic applies so long as the data is meant to be accessible from the State concerned. This is so even if it is

---

[85] *See, e.g.*, MANN 1984, at 34–38; Restatement (Third), Secs. 432–433.

[86] Convention on Cybercrime, Art. 32(b).

[87] *See also* Convention on Cybercrime, Art. 32(a); Arab Convention on Combatting Information Technology Offences, Art. 40(1); International Association of Penal Law (AIDP-IAPL), XIXth International Congress of Penal Law, Information Society and Penal Law, Sec. IV, General Report, at 19; International Association of Penal Law (AIDP-IAPL), XIXth International Congress of Penal Law, Information Society and Penal Law, Sec. IV, General Report, Final Resolution, at 8–9.

password or otherwise protected. If, for example, a State's law enforcement agency is able to obtain, under false pretences, the log-on credentials to a closed online forum hosted on servers located abroad, but meant to be accessible to one or more users from the State, that the State is exercising, in the estimation of the Experts, territorial enforcement jurisdiction when it accesses the forum from its own territory.

14.   Such cases must be distinguished from those in which data is not meant to be made available to individuals in the State. An example would be data that is stored on a private computer abroad, even if connected to the Internet, that is not meant to be accessible. Thus, as an example, if a law enforcement agency hacks into a suspected criminal's computer located in another State, it is exercising enforcement jurisdiction in that State and the activity requires the latter State's consent or a specific allocation of authority under international law.

15.   The International Group of Experts also discussed the situation in which law enforcement authorities directly contact private foreign hosting service providers to obtain extraterritorial data (usually subscriber or traffic information). The Experts agreed that the private entities involved have no legal obligation to comply with such requests. However, they were evenly split over whether the mere making of a request directly to a private entity, and not through a relevant government agency, constitutes a prohibited exercise of extraterritorial enforcement jurisdiction. Some of them were of the view that since the information that the service provider holds is not publicly available, gaining access to it requires either a specific allocation of authority under international law or consent of the State enjoying enforcement jurisdiction over the data sought. Other Experts opined that a mere request made directly to a private entity that is not accompanied by compulsion to comply on the part of the requesting State does not rise to the level of interference with the exclusive right of the other State to exercise enforcement jurisdiction on its territory.

16.   The Experts considered the issue of whether a State may conduct unilateral enforcement measures with respect to data that is stored abroad by an individual or private entity of its nationality. They agreed that the mere fact that a person or private entity bears a State's national-ity does not alone afford that State the legal authority to engage in an exercise of extraterritorial enforcement jurisdiction with respect to that data. The Experts hastened to add, however, that the State may exercise enforcement jurisdiction over the individuals or private entities them-selves if they are located in the State, based on, for instance, the failure to cooperate with authorities.

17.   Consider a situation involving a private entity domiciled in State A that stores its data in State B. State C, as part of its law enforcement activities, wants to access that data. The Experts agreed that the consent of State A is insufficient to permit remote access by State C to the data in State B. Remotely accessing the data would be an exercise of enforcement jurisdiction by State C in State B that necessitates a specific allocation of authority under international law or State B's consent. However, the Experts likewise emphasised that State A may exercise its jurisdiction over the entity and, for example, require it to provide the respective data to State C.

Rule 12 – Immunity of States from the exercise of jurisdiction

A State may not exercise enforcement or judicial jurisdiction in relation to persons engaged in cyber activities or cyber infrastructure that enjoy immunity under international law.

1.   This Rule deals only with the immunities from foreign jurisdiction that States enjoy, that is, the immunities of their organs (Rule 15), property, and assets *vis-à-vis* the exercise of enforcement and judicial jurisdiction by another State. Other limitations on jurisdiction are set forth elsewhere in this Manual, such as Rules 39, 41–42, and 44 on diplomatic and consular immunities and inviolability. This Rule also must be distinguished from Rule 5, which addresses the sovereign immunity and inviolability of sovereign immune platforms.

2.   Under customary international law, States generally enjoy immunity for non-commercial activities and transactions of an exclusively governmental nature with respect to the jurisdiction of other States. For instance, the domestic courts of one State may not, except in certain limited circumstances, such as with consent (Rule 19), entertain judicial proceedings against another State for cyber activities of a non-commercial governmental nature.

3.   For so long as they are in office, heads of State, heads of government, and various high-ranking officials, such as ministers of foreign affairs, enjoy complete personal immunity (*ratione personae*) from any exercise of enforcement jurisdiction and from proceedings before foreign domestic courts, for both private and public cyber-related acts.[88] As an example, a head of State would enjoy immunity for ordering cyber operations that violate another State's domestic law. It should be

---

[88] *Arrest Warrant* judgment, paras. 54, 58.

cautioned that the issue of precisely which high-ranking officials enjoy personal immunity is unsettled in international law.

4.   State officials enjoy functional immunity (*ratione materiae*) for official acts, including cyber-related acts, committed in their home State while holding office.[89] The International Group of Experts was unable to achieve consensus as to whether functional immunity extends to foreign State officials when they perform cyber-related official acts while they are physically present on the territory of the State seeking to exercise jurisdiction.

5.   According to the majority of the Experts, officials or other individuals representing a State who are present on the territory of another State with its consent enjoy functional immunity for official acts within the scope of the consent granted for the duration of their stay on the consenting State's territory.[90] By this view, no special agreement conferring immunity is necessary. Consider the case of a delegation of intelligence officers of a sending State that conducts joint operations with the receiving State's intelligence officers while on official mission in the receiving State's territory with the consent of that State. As part of that joint operation, they conduct operations that involve hacking into a restricted network. These Experts were of the view that the officers enjoy functional immunity for their official acts with respect to the receiving State's domestic legislation.

6.   A minority of the Experts was of the view that officials representing a foreign State do not enjoy functional immunity with respect to cyber-related acts they perform while they are present on the territory of the State seeking to exercise enforcement or judicial jurisdiction unless they fall within the category of high-ranking officials described above and thus enjoy personal immunity; are in the country with the State's consent, are acting within the scope of said consent, and enjoy immunity by virtue of a specific agreement between the State's concerned, such as a status of forces agreement; or benefit from any immunities to which personnel on a special mission are entitled (chapeau to Chapter 7).

7.   The question of whether any functional immunities foreign State officials might enjoy apply in relation to cyber activities that constitute violations of peremptory norms (Rule 19) or crimes under international law subject to the universality principle of jurisdiction (Rule 10),

---

[89] THE LAW OF STATE IMMUNITY, at 538–546 (stating the treatment of State immunity in relation to universal jurisdiction over crimes under international law).

[90] THE LAW OF STATE IMMUNITY, at 564–565.

particularly genocide, crimes against humanity, war crimes, and the crime of aggression, is unsettled. The International Group of Experts agreed that, at present, *opinio juris* and State practice has not yet fully accepted the suspension or exclusion of functional immunity between States *inter se* in relation to perceived violations of *jus cogens* norms and crimes under international law, but there is a considerable body of opinion that points in the opposite direction with respect to crimes under international law. This question is related to the scope of jurisdiction under the universality principle.[91]

8. Foreign State property entitled to immunity includes buildings, installations, vessels, aircraft, and space objects that are owned or operated by a foreign State for non-commercial exclusively governmental purposes. For instance, a State's cyber infrastructure that serves non-commercial governmental purposes may not be seized or attached by a domestic court or officials of another State. Military vessels, aircraft, and other moveable or non-moveable State property and equipment of a military nature, including military cyber infrastructure, are *ipso facto* considered to be of a non-commercial governmental nature. Foreign State aircraft or vessels and their crews and cargo that are temporarily present on another State's territory as a result of distress or emergency enjoy immunity for such time as is necessary to safely resume their journey.[92]

9. A number of multilateral, regional, and bilateral international agreements contain provisions regarding immunities that may differ in some respects from the aforementioned customary law immunities.[93] As a general matter, an immunity provision in an international agreement executed after a related customary norm has matured will prevail as between the Parties to the agreement.[94]

10. The International Group of Experts agreed that to the extent cyber activities on another State's territory are provided for in an

---

[91] A number of cases have examined this issue with differing outcomes and have led to further controversy. These cases include the *Arrest Warrant* judgment, paras. 53 *et seq.* (with separate and dissenting opinions by most of the judges on the bench); *Jurisdictional Immunities of the State (Ger. v. It., Greece intervening)* 2012 ICJ 99 (3 February); *In Re Pinochet* (HL) (15 January 1999).

[92] Law of the Sea Convention, Art. 18.

[93] Examples include the Convention on Jurisdictional Immunities; European Convention on State Immunity, May 16, 1972, ETS No. 74, and numerous bilateral conventions relating to status of forces, consular representation, etc.

[94] Vienna Convention on the Law of the Treaties, Art. 31(3)(c).

agreement, or are otherwise undertaken consensually, cyber infrastructure that is used for the agreed upon non-commercial governmental activities or purposes likewise enjoys immunity. For example, if a State consents to law enforcement cyber surveillance by a foreign State on its territory, the computers, other related equipment, software, and data used for these purposes benefit from the immunities accorded under any agreement between the States concerned (or pursuant to customary international law as discussed above).

11.   Immunity extends to cyber communications necessary for conducting the activities, such as a VPN tunnel between the individuals conducting the activities and the sending State; they may not be interfered with by the receiving State, for example, by judicial authorisation for monitoring the communications. Similar immunity may extend to a network operations centre operated by a sending State's armed forces pursuant to a basing or status of forces agreement. For discussion of the inviolability to which official diplomatic or consular correspondence is entitled, see Rule 41.

12.   Aspects of foreign State immunities are, in principle, suspended between States that are engaged as opposing belligerents in an international armed conflict (Rule 82). The relevant provisions of the law of armed conflict primarily govern the status of individuals, including State military and civilian officials, and State property, including cyber infrastructure, during the conflict. This is without prejudice to diplomatic immunities enjoyed by foreign diplomats and diplomatic premises despite the outbreak of a conflict (Rule 44). Immunities of third States not parties to an armed conflict are not suspended, but may be subject to the law of neutrality (Chapter 20). As an example, consider a diplomat of State A posted in State B during a conflict between States B and C. The diplomat engages in espionage for State C. His diplomatic immunity in State B remains intact. However, it should be noted that because he is an organ of State A, State A is in breach of its obligations under the law of neutrality (Rule 152).

13.   The previous discussion of immunity is without prejudice to the law that applies to the immunity of any official accused of a crime under international law in relation to proceedings before an international court or tribunal that has jurisdiction.[95]

---

[95] *Arrest Warrant* judgment, para 61. State immunity is excluded in the Statutes of the *ad hoc* tribunals established by the UN Security Council and under the Rome Statute. *See, e.g.,* Rome Statute, Art. 27; ICTY Statute, Art. 7(2); ICTR Statute, Art. 6(2).

Rule 13 – International cooperation in law enforcement

Although as a general matter States are not obliged to cooperate in the investigation and prosecution of cyber crime, such cooperation may be required by the terms of an applicable treaty or other international law obligation.

1. The International Group of Experts agreed that customary international law does not generally oblige States to cooperate with other States in domestic criminal law matters. This is so even if such matters have a transnational character. However, a cyber crime in relation to which cooperation is sought may fall within the scope of various treaties that require cooperation between States Parties in response thereto.

2. The term 'cyber crime' in this Rule extends both to crimes committed entirely by cyber means, such as malicious hacking, and to traditional non-cyber crimes, like terrorism, that may be facilitated or effectuated by cyber means.

3. Treaties that oblige States Parties to cooperate in the investigation and prosecution of cyber crime may be broad agreements on cooperation in criminal matters generally or specifically address cyber crime. The International Group of Experts noted, however, that an international agreement mandating cooperation may be of limited scope or set forth various grounds for refusal of cooperation requests. For instance, a treaty may limit extradition to enumerated crimes or to offences meeting a certain threshold of gravity.[96]

4. International and regional cyber crime suppression treaties sometimes include international cooperation provisions. Current examples are the Council of Europe's Convention on Cybercrime and the League of Arab States' Arab Convention on Combating Information Technology Offences. Both of these agreements provide for mutual assistance to investigations or proceedings concerning criminal offences related to computer systems and data, and for the collection of electronic evidence for any offence.[97] In addition, there exists a

[96] *See, e.g.,* Convention on Cybercrime, Art. 24; Arab Convention on Combating Information Technology Offences, Art. 31.
[97] Convention on Cybercrime Arts. 23, 25, 27; Arab Convention on Combating Information Technology Offences, Arts. 32, 34–35. *See also* Commonwealth of Independent States' Agreement on Cooperation in Combating Offences Related to Computer Information, Arts. 5–6.

wide network of bilateral conventions providing for mutual cooperation on criminal matters more broadly.[98]

5.   International agreements that are not dedicated to the issue of international cooperation in criminal matters may nevertheless contain provisions requiring cooperation. For instance, a number of terrorism conventions mandate cooperation between the Parties in combatting terrorist acts, including by means of investigative and prosecutorial action.[99] In such cases, an obligation to cooperate would attach when the activities concerned have been carried out by cyber means or electronic evidence exists as to the crime in question.

6.   States Parties to an international criminal tribunal's statute may be required to cooperate with the tribunal when it is hearing a case involving cyber activities.[100] A binding UN Security Council resolution may also require cooperation with an international tribunal.[101]

7.   Of particular importance with regard to mutual cooperation between States in combatting cyber crime are the principles of *ne bis in idem* and double criminality. According to the former, no one can be tried or convicted twice for the same act. Although its nature as a customary international law rule is somewhat contested, the principle finds application through treaty law, particularly in various extradition treaties.[102] The principle of double criminality requires that the cyber activity with respect to which the cooperation is sought be criminalised in both the requesting and requested States. For example, both the Convention on Cybercrime and the Arab Convention on Combatting Information Technology Offences include non-compliance with the principle as an optional ground for refusal to cooperate.[103] With respect to cyber activities, the principle has

---

[98]   A dispute on the interpretation and application of one such treaty was at the heart of the International Court of Justice's *Certain Questions of Mutual Assistance* judgment.

[99]   *See, e.g.,* International Convention for the Suppression of Terrorist Bombings, Art. 7(1–2), 15 December 1997, 2149 UNTS 284; International Convention for the Suppression of Acts of Nuclear Terrorism, Art. 7(1)(b), 14 September 2005, 1987 UNTS 125.

[100]   *See, e.g.,* Rome Statute, Arts. 86–87, 89, 91–93.

[101]   *See, e.g.,* SC Res. 1593, para. 2, UN Doc. S/RES/1539 (31 March 2005); SC Res. 1970, para. 5, UN Doc. S/RES/1970 (26 February 2011).

[102]   *See, e.g.,* The Bolivarian Agreement on Extradition, Art. 5, 18 July 1911, 29 Am. J. Int'l L. Supp. 282 (1935).

[103]   Convention on Cybercrime, Arts. 24(1), 25(5), 29(3–4); Arab Convention on Combating Information Technology Offences, Arts. 32(5), 37(3–4).

created practical difficulties due to gaps in the criminalisation of cyber crime in many States.[104]

8. Certain treaties include the requirement to prosecute or extradite alleged offenders.[105] For example, some cyber-specific treaties provide that if extradition is refused on the basis of the nationality of the person sought or because the requested State deems that it has jurisdiction over the offence, the requested State shall take action to prosecute.[106] These treaties also adopt traditional limits to, and grounds for refusal of, mutual law enforcement cooperation. The Convention on Cybercrime and the Arab Convention on Combating Information Technology Offences, for example, envisage such optional grounds for refusal as the offence's political character and prejudice to the requested State's sovereignty, security, *ordre public*, or other essential interests.[107] A refusal based on any of these grounds is subject to the obligation of States to act in good faith and, when provided for in the treaty in question, must be accompanied by the reason for the refusal.[108]

9. States may agree to facilitate expedited communications between Parties to a treaty. For instance, Parties to the Convention on Cybercrime are obliged to designate a point of contact that is available on an around-the-clock basis in order to ensure the provision of immediate assistance with respect to criminal investigations.[109] States may also establish legal assistance mechanisms for immediate disclosure to foreign authorities of certain information obtained during investigations.[110] International

---

[104] The 'Love Bug' illustrates the challenges of double criminality. In 2000, the 'Love Bug' malware infected millions of private and public computers worldwide, generating billions of dollars in damages. Cooperation between law enforcement agencies (in particular, between the US and Philippines) worked smoothly and quickly led to the identification of the creator and disseminator of the malware. However, at that time, the Philippine penal legislation did not criminalise virus distribution, nor illegal access to computer systems; moreover, the Philippine cooperation framework envisaged the double criminality principle. Therefore, due to lack of criminalisation of the act by both cooperating parties, extradition to the United States was disallowed.

[105] Final Report of the International Law Commission, 66th Sess., VI, The Obligation to Extradite or Prosecute (*aut dedere aut judicare*), GA Res. A/69/10 (2014), at 143.

[106] Convention on Cybercrime, Art. 24(6); Arab Convention on Combating Information Technology Offences, Art. 31(6).

[107] Convention on Cybercrime, Art. 27(3); Arab Convention on Combating Information Technology Offences, Art. 35.

[108] *Certain Questions of Mutual Assistance* judgment, paras. 145–152.

[109] Convention on Cybercrime, Art. 26(2).

[110] Convention on Cybercrime, Art. 26; Arab Convention on Combating Information Technology Offences, Art. 33.

and regional law enforcement organisations play a pivotal role in making possible interstate cooperation and coordination. For instance, the Interpol Digital Crime Centre and Europol's European Cybercrime Centre are specifically focused on cooperation in combatting cyber crime.[111]

10.   A State's domestic law may regulate how a State makes and accedes to requests for cooperation. Similarly, informal cooperation, which is common in the investigation of cyber crime, is subject to domestic guidelines.

11.   The International Group of Experts noted that international human rights law is likely to bear on mutual cooperation relating to cyber crime, especially with regard to the right to privacy (Rule 35). The Experts emphasised that any limitations to applicable human rights must be consistent with Rule 37.

---

[111] As an example of successful interagency operation, in 2015 the FBI and Europol's European Cybercrime Centre coordinated law enforcement agencies from twenty countries in the technical take down of a prominent criminal Internet forum (Darkode) and in numerous related law enforcement actions resulting in several arrests, searches, and seizures. Press Release, Europol, Cybercriminal Darkode Forum Taken Down through Global Action (15 July 2015); Press Release, US Department of Justice Office of Public Affairs, Major Computer Hacking Forum Dismantled (15 July 2015).

4

Law of international responsibility

SECTION 1: INTERNATIONALLY WRONGFUL ACTS BY A STATE

1. In this Chapter, Sections 1–3 are based on the customary international law of State responsibility, which is largely reflected in the International Law Commission's Articles on State Responsibility and upon which the Rules that follow rely in great part.[112] To the extent the Rules that follow adopt the Articles, the International Group of Experts concurred that they replicate customary international law. However, the International Group of Experts acknowledged that certain issues with respect to some Articles remain unsettled and that not all States view them as an authoritative restatement of customary international law.[113] These issues are discussed below to the extent they affect the Rules set forth in Sections 1–3.

2. Sections 1–3 pertain to the responsibility of States. On the responsibility of international organisations, see Section 4. Additionally, Sections 1–3 only address the responsibility of States under international law. The domestic legal regime of States may prescribe

---

[112] The Articles on State Responsibility are not a treaty and therefore are not binding under international law. However, they were drafted by the International Law Commission during a process that took more than half a century under the leadership of five special rapporteurs. Once completed, the UN General Assembly commended the Articles to governments. GA Res. 56/83, UN Doc. A/RES/ 56/83 (12 December 2001). By 2012, the Articles and the accompanying commentary had been cited 154 times by international courts, tribunals, and other bodies. United Nations Materials on the Responsibility of States for Internationally Wrongful Acts, UN Doc. ST/LEG/SER B/25 (2012).

[113] For instance, prior to adoption of the Articles by the International Law Commission, the United States stated, '[w]hile we welcome the recognition that countermeasures play an important role in the regime of State responsibility, we believe that the draft articles contain unsupported restrictions on their use'. US 1997 Comments, at 1. *See also* US 2001 Comments, at 1. Note that the 1997 and 2001 US comments explain at length the United States' views on the 'unsupported restrictions'.

different rules with regard to the responsibility of States for acts committed in violation of their domestic law.

3. For the purposes of this Manual, the term 'responsible State' denotes the State breaching an obligation owed to another State, whereas the State to which the obligation breached is owed is referred to as the 'injured State'. The term 'invoke' signifies the 'taking [of] measures of a relatively formal character, for example, the raising or presentation of a claim against another State or the commencement of proceedings before an international court or tribunal'[114] or engaging in countermeasures (Rule 20).[115] The term 'act' refers to both actions and omissions.

4. The International Group of Experts agreed that the customary international law of State responsibility undeniably extends to cyber activities. That body of law consists of secondary, as distinct from primary, rules of international law. Primary rules are those that set forth international law obligations. Breach of them results in State responsibility. Secondary rules lay out the general conditions for a State's responsibility, as well as the consequences of violating a primary rule. As an example, Article 2(4) of the UN Charter prohibits the use of force (Rule 68). It is a primary rule of international law. The law of State responsibility sets forth, *inter alia*, the legal criteria for attribution to a State of a cyber operation rising to the level of a use of force, as well as the international law remedies available to the injured State; these are secondary rules.

5. States may agree between themselves to a rule of responsibility specific to a particular cyber act or practice or may agree not to apply certain of the State responsibility rules thereto pursuant to the maxim *lex specialis derogat legi generali*.[116] For example, the law of armed conflict contains a number of specific rules on State responsibility in cases of violation thereof.[117]

6. A minority of the International Group of Experts took the position that international law encompasses various 'self-contained regimes'. By their interpretation, such regimes set forth specialised rules of international

---

[114] Articles on State Responsibility, Art. 42, para. 2 of commentary.

[115] Articles on State Responsibility, Art. 42, para. 2 of commentary.

[116] 'Specific law prevails over general law'. Articles on State Responsibility, General Commentary, para. 5, Art. 55.

[117] In particular, Article 3 of Hague Convention IV and Article 91 of Additional Protocol I provide for compensation when certain rules of the law of armed conflict are breached. *See also* ICRC CUSTOMARY IHL STUDY, Rules 149–150.

responsibility that result in the inapplicability of the general rules of State responsibility. For example, it is sometimes suggested that regional human rights law qualifies as a self-contained regime that provides for its own remedies.

7. The International Law Commission struggled with this issue in drafting the Articles on State Responsibility, but did not express a definitive position thereon. Instead, it emphasised the notion of *lex specialis*, styling so-called self-contained regimes as "'strong" forms of *lex specialis*'.[118] The majority of the Experts took the same approach. In their view, although treaties and customary international law may specifically address State responsibility in particular situations, such rules constitute *lex specialis* and therefore only displace general rules of State responsibility that are in direct conflict therewith. *Lex specialis* rules of responsibility are not discussed herein.

8. The law of State responsibility applies objectively to facts as they exist or do not exist. For instance, the cyber operations of a non-State actor are attributable to a State if the State factually exercises 'effective control' over that specific conduct of the non-State actor (Rule 17). Questions of burdens, standards, and methods of proof are generally a matter for judicial or other types of proceedings, to be determined by the relevant forum. Indeed, the requisite burdens, standards, and methods of proof vary depending on the purposes for which they are employed by such bodies.

9. However, in the context of unilateral self-help measures, the reality is that States must make *ex ante* determinations with respect to attribution of a cyber operation to another State before responding. Although such determinations may be subject to *post factum* review applying standards set by a judicial or other forum, as a practical matter the State may be faced with a situation to which it may have to respond in an extremely short time frame, without recourse to the full range of information that might be available in the non-cyber context.

10. With respect to *ex ante* uncertainty as to the attribution of cyber operations, the International Group of Experts agreed that as a general matter, States must act as reasonable States would in the same or similar circumstances when considering responses to them.[119] Reasonableness is always context dependent. It depends on such factors as, *inter alia*, the

---

[118] Articles on State Responsibility, Art. 55, para. 5 of commentary.

[119] The International Court of Justice, in determining the standard of review regarding Japan's whaling activities to be one of reasonableness, emphasised the objective nature of

reliability, quantum, directness, nature (e.g., technical data, human intelligence), and specificity of the relevant available information when considered in light of the attendant circumstances and the importance of the right involved. These factors must be considered together. Importantly in the cyber context, deficiencies in technical intelligence may be compensated by, for example, the existence of highly reliable human intelligence.

11.   Additionally, the International Group of Experts agreed that the severity of the cyber operations being directed against the State and the robustness of any possible response should factor into an assessment of whether attribution meriting a particular response is reasonable. To illustrate, the Experts were of the view that as a general matter the graver the underlying breach (including considerations as to the primary norm concerned), the greater the confidence ought to be in the evidence relied upon by a State considering a response.[120] This is because the robustness of permissible self-help responses (such as retorsion, countermeasures, a plea of necessity, and self-defence) grows commensurately with the seriousness of a breach.[121] However, they likewise agreed that the severity of the cyber operations directed at the injured State is a relevant consideration. For instance, a State facing low-level cyber operations that are merely disruptive may be in a position to accumulate more evidence for attribution than would a State suffering devastating cyber operations and needing to respond immediately to terminate them. Ultimately, the reasonableness of *ex ante* attribution must be assessed on a case-by-case basis, considering the aforementioned, and other relevant, factors.

12.   Although States must always act as reasonable States would in same or similar circumstances, it must be cautioned that specific rules apply to particular types of responses. For instance, as discussed in Rule 20, the majority of the International Group of Experts took the position that States taking countermeasures based on a decision that another State has breached an obligation owed to them do so at their own risk. Thus,

---

the standard. *Whaling in the Antarctic (Austl.* v. *Japan: NZ intervening),* Judgment, 2014 ICJ 226, para. 67 (31 March).

[120] *See Oil Platforms* judgment, para. 33 (separate opinion of Judge Higgins). *See also Corfu Channel* judgment, at 17; *Genocide* judgment, paras. 209–210; *Application of the Convention on the Prevention and Punishment of the Crime of Genocide (Croat.* v. *Serb.),* 2015 ICJ General List No. 118, para. 178 (3 February).

[121] The United States has expressed a view that the range of permissible countermeasures should not depend simply on the 'gravity' of the other State's breach but also on the 'degree of response necessary to induce the State responsible for the internationally wrongful act to comply with its obligations'. *See* US 2001 Comments, at 5.

while it might be reasonable to take a countermeasure in the circum-stances, for instance because significant evidence exists to support attri-bution to a State against which the cyber countermeasure is taken, if the conclusion as to attribution proves to be flawed, the wrongfulness of the State's response will not be precluded by the majority view and therefore the State itself will have committed an internationally wrongful act (Rule 14).

13.   The International Group of Experts considered the issue of whether a State bears an obligation to publicly provide evidence of the basis upon which it attributed cyber operations to another State when responding thereto pursuant to the law of State responsibility. The Experts concurred in the view that although doing so may be prudent in avoiding political and other tensions,[122] insufficient State practice and *opinio juris* (in great part because cyber capabilities are in most cases highly classified) exist to conclude that there is an established basis under international law for such an obligation. They acknowledged, however, that a few States have taken the position that there is a legal obligation to disclose evidence on which attribution is based whenever taking actions in response to cyber operations that purportedly constitute an internationally wrongful act.

14.   Rules 15–18 deal with the attribution of cyber operations to States. As a general matter, geography is of only limited relevance to the issue of attribution. In particular, States may, in order to conceal their activities, initiate cyber operations from outside their territories. An example on point would involve a State instructing (Rule 17) a non-State actor in another State to assimilate hosts located in multiple States into a botnet, and to use the botnet to target the injured State. The determinative issue is whether the non-State actor is operating pursuant to the instructions of the first State, not the location of the offending activities. As discussed in Rule 15, States from which the operations are launched, or those where the assimilated computers are located, cannot be presumed to be responsible solely because the group involved, or the bots, are located in those States. Note that failure of the territorial State to take appropriate measures to control the individuals and cyber infra-structure may raise the issue of due diligence (Rules 6–7). In such a case, the State from which the operations are mounted may be responsible on its own accord for its failure to take the requisite remedial measures, rather than through attribution of the offending cyber operations.

---

[122]   *See, e.g.,* UN GGE 2015 Report, para. 28(f).

Rule 14 – Internationally wrongful cyber acts

A State bears international responsibility for a cyber-related act that is attributable to the State and that constitutes a breach of an international legal obligation.

1. States bear 'responsibility' for their internationally wrongful acts pursuant to the law of State responsibility.[123] The International Court of Justice has confirmed the customary character of this principle on many occasions.[124] An 'internationally wrongful act' is an action or omission[125] that both: (1) constitutes a breach of an international legal obligation applicable to that State; and (2) is attributable to the State under international law.[126] The absence of either element precludes State responsibility with respect to the act in question.

2. The breach required to establish an internationally wrongful act may consist of a violation of a State's treaty obligations, customary international law, or general principles of law, 'regardless of [their] origin or character'.[127] As a result, this Rule extends to all obligations in international law that are binding on the responsible State.[128] It encompasses breaches of obligations owed by one State to another, as well as those owed to the international community as a whole (see discussion of *erga omnes* norms in Rule 30).

3. The term 'cyber-related acts' is employed in this Rule to denote the fact that a State sometimes may bear responsibility for acts other than cyber operations that it conducts or that are attributable to it. For instance, a State can make its cyber infrastructure available to non-State groups or other States, fail to take required measures to terminate cyber

---

[123] Articles on State Responsibility, Art. 1. *See also* UN GGE 2013 Report, para. 23; UN GGE 2015 Report, para. 28(f).

[124] *See, e.g., Tehran Hostages,* generally; *Nicaragua* judgment, paras. 283, 292; *Gabčíkovo-Nagymaros* judgment, para. 47. The Permanent Court of International Justice enunciated the same principle earlier. *See, e.g., Phosphates in Morocco* preliminary objections, at 28; *Wimbledon* judgment, para. 30; *Factory at Chorzow (Ger. v. Pol.),* judgment (jurisdiction), 1927 PCIJ (ser. A) No. 9, at 21 (26 July).

[125] Articles on State Responsibility, Art. 2.

[126] Articles on State Responsibility, Art. 2 and accompanying commentary. *See also Phosphates in Morocco* preliminary objections, at 28 ('[t]his act being attributable to the State and described as contrary to the treaty right of another State, international responsibility would be established immediately as between the two States'); *Tehran Hostages* judgment, para. 56.

[127] Articles on State Responsibility, Art. 12.

[128] *Rainbow Warrior* arbitral award, para. 75; *Gabčíkovo-Nagymaros* judgment, para. 47.

operations from its territory (Rules 6–7), or provide hardware or software to conduct cyber operations. Such activities, *inter alia*, fall within the scope of application of this Rule, as well as others employing the term.

4. In the realm of cyberspace, an internationally wrongful act can consist of a breach of either the rules governing peacetime or those applicable in an armed conflict. As an example, a State that conducts cyber operations during peacetime against a coastal State from a vessel located in the latter's territorial sea is in breach of the innocent passage regime (Rule 48). If a State launches cyber 'attacks' (Rule 92) against civilian objects (Rule 100) in the course of an armed conflict, it violates the law of armed conflict (Rule 99) and has thus committed an internationally wrongful act. Especially prominent among the relevant customary norms, breaches of which constitute internationally wrongful acts, are respect for sovereignty (Rule 4), the prohibition of intervention (Rule 66), and the prohibition of the use of force (Rule 68).

5. International law also imposes duties on States that require positive action on their part. Failure to comply with such a duty is an omission, which also qualifies as a breach in the sense of the law of State responsibility. An example is a State's non-compliance with the due diligence obligation (Rules 6–7). Since non-State actors such as hacktivists often launch harmful cyber operations, and, in light of the likelihood of the use of cyberspace by terrorists, a State's obligation to take measures to control cyber activities taking place on its territory looms especially large.

6. Note that the requirement that there be a breach of international law is strictly construed. State responsibility is not implicated when States engage in acts that are either expressly permitted (as in suspension of services pursuant to the International Telecommunication Union Constitution, see Rule 62) or unregulated by international law (as with cyber espionage and other forms of intelligence gathering, see Rule 32).[129] With regard to the latter, the International Court of Justice has noted that 'it is entirely possible for a particular act ... not to be in violation of international law without necessarily constituting the exercise of a right conferred by it'.[130]

7. Even though certain cyber acts by States against other States may be detrimental, objectionable, or otherwise unfriendly, if they do not constitute breaches of international law obligations, States incur no legal

---

[129] *Kosovo* advisory opinion, para. 84; *Lotus* judgment, at 18.
[130] *Kosovo* advisory opinion, para. 56.

responsibility in the sense of this Rule.[131] For example, a State's suspension of e-commerce with another State (for instance, by blocking certain commercial sites), while unfriendly and perhaps economically harmful, generally would not entail a breach of an international obligation (absent violation of a specific treaty obligation).[132]

8.   Physical damage or injury is not a precondition to the characterisation of a cyber operation as an internationally wrongful act under the law of State responsibility unless damage is an element of breach of the primary rule.[133] To illustrate, a State Party's failure to adopt legislative and other measures concerning real-time traffic data collection in accordance with Article 20 of the Council of Europe Convention on Cybercrime constitutes an internationally wrongful act with respect to other States Parties despite the absence of physical damage.[134]

9.   Intent to cause harm is not a general requirement of an internationally wrongful act.[135] However, the primary obligation purportedly breached must be examined on a case-by-case basis in order to determine whether it contains such an element, as with the prohibition of genocide, which requires an 'intent to destroy, in whole or in part, a particular group'.[136] The breach of certain obligations may require culpability, negligence, or lack of due diligence (Rules 6–7). In such cases, responsibility would only attach upon fulfillment of the specific element concerned.

10.   The concept of breach as it applies in the law of State responsibility does not extend to violations of rules found solely in the domestic legal order. Rather, international law determines whether an obligation owed another State has been breached.[137] Consider the case of military forces stationed abroad that are not exempt from the receiving State's Internet usage regulatory regime. Even if those forces fail to comply with the legal requirements of that regime, State responsibility does not attach because there has been no breach of an international legal obligation (unless the relevant basing agreement provides for compliance with the regime).

---

[131] Articles on State Responsibility, General Commentary, para. 4.
[132] For an analogous example in the non-cyber context, see *Nicaragua* judgment, para. 276.
[133] Articles on State Responsibility, Art. 2, para. 9 of commentary.
[134] Council of Europe Convention on Cybercrime, Art. 20.
[135] Articles on State Responsibility, Art. 2, para. 10 of commentary.
[136] Genocide Convention, Art. II.   [137] Articles on State Responsibility, Art. 3.

11. As a general matter, the internationally wrongful character of a cyber operation does not depend on the geographic location from which it is launched. A responsible State may engage in cyber operations constituting a breach of an international legal obligation from its own territory, that of the injured State, the territory of another State, the high seas, international airspace, or outer space. It must be cautioned that certain internationally wrongful acts are geographically dependent, particularly with respect to space, airspace, and the sea. As an example, breach of the innocent passage regime (Rule 48) requires that the vessel concerned be conducting a cyber operation in the coastal State's territorial sea at the time of the operation.

12. In addition to breaching an international legal obligation, cyber-related acts must be attributable to a State to fall within the ambit of this Rule. Attribution of actions or omissions is discussed in Rules 15–18.

Rule 15 – Attribution of cyber operations by State organs

Cyber operations conducted by organs of a State, or by persons or entities empowered by domestic law to exercise elements of governmental authority, are attributable to the State.

1. Attribution to a State occurs in a number of circumstances. The clearest case is when State organs, such as the military or intelligence agencies, commit the wrongful acts.[138] For instance, all cyber activities of US Cyber Command, the Netherlands Defence Cyber Command, the French Network and Information Security Agency (ANSSI), the Estonian Defence League's Cyber Unit, the People's Liberation Army cyber unit, and Israel's Unit 8200 are fully attributable to the respective States.

2. The concept of 'organs of a State' in the law of State responsibility is broad. All persons or entities that have that status under the State's domestic laws are State organs regardless of their function or place in the governmental hierarchy.[139] Thus, any cyber activity undertaken by the intelligence, military, internal security, customs, or other State agencies engages State responsibility if it violates an international legal obligation binding on that State.

3. The law of State responsibility infuses the term 'State organ' with broad meaning to ensure that States do not escape responsibility by

---

[138] Articles on State Responsibility, Art. 4(1).
[139] Articles on State Responsibility, Art. 4(2).

asserting an entity's non-status as its organ in domestic law. This is clear from the text of Article 4(2) of the Articles on State Responsibility, which states that '[a]n organ includes any person or entity which has that status in accordance with the internal law',[140] thereby confirming that an organ need not necessarily be designated as such under domestic legislation.[141] The International Group of Experts concurred with the International Law Commission that a State cannot avoid responsibility for the conduct of a body acting as the State's organ by denying it such status under its own law.[142]

4.   A similar approach, which the International Group of Experts found useful, was taken by the International Court of Justice in the 2007 *Genocide* judgment. There, the Court held that 'persons, groups of persons or entities may, for purposes of international responsibility, be equated with State organs even if that status does not follow from internal law, provided that in fact the persons, groups or entities act in "complete dependence" on the State, of which they are ultimately merely the instrument'.[143] The Court cautioned, 'to equate persons or entities with State organs when they do not have that status under internal law must be exceptional, for it requires . . . a particularly great degree of State control over them'.[144] The International Group of Experts agreed that it is the function of the entity and the State's intention with regard to its cyber activities that underpins characterisation as an organ.

5.   The mere fact of State ownership is not alone sufficient to characterise a corporation as an organ of a State. Although owned by a State, such entities may have purely private functions, as distinguished from those that perform, at least in part, governmental ones.[145] In such cases, the activities of the State-owned entity are assessed pursuant to Rule 17.

---

[140] Articles on State Responsibility, Art. 4(2) and para. 11 of commentary.

[141] As noted in the commentary to the Article, 'a State cannot avoid responsibility for the conduct of a body which does in truth act as one of its organs merely by denying it that status under its own law. This result is achieved by the use of the word "includes" in paragraph 2.' Articles on State Responsibility, Art. 4(2), para. 11 of commentary.

[142] Articles on State Responsibility, Art. 4, para. 11 of commentary.

[143] *Genocide* judgment, para. 392. The Court looked to the *Nicaragua* judgment in reaching this conclusion. *Nicaragua* judgment, paras. 109–110.

[144] *Genocide* judgment, para. 393.

[145] Articles on State Responsibility, Art. 8, para. 6 of commentary. Although the reference is to Article 8 commentary, the logic contained therein applies equally to determinations of qualification as an organ of a State. *See also* CRAWFORD, STATE RESPONSIBILITY, at 161–165.

6. When State organs acting in an apparently official capacity breach international obligations, the State bears responsibility even if the conduct in question is *ultra vires,* that is, it exceeds the authority granted by the State or contravenes its instructions.[146] As an example, if a member of a military cyber unit conducts unlawful cyber operations in defiance of orders to the contrary, the State incurs responsibility for any breach of obligations owed to other States.

7. It is sometimes difficult to ascertain whether the individual concerned is acting in an official capacity. In this respect, the fact that that individual harbours 'ulterior or improper motives or may be abusing public power' is irrelevant.[147] So long as the individual is acting in an apparently official capacity, or 'under colour of authority', the actions or omissions involved are attributable to the State.[148] However, attribution does not attach in cases of purely private actions or omissions, such as those involving the exploitation of access to cyber infrastructure for criminal activity leading to private gain.

8. In addition to the acts of State organs, acts committed by persons or entities that do not qualify as State organs, but that are empowered by domestic law (e.g., legislation, administrative act, or, if domestic law so provides, by contract) to exercise elements of governmental authority, are attributable to the State, provided that the person or entity is acting in that capacity in the particular instance.[149] Examples include a private corporation that has been granted legal authority by the government to conduct offensive cyber operations against another State and a private entity legally empowered to engage in cyber intelligence gathering. With respect to situations in which persons or entities are empowered by law to perform particular activities that do not qualify as elements of government authority, see Rule 17.

9. Qualifying elements of governmental authority are those that represent quintessential governmental functions. In other words, they are activities over which governments typically exercise competence, such as the conduct of foreign affairs, the levying of taxation, the operation of police forces, and border control. The exact parameters of governmental authority are not always clear. They must be assessed contextually with regard to the activity in question, the particular State

[146] Articles on State Responsibility, Art. 7.
[147] Articles on State Responsibility, Art. 4, para. 13 of commentary.
[148] Articles on State Responsibility, Art. 4, para. 13 of commentary.
[149] Articles on State Responsibility, Art. 5.

involved, the method by which the powers have been conferred, their purpose, the degree of governmental accountability for their exercise, and the history and traditions of the State concerned.[150]

10.   A paradigmatic case of a governmental function is law enforcement. Because of limitations in capabilities, States are sometimes unable to perform law enforcement functions when cyber activities are involved. They therefore may outsource them to private or voluntary entities. As an example, if a law enforcement agency lacks the technical wherewithal to engage in digital forensics for law enforcement purposes, it may contract, in accordance with domestic law, with a private company to perform that function. The fact that the forensics are not performed by a State organ does not avoid attribution of the action to the State.

11.   It is important to emphasise that attribution only occurs when the entity in question is acting in the empowered capacity. Consider the case of a State that contracts with a private company to conduct cyber defence of military networks identified by the government. While so acting, the company's activities are attributable to the State. However, when the same company performs information security services for private entities, such as corporations or non-governmental organisations, its activities are not attributable to the State. The conditions for attribution are that the acts in question are of a governmental character and the entity is empowered by the State to carry out such acts.

12.   If entities empowered to exercise elements of governmental authority engage in *ultra vires* acts that nevertheless generally fall within the scope of their duties, the State bears responsibility for said acts.[151] Consider the case of a State that lacks the capability to engage in sufficiently robust cyber defences of its governmental cyber infrastructure. It accordingly promulgates regulatory authority for a private company to defend its State networks employing passive defence measures. During an incident involving malicious cyber operations against the networks, the company engages in active cyber defence by hacking back. Despite the fact that its response is *ultra vires*, the hack-back will be attributable to the State because the activity is incidental to the company's defence of the networks. However, the State bears no responsibility for the activities of

---

[150] Articles on State Responsibility, Art. 5, para. 6 of commentary.
[151] Articles on State Responsibility, Art. 7.

such an entity when they fall outside the State's grant of authority. Thus, if personnel of the company conduct malicious operations unrelated to the obligations of the company under the regulatory authority, such as engaging in cyber crime, the activities are not attributable.

13.   Traditionally, the use of governmental assets, in particular military equipment like tanks or warships, has long constituted a nearly irrefutable indication of attribution due to the improbability of their use by persons other than State organs. This traditional rebuttable presumption cannot be easily translated into the cyber context. In particular, another State or a non-State actor may have acquired control over government cyber infrastructure and is using it to conduct cyber operations. Accordingly, the mere fact that a cyber operation has been launched or otherwise originates from governmental cyber infrastructure, or that malware used against hacked cyber infrastructure is designed to 'report back' to another State's governmental cyber infrastructure, is usually insufficient evidence for attributing the operation to that State.[152] That said, such usage can serve as an indication that the State in question may be associated with the operation.

14.   Even less compelling as an indication of State involvement is the mere fact that a harmful cyber operation has been mounted using private cyber infrastructure in a State's territory. This is a particularly important limitation in light of the possibility of creating botnets using zombie computers to mount distributed denial of service attacks. As an illustration, in 2013 an allegedly North Korean cyber operation shut down thousands of South Korean media and banking computers and servers by employing cyber infrastructure located around the world. Obviously, most, if not all, of the States in which the infrastructure was located played no direct part in the operation.

15.   To complicate matters, those involved may also try to create the impression that a particular State is behind the operation. Indeed, 'spoofing', such as impersonating organisations themselves or their IP-addresses, is a widely used cyber technique designed to feign identity. For example, in 2013, malicious cyber operations were mounted to impersonate the NATO Cooperative Cyber Defence Centre of Excellence (NATO CCD COE) and make it appear as if the organisation had defaced Ukrainian government websites. In fact, the operations did not originate

---

[152] *See also* UN GGE 2015 Report, para. 28(f), which drew on text from the original Tallinn Manual, Rule 7.

from the Centre. The true originators then directed their operations against the NATO CCD COE website, the Estonian Defence Forces, and the militaries of other NATO States, but made it appear as if the Ukrainian government had conducted them by spoofing the source IP addresses. The fact that some cyber operations necessitate an immediate response further exacerbates the difficulty of correctly attributing harmful operations to another State.

16.   Each situation must be assessed in context. A regular pattern of a non-State group taking control of governmental cyber infrastructure to launch cyber operations, for example, can be a counter-indication that a State launched a particular operation. Similarly, reliable human intelligence that indicates governmental computers will be, or have been, employed by non-State actors to conduct operations could also augur against a conclusion of State involvement. So too would the existence of friendly relations between the injured State and the purportedly responsible State.

17.   In exceptional circumstances, a State may be unable (as distinct from situations in which the State is unwilling to act or is acting in an ineffective manner) to exercise its governmental authority. In such a case, private groups or persons might engage in activities on their own initiative that involve such authority, despite the fact that the State did not empower them. As reflected in Article 9 of the Articles on State Responsibility, when this occurs and the circumstances call for the exercise of such authority, the activities are attributable to the State.[153] Consider a rootkit attack on a State's civil defence computers during a non-international armed conflict (Rule 83) that has the effect of making it impossible to conduct warnings (Rule 120) by cyber means. The State must disconnect its host from the network. Therefore, a private entity steps in to perform the organisation's functions from an uninfected host until the State can remedy the situation or find an alternative means of transmitting the warnings. The State concerned would be responsible for the actions of the private entity should the actions breach an obligation owed to another State. It must be cautioned that attribution on this basis only manifests when the situation is dire, the State is powerless to perform its governmental functions, and the 'circumstances [are] such as to call for the exercise of those elements of its authority'.[154]

---

[153] Articles on State Responsibility, Art. 9.   [154] Articles on State Responsibility, Art. 9.

Rule 16 – Attribution of cyber operations by organs of other States

Cyber operations conducted by an organ of a State that has been placed at the disposal of another State are attributable to the latter when the organ is acting in the exercise of elements of governmental authority of the State at the disposal of which it is placed.

1.   State organs are sometimes temporarily placed at the disposal of other States in order to perform specified governmental functions. Under this Rule, the conduct of the organ is attributable to the receiving State alone when two factual preconditions are met: (1) exclusivity of control; and (2) the acts are engaged in for the purposes of and on behalf of the receiving State.[155]

2.   First, the organ concerned must act under the exclusive direction and control of the receiving State. The fact that the sending State continues to fund or provide resources to the organ does not undermine the principle of responsibility set forth in this Rule, so long as the receiving State is exercising exclusive authority over the organ sent. Neither does the fact that the sending State maintains the authority to recall its organ or to direct it to cease activities on behalf of the receiving State.

3.   However, if the organ continues to receive any instructions as to its operations from the sending State, this Rule does not apply. Instead, and depending on the particular circumstances at hand, other Rules of this Section are likely to be applicable, such as Rule 15 on attribution of State organs' cyber activities and Rule 18 on aid or assistance. For instance, if one State sends members of its CERT to another State to assist it in dealing with a cyber incident, but the sending State requires the team to secure approval prior to engaging in specific actions requested by the receiving State, the exclusivity of control condition under this Rule is not satisfied.

4.   Moreover, the entity concerned must be used solely for the purposes of the receiving State, and has to be acting on behalf of that State.[156] If it operates for the purposes of both the receiving and sending State, the precondition of exclusivity of purpose under this Rule is not met. As an example, this Rule would apply in a situation in which experts from a sending State's government CERT are made available to the receiving State in order to deal with cyber operations directed at only the receiving State,

---

[155] Articles on State Responsibility, Art. 6, para. 1 of commentary.
[156] Articles on State Responsibility, Art. 6, para. 1 of commentary.

as long as the receiving State exercises exclusive direction and control over the experts. This is true even if the experts are made available only remotely, that is to say, the experts do not physically relocate to the receiving State. By contrast, if the offending cyber operations are directed at both the receiving State and the sending State, and the CERT's experts handle the incident, this Rule does not apply. The International Group of Experts recognised that in most circumstances the sending State will benefit indirectly from the efforts of the organ. The important point for the purposes of this Rule, however, is to establish that the principal object and focus of the organ's activities is to fulfil the interests and purposes of the receiving State.

5.   This Rule extends to *ultra vires* acts.[157] For instance, consider the case of a sending State that places its cyber rapid reaction team at the full disposal of a receiving State. The latter instructs the team to conduct only passive defences and mitigate any harm that has been caused by the cyber event in question. On its own accord, the team engages in active cyber defence such as hacking back or conducting denial of service operations. The receiving State bears responsibility for those actions the team conducts in violation of international law.

6.   Only in cases in which one State's organ is placed at the disposal of another State in order to exercise elements of governmental authority does the Rule apply. It would not encompass, for instance, situations in which the organ is used to facilitate or otherwise support the receiving State's commercial activities. As noted in Rule 15, the precise parameters of the notion of governmental authority are somewhat ambiguous and are situation and State specific.

7.   As to situations in which one State aids or assists another State that engages in an internationally wrongful act, see Rule 18.

Rule 17 – Attribution of cyber operations by non-State actors

Cyber operations conducted by a non-State actor are attributable to a State when:

(a) **engaged in pursuant to its instructions or under its direction or control; or**

(b) **the State acknowledges and adopts the operations as its own.**

---

[157] Articles on State Responsibility, Art. 7, para. 9 of commentary.

1. As a general rule, the cyber operations of private persons or groups are not attributable to States.[158] However, Article 8 of the Articles on State Responsibility provides that '[t]he conduct of a person or group of persons shall be considered an act of a State under international law if the person or group of persons is in fact acting on the instructions of, or under the direction or control of, that State in carrying out the conduct'.[159]

2. For the purposes of this Rule, non-State actors include both individuals and groups. Groups are considered non-State actors under this Rule whether incorporated or unincorporated; hierarchical or non-hierarchical; organised or unorganised; and possessing domestic legal personality or not. The term encompasses, *inter alia*, individual hackers; informal groups like Anonymous; criminal organisations engaged in cyber crime; legal entities such as commercial IT services, software, and hardware companies; and cyber terrorists or insurgents.

3. *Lit.* (a) articulates the legal standard for attribution of non-State actors' conduct based on the factual relationship between the person or group engaging in the cyber operations in question and the State. By this standard, 'a State may, either by specific directions or by exercising control over a group, in effect assume responsibility for their conduct. Each case will depend on its own facts'.[160]

4. Acting pursuant to instructions of a State is generally equated with conduct that is authorised by that State, but does not fall within the scope of Rule 15, which addresses entities that have been legally empowered to exercise particular elements of governmental authority.[161] 'Instructions' in the context of this Rule refers most typically to situations in which a non-State actor functions as a State's auxiliary. Consider, for instance, the case of unanticipated massive cyber operations directed against a State. The State has no standing cyber defence organisations. Therefore, the State instigates private individuals and groups to act as volunteers to help respond to the crisis. It is clear that during the incident they are acting as an auxiliary of the State in responding to the crisis; the individuals and group are an instrument of the State and acting on its behalf. Similarly,

---

[158] Articles on State Responsibility, chapeau to Chapter II of Part 1, paras. 2–3; Art. 8, para. 7 of commentary.

[159] Articles on State Responsibility, Art. 8. *See also* UN GGE 2013 Report, para. 23; UN GGE 2015 Report, para. 28(f).

[160] Articles on State Responsibility, Art. 8, para. 7 of commentary.

[161] Articles on State Responsibility, Art. 8, para. 2 of commentary.

'instructions' might apply to a private company that has been requested by the armed forces to conduct certain types of cyber operations to support ongoing kinetic operations. The operations of the company that are within the scope of the request are attributable to the State.

5.   In the commentary to the Articles on State Responsibility, the International Law Commission indicated that the terms 'instruction', 'direction', and 'control' are to be understood in the disjunctive.[162] However, courts tend to treat 'direction' and 'control' together.[163] The two terms refer to a continuing process of exercising authority over an activity such as a cyber operation. The International Group of Experts agreed that the phrase 'effective control' employed by the International Court of Justice in the *Nicaragua* and *Genocide* judgments captures the scope of the concept.[164]

6.   The International Court of Justice has explained that when a State exercises 'effective control' over a non-State actor's operations, the latter's actions are attributable to the State.[165] A State is in 'effective control' of a particular cyber operation by a non-State actor whenever it is the State that determines the execution and course of the specific operation and the cyber activity engaged in by the non-State actor is an 'integral part of that operation'.[166] Effective control includes both the ability to cause constituent activities of the operation to occur, as well as the ability to order the cessation of those that are underway. The International Court of Justice has confirmed that 'effective control' is not to be equated with the lower 'overall control' threshold used to classify armed conflicts (Rule 82).[167]

7.   As an example of effective control, consider a case in which one State plans and oversees an operation to use software updates to implant new vulnerabilities in software widely used by another State in its governmental computers. The former State concludes a confidential contract to embed the exploits with the company that produces the software and then directs the process of doing so. Such being the case, the company's behaviour is attributable to the controlling State.

---

[162] Articles on State Responsibility, Art. 8, para. 7 of commentary.
[163] CRAWFORD, STATE RESPONSIBILITY, at 146.
[164] *Nicaragua* judgment, para. 115; *Genocide* judgment, para. 400.
[165] *Nicaragua* judgment, para. 115. *See also* Articles on State Responsibility, Art. 8, para. 4 of commentary.
[166] Articles on State Responsibility, Art. 8, para. 3 of commentary.
[167] *Genocide* judgment, paras. 404–406.

8.   A State's general support for or encouragement of a non-State actor or its cyber operations is insufficient to establish attribution. In particular, 'effective control' does not involve a State merely supplementing a non-State actor's cyber activities or assuming responsibility for performing a particular function. For example, the provision of malware by a State to a non-State actor does not amount, without more, to effective control over operations conducted by the group using that malware.

9.   In the context of a non-State actor's actions, a State's preponderant or decisive participation in the 'financing, organising, training, supplying, and equipping . . ., the selection of its military or paramilitary targets, and the planning of the whole of its operation' has been found insufficient to reach the 'effective control' threshold.[168] Of course, the fact that the non-State group's cyber activities are not attributable to a State does not mean that the State would not bear responsibility for its support if such support *per se* amounts to a violation of international law. For instance, the provision of malware to the group may constitute prohibited intervention by the State (Rule 66).

10.   An interesting situation involves State-owned companies, such as an IT firm. As noted in Rule 15, State ownership of a company alone is insufficient for characterising it as an organ of the State. Companies that fail to qualify as an organ of a State or that are not exercising elements of governmental authority (Rule 15) are subject to this Rule. Therefore, if such a company's cyber operations are conducted pursuant to the State's instructions or under its effective control, the activities are attributable to the State on the basis of this Rule.[169]

11.   In contrast to Rules 15 and 16, *ultra vires* acts of non-State actors are generally not attributable to the State. The International Group of Experts cautioned that application of this general principle can prove highly complex and each case must be assessed on its own merits.[170]

12.   The notion of *ultra vires* acts with respect to non-State actors who are acting pursuant to the instructions of a State can be illustrated through three contrasting situations. In the first, the State instructs a private company that is under contract to support its armed forces to engage in a cyber operation that breaches the State's international obligations to another State. For example, the State instructs the company to

---

[168] *Nicaragua* judgment, para. 115.
[169] Articles on State Responsibility, Art. 8, para. 6 of commentary.
[170] Articles on State Responsibility, Art. 8, paras. 7–8 of commentary.

conduct operations against another State's SCADA system in order to destroy property. To do so, it introduces a destructive logic bomb into that system. The conduct is attributable to the State. In the second situation, the State instructs the company to launch cyber operations against the SCADA system as a lawful countermeasure (Rule 20) against the other State. However, the malware spreads to systems in a third State, causing damage. The company's conduct was related to the operation it was instructed to carry out; therefore, the infection of the third State's systems is attributable to the State notwithstanding that the effect on the third State did not form part of the instructions. In the third situation, the State instructs a non-State actor to introduce malware into the other State's government networks. The non-State actor misappropriates the malware to target a third State. The operation cannot be attributed to State A because it is *ultra vires*.

13. If a non-State actor who is operating under the effective control of a State engages in *ultra vires* cyber operations, it must be assessed whether the *ultra vires* acts were 'incidental to the mission'.[171] The International Group of Experts agreed that if the *ultra vires* cyber operations are extraneous or unrelated to the purpose of the operation over which the State exercises 'effective control', they are not attributable to the controlling State. This means that conduct is only attributable so long as the *ultra vires* cyber operations are 'integral' in the sense that they are an essential part of the operation over which the State exercises 'effective control'. When this is the case, attribution attaches even if the non-State actor ignores or disobeys the directions that have been provided by the State for the conduct of the particular operation.[172]

14. Consider a case in which State A is in effective control of a cyber operation by a private IT company that is to employ a particular server in State B. However, as the operation is unfolding, doing so becomes technically impossible and, without seeking authorisation from State A, the company executes the operation through a server in State C in a manner that breaches an obligation State A owes to State C. Although State A had not explicitly authorised the use of the server in State C, attribution will nevertheless result because the use of the server was incidental to the operation. By contrast, if the company, in carrying out the mission, also unlawfully gathers data on a business competitor from the server, that aspect of the operation will not be

---

[171] Articles on State Responsibility, Art. 8, para. 8.
[172] Articles on State Responsibility, Art. 8, paras. 7–8 of commentary.

attributable to State A because it is beyond the purpose of the cyber operation and is, accordingly, *ultra vires*.

15. Pursuant to *lit.* (b), acts may nevertheless be attributed to the State when the attribution requirements set forth in *lit.* (a) are not met. Article 11 of the Articles on State Responsibility provides, 'conduct which is not attributable to a State under the preceding articles shall nevertheless be considered an act of that State under international law if and to the extent that the State acknowledges and adopts the conduct in question as its own'.[173] The International Court of Justice recognised this basis as customary international law in the *Tehran Hostages* case. There the Court found that Iran bore responsibility for holding US hostages between 1979 and 1981 because '[t]he approval given to [the seizure] by the Ayatollah Khomeini and other organs of the Iranian State, and the decision to perpetuate them, translated the continuing occupation of the Embassy and detention of the hostages into acts of that State'.[174]

16. Note that the standard set out in *lit.* (b) is to be narrowly applied. Not only are the conditions of 'acknowledgement' and 'adoption' cumulative, but they also require more than mere endorsement or tacit approval of the non-State actor's cyber operations, albeit not express endorsement.[175] By contrast, the standard entails, whether in the form of words or conduct, an identification of a particular factual situation ('acknowledgement') that the State concerned makes its own ('adoption').[176] Consider the case of cyber operations conducted by a non-State actor against a State. If another State later merely expresses approval of them, attribution does not attach. However, if the other State adopts them, for instance by intentionally employing its cyber capabilities to protect the non-State actor against counter-cyber operations so as to facilitate their continuance as acts of that State, the requirements for attribution have been met.

17. States may acknowledge and adopt only some of the acts of a non-State group, a point reflected in the 'if and to the extent' phrasing in Article 11. For instance, consider a hacker group that engages in various types of operations, or operations against different targets. The State might acknowledge and adopt operations by the group against

---

[173] Articles on State Responsibility, Art. 11.   [174] *Tehran Hostages* judgment, para. 74.
[175] Articles on State Responsibility, Art. 11, paras. 6, 9 of commentary. *See also Lighthouses Arbitration (Fr. v. Greece)*, 12 RIAA 155, 198 (1956).
[176] Articles on State Responsibility, Art. 11, paras. 6, 8 of commentary.

another State's government agency, but not those that the group is directing against the families of State officials.

18.   A few of the Experts were of the view that *lit.* (b) only applies prospectively. By that view, Article 11 of the Articles on State Responsibility is based on a misreading of the judgment in the *Tehran Hostages* case. For the proponents of this view, the International Court of Justice determined that the attitude taken by the Iranian authorities had only prospectively, not retroactively, transformed the conduct of the students into that of the State of Iran.

19.   This Rule applies solely to attribution for the purposes of State responsibility. However, a State's involvement with a non-State actor or another State may itself constitute a violation of international law, even in cases where the cyber operations of the non-State actor or the other State cannot be attributed to the State. For instance, if a State provides hacking tools to an insurgent group operating on another State's territory that are subsequently employed by the group on its own initiative against the State where the group is based, the mere provision of these tools is insufficient to attribute the group's operation to the supplying State. Nevertheless, the provision of the hacking tools may itself constitute a violation of international law (see Rule 66 on intervention and 68 on the use of force).

Rule 18 – Responsibility in connection with cyber operations by other States

With respect to cyber operations, a State is responsible for:

(a) its aid or assistance to another State in the commission of an internationally wrongful act when the State provides the aid or assistance knowing of the circumstances of the internationally wrongful act and the act would be internationally wrongful if committed by it;

(b) the internationally wrongful act of another State it directs and controls if the direction and control is done with knowledge of the circumstances of the internationally wrongful act and the act would be internationally wrongful if committed by it; or

(c) an internationally wrongful act it coerces another State to commit.

1.   A State is responsible for its acts related to an internationally wrongful act by another State in the three circumstances set forth in this Rule. This is so whether that act is cyber or non-cyber in nature.

Moreover, responsibility may arise when the State engages in non-cyber activities in support of the other State's wrongful cyber operation.[177]

2. The actions encompassed in this Rule must breach an obligation owed by the State engaging in them to the injured State. As an example, consider a case in which State A conducts a cyber operation that breaches a treaty obligation it owes to State B. State A is assisted by State C, which is not a Party to the treaty. Only State A bears responsibility because State C does not owe such an obligation to State B. In this case, it must be cautioned that State C may nevertheless be subject to other treaty or customary law obligations with respect to State B and shoulder responsibility on the basis of their breach.

3. Regarding *lit.* (a), a State that aids or assists (the 'assisting State') the commission of an internationally wrongful act by another (the 'assisted State') will bear responsibility for such aid or assistance if: (1) the assisting State does so knowing the circumstances surrounding the unlawful act; (2) the aid or assistance is provided with the intention of facilitating the internationally wrongful act (and it does so facilitate the act); and (3) the act would have been wrongful if committed by the assisting State.[178] For example, allowing the assisted State to use the assisting State's cyber infrastructure, such as an ISP under its control, to mount a wrongful cyber operation could give rise to responsibility for the assisting State. Similarly, an assisting State may bear responsibility for financing an assisted State's wrongful cyber operation.

4. The requirement that the State actually be aware of the circumstances of the breach of the international legal obligation is critical in this regard.[179] For instance, if one State finances the acquisition of cyber capabilities by another State without knowing that those capabilities will be used to conduct internationally wrongful acts, it will bear no responsibility since it was unaware of the latter State's intentions.

5. There is no generally accepted definition of the term 'aid or assistance', drawn from Article 16 of the Articles on State Responsibility.[180] Nevertheless, the International Group of Experts agreed that

---

[177] Articles on State Responsibility, Arts. 16–18; *Genocide* judgment, para. 420.

[178] Articles on State Responsibility, Art. 16 and Art. 16, para. 3 of commentary. With respect to the wrongfulness requirement *vis-à-vis* the assisting State, note that a State is not bound by the obligations of another State with regard to third States. *See, e.g.*, Vienna Convention on the Law of Treaties, Arts. 34–35.

[179] Articles on State Responsibility, Art. 16, para. 4 of commentary.

[180] Note that the International Law Commission did not distinguish between 'aiding' and 'assisting'; nor did the International Court of Justice in *Genocide* judgment, para. 420.

aiding or assisting is a threshold that falls below that of jointly conducting an act and lies above participation that is merely tangential to the
act.[181] In its commentary, the International Law Commission indicated
that the aid or assistance must contribute 'significantly' to the act in
question.[182] Earlier, it had stated that the aid or assistance 'must have the
effect of making it materially easier for the State receiving the aid or
assistance in question to commit the internationally wrongful act'.[183] The
Experts concurred with these characterisations and therefore concluded
that the aid or assistance, irrespective of the form it takes, must materially
and causally contribute to the aided or assisted State's internationally
wrongful act. They cautioned that, since a degree of ambiguity remains,
each situation must be addressed contextually.

6.   It is important to distinguish between responsibility under *lit.*
(a) and that which attaches under *lit.* (b) and (c). In the case of *lit.*
(a), the State that provides aid or assistance is responsible solely for
the contribution to the internationally wrongful act made by virtue of
the aid or assistance, not for the entirety of the internationally wrongful act of the State receiving the aid or assistance.[184] To illustrate, take
the case of an assisting State merely providing some of the financing
for another State's wrongful cyber operation. The assisting State is
only responsible to the extent its financing caused or contributed to
the internationally wrongful act. By contrast, in *lit.* (b) and (c) situations a State that directs and controls, or coerces, another State is
responsible for the resulting internationally wrongful conduct of the
latter.

7.   The International Group of Experts noted that in some circumstances a State's aid or assistance may be such an essential and integral
aspect of the assisted State's operation that the former will in fact be
responsible for the entire internationally wrongful act.[185] For instance,
if a State provides uniquely effective and indispensable decryption
capabilities to another State to enable the latter to conduct a harmful
cyber operation, and without which the operation could not be
mounted, the assisting State will be responsible for the harm caused
to the injured State. In cases where more than one State is responsible

---

[181] CRAWFORD, STATE RESPONSIBILITY, at 401–403.
[182] Articles on State Responsibility, Art. 16, para. 5 of commentary.
[183] International Law Commission Yearbook, vol. 2(2) (1998), at 99.
[184] Articles on State Responsibility, Art. 16, paras. 1, 10 of commentary.
[185] Articles on State Responsibility, Art. 16, para. 10 of commentary.

for the same internationally wrongful act, the responsibility of each may be invoked by the injured State.[186]

8.   *Lit.* (b) sets forth a second basis of responsibility for another State's wrongful cyber operation – directing and controlling the latter's commission of an operation in the knowledge that it is wrongful with respect to its own obligations.[187] The State mounting the operation essentially serves as a surrogate; therefore, the State exercising direction and control is fully responsible for its surrogate's actions. *Lit.* (b) situations are distinguished from those provided for by *lit.* (a) in the sense that, whereas the latter involves a contribution to another State's wrongful act and therefore responsibility only attaches for the extent of that contribution, *lit.* (b) refers to those in which a State completely controls the act of another State and therefore is responsible for the controlled State's wrongful act.[188] It must be cautioned that the controlled State is not, unlike the situations referred to in *lit.* (c), excused from responsibility for its wrongful act, unless it can rely on any of the circumstances precluding wrongfulness cited in Rule 19. Situations falling within *lit.* (b) are rare, given that States, while perhaps subject to other States' influence, interference, oversight, or incitement, are seldom in their control. Occupation is the most relevant contemporary illustration of such control.

9.   Coercion, provided for in *lit.* (c), is the third basis for rendering a State responsible for another State's wrongful acts.[189] The degree of coercive effect must be extremely high; '[n]othing less than conduct which forces the will of the coerced State will suffice, giving it no effective choice but to comply with the wishes of the coercing State'.[190] Because the coerced State has no option other than to act pursuant to the coercing State's will, as a general matter, it will not be responsible *vis-à-vis* the injured State.[191] As an example, State A might threaten to take devastating economic measures against State B if the latter does not engage in a particular cyber operation, such as altering critical data of State C stored on servers located in State B. State A, not State B, is responsible for the alteration of the data and any foreseeable consequences thereof.

---

[186] Articles on State Responsibility, Art. 47(1).
[187] Articles on State Responsibility, Art. 17.
[188] Articles on State Responsibility, Art. 17, para. 1 of commentary.
[189] Articles on State Responsibility, Art. 18.
[190] Articles on State Responsibility, Art. 18, para. 2 of commentary.
[191] Articles on State Responsibility, Art. 18, para. 4 of commentary.

10.   The International Group of Experts acknowledged, but did not concur with, a view by which the Articles on State Responsibility underlying *lit.* (b) and (c) constitute progressive development of the law and not a reflection of customary international law.

Rule 19 – Circumstances precluding wrongfulness of cyber operations

The wrongfulness of an act involving cyber operations is precluded in the case of:

(a) consent;
(b) self-defence;
(c) countermeasures;
(d) necessity;
(e) *force majeure*; or
(f) distress.

1.   This Rule is based on the grounds set forth in Part One, Chapter V, of the Articles on State Responsibility. Should one of the enumerated circumstances exist, the action or omission in question will not be 'wrongful' and, therefore, the State engaging in the, or omitting required, conduct will not bear responsibility for what would otherwise be a wrongful breach of an obligation owed to the injured State. As will be discussed, the circumstances merely excuse non-performance of the obligation while the condition exists; they do not extinguish the obligation altogether.[192]

2.   By *lit.* (a), a State's consent to a cyber operation by another State bars the former from claiming that the operation breached an obligation it was owed.[193] For example, one State may allow another State temporarily to take control of certain elements of its cyber infrastructure in order to allow the latter to identify and respond to malicious activities occurring therein. Should this occur, the former may not claim that it has suffered a breach of an obligation, such as respect for sovereignty (Rule 4) or non-intervention (Rule 66), that it is owed by the latter.

3.   Consent to a cyber operation only precludes the wrongfulness of an action or omission to the extent the consent is valid as a matter of law.

---

[192] *Gabčíkovo-Nagymaros* judgment, paras. 47–48. *See also Rainbow Warrior* arbitral award, para. 79.

[193] Articles on State Responsibility, Art. 20. *See also Armed Activities* judgment, paras. 45–46.

Valid consent is that which is freely given, in other words, consent that is not the result of threat or coercion.[194] Additionally, the cyber operation in question may not exceed the scope of the State's consent, that is, does not go beyond the action or omission for which consent was granted.[195] As an illustration, consider a case in which a State consents to another State's use of its cyber infrastructure to conduct joint intelligence operations. If the latter uses the access in order to mount cyber operations against its partner, the scope of consent has been exceeded and the consent cannot be relied upon to escape responsibility.

4. Generally, consent is only valid when given by a competent State organ that, or a particular individual who, is authorised to grant consent on the State's behalf. The authority to grant consent depends on the specific rule of international law that would otherwise be breached. Different officials or agencies enjoy the authority to consent in different contexts. For instance, whereas a head of mission may have the authority to consent to entry into diplomatic premises,[196] that diplomat would not enjoy authority to consent to manipulation of cyber infrastructure within his or her own State's territory.

5. In certain cases, an official of one State might consent, without the domestic authority to do so, to another State's cyber activities. If the latter State subsequently relies on such an apparent grant of consent, the consent will preclude wrongfulness so long as that State acted in good faith in the belief that the former State had validly consented. The question will be whether the State engaging in the act that breaches an obligation owed to the first State had reason to know of the absence of authority.[197]

6. The consent envisioned in this Rule is that of the State. In some limited cases, the consent of individuals or entities such as private companies may nevertheless influence the determination of whether consent precludes wrongfulness.[198] For example, a State may be acting in collaboration with an information technology company based abroad that has 'consented' to the activities (which would otherwise breach an obligation it owes the other State) through contract. If the State is acting

---

[194] Articles on State Responsibility, Art. 20.
[195] Articles on State Responsibility, Art. 20. The Article refers to 'a given act' and emphasises that consent only precludes wrongfulness 'to the extent that the act remains within the limits of that consent'. *See also Armed Activities* judgment, para. 52.
[196] Vienna Convention on Diplomatic Relations, Art. 22(1).
[197] Articles on State Responsibility, Art. 20, para. 4 of commentary.
[198] Articles on State Responsibility, Art. 20, para. 10 of commentary.

in a good faith belief that the company enjoyed authority under domestic law to consent to the action, that fact will bear on the determination of whether the action constituted an internationally wrongful act on the part of the State.

7.   Consent need not always be express. Implicit consent may sometimes suffice.[199] Take the earlier example of a State that is engaged in joint cyber operations with another State involving use of cyber infrastructure on the latter's territory. If no express agreement sets forth the precise parameters of the joint operations, a question might arise as to whether particular acts of the former were consented to by the latter. The issue is whether the former acted in good faith in the reasonable belief that the latter had impliedly consented to those aspects of the operation that are in question. It must be cautioned that consent cannot be 'merely presumed on the basis that the State would have consented if it had been asked'.[200]

8.   The timing of the injured State's consent is critical. This Rule only operates *vis-à-vis* consent granted prior to the conduct or omission or while that conduct or omission is underway.[201] Purported consent granted following the action or omission in fact amounts to waiver or acquiescence,[202] not a circumstance precluding wrongfulness. In such cases, the State is essentially renouncing a right to invoke State responsibility against the State engaging in the internationally wrongful act.

9.   In some cases, cyber operations result in unforeseen consequences. So long as those consequences are the result of the specific act consented to, the consent remains valid despite their unforeseeability. Yet, if the consequences are foreseen by the acting State and reasonably unforeseeable by the consenting State, the consent may be invalid because it was fraudulently solicited, as discussed below. Consider the case of cyber operations being conducted by one State in another's territory with the latter's consent. The former knows of a flaw in the malware it is using that will have negative effects on systems that are not the target of the operation. It intentionally fails to inform the latter. The consent would not preclude any wrongfulness of the conduct in question because the

---

[199]   *The Savakar Case (Gr. Brit. v. Fr.)*, 11 RIAA 243, 252–255 (1911); *Russian Indemnity* arbitral award, at 446.

[200]   Articles on State Responsibility, Art. 20, para. 6 of commentary. *See also Armed Activities* judgment, para. 99.

[201]   *Armed Activities* judgment, paras. 45–46, 96.

[202]   Articles on State Responsibility, Art. 45.

former knew that the operation would have deleterious consequences for the latter and the latter was unaware of those consequences at the time it agreed to the operation.

10.   The International Group of Experts agreed that, as a general matter, the rules set forth in the Vienna Convention on the Law of Treaties, albeit not universally considered fully reflective of customary international law, are useful by analogy in grasping the notion of invalidity of consent, even in cases not involving a treaty norm. Pursuant to that treaty, the bases for invalidity are: violation of internal law when the violation was 'manifest and concerned a rule of its internal law of fundamental importance'; express withdrawal of an official's authority to consent when said withdrawal was notified to the other party; error; fraud; corruption of the representative of the State; coercion of the representative of the State; coercion of the State; and conflict with a peremptory norm of general international law (*jus cogens*).[203]

11.   Pursuant to *lit.* (b), cyber operations that qualify as self-defence against an armed attack, whether executed by cyber or kinetic means, in the *jus ad bellum* context (Rule 71) do not amount to internationally wrongful acts.[204] In this regard, it is not only the wrongfulness of using force (Rule 68) that is precluded. For instance, qualification of an action as self-defence would also preclude its characterisation as a violation of the sovereignty (Rule 4) of the State that conducted the armed attack.

12.   In the event an armed attack initiates an armed conflict (Rules 82–83), the fact that the response qualifies as lawful self-defence does not preclude the wrongfulness of any law of armed conflict violations that may occur. For instance, defensive measures may not include conducting cyber attacks against civilians (Rule 94) or civilian objects (Rule 98). Similarly, the fact that operations are conducted in self-defence does not necessarily preclude the wrongfulness of the conduct with respect to applicable human rights obligations (Rule 35) from which the State has not derogated (Rule 38).[205]

13.   *Lit.* (c) acknowledges that the qualification of a cyber operation as a countermeasure precludes the wrongfulness of the operation.[206]

---

[203] Vienna Convention on the Law of Treaties, Arts. 46–53.
[204] Articles on State Responsibility, Art. 21.
[205] *Nuclear Weapons* advisory opinion, para. 30. The International Court of Justice made this point in the context of international environmental law.
[206] Articles on State Responsibility, Art. 22.

However, as with self-defence, a countermeasure taken against one State does not necessarily preclude its wrongfulness *vis-à-vis* other States.[207] On countermeasures, see Section 2 of this Chapter.

14.   *Lit.* (d) addresses situations in which the wrongfulness of a State's act is precluded by virtue of necessity. The plea of necessity is discussed in Rule 26.

15.   *Lit.* (e) deals with *'force majeure'* situations. The term refers to circumstances that involve 'the occurrence of an irresistible force or of an unforeseen event, beyond the control of the State, making it materially impossible in the circumstances to perform the obligation'.[208] In essence, the action or omission that would otherwise qualify as an internationally wrongful act is involuntary. A force is irresistible when it amounts to 'a constraint that the State was unable to avoid or oppose by its own means'.[209] To preclude wrongfulness, the irresistible force or event must be the cause of the material impossibility of performing the obligation.[210] Take the case of a State that has a treaty obligation with another State allowing the latter to use a specific server park located on its territory. The server park is destroyed in a hurricane, putting the former State in breach of its treaty obligation. In this case, *force majeure* precludes the wrongfulness of the breach of the treaty's terms.

16.   *Force majeure* does not extend to situations in which the performance of the obligation is merely rendered more onerous, such as an increase in cost or the causation of political or economic consequences.[211] Neither does it encompass situations in which the responsible State is unable to comply with its obligation due to its own conduct, especially negligent conduct.[212] In the case above involving

---

[207] Articles on State Responsibility, Art. 22, paras. 4–5 of commentary.

[208] Articles on State Responsibility, Art. 23.

[209] Articles on State Responsibility, Art. 23, para. 2 of commentary.

[210] *See, e.g., Gould Marketing, Inc.* v. *Ministry of Defence of Iran*, Interlocutory Award No. ITL 24-49-2, 3 Iran–US CTR 147, 153 (27 July 1983); *Anaconda-Iran, Inc.* v. *Iran* et al., Interlocutory Award No. ITL 65-167-3, 13 Iran–US CTR 199, 213 (10 December 1986). The US–Iran Claims Tribunal has, for instance, cited 'social and economic forces beyond the power of the state to control through the exercise of due diligence' and 'strikes, riots and other civil strife in the course of [the Iranian] Revolution' as examples of *force majeure*.

[211] *Russian Indemnity* arbitral award, at 39–40; *Sempra* v. *Argentina* arbitral award, para. 246; *Rainbow Warrior* arbitral award, para. 77.

[212] Articles on State Responsibility, Art. 23(2)(a); *Libyan Arab Foreign Investment Company* v. *Burundi*, 96 ILR 279, 318 (1994).

the hurricane, assume the State had ample warning, but failed to take reasonable measures to back up the data resident in the server park in a safe location. The State may not claim *force majeure* as a ground for precluding the wrongfulness of its breach. Along the same lines, a State invoking the responsibility of another State may not do so if it has materially contributed to the situation amounting to *force majeure*. Consider a case in which a State is providing assistance to a rebellion in another State. A treaty requires the latter to sell particular computer equipment to the former. The rebels seize control of territory on which the equipment is stored. The former may not invoke the responsibility of the latter because it has contributed to the *force majeure* situation that makes it impossible for the former to comply with its treaty obligation. Additionally, the preclusion of wrongfulness based upon *force majeure* does not operate when the injured State has assumed the risk of *force majeure* in a provision of the treaty in question.[213]

17. *Force majeure* must be distinguished from supervening impossibility of performance of an international obligation. The latter principle, which is set forth in Article 61 of the Vienna Convention on the Law of Treaties, only deals with the termination or suspension of a treaty obligation. Article 61 provides that 'permanent disappearance or destruction of an object indispensable for the execution' of a relevant treaty provision precludes the wrongfulness of a breach of that provision.[214] In the example above, the destruction of the server park specified in the treaty would permit suspension or termination of the treaty, should one of the Parties desire to do so. Similarly, if during a non-international armed conflict, rebel forces destroyed that server park, the State shouldering the obligation to make available its use may suspend or terminate the treaty. Note that suspension or termination is only permissible when an object indispensable to the performance has disappeared. Therefore, the State could not suspend or terminate the treaty on the basis of, for instance, significantly increased cost of maintaining the server park.

18. *Lit.* (f) provides that distress precludes wrongfulness in situations in which a person whose actions are attributable to the State has 'no other reasonable way... of saving [his or her] life or the lives of other persons entrusted to [his or her] care'.[215] This ground for preclusion differs from

---

[213] Articles on State Responsibility, Art. 23(2)(b).
[214] Vienna Convention on the Law of Treaties, Art. 61.
[215] Articles on State Responsibility, Art. 24(1).

force majeure in that whereas the former applies only in situations that are beyond the State's control, options exist in cases of distress but the only reasonable course of action is to select a specific one.

19.   Distress is limited to situations that involve a threat to life; it does not extend to the breach of any obligation that is unnecessary to safeguard the life of the individual or others.[216] As an illustration, assume a State has agreed by treaty to allow another State to use its satellite navigation services. Distress would be exemplified if the former suspends its navigation services due to the risk of malware infection from a third State that would alter navigational data and pose a grave risk to vessels and aircraft relying upon the system.

20.   As with *force majeure*, distress does not preclude wrongfulness in situations in which the State levelling a claim of responsibility against another has contributed to the situation of distress. Additionally, an act may not be justified on the basis of distress if it can reasonably be expected to result in comparable or greater harm than compliance with the obligation in question.[217] In the example above regarding navigation, this would be the case if infection by the malware would be less dangerous than interrupting the satellite services.

21.   The International Group of Experts noted that a cyber operation authorised by the UN Security Council under Chapter VII of the UN Charter is lawful *ab initio* (Rule 76). Therefore, in such situations, there is no wrongfulness to be precluded. In this regard, note that Article 103 of the UN Charter provides for the supremacy of United Nations Charter obligations over other international legal obligations for members of the organisation. Article 59 of the Articles on State Responsibility acknowledges this hierarchy.

22.   Under no circumstances may the wrongfulness of a violation of a peremptory norm by cyber means be precluded. A peremptory norm is one that is 'accepted and recognised by the international community of States as a whole as a norm from which no derogation is permitted and which can be modified only by a subsequent norm of general international law having the same character'.[218] This principle, set forth in Article 53 of the Vienna Convention on the Law of Treaties, undoubtedly applies as a matter of customary international

---

[216] *Kate A. Hoff, Administratrix of the Estate of Samuel B. Allison, Deceased (USA)* v. *United Mexican States*, 4 RIAA 444 (1929).
[217] Articles on State Responsibility, Art. 24(2).
[218] Vienna Convention on the Law of Treaties, Art. 53.

law.[219] Although it is unsettled whether certain norms are peremptory in character, the status of some norms as peremptory is unquestioned. Prominent among these are the prohibitions of aggression, genocide, and torture.

23. In situations in which the circumstances precluding the wrongfulness of a cyber action or omission cease or fade over time, the State concerned must resume compliance with its obligations to the extent it can still do so.[220]

SECTION 2:   STATE COUNTERMEASURES AND NECESSITY

Rule 20 – Countermeasures (general principle)

A State may be entitled to take countermeasures, whether cyber in nature or not, in response to a breach of an international legal obligation that it is owed by another State.

1. The wrongfulness under international law of an injured State's cyber operation is precluded if the operation qualifies as a countermeasure. Only available in response to internationally wrongful acts, countermeasures are actions or omissions by an injured State directed against a responsible State that would violate an obligation owed by the former to the latter but for qualification as a countermeasure. Both the International Court of Justice and arbitral tribunals have recognised countermeasures as lawful under international law.[221]

2. In the first half of the twentieth century, countermeasures were labelled 'peacetime reprisals', a term that is no longer used. The historical notion of reprisals was broader than that of countermeasures in that it included both non-forcible and forcible actions.[222] As noted in Rule 22,

---

[219] See also Furundžija judgment, paras. 144–155.
[220] Articles on State Responsibility, Art. 27(a); Gabčíkovo-Nagymaros judgment, para. 101 (with respect to necessity).
[221] Nicaragua judgment, para. 249; Gabčíkovo-Nagymaros judgment, paras. 82–83. See also Naulilaa arbitral award, at 1025–1026; Responsabilité de l'Allemagne en raison des actes commis postérieurement au 31 juillet 1914 et avant que le Portugal ne participât à la guerre ('Cysne') (Port. v. Ger.), 2 RIAA 1035 (1930), at 1052; Air Services arbitral award, paras. 80–96.
[222] See, e.g., PEARCE HIGGINS, HALL'S INTERNATIONAL LAW, 433–434 (8th edn, 1924); T. J. LAWRENCE, THE PRINCIPLES OF INTERNATIONAL LAW, 311–315 (7th edn, 1910).

the qualification of a forcible action as a countermeasure is an unsettled issue. However, forcible peacetime reprisals have today been broadly subsumed into the UN Charter's use of force paradigm, which allows States to resort to force in self-defence in response to armed attacks (Rule 71).

3. Countermeasures must be distinguished from 'belligerent reprisals'. Belligerent reprisals comprise certain actions taken during an armed conflict that would ordinarily violate the law of armed conflict but for the enemy's prior unlawful conduct (Rule 108). The concept of countermeasures is not applicable to actions taken against the enemy during armed conflict that have a nexus to the conflict. However, countermeasures, whether cyber or non-cyber in nature, are available as a response to actions taken by a party to an international armed conflict with respect to violations of legal regimes other than the law of armed conflict.

4. The fact that countermeasures involve acts that would otherwise be unlawful also distinguishes them from retorsion. Retorsion refers to the taking of measures that are lawful, albeit 'unfriendly'.[223] A State may, for instance, employ an access control list to prevent communications from another State because the former enjoys sovereignty over the cyber infrastructure on its territory (Rule 2). The action would be lawful even if detrimental to the interests of the latter so long as it violates no treaty obligation or applicable customary law norm.

5. Countermeasures may only be conducted by an injured State to induce or cause the responsible State to resume compliance with its international legal obligations. In that countermeasures contemplate actions that would otherwise be unlawful, international law places strict restrictions on their use. These restrictions, discussed in Rules 21–23, concern their purpose, relationship with other legal rights and duties, means and scope of execution, originators, and targets. Such limitations on the taking of countermeasures are the reason the term 'may be' is used in lieu of 'is' in this Rule.

6. The targets of a countermeasure need not be State organs or State cyber infrastructure, although a State must be the 'object' of the countermeasure. Consider a situation in which organs of a responsible State are conducting cyber operations resulting in loss of functionality of private cyber infrastructure in the injured State. The injured State responds in

---

[223] Articles on State Responsibility, chapeau to Chapter II of Part 3, para. 3 of commentary.

kind. Since the responsible State has itself engaged in an internationally wrongful act, the cyber countermeasure is lawful; as a matter of law, the State is the object of the countermeasure, which is designed to put an end to that State's wrongful activity. By contrast, assume that a private firm in the first State is engaging in harmful cyber operations against a competitor in the second State. In such a case, it would be inappropriate for the second State to launch countermeasures against the firm unless the firm's action can be attributed to the first State (Rules 15 and 17) or that State has wrongfully failed to control the activities of the firm and therefore breached its due diligence obligation to control its territory once it became aware of the operations (Rules 6–7).

7. It is important to emphasise that countermeasures are not available in response to a cyber operation conducted by a non-State actor unless the operation is attributable to a State (Rules 15 and 17). Consider a situation in which a hacktivist group located in one State exploits a buffer overflow vulnerability in a SCADA system located in another. Whether the latter may launch a remote take-down operation against the hacktivist group's server as a countermeasure depends, *inter alia*, on whether the group's activities are attributable to the former (or in certain cases discussed in Rules 6–7, operation of the due diligence principle).

8. The International Group of Experts acknowledged a view by which countermeasures may be taken against non-State actors. According to this view, non-State entities may engage in cyber operations that breach obligations they purportedly owe States, such as compliance with the prohibition of the use of force and the requirement to respect their sovereignty. By this view, to the extent non-State actors owe States legal obligations, the 'injured' States are entitled to take countermeasures against the non-State actors in the event they breach such obligations.

9. For its advocates, this approach is especially appropriate in situations in which no State is responsible for the malicious cyber operation in question. Consider a case in which a terrorist group situated in one State engages in cyber operations against another State, and the operations result in physical damage to hardware on the territory of the latter. Had the operations been conducted by a State, they would at least have violated the latter's sovereignty (Rule 4). The first State takes all feasible measures to terminate the group's cyber operations originating in its territory, in line with its duty to exercise due diligence (Rules 6–7), but ultimately fails and the operations persist. The target State, continuing to suffer harm from the group's activities, may, according to proponents of the approach, take

countermeasures against the group, even though those measures might infringe upon the first State's sovereignty.

10.   The Experts disagreed with the approach both on the basis that countermeasures are limited to measures directed against responsible States and that only States are subject to the international law prohibitions cited by its advocates. They emphasised that their view should not be taken to suggest that such non-State actors' cyber operations are lawful; in all likelihood, they would violate the target State's domestic law. However, the Experts pointed out that other circumstances precluding wrongfulness (Rule 19), such as the plea of necessity (Rule 26) or self-defence (Rule 71), may permit States to take measures in response to non-State actor cyber operations.

11.   Recommendations made and measures imposed by the Security Council pursuant to Chapter VII of the UN Charter do not qualify as countermeasures because the Council's powers render them lawful *ab initio* (Rule 76). For example, Article 41 of the UN Charter describes interruption of communications as a non-forcible measure that may, in accordance with a decision of the Security Council, be taken to address a threat to the peace, breach of the peace, or act of aggression.[224] Thus, interference by one State with another State's cyber capabilities that has been authorised by a Security Council resolution under Chapter VII of the Charter is lawful and, hence, not a countermeasure because there is no wrongfulness that needs be precluded.

12.   Countermeasures must also be distinguished from actions taken based on a plea of necessity (Rule 26). The former differ from the plea in two main ways. First, there must be an underlying internationally wrongful act to justify countermeasures, whereas necessity has no such condition precedent. In other words, the act that precipitates a countermeasure must be attributable to a State, while acts pursuant to the plea of necessity may be taken in response to the cyber operations of non-State actors (or even when the author of the act is unidentified). Second, mere international wrongfulness suffices to trigger the right to take countermeasures; action based on necessity is only permissible when the situation amounts to a grave and imminent peril to an essential interest of the acting State.

13.   Application of the law of treaties can affect the permissibility of countermeasures. As a general matter, a State may respond to the breach

---

[224] UN Charter, Art. 41.

of a treaty obligation constituting an internationally wrongful act through countermeasures. However, note that some treaties may bar countermeasures in particular situations and instead impose a requirement to resort to specific means of dispute resolution.[225] For example, a bilateral treaty may prohibit countermeasures in response to breaches of the treaty's terms and require recourse to a regional organisation to address breaches thereof. In such a case, the injured State Party may not take cyber or other countermeasures in response to the breach, at least not until efforts to resolve the matter through the regional organisation have been exhausted.

14.   The aforementioned situation must be distinguished from one in which a Party to a treaty suspends or terminates its operation based on a material breach of the treaty's terms by another Party.[226] Material breach refers to a violation of a provision in the treaty that is 'essential to the accomplishment of the object or purpose of the treaty'.[227] As an example, assume one State executes an international agreement with another to store its critical data on the servers of the latter for purposes of redundancy. If the latter State subsequently refuses to allow the data to be so stored, it has materially breached the treaty because the treaty's primary purpose is the storage of the data. Although the Parties need no longer comply with their obligations under the treaty once it has been suspended or terminated, the injured Party may take countermeasures to cause the responsible Party to make reparation (Rule 28).

15.   As discussed in the chapeau to Section 1 of this Chapter and Rule 15, it is often difficult to attribute cyber activities to a particular State or actor with unqualified certainty. In particular, cyber operations can be designed to mask or spoof the originator. Consider a case in which State A takes control of State B's cyber infrastructure and uses it to mount harmful operations against State C to make State C believe that State B is conducting them. State C arrives at that conclusion and launches countermeasures against State B. The urgency of this situation does not allow State C the time to notify State B of its intent to launch

---

[225] Articles on State Responsibility, Art. 50, para. 10 of commentary.

[226] Vienna Convention on the Law of Treaties, Arts. 60, 70(b), 72.

[227] Vienna Convention on the Law of Treaties, Art. 60(3)(b). *See also Legal Consequences for States of the Continued Presence of South Africa in Namibia (South West Africa) notwithstanding Security Council Resolution 276 (1970)*, advisory opinion, 1971 ICJ 16, para. 95 (21 June); *Gabčíkovo-Nagymaros* judgment, para. 106.

countermeasures (Rule 21). The International Group of Experts was split on the lawfulness of State C's countermeasure.

16.   A few of the Experts believed that although State C's determination that State B launched the operations is mistaken, if that mistake was reasonable in the attendant circumstances, State C's purported countermeasure, so long as all other requirements for countermeasures have been met, was lawful. The majority, however, agreed with the commentary to Article 49 of the Articles on State Responsibility to the effect that States taking countermeasures do so at their own risk, that is, the wrongfulness of their actions will not be precluded if they mistakenly attribute the cyber activities to a State that is not responsible.[228] These Experts emphasised the desirability of preventing a proliferation of countermeasures and the fact that countermeasures, despite being designed to resume lawful relations between the States concerned, nevertheless present a risk of escalation.

17.   The location from which a cyber or non-cyber countermeasure is launched does not affect its qualification as a countermeasure. However, location may implicate various aspects of international law. If, for example, agents of injured State A travel into State B without consent and launch a cyber operation against responsible State C, State A's agents may have violated the sovereignty of State B, but their action may nevertheless be a lawful countermeasure with respect to State C.

Rule 21 – Purpose of countermeasures

Countermeasures, whether cyber in nature or not, may only be taken to induce a responsible State to comply with the legal obligations it owes an injured State.

1.   The purpose of countermeasures is to cause the responsible State to cease its unlawful action or omission, and, where appropriate, provide assurances or guarantees (Rule 27) and make reparation (Rule 28).[229] They are a remedy designed to lead to a return to lawful relations between the States concerned. Punishment and retaliation are impermissible purposes.

---

[228] Articles on State Responsibility, Art. 49, para. 3 of commentary.

[229] Articles on State Responsibility, Art. 49(1). In the *Archer Daniels* arbitral award, Mexico's argument that a tax was lawful as a countermeasure was rejected on the basis that Mexico did not impose it in order to cause the United States to comply with its obligations. *Archer Daniels* arbitral award, paras. 134–151.

2.   Since their purpose is to incentivise the resumption of lawful interactions, that is, to lead to the cessation of a continuing wrongful act, the risk of escalation must be taken into account when deciding whether, and how, to engage in countermeasures. Relatedly, a measure that will only exacerbate the situation is mere retaliation and, as such, impermissible. As noted in the *Air Service* arbitration, '[c]ounter-measures ... should be a wager on the wisdom, not on the weakness of the other Party. They should be used with a spirit of great moderation and be accompanied by a genuine effort at resolving the dispute.'[230] This cautionary note is especially relevant with regard to cyber countermeasures because the speed with which the precipitating wrongful cyber operations may unfold poses a particular risk of a rapid retaliatory exchange that leaves little time for the careful consideration of possible consequences.

3.   The condition that the purpose of a countermeasure be to induce a return to compliance with international law does not exclude the possibility that a countermeasure by the injured State designed to achieve that objective may directly achieve compliance with an international legal obligation breached by the responsible State. For example, consider the case of two States that have just ended an international armed conflict (Rule 82). The first State maintains and regularly updates a database regarding the location of civilians who have been displaced by the armed conflict in the border region between the States. In contravention of its obligation under the law of armed conflict to facilitate the reunification of families following armed conflict,[231] that State refuses to release the information to the other. As a countermeasure, the second State hacks into the first State's government computer network, copies the database, and uses the information to enable the reunification of families. In view of the first State's continuing refusal to provide the information, the second State continues to exfiltrate updated information from the database on a regular basis. To the extent they might otherwise be unlawful, the second State's cyber operations are permissible as a countermeasure even though not designed to compel the first to provide the information itself.

4.   The International Group of Experts was divided on the issue of whether there is a requirement to attempt lesser means of convincing another State to desist in its internationally wrongful conduct before

---

[230] *Air Services* arbitral award, para. 91.
[231] Geneva Convention IV, Art. 26; Additional Protocol I, Art. 74; ICRC CUSTOMARY IHL STUDY, Rule 105.

turning to countermeasures. The majority of the Experts was of the view that there is no such obligation because the notification requirement (see below) offers adequate safeguards against the risk of escalation. However, some of the Experts took the opposite position. By their approach, for instance, an injured State would be required to attempt available acts of cyber retorsion before taking cyber countermeasures if they would likely cause the responsible State to comply with its obligations.

5.   Countermeasures, being intended to cause a responsible State to comply with its legal obligations, are by nature reactive, not prospective. As the International Court of Justice observed in the *Gabčíkovo-Nagymaros* judgment, they 'must be taken in response to a previous internationally wrongful act of another State'.[232] There is no countermeasure equivalent to anticipatory self-defence against an imminent cyber or kinetic armed attack (Rule 71). Nor may countermeasures be employed for preventive purposes. Take the case of a State involved in a non-international armed conflict. A neighbouring State that supports the anti-government forces could use social media websites to incite further violence against the government, such that it would violate the prohibition of intervention (Rule 66). The State involved in the conflict may not engage in preventive countermeasures prior to the social media's use by its neighbour.

6.   As they are designed to cause a responsible State to meet its legal obligations, countermeasures may not be taken in response to an internationally wrongful act that has ended, is unlikely to be repeated, and regarding which reparation (Rule 28) and assurances or guarantees (Rule 27), where appropriate, have been provided.[233] In this regard, note that countermeasures remain available to secure reparation.

7.   When a cyber operation in question is but one in a series of on-going actions that, for the purposes of State responsibility constitute a single internationally wrongful act, countermeasures remain available.[234] To illustrate, from late 2012 through early 2013 the US banking system was the target of DDoS operations that appeared to be related and from the same source.[235] If, as is suspected, the operations

---

[232] *Gabčíkovo-Nagymaros* judgment, para. 83.
[233] Articles on State Responsibility, Art. 49(1).
[234] Articles on State Responsibility, Art. 15.
[235] *See, e.g.*, Nicole Perlroth and Quentin Hardy, Bank Hacking Was the Work of Iranians, Officials Say, NY TIMES, 8 January 2013.

were conducted by another State, the United States would have been entitled to conduct countermeasures throughout the period of those operations to cause the responsible State to desist from its pattern of conduct.

8.   Countermeasures are generally characterised as temporary measures and therefore, according to the International Law Commission, 'must be as far as possible reversible in their effects in terms of future legal relations between the two States'.[236] Reflecting this purpose, the International Court of Justice has confirmed that countermeasures should, to the extent feasible, be taken in such a way as to permit the resumption of performance of the breached obligations underlying the countermeasures.[237] As an example, a DDoS operation is typically reversible, whereas deletion of data that the State taking the countermeasures knows has not been backed up cannot be reversed. The International Group of Experts agreed that the requirement of reversibility is broad and not absolute, as reflected in the caveat that they need only be so to the extent possible. For instance, a DDoS countermeasure can be terminated and service restored, but the activities that were disrupted may not be able to be performed at a later date. This would not bar the countermeasure.

9.   The International Group of Experts could achieve no consensus on whether States need to select the cyber countermeasure option that is most easily reversed or simply one that is, in fact, reversible. Consider a situation in which a State has a choice between a DDoS operation that it can terminate and a cyber operation that will require the target State to reconfigure its affected cyber infrastructure. Both options are equally likely to force the responsible State back into compliance with its international legal obligation. The question is whether the State conducting the countermeasure is required as a matter of law to opt for the former. A majority of the Experts was of the view that so long as both countermeasures complied with all other requirements for countermeasures, particularly that of proportionality (Rule 23), the State may select either option. A few Experts took the opposite view on the basis international law generally favours resolution in the manner least likely to exacerbate relations between States.

---

[236] Articles on State Responsibility, chapeau to Chapter II of Part 3, para. 6.
[237] *Gabčíkovo-Nagymaros* judgment, para. 87; Articles on State Responsibility, Art. 49(3).

10. In the view of the International Group of Experts, a further requirement that derives from their underlying purpose is that a State intending to take countermeasures must notify the responsible State that it is invoking responsibility, has decided to take countermeasures, and offer to negotiate.[238] A single notification to this effect can suffice to satisfy the requirement.[239]

11. In the case of cyber operations, this requirement is especially apropos because the originator of a cyber operation might be spoofed. The Experts cautioned that the notification requirement is not categorical. In certain circumstances it may be necessary for an injured State to act immediately in order to preserve its rights and avoid further injury. When such circumstances arise, the injured State may launch 'urgent countermeasures' without notification of its intent to do so.[240] Given the speed with which the consequences of a cyber operation manifest, this situation is highly likely.

12. Similarly, the Experts agreed that if notification of intent to take a countermeasure would likely render that measure meaningless, notice need not be provided.[241] As an example, assume that serious internationally wrongful cyber operations are underway against a State. The injured State intends to respond by blocking all electronic access to the responsible State's bank accounts. Notifying the responsible State of its intent to do so would afford that State an opportunity to transfer assets out of the country, thereby effectively depriving the injured State of the option of taking that countermeasure.

13. A minority of the Experts also took the position that customary international law requires the injured State to seek negotiations before taking countermeasures. Such a requirement is suggested in the Articles on State Responsibility.[242] The majority of the Experts rejected the purported requirement, asserting that an injured State may engage in countermeasures before seeking negotiations and that countermeasures are permissible during negotiations. They argued that such a requirement

---

[238] Articles on State Responsibility, Art. 52(1). *See also Gabčíkovo-Nagymaros* judgment, para. 84; *Air Services* arbitral award, paras. 85–87.

[239] Articles on State Responsibility, Art. 52, para. 5 of commentary.

[240] Articles on State Responsibility, Art. 52(2).

[241] Agreement was based on Articles on State Responsibility, Art. 52, para. 6 of commentary. Although the commentary refers to urgent countermeasures, the Experts concurred that the same logic applies in the case of any countermeasure that may be frustrated if notification is provided, a highly likely possibility in the cyber context.

[242] Articles on State Responsibility, Art. 52, para. 5 of commentary.

would permit the responsible State to control the duration and impact of its breach by deciding when and for how long to conduct 'good faith negotiations'.[243]

14.   The majority of the International Group of Experts agreed that countermeasures may not be taken, and if already taken must be suspended, if the dispute in question is pending before a 'court or tribunal' that may issue a binding decision in the matter and the internationally wrongful activity has ceased.[244] The phrase 'court or tribunal' refers to 'any third-party dispute settlement procedure, whatever its designation'. The court or tribunal must have the power to order interim measures that are capable of protecting the purportedly injured State.[245] The prohibition applies only once the case is *sub judice*.[246] Furthermore, the International Group of Experts agreed that even if the internationally wrongful act has not ceased, if it is not continuing to cause injury and on-going negotiations between parties are being conducted in good faith, countermeasures are also prohibited.[247]

15.   A minority of the Experts disagreed with the imposition of an 'absolute rule' that countermeasures are impermissible in these situations. Instead, these Experts held the view that whether a party must avoid countermeasures depends on whether the tribunal, *inter alia*, orders equivalent interim measures of protection to replace countermeasures in protecting the rights of the injured State. The determination of whether a particular court or tribunal has the ability to sufficiently do so must be assessed on a case-by-case basis; thus, for them, an absolute rule is inappropriate.[248]

16.   The International Group of Experts also considered whether, as a general matter, cyber or non-cyber countermeasures may be taken when the internationally wrongful act to which they would respond is not yet

---

[243]   *See, e.g.,* US 1997 Comments, at 3. In support of this position, the United States cited *Air Services* arbitral award. *See Air Services* arbitral award, paras. 84–99.

[244]   Articles on State Responsibility, Art. 52(3).

[245]   Articles on State Responsibility, Art. 52, para. 8 of commentary. The term 'court or tribunal' refers to arbitration and judicial proceedings, but does not include cases that have been referred to political entities such as the UN Security Council.

[246]   *Air Services* arbitral award, para. 95. Additionally, the court or tribunal must exist at the time and enjoy jurisdiction over the matter. For instance, the limitation does not apply to an *ad hoc* tribunal established by treaty, which has not yet been formed. Articles on State Responsibility, Art. 52, para. 8 of commentary.

[247]   *See Lac Lanoux (Fr. v. Sp.),* 12 RIAA 281, 306–307 (16 November 1957); *Air Services* arbitral award, para. 91.

[248]   *See, e.g.,* US 2001 Comments, at 6.

pending before a court or tribunal, but is subject to a dispute settlement procedure that is related to the dispute in question. For example, an international agreement that allegedly is being breached by one of the Parties may provide for a dispute resettlement mechanism in the event a breach by a Party is alleged by another Party.[249] Some of the Experts were of the view that only the procedure, and not countermeasures, may be employed by the purportedly injured State to compel the responsible State to honour its obligations.[250] They likewise took the position that, in cases where no such mechanism exists, the countermeasure itself may not involve activity subject to a compulsory dispute settlement procedure.[251]

17.   Although these Experts agreed that there must be resort to compulsory dispute resolution mechanisms when specifically required by international law, they could not achieve consensus as to whether exceptional circumstances exist that would permit the taking or maintaining of cyber or non-cyber countermeasures while such mechanisms are being used. In particular, they were sensitive to a situation in which the proceedings are protracted and the dispute resolution mechanism lacks the authority to impose provisional measures to safeguard the rights of the injured State. Within this group, most suggested that countermeasures would be appropriate in such cases, whereas the others in the group would adhere strictly to the compulsory nature of the mechanism and disallow countermeasures.

18.   The remaining Experts, consistent with their approach to the permissibility of countermeasures during negotiations and the pendency of proceedings before a tribunal, asserted that there is, as a matter of *lex lata*, no prohibition of taking or maintaining cyber or non-cyber countermeasures when an issue has been submitted to a compulsory dispute resolution mechanism, at least not when the countermeasures are 'provisional and urgent'.[252]

Rule 22 – Limitations on countermeasures

Countermeasures, whether cyber in nature or not, may not include actions that affect fundamental human rights, amount to prohibited

---

[249] Articles on State Responsibility, Art. 50(2)(a).
[250] *Appeal Relating to the Jurisdiction of the ICAO Council (India v. Pak.)*, 1972 ICJ 46, para. 16 (18 August).
[251] Articles on State Responsibility, Art. 50, para. 12 of commentary.
[252] *See* US 2001 Comments, at 5–6.

belligerent reprisals, or violate a peremptory norm. A State taking countermeasures must fulfil its obligations with respect to diplomatic and consular inviolability.

1.   An internationally wrongful act by a responsible State does not allow the injured State to respond with countermeasures that involve certain breaches of its own obligations. This Rule, drawn from Article 50(1) of the Articles on State Responsibility, sets forth those obligations that may not be so breached. The issue of whether countermeasures may breach the prohibition of the use of force (Rule 68) is discussed below in this commentary.

2.   The International Group of Experts acknowledged that at least one State has objected to the inclusion of Article 50(1) in the Articles on State Responsibility.[253]

3.   The Experts agreed that the reference to fundamental human rights obligations set forth in Article 50(1)(b) of the Articles on State Responsibility reflects customary international law.[254] However, the scope of Article 50(1)(b) is the subject of some disagreement.[255] It is incontestable that it encompasses peremptory (see discussion below) human rights norms. Examples cited by the International Law Commission in the commentary to the Article include the prohibitions of aggression, genocide, slavery, racial discrimination, crimes against humanity, and torture.[256] Additionally, the International Group of Experts agreed that the term may encompass human rights that may not be derogated from during periods of national emergency or armed conflict.[257]

4.   The open question is the degree to which the prohibition extends to other human rights. For instance, cyber activities raise concerns

---

[253] *See* US 1997 Comments, at 6.

[254] *See also* the findings of the 1928 *Naulilaa* arbitration, which barred countermeasures that 'do not meet the requirements of humanity'. *Naulilaa* arbitral award, at 1026.

[255] *See, e.g.*, US 2001 Comments, which in recommending that the Article in question be deleted from the draft noted

> There is no consensus, for example, as to what constitutes 'fundamental human rights.' In fact, no international legal instrument defines the phrase 'fundamental human rights,' and the concept underlying this phrase is usually referred to as 'human rights and fundamental freedoms.' Likewise, the content of peremptory norms in areas other than genocide, slavery and torture is not well-defined or accepted.

US 2001 Comments, at 3.

[256] Articles on State Responsibility, Art. 26, para. 5 of commentary; Art. 40, paras. 4–5 of commentary.

[257] For instance, see the list of non-derogable rights set forth in ICCPR, Art. 4(2).

regarding the right to privacy (Rule 35), thereby begging the question of whether a cyber operation that affects this right may qualify as a countermeasure or, instead, is precluded on the basis that the right is 'fundamental', as that term is understood with respect to Article 50(1)(b). The International Group of Experts could achieve no consensus on this point. A further issue is the extraterritorial applicability of human rights norms. As discussed in Rule 34, whether or how human rights apply extraterritorially is unsettled and controversial.

5.   The Articles on State Responsibility further prohibit States seeking to engage in countermeasures from taking actions that qualify as unlawful belligerent reprisals under the law of armed conflict (Rule 108).[258] In other words, an act that constitutes a prohibited belligerent reprisal cannot be justified as a countermeasure. For example, during an armed conflict it would be forbidden to conduct cyber attacks (Rule 92) against the enemy's wounded personnel by cutting electricity to a medical facility in a manner that would affect their treatment in response to a kinetic or cyber attack on one's own wounded soldiers.

6.   Countermeasures may not include actions that violate peremptory norms, such as the prohibition of genocide.[259] According to Article 53 of the Vienna Convention on the Law of Treaties,

> a peremptory norm of general international law is a norm accepted and recognised by the international community of States as a whole as a norm from which no derogation is permitted and which can be modified only by a subsequent norm of general international law having the same character.

7.   Thus, using cyber or non-cyber means to incite genocide, for instance by manipulating the content of news reports that are distributed by cyber means, cannot qualify as a countermeasure. According to a judgment of the International Criminal Tribunal for the former Yugoslavia, most norms of the law of armed conflict would likewise be encompassed in the peremptory category.[260] Although the majority of the International Group of Experts agreed, some members took the position that this statement inaccurately characterises customary law, or at least is overbroad.

---

[258] Articles on State Responsibility, Art. 50(1)(c).
[259] Articles on State Responsibility, Art. 50(1)(d).
[260] *Prosecutor* v. *Kupreskic*, Case No. IT-95-16, judgment (Int'l Crim. Trib. for the Former Yugoslavia 14 January 2000), para. 520.

8. Countermeasures infringing diplomatic or consular inviolability (Rules 39 and 41) are proscribed.[261] As an example, launching ransomware against an embassy's computer system and then demanding that the sending State discontinue an internationally wrongful act cannot qualify as a countermeasure. This prohibition includes situations in which the precipitating internationally wrongful act to which the countermeasure would respond is committed by a member of the diplomatic service or otherwise involves the abuse of diplomatic privileges.[262]

9. A contentious issue with respect to limitations on countermeasures is whether they may consist of actions that amount to a use of force under Article 2(4) of the UN Charter and customary international law. In the cyber context, the critical issue in this regard is the point at which a cyber operation amounts to a use of force. Qualification of a cyber operation as a use of force is addressed in Rule 68.

10. Although all of the members of the International Group of Experts agreed that a countermeasure may not rise to the level of an armed attack (Rule 71), they were divided over whether cyber countermeasures crossing the use of force threshold, but not reaching that of an armed attack, are lawful. In light of this disagreement, no such limitation is included in this Rule.

11. According to the majority of the International Group of Experts, the obligation to refrain from the use of force is a key limitation on an injured State when conducting countermeasures.[263] This position is consistent with the jurisprudence of the International Court of Justice[264] and is replicated in Article 50(1)(a) of the Articles on State Responsibility.

12. A minority of the Experts asserted that forcible countermeasures are appropriate in response to a wrongful use of force that itself

---

[261] Articles on State Responsibility, Art. 50(2)(b). *See also Tehran Hostages* judgment, paras. 83, 86; Vienna Convention on Consular Relations, Arts. 33, 35.

[262] The International Court of Justice noted in the *Tehran Hostages* judgment that diplomatic law is a 'self-contained regime which, on the one hand, lays down the receiving State's obligations regarding the facilities, privileges and immunities to be accorded to diplomatic missions and, on the other, foresees their possible abuse by members of the mission and specifies the means at the disposal of the receiving State to counter any such abuse.' *Tehran Hostages* judgment, para. 86.

[263] Articles on State Responsibility, Art. 50(1)(a). *See also* Arbitral Tribunal Constituted Pursuant to Article 287, and in Accordance with Annex VII, of the United Nations Convention on the Law of the Sea (*Guy. v. Surin.*), award, para. 446 (Perm. Ct. Arb. 2007).

[264] *Corfu Channel* judgment, at 35; *Nicaragua* judgment, para. 249.

does not qualify as an armed attack (whether by cyber means or not). They did so on the basis that the majority view would mean that a State facing a cyber use of force not reaching the armed attack threshold would be unable to respond with its own forcible cyber (or non-cyber) operations. In other words, the injured State would be limited to responding with cyber countermeasures below the use of force level and thereby deprived of a proportionate response.

13.   These Experts were swayed by the position of Judge Simma in his separate opinion in the *Oil Platforms* case. There, Judge Simma suggested:

> But we may encounter also a lower level of hostile military action, not reaching the threshold of an 'armed attack' within the meaning of Article 51 of the United Nations Charter. Against such hostile acts, a State may of course defend itself, but only within the more limited range and quality of responses (the main difference being that the possibility of collective self-defence does not arise, cf. *Nicaragua*) and bound to necessity, proportionality and immediacy in time in a particular strict way.[265]

14.   The reference to the inadmissibility of collective action, which, in part, distinguishes countermeasures from self-defence, confirms that Judge Simma supported a limited right to take forcible countermeasures in the face of a wrongful cyber operation falling within the gap between less grave uses of force and those that qualify as an armed attack for the purposes of the law of self-defence. What this approach might mean in the cyber context will remain an open question until uncertainty as to the use of force and armed attack thresholds is resolved. It should be reemphasised, however, that all of the Experts agreed that cyber countermeasures may not rise to the level of an armed attack.

15.   Some States reject the notion of a gap between actions that amount to a use of force and those that qualify as an armed attack (Rule 71). For States adopting this interpretation, the dilemma underlying the minority's concern does not present itself. A State subjected to a wrongful use of force has, by the no-gap interpretation, equally been the object of an armed attack. Therefore, it may respond with its own use of force, whether cyber or non-cyber in nature, pursuant to the law of self-defence.

---

[265] *Oil Platforms* judgment, para. 13 (separate opinion of Judge Simma).

Rule 23 – Proportionality of countermeasures

Countermeasures, whether cyber in nature or not, must be proportionate to the injury to which they respond.

1. Countermeasures must, as reflected in Article 51 of the Articles on State Responsibility, be proportionate, that is, 'commensurate with the injury suffered, taking into account the gravity of the internationally wrongful act and the rights in question'.[266] A countermeasure that is disproportionate to the injury suffered amounts to punishment or retaliation and is therefore contrary to the object and purpose of the law governing countermeasures (Rule 21). Consequently, the wrongfulness of the breach is not precluded.

2. The term 'injury' is not to be understood to require damage. Instead, simple breach of an international legal obligation suffices to make proportionate countermeasures available to the injured State. The question of damage relates instead to the primary rule, the breach of which constitutes the internationally wrongful act.[267] For instance, if the prohibition of the use of force (Rule 68) is interpreted as requiring physical damage or injury, a cyber operation that does not generate such consequences would not, on the basis of that prohibition, constitute an internationally wrongful act. That being so, countermeasures in response to the operation would be impermissible unless a separate basis of international wrongfulness exists (such as failure to respect sovereignty, Rule 4).

3. Proportionality in the context of countermeasures must be distinguished from *jus ad bellum* proportionality (Rule 72), which refers to the degree of force required for a State to defend itself effectively against an armed attack. Countermeasures proportionality must also be distinguished from the rule of proportionality in the law of armed conflict (Rule 113), which assesses the harm expected to be caused to civilians or civilian objects in light of an attack's (Rule 92) anticipated military advantage.

---

[266] Articles on State Responsibility, Art. 51; *Gabčíkovo-Nagymaros* judgment, para. 85. This principle was set forth in the 1928 *Naulilaa* arbitral award: 'Even if one were to admit that the law of nations does not require that the reprisal should be approximately in keeping with the offense, one should certainly consider as excessive and therefore unlawful reprisals out of all proportion to the act motivating them'. *Naulilaa* arbitral award, at 1028.

[267] Articles on State Responsibility, Art. 2, para. 9 of commentary.

4.   The issues with respect to the proportionality of countermeasures, by contrast, are the injury suffered (i.e., the extent of harm), the gravity of the wrongful act (i.e., the significance of the primary rule breached), the rights of the injured and responsible State (and interests of other States) that are affected, and the need to effectively cause the responsible State to comply with its obligations.[268]

5.   With regard to the significance of the primary norm involved, appraisal of proportionality is not merely a matter of quantitative comparison of consequences; the objective is to ensure that there is no patent imbalance between the underlying internationally wrongful act and the countermeasure.[269] To illustrate, consider the case of countermeasures that affect the operability of the responsible State's governmental cyber communications systems in a manner that would otherwise amount to a violation of the responsible State's sovereignty (Rule 4). Not only will the actual consequences of the responsible State's wrongful cyber operation factor into the proportionality assessment, but so too will the significance of the principle of sovereignty.[270]

6.   The interconnected and interdependent nature of cyber systems can render it difficult to determine accurately the consequences likely to result from cyber countermeasures. States must therefore exercise considerable care when assessing whether their countermeasures will be proportionate. Conducting a full assessment may require, for instance, mapping the targeted system or reviewing relevant intelligence. Whether the assessment is adequate depends on the foreseeability of potential consequences and the feasibility of the means that can be used to conduct it.

7.   Proportionality does not imply reciprocity; there is no requirement that an injured State's countermeasure breach the same obligation violated by the responsible State. Nor is there any requirement that countermeasures be of the same nature as the underlying internationally wrongful act that justifies them. Non-cyber countermeasures may be used in response to an internationally wrongful act involving cyber operations, and *vice versa*. However, as a general

---

[268] Articles on State Responsibility, Art. 51, para. 6 of commentary; CRAWFORD, STATE RESPONSIBILITY, at 699.

[269] *Air Services* arbitral award, para. 83.

[270] The International Court of Justice confirmed this approach in *Gabčíkovo-Nagymaros*. *Gabčíkovo-Nagymaros* judgment, paras. 85–87. In doing so, the Court looked to the Permanent Court of Justice's judgment in *Territorial Jurisdiction of the International Commission of the River Oder*, 1929 PCIJ (ser. A-No. 23) No. 16, at 27 (10 September).

matter, the requirement of proportionality is less likely to be contravened, or at least to be assessed as having been contravened, when a countermeasure is in kind.[271]

8. Relatedly, there is no requirement of numerical congruency. A single internationally wrongful cyber operation by a responsible State may be responded to by countermeasures that would otherwise breach numerous obligations. An injured State may respond, for instance, with a series of different cyber countermeasures, none of which would alone be sufficient to cause the responsible State to desist, but that would do so collectively, so long as they are proportionate. The question in such a case is whether the combined countermeasures are proportionate to the injury suffered.

9. The International Group of Experts agreed that there is no procedural requirement that an injured State take measures to mitigate harm it is suffering before taking countermeasures. Nor does the lack of mitigation affect the proportionality of the countermeasures in question. Suppose a State suffers a series of data deletions from another State's remotely executed cyber operations that violate a legal obligation owed the target State. Although the injured State could black- or whitelist network traffic, take the system offline, shut the system down, or engage in other measures to prevent further damage, it does not do so. That fact has no bearing on the proportionality on those countermeasures it takes against the responsible State because the law of State responsibility does not require a State to mitigate harm. Note, however, that the injured State's failure to mitigate may bear on the issue of reparation (Rule 28).

10. There is no requirement that a countermeasure be directed at the activity constituting the breach of a responsible State's obligation. Rather, the key is that the countermeasure be designed to cause the responsible State to comply with its legal obligations. In many cases, countermeasures wholly unrelated to the precipitating conduct may prove most effective in convincing the responsible State to desist in its wrongful conduct. Consider the case of a coastal State being targeted by DDoS attacks launched by another State in a manner that violates the former's sovereignty. Instead of attempting to take the botnet down by means that would otherwise be unlawful *vis-à-vis* the responsible State, the coastal State may take the countermeasure of closing its territorial sea to innocent passage by the responsible State's vessels.

---

[271] Articles on State Responsibility, chapeau to Chapter II of Part 3, para. 5.

11.   As discussed in Rule 7, and subject to the caveats set forth in that Rule, the failure of a State to exercise due diligence by taking feasible measures to terminate harmful cyber operations originating in its territory constitutes an internationally wrongful omission by that State. Injured States taking countermeasures based on such a breach must be cautious. In particular, the proportionality of the countermeasure will be determined with respect to the responsible State's omission, not *vis-à-vis* the severity and consequences of the cyber operations that the responsible State had a duty to terminate.

12.   For instance, assume non-State actors unaffiliated with a State are conducting cyber operations in that State against another State. The operations have caused widespread disruption and damage throughout the target State. The State in which the non-State actors are located took some measures to put an end to the non-State actors' activities from its territory, but reasonably could have done more. Its failure to take all feasible measures in compliance with its due diligence duty (Rule 7) amounts to an internationally wrongful act. The proportionality of any countermeasures will be assessed against the failure to take the appropriate measures rather than the injury caused by the non-State actors' operations.

Rule 24 – States entitled to take countermeasures

Only an injured State may engage in countermeasures, whether cyber in nature or not.

1.   The term 'injured State' is defined in the chapeau to Section 1 of this Chapter.

2.   Only States may take countermeasures. For example, an information technology firm may not act on its own initiative in responding to a harmful cyber operation targeting it by styling its response as a countermeasure. To illustrate, when Sony was the subject of malicious cyber operations in 2014 allegedly conducted by, or attributable to, North Korea, it was not entitled to 'hack back' as a countermeasure under the law of State responsibility. Instead, the right to respond by countermeasures was reserved to the United States, assuming the operation against Sony could properly be characterised as an internationally wrongful act (Rule 14) by North Korea against the United States, for instance, on the basis of a violation of sovereignty (Rule 4). It should be noted that had Sony hacked back, it would have violated no customary rule of general international law (Rule 33); however, doing so might have raised the

issue of due diligence on the part of the United States (Rules 6–7). On the attribution of cyber operations by non-State actors, see Rules 15 and 17.[272]

3. There is no prohibition against injured States turning to a private firm, including foreign companies, to conduct cyber countermeasures on their behalf against responsible States. In such a case, the company's operations would generally be attributable to the injured States (Rule 17). The cyber operations in question would be subject to all relevant restrictions and conditions on countermeasures.

4. Pursuant to Article 48(1) of the Articles on State Responsibility, '[a]ny state . . . is entitled to invoke the responsibility of another state . . . if (a) the obligation breached is owed to a group of States including that State, and is established for the protection of a collective interest of the group; or (b) the obligation breached is owed to the international community as a whole'. Subparagraph (a) refers to an obligation found in an integral treaty, such as a multilateral arms control treaty. Subparagraph (b) situations involve obligations *erga omnes* (Rule 30). Acting on either of these two bases is subject to numerous restrictions.[273]

5. It is unsettled whether States referred to in Article 48(1), but not directly injured by a responsible State's internationally wrongful act, may resort to countermeasures, as distinct from lawful measures, such as retorsion, to ensure cessation of the breach and reparation in the interest of the injured State or the beneficiaries of the obligation.[274] The International Group of Experts could achieve no consensus on this issue.

6. The International Group of Experts noted that States routinely cooperate with other States, bilaterally and multilaterally, to strengthen their cyber security, increase their cyber defence capabilities, and provide support and coordination in response to cyber operations directed against them. The Asia Pacific Computer Emergency Response Team and the NATO Rapid Reaction Team (RRT) are examples of existing multilateral arrangements to provide support to States as they are coping with hostile cyber operations. So long as the activities they engage in do not constitute internationally wrongful acts, international law bars no such initiatives. This, however, begs the questions of

---

[272] As noted in the commentary to Rule 20, the International Group of Experts acknowledged the existence of a view that non-State actors may be the object of countermeasures. The International Group of Experts did not agree with this assertion.

[273] Articles on State Responsibility, Art. 48(1)(a–b), paras. 6–10 of commentary.

[274] Articles on State Responsibility, Art. 54, paras. 6–7 of commentary; Art. 22, para. 6 of commentary.

whether a State or group of States may conduct countermeasures on behalf of another State, as well as whether they may assist a State that is conducting countermeasures.

7.   A few of the Experts were of the opinion that a non-injured State may conduct countermeasures as a response to an internationally wrongful act committed against an injured State so long as the latter requests that it do so. They based their view on certain State practice, such as that identified by the International Law Commission.[275] The majority of the Experts, however, took the position that, as set forth in the *Nicaragua* judgment, purported countermeasures taken on behalf of another State are unlawful.[276] These Experts noted that the International Law Commission styled the above mentioned practice as 'sparse and involv[ing] a limited number of States'.[277]

8.   Although the majority was of the view that States may not lawfully take countermeasures on behalf of another State, members thereof were split over whether a State may assist another State in conducting the latter's countermeasures. This issue would be raised, for instance, if one State provided guidance on how to conduct a hack-back qualifying as a countermeasure or shared information regarding vulnerabilities in the responsible State's cyber infrastructure.

9.   There were three views. Some of the Experts took the position that taking measures designed to facilitate another State's countermeasures cannot be differentiated from countermeasures taken on behalf of another State. Others took the position that the lawfulness of such measures depends on whether they would violate a legal obligation owed to the State against which the countermeasure is directed by the State providing assistance. In other words, a State may provide assistance to a State taking lawful countermeasures if the acts comprising the assistance do not violate any specific obligation that the assisting State separately owes to the responsible State. A third group of Experts was of the view that providing assistance to an injured State engaged in countermeasures is lawful on the basis that such activity must be distinguished from taking countermeasures on behalf of another State. All of the Experts concurred, however, that a State that aids or assists a cyber operation that fails to qualify as a countermeasure may be held responsible for aiding or assisting an internationally wrongful act (Rule 18).

---

[275] Articles on State Responsibility, Art. 54, paras. 3–4 of commentary.
[276] *Nicaragua* judgment, para. 249.
[277] Articles on State Responsibility, Art. 54, para. 6 of commentary.

10. If a State's cyber operation breaches an obligation owed to multiple States, each may respond with countermeasures. They may also coordinate their actions so long as the measures taken by any one State are proportionate to the injury it has suffered and the rights in question (Rule 23), and that any collaborative countermeasures are proportionate overall. This is a particularly important observation because of the interconnectivity and interdependency that characterises cyberspace.

Rule 25 – Effect of countermeasures on third parties

A countermeasure, whether cyber in nature or not, that violates a legal obligation owed to a third State or other party is prohibited.

1. The fact that a cyber operation by an injured State qualifies as a countermeasure against a responsible State does not preclude the wrongfulness of a breach of the injured State's obligations towards third States or other parties. Of particular note in this regard is the fact that, in light of the interconnectedness of computer networks across borders, the effects of a countermeasure may reverberate throughout trans-border networks. When this occurs, the question is whether those effects violate obligations owed to third States or other parties.

2. The Rule refers to 'other parties'. Although most international law obligations are owed to States, contemporary international law imposes certain obligations on States with respect to non-State actors, including international organisations and individuals.[278] The wrongfulness of a breach of such an obligation is not precluded by the fact that the act is a valid countermeasure against the responsible State. This is of particular relevance in the case of international human rights law (Chapter 6).

---

[278] As noted in *Archer Daniels*, an arbitral decision addressing the subject,

> [I]nternational law may under specific circumstances confer direct rights on individuals, the breach of which may amount to an international wrongful act if attributable to the State in question. Thus, the responsibility of a State may be invoked not just by other States, but also in certain areas, such as foreign investor protection, human rights and environmental protection, where there may be a significant role for individuals and non-state entities to assert state responsibility before international dispute settlement bodies.

Archer Daniels arbitral award, para. 170.

3. The International Law Commission has observed that counter-measures are lawful if they have only an incidental effect on third States or other parties.[279] The critical distinction is between the breach of a legal obligation and merely affecting interests that are not protected by international law.[280] Given the fact that the government, private entities and individuals share the use of most cyber infrastructure, the exclusion of collateral effects that do not amount to violations of international law is especially important in the cyber context.

4. Where a cyber countermeasure affects only an interest of third States or other parties, it will be lawful with regard to them. However, if it breaches a legal obligation owed a third State or other party, the wrongfulness of the action or omission is not precluded *vis-à-vis* them by the fact that the action or omission is a countermeasure taken against the responsible State. To illustrate, consider a counter-measure involving introduction of a highly targeted computer worm into an industrial control system of a responsible State's tanker loading facility. As a result, tanker loading is brought to a halt. Contrary to the plans of the injured State, the malware escapes the computer systems of the tanker loading facility and spreads globally. However, because it is programmed to only have effects on that specific tanker loading facility, the impact on other States is simply the fact that the malware is present in their computer systems without causing any effects therein. Even though the operation negatively affects the interest of third States in not having suspicious malware in their systems, the injured State has not violated this Rule because the mere presence of the malware does not breach any international law obligations the injured State owes third States.

5. An injured State must immediately end a countermeasure that is violating the rights of third States or other parties once it becomes aware of this effect.[281] Consider the case of malware that is inserted during a close-access operation into what the injured State believes is a closed and virtually air-gapped network of the responsible State. After insertion, the injured State learns that the targeted network is connected to the Internet and the malware is likely to have damaging effects in third States. The injured State must immediately deactivate the malware.

---

[279] Articles on State Responsibility, Art. 49, para. 5 of commentary.
[280] Articles on State Responsibility, Art. 49, para. 4 of commentary.
[281] Articles on State Responsibility, Art. 30(a).

Rule 26 – Necessity

A State may act pursuant to the plea of necessity in response to acts that present a grave and imminent peril, whether cyber in nature or not, to an essential interest when doing so is the sole means of safeguarding it.

1. The wrongfulness under international law of an act is precluded if the operation is undertaken in a situation of 'necessity', whether caused by cyber means or not. Necessity refers to a circumstance in which a State's 'essential interest' faces 'grave and imminent peril' and the sole means of averting that peril is temporary non-compliance by the State with its international obligations of 'lesser weight or urgency'.[282] Set forth in Article 25 of the Articles on State Responsibility, the precise nature and scope of the plea of necessity, beyond the aspects reflected in this Rule, remain controversial. However, in light of its acceptance by the International Court of Justice and other bodies,[283] the International Group of Experts agreed that as a general matter, and as described below, the plea is customary in nature and can be applied in the cyber context. Yet, it must be emphasised that the threshold for invocation of necessity is extremely high; it may only be relied upon as a circumstance precluding wrongfulness (Rule 19) in exceptional cases.[284] Acting on the basis of necessity is only permissible when a State's essential interests are gravely threatened.

2. The notion of 'essential interest' is vague in international law; there is no accepted definition thereof.[285] The International Group of Experts agreed that an essential interest is one that is of fundamental and great importance to the State concerned. The determination of whether an interest is essential is always contextual. Essentiality of a particular interest is also, to an extent, likely to vary from State to State. In this regard, the International Group of Experts took note of the tendency of States to designate certain infrastructure, including cyber infrastructure, as 'critical', which is suggestive of their characterisation of an interest as

---

[282] Articles on State Responsibility, Art. 25, para. 1 of commentary.

[283] Necessity (or phraseology clearly referring to necessity) has been cited in many contexts. *See, e.g., Wall* advisory opinion, para 140; *Rainbow Warrior* arbitral award, para. 78; *LG&E Energy Corp.* v. *Argentina* decision on liability, paras. 201–266; *CMS* v. *Argentina* arbitral award, paras. 304–394; *Enron* v. *Argentina* award, paras. 288–345; *Sempra* v. *Argentina* arbitral award, paras. 325–397.

[284] Articles on State Responsibility, Art. 25(1); *Gabčíkovo-Nagymaros* judgment, para. 51.

[285] Articles on State Responsibility, Art. 25, para. 15 of commentary.

essential.[286] However, designation as such does not necessarily deprive other infrastructure of its essentiality, nor is a State's unilateral description of infrastructure as critical determinative of the issue.

3.   The International Group of Experts agreed that whether an interest of the international community as a whole may qualify as essential for the purposes of this Rule remains unsettled. The majority concurred that only interests of States are protected by operation of the plea of necessity in the present state of the law. However, the Experts also acknowledged that there might be extreme cases where a State may use cyber means to respond to cyber acts that gravely threaten the essential interests of the 'international community as a whole' (obligations *erga omnes*, Rule 30). Consider a case in which a non-State group successfully incites genocide via the Internet in another State. Where the other conditions for necessity are met, a State may use cyber means to bring such incitement to an end pursuant to the plea of necessity.

4.   The mere fact that a cyber operation targets an essential interest is insufficient to invoke the plea of necessity. In addition, the potential harm posed to that interest must be 'grave'. The Experts agreed that a peril is grave when the threat is especially severe. It involves interfering with an interest in a fundamental way, like destroying the interest or rendering it largely dysfunctional. As with the notion of 'essential interest', the gravity of the peril depends heavily on the attendant circumstances. Although the peril need not risk physical damage or injury, mere inconvenience, irritation, or minor disruption never suffice.

5.   A number of examples may serve to illustrate situations in which essential interests are gravely and imminently threatened. Most of the Experts agreed that, for instance, a cyber operation that would debilitate the State's banking system, cause a dramatic loss of confidence in its stock market, ground flights nation-wide, halt all rail traffic, stop national pension and other social benefits, alter national health records in a manner endangering the health of the population, cause a major environmental disaster, shut down a large electrical grid, seriously disrupt the national food distribution network, or shut down the integrated air defence system would provide the basis for the application of this Rule. They concurred that it is most clearly

---

[286] For analysis of whether the interests facing 'grave and imminent peril' qualify as 'essential' in the economic context, see *LG&E Energy Corp.* v. *Argentina* decision on liability, para. 251; *CMS* v. *Argentina* arbitral award, para. 320; *Enron* v. *Argentina* award, para. 306; *Sempra* v. *Argentina* arbitral award, para. 351.

implicated when critical infrastructure is targeted in a manner that may have severe negative impact on a State's security, economy, public health, safety, or environment.

6. States may act pursuant to the plea of necessity even if its response to the peril in question violates the rights of non-responsible States. For example, the plea of necessity may be invoked in the face of a non-State actor's cyber operation in circumstances where no State is responsible for the operation. In such cases, action pursuant to the plea of necessity may be permissible irrespective of the effects that manifest in non-responsible States, except as explained below.[287]

7. Consider the following scenario. State A conducts an internationally wrongful cyber operation against State B. State B takes a countermeasure (Rule 20) against State A. If the countermeasure has bleed-over effects into State C, and those effects violate an obligation State B owes State C, the response's wrongfulness is not precluded as a countermeasure because State C was not a responsible State *vis-à-vis* State B (Rule 25). However, if State B's essential interests are gravely affected and the action taken is the only means of protecting those interests, the wrongfulness of the cyber response as to State C (as well as State B) is precluded on the basis of necessity.

8. A key limitation in this regard is that a State invoking the plea of necessity may not engage in cyber operations that seriously impair the essential interests of affected States.[288] Take the case of a State that is the victim of cyber operations conducted by non-State actors using cyber infrastructure located in another State and causing major damage to the former's critical infrastructure. The victim State has the technical ability to respond with operations to shut down the infrastructure used. If doing so would affect the essential interests of other States, the operations are prohibited despite the magnitude of the harm that the victim State is suffering or about to suffer.

9. Unlike countermeasures (Rule 20), necessity is not dependent on the prior unlawful conduct of another State. The state of necessity may be caused by a natural disaster or other situation that does not implicate international legal norms.

10. This is of exceptional importance in the cyber context because the plea of necessity will lie when individuals or non-State groups such as companies, activist groups, or terrorists, conduct cyber operations that

---

[287] Articles on State Responsibility, Art. 25, para. 17 of commentary.
[288] Articles on State Responsibility, Art. 25(1)(b).

satisfy the standard set forth in this Rule. There is no need to attribute the underlying conduct to a State. Therefore, in cases where a non-State actor has launched a cyber operation that falls below the armed attack threshold, the plea of necessity may present the sole option for a response that would otherwise be unlawful.

11.   In situations in which the exact nature or origin of a cyber incident is unclear, cyber measures may be justified on the basis of the plea of necessity. For example, a State faced with a perplexing cyber incident that endangers its essential interests may in some cases shut down certain cyber infrastructure while it assesses the situation and potential remedial action, even when doing so affects cyber systems or activities in other States and breaches an agreement with those States regarding shared access to the infrastructure. Similarly, if significant cyber operations of unknown origin target its critical infrastructure, the plea of necessity could justify a State's resort to counter-hacking.

12.   A State resorting to action based on the plea of necessity need not face a peril that has materialised at the time it takes action, a fact illustrated by the reference to 'imminent peril' in Article 25 of the Articles on State Responsibility. Such imminence must be 'objectively established and not merely apprehended as possible'.[289] The decision that measures are required at the time taken must be 'clearly established on the basis of the evidence reasonably available at the time'.[290]

13.   A rule of reason applies with respect to imminence. In other words, a State may only act when a reasonable State in the same or similar circumstances would act prior to the advent of the harm that will be caused by the cyber operation. This standard allows some degree of uncertainty as to whether the offending operation will occur, whether sufficient harm will ensue to justify a plea of necessity, and the identity of the originator of the operation.

14.   Imminence is not judged solely by temporal standards. The International Court of Justice confirmed this point in its *Gabčíkovo-Nagymaros* judgment, acknowledging that the harm in question could occur 'in the long term' so long as that fact did not render the harm 'less certain and inevitable'.[291] The analogy to cyber activities is clear. When a State is facing harm to essential interests from cyber operations that constitute, whether immediately or over time, 'grave peril', it may take

---

[289] Articles on State Responsibility, Art. 25, para 15 of commentary.
[290] Articles on State Responsibility, Art. 25, para 16 of commentary.
[291] *Gabčíkovo-Nagymaros* judgment, para. 54.

those measures required to forestall that harm so long as the measures are the sole means available to avert the peril. Thus, for instance, a cyber operation targeting the banking system or stock market may have certain immediate effects, but the loss of confidence in the longer term may be the factor that qualifies as 'grave and imminent peril'.

15.   In terms of timing, the International Group of Experts agreed that peril is always imminent when the 'window of opportunity' (see also discussion in Rule 73) to take action to prevent it is about to close. Consider the case of a State that has reliable intelligence that a non-State group is going to launch cyber operations on a particular date that will significantly degrade its critical infrastructure. The State may act anticipatorily against the non-State group once its failure to do so will risk losing the chance to effectively prevent the operations from occurring.[292]

16.   Although Article 25 is framed in terms of prospective harm, the International Group of Experts agreed that the preclusion of wrongfulness on the basis of necessity applies equally when the cyber operations in question are underway and the harm is manifesting. In other words, the plea of necessity applies to cyber operations that are continuing, as in the case of a series of related cyber operations. It would also apply after the cyber operations have ceased if the harm is still unfolding and the measures in question are the only way to prevent further qualifying harm. This might be the case, for instance, when steps must be taken to eradicate a virus that was previously present in cyber infrastructure outside of the State's territory, but that is now spreading rapidly into the State's systems.

17.   Since acting based on necessity is an exceptional measure, doing so is only permissible when no other way to address the situation exists.[293] In determining whether alternatives exist, cost and inconvenience alone are not decisive factors. As an example, if particular cyber infrastructure relied upon by the State is being targeted from abroad by non-State actors, but that State can viably shift operations to other infrastructure while the situation is being resolved, it must do so rather than hack back in a manner that would violate the sovereignty of other States (Rule 4).

---

[292] Should the imminent cyber operation rise to the level of an armed attack, anticipatory action consistent with the right of self-defence would be lawful (Rule 73).

[293] See, e.g., Wall advisory opinion, para. 140; The M/V 'Saiga' (No. 2) (St. Vincent v. Guinea), judgment (ITLOS 1999), para. 134; ICSID, CMS v. Argentina arbitral award, paras. 323–324.

18.   It should be cautioned that whether measures based on the plea of necessity may involve forcible action is unsettled in international law.[294] The International Group of Experts was split on this issue. Some of the Experts took the position that the use of force in response to a harmful cyber operation is only permissible pursuant to the law of self-defence (Rule 71). In their view, the primary rule of international law prohibiting the use of force is subject to specific exclusive exceptions – authorisation from the Security Council (Rule 76) and self-defence. The other Experts countered that prohibiting forcible measures in necessity would mean that States facing cyber operations, the consequences of which are comparable to a cyber use of force, could find themselves in a situation in which the only effective response is a use of force that is unavailable unless and until those operations reach the threshold of an armed attack.

19.   If the State facing grave and imminent peril has substantially contributed to the situation, it may not justify its response on the basis of necessity.[295] However, its contribution must be more than marginal. The International Group of Experts agreed that mere failure to take preventive measures to protect a State's cyber infrastructure from harmful cyber operations amounting to 'grave and imminent peril' does not bar measures based on necessity. Consider a case in which one State encourages private individuals to conduct malicious cyber operations against another State. Private citizens of the target State respond in kind, in a manner that affects the essential interests of the former. The former, on the basis of necessity, cannot justify any subsequent measures taken, even though it is in fact facing a grave and imminent peril. Although this scenario raises issues of attribution (Rule 17) and due diligence (Rules 6–7) on the part of the first State, those issues have no bearing on whether this Rule applies.

20.   The notion of contribution in this context does not generally extend to actions that are lawful under international law and fall within the *domaine réservé* (as discussed in Rule 66) of the State concerned. Take a case in which national elections bring representatives of a particular ethnic group to power. Individuals in another State of different

---

[294] Articles on State Responsibility, Art. 25, para. 21 of commentary. In its commentary to Article 25, the International Law Commission expressed no opinion on the subject, indicating that it was a matter to be determined by reference to the proper interpretation to be given to the primary rule.

[295] Articles on State Responsibility, Art. 25, para. 20 of commentary.

ethnicity launch cyber operations of the requisite severity against the first State's critical infrastructure. The first State is not precluded from taking measures based on necessity on the grounds that it contributed to the situation. This is because selection of its government is a matter of *domaine réservé*.

21.   The International Group of Experts could not agree on whether the possibility of cooperation with other States or with international organisations qualifies as an alternative means of addressing situations of necessity, such that the plea of necessity's 'only means for the State to safeguard an essential interest' criterion is not satisfied. The majority took the position, shared by the International Law Commission,[296] that so long as there is a feasible prospect of resolving the situation through such cooperation, the plea of necessity is unavailable. To illustrate, assume that a State is the target of cyber operations at the necessity threshold. The cyber infrastructure used for those cyber operations is, in part, located in a friendly State. The target State could resort to that State's CERT, with sophisticated cyber means at its disposal, to address the situation and disable that infrastructure. By the majority view, the victim State would have to, if time permits and doing so is otherwise feasible in the circumstances, solicit the assistance of the CERT before invoking the plea of necessity.

22.   A minority of the Experts countered that the notion of alternative means only refers to means that are within the exclusive control of the State claiming necessity as the basis for its actions. In light of the speed at which harmful cyber operations can manifest, their often confusing factual setting, and the common practical need for immediate remedial response once a harmful cyber operation is discovered, these Experts opined that an obligation to cooperate with other States or international organisations would amount to an undue burden on States facing grave and imminent peril to their essential interests.

23.   Necessity must be distinguished from *force majeure* (Rule 19). In the latter case, performance of the obligation is rendered impossible by the circumstances. With necessity, the State concerned may comply with the obligation (e.g., to respect the sovereignty of the State from which the harmful cyber operations are emanating), but doing so would result in grave harm to its essential interests. In other words, with respect to necessity, the acting State retains the choice of continuing to comply

---

[296] Articles on State Responsibility, Art. 25, para 15 of commentary.

with its obligations, but compliance would entail severe hardship for that State. Necessity also differs from distress as a circumstance precluding wrongfulness (Rule 19) in that the interest protected need not be human life. It need only qualify as 'essential'.

SECTION 3:   OBLIGATIONS OF STATES FOR INTERNATIONALLY WRONGFUL ACTS

Rule 27 – Cessation, assurances, and guarantees

A responsible State must cease an internationally wrongful act committed by cyber means and, if appropriate, provide assurances and guarantees of non-repetition.

1.   When a State's cyber operation has 'injured' another State through commission of an internationally wrongful act, the injured State or States may invoke the international responsibility of the responsible State and demand cessation, assurances and guarantees of non-repetition, subject to a number of limitations discussed below.[297] Additionally, the injured State may demand reparation from the responsible State (Rule 28). The term 'responsible State' is defined in the chapeau to Section 1 of this Chapter.

2.   In light of the interconnectedness and interdependency of cyber activities and cyber infrastructure, an internationally wrongful cyber action or omission by a responsible State will sometimes breach obligations owed to more than one other State. When such a breach occurs each of the States that is injured may separately invoke responsibility.[298] Consider the case of a State that launches damaging malware into a classified network used for information sharing that links the intelligence systems of close allies. Each of the injured States are, as a general matter, entitled to demand cessation, assurances, guarantees, and reparation (Rule 28).

3.   A responsible State is legally obliged to cease an ongoing internationally wrongful cyber operation (or rectify an omission).[299] The obligation of cessation also applies in situations of repeated conduct, as in a series of cyber operations, each of which breaches an obligation owed.

---

[297] Articles on State Responsibility, Arts. 30–31, 34–37, 42, 48(1).
[298] Articles on State Responsibility, Arts. 42, 46.
[299] Articles on State Responsibility, Art. 30.

4. The International Group of Experts was of the view that, consistent with the Articles on State Responsibility, a responsible State may be required to 'offer appropriate assurances and guarantees of non-repetition if circumstances so require'.[300] Assurances and guarantees bear on future conduct and are designed to restore confidence in the fulfilment of the obligation as between the parties concerned.

5. 'Assurances' generally refers to communications, such as a diplomatic note or public pronouncement. By contrast, guarantees of non-repetition involve taking measures to ensure the internationally wrongful act is not repeated. Consider a case in which a State has failed to comply with its obligation of exercising due diligence (Rules 6–7) to ensure that harmful cyber operations do not emanate from its territory. It may be insufficient for the responsible State merely to assure the injured State that it will meet its obligations to do so in the future. Rather, that State may need to adopt technical, operational, or legislative means of ensuring that its offending cyber operations do not recur, as in addressing vulnerabilities in its cyber infrastructure that were exploited. The responsible State generally retains discretion in how to comply with its international law obligations in this regard.

6. Unlike cessation, assurances and guarantees are not required in every case, but only in those in which the injured State is reasonably concerned that it will not be protected by simple cessation of the internationally wrongful action or omission. As an example, if a State has repeatedly used cyber operations to violate the sovereignty of another State in violation of Rule 4, the latter may not only demand the course of conduct cease, but also seek guarantees from the responsible State that it will henceforth respect the injured State's sovereignty.

7. Whether it is reasonable to demand assurances and guarantees will depend on the attendant circumstances, as well as the nature of the obligation and the breach in question. To illustrate, no assurances may be appropriate in the case of a State enjoying otherwise favourable relations with the injured State or one in which the breach is of a technical and minor nature. When relations are generally poor, but where, for example, the responsible State has so far conducted only a single wrongful cyber operation and exercises reasonable control over its State organs and cyber infrastructure, a demand for an assurance may be appropriate, but insistence on a guarantee would be excessive.

---

[300] Articles on State Responsibility, Art. 30.

8.   The International Group of Experts acknowledged the existence of a view that 'assurances and guarantees of non-repetition cannot be formulated as a legal obligation, have no place in the draft articles on state responsibility, and should remain an aspect of diplomatic practice'.[301] However, the Experts noted that a requirement to offer assurances and guarantees in appropriate circumstances is consistent with, and supportive of, the object and purpose of the law of State responsibility, in particular that of ensuring the interests of injured States are safeguarded against the possibility of further breaches of the obligations they are owed by responsible States.

Rule 28 – Reparation (general principle)

A responsible State must make full reparation for injury suffered by an injured State as the result of an internationally wrongful act committed by cyber means.

1.   Responsible States must, in appropriate circumstances, make reparation for injury caused by their cyber operations.[302] As noted by the Permanent Court of International Justice, the objective of reparation is to, 'as far as possible, wipe out all the consequences of the illegal act and re-establish the situation which would, in all probability, have existed if that act had not been committed'.[303] To achieve this objective, reparation should include '[r]estitution in kind, or, if this is not possible, payment of a sum corresponding to the value which restitution in kind would bear'.[304]

2.   'Injury' refers to any material or moral damage caused by an internationally wrongful cyber operation.[305] Material damage includes property damage and harm affecting other interests of the injured State when said harm can be assessed in financial terms. The nature and extent of material harm is especially relevant with respect to the type and amount of reparation. In the context of cyber operations, the International Group of Experts agreed that interference with cyber operations or the loss of data that results in financial loss qualifies as material damage. The International Group of Experts further agreed that mere distress over having temporarily lost access

---

[301] US 2001 Comments, at 11.   [302] Articles on State Responsibility, Art. 31.
[303] *Factory at Chorzow* judgment, at 47.   [304] *Factory at Chorzow* judgment, at 47.
[305] Articles on State Responsibility, Art. 31(2).

to the Internet or losing personal e-correspondence that lacks pecuniary impact does not qualify as material damage.

3. 'Moral damage' refers to other forms of harm, such as damage 'of a moral, political and legal nature, resulting from an affront to the dignity and prestige' of the injured State.[306] It includes 'such items as individual pain and suffering, loss of loved ones or personal affront associated with an intrusion on one's home or private life'.[307] As an example, a cyber operation that manipulates information posted on a governmental website may undermine confidence in the government. Such effects qualify as moral damage and satisfaction therefor may take the form of pecuniary payment. Similarly, breach of a 'no-spying' agreement by conducting a cyber operation against a State official could result in moral damage by this definition. The International Group of Experts agreed that moral damages do not include punitive damages.

4. In the cyber context, injury resulting from an internationally wrongful act may befall individuals or entities other than the State, such as its nationals or companies. For the purposes of State responsibility, such injury also qualifies as the injury of the State (see also discussion in Rule 29 on compensation).[308]

5. The damage underlying the requirement to make reparation need not be readily quantifiable or easily determined. For instance, a State's wrongful cyber operation that releases pollutants may cause long-term harm to another State's enjoyment of the environment. These consequences may be difficult to quantify, but the harm would qualify as an injury meriting reparation. Or, for example, a DDoS operation against a State's banking system may disrupt financial transactions and result in a loss of confidence in the State's financial sector. Despite the difficulty of precisely calculating the harm in these and other cases, the right to reparation survives in principle.

6. The obligation to make reparation only lies when the internationally wrongful cyber operation has 'caused' the injury. Injury caused does not include 'any and all consequences flowing' from the act; the damage that is 'remote' or 'consequential' does not qualify.[309] Rather, the underlying injury should be assessed in terms of factors such as directness,

---

[306] Articles on State Responsibility, Art. 31, paras. 5, 7 of commentary; *Rainbow Warrior* arbitral award, paras. 109–110.
[307] Articles on State Responsibility, Art. 31, para. 5 of commentary.
[308] Articles on State Responsibility, Art. 31, para. 5 of commentary.
[309] Articles on State Responsibility, Art. 31, para. 10 of commentary.

proximity, and foreseeability.[310] Consider a DDoS operation against a State's information systems portal that provides various e-services to the population, including the issuance of e-prescriptions. The negative effects of the operation on the health of the population are direct. However, the fact that the day-to-day operations of some private companies are hampered because their employees had delayed access to medication and are thus temporarily absent due to sickness is an insufficiently direct consequence to merit reparation.

7.   A particular challenge in this regard is that unforeseeable or remote effects are highly likely in the cyber context. The networked nature of cyber infrastructure and activities can make it difficult to anticipate the impact of a cyber operation. As an example, although some malware is very specific to particular cyber infrastructure, other malware is highly 'contagious' and can easily spread into other systems to which the target infrastructure is linked or be inadvertently trans-mitted by means such as memory sticks. Moreover, a State may be unable to map adequately the network into which it is launching a cyber operation and, therefore, be unaware of its likely effects on other systems. This reality complicates the assessment of whether the injury upon which reparation might be based was 'caused' by the cyber operations in question.

8.   The injured State's ability to mitigate the damage caused by a wrongful cyber operation is a relevant factor in determining the scope of reparation. In this regard, it is important to note that under general international law, the injured State has no duty to mitigate. However, if it could have reasonably acted to mitigate harm, but failed to do so, that failure bears on the reparation the responsible State must make. It will not be entitled to reparation based on injury that it could have avoided by taking reasonable measures of mitigation.[311] Thus, as an example, if an injured State could have easily taken the affected cyber systems offline to prevent further damage from a destructive cyber operation, the damage that was caused to the systems following the point at which that State could have done so will not be part of the reparations calculation. However, had the State done so, the harm caused by the fact that those systems were unavailable to the injured State is a reasonable consider-ation in determining the extent of injury.

---

[310] Articles on State Responsibility, Art. 31, para. 10 of commentary. *See also Naulilaa* arbitral award, para. 1031.
[311] *Gabčíkovo-Nagymaros* judgment, para. 80.

9. Wilful or negligent actions or omissions of the injured State that contributed to the damage resulting from a cyber operation are taken into account when determining the reparation due.[312] Negligence in such cases is understood as a lack of due care on the part of the victim in the attendant circumstances. There is no requirement that the negligence rise to a particular level (e.g., gross negligence).[313] Rather, it is the degree to which the negligence contributed to the injury that is relevant in determining the appropriate form of reparation.

10. As an example, assume a responsible State's internationally wrongful cyber operation causes damage, but the injured State acts negligently in attempting to address the situation such that its efforts exacerbate the damage. In this case, the responsible State will not be obliged to make reparation for the latter damage. It must be cautioned in this regard that the injured State may take actions that exacerbate the harm, but that are not negligent. For instance, at the time the offending cyber operation is launched, the injured State may not fully understand its nature and accordingly take reasonable, albeit incorrect, steps to contain the damage. Since its actions are not negligent, and response by the injured State is the normal response to a harmful cyber operation, the responsible State has to make reparation for the resulting additional harm caused by the injured State's actions.

11. When States act together in the commission of a single integrated cyber operation, they are subject to the remedies set forth in this Section, although the reparation to the injured State from the responsible States may not exceed the injury caused by the internationally wrongful act.[314] Consider the case of one State that allows the security agencies of another to use its cyber infrastructure in order to conduct a specific cyber operation or that shares cyber intelligence in order to mount particular joint operations. Both States may be responsible for the same internationally wrongful act that ensues, and if so, the two are subject to reparation since the injury suffered is due to their joint action. Exceptions to this general rule exist as *lex specialis* in certain treaty law, as is the case with respect to damage to space objects (Rule 60).

---

[312] Articles on State Responsibility, Art. 39. *See also LaGrand (Ger.* v. *US)*, Merits, 2001 ICJ 466, paras. 57, 116 (27 June).
[313] Articles on State Responsibility, Art. 39, para. 5 of commentary.
[314] Articles on State Responsibility, Art. 47; *Certain Phosphate Lands in Nauru*, 1992 ICJ 240, para. 48 (26 June).

12.   Sometimes, responsible States act towards a common end, albeit not in the form of joint operations. For instance, the security agencies of two States may agree separately to target cyber infrastructure of a third State's government. In such a case, each internationally wrongful act and the resulting damage is clearly allocable to one or the other party. The States are conducting distinct acts and will only bear responsibility and the consequent obligation to make reparation on the basis of their own wrongful acts.

13.   Similarly, a number of States may separately engage in wrongful, but distinct, conduct (or omissions) that combines to cause the resulting injury.[315] Consider the case of a cyber operation by one State against another's cyber infrastructure that was mounted from a third State. The operation would have been stopped had the third State been exercising due diligence over cyber activities on its territory, but that State failed to do so (Rules 6–7). The reparation that the responsible States must make will be determined individually based on their respective breaches and resultant injury.

14.   To invoke responsibility, an injured State must give notice of its claim of an internationally wrongful cyber action or omission to the responsible State, specifying the conduct that the responsible State should take to end the conduct and the form of any reparation.[316] There is no requirement that the notice be in a particular form or format; the key is simply that the notice be effective. Nor is a claim for particular measures necessarily binding on the responsible State, for the nature of reparation is governed by the law restated in Rule 29 below. The injured State's failure to issue a claim does not relieve a responsible State of its responsibility or of its obligation to make reparation; giving notice of its claim is the practical means of invoking the other State's responsibility.

Rule 29 – Forms of reparation

Reparations for injury suffered by an injured State as the result of an internationally wrongful act committed by cyber means may take the form of restitution, compensation, and satisfaction.

1.   This Rule sets forth the various forms of reparation. They include restitution, compensation, and satisfaction, either individually or in

---

[315] *See Tehran Hostages*, paras. 57–68; *Corfu Channel* judgment, at 17–23.
[316] Articles on State Responsibility, Art. 43.

combination, based on the circumstances.[317] Note that the obligation to make reparation is a distinct legal obligation of the responsible State that arises from the underlying internationally wrongful act. Failure to make reparation is itself an internationally wrongful act.

2. Restitution involves the re-establishment of the situation that existed prior to the internationally wrongful act.[318] It is the first, and primary, form of reparation. Only if restitution does not suffice to remedy the situation caused by the responsible State's wrongful cyber operation do other forms of reparation come into play.[319]

3. The concept of restitution differs from that of simple cessation of an internationally wrongful cyber operation (Rule 27). The former is designed to return the situation to the *status quo ante*, whereas the latter merely refers to ceasing the offending conduct (or omission). For instance, if one State is conducting hostile cyber operations against another in violation of a treaty obligation, cessation requires that the operations cease. Restitution, by contrast, might include providing information on the malware used such that the injured State can neutralise the effects of malware already emplaced on its systems. In many cases, however, such as cessation of a DDoS operation, the two obligations are indistinguishable.

4. Restitution may be inappropriate in cases in which the acts necessary to restore the situation to the *status quo* 'involve a burden out of all proportion to the benefit deriving from restitution instead of compensation'.[320] Despite the vagueness inherent in the standard, some situations will be clear. Consider a case in which a State is obliged by treaty to allow the use of certain State cyber infrastructure by another State for a set period. Technological advances subsequently necessitate modification of that cyber infrastructure lest it be rendered ineffective. However, the modifications are unavoidably incompatible with the cyber activities of the latter State absent significant and prohibitively expensive alterations. The failure to provide the use of the systems will likely constitute an internationally wrongful act, but restitution would not be required because of the disproportionate burden of doing so relative to the benefit to the injured State. Instead, compensation and satisfaction (discussed below) may instead be the

---

[317] Articles on State Responsibility, Art. 34.   [318] Articles on State Responsibility, Art. 35.
[319] Articles on State Responsibility, Art. 35, para. 3 of commentary, citing *Factory at Chorzow* judgment, at 48.
[320] Articles on State Responsibility, Art. 35(b).

appropriate remedies. It must be cautioned that the mere fact that burden in some degree outweighs benefit does not preclude restitution. Rather, the disproportionality must be 'grave'; close cases are assessed in favour of the injured State.[321]

5. The fact that restitution is difficult does not justify its avoidance; nor does the fact that the act of restitution would violate domestic law or regulations. On the contrary, 'special efforts' to make restitution are sometimes merited.[322] However, if restitution is 'materially impossible', for instance where the injury caused by the cyber operation cannot be reversed or the cyber infrastructure targeted by the operation has been destroyed and cannot be replaced, compensation and satisfaction may be appropriate.[323] Similarly, restitution will not entirely return the *status quo ante* in certain situations. For instance, a DDoS operation could result in down-time for other systems or financial loss. Merely restoring service (restitution) would not account for the injury caused by the responsible State's wrongful cyber operation; again, compensation and satisfaction may be additionally required.

6. Compensation involves payment for injury caused by an internationally wrongful act that is not made good by restitution and that is financially assessable.[324] It is intended to address actual financial loss, thereby ensuring the injured State is 'made whole' by the reparation. Despite their differing purposes, the injured State may agree with the responsible State to accept compensation in lieu of restitution.

7. The notion of compensation is broad. It extends not only to financial loss and damage suffered by the injured State, but also to that of its nationals, including companies. Compensation can encompass recovery for lost profits that are relatively identifiable, although such awards are less common than those for accrued losses.[325] For example, a DDoS operation against a commercial site may result in lost advertising revenue that is relatively easy to assess.

---

[321] Articles on State Responsibility, Art. 35, para. 11 of commentary.

[322] Articles on State Responsibility, Art. 35, para. 8 of commentary.

[323] Articles on State Responsibility, Art. 35(a).

[324] Articles on State Responsibility, Art. 36. *See also Gabčíkovo-Nagymaros* judgment, para. 152; *Pulp Mills on the River Uruguay* (*Arg.* v. *Uru.*), judgment, 2010 ICJ 14, para. 273 (20 April); *Ahmadou Sadio Diallo* judgment, para. 161.

[325] Articles on State Responsibility, Art. 36, paras. 27, 32 of commentary, citing the examples of *Cape Horn Pigeon* judgment (*US* v. *Russ.*), 9 RIAA 63 (1902); *Sapphire Int'l Petroleums Ltd.* v. *Nat'l Iranian Oil Co.*, 35 ILR 136, 187–189 (1963).

8.   Assessment of loss includes costs naturally associated with the injury concerned.[326] To illustrate, if a wrongful cyber operation against a private company results in employees receiving unemployment benefits from the injured State while the systems on which they work are inoperative, such benefits would be subject to compensation. In the same sense, permanent diminished value of national companies caused by a cyber operation against economic targets would be compensable, as would costs associated with responding to and resolving the consequences of a wrongful cyber operation.[327] However, punitive or exemplary damages are not compensable.[328]

9.   Satisfaction consists of 'an acknowledgment of the breach, an expression of regret, a formal apology or other appropriate modality'.[329] It is only appropriate when restitution and compensation cannot make good the injury, as in a non-material affront to a State. It is a response to the breach of the responsible State's obligation, not to the material loss the injured State has suffered. Satisfaction is not meant to be punitive, nor should it be 'humiliating'.[330]

10.   An expression of satisfaction need not be formal or public. The requirement could be met, for instance, through formal inquiry into a breach of the responsible State's international legal obligations with respect to cyber operations by agents of the State, like the personnel of its intelligence organs. Discipline of individuals who conducted the offending operation, especially in cases where the breach for which the State is responsible was of an *ultra vires* nature (Rule 15), may also qualify as satisfaction.

11.   There is significant State practice of claims for satisfaction that is relevant in the cyber context. For example, claims have been made for insulting a national symbol such as a flag, violations of sovereignty, and violations of diplomatic premises.[331] By analogy, States could make

---

[326] In the *Corfu Channel* judgment, as an illustration, the International Court of Justice held that compensation was due not only for damage to the two British warships harmed by the mines in Albanian waters, but also for the pensions and other survivor benefits owed to the victims and their survivors. *Corfu Channel* case (compensation) (*UK* v. *Alb.*), 1949 ICJ 244, at 249 (15 December).

[327] Analogously, courts in the environmental arena have also awarded compensation for lost value and clean-up. See discussion in Articles on State Responsibility, Art. 36, para. 15 of commentary.

[328] Articles on State Responsibility, Art. 36, para. 4 of commentary.

[329] Articles on State Responsibility, Art. 37(2).

[330] Articles on State Responsibility, Art. 37, para. 8 of commentary.

[331] Articles on State Responsibility, Art. 37, para. 4 of commentary.

claims for defacement of national websites, violations of sovereignty by cyber operations (Rule 4), and using cyber means to target official diplomatic correspondence (Rule 41).

Rule 30 – Breach of obligations owed to the international community as a whole

Any State may invoke the responsibility of a State that has conducted cyber operations breaching an *erga omnes* obligation owed to the international community as a whole.

1. All States may invoke the responsibility of a State that has breached an *erga omnes* norm.[332] With respect to the invocation of responsibility for breach of an *erga omnes* norm by way of countermeasures, see Rule 24. As to application of the plea of necessity to violations of obligations *erga omnes*, see Rule 26. Note that this Rule does not address norms that are *erga omnes inter partes*, which address obligations owed to members of a particular legal regime, such as that applying to members of a regional organisation.

2. Obligations *erga omnes* are 'obligations of a State towards the international community as a whole'.[333] In its *Barcelona Traction* judgment, the International Court of Justice confirmed, '[b]y their very nature [obligations *erga omnes*] are the concern of all States. In view of the importance of the rights involved, all States can be held to have a legal interest in their protection'.[334] The Court cited the prohibitions of aggression, genocide, slavery, and racial discrimination as examples.[335] In the *Wall* advisory opinion, the Court added self-determination and certain obligations under international humanitarian law to its catalogue of obligations *erga omnes*,[336] whereas in the *Obligation to Prosecute or Extradite* judgment, the Court regarded the prevention of acts of torture as among obligations *erga omnes (partes).*[337]

3. Any State may invoke State responsibility with regard to breach of an obligation that 'is owed to the international community as a whole'. It must be cautioned that reparation (Rule 28) is limited to States that actually suffer injury, although other States may demand reparation on

---

[332] Articles on State Responsibility, Art. 48(1)(b).
[333] *Barcelona Traction* judgment, para. 33.   [334] *Barcelona Traction* judgment, para. 33.
[335] *Barcelona Traction* judgment, para. 34.   [336] *Wall* advisory opinion, para. 155.
[337] *Questions Relating to the Obligation to Prosecute or Extradite (Belg. v. Sen.),* judgment, 2012 ICJ 422, para. 68 (20 July).

their behalf as well as on behalf of individuals who are the beneficiaries of the obligation concerned.[338] All States may demand cessation of the internationally wrongful act and assurances and guarantees of non-repetition (Rule 27).[339] To illustrate, consider the case of a State that successfully incites genocide via the Internet in another State. All other States, albeit unaffected by the genocide, may invoke the first State's responsibility. However, they may not seek reparation for themselves since the obligation involved is of an *erga omnes* character and they have suffered no damage.

4.   The majority of the International Group of Experts concluded that the source of the obligation *erga omnes*, be it based in customary or treaty law, does not determine the right of a State to invoke the responsibility of the State breaching it. A few of the Experts took the view that the present state of the law was such that only obligations *erga omnes partes* (under treaties) may be invoked in such a manner.

SECTION 4:   RESPONSIBILITY OF INTERNATIONAL ORGANISATIONS

1.   International organisations bear international legal responsibility for their cyber activities and cyber-related omissions that constitute internationally wrongful acts. In assessing the circumstances under which legal responsibility attaches to an international organisation, the International Group of Experts was, in part, informed by the International Law Commission's Articles on the Responsibility of International Organizations.[340] The Commission acknowledged the limited practice concerning the responsibility of international organisations, as well as the fact that the Commission's approach has reflected

---

[338]   Articles on State Responsibility, Arts. 42(b)(i) and para. 12 of commentary, 48(2)(b) and para. 11 of commentary.

[339]   Articles on State Responsibility, Art. 48(2)(a).

[340]   As with the Articles on State Responsibility, the Articles on the Responsibility of International Organizations are not a treaty and therefore non-binding. In Resolution A/69/126 (10 December 2014), the General Assembly took note of the Articles on the Responsibility of International Organizations, the text of which was annexed to the resolution, and commended them to the attention of governments and international organisations without prejudice to the question of their future adoption as a treaty or other appropriate action. The General Assembly further decided to return to the topic at its seventy-second session, in 2017.

progressive development more than in other areas of its codification of international law.[341] However, the Experts nevertheless agreed that some elements of the Articles on the Responsibility of International Organizations reflect customary international law and therefore used them as a point of reference.[342]

2.   The International Group of Experts carefully considered, as did the International Law Commission, the inherent differences between international organisations and States. It also noted the great diversity exhibited among international organisations with respect to their degree of international legal personality, powers and functions, size of membership, relations with their Members, procedures for deliberation, structure and facilities, and primary rules that bind them. Accordingly, the Experts proceeded cautiously in crafting this Section.

3.   The Experts relied on the broad definition of an 'international organisation' adopted in Article 2 of the Articles on the Responsibility of International Organizations, according to which an international organisation is one 'established by a treaty or other instrument governed by international law and possessing its own international legal personality'. States, as well as other entities, may be members of international organisations.[343]

4.   International organisations are bound in their cyber activities by rules that apply to them as a matter of their constitutive documents, any treaties to which they are Parties, and general international law.[344] The obligations set forth therein may be owed to States and other international organisations.

5.   The International Group of Experts agreed with the general principle that international organisations are subject to customary

---

[341] Articles on the Responsibility of International Organizations, General commentary, para. 5.

[342] *See, e.g.*, International Law Association Study Group, Report on the Responsibility of International Organizations to the Sofia Conference (2012), at 7–8, 11.

[343] *E.g.*, the European Union is a member of the World Trade Organization, the Food and Agricultural Organization, and various fisheries organisations. With respect to territories, Taiwan, Hong Kong and Macau, for example, are 'separate customs territories' that are Members of the World Trade Organization, while Taiwan and Hong Kong are separate 'economies' for the purposes of their participation in the Asia-Pacific Economic Cooperation (APEC) grouping. As an example of private entity membership in an international organisation, trade unions are Members of the International Labour Organization.

[344] *See, e.g., Interpretation of the Agreement of 25 March 1951 between the WHO and Egypt*, Advisory Opinion, 1980 ICJ 73, para. 37 (20 December).

international law. They acknowledged, however, that the binding nature of many customary norms *vis-à-vis* international organisations is unsettled, and therefore did not proffer a catalogue of those primary rules of customary international law that apply to international organisations. Nevertheless, the Experts concurred that to the extent a customary primary norm applies to an international organisation in the non-cyber context, it does so fully in the cyber context as well.

6.   With the exception of peremptory norms (*jus cogens*), Member States of an international organisation may, *inter se*, agree upon a specialised legal regime involving cyber activities that departs from the customary international law that would otherwise be applicable to them. For example, as discussed in Rule 9, States enjoy the sovereign right to exercise prescriptive jurisdiction over particular cyber activities occurring on their territory. Thus, they may determine the technical criteria that electronic signatures have to meet as a matter of domestic law. However, Member States of a regional organisation may surrender the exercise of this sovereign right to the organisation by allowing it to prescribe such criteria. The regional organisation then performs the function even though customary international law affords no basis for its exercise of prescriptive jurisdiction over cyber activities occurring on the territory of any Member State.

7.   While some international organisations rely heavily on the cyber infrastructure of Member States and have limited capacity of their own, others own and operate significant cyber infrastructure. Furthermore, while some international organisations are limited to cyber defence, others may be in a position to conduct offensive cyber operations, using either assets of Member States or those owned or controlled by the organisation itself.

8.   Ultimately, the key questions for international organisations are the extent to which customary international law regulates their own cyber operations and the degree to which it protects them from hostile cyber operations. The Experts agreed that the lawfulness under international law of each cyber operation by or against an international organisation must be assessed on its own merits and with sensitivity to the specific nature of the organisation, including its powers and functions.

9.   Consider a situation in which an international organisation's cyber infrastructure is the target of a destructive cyber operation conducted by a State. The Experts agreed that as international organisations do not enjoy sovereignty (Rule 1), the organisation may not claim a violation of its sovereignty and thus resort to any remedial measures

under international law on that basis. However, the State in which such infrastructure is located may assert a violation of its own sovereignty (Rule 4) by virtue of the operation's destructive effects that manifest on its territory and respond to that breach as set forth in this Manual (for instance, by resorting to countermeasures, Rule 20). If the cyber operation rises to the level of an armed attack, the Experts concurred that the territorial State may use force to respond in self-defence (Rule 71). Although they also agreed that the international organisation may be the means by which the territorial State exercises its inherent right of collective self-defence, they could not achieve consensus as to whether the organisation itself enjoys a right to self-defence separate from that of the State (see further discussion in Rule 31).

10.   Or consider a situation in which an international organisation mounts coercive cyber operations in order to influence elections in a State. The International Group of Experts agreed that international organisations are subject to the prohibition of intervention (Rule 66), a conclusion supported, in part, by the prohibition of United Nations intervention set forth in Article 2(7) of the UN Charter (Rule 67). That Article provides that the United Nations 'has no authority to intervene in matters which are within the domestic jurisdiction of any State'. Note, in this regard, that to the extent an international organisation may violate the prohibition of intervention, it is logical to conclude that acts of international organisations may also violate the sovereignty of States. This is because the prohibition of intervention derives from the principle of sovereignty (Rules 1–3).

11.   By contrast, a State's cyber operation directed against an international organisation does not violate the prohibition of intervention because said prohibition is designed to safeguard certain key aspects of sovereignty, which only States enjoy. The Experts noted, in this regard, that it may be difficult in practice to differentiate between an operation directed against an international organisation as such from one that is directed at its Member States, particularly when the organisation relies on a Member State's cyber infrastructure. The conclusion that the cyber operation does not constitute prohibited intervention is without prejudice to application of other Rules set forth in this Manual that might bar it, as well as any treaty obligations the State might owe the international organisation.

12.   The International Group of Experts agreed that Article 2(4) of the UN Charter as such does not bind international organisations; textually, it only applies on to 'Members' of the organisation. They

refrained from taking a position as to whether the customary law prohibition of the threat or use of force binds international organisations with respect to their cyber operations. However, the Experts drew attention to the general rule that a State incurs international responsibility if it causes an international organisation of which it is a Member to commit an act that, if committed by that State, would constitute a breach of an international obligation binding it.[345]

Rule 31 – General principle

An international organisation bears international legal responsibility for a cyber operation that breaches an international legal obligation and is attributable to the organisation.

1.   The International Group of Experts agreed that this Rule reflects an established principle of the international law governing international organisations, according to which international organisations are responsible for their internationally wrongful acts (on the notion of an 'internationally wrongful act', see also discussion in Rule 14).[346] An international organisation may breach an international legal obligation through an action or omission, including one that involves cyber activities.[347] For instance, if a cyber operations unit constituted within the structure of a regional security organisation, and thereby qualifying as an organ of the organisation, conducts a cyber operation against a State that amounts to prohibited intervention (see discussion in the chapeau to this Section), the organisation has breached an international legal obligation. It must be cautioned that the question of whether intent or damage need be established in order to determine the existence of a breach is answered by reference to the specific primary rule implicated by the cyber operation in question.

2.   Cyber operations or other cyber activities must be attributable to an international organisation under international law for that organisation to bear international responsibility for them. When conducted by

---

[345] Articles on the Responsibility of International Organizations, Art. 61(1).

[346] Articles on the Responsibility of International Organizations, Art. 3; *Immunity of a Special Rapporteur* advisory opinion, para. 66 (addressing the responsibility of the United Nations for compensating injured parties for acts performed by it, or its agents acting in their official capacity).

[347] Articles on the Responsibility of International Organizations, Arts. 4, 5, 10(1), 11.

organs or agents of an international organisation in the performance of their functions, such operations are attributable, that is, constitute acts of the organisation under international law.

3. 'Organs' of an international organisation are entities that are assigned specific competences by that organisation's constitutive instrument, other rules of the organisation, or practice.[348] As an example, the General Assembly, Security Council, and International Court of Justice are organs of the United Nations.[349] Similarly, the North Atlantic Council is an organ of NATO, the ECOWAS Council is an organ of ECOWAS, and the Mercosur Common Market Council is an organ of Mercosur.

4. An 'agent' is any person who has been charged by an organ of the organisation with carrying out, or helping to carry out, one of its functions – in short, any person through whom the organisation acts. This is so irrespective of whether the individual is a paid official or not, or permanent employee or not, of the organisation.[350] Persons or entities that, albeit not organs of the organisation, act under the instructions, or the direction or control, of an international organisation are also agents of the organisation.[351] The International Group of Experts agreed that the explanation of the terms 'instructions' and 'direction or control' in Rule 17 applies *mutatis mutandis* to this Rule. A cyber operation planned by an international organisation and entrusted to an agent is attributable to that international organisation and, in the event of a breach of an international legal obligation, entails the responsibility of the organisation.

5. Of particular note in the cyber context are private persons and entities, such as companies, engaging in cyber operations. Although not organs of an international organisation, their operations are attributable to an international organisation whenever they qualify as agents of the organisation, as discussed above.

---

[348] Articles on the Responsibility of International Organizations, Art. 2(b–c).

[349] UN Charter, Art. 7(1).

[350] *Reparation for Injuries Suffered in the Service of the United Nations*, advisory opinion, 1949 ICJ 174, at 177 (11 April). *See also Immunity of a Special Rapporteur* advisory opinion, para. 66; Articles on the Responsibility of International Organizations, Art. 6, para. 4 of commentary (citing a decision of the Swiss Federal Council, according to which 'one attributes to an international organisation acts and omissions of its organs of all rank and nature and of its agents in the exercise of their competences'.).

[351] Articles on the Responsibility of International Organizations, Art. 6, para. 11 of commentary.

6. Attribution of the conduct of organs or agents of an international organisation is limited to acts or omissions in the performance of their functions for the organisation. Conduct undertaken in their private capacity is not attributable to the organisation.[352] For example, a United Nations special envoy's cyber activities for private gain would not be attributable to the organisation. As a general matter, the particular rules of the organisation will establish which functions are entrusted to each organ or agent.[353]

7. The International Group of Experts agreed that this Rule extends to the *ultra vires* conduct of organs or agents.[354] As is also the case with respect to State responsibility (Rule 15), the notion of *ultra vires* acts encapsulates conduct that, albeit falling within the functions of the organ or agent, exceeds their authority. Thus, even if the organ or agent, acting in an apparently official capacity, exceeds the authority granted by, or contravenes the instructions of, the international organisation, the organisation will bear responsibility. For example, if an international organisation's peacekeeping force (on peacekeeping operations, see also Rule 78) violates the organisation's rules of engagement by conducting particular proscribed cyber operations, the international organisation will nevertheless be responsible for that conduct.

8. International organisations routinely depend on the organs of States or the organs or agents of other international organisations to perform their functions. If the organs or agents have been fully seconded to the international organisation, they are treated as organs or agents of the receiving organisation and their cyber activities are attributable solely to it.[355]

9. However, if an organ or agent of a State or another international organisation is not fully seconded and continues to act as an organ or agent of the seconding State or organisation, its acts will only be attributed to the receiving organisation if the latter exercises effective control over the conduct in question (on the notion of 'effective control', see also

---

[352] Articles on the Responsibility of International Organizations, Art. 6, para. 7 of commentary; Art. 8, para. 4 of commentary.

[353] Articles on the Responsibility of International Organizations, Art. 6(2). *See also* Articles on the Responsibility of International Organizations, Art. 2, para. 16 of commentary; Art. 6, para. 9 of commentary.

[354] Articles on the Responsibility of International Organizations, Art. 8.

[355] Articles on the Responsibility of International Organizations, Art. 7, para. 1 of commentary.

discussion in Rule 17).[356] The International Group of Experts agreed that attribution in these cases is based on the factual control that is exercised over the specific cyber conduct engaged in by the seconded organ or agent.[357] For example, if information technology specialists employed by a State's criminal investigation body are placed at the disposal of an international organisation, the seconding State may retain disciplinary powers and criminal jurisdiction over them pursuant to an agreement with the international organisation.[358] Despite retention of some residual control by the seconding State, the receiving organisation is responsible for the conduct of the specialists if the conduct in question is undertaken pursuant to the orders of the receiving organisation. In such situations, the State providing the specialists may bear separate responsibility for their acts pursuant to Rule 15, for instance, when the State tasks them to engage in offensive cyber operations *vis-à-vis* another State while deployed at the international organisation.

10.   If a State or organisation seconds its organ or agent pursuant to an agreement to that effect, such an agreement generally governs only the relations between the Parties; it usually does not have the effect of depriving a third party of any rights that might arise in case of a breach by the seconded organ or agent of an international legal obligation.[359] Such a situation might arise in the cyber context, for instance, if a State seconds a highly specialised team of IT specialists to an international organisation pursuant to an agreement between the State and the organisation, and the team engages in conduct that violates international law *vis-à-vis* a third State.

---

[356] Articles on the Responsibility of International Organizations, Art. 7.

[357] Articles on the Responsibility of International Organizations, Art. 7, para. 4 of commentary. *See also* Report of the Commission of Inquiry Established Pursuant to Security Council Resolution 885 (1993) to Investigate Armed Attacks on UNOSOM II Personnel Which Led to Casualties Among Them, UN Doc. S/1994/653, paras. 243–244 (24 February 1999); Report of the Secretary-General on Third-party Liability arising from Peacekeeping Operations, UN Doc. A/51/389, paras. 17–18 (1996); *Behrami and Behrami* v. *France*; *Saramati* v. *France, Germany and Norway*, Apps. No. 71412/01 and No. 78166/01, ECtHR, para. 133 (2007) (endorsing an even lower standard of 'ultimate authority and control'); *Al-Jedda* v. *United Kingdom*, App. No. 27021/08, ECtHR, para. 84 (2011).

[358] Articles on the Responsibility of International Organizations, Art. 7, para. 1 of commentary.

[359] The International Law Commission uses the example of the model contribution agreement relating to military contingents placed at the disposal of the United Nations by its Member States. Articles on the Responsibility of International Organizations, Art. 7, para. 3 of commentary.

11.   An international organisation may be held responsible in connection with an internationally wrongful act of a State or another international organisation when it (1) aids or assists, (2) directs or controls, or (3) coerces a State or another organisation to commit an internationally wrongful act.[360] These situations are discussed individually below. The legal analysis applicable to analogous situations involving the responsibility of States (Rule 18) applies *mutatis mutandis* in these cases. Therefore, the commentary that follows is abbreviated and reference should be made to the fuller discussion of the issues in Rule 18.

12.   An international organisation is responsible for its aid or assistance when it engages in cyber activities related to an internationally wrongful act of a State or another international organisation irrespective of whether the unlawful act is cyber or non-cyber in nature.[361] Consider a case in which an international organisation provides VSAT devices to a State to access the Internet for the purpose of facilitating a wrongful use of force (Rule 68) by that State against another State. The organisation is responsible for its aid. Responsibility also arises when an international organisation engages in non-cyber activities in support of a wrongful cyber operation of a State or another international organisation. This will be the case, for example, if an international organisation gathers biometric data on individuals located in a State through non-cyber means, and then provides that information to another State that uses the information to obtain access to military computer networks and then launches wrongful cyber operations against them. As distinguished from cases of direction and control, and coercion, an international organisation providing aid or assistance to an internationally wrongful act is not responsible for the underlying wrongful act, but rather only for the aid or assistance provided.[362]

13.   In such cases, the international organisation concerned must have knowledge that the action or omission of the State or the other international organisation constitutes an internationally wrongful act.[363] In other

---

[360]   Articles on the Responsibility of International Organizations, Arts. 14–16, respectively. *See also Genocide* judgment, para. 420.

[361]   Articles on the Responsibility of International Organizations, Art. 14.

[362]   Note that the text of Article 14 of the Articles on the Responsibility of International Organizations differs from that of Articles 15 and 16 in this regard. Article 14 includes the phrase 'for doing so' (referring to aiding or assisting), whereas Articles 15 and 16 use 'for the act'.

[363]   Articles on the Responsibility of International Organizations, Art. 14, para. 3 of commentary. *See also* Art. 15, para. 6 of commentary and Art. 16, para. 3 of commentary

words, if the international organisation is asked to provide cyber or non-cyber aid to a State or another international organisation, but is unaware that the assisted State or international organisation intends to engage in an internationally wrongful cyber or non-cyber act, the organisation bears no responsibility for having provided such assistance. As an example, an international organisation is not responsible for the act of a State or another international organisation to which it has provided computer hardware if the organisation is unaware that the hardware will be used to engage in internationally wrongful conduct, such as developing and deploying destructive malware against a State.

14.   Furthermore, the aiding or assisting international organisation is only responsible if the act which it aids or assists would be unlawful if committed by that organisation itself.[364] Responsibility is thus linked to the breach of an obligation binding on the international organisation, and is engaged when that international organisation contributes to the breach.

15.   The International Group of Experts took the view that aid or assistance must contribute 'significantly' to the commission of the internationally wrongful act such that a clear causal link exists between the aid or assistance and the act.[365] Consider the case of an international organisation that provides a zero-day exploit to a State to afford it the capacity to penetrate the computer network of another State. The former State uses its access to damage the latter State's telecommunication infrastructure in a manner that constitutes an internationally wrongful act. The first State is responsible for the act, whereas the organisation is responsible for its aid to the State.

16.   The second basis for international organisation responsibility is direction and control. An international organisation is responsible for an internationally wrongful cyber act committed by a State, whether a Member or not, or another international organisation under its direction and control.[366] For example, if a regional organisation passes a binding resolution requiring its Members to acquire access to networks inside a State so that the access can be used to facilitate a prohibited intervention

---

with respect to the knowledge requirements that attach to direction or control and coercion, respectively.

[364] Articles on the Responsibility of International Organizations, Art. 14, para. 5 of commentary.

[365] Articles on the Responsibility of International Organizations, Art. 14, para. 4 of commentary (citing Articles on State Responsibility, Art. 16, para. 5 of commentary).

[366] Articles on the Responsibility of International Organizations, Art. 15.

against that State, the organisation cannot escape responsibility on the basis that the operations were conducted by the national cyber assets of Member States.[367]

17.   A third basis for the responsibility of an international organisation is coercion of a State or another international organisation in the commission of an internationally wrongful act.[368] Consider the case of an international organisation's peacekeeping force commander who threatens to use previously acquired access to a State's infrastructure to shut down the State's electrical power grid if its security forces do not engage in cyber operations constituting a use of force (Rule 68) against a neighbouring State. The international organisation will be responsible under international law for the cyber use of force. In contrast to situations involving aid or assistance or direction and control, it is irrelevant whether the international organisation is bound by the primary rule that is violated as a result of the coercion. In other words, coerced acts that are unlawful for either the coerced State or international organisation are attributable to the coercing international organisation regardless of the breached primary norm's binding nature upon the organisation.[369] The International Group of Experts observed, however, that the preconditions to satisfaction of the coercion requirement (see Rule 18 as applied *mutatis mutandis* here) render such situations unlikely.

18.   International organisations may not escape international responsibility by adopting a decision requiring Member States or other international organisations to engage in cyber operations that would be internationally wrongful if the international organization conducted them.[370] Doing so is known as 'circumvention', a term that denotes 'an intention on the part of the international organisation to take advantage of the separate legal personality of its members in order to avoid compliance with an international obligation'.[371] The responsibility of the international organisation does not depend on whether the Member States or other international organisations concerned breach any international

---

[367] On this example, see Articles on the Responsibility of International Organizations, Art. 15, para. 4 of commentary.
[368] Articles on the Responsibility of International Organizations, Art. 16.
[369] Articles on the Responsibility of International Organizations, Art. 16, para. 3 of commentary.
[370] Articles on the Responsibility of International Organizations, Art. 17.
[371] Articles on the Responsibility of International Organizations, Art. 17, para. 4 of commentary.

obligation themselves.[372] This is without prejudice to the effect of binding resolutions adopted by the UN Security Council under Chapter VII (see also Rule 76).

19.   Take, for example, a situation in which an international organisation is engaged in a consensual peacekeeping mission in a non-Member State (Rule 78). The agreement with the non-Member host State specifies that the organisation shall not conduct acts of cyber espionage against the host State. The organisation will incur responsibility if it authorises a Member State to hack into the telecommunication infrastructure of the host State and conduct espionage, even if such espionage is not unlawful as between the host State and the State conducting the cyber espionage (Rule 32).

20.   Member States enjoy a considerable scope of appreciation for the actions they take to implement binding decisions of international organisations. However, if an international organisation adopts a binding decision *vis-à-vis* its Members that can be complied with lawfully, the organisation will not be responsible should they choose to comply with that decision in a manner that breaches an obligation owed by the organisation. It is only when the decision leaves the Member concerned with no discretion to engage in a lawful course of action in order to satisfy the decision that responsibility attaches.[373]

21.   For instance, an international organisation might require its Members to take action to deprive an international terrorist group of financing. One of the Members then conducts destructive cyber operations into a non-Member's territory that the terrorist group controls to disrupt the terrorist group's ability to export oil from the area, such that the cyber operation violates the target State's sovereignty (Rule 4). The Member State does so to deny the terrorist group of profits from the export. If the Member State could have complied with the binding decision by conducting other operations, such as closing its border to the oil transshipments, without otherwise violating the territorial State's sovereignty, only the Member State will be responsible, and not the international organisation, because the State did not need to violate international law to comply with the international organisation's decision.

---

[372] Articles on the Responsibility of International Organizations, Art. 17, para. 3 of commentary.

[373] *Bosporus Hava Yollari Turizm ve Ticaret Anonim Şirketi* v. *Ireland*, App. No. 45036/98, ECtHR, para. 157 (2005).

22. The International Group of Experts carefully considered the issue of whether an international organisation bears responsibility for merely authorising, as distinct from requiring, its Members to engage in cyber activities that would breach the international organisation's obligations under international law. The Experts could identify no practice and insufficient *opinio juris* to conclude that such a rule of responsibility exists as a matter of customary international law. Accordingly they concluded that the organisation would not bear responsibility for a breach in such circumstances.[374]

23. The Experts could arrive at no consensus as to whether all of the circumstances that preclude the wrongfulness of a State's action or omission (Rule 19) also exist for an international organisation. A minority of them took the position, as did the International Law Commission in the Articles on the Responsibility of International Organizations, that six grounds preclude the wrongfulness of an action or omission by an international organization: (1) consent, (2) self-defence, (3) countermeasures, (4) *force majeure*, (5) distress, and (6) necessity (to safeguard the essential interests of Member States, not of the organisation).[375] For these Experts, it would be incongruent to accept that the premise that international legal responsibility attaches to international organisations, but exclude what are otherwise well-accepted grounds for precluding the wrongfulness of actions or omissions on the basis that the actor is an international organisation. However, they acknowledged that the precise parameters of those grounds are not well developed *vis-à-vis* international organisations in customary international law, and that said parameters are accordingly not necessarily identical to the ones set forth for States in Rules 19–26 of this Manual.

24. A majority of the Experts was of the view that the wrongfulness of actions or omissions by an international organisation may be precluded, but were hesitant to characterise all six grounds as customary in nature. These Experts took notice of the fact that the Articles on the Responsibility of International Organizations were acknowledged by the International Law Commission in part to represent progressive development of the law. They also emphasised the limited practice and expressions of *opinio juris* on the matter.

---

[374] In this regard, the International Group of Experts took note of the International Law Commission's assertion to the contrary. Articles on the Responsibility of International Organizations, Art. 17, paras. 2, 8 of commentary.

[375] Articles on the Responsibility of International Organizations, Arts. 20–25, respectively.

25.   The Experts in the majority were willing to accept that consent is a valid ground for preclusion of the wrongfulness of the acts of international organisations on the basis that what limited practice exists appears to support its validity.[376] By contrast, they could not discern sufficient practice in relation to either *force majeure* or distress to conclude that those grounds apply in the case of international organisations. Similarly, the majority concluded that insufficient State practice exists to extend the right of self-defence to international organisations.

26.   Those Experts in the majority adopted a more nuanced approach with regard to both the plea of necessity and countermeasures. As to the former, some of them took the position that although an international organisation may not invoke the plea of necessity to safeguard its own essential interests against a grave and imminent peril, it may do so to safeguard an essential interest of its Member States.[377] The other Experts in the majority pointed to the paucity of practice acknowledged even by the International Law Commission. They also emphasised that the plea of necessity is an exceptional remedy and that in light of the close relationship between the plea and State sovereignty it would be inappropriate to extend it to an entity that does not itself enjoy sovereignty.[378]

27.   The Experts comprising the majority were similarly divided on the question of whether an international organisation may resort to cyber or non-cyber countermeasures in order to induce a State (including, in some situations, Member States[379]) or another international organisation that is in breach of an international legal obligation to desist from that breach. Though little practice exists, some of them were willing to agree with the minority, as well as the International Law Commission, that international organisations may

---

[376] See the invitation given by the Government of Indonesia to the European Union and seven contributing States to deploy the Aceh Monitoring Mission within Indonesian territory. *See* European Union Council Joint Action 2005/643/CFSP of 9 September 2005 on the European Union Monitoring Mission in Aceh (Indonesia) (Aceh Monitoring Mission — AMM), pmbl. (10 September 2005).

[377] Articles on the Responsibility of International Organizations, Art. 25, para. 4 of commentary (explaining that the scarcity of relevant practice, as well as the heightened risk entailed by the invocation of necessity by international organisations, militates in favour of stricter conditions in such cases.).

[378] Articles on the Responsibility of International Organizations Comments and Observations Received from Governments, International Law Commission, A/CN.4/636, at 23–24 (14 February 2011).

[379] Articles on the Responsibility of International Organizations, Art. 22(3).

take countermeasures and be the subject thereof.[380] They cautioned that the conditions for taking countermeasures differ somewhat from those applicable to States (Rules 20–25), particularly with respect to Member States, a point that is evident in the relevant Articles on the Responsibility of International Organizations.[381] Other Experts in the majority did not subscribe to this view, again citing the lack of practice in the area.

---

[380] Articles on the Responsibility of International Organizations, Arts. 22, 51–56. *See also* Articles on the Responsibility of International Organizations, Art. 51, paras. 2 (citing submissions made by the WHO, UNESCO, and the OSCE), 3 (citing the submissions of Denmark on behalf of the five Nordic countries, Malaysia, Japan, the Netherlands, Switzerland, and Belgium) of commentary.

[381] For instance, Article 22(2)(c) of the Articles on the Responsibility of International Organizations requires that 'no appropriate means are available for otherwise inducing compliance with the obligations' in question, whereas no such requirement exists with regard to countermeasures by States against other States.

5

Cyber operations not *per se* regulated by international law

Rule 32 – Peacetime cyber espionage

Although peacetime cyber espionage by States does not *per se* violate international law, the method by which it is carried out might do so.

1.   This Rule applies only to cyber espionage conducted outside the context of an armed conflict. With respect to cyber espionage during armed conflict and the issue of spies, see Rule 89.

2.   As used in this Rule, the term 'cyber espionage' refers to any act undertaken clandestinely or under false pretences that uses cyber capabilities to gather, or attempt to gather, information.[382] Cyber espionage involves, but is not limited to, the use of cyber capabilities to surveil, monitor, capture, or exfiltrate electronically transmitted or stored communications, data, or other information. It should be cautioned that the term is proffered here for the purposes of the Rule and has no independent legal significance.

3.   This Rule is limited to cyber espionage by or otherwise attributable to States (Rules 15–18). For activities conducted by non-State actors, see Rule 33. Cyber espionage includes that which is directed at States, as well as commercial entities (e.g., so-called industrial espionage or economic espionage). The operations can target specific information or involve long-term bulk collection.

4.   Cyber espionage can differ in both speed and volume from more traditional methods of espionage. Moreover, cyber techniques will often alleviate the need for physical presence in a State due to the possibility of remote access operations. Each of the three layers of cyberspace (as discussed in Rule 1) can facilitate cyber espionage. In the physical layer, for instance, code can be inserted on hardware during the manufacturing process that would subsequently permit remote access, or data

---

[382] Note that in some languages 'espionage' by definition means an unlawful activity. The term is not used in this sense in this Manual.

that is transmitted over communications cables can be redirected through specific countries for tapping purposes. Vulnerabilities in the logical layer can be exploited by malware designed to monitor communications. Finally, social engineering techniques such as phishing, spear-phishing, and whaling can be employed in the social layer to gather access credentials to facilitate seemingly authorised access to information that possesses intelligence value.

5.   The International Group of Experts agreed that customary international law does not prohibit espionage *per se*.[383] Whereas the Wikileaks, Snowden, and other disclosures of cyber espionage by States against other States and commercial entities have sparked debate as to whether cyber espionage has become so pervasive and detrimental that a new customary international law norm prohibiting it has crystallised, the Experts concurred that insufficient State practice and *opinio juris* on the matter exist to so conclude.[384] On the contrary, a number of States have by domestic law authorised their security services to engage in espionage, including cyber espionage.[385] The Experts cautioned that States may commit themselves to restricting or banning cyber espionage activities *inter se*.[386]

---

[383] *See, e.g*, DoD Manual, para. 16.3.2.

[384] One of the few examples of *opinio juris* to this effect is the Statement by Brazilian President H. E. Dilma Rousseff on 24 September 2013 at the Opening of the General Debate of the 68th session of the United Nations General Assembly. Translated reprint, at 2, gadebate.un.org/sites/default/files/gastatements/68/BR_en.pdf.

[385] *See, e.g.*, Lag om signalspaning i försvarsunderrättelseverksamhet (2008:717), Secs. 1–2 (Swed.); BND-Gesetz (20 December 1990), Sec. 2(1)(40) (Ger.); Wet op de inlichtingen – en veiligheidsdiensten (WIV) (7 February 2002), Arts. 6.2.d, 7.2.a.1˚, 7.2.e, 27(1) (Neth.); Regulation of Investigatory Powers Act (RIPA) (2000), Sec. 8(4) (UK); Bundesgesetz über die Zuständigkeiten im Bereich des zivilen Nachrichtendienstes (3 October 2008), Art. 1.a (Switz.); Bundesgesetz über Aufgaben und Befugnisse im Rahmen der militärischen Landesverteidigung (Militärbefugnisgesetz – MBG) (27 April 1999), Sec. 20(a) (Austria).

[386] See the commitment between the United States and China to the effect that neither State's government will engage in or support cyber-enabled theft of intellectual property (25 September 2015), www.whitehouse.gov/the-press-office/2015/09/25/fact-sheet-president-xi-jinpings-state-visit-united-states. The commitment prohibits cyber espionage targeting trade secrets or other confidential business information that is conducted in order to provide a competitive advantage to their companies or commercial sectors. The undesirability (but not unlawfulness) of this type of cyber espionage was also expressed by the G20 leaders in 2015 when they affirmed that 'no country should conduct or support ICT-enabled theft of intellectual property, including trade secrets or other confidential business information, with the intent of providing competitive advantages to companies or commercial sectors.' G20 Leaders' Communiqué (16 November 2015),

6.   While the International Group of Experts agreed that there is no prohibition of espionage *per se*, they likewise concurred that cyber espionage may be conducted in a manner that violates international law due to the fact that certain of the methods employed to conduct cyber espionage are unlawful. The Experts noted in particular that this may be the case with regard to respect for the principle of sovereignty (Rule 4) and the prohibition of intervention (Rule 66). In other words, if an aspect of a cyber espionage operation is unlawful under international law, it renders the cyber espionage unlawful. By styling a cyber operation as a 'cyber espionage operation', a State cannot therefore claim that it is by definition lawful under international law; its lawfulness depends on whether the way in which the operation is carried out violates any international law obligations that bind the State. For instance, if organs of one State, in order to extract data, hack into the cyber infrastructure located in another State in a manner that results in a loss of functionality, the cyber espionage operation violates, in the view of the Experts, the sovereignty of the latter. Similarly, if cyber operations that are undertaken for espionage purposes violate the international human right to privacy (Rule 35), the cyber espionage operation is unlawful.

7.   The International Group of Experts took particular note of the bulk collection of Internet traffic and cyber surveillance, which may implicate international law norms addressed elsewhere in this Manual. As an example, the lawfulness of tapping a submarine communication cable depends, *inter alia*, on whether the operation is conducted within or beyond the territorial sea of a coastal State (Rule 54). Surveillance of diplomatic correspondence is subject to Rule 41. The rules set forth in international human rights law (Chapter 6) are implicated by cyber surveillance conducted in a State's own territory and, under certain circumstances, also extraterritorially. Therefore, every cyber surveillance operation must be assessed on its individual merits.

8.   The Experts were incapable of achieving consensus as to whether remote cyber espionage reaching a particular threshold of severity violates international law.[387] For example, consider a situation in which a

---

para. 26, g20.org.tr/g20-leaders-commenced-the-antalya-summit/. *See also* UK–China Joint Statement 2015 (22 October 2015), www.gov.uk/government/news/uk-china-joint-statement-2015; Statement on the Occasion of the 4th German-Chinese Intergovernmental Consultations (13 June 2016), www.china.diplo.de/contentblob/4842162/Daten/668889/160704erklaerungold.pdf.

[387] The Experts noted, for instance, that mass surveillance, an activity engaged in by some States, has been condemned by at least one State as a violation of sovereignty (Rule 4).

State remotely accesses another State's military cyber systems without consent and exfiltrates gigabytes of classified data over an extended period. The majority of the Experts was of the view that exfiltration violates no international law prohibition irrespective of the attendant severity. They suggested that the legal issue is not severity, but instead whether the method employed is unlawful. A few Experts took the position that at a certain point the consequences suffered by the target State are so severe (e.g., the exfiltration of nuclear launch codes) that the operation is a violation of sovereignty (Rule 4). The majority countered by stating that this position is not reflective of *lex lata*.

9.   Neither could the Experts agree on the lawfulness of close access cyber espionage operations, such as the insertion of a USB flash drive into a computer located on one State's territory by an individual acting under the direction or control (Rule 17) of another State. The majority viewed such activity as a violation of sovereignty, not because cyber espionage is involved, but rather by virtue of the fact that the individual is on another State's territory while non-consensually engaging in the operation. A few of the Experts took the view that this activity would not be unlawful, suggesting that acts of espionage represent an exception to the prohibitions of violation of sovereignty (Rule 4) and intervention (Rule 66).[388]

10.   The majority of the Experts agreed that although acts of cyber espionage may not be unlawful standing alone, they can nevertheless constitute an integral and indispensable component of an operation that violates international law. Consider the case of a State that executes a single plan in which it employs cyber espionage to acquire the credentials necessary to access the industrial control system of a nuclear power plant of another State with the intent of threatening to conduct cyber operations against the system in a manner that will cause significant damage or death unless the former ends particular military operations abroad. The majority was of the view that, once the threat has been communicated, the action in its entirety, including the integrated cyber espionage, constitutes an unlawful threat of the use of force (Rule 68). A minority of

---

See Statement by Brazilian President H. E. Dilma Rousseff on 24 September 2013 at the opening of the general debate of the 68th session of the United Nations General Assembly, gadebate.un.org/sites/default/files/gastatements/68/BR_en.pdf.

[388] *See, e.g.*, Ashley Deeks, *An International Legal Framework for Surveillance*, 55 Va. J. Int'l L. 291, 302 (2015) ('In this view, ideas such as non-intervention and sovereignty developed against a background understanding that states do and will spy on each other, thus establishing a carve-out for espionage within those very concepts.').

the Experts, however, maintained that the two aspects of the operation must be assessed separately and that the acquisition of the access credentials, as distinct from the threat of the use of force, does not violate international law.

11.   By contrast, take a case in which one State employs cyber espionage to acquire information about another State's defensive capabilities and posture. Later, relations between the two States deteriorate, and the first develops and executes a plan to use the previously gathered intelligence to facilitate an unlawful kinetic attack in violation of the prohibition of the use of force. Despite the unlawfulness of the attack, all of the Experts concurred that the gathering of the intelligence during the earlier operation, even though ultimately used to support the unlawful action, was not itself unlawful. The two acts are distinct and their permissibility under international law must be assessed separately.

12.   Sometimes, other cyber operations are employed to enable cyber espionage operations. Such operations must be assessed on their own merits irrespective of the fact that they are designed to facilitate internationally lawful cyber espionage. In other words, the fact that the ultimate objective is to conduct cyber espionage has no bearing on the first operation's lawfulness. As an example, a tactic of signals intelligence is to force adversaries to use forms of communication that are less secure so information can be collected. This driving, or 'herding', of enemy communications from a platform not susceptible to exploitation to a less secure one from which intelligence can be collected might be accomplished by physical damage to the former. Similarly, consider a case in which a military unit in one State has been communicating using a Voice over Internet Protocol (VoIP) system that has been penetrated and is being monitored by the intelligence service of another State. The unit switches to a standalone, custom designed secure voice communications system. Knowing that there is no ready stock of replacement equipment, the intelligence service introduces malicious code into a SCADA device causing an electrical spike, thereby physically damaging the new communications hardware. As a result, the unit is forced to revert to VoIP communications, which again enables the espionage operations. The fact that the cyber operation was conducted with the purpose of enabling cyber espionage does not mean that it was necessarily lawful under international law; indeed, in this case the causation of damage qualifies the operation at least as a violation of sovereignty (Rule 4).

13.   It must be cautioned that it can be challenging for a target State to distinguish cyber espionage activities from other cyber operations,

including offensive cyber operations. For example, both cyber espionage and offensive cyber operations usually require penetration of a system, often by the introduction of malware or a successful phishing operation. Such access may allow for further manoeuvre through the compromised system to engage in espionage or, alternatively, degradation, disruption, or destruction of the targeted system or the data stored within, or being transmitted through, it. Should the target State discover the malware, it may have difficulty in expeditiously ascertaining the malware's precise functions. Technical realities like this contribute to the risk that an act of cyber espionage will be misconstrued as another type of activity, such as a cyber use of force (Rule 68) or even an imminent armed attack (Rules 71 and 73). The International Group of Experts agreed that this dilemma is addressed by the various requirements regarding certainty that apply with respect to State responses to cyber operations (see discussion in chapeau to Section 1 of Chapter 4, Rule 15, and Rule 71).

14.   If a cyber espionage operation causes unintended consequences, the lawfulness of the operation is assessed by reference to the primary norms involved. For example, during the course of installing a backdoor in a network so that it can later be accessed for cyber espionage, the target operating system can become corrupted and damage can result to equipment controlled by the system. As discussed in Rule 4, a State's cyber operation can violate the sovereignty of another State even based on the operation's unintended consequences. Therefore, in the aforementioned case, the operation qualifies at least as a violation of sovereignty.

15.   States sometimes create honeypots based upon the assumption that other States will conduct cyber espionage activities against them. The honeypots consist of seemingly valuable data or network segments, whereas in reality they possess no intelligence value. Honeypots are used for various purposes. In some cases, a State sets one up as a form of counter-intelligence to monitor how another State conducts its operations inside the honeypot, thereby providing valuable information as to that State's behavioural patterns and cybes capabilities. In other cases, a State might store files in the honeypot that, once exfiltrated, will report back with information about their destination in order to determine which States engage in cyber espionage activities against it. The exfiltrated files might also include the capability to monitor activities in their new destination and report back on them. The International Group of Experts agreed that these operations do not amount to violations of international law. The first is merely an exercise of sovereign rights by the State that created the honeypot in its own territory. The second does

not constitute a breach of a customary international law norm (for instance, a violation of sovereignty, Rule 4) owed to the exfiltrating State because it constitutes mere cyber espionage; indeed, there would be no breach had the State itself transmitted the files into the exfiltrating State's cyber infrastructure.

16.   A more complicated situation involves a honeypot that contains weaponised files that, once exfiltrated, will cause significant disruption or damage in the target system. The International Group of Experts was divided with respect to these operations, although they agreed that the legal issue was one of attribution. The minority was of the view that the operation is attributable to the State creating the honeypot pursuant to the law of State responsibility (Rule 15) because that State set it in motion and the operation will culminate as anticipated by it. Thus, these Experts opined that such an operation at least violates the sovereignty (Rule 4) of the target State because the destructive nature of the operation qualifies it as such. In other words, for the minority, the State that placed the weaponised files into the honeypot has committed an internationally wrongful act (Rule 14). The majority took the position that the organs of the State that penetrated the honeypot factually transmitted the infected files into their own cyber infrastructure; therefore, the State that laid the trap did not conduct the actual activity (transmitting destructive malware into the target State's cyber infrastructure) causing the harm and thus the operation is not attributable to it pursuant to Rule 15.

17.   Despite the absence of an international law prohibition of espionage, States are entitled to, and have, enacted domestic legislation that criminalises cyber espionage carried out against them. The exercise of prescriptive, enforcement, and judicial jurisdiction must be consistent with Chapter 3.

18.   With respect to espionage from diplomatic missions and consular posts, and the activities of diplomatic agents and consular officials, see the chapeau to Chapter 7 and Rule 43.

Rule 33 – Non-State actors

International law regulates cyber operations by non-State actors only in limited cases.

1.   Apart from specific areas of the law directed at the rights and obligations of individuals or other non-State actors (as in the case of

human rights law, the law of armed conflict, and international criminal law), international law by and large does not regulate cyber operations conducted by non-State actors, such as private individuals or companies.

2.   The International Group of Experts agreed that cyber operations conducted by non-State actors that are not attributable to States (Rules 15 and 17) do not violate the sovereignty of the State into which they are launched (Rule 4), constitute intervention (Rule 66), or amount to a use of force (Rule 68) because these breaches can be committed only by States. This is so irrespective of any consequences caused by such operations. With respect to a violation of sovereignty, in Rule 4, the Experts acknowledged the existence of a contrary view.

3.   Resultantly, States cannot resort to countermeasures in response to cyber operations by non-State actors unless those operations are attributable to another State. However, in some cases, the failure of a State to terminate cyber operations conducted by non-State actors on its territory will constitute a breach of the requirement to exercise due diligence (Rules 6–7). Additionally, certain non-State cyber operations permit the target States to directly respond against the non-State actors abroad conducting them. As discussed in Rule 26, the plea of necessity is available even in situations in which the originator cannot reliably be identified as another State or is known to be a non-State actor. Furthermore, responses directed against non-State actors may be permissible pursuant to the law of self-defence (Rule 71).

4.   Non-State actors are not entitled to engage in the responses that States may conduct under the law of State responsibility when facing hostile cyber operations by or attributable to other States. In particular, cyber responses by non-State actors cannot qualify as countermeasures (Rule 24), although as explained in Rules 15 and 17, non-State actors may be empowered by States to act on their behalf. This is so even though such non-State actors may be the direct target of cyber activities by States and despite the fact that the non-State actor concerned may possess cyber capabilities that are robust, in some cases exceeding those of States.

5.   States enjoy the authority to establish specific legal regimes governing cyber activities by non-State actors and cooperative arrangements may be set up to address particular cyber issues. For instance, with respect to the latter, a global multi-stakeholder community, which includes both States and non-State actors, manages the Internet's naming system. This Rule is without prejudice to such regimes.

6.   When non-State actors engage in cyber operations related to an armed conflict, their activities are subject to the law of armed conflict

(Part IV). In certain cases, an organised armed group engaging in cyber operations may become a party to a non-international armed conflict (Rule 83).

7.   In some circumstances, non-State actors may engage in cyber operations that are contrary to international human rights law or the law of armed conflict such that individual criminal responsibility attaches pursuant to international criminal law (Rule 84).

8.   Non-State actors and their cyber operations will always be subject to the jurisdiction of one or more States pursuant to Chapter 3.

PART II

Specialised regimes of international law
and cyberspace

6

International human rights law

1. It is widely accepted that many of the international human rights that individuals enjoy 'offline' are also protected 'online'.[389] This Chapter articulates Rules indicating the scope of application and content of international human rights law bearing on cyber activities. Although the International Group of Experts agreed that both treaty and customary international human rights law apply to cyber-related activities, they cautioned that it is often unclear as to whether certain human rights reflected in treaty law have crystallised as rules of customary law. Moreover, aspects of international human rights treaty law are subject to variance when States and regional bodies interpret them *vis-à-vis* cyber activities. The Experts further noted that States may, under specific circumstances (Rule 37), limit the exercise and enjoyment of certain rights in accordance with international human rights law.

2. The Universal Declaration of Human Rights is often cited as reflective of certain key customary norms.[390] Many provisions of international human rights treaty law, including certain of those found in the

---

[389] *See, e.g.*, The Promotion, Protection and Enjoyment of Human Rights on the Internet, para. 1, UN Doc. A/HRC/32/L.20 (27 June 2016); The Right to Privacy in the Digital Age, GA Res. 68/167, para. 3, UN Doc. A/RES/68/167 (18 December 2013); EU Human Rights Guidelines on Freedom of Expression Online and Offline, Council of the European Union, para. 6 (12 May 2014); UN GGE 2013 Report, para. 21; UN GGE 2015 Report, paras. 13(e), 26; NATO 2016 Warsaw Summit Communiqué, para. 70; Convention on Cybercrime, pmbl., Art. 15.1; Deauville G8 Declaration: Renewed Commitment for Freedom and Democracy, para. II(10) (26–27 May 2011); Agreement between the Governments of the Member States of Shanghai Cooperation Organization on Cooperation in the field of International Information Security, Art. 4(1), 16 June 2009.

[390] UN International Conference on Human Rights, Final Outcome Document, para. 2, UN Doc. A/CONF.32/41 (13 May 1968). ('[T]he Universal Declaration of Human Rights ... constitutes an obligation for the members of the international community'.). For an example of one State's view as to those international human rights law norms that are customary in nature, see Restatement (Third), Sec. 702.

ICCPR and the ICESCR, are also regarded as reflective of customary international law. However, no definitive catalogue of customary international human rights law exists. Additionally, not all States are Parties to the same international human rights law treaties and the rights accorded to individuals under regional human rights instruments, and the scope of those rights, vary. Even within regional systems, there is often a margin of appreciation that reflects respect for differences in, *inter alia*, capacity and national legal tradition. Finally, some treaties allow States to issue reservations to their provisions when they become Parties thereto or subsequently derogate (Rule 38) from their obligations under the treaty in exceptional circumstances provided for in the instrument.

3. This Chapter relies heavily upon various human rights treaties, as well as case law interpreting and applying them. Such instruments are directly binding only on Parties thereto and it is inappropriate to freely generalise from one treaty regime to another. Nevertheless, the Experts agree that treaty provisions shed light, in a general sense, on the scope of applicability and content of corresponding customary international human rights norms. In particular, whenever multiple treaties and case law adopt the same or a similar position regarding a particular human right, the International Group of Experts agreed that such congruence may support, but does not necessarily do so definitively, a conclusion that customary international law exists to that effect. Accordingly, the Experts took a conservative approach in drafting the Rules that follow.

4. Although the Experts concluded the Rules set forth in this Chapter are meant to apply globally, they also agreed with the assertion that 'the realisation of human rights must be considered in the regional and national context bearing in mind different political, economic, legal, social, cultural, historical and religious backgrounds'.[391] This point is especially relevant in the cyber context given differing levels of cyber development, economic wherewithal, national and regional security concerns, and the like. However, the Experts concurred that such factors do not relieve States of their customary human rights law obligations, except in accordance with the limitations set forth in Rule 37 or a treaty provision permitting derogation (Rule 38). Rather, these factors are to be considered when assessing how the right in question applies to a

[391] ASEAN Human Rights Declaration, Art. 7.

situation, as well as the nature of the limitations, if any, that a State may impose on its exercise or enjoyment.

5. The International Group of Experts was in accord that States must not only respect human rights, but also protect (i.e., ensure respect for) them. The obligation to respect denotes a duty to refrain from unlawfully interfering with human rights that individuals enjoy. In other words, it applies with regard to the activities of a State *vis-à-vis* each individual enjoying the human right in question. By contrast, the obligation to protect refers to the legal requirement to take measures to ensure third parties do not interfere with the enjoyment of human rights. The parameters of these two obligations, and limitations thereon, are dealt with in Rule 36.

6. The precise interplay between the law of armed conflict (Part IV) and international human rights law remains unsettled and is determined with respect to the specific legal rules in question. Nevertheless, the International Group of Experts was unanimous in the view that both the law of armed conflict and international human rights law apply to cyber-related activities in the context of an armed conflict, subject to the application of the principle of *lex specialis*.[392] For instance, although human rights treaty provisions prohibiting arbitrary deprivation of life are non-derogable,[393] whether a cyber attack (Rule 92) during an armed conflict violates that prohibition is determined primarily by reference to the *lex specialis* law of armed conflict rules regarding the conduct of hostilities (Chapter 17).

7. Rule 34 affirms the general premise that individuals enjoy customary international human rights law protections with respect to their cyber-related activities. The following Rule examines some of the key international human rights that individuals enjoy with respect to such cyber-related activities. It must be cautioned that although a State's activity may interfere with a specific international human right, such as the right to privacy, this fact does not answer the question of whether that right has been violated. Violation is a separate issue. In this regard, human rights law

---

[392] *Nuclear Weapons* advisory opinion, para. 25; *Wall* advisory opinion, paras. 106, 142. *See also* General Comment No. 31, para. 11. Some of the Experts emphasised that *lex specialis* is not to be understood as only a matter of the law of armed conflict overriding international human rights law. Rather, *lex specialis* is a means of interpretation and conflict resolution in the event a specific rule within one legal regime conflicts with a rule from another; it is but part of a system of legal methodology and interpretation.

[393] *See, e.g.,* ICCPR, Arts. 4(2), 6(1); ACHR, Arts. 4, 27(2); African Charter, Art. 4; ECHR, Arts. 2, 15(2).

obligations, with the exception of absolute rights, are subject to limitation by the State in certain circumstances. Furthermore, most human rights treaties allow for States to derogate from some of their obligations, albeit only to the extent delineated by those instruments and in accordance with international law. This means that a State has only violated international human rights law if (1) it owes international human rights law obligations to the person in question (Rule 34); (2) the person's cyber-related activity falls within the scope of a particular international human right (Rule 35); (3) the State engages in an act that interferes with the international human right in question; and (4) the State has not imposed lawful limitations (Rule 37) on, or derogated from (Rule 38), the right in question.

Rule 34 – Applicability

International human rights law is applicable to cyber-related activities.

1. The International Group of Experts agreed that international human rights law, whether found in customary or treaty law, applies in relation to cyber-related activities. As noted in the chapeau to this chapter, the principle that the same rights people have offline are to be protected online has been asserted repeatedly in numerous multilateral and multi-stakeholder fora. Indeed, at the time international human rights law norms emerged it was recognised, for example, that the right to freedom of expression (Rule 35) extended to 'any' media, a reference that accommodates technological advancements, such as the emergence of cyber-enabled expression.[394] However, the International Group of Experts acknowledged that State understandings concerning the precise scope of certain human rights entitlements in the cyber context, as well as those of human rights tribunals and other relevant human rights bodies, vary.

2. States bear responsibility for international human rights law violations that they themselves commit (*lit.* (a) of Rule 36).[395] Additionally, if the activities of a non-State actor or another State interfere with the ability of individuals to engage in cyber activities protected by international human rights law, States may shoulder an obligation to ensure that the individuals entitled to benefit from the rights in question can do so (*lit.* (b) of Rule 36).

---

[394] UDHR, Art. 19. *See also* ICCPR, Art. 19(2); ECHR, Art. 10(1); ACHR, Art. 13(1).
[395] *See, e.g., Genocide* judgment, paras. 207–208.

3. The Experts noted that the issue of whether entities other than States are bound by international human rights law and, if so, the extent to which they are so bound, is unsettled and controversial. However, they agreed that international organisations, as legal persons, may be bound by customary international human rights law.[396]

4. The International Group of Experts was of the view that although certain human rights regimes, such as that of the Council of Europe,[397] afford various human rights to legal persons, customary international human rights attach only to natural persons.[398] For instance, if a hostile cyber operation is directed against the website of a human rights organisation, the customary law human rights potentially implicated are those of the organisation's members, not the organisation itself.[399]

5. With regard to the applicability of customary international human rights law, the International Group of Experts concurred that such law applies to all persons on a State's territory irrespective of where the State's cyber activities that implicate the human right in question occur.[400] For instance, a State's human rights law obligations attach when the communications of an individual who is located in its territory are

[396] *See, e.g.*, United Nations Safety Convention, Art. 20(a); Optional Protocol to the United Nations Safety Convention, Art. II(1); Decision No. 2005/24 of the Secretary-General's Policy Committee on Human Rights in Integrated Missions (2005); Capstone Doctrine, at 14–15, 27.

[397] For instance, the European Court of Human Rights has held that the freedom of expression in Art. 10 of the ECHR applies to commercial entities. *See, e.g., Autronic AG v. Switzerland*, 12 EHRR 485 para. 47 (2 May 1990).

[398] *See, e.g.*, Human Rights Council, Implementation of General Assembly Resolution 60/251 of 15 March 2006 Entitled 'Human Rights Council': Report of the Special Representative of the Secretary-General (SRSG) on the Issue of Human Rights and Transnational Corporations and Other Business Enterprises, para. 38, UN Doc. A/HRC/4/035 (9 February 2007).

[399] The Inter-American Court has afforded legal persons a margin of protection when they are the mechanisms through which natural persons enjoy their human rights. In *Granier and others (Radio Caracas Televisión) v. Venezuela*, a television channel received a degree of protection because it was a mechanism by which its owners exercised their right to freedom of expression. Such a holding is especially relevant in the cyber context as companies that operate online are frequently used as a mechanism by which the right is exercised. Case of *Granier and others (Radio Caracas Televisión) v. Venezuela*, Judgment, Inter-Am. C.H.R., para. 22 (22 June 2015).

[400] *See, e.g.*, ICCPR, Art. 2(1); ECHR, Art. 1; ACHR, Art. 1(1) (note that the jurisdictional clauses in these instruments differ to a degree with respect to scope of application). *See also* General Comment No. 31, para. 10; *López Burgos v. Uruguay*, para. 12.3, UN Doc. Supp. No. 40 (A/36/40) (29 July 1981).

intercepted abroad by that State or when the State acquires access to the individual's data that is stored electronically beyond its borders.

6. The Experts agreed that, as a general principle, customary international human rights law applies in the cyber context beyond a State's territory in situations in which that State exercises 'power or effective control', as it does offline.[401] Power or control may be over territory (spatial model)[402] or over individuals (personal model). A State may be, for example, in effective control of foreign territory (that is, the territory is under the authority of the hostile army) during a belligerent occupation (chapeau to Chapter 19), whether that occupation be lawful or unlawful,[403] or if it leases territory from another State and is granted the right of exclusive control over that territory. With regard to application of the personal model, the Experts agreed that individuals abroad who are physically in the power or effective control of the State, as with those detained by the State, are entitled to have their human rights respected by the State concerned.[404] However, in this latter situation, it may be that only those specific rights relevant to the situation will be engaged.[405]

7. The International Group of Experts acknowledged a viewpoint by which customary international human rights law does not apply at all beyond a State's borders, irrespective of whether the State is exercising power or effective control, but disagreed with that position. The Experts also acknowledged that a number of States accepting the

---

[401] The term 'power or effective control' is drawn from General Comment No. 31, para. 10. The same concept is expressed somewhat differently in different human rights regimes. For instance, with regard to interpretation of the ECHR in this context, see Al-Skeini judgment, paras. 130–139; Catan v. Moldova and Russia, judgment, App. Nos. 43370/04, 8252/05, and 18454/06, ECtHR, para. 105 (2012).

[402] With respect to the ICCPR, see General Comment No. 31, paras. 3, 10. As to the ECHR, see Loizidou v. Turkey, App. No. 15318/89, preliminary objections, 310 ECtHR., paras. 61–62 (ser. A) (1995). On the American Declaration of the Rights and Duties of Man, see Armando Alejandre Jr. et al. v. Cuba, Case 11.589, Rep. No. 109/99, para. 23 (1999).

[403] See Wall advisory opinion, para. 109; Armed Activities judgment, para. 173. The International Group of Experts noted recent case law of the European Court of Human Rights that emphasises the importance of de facto control and notes that not all instances of occupation entail sufficient control for the ECHR rights to apply in toto. Al-Skeini judgment, para. 139.

[404] See, e.g., Delia Saldias de López v. Uruguay, Human Rights Committee, Comm. No. 52/ 1979, para. 12, UN Doc. CCPR/C/OP/1 (1984); Ocalan v. Turkey, App. No. 46221/99, ECtHR, para. 91 (2005); Isaak and others v. Turkey, App. No. 44587/98, ECtHR, para. 115 (2006).

[405] Al-Skeini judgment, para. 137.

extraterritoriality of customary international human rights law disagree with application of the 'power or effective control' standard. For these States, the standard is limited to specific treaty law. As an example, it applies under the ECHR, but not all States are Parties to the instrument. In the view of these States, it is inappropriate to extend the notion beyond the specific treaties and in the context in which it applies.

8.   The International Group of Experts could achieve no consensus as to whether State measures that do not involve an exercise of physical control may qualify as 'power or effective control' in the sense of this Rule. In particular, no consensus could be reached as to whether State activities conducted through cyberspace can give rise, as a matter of law, to power or effective control over an individual located abroad, thereby triggering the extraterritorial applicability of that State's international human rights law obligations.

9.   On this issue, the Experts were split. The majority was of the view that, in the current state of the law, physical control over territory or the individual is required before human rights law obligations are triggered.[406] These Experts asserted that the premise of exercising power or effective control by virtual means such that human rights obligations attach runs contrary to both extensive State practice and the paucity of expressions of *opinio juris* thereon. As an example, there is little evidence that when States conduct signals intelligence programmes directed at foreigners on foreign territory, they consider that their activities implicate the international human right to privacy (Rule 35).

10.   A few of the Experts took the position that so long as the exercise or enjoyment of a human right in question by the individual concerned is within the power or effective control of a State, that State has power or effective control over the individual with respect to the right concerned. In other words, if an individual cannot exercise a human right or enjoy the protection of one because of a State's action, international human rights law applies extraterritorially. As an illustration of this view, consider the case of a State that interferes with the ability of an individual located abroad to engage in electronic communications, for instance by hacking into the person's email account and changing its password such that the individual no longer

---

[406]   *Al-Skeini* judgment, para. 136.

has access to the account. Because the State's cyber operation restricts the individual's ability to exercise the right to freedom of expression (Rule 35), the State is in power or effective control of the individual with respect to the freedom of expression (but not, for instance, with respect to the right to liberty of movement[407]). Note, however, that this only means that the rights are implicated; whether they have been violated is a separate determination.

11.   All of the Experts also agreed that international human rights law treaty provisions setting forth the scope of the applicability of the instrument in question govern the issue of extraterritorial application. For example, there is some disagreement over whether the ICCPR applies extraterritorially.[408] The issue is whether Article 2(1)'s scope provision, which extends protection to 'individuals within its territory and subject to its jurisdiction', is meant to extend the Covenant's obligations abroad. Irrespective of the existence of differing positions on this question, all of the Experts agreed that, as a scope provision, Article 2(1) governs the treaty's extraterritorial applicability, or lack thereof. This observation is fundamental for those assessing the application of international human rights law in the cyber context because the bulk of such law is found in treaties governing the activities of the Parties thereto and because the precise scope of many aspects of customary international human rights law is unclear.

12.   The International Group of Experts was split on the issue of whether an international human rights treaty that does not address the issue of extraterritoriality should be interpreted as applying extraterritorially or as limited to the territories of the States Parties to the instrument. Some of the Experts were of the view that unless a treaty so provides, the provisions thereof do not apply extraterritorially. They took the position on the basis that treaty provisions should not be interpreted so as to impose obligations on Parties to which they did not expressly agree. The others would apply the treaty provisions extraterritorially unless the treaty provides otherwise. This approach, in their opinion, better reflects the underlying object and purpose of international human rights law.

---

[407] ICCPR, Art. 12(1).

[408] *See, e.g.*, UN Human Rights Committee, Consideration of Reports Submitted by States Parties under Article 40 of the Covenant, Third Periodic Reports of States Parties, United States of America, para. 3, UN Doc. CCPR/C/USA/3, Annex I (28 November 2005); *Wall* advisory opinion, paras. 109–111.

13. For a discussion of extraterritoriality in the context of a State's obligation to protect individuals from violations of their international human rights, see *lit.* (b) of Rule 36.

Rule 35 – Rights enjoyed by individuals

Individuals enjoy the same international human rights with respect to cyber-related activities that they otherwise enjoy.

1. The application of treaty and customary international human rights law to cyber-related activities encompasses civil, political, economic, social, and cultural rights, that is, all international human rights. The commentary that follows examines certain rights that the International Group of Experts found especially relevant in the cyber context.[409] These include the rights to freedom of expression, privacy, freedom of opinion, and due process. The omission of a purported international human right in this commentary is not to be understood as indicating that the Experts concluded it was not customary in nature.

2. Freedom of expression[410] is an international human right often implicated in the cyber context. This is not only because it is a right in itself, but also because an ability to exercise the right is sometimes necessary for the enjoyment of other human rights. The International Group of Experts agreed that the right of freedom of expression is the 'freedom to seek, receive and impart information and ideas of all kinds, regardless of frontiers, either orally, in writing or in print, in the form of art, or through any other media of his choice'.[411]

3. Consider State cyber operations directed at online forums, chatrooms, social media, and other websites. Such operations are likely to

---

[409] The International Group of Experts noted that the enumerated rights in this Rule are not exhaustive. For instance, other rights that may be relevant in the cyber context include the right of association and peaceful assembly (UDHR, Art. 20; ICCPR, Arts. 21–22); liberty and security (UDHR, Art. 3; ICCPR, Art. 9); and protection from defamation (UDHR, Art. 12; ICCPR, Art. 17).

[410] UDHR, Art. 19; ICCPR, Art. 19(2); ECHR Art. 10; ACHR, Art. 13; ACHPR, Art. 9. *See also* General Comment No. 34, para. 12; Report of the Special Rapporteur on the Promotion and Protection of the Right to Freedom of Opinion and Expression, paras. 20–22, UN Doc. A/HRC/17/27 (16 May 2011); Report of the Special Rapporteur on the Promotion and Protection of the Right to Freedom of Opinion and Expression, para. 11, UN Doc. A/HRC/29/32 (22 May 2015); EU Human Rights Guidelines on Freedom of Expression Online and Offline, Council of the European Union, paras. 16, 18 (12 May 2014).

[411] ICCPR, Art. 19(2). *See also* UDHR, Art. 19; General Comment No. 34, para. 11; ECHR, Art. 10(1); ACHR, Art. 13(1); African Charter, Art. 9.

implicate the right of freedom of expression, for instance when the websites targeted are those of bloggers, journalists, or other individuals that disseminate information embarrassing to the State or to powerful individuals therein. If the expression is of a protected nature, States may only conduct the operations if they are designed to enforce lawful limitations (Rule 37) the State has imposed on the freedom of expression. Similarly, a State could block individuals seeking to express themselves from accessing specific IP addresses or domain names, take down websites, employ filtering technologies to deny access to pages containing keywords or other specific content, or obstruct the sending of email, text, and other forms of point-to-point or group communications. These activities infringe upon the right to freedom of expression when not in accordance with Rule 37. It must be noted that such actions might also violate other rights, such as the freedoms of peaceful assembly and association.[412]

4.   Although it could achieve no consensus on the precise parameters of the right to freedom of expression, the International Group of Experts noted that restrictions on certain categories of expression, whether offline or online, are subject to particular scrutiny from an international human rights law perspective. Examples of these categories include discussion of government policies, politics, and elections, as well as reporting on human rights, government activities, and corruption in government.[413]

5.   Related to freedom of expression is the separate right to freedom of opinion. States must respect the right of individuals to hold opinions without interference.[414] Although the right to hold an opinion and freedom of expression are closely related, the International Group of Experts agreed that there is a distinction between the two. The right to hold an opinion freely is a guarantee so central to the object and purpose of international human rights law that, unlike the freedom of expression, its exercise may not be restricted. State conduct that interferes with the freedom of opinion includes online incitement against protected persons,

---

[412] UDHR, Art. 20; ICCPR, Arts. 21–22.

[413] Promotion and Protection of all Human Rights, Civil, Political, Economic, Social and Cultural Rights, including the Right to Development, Human Rights Council Res. 12/16, para. 5(p)(i), UN Doc. A/HRC/RES/12/16 (12 October 2009); Report of the Special Rapporteur on the Promotion and Protection of the Right to Freedom of Opinion and Expression, para. 42, UN Doc. A/HRC/17/27 (16 May 2011). *See also* General Comment No. 34, para. 23.

[414] UDHR, Art. 1; ICCPR, Art. 19(1); ASEAN Human Rights Declaration, Art. 22.

online intimidation, or other forms of harassment conducted on the basis of a person's views, such as political or religious views that are evidenced by membership in a political party or a religious denomination. The Experts noted that once an opinion is expressed, that expression is subject to limitations by the State in accordance with Rule 37.

6. The right to be free from arbitrary interference with one's privacy is of central importance in the cyber context.[415] The International Group of Experts concluded that the right is of a customary international law character,[416] but cautioned that its precise scope is unsettled and that a number of States that accept the existence of the right take the position that it does not extend extraterritorially (Rule 34). The Experts further noted that privacy is not an absolute right and may be subject to limitations, as discussed in Rule 37. They also acknowledged the existence of a view that the right to privacy has not yet crystallised into a customary norm.

7. All of the Experts agreed that the right to privacy encompasses the confidentiality of communications.[417] As a general matter, communications such as email must be 'delivered to the addressee without interception and without being opened or otherwise read'.[418] For instance, an email sent by one individual to another falls within the scope of the right to privacy. That right is implicated if a State accesses the content of the

---

[415] UDHR, Art. 12; ICCPR, Art. 17; CRC, Art. 16; CRPD, Art. 22; International Convention on the Protection of the Rights of All Migrant Workers and Members of their Families, Art. 14, 18 December 1990, 2220 UNTS 39481. *See also* ECHR, Art. 8; ACHR, Art. 11; Convention for the Protection of Individuals with regard to Automatic Processing of Personal Data, Art. 1, 1 October 1985, ETS No. 108; Report of the Special Rapporteur on the Promotion and Protection of the Right to Freedom of Opinion and Expression, para. 23, UN Doc. A/HRC/23/40 (17 April 2013); The Right to Privacy in the Digital Age, para. 14; Council of Europe, Declaration on Freedom of Communication on the Internet, princ. 7 (2003); *R v. Spencer*, 2014 SCC 43, para. 62.

[416] *See, e.g.,* G20 Leaders' Communiqué, Antalya Summit, 15–16 November 2015; Council of Europe, Parliamentary Assembly, Resolution 2045, paras. 4, 10 (21 April 2015); ASEAN Human Rights Declaration, Art. 21; The Right to Privacy in the Digital Age, GA Res. 69/166, pmbl., UN Doc. A/RES/69/166 (10 February 2016).

[417] *See, e.g.,* The Right to Privacy in the Digital Age, para. 17; Report of the Special Rapporteur on the Promotion and Protection of Human Rights and Fundamental Freedoms while Countering Terrorism, paras. 16–18; *Copeland v. United Kingdom*, judgment, App. No. 62617/00, ECtHR, para. 43 (2007). Article 17 of the ICCPR includes the right to be free from arbitrary or unlawful interference with both privacy and correspondence. The International Group of Experts agreed that the latter is an aspect of the right to privacy and therefore did not treat it separately. The Experts also agreed that use of the term communication is more appropriate in the cyber context than correspondence.

[418] General Comment No. 16, para. 8.

communication. In this regard, the Experts agreed that it is irrelevant whether the communication includes sensitive information.[419]

8.   Although the International Group of Experts concurred that human inspection of content implicates the right to privacy, it was divided on the applicability of the right to machine inspection by algorithmic analysis. The Experts were of the view that machine inspection of a communication's content undertaken solely for the efficient and secure operation of a network either does not implicate the right to privacy, or implicates it, but is generally justified (Rule 37). Yet, they could reach no agreement on the circumstances that fell between these examples, such as where a machine engages in the inspection of content to filter for terms that will result in subsequent human inspection.

9.   The Experts discussed a scenario in which a State merely collects communications without examining them by either human means or machine, or a combination thereof. The majority position was that the right to privacy is not implicated until such time as the State accesses the content of the communications or, as discussed below, processes personal data found in them. A minority of Experts was of the view that the mere collection of communications, even without accessing them, constitutes an interference with the right of privacy; in such cases, whether it constitutes a violation thereof depends on Rules 37 and 38.[420]

10.   The International Group of Experts agreed that the right to privacy with respect to the confidentiality of communications is not implicated when a State accesses publicly available website postings, openly accessible social media sites, or other sources that are generally

---

[419] *See, e.g.,* Court of Justice of the European Union, *Digital Rights Ireland and Seitlinger and Others,* judgment in joined cases C-293/12 and C-594/12, 2014 ECR 238 (8 April 2014), para. 33.

[420] *See, e.g., Leander* v. *Sweden,* judgment, App. no. 9248/81, ECtHR, para. 48 (1987), in which the Court first held that the storing of information alone can constitute an interference with the right to privacy under the ECHR. *See also* The Right to Privacy in the Digital Age, para. 20. The storing of personal data (see discussion below) is also considered to fall within the scope of the right to privacy under European Union legislation because it constitutes the 'processing of personal data'. Therefore, to the extent the communications that a State stores include personal data, the right to privacy is implicated. *See, e.g.,* Directive 95/46/EC of the European Parliament and of the Council on the protection of individuals with regard to the processing of personal data and on the free movement of such data, Art. 2(b) (24 October 1995); Regulation (EU) 2016/679 of the European Parliament and of the Council on the Protection of Natural Persons with Regard to the Processing of Personal Data and on the Free Movement of Such Data, and Repealing Directive 95/46/EC, Art. 4(2) (27 April 2016) (in effect as of 25 May 2018).

available to the public. By contrast, the use of social media to communicate or share material among a small closed group, as in Facebook messaging or use of a limited access cloud drive, is more likely to implicate the right of privacy. The Experts could identify no clear threshold at which the right to privacy is implicated on the basis of the accessibility of communications. Factors other than size of the group that has access may be relevant. For example, if the terms of participation in the closed group provide that communications may not be shared with those beyond the group, the right to privacy is more likely to be implicated by a State accessing them.

11. The Experts discussed whether the right to privacy under customary international law with respect to a communication is dependent upon a reasonable expectation of the parties thereto that the content will not be made known to, or seen by, others. Some of them reasoned that absent such an expectation, there is no colourable basis for asserting that a State has violated an individual's privacy. Other Experts suggested that such a standard is unhelpful because in those cases in which an individual knows the State is conducting operations that intrude into his or her communications, for instance because it has been reported on the media that the State engages in particular large-scale surveillance operations, the individual may not logically harbour any expectation that the communications will remain confidential. For these Experts, therefore, imposing such an expectation would be an overbroad exclusion of the right.

12. The International Group of Experts agreed that in addition to the confidentiality of communications, the right to privacy generally protects the personal data of individuals.[421] It acknowledged that the precise definition of 'personal data' is a matter that has generated a degree of controversy with respect to regional human rights regimes and national laws.[422] The Experts were likewise unable to articulate the precise scope of the concept in the more ambiguous environment of customary international law. Nevertheless, certain examples are clear. Information

---

[421] See, e.g., ASEAN Human Rights Declaration, Art. 21; General Comment No. 16, para. 10; Convention for the Protection of Individuals with regard to Automatic Processing of Personal Data, Art. 1, 1 October 1985, ETS No. 108.

[422] In this regard, personal data is sometimes referred to as personally identifiable information. The Experts noted that in regional human rights regimes the protection of personal data is occasionally treated as a right distinct from that of privacy. For example, the Charter of Fundamental Rights of the European Union provides for the 'right to respect for . . . communications' in Article 7 and 'right to the protection of personal data' in Article 8.

contained in health records or that is submitted to acquire security clearances, for example, is of such a personal nature that it unambiguously qualifies. Whether a State that accesses, copies, or extracts such data relating to individuals located on another State's territory has violated the concerned individuals' international human right to privacy depends on (1) extraterritorial application (Rule 34) of the right, and (2) whether the activity was consistent with the lawful limitations on, and derogations from, that right (Rules 37–38).

13.   The Experts considered the issue of whether the collection and processing of metadata by a State is encompassed within the scope of the right to privacy, either as personal data or as a part of a communication. In their view, metadata may constitute personal data if the captured metadata is subsequently linked to an individual and relates to that individual's private life. They suggested, for example, that if a State, based on an individual's web browsing metadata, is able to ascertain aspects of that individual's health or personal relationships, the right to privacy is implicated. In drawing these conclusions, the Experts felt the need to emphasise that State practice and *opinio juris* on this matter are limited.

14.   Despite consensus that metadata qualifying as personal data is protected by the right to privacy, the Experts did not reach agreement regarding other types of metadata. A minority of the Experts took the position that all metadata associated with confidential communications constitutes an integral element thereof and is thus protected as a communication.[423] The majority countered that the meaning of the notion of 'communications' that falls within the right to privacy is only to be understood as extending to the content thereof, such as the body of an email, and not the associated metadata. For them, metadata *per se* is not protected as an element of a confidential communication, but, as discussed, may be protected as personal data. To illustrate, metadata indicating the sender and recipient of an email implicates the right to privacy because it is likely to constitute, by this approach, personal data, but metadata that denotes whether a confidential email communication employed an IMAP or POP3 email protocol does not.

15.   The Experts noted that States frequently engage in cyber espionage (Rule 32), both within and beyond their territories. Although questions might arise as to the extraterritorial application of international

---

[423] *See, e.g., Malone* v. *United Kingdom*, App. No. 8691/70, 82 ECtHR (ser. A), para. 84 (1984).

human rights law (Rule 34) with respect to espionage, the Experts were aware of no *opinio juris* suggesting that States consider espionage *per se* to fall beyond the bounds of their international human rights law obligations concerning the right to privacy. As such, the Experts concluded that, notwithstanding State practice, espionage remains subject to States' applicable human rights law obligation to respect the right to privacy.

16.   With respect to the right to due process,[424] the International Group of Experts concurred that individuals who are suspected or convicted of committing cyber crimes enjoy the protection of the same international human rights law norms pertaining to law enforcement and judicial processes that are due individuals suspected or convicted of committing non-cyber crimes. The Experts were of the view that there is no justification for a relaxation of the established norms for independent and impartial investigation, due process in relation to any arrest and subsequent pre-trial detention, fair and independent trial procedures, and standards of treatment in post-conviction detention in the case of cyber crime.

17.   The Experts took particular note of the increasing importance of electronic sources of evidence in the investigation and prosecution of criminal activity, the seizure of which may raise international human rights issues. For example, if an individual is accused of maliciously hacking into the website of a business, law enforcement officials may want to gain access to some of the individual's data, such as personal electronic communications, to establish guilt. In this regard, the limitations on a State's searches deriving from international human rights law that regulate other types of searches, including the obligation to respect the right to privacy, apply *mutatis mutandis* to remote searches of an individual's networks or online storage. The Experts noted in this regard that States are promulgating domestic laws regarding remote access by cyber means for law enforcement and other purposes.[425] With regard to the lawfulness of a law enforcement agency's unilateral acquisition of electronic evidence from cyber infrastructure located abroad, see Rule 11.

---

[424] UDHR, Arts. 9–11; ICCPR, Arts. 9–11, 14–15. *See also, e.g., Premininy* v. *Russia,* judgment, App. No. 44973/04, ECtHR, paras. 119–124 (2011).

[425] *See, e.g.,* Search and Surveillance Act 2012, Public Act 2012 No. 24 (5 April 2012), Secs. 111, 114 (N.Z.).

18. As with the aforementioned civil and political rights, the International Group of Experts agreed that the enjoyment of certain economic, social, and cultural rights is increasingly dependent on cyber activities. These rights include, *inter alia*, the right to an adequate standard of living, including adequate food, the right to the enjoyment of the highest attainable standard of physical and mental health, the right to work, the right to education, and the right to take part in cultural life.[426] For instance, the Committee on Economic, Social and Cultural Rights has stated that the enjoyment of the highest attainable standard of physical and mental health includes 'the right to seek, receive and impart information and ideas concerning health issues'.[427] A State's cyber activities that prevent access to valid health information or services on the Internet implicate this right. Online surveillance activities may also implicate the right if, for example, an individual refrains from seeking or communicating sensitive health-related information out of fear that his or her condition may be revealed to others.

19. The Experts noted that the customary status of particular economic, social, and cultural rights is unsettled. Indeed, some States take the position that no such rights are customary in nature and that they are instead exclusively treaty commitments of States that are Parties to the relevant instruments. The Experts also noted that a State's obligations in the realm of these rights, if and to the extent they reflect customary international law, are variable; in particular, they may depend on the resources available to the State.[428]

20. The International Group of Experts discussed whether there is a so-called 'human right to anonymity' *per se* and agreed that international law has not crystallised with respect to a right to be anonymous on the Internet. Therefore, they took the position that although actions to prohibit, restrict, or undermine access to devices

---

[426] ICESCR, Arts. 6, 11–13, 15; UDHR, Arts. 23, 25(1), 26–27; CERD, Art. 5; CEDAW, Arts. 10–13; CRC, Arts. 2, 17, 23–24, 28–29, 31; European Social Charter, Arts. 1, 11, 21, 29, 3 May 1996, ETS No. 163; African Charter, Arts. 15, 16–17, 22; Additional Protocol to the American Convention on Human Rights, Arts. 6, 10, 12–14, 17 November 1988, OASTS No. 69.

[427] Office of the High Commissioner for Human Rights, CESCR General Comment No. 14: The Right to the Highest Attainable Standard of Health (Art. 12), para. 12(b), UN Doc. E/C.12/2000/4 (11 August 2000).

[428] ICESCR, Art. 2(1). *See also* CESR General Comment No. 3: The Nature of State Parties' Obligations (Art. 2(1) of the Covenant), para. 10, UN Doc. E/1991/23 (14 December 1990).

or technology that foster anonymity may, as a practical matter, reduce the exercise or enjoyment of international human rights online, such actions do not in themselves necessarily implicate international human rights law as a matter of *lex lata* on the basis of infringement with or loss of anonymity.

21.   That said, the Experts noted that an ability to be anonymous in cyberspace may bear on the exercise of the freedom of expression and the enjoyment of the right to privacy. Consider a situation in which a State requires individuals who post material protected by the right to freedom of expression on the Internet to identify themselves. The requirement effectively deters them from engaging in protected expression and, thus, in the view of the Experts, constitutes an interference with that right. Accordingly, any such requirement would need to be justified pursuant to one of the grounds set forth in Rule 37. The same legal reasoning applies in the case of the right to privacy. For instance, a State may not process metadata to identify participants in an anonymous online survey that collects personal health data unless the processing complies with that Rule.

22.   In the view of the International Group of Experts, 'access to the Internet' is also not an international human right in itself as a matter of customary international law; technology is an enabler of rights, not a right as such. Nevertheless, State measures limiting access to or use of the Internet must be consistent with the exercise or enjoyment of international human rights, such as those cited earlier in this commentary. A State that blocks access to the Internet throughout the country during civil disturbances is, for instance, in violation of the right to freedom of expression if the limitations on the exercise of that right caused by the blockage are not in compliance with the criteria set forth in Rule 37.

23.   The International Group of Experts further agreed that no customary international human 'right to be forgotten' currently exists. A purported right of individuals to have certain data removed from the Internet has been asserted in litigation.[429] While such litigation may have

---

[429]   For instance, in *Google* v. *Spain*, the Grand Chamber of the Court of Justice of the European Union ruled that Google is a data controller for the purposes of the European Union's Data Retention Directive. As a result, Google was obliged to protect the fundamental rights of the owner of that data, in particular, the 'right to be forgotten', by responding to requests that certain dated data be removed from the Internet. *Google Spain SL, Google Inc.* v. *Agencia Espanola de Proteccion de Datos and Mario Costeja Gonzalez* (case C-131/12), ECR, 13 May 2014; Judgment of Judge

ramifications for future regulation of search engines and Internet service providers, the Experts were of the view that, at present, there is no customary international human rights law-based obligation of States to require third parties to remove personal data or links to that data from the Internet on the basis of a 'right to be forgotten'.

Rule 36 – Obligations to respect and protect international human rights

With respect to cyber activities, a State must:

(a) respect the international human rights of individuals; and
(b) protect the human rights of individuals from abuse by third parties.

1.   International human rights law requires States to respect, as well as to protect (i.e., ensure respect for), human rights.[430] The International Group of Experts agreed that these obligations apply in cyberspace.[431] An obligation to 'fulfil' is not included in this Rule for the reasons set forth below.

2.   Pursuant to *lit.* (a), States must refrain from activities that violate the human rights individuals enjoy in cyberspace. Some of the key rights are discussed in Rule 35. The obligation extends to human rights that apply extraterritorially (Rule 34). If, however, a State interferes with or curtails the exercise or enjoyment of a human right in accordance with Rule 37 on lawful limitations on human rights, or Rule 38 on derogation, it has not violated *lit.* (a).

Nobuyuki Seki of the Tokyo District Court on 9 October 2014 (unreported), (taking into account the *Google* v. *Spain* ruling to support the finding that Google had the obligation to remove search results referring to crimes the complainant might have been involved in over a decade earlier because such search results allegedly threatened his life and privacy.). *See also* Loi No. 78-17 relative à l'informatique, aux fichiers et aux libertés (6 January 1978), Art. 40(I) (Fr.).

[430] Although employing different terminology, this is apparent in ICCPR, Art. 2(1); ICESCR, Art. 2. *See also* General Comment 31, para. 6.

[431] *See, e.g.*, The Right to Privacy in the Digital Age, GA Res. 69/166, para. 4(a), UN Doc. A/RES/69/166 (10 February 2015); UN GGE 2015 Report, para. 28(b); Council of Europe Recommendation CM/Rec(2014)6 of the Committee of Ministers to Member States on a Guide to Human Rights for Internet Users, para. 2 (16 April 2014).

3. A duty to respect human rights is also triggered when a non-State entity's cyber activities are attributable to a State (Rules 15 and 17). For example, a State that instructs, or directs or controls, third parties, like private companies, to collect, retain, or disclose personal data will be responsible for human rights violations that occur in the course of that conduct.

4. *Lit.* (a) must be distinguished from *lit.* (b), which addresses the obligation to protect the international human rights of individuals from abuse by third parties. The International Group of Experts agreed that, pursuant to *lit.* (b), international human rights law entails a general positive obligation requiring States to take action to protect the enjoyment or exercise of rights of those within their territories or territories under their exclusive governmental control, that is, to 'ensure respect' for said rights by others.[432] The Experts concurred that *lit.* (b) obliges States to take action in relation to third parties that is necessary and reasonable in the circumstances to ensure that individuals are able to enjoy their rights online, but that States have discretion with respect to which measures to take in order to satisfy the obligation. For example, assume a third party threatens an individual who expresses certain protected views online. The State where the individual is located has an obligation to protect the individual from the third party's threatened action.

5. The International Group of Experts observed that some States hold the position that the obligation to protect is limited and cannot be characterised as a general obligation of customary international human rights law.[433] Nevertheless, the Experts noted that while, as explained below, the precise parameters of the obligation may be contested, it is reflected in most major international human rights law treaties.[434] The obligation to protect is further recognised in case law, as indicated below

---

[432] ICCPR, Art. 2(1). *See also* ACHR, Art. 1(1); General Comment No. 3, para. 1; General Comment No. 31, para. 7. *See also, e.g.*, application of the duty to protect in the context of the ECHR in *Case of Osman* v. *United Kingdom* (87/1997/871/1083), judgment, paras. 115–122 (28 October 1998), and of the ACHR in *Velasquez Rodriguez* case, judgment, Inter-AmCtHR (ser. C) No. 4, paras. 166–167 (1988).

[433] *See, e.g.*, Letter from David Bethlehem QC, Legal Adviser, Foreign and Commonwealth Office, to John Ruggie, Special Representative on Human Rights and Transnational Corporations and Other Business Enterprises, Office of the High Commissioner for Human Rights (9 July 2009); Department of State, US Observations on Human Rights Committee General Comment 31, paras. 10–18, 27 December 2007.

[434] *See, e.g.*, ICCPR, Art. 2(1); ACHR, Art. 1(1).

in the commentary. The International Group of Experts was accordingly comfortable in concluding that the obligation is customary in nature.

6.   The Experts could not achieve consensus on the precise territorial circumstances in which a State has an obligation to protect a particular individual's human rights from interference by third parties. To illustrate, consider the case of an individual outside a State who hosts his or her website on servers located in the State. Another State hacks into the web server and corrupts the website, thereby interfering with the individual's freedom of expression (Rule 35). A majority of the Experts was of the view that the State shoulders an obligation to protect only when the individuals concerned are within the territory of the State or in territory under its effective control (Rule 34). The remaining Experts took the position that the obligation to protect is also triggered if the international human right concerned is being exercised within territory under the State's effective control, irrespective of whether the individual is located within that territory.

7.   Encompassed within the obligation to protect is the duty of States to safeguard individuals from human rights abuses that are initiated in cyberspace, but may affect their rights offline. In complying with this duty, States may, for instance, criminalise conduct and expression, including cyber activities, that harm the rights of others, as in the case of direct and public incitement to genocide;[435] child pornography;[436] and incitement to national, racial, or religious hatred that constitutes incitement to violence.[437] In that regulation in each of these areas restricts the right of freedom of expression (Rule 35), it must comply with the international human rights law obligations relating to limitations discussed in Rule 37.

8.   The obligation to protect entails taking measures that are preventive in nature. It is not limited to those necessary to terminate an on-going abuse of human rights by third parties or the taking of appropriate measures against those who have committed such abuse. Accordingly, States are equally obliged to take those feasible measures that are

---

[435] Genocide Convention, Art. III; Rome Statute, Arts. 3(e), 25; ICTY Statute, Arts. 3(c), 4; ICTR Statute, Arts. 2, 3(c).

[436] Optional Protocol to the Convention on the Rights of the Child on the Sale of Children, Child Prostitution and Child Pornography, Art. 3, 25 May 2000, 2171 UNTS 227; Report of the Special Rapporteur on the Sale of Children, Child Prostitution and Child Pornography, para. 2, UN Doc. A/HRC/12/23 (13 July 2009). *See also* Convention on Cybercrime, Art. 9.

[437] ICCPR, Art. 20.

reasonable in the circumstances to prevent an abuse of human rights by third parties if there are reasonable grounds to believe that such abuse will occur.[438] As an example, if a certain ethnic group living in a defined territory in a State has been the target of repeated malicious cyber operations that interfere with the group's members' right to express themselves on political matters on the Internet, the State concerned is obligated to take measures that are feasible and reasonable in the circumstances to preclude future malicious operations of the same nature.

9.   The Internet has been used for terrorist purposes, such as recruitment for, incitement of, and the financing of terrorism.[439] The International Group of Experts agreed that 'States have both a right and a duty to take effective measures to counter the destructive impact of terrorism on human rights', even though some measures taken by the State may affect human rights such as the freedom of expression and the right of privacy.[440] Any such measures must comply with Rule 37.[441]

10.   The International Group of Experts could achieve no consensus as to whether States have an obligation to ensure access to cyberspace and cyber infrastructure, if such access is the only way to exercise a human right.[442] Consider a situation in which a State has an electoral

---

[438] *See, e.g., Velasquez Rodriguez* case, judgment, Inter-AmCtHR (ser. C) No. 4, paras. 172, 174–175 (1988).

[439] *See, e.g.,* Letter dated 2 September 2015 from the Chair of the Security Council Committee established pursuant to Resolution 1373 (2001) concerning Counter-terrorism addressed to the President of the Security Council, S/2015/683, at 7–12 (2 September 2015).

[440] United Nations Office on Drugs and Crime, The Use of the Internet for Terrorist Purposes, paras. 33, 80–8 (September 2012); SC Res. 2178, para. 2, UN Doc. S/RES/ 2178 (24 September 2014) (encouraging 'Member States to employ evidence-based traveller risk assessment and screening procedures including collection and analysis of travel data, without resorting to profiling based on stereotypes founded on grounds of discrimination prohibited by international law'.) *See also Brogan and others* v. *United Kingdom,* judgment, App. No. 11209/84, ECtHR, para. 61.3 (1988); International Code of Conduct for Information Security, Art. 2(4), UN Doc. A/69/723 (13 January 2015); Information Technology Act (9 June 2000), Art. 66F (India); Anti-cyber Crime Law, Royal Decree No. M/17, 8 Rabi 11428 (26 March 2007), Art. 7 (Saudi Arabia).

[441] Inter-American Commission on Human Rights, Report on Terrorism and Human Rights, OEA/Ser.L/V/II.116, Doc. 5 rev. 1 corr., para. 36 (2002); General Comment No. 34, para. 46.

[442] For instance, the obligation to provide access is only framed in hortatory and aspirational terms in the Inter-American Commission on Human Rights, Freedom of Expression and the Internet, para. 37, OEA/ser.L/V/II (31 December 2013).

system requiring individuals to vote online. The Experts were unable to agree if the State is obliged to provide the necessary access to enable individuals who cannot otherwise do so to exercise their right to vote.

11. In order to give effect to the obligation to protect, States have created additional obligations through treaty law. International human rights treaty regimes sometimes obligate States to conduct prompt, effective, thorough, independent, and impartial investigations of alleged human rights violations.[443] A number of treaties require notification and reporting,[444] measures of accountability, and effective remedies for victims of human rights violations.[445] In situations where such obligations exist, any remedies must be known and accessible to those who claim a violation of their rights. All of the Experts recognised that these treaty obligations apply equally to alleged violations of international human rights law perpetrated by cyber means.

12. The Experts did not agree, however, on whether the obligation to provide remedies to victims of international human rights law violations is of a customary nature.[446] The majority was of the view that no such obligation has crystallised, whereas the minority took the opposite position.[447]

13. A few Experts went so far as to assert that the purported customary law obligation to provide an effective remedy for violations of international human rights law that might occur during the collection of electronic communications and personal data through surveillance

---

[443] See Basic Principles and Guidelines on the Right to a Remedy and Reparation for Victims of Gross Violations of International Human Rights Law and Serious Violations of International Humanitarian Law, GA Res. 60/147, UN Doc. A/RES/60/147 (16 December 2005); General Comment No. 31, paras. 8, 15. See also UDHR, Art. 8; ICCPR, Art. 2(3); ACHR, Art. 25; ECHR, Art. 13.

[444] See, e.g., ICCPR, Art. 40 on the periodic reporting requirements of States Parties.

[445] ICCPR, Art. 2(3)(a–b). See also General Comment No. 16, para. 11; General Comment No. 31, paras. 8, 15; UN Human Rights Committee, *Dmitriy Vladimirovich Bulgakov* v. *Ukraine*, Communication No. 1803/2008, paras. 9–10, UN Doc. CCPR/C/106/D/1803/2008 (29 November 2012).

[446] See, e.g., UN Guiding Principles on Business and Human Rights, Human Rights Council, para. 25, UN Doc. A/HRC/17/31 (16 June 2011). Though the Report is guiding principles, para. 25 provides that 'as part of their *duty* to protect against business-related human rights abuse, States *must* take appropriate steps to ensure . . . those affected have access to effective remedy.' (emphasis added).

[447] UDHR, Art. 8; Basic Principles and Guidelines on the Right to a Remedy and Reparations for Victims of Gross Violations of International Human Rights Law and Serious Violations of International Humanitarian Law, Arts. 1(b), 2, GA Res. 60/147, UN Doc. A/RES/60/147 (16 December 2005).

programmes necessitates an 'independent oversight body . . . governed by sufficient due process guarantees and judicial oversight, within the limitations permissible in a democratic society,'[448] to monitor such programmes in the State concerned. The other Experts countered that international human rights law has not developed to the point where any such obligation exists. Rather, the obligation to provide remedies, if any, solely attaches as to individuals to whom human rights obligations are owed and do so only once the violation has taken place. For them, *ex ante* preventive monitoring measures far exceed the requirements of current customary international human rights law.

14. As mentioned above, the text of this Rule incorporates no obligation of States to fulfil human rights, that is, to take measures to ensure that individuals can realise their rights. This is because the International Group of Experts was unable to reach consensus on whether the obligation to fulfil is of a customary nature. However, the Experts noted that some human rights treaties contain an obligation of States Parties to fulfil certain international human rights, in other words, to take measures beyond those required by the obligations to respect and protect. They pointed to the fact that treaty regimes may impose a special obligation to ensure the realisation of human rights by cyber means. For instance, States Parties to the Convention on the Rights of Persons with Disabilities are under a specific obligation to 'promote the availability and use of new technologies, including information and communications technologies . . . suitable for persons with disabilities, giving priority to technologies at an affordable cost,'[449] and to 'promote access for persons with disabilities to new information and communications technologies and systems, including the Internet.'[450]

Rule 37 – Limitations

The obligations to respect and protect international human rights, with the exception of absolute rights, remain subject to certain

---

[448] 'Joint Declaration on Surveillance Programs and their Impact on Freedom of Expression', issued by the Special Rapporteur on the Promotion and Protection of the Right to Freedom of Opinion and Expression and the Special Rapporteur for Freedom of Expression of the Inter-American Commission on Human Rights, para. 9 (2013). *See also* The Right to Privacy in the Digital Age, para. 41.
[449] CRPD, Art. 4(1)(g).   [450] CRPD, Art. 9 (2)(g).

limitations that are necessary to achieve a legitimate purpose, non-discriminatory, and authorised by law.

1.   The International Group of Experts agreed that, as a general matter, the basis for a limitation on the enjoyment or exercise of an international human right must be provided for in international law; the limitation must be necessary to achieve a legitimate purpose; and the limitation must be non-discriminatory. In this regard, international human rights law allows States to limit the enjoyment or exercise of certain human rights in order to protect other rights and to maintain national security and public order,[451] including with respect to activities in cyberspace. For instance, restrictions on the right to seek, receive, and impart information pursuant to Article 19 of the ICCPR must satisfy a tripartite test: they must be provided for by law under the clearest and most precise terms possible, foster a legitimate objective recognised by international law, and be necessary to achieve that objective.[452]

2.   This Rule extends to both the obligations to respect and to protect (Rule 36). For instance, if a State gains access to the electronic health records of its citizens, such activity must be based on a recognised limitation to the right of privacy. Similarly, if one State allows another State to remotely examine health records to which it has access, there must be a legitimate basis for doing so, such as a shared national security concern.

3.   The International Group of Experts cautioned that the criteria for limitations can vary based on the right or treaty concerned. Therefore, with respect to limitations on treaty rights, first recourse must always be to the treaty itself.

4.   International human rights that are absolute in nature are not subject to the limitations set forth in this Rule. The term 'absolute rights', as used in the Rule, refers to those rights that may not be limited by States in any circumstance or for any purpose, such as the freedoms from torture and slavery and the freedom to hold an opinion (Rule 35). The impermissibility of limitations is distinct from the notion of non-derogability (Rule 38). For example, although the freedom to manifest one's religion and the freedom from arbitrary deprivation of life are,

---

[451]   *See, e.g.,* UDHR, Art. 29(2); ICCPR, Arts. 18–19, 21; ASEAN Human Rights Declaration, Art. 8.

[452]   ICCPR, Art. 19(3)(b); General Comment No. 34, paras. 21–36.

pursuant to certain treaties,[453] non-derogable in time of public emergency, they are not absolute rights in the sense of this Rule.

5. Limitations are lawful only if they serve a legitimate purpose. Such purposes include the protection of rights and reputations of others, national security, public order, public health, or morals.[454] For instance, countering terrorism is a legitimate purpose that allows States to monitor particular online communications without thereby violating the right to privacy. By contrast, the purpose of putting an end to criticism of the government, whether that criticism manifests online or offline, will seldom, if ever, qualify as a legitimate State purpose justifying interference with the right to freedom of expression.[455]

6. A restriction on cyber activities that might otherwise be protected by international human rights law must be 'necessary', although States enjoy a margin of appreciation in this regard.[456] To illustrate, it is generally considered necessary to restrict the exercise of freedom of expression online or the enjoyment of the right to privacy (Rule 35) in order to eliminate child pornography and child exploitation,[457] protect intellectual property rights,[458] and stop incitement to genocide.[459] The

---

[453] See, e.g., ICCPR, Arts. 4(2), 6, 18(3).

[454] Human Rights Council, Report of the Special Rapporteur on the Promotion and Protection of the Right to Freedom of Opinion and Expression, para. 33, UN Doc. A/HRC/29/32 (22 May 2015). Treaties set forth the allowable limitations for particular rights. As an example, the ACHR acknowledges the appropriateness of restricting freedom of expression as necessary to ensure 'respect for the rights or reputations of others'; 'the protection of national security, public order, or public health or morals'; 'the moral protection of childhood and adolescence'; and to counter 'propaganda for war and any advocacy of national, racial, or religious hatred that constitute incitements to lawless violence . . .'. ACHR, Art. 13.

[455] See General Comment No. 34, paras. 3, 43.

[456] With regard to the European system, see Handyside v. United Kingdom, judgment, App. No. 5493/72, ECtHR, para. 48 (1976). See also Chaparro Alvarez v. Ecuador, 2007 Inter-AmCtHR (ser. C) No. 170, para. 93 (2007).

[457] See, e.g., Convention on Cybercrime, Art. 9; Council of Europe Convention on the Protection of Children Against Sexual Exploitation and Sexual Abuse, Art. 20(f), 1 July 2010, CETS No. 201; Directive 2011/92/EU of the European Parliament and of the Council of 13 December 2011 on Combating the Sexual Abuse and Sexual Exploitation of Children and Child Pornography, and replacing Council Framework Decision 2004/68/JHA, Arts. 18–20 (13 December 2011).

[458] Convention on Cybercrime, Art. 10; WIPO Copyright Treaty, Art. 11, 20 December 1996; Agreement Establishing the Word Trade Organization, Annex 1C: Agreement on Trade-Related Aspects of Intellectual Property Rights, Art. 7, 15 April 1994.

[459] Genocide Convention, Art. III. See also Report of the Special Rapporteur on the Promotion and Protection of the Right to Freedom of Opinion and Expression, paras. 23–25, UN Doc. A/HRC/17/27 (16 May 2011).

International Group of Experts noted that with respect to the mass collection of electronic communications that is not directed at particular individuals, the requirement that the surveillance be a necessary limitation on the right to privacy looms large.[460]

7. While the International Group of Experts agreed that any limitation on international human rights must be necessary for the achievement of a legitimate purpose, the Experts were divided as to whether such measures must also be proportionate as a matter of customary international law. The purported proportionality condition of international human rights law requires that the need for any State interference with human rights in order to meet a legitimate State objective be assessed against the severity of the infringement on human rights.[461] Moreover, proportionality requires that the restriction be the least intrusive means available to achieve that objective.[462] By the notion of proportionality, the mass collection of those individuals' electronic communications to whom the State owes human rights law obligations (Rule 34), as an example, may not be conducted if the State can achieve its legitimate objective by other means that do not implicate international human rights or that are more limited in the extent to which they do so. Nor may the mass collection of data be conducted if its effect on the enjoyment of rights such as privacy is disproportionate relative to the specific purpose for which it is conducted.

8. A few of the Experts held the view that while the principle of proportionality is common to various regional international human rights systems and domestic legal regimes, it has not matured into a requirement of customary international human rights law. They pointed to the objection of some States as to whether limitations on the right to privacy are subject to the requirement of proportionality.[463]

---

[460] See, e.g., Uzun v. Germany, judgment, App. No. 35623/05, ECtHR, para. 61 (2010). See also The Right to Privacy in the Digital Age, para. 25; Report of the Special Rapporteur on the Promotion and Protection of Human Rights and Fundamental Freedoms while Countering Terrorism, para. 59.

[461] See, e.g., General Comment No. 27, paras. 14–16; General Comment 34, para. 34; Leander v. Sweden, Judgment, App. no. 9248/81, ECtHR, para. 59 (1987).

[462] Wall advisory opinion, para. 136; General Comment No. 27, para. 14; General Comment No. 34, para. 34.

[463] See, e.g., Ambassador Keith Harper, Explanation of Position by the Delegation of the United States of America on Resolution Entitled 'The Right to Privacy in the Digital Age', A/HRC/28/L.27, Human Rights Council 28th Sess., 26 March 2015.

Moreover, these Experts noted the practice of various States of imposing limitations on international human rights that, while possibly advancing a legitimate State purpose, appear to be a greater infringement on human rights than justified by that need. An example is the broad banning of NGO activities in response to domestic terrorism that limits, *inter alia*, the freedom of expression. In these Experts' view, a customary international law requirement of proportionality with regard to international human rights limitations may constitute *lex ferenda*, but not, in the current state of affairs, *lex lata*.

9.   The majority of the Experts, however, accepted a condition of proportionality. In doing so, they relied heavily on the interpretation given to these norms by the independent bodies created through human rights treaties to monitor their sound application.[464] These Experts emphasised that necessity alone does not suffice to justify limiting obligations under international human rights law. They asserted that it would be incongruent with the object and purpose of limitations on international human rights law to permit a restriction that is necessary, but disproportionate to the State's interest in question. Thus, the least restrictive means must be used to limit a human right, although, again, these Experts agreed that States enjoy a margin of appreciation in this regard.

10.   It must be cautioned that measures that are necessary (and proportionate, by the majority criterion) to achieve one legitimate aim may not be so for the purposes of another.[465] To illustrate, temporarily suspending general access to the Internet might be permissible in response to a national security emergency involving widespread cyber operations targeting critical infrastructure (see also Rule 62), but would not be allowable in order to preclude the Internet transmission of, for example, material that infringes on copyright or to impede protests protected by the freedom of expression.[466]

---

[464]   *See, e.g.*, General Comment 34, paras. 34–35. On the requirement of proportionality, *see also Ahmadou Sadio Diallo* judgment, para. 67; *Francesco Madafferi* v. *Australia*, Communication No. 1011/2001, para. 9.2, UN Doc. CCPR/C/81/D/1011/2001 (2004); *M.G.* v. *Germany*, UN Human Rights Committee, Communication No. 1482/2006, para. 10, UN Doc. CCPR/C/93/D/1482/2006 (2008); Report of the Special Rapporteur on the Promotion and Protection of Human Rights and Fundamental Freedoms while Countering Terrorism, paras. 15, 17; Report of the Special Rapporteur on the Promotion and Protection of the Right to Freedom of Opinion and Expression, para. 24, UN Doc. A/HRC/17/27 (16 May 2011).

[465]   The Right to Privacy in the Digital Age, para. 27.

[466]   Report of the Special Rapporteur on the Promotion and Protection of the Right to Freedom of Opinion and Expression, para. 49, UN Doc. A/HRC/17/27 (16 May 2011).

11.   Restrictions on cyber activities that are otherwise protected by international human rights law must be non-discriminatory.[467] Discrimination could include distinctions, exclusions, restrictions, or preferences that are based on race, colour, sex, language, religion, political or other opinion, national or social origin, property, birth, or other status that has the purpose or effect of nullifying or impairing the recognition, enjoyment, or exercise, on an equal footing, of rights and freedoms.[468] As an illustration, it would be discriminatory to block Internet services to a region populated by a particular ethnic group or to charge users in that area much more for access than users located elsewhere, at least without a legitimate reason such as those discussed earlier.

12.   Not every instance of difference in treatment *ipso facto* constitutes discrimination, but differentiation requires an objective and reasonable justification.[469] Consider a case in which unrest and violence has been occurring in an area populated by a particular ethnic group. Social media is being used to orchestrate the violent events. In such a situation, the fact that the measures the State takes to limit access to the social media affect the ethnic group more than other individuals in the State does not constitute unlawful discrimination.

13.   The UN Human Rights Committee has noted that '[n]o interference [with a right] can take place except in cases envisaged by the law … [and] relevant legislation must specify in detail the precise circumstances in which such interferences may be permitted'.[470] In the same vein, the International Group of Experts was of the view that any

---

[467] UN Charter, Arts. 1, 55; UDHR, Art. 2(1); ICCPR, Arts. 2(1), 26; ICESCR, Art. 2(2); CERD, Art. 2; CEDAW, Art. 2; ACHR, Arts. 1(1), 24; ECHR, Art. 14; ASEAN Human Rights Declaration, Art. 9. *See also* General Comment No. 18, paras. 1–4; Committee on Economic, Social and Cultural Rights, General Comment No. 20: 'Non-Discrimination in Economic, Social and Cultural Rights (Art. 2, para. 2, of the ICESCR)', paras. 2, 7–35, UN Doc. E/C.12/GC/20 (2 July 2009); *Carson and others* v. *United Kingdom*, judgment, App. No. 42184/05, ECtHR, paras. 70–71 (2010); *Juridical Condition and Rights of the Undocumented Migrants*, advisory opinion, OC-18/03, Inter.-AmCtHR (ser. A) No.18, para. 101 (17 September 2003); Inter-American Commission on Human Rights, Freedom of Expression and the Internet, paras. 20–21 (*inter alia*) (13 December 2013); Concluding Observations on the Fourth Periodic Report of the United States of America, Human Rights Committee, UN Doc. CCPR/C/USA/CO/4, para. 22 (23 April 2014). *See also* The Right to Privacy in the Digital Age, para. 36.
[468] UDHR, Art. 1(1); ICCPR, Arts. 2(1), 26; ICESCR, Art. 2(2); CERD, Art. 1(1); CEDAW, Art. 1; CPRD, Arts. 1, 5; ACHR, Art. 24; ECHR, Art. 14; General Comment 18, paras. 6–7.
[469] General Comment No. 29, para. 7.   [470] General Comment No. 16, paras. 3, 8.

basis for a restriction must be 'provided', 'established', or 'prescribed by law',[471] and must be precise and clear enough to place affected individuals on notice as to its effect. It must also be accessible to the public.[472] Thus, for instance, legislative restrictions on the exercise of freedom of speech on websites, blogs, and via private electronic communications must be sufficiently descriptive to place those who might be affected by them on notice. Likewise, a law or directive upon which online surveillance is based has to outline the conditions under which the State may engage in the surveillance that implicates the right to privacy.

14.   The Experts did not agree, however, as to whether the condition that a limitation be provided or prescribed by law necessarily requires that law to be domestic in character. Some of the Experts were of the view that international law may itself provide or prescribe the grounds for limitation. Other Experts took the position that the limitations must be set forth in domestic law.

Rule 38 – Derogation

A State may derogate from its human rights treaty obligations concerning cyber activities when permitted, and under the conditions established, by the treaty in question.

1.   Some human rights treaties permit States to derogate, that is, to temporarily release themselves, in full or in part, from the binding nature of certain obligations contained therein in times of public emergency. The precise conditions under which derogation is permitted are defined by the treaty in question; they are generally narrow. For example, the ICCPR permits derogations from some of its provisions 'in time of public emergency which threatens the life of the nation and the

---

[471] *See, e.g.*, ICCPR, Arts. 9(1), 12(3), 18(3), 19(3), 22(2); ECHR, Arts. 8–11; ASEAN Human Rights Declaration, Art. 8; UN Commission on Human Rights, The Siracusa Principles on the Limitation and Derogation Provisions in the International Covenant on Civil and Political Rights, paras. 15–18, E/CN.4/1985/4 (28 September 1984). *See also* General Comment No. 16, para. 4; Human Rights Committee, *Antonius Cornelis Van Hulst* v. *Netherlands*, paras. 7.3, 7.7, UN Doc. CCPR/C/82/D/903/1999 (5 November 2004); *Ahmet Yildirim* v. *Turkey*, judgment, App. No. 3111/10, ECtHR, paras. 56–57 (2012).

[472] General Comment No. 34, paras. 24–25. *See also Sunday Times* v. *United Kingdom*, judgment, App. No. 6538/74, ECtHR, para. 49 (1979). The European Court of Human Rights has confirmed this requirement in the context of government surveillance of telephone communications without judicial authorisation. *Zakharov* v. *Russia*, judgment, App. No. 47143/06, ECtHR, para. 236 *et seq.* (2015).

existence of which is officially proclaimed'.[473] Similarly, the ECHR permits derogation from particular provisions 'in time of war or other public emergency threatening the life of the nation'.[474] The ACHR permits derogation in broader circumstances than permitted by the ICCPR and ECHR, that is, '[i]n time of war, public danger, or other emergency that threatens the independence or security of a State Party' with respect to certain of the rights set forth therein.[475] The International Group of Experts agreed that a treaty's derogation provisions apply to cyber activities for Parties thereto. As an example, if a State derogates from a provision involving freedom of expression in full compliance with the terms of the particular treaty in question, it may, to the extent necessary, block access to or remove online posts that might exacerbate a situation of emergency.

2.   Some treaties prohibit derogation that is not strictly required by the exigencies of the situation.[476] For instance, in the situation above, placing some limits on the freedom of expression exercised by cyber means may be acceptable, but, depending on the situation, blocking all such expression may not be permissible. Additionally, the ICCPR prohibits derogations that discriminate solely on the basis of race, colour, sex, language, religion, or social origin.[477] The ICCPR, ACHR, and ECHR also bar derogations that are inconsistent with the States Parties' other international legal obligations.[478]

3.   The treaty in question may explicitly exempt certain human rights obligations contained therein from derogation. For instance, the ICCPR prohibits derogation from provisions protecting, *inter alia*, the prohibition of the arbitrary deprivation of life, the prohibition against torture and slavery, the right to recognition as a person before the law, and the right to freedom of thought, conscience and religion.[479] Additionally, the ECHR prohibits derogation from the prohibition of punishment without law even during times of emergency.[480]

---

[473] ICCPR, Art. 4(1).   [474] ECHR, Art. 15(1).
[475] ACHR, Art. 27. However, the list of non-derogable ACHR provisions is broader than those of the ICCPR and ECHR.
[476] *See, e.g.,* ICCPR, Art. 4(1); ECHR, Art. 15(1).   [477] ICCPR, Art. 4(1).
[478] ICCPR, Art. 4(1); ECHR, Art. 15(1); ACHR, Art. 27(1).   [479] ICCPR, Art. 4(2).
[480] ECHR, Art. 15(2).

7

Diplomatic and consular law

1. This Chapter sets out the international law governing diplomatic and consular relations applicable to State conduct in cyberspace. Diplomatic and consular law rests heavily on the 1961 Vienna Convention on Diplomatic Relations and the 1963 Vienna Convention on Consular Relations. The International Group of Experts agreed that these treaties substantially reflect customary international law.[481] Therefore, the Rules that follow significantly draw upon them.

2. The term 'receiving State' refers to the State to which a diplomatic mission or consular post is accredited. 'Sending State' is the State that the mission or post represents. It should be noted that a head of mission or other member of the diplomatic staff may be accredited to several States.[482] In such cases, the reference to 'receiving State' applies to all States to which the individual has been accredited.

3. As used in this Chapter, the term 'diplomatic mission' refers to a State's diplomatic presence in another State, established with the consent of the latter, for the purpose of representing the sending State in the receiving State and performing other functions set out in international law. 'Premises of a mission' refers to 'the buildings or parts of buildings and the land ancillary thereto, irrespective of ownership, used for the purposes of the mission'. The term includes the residence of the head of the mission.[483] A 'diplomatic agent' is the head of the mission or a member of the diplomatic staff of the mission.[484]

4. 'Consular post' denotes any consulate-general, consulate, vice-consulate, or consular agency of a sending State in a receiving State, established with the consent of the latter, for the purpose of performing

---

[481] *Tehran Hostages* judgment, paras. 62, 69.
[482] Vienna Convention on Diplomatic Relations, Art. 5.
[483] Vienna Convention on Diplomatic Relations, Art. 1(i).
[484] Vienna Convention on Diplomatic Relations, Art. 1(a), (d–e).

consular functions.[485] 'Consular premises' refers to the 'buildings or parts of buildings and the land ancillary thereto, irrespective of ownership, used exclusively for the purposes of the consular post'.[486] A 'consular officer' is 'any person, including the head of a consular post, entrusted in that capacity with the exercise of consular functions'.[487] A diplomatic mission may perform consular functions; no consent of the receiving State is required in these cases.[488] Although consular officers may in certain circumstances be authorised to perform diplomatic acts, doing so does not confer upon them any right to claim diplomatic privileges and immunities (Rule 44).[489]

5.   The law that governs international organisations is not specifically addressed in this Chapter. However, major international organisations such as the United Nations and its specialised agencies enjoy immunities and privileges by treaty that are akin to those to which diplomatic missions are entitled. For example, they are entitled to inviolability of premises and communications, and representatives to these organisations benefit from privileges and immunities analogous to those afforded to diplomats or consular officers.[490] The law governing the privileges and immunities accorded to international organisations and their staff differs for each organisation and can be found in the constitutive treaties or other instruments that establish the organisations, as well as in agreements that the organisations conclude with their host States and other States where they need privileges or immunities for the performance of their functions.[491]

6.   Similarly, the law governing special missions is not specifically dealt with in this Chapter. The 1969 Convention on Special Missions addresses the privileges and immunities that apply to 'special missions', that is, temporary missions representing a sending State in a receiving

---

[485] Vienna Convention on Consular Relations, Art. 1(1)(a).
[486] Vienna Convention on Consular Relations, Art. 1(1)(j).
[487] Vienna Convention on Consular Relations, Art. 1(1)(d).
[488] Vienna Convention on Diplomatic Relations, Art. 3(2); Vienna Convention on Consular Relations, Arts. 3, 70.
[489] Vienna Convention on Consular Relations, Art. 17.
[490] See, e.g., UN Charter, Art. 105(1–2).
[491] See, e.g., Convention on the Privileges and Immunities of the United Nations, 13 February 1946, 1 UNTS 15; Agreement Between the United Nations and the United States Regarding the Headquarters of the United Nations, 26 June 1947, 11 UNTS 147; Rome Statute, Art. 48; Headquarters Agreement between the International Criminal Court and the Host State, 7 June 2007, ICC-BD/04-01-08.

State with the consent of the latter for the purpose of dealing with it on specific questions or to perform a specific task.[492] Although the Convention has not been widely ratified and operates only with the consent of the receiving State, the International Group of Experts acknowledged support among States for the position that members of special missions enjoy immunity and inviolability as a matter of customary law, particularly in light of State practice affording special missions the privileges and immunities stipulated in the Convention. The Experts noted that when special missions make use of the facilities of their State's diplomatic missions, the inviolability of the premises and cyber infrastructure therein would protect their cyber activities as discussed in this Chapter irrespective of the applicability of the privileges and immunities to which special missions are entitled.

7. Many of the immunities set out in this Chapter apply to a more limited extent to family members of a diplomatic mission's or consular post's personnel, as well as to the administrative and technical staff of a mission or post and their families.[493] However, the commentary that follows does not address these immunities. The Vienna Convention on Diplomatic Relations, the Vienna Convention on Consular Relations, and the Convention on Special Missions set forth the specific scope of such immunities afforded to these individuals and should be consulted in this regard. With respect to the immunity of States and State officials under general international law, see Rule 12.

8. The International Group of Experts noted that the interrelationship of diplomatic and consular law with the rules of the law of State responsibility involving circumstances precluding wrongfulness (Rule 19) is especially complex. In particular, the Experts agreed that as set forth in Rule 22, countermeasures that would breach the inviolability (including the jurisdictional immunity) of diplomatic or consular agents (Rule 44), premises (Rule 39), or archives or documents (Rule 41) are prohibited.[494] Take the example of a sending State that is using the cyber infrastructure of a diplomatic mission to transmit espionage malware into computers in the receiving State. Doing so is an abuse of the diplomatic function[495] and therefore an internationally wrongful

---

[492] Convention on Special Missions, Art. 1, 8 December 1969, 1400 UNTS 23431.
[493] See, e.g., Vienna Convention on Diplomatic Relations, Arts. 37–38; Vienna Convention on Consular Relations, Arts. 43.
[494] Articles on State Responsibility, Art. 50(2)(b) and paras. 14–15 of commentary.
[495] Vienna Convention on Diplomatic Relations, Art. 3(1).

act (Rule 14). Nevertheless, the receiving State is not allowed to engage in cyber operations directed at cyber infrastructure in the premises as a countermeasure.

9.   The Experts agreed that pursuant to the principle of reciprocity, a receiving State may provide, with respect to a sending State's cyber-related activities, less favourable treatment to the sending State than it provides to other sending States when its mission or post is subjected to similar treatment in the sending State. They cautioned, nevertheless, that the receiving State may not act in a manner that violates diplomatic or consular law.[496] The Experts took note of the view, which none of them held, that a receiving State acting in violation of the provisions of diplomatic or consular law may be subject to a proportionate denial of reciprocal rights.

10.   The International Group of Experts agreed that this Chapter generally applies during periods of armed conflict. In this regard, Article 45(a) of the Vienna Convention on Diplomatic Relations provides: 'The receiving State must, even in case of armed conflict, respect and protect the premises of the mission, together with its property and archives.' Article 27(1)(a) of the Vienna Convention on Consular Relations sets forth an equivalent protection for consular premises, property, and archives. Moreover, the two instruments state that the functions of a person enjoying diplomatic privileges and immunities subsist during a period of armed conflict until the person leaves the receiving State, or upon expiry of a reasonable period in which to do so.[497]

Rule 39 – Inviolability of premises in which cyber infrastructure is located

Cyber infrastructure on the premises of a diplomatic mission or consular post is protected by the inviolability of that mission or post.

1.   Inviolability of the premises of a diplomatic mission is a bedrock principle of diplomatic law. By the principle, the premises may not be entered absent consent.[498] Additionally, property on the premises of a

---

[496] Vienna Convention on Diplomatic Relations, Art. 47(2); Vienna Convention on Consular Relations, Art. 72(2). *See also* DENZA, DIPLOMATIC LAW, at 406–408.

[497] Vienna Convention on Diplomatic Relations, Art. 39(2); Vienna Convention on Consular Relations, Art. 53(3).

[498] Vienna Convention on Diplomatic Relations, Art. 22(1).

diplomatic mission is immune from search, requisition, attachment, or execution by the receiving State's agents without the sending State's consent.[499]

2. The International Group of Experts agreed that this Rule extends to the premises of a consular post, but the protection only encompasses those areas that are used exclusively for the purposes of the consular post.[500]

3. With respect to the application of this Rule, the International Group of Experts was divided over the lawfulness of remotely intruding into cyber infrastructure located in a sending State's diplomatic or consular premises, or otherwise disrupting or altering data therein. The majority of the Experts agreed that the Rule prohibits a receiving State from doing so on the basis that cyber operations manifesting on cyber infrastructure in the premises amount to unconsented-to entry into the premises. The Experts' conclusion is further supported by the receiving State's special duty to take all appropriate steps to protect the premises of a diplomatic mission against any intrusion or damage (Rule 40),[501] and its obligation to facilitate the full performance of the mission.[502]

4. A few of the Experts, however, were of the view that a violation of this Rule requires the receiving State's physical presence in the mission or post. For them, conducting a close-access cyber operation would, for example, satisfy this standard. They were also willing to characterise the remote causation of physical consequences in a diplomatic mission or consular post by cyber means as a violation of this Rule. To the extent the Rule protects the premises of diplomatic missions against non-consensual physical entry, the remote causation of physical consequences effectively amounts to physical presence therein for these Experts.

5. It must be cautioned that activities conducted remotely against a diplomatic mission's or consular post's cyber infrastructure or activities might violate other Rules set forth in this Chapter, such as that protecting diplomatic archives, documents, and official correspondence (Rule 41). In other words, the fact that a receiving State's cyber

---

[499] Vienna Convention on Diplomatic Relations, Art. 22(3).
[500] Vienna Convention on Consular Relations, Art. 31.
[501] Vienna Convention on Diplomatic Relations, Art. 22(2).
[502] Vienna Convention on Diplomatic Relations, Art. 25; DENZA, DIPLOMATIC LAW, at 171–172.

operation does not violate this Rule does not necessarily render it lawful under diplomatic and consular law.

6.   The International Group of Experts was divided as to whether a State other than the receiving State has an obligation to respect the inviolability of the premises of a diplomatic mission or consular post situated in the receiving State. Consider a case in which State A conducts a cyber operation to exfiltrate data from the cyber infrastructure in State B's embassy that is located in State C in order to determine the positions of State B's diplomatic personnel. The International Group of Experts was evenly split over this example. Some Experts took the position that State A has violated this Rule, noting that its behaviour is inconsistent with the object and purpose of the principle of inviolability, as well as the fact that remote access to cyber infrastructure is increasingly a mere technical matter. The other Experts adopted the contrary position on the ground that legal obligations in diplomatic law arise primarily from the relationship between sending and receiving States. They also pointed out that the specific obligations imposed on third parties in the relevant treaty texts are generally confined to the inviolability of official correspondence and communications that are in transit (Rule 41).[503]

7.   The Experts concurred that a receiving State *in extremis* may take actions against the premises, or cyber infrastructure therein, of a diplomatic mission or consular post in self-defence (Rule 71).[504] For instance, if cyber infrastructure in a mission is being used to transmit critical information about the receiving State's armed forces for use in an imminent armed attack by the sending State, the receiving State may conduct operations, including at the use of force level, against that cyber infrastructure. The Experts acknowledged a view, which none of them held, by which the inviolability of the premises of a mission or post is absolute. Proponents of this view assert that the remedies available to a receiving State in such a scenario are those contained in diplomatic and consular law, such as the termination or suspension of diplomatic or consular relations, as well as the use of force in self-defence against targets other than the premises of the mission.

---

[503] Vienna Convention on Diplomatic Relations, Art. 40(1) and (3); Vienna Convention on Consular Relations, Art. 54(1) and (3).

[504] First report from the Foreign Affairs Committee, Session 1984–85: the abuse of diplomatic immunities and privileges, paras 88–95. *See also* Yearbook of the International Law Commission, Vol. II (1958), at 97; DENZA, DIPLOMATIC LAW, at 223.

8. A separate question involves the protection of a diplomatic mission's property that is not on its premises, such as official mobile phones or laptops that are removed from the premises. The International Group of Experts was divided also on this question.

9. A majority of the Experts was of the view that such property enjoys inviolability under this Rule. Most of the Experts among the majority took the view that it is inviolable, as discussed above. Therefore, the sending State may not undertake cyber operations against it. For these Experts, extending inviolability to property that is located outside of the premises is in line with the object and purpose of the law governing diplomatic and consular inviolability. They noted that such property also is likely to qualify as inviolable 'archives' of a diplomatic mission under Rule 41, as there will usually be official diplomatic material stored on it. Finally, the Vienna Convention on Diplomatic Relations provides that the movable personal property of diplomatic agents is inviolable, subject only to exceptions for certain civil or administrative actions.[505] Therefore, for these Experts, it would be incongruent to conclude that property of a diplomatic mission is violable once removed from the premises, whereas the private property of a diplomatic agent enjoys inviolability, wherever located.

10. Some of the Experts among the majority concluded that such property is only immune from cyber operations that would constitute a search, requisition, attachment, or execution. They based their view on the fact that property on the diplomatic premises enjoys these forms of protection.[506] These Experts also observed that the Vienna Convention on Diplomatic Relations extends the same immunity to means of transport,[507] one of the principal forms of movable property at the time of its drafting. They further noted the emerging practice of recognising immunity from attachment of diplomatic bank accounts.[508]

11. A few of the Experts who were not in accord with the majority position opined that such property is not protected at all under this Rule,

---

[505] Vienna Convention on Diplomatic Relations, Art. 30(2); Yearbook of the International Law Commission, Vol. II (1958), at 98.

[506] Vienna Convention on Diplomatic Relations, Art. 22(3).

[507] Vienna Convention on Diplomatic Relations, Art. 22(3).

[508] *Alcom* v. *Republic of Colombia* AC 580 (12 April 1984) (UK); *Republic of 'A' Embassy Bank Account* Case, 77 ILR 489 (1986) (Austria); *MK* v. *State Secretary for Justice*, 94 ILR 357 (1988) (Neth.); *In the Matter of the Application of Liberian Eastern Timber Corp.* v. *The Government of Liberia*, 89 ILR 360 (1987) (US). *See also* the Convention on Jurisdictional Immunities, Art. 21; US Department of State Office of the Legal Advisor, Digest of United States Practice in International Law (2000), at 548.

citing the language in the Vienna Convention on Diplomatic Relations, which provides immunity from search, requisition, attachment, or execution only to the 'premises of the mission, their furnishings and other property thereon'.[509]

12. Given the complexity of the issue of property that is not on the premises of diplomatic missions, the Experts could come to no conclusion as to property removed from consular posts.

13. For a discussion of the placement of listening devices by the receiving State on the premises of a diplomatic mission, see Rule 41.

14. The International Group of Experts considered the announcements of a few States that they have established 'virtual embassies'. For example, the United States has launched websites that it describes as 'virtual embassies' in Iran and Syria, while Estonia has announced that it will establish a 'data embassy' in order to back up critical government data on servers located in friendly States. Given the contexts in which the United States and Estonia have invoked the terms 'virtual embassy' and 'data embassy', the Experts agreed that these entities, solely by virtue of the use of the term 'embassy', do not qualify as premises of a diplomatic mission. The Experts further pointed to the fact that mutual consent is required to establish diplomatic relations between States, and, in particular, to establish permanent diplomatic missions.[510] In the absence of such consent, a 'virtual embassy' is not entitled to special protection under diplomatic law. It should be noted that if the cyber infrastructure (such as computers, servers, or other network devices) upon which a so-called virtual or data embassy relies is located on the premises of a diplomatic mission, it falls under the protection set forth in this Rule. Furthermore, data relating to the 'virtual embassy' or 'data embassy' that also qualifies as official diplomatic correspondence or the archives or documents of the diplomatic mission (Rule 41) is protected as such.

15. The Experts likewise considered the 'online presences' of diplomatic missions. For example, it is now commonplace for diplomatic missions to create official accounts on social media platforms, such as Facebook. The International Group of Experts concluded that the inviolability of a diplomatic mission's premises does not apply to such a virtual presence. On the contrary, the premises of a diplomatic mission have been traditionally understood to imply physical presence.

[509] Vienna Convention on Diplomatic Relations, Art. 22(3).
[510] Vienna Convention on Diplomatic Relations, Art. 2.

Indeed, premises are defined in Article 1 of the Vienna Convention on Diplomatic Relations as 'buildings or parts of buildings and the land ancillary thereto'.[511] As with a 'virtual' or 'data embassy', however, the Experts acknowledged that if the online presence relies upon cyber infrastructure located in the physical premises of a diplomatic mission, said infrastructure falls within the scope of the protection established under this Rule. Moreover, the archives, documents, and official correspondence associated with the operation of the online presence may fall within the protective scope of Rules 41 and 42.

Rule 40 – Duty to protect cyber infrastructure

A receiving State must take all appropriate steps to protect cyber infrastructure on the premises of a sending State's diplomatic mission or consular post against intrusion or damage.

1.   A receiving State has a 'special duty' to protect the premises of a diplomatic mission or consular post against intrusion or damage, irrespective of the source of the operation in question.[512] For instance, if the security services of the receiving State become aware that the sending State's cyber infrastructure within the premises of a diplomatic mission is being targeted by cyber operations, the receiving State must engage in all reasonable efforts to terminate the offending operations, including, where appropriate, notifying the sending State of the operations. Likewise, if the security services have information that the mission's cyber infrastructure is about to be targeted by cyber operations, the receiving State must take law enforcement or other measures that are proportionate and appropriate to the threat to prevent the operations.

2.   The obligation set forth in this Rule is not absolute. The receiving State need only take 'all appropriate steps' to protect the premises.[513] As a general proposition, the extent of protection owed is based on, *inter alia*, the magnitude of the threat to the premises, the extent to which the

---

[511] *See also* Vienna Convention on Diplomatic Relations, Art. 21(1).

[512] Vienna Convention on Diplomatic Relations, Art. 22(2); *Tehran Hostages* judgment, paras. 61–66; Vienna Convention on Consular Relations, Art. 31(3). With respect to the premises of a diplomatic mission, *see also* Yearbook of the International Law Commission, Vol. II (1958), at 78, 95 (stating that a receiving State 'must, in order to fulfil this obligation, take special measures – over and above those it takes to discharge its general duty of ensuring order').

[513] Vienna Convention on Diplomatic Relations, Art. 22(2); Vienna Convention on Consular Relations, Art. 31(3).

receiving State is aware of a specific threat, and the capacity of the receiving State to take action in the circumstances. The receiving State enjoys the discretion to select the particular measures it will take to fulfil this duty.[514]

3. The International Group of Experts took notice of the fact that cyber operations targeting the premises of diplomatic missions or consular posts are often likely to originate from abroad, but could achieve no consensus as to whether a receiving State has a duty to seek assistance from those other States when necessary to protect premises on its territory. The majority was of the view that the receiving State bears no obligation to seek assistance under diplomatic and consular law; the duty to take 'appropriate steps' is limited to measures that involve the exercise of its sovereign authority. These Experts also took note of the apparent absence of State practice supporting the existence of such a duty. The minority was of the view that given the common benefit of maintaining diplomatic relations among States generally, it is reasonable to interpret this Rule as including a duty to seek assistance from other States when such assistance is likely to help put an end to the intrusive or damaging cyber operations.

4. The Experts agreed that there is no duty to take preventive measures to protect a diplomatic mission or consular post's premises and the cyber infrastructure therein until the receiving State is aware of a particular threat. In adopting this position, the Experts pointed to the common practice of receiving States in only providing special security personnel to protect the premises of a mission or post when there is a known security risk and, even then, only if requested by the head of a mission or post.[515] They further noted that, as a practical matter, the sending State is likely to rely on its own security measures to protect the cyber infrastructure on the premises of a mission or post, rather than those of the receiving State.

5. A receiving State is, however, obliged to take all appropriate steps to 'prevent any disturbance of the peace' of a diplomatic mission or consular post or the 'impairment of [their] dignity'.[516] Although this is an ill-defined

---

[514] *See, e.g., Ignatiev v. United States*, 238 F.3d 464 (D.C. Cir. 2001).

[515] *See, e.g.,* Australian Government, Department of Foreign Affairs and Trade, Protocol Guidelines, para. 12.2; Anthony Minnaar, *Protection of Foreign Missions in South Africa*, 9 AFRICAN SECURITY REVIEW 67, 72 (2000).

[516] Vienna Convention on Diplomatic Relations, Art. 22(2); Vienna Convention on Consular Relations, Art. 31(3).

duty, the Experts agreed that the receiving State has no obligation to take steps against mere online expressions of criticism of a diplomatic mission or consular post or the sending State. Rather, the obligation is satisfied so long as the receiving State ensures that the actual functioning of the mission or post and the cyber infrastructure therein is not impaired. They observed that, in practice, States tend to balance the duty to prevent disturbance or impairment against the human rights of expression and assembly (Rule 35), and that although many States will impose certain restrictions on demonstrations in the immediate vicinity of embassies, they usually will refrain from prohibiting all speech in a particular medium that is critical of a sending State or its mission or post.[517]

6. This Rule should be read in conjunction with the other Rules set forth in this Chapter, especially that on the obligation to protect the free communication of a diplomatic mission or consular post (Rule 42), as well as applicable Rules set forth elsewhere in the Manual, such as those on due diligence (Rules 6–7).

Rule 41 – Inviolability of electronic archives, documents, and correspondence

Archives, documents, and official correspondence of a diplomatic mission or consular post that are in electronic form are inviolable.

1. International law affords broad inviolability to a diplomatic mission's or consular post's archives, documents, and official correspondence, including in electronic form.[518] The International Group of Experts agreed that 'inviolability' means that these materials are free from seizure, cyber espionage (see also Rule 32), enforcement, or judicial action, or any other form of interference by a State. The purpose of this protection is to ensure confidentiality.

2. Only States are bound by the Rule. It is not violated by the actions of private entities unless said actions are attributable to a State (Rules 15 and 17).

---

[517] *See, e.g., Finzer* v. *Barry,* 798 F.2d 1450 (D.C. Cir. 1986) (US); *Minister for Foreign Affairs and Trade and others* v. *Magno and another,* 112 ALR 529 (1992) (Austl.).

[518] Vienna Convention on Diplomatic Relations, Arts. 24, 27(2); Vienna Convention on Consular Relations, Arts. 33, 35(2). Note that the archives and documents of a consular post headed by an honorary consular officer shall be inviolable, but only if they are kept separate from other papers and documents. Vienna Convention on Consular Relations, Art. 61.

3.   The International Group of Experts was of the view that 'archives', for the purposes of this Rule, include external hard drives, flash drives, and other media on which electronic documents are stored.[519] The term 'documents' includes not only final materials in electronic form, but also related drafts, negotiating documents, and other similar material that are amassed and deliberately preserved by diplomatic missions or consular posts in the course of their activities. 'Official correspondence' includes emails, demarches, cables, and other messages that relate to a diplomatic mission or consular post or the functions thereof.

4.   The International Group of Experts was split over the issue of whether private submissions to a mission or post via email or through an online presence qualify as the archives, documents, or official corres-pondence protected by this Rule. For instance, the website of a diplo-matic mission or consular post may allow nationals of the receiving State to submit online applications for visas to travel to the sending State. A majority of the Experts was of the view that the extension of inviol-ability in these circumstances is consistent with the object and purpose of diplomatic and consular law, and that once submitted for an official purpose, the information at least becomes part of the archives and documents of the mission or post. A few of the Experts took the contrary view that such private submissions are outside the scope of this Rule because diplomatic and consular law is limited to relations between States. However, all of the Experts agreed, for instance, that if a citizen of the receiving State posts a comment to the mission's most recent entry on a social media website, the comment is not protected by this Rule because it is publicly available.

5.   In addition to the electronic archives, documents, and official correspondence of a diplomatic mission expressly cited in the Rule, inviolability encompasses the private papers and correspondence of diplomatic agents.[520] Inviolability does not, however, extend to the private papers and correspondence of consular officers or the staff of a consular post.[521]

---

[519] *See also* Vienna Convention on Consular Relations, Art. 1(1)(k) (defining 'consular archives' to include all the papers, documents, correspondence, books, films, tapes and registers of the consular post, together with the ciphers and codes, the card-indexes and any article of furniture intended for their protection or safe keeping).

[520] Vienna Convention on Diplomatic Relations, Art. 30(2).

[521] This conclusion is also supported by the fact that there is no comparable provision to Art. 30(2) of the Vienna Convention on Diplomatic Relations in the Vienna Convention on Consular Relations.

6. The inviolability of the archives and documents of a diplomatic mission or consular post attaches, in the view of the International Group of Experts, 'at any time and wherever they may be'.[522] Accordingly, electronic archives and documents of a mission or post are entitled to inviolability even when they are outside of the receiving State. To illustrate, if a diplomatic mission's archives are stored on a government server beyond the receiving State's territory, such as the sending State's Ministry of Foreign Affairs server, they remain inviolable. Similarly, if the material is stored on private cyber infrastructure, like a private email server or private cloud infrastructure, it remains protected so long as the sending State intends the material to remain confidential and it has not been disclosed to a third party with the consent (Rule 19) of the sending State.

7. The Experts agreed that treaty and customary law require all States – not just the receiving State – to accord official diplomatic and consular correspondence and other official communications 'in transit … the same freedom and protection as the receiving State is bound to accord.'[523] Thus, they took the position that both the receiving and third States are prohibited from intercepting the electronic communications of diplomatic missions and consular posts that are in transit. In doing so, they noted that the confidentiality of diplomatic and consular communications is essential and central to the function of a diplomatic mission or consular post.

8. However, the Experts were divided over the question of whether all States, and not just the receiving State, are obliged to respect the inviolability of the sending State's diplomatic and consular material when that material is at rest as opposed to in transit. They noted that when the material is stored on the premises of a diplomatic mission or consular post, it may be protected by the premises' inviolability (see discussion in Rule 39). When that material is outside the mission or post, as in the case of data stored on a private cloud server, the Experts were divided. A minority of them took the view that extending the

---

[522] Vienna Convention on Diplomatic Relations, Art. 24; Vienna Convention on Consular Relations, Art. 33.

[523] Vienna Convention on Diplomatic Relations, Art. 40(3); Vienna Convention on Consular Relations, Art. 54(3). Third parties are also obliged to honour the inviolability of other categories of diplomatic and consular material in transit, such as the diplomatic or consular bag. Vienna Convention on Diplomatic Relations, Art. 40(3); Vienna Convention on Consular Relations, Art. 54(3). See also, generally, International Law Commission, Draft Articles on the Status of the Diplomatic Courier and the Diplomatic Bag Not Accompanied by Diplomatic Courier and Draft Optional Protocols (1989).

obligation to third States is consistent with the object and purpose of the principle of inviolability, particularly in light of the ease with which States can now access electronic data outside of their territory. The majority of the Experts adopted the contrary position on the ground that the specific obligations imposed on third parties in the relevant treaty texts are expressly confined to the inviolability of official correspondence and other communications in transit and thus do not extend to diplomatic or consular material that is at rest.

9.   The Experts disagreed on the precise scope of the prohibition of electronic surveillance by third States of diplomatic communications. Specifically, they differed over whether the material that is protected from interception by a third State is confined to communications between a diplomatic mission and its sending government, or if it includes communications between the sending State and the receiving State, as well as between the mission of the sending State and the missions of other States in the receiving State.

10.   A majority of the Experts was of the view that the prohibition extends to all such communications, citing the broad inviolability official correspondence enjoys in general; the fact that such communications come within the scope of 'all correspondence relating to the mission and its functions';[524] and the negotiating history of the Vienna Convention on Diplomatic Relations, which suggests that the principle of free communication (Rule 42) was not intended to be confined to communication between a diplomatic mission and its sending government, but rather was meant to extend to all official correspondence, including communication between the diplomatic mission of a sending State and the government of the receiving State or the diplomatic missions of other States.[525] In other words, the majority concluded that diplomatic law is, as a general matter, meant to foster the confidentiality of diplomatic communications and saw no reason to carve out an exception for this category. A few of the Experts took the position that the prohibition only encompasses the communications of a diplomatic mission with its sending government. They cited the absence of clear language prohibiting the interception of other types of communications and asserted that a fundamental object and purpose

---

[524] Vienna Convention on Diplomatic Relation, Arts. 27(1), 40(3) (suggesting the protection of official correspondence from interception by third parties, when taken together.).

[525] Yearbook of the International Law Commission Vol. II (1957), at 137–138.

of diplomatic law is to safeguard the ability of a mission to securely communicate with its own government.

11.   The International Group of Experts noted that States appear to frequently have violated the aforementioned prohibitions, with numerous reports of surveillance by receiving States of the diplomatic communications of sending States and the placement of listening devices in the diplomatic missions of sending States. Even so, the Experts observed that in these instances sending States continue to object to surveillance as a violation of international law; condemnation of the practice usually goes unanswered, at least on the basis of international law, by States accused of such activities.[526] As a consequence, the Experts concluded that *opinio juris* has not formed in favour of regarding such surveillance as lawful. In other words, the extant international law prohibition of the surveillance of diplomatic material is undiminished.[527]

12.   The materials encompassed by the Rule are protected on an indefinite basis. This is so even in the event of closure of the mission, severance of diplomatic relations, or armed conflict (Rules 82–83). Indeed, both the Vienna Convention on Diplomatic Relations and the Vienna Convention on Consular Relations require the receiving State to 'respect and protect' the property and archives of a mission following breach of relations or recall of a mission's or post's personnel.[528]

13.   The Experts were of the view that the inviolability of a diplomatic mission's or consular post's archives, documents, and official correspondence survives even if the material is stolen or obtained by a third party (including another State) using improper means and then provided, or otherwise made available, to a State obligated to respect its inviolability. Thus, States may not escape the obligation to respect the inviolability of diplomatic or consular material by employing or otherwise resorting to an intermediary who initially acquires the protected material. The Experts emphasised that the rules of attribution in the law of State responsibility (Rules 15–18) apply to this question.

---

[526] *See, e.g., China demands U.S. explain spying allegations linked to Australian missions,* REUTERS, 31 October 2013; *Et Tu, UK? Anger Grows over British Spying in Berlin,* SPIEGEL ONLINE, 5 November 2013; *MI5 Tried to Bug London Embassy, says Pakistan,* KUWAIT NEWS AGENCY, 6 November 2003.

[527] *See also Nicaragua* judgment, para. 186.

[528] Vienna Convention on Diplomatic Relations, Art. 45; Vienna Convention on Consular Relations, Art. 27(a).

14.   On the question of whether inviolability survives if diplomatic or consular material is obtained by a third party (including another State) and then made available by the third party to members of the public, the International Group of Experts was divided. As an example, the material may be stolen or otherwise acquired improperly and posted on the Internet, as in the case of the Wikileaks incident. The majority took the position that this Rule no longer applies since its object and purpose of ensuring the confidentiality of the material has been defeated. In other words, if the material is openly accessible, it is not confidential as a matter of fact.[529]

15.   A minority of the Experts was of the view that this Rule continues to apply in such cases. These Experts observed that continuing to respect inviolability insofar as is possible in the circumstances may assist in restoring the confidential nature of the material or preventing inferences being drawn from it that are adverse to the sending State or its diplomats. Furthermore, the sending State may wish to maintain the inviolability of the material with respect to States that have not yet accessed the information, while taking legal action against those within whose possession the material has come. Finally, these Experts pointed to the breadth of the norm of inviolability and its centrality to diplomatic relations, and thus interpreted the 'wherever they may be'[530] protective scope of documents as encompassing the public domain.

16.   States are increasingly turning to an online presence to conduct certain diplomatic and consular functions, such as providing information about the receiving State's security situation for its citizens in the receiving State. In this regard, the International Group of Experts concluded that information or material made publicly available by the sending State is not entitled to the protection of this Rule because the object and purpose of the Rule is primarily to ensure the confidentiality of diplomatic and consular material. For instance, if one State defaces another State's diplomatic mission's website, this Rule is not implicated, although such action might violate a different Rule set forth in this Chapter, such as the inviolability of cyber infrastructure on diplomatic premises (Rule 39).

---

[529] *See, e.g., R (Bancoult) v. Secretary of State for Foreign and Commonwealth Affairs*, Court of Appeal Judgment [2014] EWCA Civ 708, para. 58 (finding a cable that had been leaked to the press containing diplomatic communications admissible in court).

[530] Vienna Convention on Diplomatic Relations, Art. 24; Vienna Convention on Consular Relations, Art. 33.

17. The International Group of Experts agreed that there is presently no requirement in customary international law for the electronic archives, documents, or official correspondence of a diplomatic mission or consular post to be marked as such for inviolability to attach. The Experts cited the absence of State practice to that effect and took note of the negotiating history of the Vienna Convention on Diplomatic Relations, during which proposals to impose such a condition on physical archives were rejected.[531]

18. The International Group of Experts noted the increasing use of honorary consular officers. In an effort to encourage economic ties while reducing the costs of establishing consular posts, many States employ businessmen and -women or other professionals to act as consular representatives on a part-time basis. Although the documents, correspondence, and archives of a consular post headed by an honorary consular officer are inviolable, this protection is conditional on the materials being kept separate from materials relating to the honorary consular officer's other professional activities.[532]

Rule 42 – Free communication

A receiving State must permit and protect the free cyber communication of a diplomatic mission or consular post for all official purposes.

1. International law provides that a receiving State must permit and protect the 'free communication' on the part of a sending State's diplomatic mission or consular post for all official purposes.[533] The International Group of Experts agreed that this provision reflects customary international law.

2. With respect to consular posts, of particular note is the right of consular officers to communicate freely with the sending State's nationals.[534] Therefore, the receiving State may not, for instance, interfere with

---

[531] United Nations Conference on Diplomatic Intercourse and Immunities, *United States of America: amendment to article 22*, A/CONF.20/C.1/L.153 (14 March 1961); United Nations Conference on Diplomatic Intercourse and Immunities, Official Records, A/CONF.20/14, at 149 (21 March 1961).

[532] Vienna Convention on Consular Relations, Art. 61.

[533] Vienna Convention on Diplomatic Relations, Art. 27(1); Vienna Convention on Consular Relations, Art. 35(1).

[534] Vienna Convention on Consular Relations, Art. 36(1)(a).

email communications between consular officers and the sending State's nationals regarding official consular matters.

3.   The Experts noted that the Vienna Convention on Consular Relations uses the term 'permit and protect freedom of communication' in lieu of 'freedom communication', which more clearly conveys the object and purpose of the provision. For the Experts, the term 'permit' and the reference to 'freedom' mean that receiving States may not impede the capability of a diplomatic mission or consular post to communicate through cyber or other electronic means. For instance, they may not interfere with access to a diplomatic mission's or consular post's website that is used to convey essential information to its citizens in the country, interrupt or slow the Internet connection of a diplomatic mission or consular post, or block or interfere with its cell phones or other telecommunications equipment. The term 'permit' is not meant to imply that the sending State must seek the approval of the receiving State to engage in cyber communication.

4.   The obligations of a receiving State go beyond permitting the free cyber communication of a diplomatic mission or consular post. The receiving State must also take action to 'protect' their communications from interruption by others. The International Group of Experts was of the view that the same standard that applies to the duty to protect cyber infrastructure on the premises of a mission or post (Rule 40) extends to the protection of free cyber communication; a receiving State must take 'all appropriate steps' to ensure said protection. As with the protection of the cyber infrastructure, this is not an absolute duty. The specific obligation is proportionate to the risk and the dangers threatening the cyber communications.

5.   On the basis of the duty to protect, the Experts concurred that, for instance, should the authorities of the receiving State learn, from the sending State or any other source, that the sending State's cyber communications are being impeded, it must take appropriate steps to terminate the impediment. They also agreed that the receiving State is likewise obligated to take such measures to stop the interception of diplomatic cyber communications, including by other States (Rule 41), occurring on its territory.[535]

---

[535] Cyber communications present special challenges with regard to the obligation to protect. Consider the 2002 case in which unknown persons intercepted politically sensitive emails sent by the European Union's ambassador to Turkey, which were then shared with and published by a Turkish magazine. The Turkish government promised to investigate the incident and prosecute those involved, and after several days banned further publication of the emails, but it also observed that Internet surveillance is a widespread problem for which no State has been able to develop an effective response.

6. The Experts emphasised that the obligations of a receiving State to 'permit' and 'protect' are limited to cyber communications that are 'official'. For instance, if hackers in the receiving State are targeting a mission's or a post's official website, the receiving State must take those measures that are reasonably available to terminate the activity. Yet, a receiving State would not be obliged to permit and protect the capacity of diplomatic agents to engage in personal communications, for instance, through personal email accounts. The Experts acknowledged that it is sometimes difficult to distinguish between official and unofficial functions. This is particularly the case with regard to public diplomacy, which is directed at the receiving State's population. In the absence of *opinio juris* in this area, the Experts were unable to come to a definitive conclusion on this matter.

7. The International Group of Experts considered whether a receiving State is in violation of this Rule when it prohibits a diplomatic mission from establishing and operating an online presence, such as a website or social media account, on the basis that official business with the receiving State is required to be conducted with or through the Ministry for Foreign Affairs, or such other ministry as may be agreed, as set forth in Article 41(2) of the Vienna Convention on Diplomatic Relations. The Experts agreed that the requirement in Article 41(2) is only meant to clarify who within the receiving State's government should be the primary formal point of contact for official business between the sending and the receiving State. The Experts noted that many official business activities undertaken by foreign diplomatic agents in receiving States occur outside of these official channels; that it is customary for ambassadors and other diplomatic agents to give speeches to private audiences, hold roundtables, and otherwise interact on an official basis with private parties in the receiving State; and that these are accepted methods of exercising the diplomatic functions of representing the sending State, ascertaining conditions and developments in the receiving State, and promoting friendly relations between sending and receiving States.

Rule 43 – Use of premises and activities of officials

(a) **The premises of a diplomatic mission or consular post may not be used to engage in cyber activities that are incompatible with diplomatic or consular functions.**

(b) Diplomatic agents and consular officials may not engage in cyber activities that interfere in the internal affairs of the receiving State or are incompatible with the laws and regulations of that State.

1.   The premises of a diplomatic mission may not be used in any manner incompatible with the functions of a diplomatic mission.[536] Such functions include, but are not limited to:

(a) Representing the sending State in the receiving State;
(b) Protecting the interests of the sending State and of its nationals in the receiving State, within the limits permitted by international law;
(c) Negotiating with the Government of the receiving State;
(d) Ascertaining by all lawful means conditions and developments in the receiving State, and reporting thereon to the Government of the sending State; and
(e) Promoting friendly relations between the sending State and the receiving State, and developing economic, cultural, and scientific relations.[537]

2.   Similarly, consular posts may not be used in any manner incompatible with consular functions.[538] Consular functions of relevance to cyber activities include, but are not limited to:

(a) Protecting in the receiving State the interests of the sending State and of its nationals (both individuals and legal persons), within the limits permitted by international law;
(b) Furthering the development of commercial, economic, cultural, and scientific relations between the sending State and the receiving State;
(c) Ascertaining conditions and developments in the commercial, economic, cultural, and scientific life of the receiving State and reporting thereon to the sending State, as well as providing such information to interested persons;
(d) Issuing passports and travel documents to nationals of the sending State, and visas or appropriate documents to persons wishing to travel to the sending State;
(e) Assisting nationals, both individuals and bodies corporate, of the sending State; and

---

[536] Vienna Convention on Diplomatic Relations, Art. 41(3).
[537] Vienna Convention on Diplomatic Relations, Art. 3.
[538] Vienna Convention on Consular Relations, Art. 55(2).

(f) Transmitting judicial and extrajudicial documents or executing letters rogatory or commissions to take evidence for the courts of the sending State.[539]

3. For instance, a sending State may not use the premises of its diplomatic mission to engage in cyber espionage against the receiving State (see also discussion in Rule 41). Using a diplomatic mission's cyber infrastructure to engage in commercial activity, such as e-commerce, would likewise fail to qualify as a diplomatic function.

4. A separate issue is whether it is permissible for a sending State to use the premises of its diplomatic mission or consular post, without the consent of the receiving State, as a base to engage in cyber espionage directed at a third State, whether that espionage occurs against the third State's organs located in the receiving State or beyond it. A majority of the International Group of Experts concluded that such practices are prohibited by *lit.* (a) of this Rule since they are inconsistent with accepted diplomatic functions. A few of the Experts countered that diplomatic relations are bilateral in character and do not bring about obligations *vis-à-vis* third States. Furthermore, they suggested that insufficient State practice and expressions of *opinio juris* exist to conclude that such a prohibition has crystallised into customary international law. They pointed in particular to long-standing allegations of State practice to the contrary.

5. Reflected in *lit.* (b) is the fact that it is the duty of diplomatic agents and consular officers 'to respect the laws and regulations of the receiving State'.[540] For example, in most instances it would be a violation of *lit.* (b) for a diplomatic agent to engage in online piracy of intellectual property while in the receiving State because such activities are likely to violate the receiving State's laws and regulations.

6. Pursuant to *lit.* (b), diplomatic agents and consular officials are also prohibited from interfering in the internal affairs of the receiving State.[541] For instance, diplomatic agents may not use social media to plot the removal of the receiving State's government or participate 'in political campaigns'. On the other hand, they may engage in cyber activities 'for the purpose of protecting the interests of the diplomatic agent's country or of its nationals in accordance with international

---

[539] Vienna Convention on Consular Relations, Art. 5.
[540] Vienna Convention on Diplomatic Relations, Art. 41(1); Vienna Convention on Consular Relations, Art. 55(1).
[541] Vienna Convention on Diplomatic Relations, Art. 41(1); Vienna Convention on Consular Relations, Art. 55(1).

law'.[542] As an illustration, the Experts agreed that they may use social media to urge the release of their citizens from detention by the receiving State on the grounds that the detention is unlawful or otherwise inappropriate; they acknowledged a view that doing so constitutes interference in internal affairs, but disagreed with it.

7.   Due to their immunity from the receiving State's criminal, civil, and administrative process (Rule 44), diplomatic agents may not be subjected to enforcement or judicial jurisdiction (Rules 8–9) for engaging in activities that violate this Rule. They may be declared *persona non grata*, which would require the sending State to withdraw them.

8.   Both the Vienna Convention on Diplomatic Relations and the Vienna Convention on Consular Relations provide that a diplomatic mission and a consular post, respectively, may install and use a 'wireless transmitter' only with the consent of the receiving State.[543] At the time of the drafting of the Conventions, wireless transmitters were primarily used for radio transmissions. The International Group of Experts opined that this treaty language is to an extent dated and its precise translation to cyber technologies is not entirely clear. In particular, the Experts took the view that equipment that generally emits radio frequency signals only within the perimeter of a diplomatic mission or consular post, such as a wireless router, falls outside of the rule. But the Experts did agree that as new forms of wireless technology emerge, this principle should continue to require the receiving State's consent for the installation and use of equipment that allows the diplomatic mission or consular post to transmit communications beyond its premises. This would include the installation of all types of wireless communication equipment (e.g., for satellite communications) when their use is capable of causing harmful interference with wireless communications in the receiving State (on harmful interference, see also Rule 63).

Rule 44 – Privileges and immunities of diplomatic agents and consular officers

To the extent diplomatic agents and consular officers enjoy immunities from criminal, civil, and administrative jurisdiction, they enjoy the immunities with regard to their cyber activities.

---

[542] Yearbook of the International Law Commission, Vol. II (1958), at 104.

[543] Vienna Convention on Diplomatic Relations, Art.27(1); Vienna Convention on Consular Relations, Art. 35(1).

1.   This Rule sets forth the immunities enjoyed by diplomatic agents and consular officers. Such immunities may always be waived by the sending State.[544]

2.   Diplomatic agents are entitled to immunity from the criminal jurisdiction of the receiving State for any activity that qualifies as cyber crime under the receiving State's domestic laws while present in the country.[545] This diplomatic immunity is absolute and unqualified. They also enjoy immunity from arrest and are exempt from the obligation to give evidence as a witness.[546] Following completion of their diplomatic functions and departure from the receiving State, the privileges and immunities normally cease, although immunity for acts performed in the exercise of official functions continues (Rule 12).[547]

3.   Diplomatic agents also enjoy immunity from the receiving State's civil and administrative jurisdiction with respect to their cyber activities, except in the case of certain actions relating to 'private immovable' (or 'real') property, succession, and any of the diplomatic agent's professional or commercial activities that were engaged in while in the receiving State and outside his or her official functions.[548] For example, a diplomatic agent might not enjoy immunity from civil or administrative jurisdiction for selling goods online as a personal business.

4.   Consular officers are entitled to more limited immunity from the criminal and civil jurisdiction of the receiving State for their cyber activities.[549] In particular, they do not enjoy absolute immunity from the receiving State's criminal jurisdiction; however, they are not liable to arrest or detention pending trial, except in the case of a grave crime, and pursuant to a decision by a competent judicial authority.[550]

---

[544] Vienna Convention on Diplomatic Relations, Art. 32(1); Vienna Convention on Consular Relations, Art. 45(1).
[545] Vienna Convention on Diplomatic Relations, Art. 31(1). Members of the family of a diplomatic agent, administrative, and technical staff, and others associated with the mission are entitled to specific privileges and immunities. Vienna Convention on Diplomatic Relations, Art. 37.
[546] Vienna Convention on Diplomatic Relations, Arts. 29, 31(2).
[547] Vienna Convention on Diplomatic Relations, Art. 39(2).
[548] Vienna Convention on Diplomatic Relations, Art. 31(1).
[549] Compare Vienna Convention on Diplomatic Relations, Art. 29, with Vienna Convention on Consular Relations, Arts. 41, 43–44.
[550] Vienna Convention on Consular Relations, Art. 41. Note that honorary consular officers do not enjoy immunity from criminal proceedings. Vienna Convention on Consular Relations, Art. 63.

8

Law of the sea

1.   The international law of the sea provides normative guidance on operations that emanate from or are carried out at sea. The International Group of Experts agreed that it is applicable to cyber operations conducted from or through cyber infrastructure located in seas (for the purposes of this Manual, the term 'seas' is interpreted to include oceans). Cyber operations may be mounted from ships and submarines (hereinafter collectively referred to as 'vessels') at sea, aircraft above the seas, offshore installations, or through submarine communication cables, both in peacetime and during armed conflict.

2.   To a great extent, the rules of the customary international law of the sea are reflected in the Law of the Sea Convention. Even States that are not Parties to the Law of the Sea Convention adhere to the terms of the treaty in most respects.[551] This Chapter draws heavily on those provisions of the Convention that the Experts agreed restate customary international law.

3.   With limited exceptions, vessels on the high seas (see definition in Rule 45) are subject to the principle of 'exclusive flag State jurisdiction'.[552] Exclusive flag State jurisdiction is a cardinal doctrine of the law of the sea. It provides that the flag State has full jurisdiction (Rule 8) over vessels flying its flag.[553] The Experts concurred that such jurisdiction includes jurisdiction over cyber operations conducted from the vessels.

4.   Flag States may, however, consent to the exercise of enforcement jurisdiction by other States aboard vessels flying its flag. Such consent may be expressed through an international agreement or on an *ad hoc*

---

[551] *See, e.g.*, Statement by the President, United States Ocean Policy, 10 March 1983; Communication of the Government of Turkey, 21 December 1995, 30 Law of the Sea Bulletin 9.

[552] Law of the Sea Convention, Arts. 92, 94.

[553] Law of the Sea Convention, Arts. 91–92.

basis (on consent, see also Rule 19). Vessels may also be subject to coastal State jurisdiction depending on their location, activity, and whether they are shielded from coastal State jurisdiction due to their sovereign immune status (Rule 5). Additionally, individuals engaged in cyber activities aboard vessels are subject to prescriptive jurisdiction on the bases set forth in Rule 10.

5. The international law of the sea is a peacetime regime. Although it generally applies *mutatis mutandis* during periods of armed conflict (Rules 82–83), there are a number of permissive rules and prohibitions, and some nuances, that are imposed by the law of naval warfare as between belligerent States, and between belligerent and neutral States. Consequently, parties to an armed conflict do not forfeit their rights as flag States, port States, or coastal States under the international law of the sea, or become released from their duties and obligations, except insofar as certain provisions of the law of the sea are modified or supplanted by particular rules of the law of naval warfare. One example is that States engaged in an armed conflict at sea may exercise 'mere passage' (Rule 49) through neutral State territorial seas, as distinct from the peacetime regime of 'innocent passage' (Rule 48). The regime of mere passage contains armed conflict and neutrality specific nuances that restrict or regulate conduct that would otherwise be permissible pursuant to the regime of innocent passage.

Rule 45 – Cyber operations on the high seas

Cyber operations on the high seas may be conducted only for peaceful purposes, except as otherwise provided for under international law.

1. As used in this Rule, the 'high seas' refers to 'all parts of the sea that are not included in the exclusive economic zone, in the territorial sea, or in the internal waters of a State, or in the archipelagic waters of an archipelagic State'.[554] A special legal regime attaches to the exclusive economic zone (EEZ) and is dealt with in Rule 47. With respect to cyber operations in territorial seas and archipelagic waters, see Rules 48 and 53, respectively.

2. Pursuant to Article 88 of the Law of the Sea Convention, which the International Group of Experts considered reflective of customary international law, the high seas are reserved for 'peaceful purposes'. The

---

[554] Law of the Sea Convention, Art. 86.

term 'peaceful purposes' in this Rule is defined by reference to Article 301 of the Convention, which restates the prohibition of the threat or use of force (Rule 68).[555]

3. The International Group of Experts agreed that there is no rationale for excluding cyber activities from the scope of the notion of 'high seas freedoms'[556] and other lawful uses of the seas. Of particular note in the cyber context are the high seas freedoms of navigation, overflight, and the laying of submarine cables.[557] Based on, for example, the first two freedoms, both aircraft and vessels are entitled to conduct cyber operations over and in the high seas so long as they do not violate applicable international law. The freedom to lay submarine communication cables is dealt with in Rule 54. In the high seas, these freedoms must be exercised with due regard for the exercise of high seas freedoms by other States.[558]

4. As noted in Article 58(1) of the Law of the Sea Convention, a number of these freedoms, including the three previously mentioned, are also available in the EEZ. In light of the requirement for due regard with respect to coastal State interests, which caveats the exercise of these freedoms in the EEZ, the EEZ is treated separately in this Chapter (Rule 47).

5. The Experts concurred that military cyber operations *per se* do not violate this Rule. They saw no reason to deviate from the general principle that military activities not involving a prohibited use of force are within the scope of high seas freedoms and other internationally lawful uses of the sea, as set forth in Article 87(1) of the Law of the Sea Convention.[559] However, the Experts also noted that, on a more limited geographic scale, certain specific military operations – including cyber operations – could constitute a breach of a treaty commitment in relation to a sea area (including parts of the high seas). One example is the Antarctic Treaty regime, which prohibits military operations in that region for Parties thereto.[560] Such treaties are binding solely on the Parties to them.

6. The International Group of Experts agreed that establishment of undersea data centres in the high seas is lawful. In the EEZ or territorial

---

[555] The term 'peaceful purposes' is also referenced in the Law of the Sea Convention, Arts. 141, 143(1), 147(2)(d), 155(2), 240(a), 242(1), 246(3), 301.
[556] Law of the Sea Convention, Art. 87.   [557] Law of the Sea Convention, Art. 87(1)(a–c).
[558] Law of the Sea Convention, Art. 87(2).   [559] *Nicaragua* judgment, para. 227.
[560] Antarctic Treaty, Art. I, 1 December 1959, 402 UNTS 71.

sea, such centres may be established with the consent of the coastal State only and their operation is subject to regulation by, and the jurisdiction of (Rule 9), that State.[561]

7.   The caveat 'except as otherwise provided for under international law' in this Rule is intended to emphasise that the law of naval warfare permits certain cyber operations on the high seas within the context of an international armed conflict (Rule 82) that would otherwise be prohibited during peacetime. To illustrate, military cyber operations may be conducted in support of a blockade (Rule 128). Similarly, a cyber attack (Rule 92) upon a merchant vessel reasonably believed to be breaching a blockade is lawful if the vessel, 'after prior warning, clearly resist[s] capture'.[562]

8.   Only States are bound by this Rule in their cyber operations. Activities of non-State actors at sea may be unlawful as a crime under international or domestic law, but they do not implicate the restriction reflected in this Rule unless they are attributable to a State (Rules 15 and 17). The International Group of Experts acknowledged, however, a view according to which non-State actors can violate various prohibitions bearing on activities at sea.

Rule 46 – The right of visit and cyber operations

A warship or other duly authorised vessel may exercise the right of visit to board a vessel without flag State consent on the high seas or within an exclusive economic zone if it has reasonable grounds for suspecting the vessel is utilising cyber means to engage in piracy, slave trading, or unauthorised broadcasting; appears to be without nationality; or is of the nationality of the visiting vessel.

1.   Due to the principle of exclusive flag State jurisdiction (chapeau to this Chapter), warships or other duly authorised vessels may generally not interfere, absent flag State consent, with vessels that are not of their nationality on the high seas. However, in certain specified situations they may do so. The International Group of Experts agreed that the

---

[561] The consent of the coastal State is required for establishment in the territorial sea as it exercises sovereignty over that area and its seabed (Rule 2). As to establishment in the EEZ, *see* Law of the Sea Convention, Art. 60(1–2), specifically the reference to installations and structures for economic purposes.

[562] SAN REMO MANUAL, Rule 98.

'right of visit' set forth in Article 110 of the Law of the Sea Convention reflects customary international law. It provides warships or other duly authorised vessels the legal authority to board foreign non-sovereign immune vessels that they encounter on the high seas when there is a 'reasonable ground for suspecting' that any of the five situations set forth in this Rule is present – the vessel is engaged in piracy, slave trading, or unauthorised broadcasting; the vessel appears to be without nationality; or the vessel is of the nationality of the visiting vessel, even when flying a foreign flag or refusing to show its flag. The same customary law right is codified in Article 58 for an EEZ.

2.   The term 'duly authorised vessel' denotes a vessel authorised by the flag State to engage in enforcement action and clearly recognisable as such.

3.   The International Group of Experts noted that social media could contribute to a finding of reasonable grounds for suspecting a vessel of conduct giving rise to a right of visit. For instance, if persons on board the vessel publish a Twitter post concerning their intention to commit acts of piracy, this could heighten suspicion as to the vessel's conduct.

4.   The scope of the actions the boarding State may subsequently take depends on the circumstances, including which of the five situations is involved. The Experts agreed that the three most relevant to cyber activities are piracy, unauthorised broadcasting, and disguising nationality.

5.   With respect to 'piracy', a warship or other duly authorised vessel may seize a vessel on the high seas or in the EEZ that is engaged in that unlawful activity and arrest persons suspected of being inudved.[563] In order to do so, it may board the vessel in the exercise of its right of visit.[564] Cyber means could be used to facilitate an act of piracy.[565] For instance, they might be used to render a vessel immobile or unable to communicate with warships that could come to its assistance. Should there be reasonable grounds for suspecting that these or other piracy-related cyber activities are taking place, the right of visit would apply.

6.   'Unauthorised broadcasting' is defined as 'the transmission of sound, radio or television broadcasts from a ship or installation on the high seas intended for reception by the general public contrary to

---

[563] Law of the Sea Convention, Arts. 101, 105.
[564] Law of the Sea Convention, Art. 110(1)(a).
[565] Law of the Sea Convention, Art. 101(c).

international regulations, but excluding the transmission of distress calls'.[566] A warship or other duly authorised vessel is entitled to visit and put an end to unauthorized broadcasting so long as it enjoys jurisdiction for that specific purpose.[567] Such vessels include those of 'any State where the transmissions can be received' or 'any State where authorised radio communication is suffering interference'.[568] The phenomenon of streaming radio and television content from aboard a vessel on the high seas or in the EEZ via the Internet arguably supports application of this authority in the cyber context. The Experts noted, however, that the prohibition is limited to broadcasting designed for public consumption.

7. The International Group of Experts considered the issue of whether using other online means to disseminate information from aboard vessels on the high seas or in the EEZ, such as on social media platforms like Twitter, Vkontakte.ru, or Facebook, qualifies as broadcasting for the purposes of this Rule. The Experts rejected any such extension of the prohibition. They pointed to the prohibition's object and purpose, which is primarily focused on broadcasting that is not in compliance with international regulation, such as the regulation of broadcasting frequencies under international telecommunication law (see also Rule 63), and that produces negative effects on maritime and air communications. Posting of online material from the high seas poses no such risks. The Experts also observed that whether online material is posted from a vessel on the high seas or in the EEZ or from a city a continent away, the end result is identical. Therefore, they would limit the prohibition to those forms of broadcasting expressly set forth in the definition above.[569]

8. All warships and other duly authorised vessels enjoy the right of visit with respect to vessels that appear to be without nationality, even in situations in which they are feigning a particular nationality.[570] Sometimes a vessel may display or transmit no indications of nationality.

[566] Law of the Sea Convention, Art. 109(2). The Experts noted that, with respect to the reference to 'international regulations' in Article 109(2), no such regulations had been adopted at the time of adoption of the Manual.
[567] Law of the Sea Convention, Arts. 110(1)(c), 58(2).
[568] Law of the Sea Convention, Art. 109(3–4).
[569] Note also that the Experts agreed that as a general matter, the transmission of propaganda does not constitute a prohibited intervention as it is not coercive in nature (Rule 66).
[570] Law of the Sea Convention, Art. 110(1)(d).

A suspicious electronic nationality indicator could also provide the requisite suspicion to permit a right of visit on this basis.

9.   If there are reasonable grounds for suspecting that a vessel, though flying a foreign flag or refusing to show its flag, is of the same nationality as the warship or other duly authorised vessel, the latter may exercise its right of visit to verify the vessel's nationality.[571] For instance, cyber means could be employed to hide the vessel's true identity and nationality, such as by providing a false automatic identification system (AIS) identity.

10.   The International Group of Experts was split with respect to whether the right of visit can be carried out virtually. Some Experts were of the view that such a 'virtual visit' is a reasonable exercise of the traditional right of visit. As an example, eligible vessels may use cyber means to verify the nationality of the vessel concerned by monitoring its communications or inspect its cyber infrastructure remotely when suspicion remains that the vessel is engaged in the activities set forth in this Rule. These Experts opined that a virtual visit is less intrusive than a physical visit and, therefore, appropriately encompassed in the notion of 'right of visit'. Moreover, they suggested that a virtual inspection is consistent with the object and purpose of the right of visit and that Article 110 does not restrict the means used to conduct a visit. The Experts noted that if the right of visit can be exercised both physically and virtually, the ability to conduct a virtual visit does not prejudice the right to engage in a physical one.

11.   The other Experts noted that the examination envisioned in Article 110(2) following the checking of the vessel's documents is one that occurs 'on board the ship'. In their view, to extend the inspection to encompass cyber means would run counter to the plain text of the Article. They therefore rejected the possibility of a right to conduct a virtual visit. Moreover, these Experts took the position that virtual inspection would likely be more intrusive than conducting an inspection of documents aboard the vessel since it would presumably involve access to more information than necessary to verify nationality. Although the vessel's communications may be of a nature to confirm or rebut a claim of nationality, they may also be unrelated to that issue. If at all, these Experts would recognise the lawfulness of exercising the right of visit

---

[571] Law of the Sea Convention, Art. 110(1)(e), 110(2).

virtually if the visit is limited to accessing information that is subject to physical inspection under the right of visit.

12. This Rule is without prejudice to other bases under international law for boarding a vessel, such as consent of the flag State or UN Security Council authorisation.

Rule 47 – Cyber operations in the exclusive economic zone

In the exercise of its rights and duties, a State conducting cyber operations in the exclusive economic zone of another State must have due regard to that State's rights and duties in the zone and the cyber operations must be conducted for peaceful purposes, except as otherwise provided for under international law.

1. The exclusive economic zone is an area beyond the territorial sea that may not extend more than 200 nautical miles seaward of the respective State's baselines.[572] Within the EEZ, the coastal State has sovereign rights and jurisdiction for the purposes of exploration, exploitation, management, and conservation of the natural resources of the water column, seabed, and subsoil of the zone, as well as for the production of energy from the water, currents, and winds.[573] In their EEZ, States may also exercise jurisdiction over the establishment and use of artificial islands, installations, and structures having economic purposes; marine scientific research;[574] and certain incidents of vessel source pollution.[575] For example, cyber activities that interfere with energy production facilities lying within the EEZ, such as wind farms or tidal current turbines, would be within the jurisdictional competence of the coastal State.

2. All States enjoy the high seas freedoms of navigation and overflight, and of laying submarine cables (Rule 54) and pipelines, within an EEZ, as well as other internationally lawful uses of the sea related to these freedoms.[576] Thus, for instance, aircraft and vessels may rely on cyber capabilities for navigational and communication purposes while in another State's EEZ and States are free to lay, or authorise companies over which they exercise jurisdiction to lay, submarine communication cables on the seabed of another State's EEZ, so long as due regard is paid to the coastal State's EEZ rights and duties.

---

[572] Law of the Sea Convention, Art. 57.   [573] Law of the Sea Convention, Arts. 55–56.
[574] Law of the Sea Convention, Art. 56(1)(b).   [575] Law of the Sea Convention, Art. 211.
[576] Law of the Sea Convention, Arts. 58(1), 87.

3.   A coastal State enjoys certain specified sovereign rights in its EEZ (that are primarily related to resources). The majority of the International Group of Experts agreed that vessels and aircraft of all nationalities enjoy those high seas freedoms in the EEZ that do not unduly impinge upon any of the enumerated sovereign rights of the coastal State therein, or that otherwise violate its rights. These Experts pointed out that the Convention fails to mention any security interest in the EEZ and, indeed, requires due regard only to the coastal State's 'rights and duties', rather than to its interests more generally. Accordingly, military activities, such as overflight by military aircraft, naval task force manoeuvring, military exercises, surveillance, survey activities, reconnaissance and intelligence collection, and ordnance testing and firing, are permissible in another State's EEZ, subject to due regard for coastal States rights. In particular, warships and military aircraft that have cyber operations capabilities are free to navigate and operate in and through an EEZ. Consent of the coastal State is not required.

4.   A few of the Experts took the position that some military activities, including activities associated with intelligence functions and cyber operations, may not be conducted within the EEZ of a coastal State without that State's consent. They noted that Article 58(3) of the Law of the Sea Convention emphasises that due regard must be paid to rights and duties of the coastal State, which they understood as including security. The majority responded that military activities typically have no bearing on the enjoyment of the limited sovereign rights and jurisdiction enjoyed by the coastal State in the EEZ. However, all of the Experts agreed that marine scientific research intended for the 'benefit of all mankind', including that conducted by the military, requires consent due to express language to that effect in the Law of the Sea Convention.[577]

5.   The phrase 'except as otherwise provided for under international law' in this Rule is intended to emphasise that, for instance, the concept of 'peaceful purposes' (Rule 45) does not prohibit the taking of countermeasures, including cyber countermeasures, from within an EEZ. Nor does it prohibit States from conducting belligerent operations against each other, in accordance with the law of naval warfare, in an EEZ.[578] Belligerent operations must comply, however, with the rules of naval

---

[577] Law of the Sea Convention, Arts. 56(1)(b)(ii), 246(3).
[578] Article 58(2) of the Law of the Sea Convention applies the principle of peaceful purposes to the EEZ.

warfare, as well as with the requirement of due regard to the coastal State's rights and duties when that State is neutral in the conflict.[579]

Rule 48 – Cyber operations in the territorial sea

In order for a vessel to claim the right of innocent passage through a coastal State's territorial sea, any cyber operations conducted by the vessel must comply with the conditions imposed on that right.

1. Coastal States are entitled to claim a territorial sea that extends up to 12 nautical miles from baselines determined in accordance with international law as reflected in the Law of the Sea Convention.[580] States enjoy sovereignty over the territorial sea, the seabed below it, and the airspace above it.[581] As a result, they enjoy, *inter alia*, the rights set forth in Rule 2.

2. In parallel with coastal State sovereignty over the territorial sea, vessels of all States, including warships, enjoy the right of innocent passage through that area. The innocent passage regime requires continuous and expeditious transit through the territorial sea. It also encompasses transit through those waters when proceeding to or from that coastal State's internal or archipelagic waters.[582] Submarines must transit on the surface and show their flag in order to claim the right of innocent passage.[583] Aircraft do not enjoy the right of innocent passage (Rule 55).

3. The International Group of Experts agreed that the right of innocent passage is not dependent upon prior consent by, or notification to, the coastal State. However, the Experts acknowledged that certain States take the position that transit through a territorial sea by warships requires the consent of, or notification to, the coastal State.[584]

4. The regime of innocent passage does not apply in waters seaward of the territorial sea or in internal waters. Sovereign immune vessels

---

[579] SAN REMO MANUAL, Rule 34.   [580] Law of the Sea Convention, Art. 3.
[581] Law of the Sea Convention, Art. 2.   [582] Law of the Sea Convention, Arts. 17–18.
[583] Law of the Sea Convention, Art. 20.
[584] *See, e.g.*, Law on the Territorial Sea and the Contiguous Zone of the Republic of China, Arts. 6, 7 (25 February 1992); Act on the Marine Areas of the Islamic Republic of Iran in the Persian Gulf and the Oman Sea, Art. 9 (2 May 1993). A number of other States also seek to impose this requirement on warships. For a collection of maritime claims in this and other regards, see, Maritime Claims Reference Manual, DoD Representative for Ocean Policy Affairs, 5 November 2014.

242   SPECIALISED REGIMES

generally require diplomatic clearance from the coastal State for entry into internal waters from the territorial sea or archipelagic waters.

5.   A coastal State may temporarily suspend innocent passage in specified areas if such suspension is essential for the protection of its security; suspension must be non-discriminatory among foreign vessels.[585] For instance, a State may suspend passage temporarily in order to conduct military exercises involving cyber operations if the presence of other vessels may present a cyber security risk.

6.   Passage remains innocent so long as it is not prejudicial to the peace, good order, or security of the coastal State.[586] The International Group of Experts agreed that the various bases for precluding passage as 'innocent' set forth in Article 19(2) of the Law of the Sea Convention reflect customary international law. For example, the following cyber activities based on certain aspects of the Article would render passage non-innocent:

(1) the unlawful threat or use of force by cyber means (Rule 68) against the coastal State;
(2) exercise or practice involving cyber-enabled weapons that is not limited solely to the ship and its systems;[587]
(3) cyber activities designed to collect information prejudicial to the security of the coastal State;
(4) propaganda distributed by cyber means bearing on the defence or security of the coastal State;
(5) the launching, landing, or taking on board of aircraft or other military devices, including those that engage in, or are capable of conducting, cyber operations;
(6) research or survey activities, including those conducted through cyber or cyber facilitated means;
(7) cyber operations intended to interfere with communication systems or other facilities or installations of the coastal State; and
(8) any other cyber activity having no direct bearing on passage.

7.   This list is not exhaustive. For example, the International Group of Experts agreed that providing wireless access points to an insurgent

[585] Law of the Sea Convention, Art. 25(3).   [586] Law of the Sea Convention, Art. 19(1).
[587] The text 'that is not internal to the ship and its systems' acknowledges that cyber weapons testing may be limited to the vessel itself, specifically the cyber infrastructure therein. The International Group of Experts agreed that since such an activity had no effect beyond the vessel, it does not render passage non-innocent.

group whose communications are being blocked by the coastal State would also be prohibited. The activity is clearly prejudicial to the security of the coastal State.

8.   The Experts discussed situations involving passive (non-intrusive) assessments of wireless networks by vessels in innocent passage. A majority of them was of the view that such activities are consistent with the innocent passage regime because they are passive in nature. The minority was of the opposite view on the basis that such assessments have little to do with passage and are accordingly contrary to the interests of the coastal State.

9.   The Experts also discussed the issue of conducting cyber operations directed at third States, or non-State actors located in third States, while transiting the territorial sea. The majority concluded that cyber activities undertaken while in innocent passage must not prejudice the security or good order of the coastal State, including its relations with other States and its duties with respect to those States. To illustrate, hacking into a third State's defence network would be, for them, incompatible with innocent passage and could compromise the good order of the coastal State by affecting its relations with other States.

10.   The minority took the position that each case must be assessed on its merits, emphasising in particular that the object and purpose of the innocent passage regime is to safeguard key interests of the coastal State, not third States or non-State actors. They opined that cyber operations against third States or non-State actors do not directly run afoul of the innocent passage regime in that regard. As to affecting the coastal State's relations with other States, these Experts suggested that an array of factors must be considered to determine whether the cyber operations in fact were detrimental to the coastal State's good order and security. In particular, the nature of the cyber operations, the extent to which they are overt, and the current state of relations between the coastal State and the third State or non-State actors are relevant factors.

11.   The International Group of Experts agreed that vessels engaged in innocent passage may undertake cyber activities that are necessary to ensure their safety and security (and that of any vessels that they are accompanying), so long as the activities do not prejudice the peace, good order, or security of the coastal State. For instance, a vessel may monitor its cyber infrastructure in order to ensure that it is not being subjected to hostile cyber operations and receive patches to fix vulnerabilities. Moreover, in the event the vessel is the target of hostile cyber operations,

it may take actions to terminate them by cyber means that are otherwise consistent with international legal regimes, including, when appropriate, self-defence (Rule 71). As an example, if a coastal State conducts cyber operations that violate its obligation not to hamper the innocent passage of a warship, thereby committing an internationally wrongful act (Rule 14), the flag State may respond, *inter alia*, with countermeasures (Rule 20).

12.   Vessels lacking sovereign immunity (Rule 5) that are engaged in innocent passage are required to comply with certain laws and regulations of the coastal State. Coastal States may sometimes exercise civil and criminal jurisdiction over such vessels.[588] For example, the coastal State may adopt laws and regulations in respect of the safety of navigation that bear on cyber activities.[589] Additionally, the coastal State may promulgate laws and regulations regarding the protection of submarine communication cables (Rule 54) passing through the territorial sea that apply to vessels in innocent passage.[590]

13.   This Rule applies *mutatis mutandis* to innocent passage through archipelagic waters that are not within archipelagic sea lanes[591] or, where archipelagic sea lanes have not been designated, 'routes normally used for international navigation'.[592] In exercising the right of archipelagic sea lanes passage (Rule 53), however, transit may be conducted in 'normal mode'.[593]

14.   While the coastal State may assert certain criminal and civil jurisdiction over non-sovereign immune vessels engaged in non-innocent passage, such jurisdiction is unavailable to the coastal State with respect to sovereign immune vessels. If a sovereign immune vessel is conducting cyber activities that are inconsistent with the right of innocent passage, the coastal State's remedy is to 'require' the vessel immediately to depart.[594] The International Group of Experts agreed that doing so can ultimately include forceful measures. Thus, the use of forcible cyber operations designed to compel the recalcitrant sovereign immune vessel to depart the territorial sea is a permissible measure available to the coastal State. The Experts acknowledged a view by which States may not resort to force, including cyber force, in such circumstances.

---

[588] Law of the Sea Convention, Arts. 27–28.   [589] Law of the Sea Convention, Art. 22.
[590] Law of the Sea Convention, Art. 21(1).   [591] Law of the Sea Convention, Art. 52.
[592] Law of the Sea Convention, Art. 53(12).   [593] Law of the Sea Convention, Art. 53(3).
[594] Law of the Sea Convention, Art. 30. *See also* Arts. 25, 95–96.

15. This Rule is without prejudice to any other applicable international law prohibitions on cyber operations, such as those prohibiting the violation of sovereignty (Rule 4) or intervention (Rule 66).

Rule 49 – Cyber operations in the territorial sea during armed conflict

During an international armed conflict, a neutral coastal State may not discriminate between the belligerents with respect to cyber operations in that State's territorial sea.

1. During periods of international armed conflict (Rule 82), the laws of naval warfare and neutrality (Chapter 20) overlay the peacetime law of the sea regime. The law of neutrality prohibits belligerents from using neutral ports and waters as a base of operations against their adversaries.[595] However, neutral coastal States may permit, but are not obligated to allow, 'mere passage' through their territorial sea by belligerent warships.[596] They may also impose conditions and restrictions on such passage, but if they do so, they must apply them equally to the warships of all the belligerents.[597]

2. During mere passage, warships may not use the neutral waters 'as a base of naval operations against their adversaries'[598] or otherwise engage in belligerent activities (i.e., activities related to the armed conflict). This includes conducting cyber operations against adversaries while transiting the territorial sea of a neutral State, although warships engaged in mere passage may conduct cyber operations to ensure the security of the vessel. Moreover, belligerent States may not mount cyber operations from outside a neutral's territorial waters against enemy warships engaged in mere passage.

3. It will often be difficult for the neutral State to 'observe' belligerent cyber operations emanating from, or directed against, a vessel in its territorial sea. Should such activities nevertheless come to the notice of that State, the law of neutrality requires that it take action to end them. This may be accomplished by, but need not be limited to, cyber means.

4. The 1907 Hague Convention XIII prohibits a belligerent from erecting 'any apparatus for the purpose of communicating with the

---

[595] Hague Convention XIII, Art. 5.   [596] Hague Convention XIII, Arts. 9–10.
[597] Hague Convention XIII, Art. 9.   [598] Hague Convention XIII, Art. 5.

belligerent forces on land or sea' in neutral territory or waters.[599]
The International Group of Experts agreed that the Rule would
prohibit the emplacement of cyber infrastructure not already aboard
a warship in these areas.

Rule 50 – Exercise of jurisdiction in relation to foreign vessels in the territorial sea

A coastal State may exercise enforcement jurisdiction on-board vessels in the territorial sea with respect to criminal activities involving cyber operations if: the consequences of the crime extend to the coastal State; the crime is of a kind to disturb the public order and security of the coastal State or the good order of the territorial sea; the master of the vessel or the flag State has requested the assistance of the coastal State's authorities; or as necessary to counter drug trafficking.

1.   This Rule is based on Article 27 of the Law of the Sea Convention,
which the International Group of Experts agreed reflects customary
international law. As a general matter, authorities of the coastal State
may not arrest individuals or conduct investigations on-board a vessel
flagged by another State whilst that vessel is in the coastal State's territorial waters. The Rule sets forth four well-accepted peacetime exceptions
to this prohibition.[600]

2.   The International Group of Experts acknowledged a debate as to
whether the list of grounds contained in Article 27 is exhaustive.[601] Since
general consensus only exists as to the four enumerated grounds, the
Experts limited the text of the Rule to those.

3.   The notion of 'consequences extending', which has been
adopted in this Rule, is undefined in the Law of the Sea Convention.
The International Group of Experts agreed, however, that the coastal
State may exercise enforcement jurisdiction on-board a vessel in its
territorial sea if cyber operations or activities emanating from it violate
the criminal law of the coastal State and manifest on that State's

---

[599] Hague Convention XIII, Art. 5.   [600] Law of the Sea Convention, Art. 27(1)(a–d).

[601] *See, e.g.,* UNITED NATIONS CONVENTION ON THE LAW OF THE SEA 1982: A COMMENTARY,
University of Virginia Center for Oceans Law and Policy (Myron H. Nordquist, *et al.,*
eds. 2011) (limiting the grounds to the four enumerated in Article 27.). *But see*
R. R. CHURCHILL & A. V. LOWE, THE LAW OF THE SEA 97 (3rd edn 1999) (suggesting that
use of the term 'should not be exercised' in the Article was intended to indicate that the
grounds therein are not exhaustive).

territory, including its territorial waters. For instance, a DDoS operation initiated from aboard a vessel against cyber infrastructure
located in the coastal State that violates the coastal State's domestic
law would qualify.

4. The Experts were divided as to whether the consequences that
manifest must be significant in scale. A minority of the Experts was of the
view that consequences that are *de minimis* or trivial do not open the
door to coastal State criminal enforcement jurisdiction. By contrast,
the majority was of the view that any violation of the coastal State's law
sufficed for attachment of the coastal State's jurisdiction.

5. The International Group of Experts agreed that any cyber
operation conducted from a foreign vessel in the territorial sea that
has widespread effects and is therefore disruptive in the coastal State
would also entitle that State to exercise enforcement jurisdiction
aboard the vessel concerned. Breaches of the 'good order of the
territorial sea' could include using cyber means to interfere with the
navigational systems of other vessels in the territorial sea and interfering with communications between them or with shore stations that
are necessary for safe navigation (see also Rule 63 on harmful
interference).

6. Cyber activity related to illegal narcotic drug trafficking provides a
further basis for the exercise of criminal enforcement jurisdiction aboard
foreign vessels in the territorial sea. Consider the situation of a State
monitoring cyber communications in certain vessels located in its territorial sea based on leads provided to law enforcement authorities. Should
the authorities identify any communications indicating the vessel is being
used for the illegal transportation of drugs, they may use cyber means to
facilitate halting the vessel.

7. If a crime involving cyber activity occurs on-board an
offending non-sovereign immune vessel before it departs the coastal
State's internal waters, the State may engage in enforcement jurisdiction aboard the vessel, as provided for in its own domestic law, while
the vessel is located in the territorial sea.[602] With certain exceptions,
coastal State authorities may not assert enforcement jurisdiction over
vessels in the territorial sea in relation to offences involving cyber
activities committed before the vessel entered the territorial sea.
This remains the case so long as the vessel is engaged in innocent

---

[602] Law of the Sea Convention, Art. 27(2).

passage through the territorial sea without at any time entering the internal waters of the coastal State.[603]

8. As distinct from criminal enforcement jurisdiction, coastal States may not exercise civil enforcement jurisdiction over cyber activities or those involved in cyber activities by stopping or diverting foreign vessels passing through the State's territorial sea.[604] Although innocent passage cannot be impeded or interrupted in order to exercise civil jurisdiction over a person on-board a foreign vessel in the territorial sea, this Rule does not prevent the coastal State or any other legal person from filing civil suit against the vessel, a member of the crew, or a passenger in a subsequent proceeding. Moreover, the limitation on exercising civil enforcement jurisdiction does apply to situations in which the vessel itself assumed or incurred the obligations or liabilities in the course, or for the purpose, of transit through the territorial sea.[605]

9. As noted above, this Rule is without prejudice to the application of reciprocal treaty rights and obligations that may be accepted by coastal and flag States. It is also without prejudice to the fact that during an international armed conflict, a neutral coastal State must take those actions that are necessary to ensure warships in 'mere passage' are complying with their obligation to refrain from belligerent cyber activities (Rule 49). Additionally, as provided for in Rule 76, the existence of a relevant UN Security Council Chapter VII mandate or authorisation can permit cyber operations in the territorial sea, even if those operations would otherwise be characterised as a breach of innocent passage.

Rule 51 – Cyber operations in the contiguous zone

With respect to vessels located in a coastal State's contiguous zone, that State may use cyber means to prevent or address violations within its territory or territorial sea of its fiscal, immigration, sanitary, or customs laws, including violations perpetrated by cyber means.

---

[603] Law of the Sea Convention, Art. 27(5). In such a case, however, authorities may act nonetheless to enforce exceptions contained in Part XII of the Law of the Sea Convention concerning certain criminal matters relating to marine environmental protection, as well as criminal matters relating to living and non-living resources – most prominently fishing – in the EEZ.

[604] Law of the Sea Convention, Art. 28.   [605] Law of the Sea Convention, Art. 28(3).

1.   States may claim a contiguous zone that extends from the limit of the territorial sea up to twenty-four nautical miles from their baselines.[606] In the area of the zone seaward of the territorial sea, the coastal State enjoys two extensions of its authority. The first is the sovereign right to enforce its fiscal, immigration, sanitary, and customs laws (the 'FISC' powers) against vessels that are suspected of having breached them while in the coastal State's internal waters or territorial sea.[607]

2.   Should a vessel that has breached a FISC law, whether by cyber or other means, be in the contiguous zone, the coastal State may interdict the vessel prior to its departure therefrom (or in hot pursuit if done in accordance with international law[608]) and return it to port for investigation and prosecution. The coastal State may use cyber means as part of the interdiction operation. For example, it may take control of the movement of the delinquent vessel by cyber means and steer it back towards law enforcement vessels.

3.   The other authority accorded the coastal State in relation to FISC issues in the contiguous zone is that of prevention.[609] This authority allows the coastal State to use cyber means to warn and prevent a vessel in the contiguous zone from carrying out a FISC-related breach that it is reasonably suspected of being about to commit in the State's territory or territorial sea.

Rule 52 – Cyber operations in international straits

Cyber operations in a strait used for international navigation must be consistent with the right of transit passage.

1.   This Rule is based on Part III, Section 2, of the Law of the Sea Convention, which the International Group of Experts agreed reflected customary international law. Straits used for international navigation ('international straits') are those routes through a State's territorial sea, or through the overlapping territorial seas of two or more States, that connect one area of the high seas or an EEZ to another area of the high seas or an EEZ, and that are used for international navigation. The seabed and waters in an international strait are subject to the sovereignty of the bordering State or States, and those States generally enjoy the

---

[606] Law of the Sea Convention, Art. 33(2).
[607] Law of the Sea Convention, Art. 33(1)(b).   [608] Law of the Sea Convention, Art. 111.
[609] Law of the Sea Convention, Art. 33(1)(a).

rights and bear the obligations that apply in the territorial sea, subject to the right of transit passage enjoyed by the vessels and aircraft of other States.[610]

2. The right of transit passage exists throughout the entire strait (shoreline-to-shoreline[611]) and its approaches. Passage through the strait by vessels and aircraft must be continuous and expeditious and has to be conducted without delay.[612] As distinct from innocent passage, transit passage may not be suspended by the coastal State(s). Additionally, vessels and aircraft may transit in their 'normal mode', that is, submarines may transit submerged and aircraft may overfly the strait.[613]

3. Vessels and aircraft in the strait may not claim the right if they engage in cyber activities that are inconsistent with the regime of transit passage. For example, airborne intelligence collection of cyber communications from a bordering State is inconsistent with the transit passage regime, as is transmitting anti-government propaganda by cyber means into the State.[614]

4. Vessels and aircraft engaged in transit passage may undertake cyber activities necessary to ensure their safety and security, and that of any vessels or aircraft they are accompanying. Belligerent military operations, including cyber operations, whilst engaged in transit passage through a neutral strait during an armed conflict are not permitted.[615]

5. Vessels or aircraft in transit passage are not subject to the laws and regulations of the States bordering the strait, except for those relating to safety of navigation, regulation of pollution, fishing activities, and FISC.[616] Such laws and regulations might address, for instance, cyber activities that are conducted in order to transmit navigational safety instructions or regulate traffic passing through the straits. All vessels and aircraft in transit passage must abide by them.

6. Although vessels and aircraft enjoying sovereign immunity might conduct cyber activities that violate coastal State laws and regulations during transit passage, the coastal State may not assert enforcement jurisdiction over them (Rule 9). However, as noted in Rule 48, the coastal State has the authority to 'require' a sovereign immune vessel (Rule 5) to

---

[610] Law of the Sea Convention, Art. 34.

[611] But only on the seaward side of any baseline; there is no right of transit passage in internal waters. Law of the Sea Convention, Art. 35(a).

[612] Law of the Sea Convention, Arts. 38(2), 39(1)(a).

[613] Law of the Sea Convention, Art. 39(1)(c).   [614] Law of the Sea Convention, Art. 39.

[615] SAN REMO MANUAL, Rule 30. *See also* DoD MANUAL, para. 15.8.1.

[616] Law of the Sea Convention, Art. 42(1).

cease its offending activity and to depart the strait.[617] Additionally, the flag State of the sovereign immune aircraft or vessel bears 'international responsibility for any loss or damage' that flows from non-compliance with coastal State laws and regulations.[618] It also will bear responsibility if the activity constitutes an internationally wrongful act (Rule 14).

7.   Other 'straits' regimes in which there are varying sets of obligations also exist. One example is a strait with respect to which a specific treaty regime applies, like the Turkish Straits provided for in the Montreux Convention.[619] Such particularised regimes might affect warship passage and requirements in relation to cyber activities and must be analysed on a case-by-case basis. Another example is straits used for international navigation between the high seas or an EEZ and the territorial sea of another State. In these straits, a regime of non-suspendable innocent passage applies[620] and reference should thus be made to Rule 48.

Rule 53 – Cyber operations in archipelagic waters

Cyber operations in archipelagic waters must be consistent with the legal regime applicable therein.

1.   An archipelagic State is one that is comprised wholly of one or more groups of islands (archipelagos), such as the Philippines or Indonesia.[621] Archipelagic States may, within certain limitations, draw straight archipelagic baselines joining the outermost points of the outermost islands of the archipelago(s). Waters enclosed within the archipelagic baselines are archipelagic waters.[622] The territorial sea and EEZ are measured seaward from the archipelagic baselines. A State enjoys sovereignty (Rule 1) over its archipelagic waters, the airspace above the waters, and the seabed and subsoil lying below them.[623]

2.   Archipelagic States may designate archipelagic sea lanes and air routes suitable for the continuous and expeditious international

---

[617] By virtue of the operation of, *inter alia*, the Law of the Sea Convention, Arts. 34, 38(3).

[618] Law of the Sea Convention, Art. 42(5).

[619] Montreux Convention Regarding the Regime of the Straits, Arts. 8–22, 20 July 1936, 173 LNTS 213.

[620] Law of the Sea Convention, Art. 45.

[621] The ratio of water to land within the baselines must be between 1:1 and 9:1. Law of the Sea Convention, Art. 47(1).

[622] Law of the Sea Convention, Art. 49(1).   [623] Law of the Sea Convention, Art. 49(2).

navigation of foreign vessels and aircraft through or over their archipelagic waters.[624] If an archipelagic State does not designate such
archipelagic sea lanes, the right of archipelagic sea lanes passage may
nonetheless be exercised by foreign vessels and aircraft through the
routes normally used for international navigation.[625]

3. In archipelagic waters outside of such archipelagic sea lanes (or,
where archipelagic sea lanes have not been designated, those routes
normally used for international navigation), the right of innocent passage
(Rule 48) applies.[626] In this regard, note that there is no right of innocent
passage for aircraft and that submarines are required to navigate on the
surface and show their flag in order to claim the right of innocent
passage.

4. Cyber activities by foreign vessels and aircraft in designated archipelagic sea lanes or, in the absence thereof, routes normally used for
international navigation, must be consistent with the archipelagic sea
lanes passage regime in order for the vessel or aircraft to claim the right
of archipelagic sea lanes passage. For the purposes of this Rule, archipelagic sea lanes passage is substantially similar to transit passage (Rule 52).

5. Vessels and aircraft engaged in archipelagic sea lanes passage may
undertake cyber activities necessary to ensure their safety and security
and those of any vessels or aircraft that they are accompanying. On this
issue, see Rule 48, including the commentary on the right of the coastal
State to require delinquent sovereign immune vessels to cease their
offending conduct and to depart from the State's territorial waters.[627]

Rule 54 – Submarine communication cables

**The rules and principles of international law applicable to submarine
cables apply to submarine communication cables.**

1. The International Group of Experts agreed that existing international law applying to submarine cables, including submarine communication cables, and the operation thereof, generally reflects customary

---

[624] Law of the Sea Convention, Art. 53(1). If the archipelagic State does not designate such
sea lanes, the right of archipelagic sea lanes passage may nonetheless be exercised by all
States through routes normally used for international navigation and overflight. The
archipelagic sea lanes passage regime is dealt with in the Law of the Sea Convention,
Arts. 53–54.

[625] Law of the Sea Convention, Art. 53(12).   [626] Law of the Sea Convention, Art. 52.

[627] By virtue of, *inter alia*, the Law of the Sea Convention, Arts. 49, 52.

international law.[628] For the purposes of this Rule, the term 'submarine communication cable' refers to any cable owned, operated, or laid by a State, as well as privately owned cables, the laying of which has been authorised by a State for international telecommunications and data traffic.

2. Submarine communication cables currently carry a majority of the world's international voice, data, and video traffic; they are a key component of the international telecommunication and data traffic cyber infrastructure. Although employed for both commercial and governmental purposes, most cables and cable networks are owned and operated by consortia of private carriers. Such cables are vulnerable to a number of threats. They may be physically damaged, resulting in degradation, interruption, or termination of data transmission. Additionally, submarine communication cables are susceptible to being physically tapped, for instance by purpose-built submarines, such that any traffic transmitted through them can be collected, altered, or jammed.

3. The enjoyment of coastal State territorial sovereignty extends to submarine communication cables laid on the seabed of the territorial sea (and internal waters). In this sense, they generally are treated in the same fashion as cyber infrastructure located on land territory (Rule 2). Therefore, in their territorial sea, States have the right to regulate the laying, maintenance, repair, and replacement of submarine communication cables and to adopt laws and regulations in respect of their protection (in this regard, see also Rule 61).

4. In the territorial sea, coastal States may 'adopt laws and regulations' for 'the protection of [submarine] cables'. Such laws may not impose restrictions that impede innocent passage (Rule 48). Likewise, coastal States may regulate activities involving submarine communication cables in international straits unless doing so impedes or hampers transit passage (Rule 52) through them.[629]

5. Subject to the rights of innocent passage and archipelagic sea lanes passage, an archipelagic State has the right to regulate the laying,

---

[628] Law of the Sea Convention, Arts. 112–113. The International Group of Experts also looked to the 1884 Cable Convention. In this regard, they noted that the Convention may not reflect customary international law in its entirety. Nevertheless, it contributed to their assessment of the customary nature of the Law of the Sea Convention provisions.

[629] Law of the Sea Convention, Arts. 21(1)(c), 34(1).

maintenance, repair, and replacement of submarine communication cables in its archipelagic waters and territorial sea. An archipelagic State must respect existing cables 'laid by other States and passing through [their] waters without making a landfall'.[630] It shall, moreover, 'permit the maintenance and replacement of such cables upon receiving due notice of their location and the intention to repair or replace them'.[631]

6.   States may lay submarine communication cables in the EEZ of another State, but must pay due regard to the rights and duties of the coastal State.[632] Coastal States may not regulate or impede the laying of submarine communication cables in their EEZ or on their continental shelf and shall exercise due regard with respect to the rights and duties of other States to lay submarine communication cables.[633]

7.   The juridical continental shelf of a coastal State consists of the seabed and subsoil of the submarine areas that extend beyond its territorial sea to the outer edge of the continental margin, or to a distance of 200 nautical miles from the baseline used to measure the width of the territorial sea where the continental margin does not extend to that distance.[634] States may lay submarine cables on another State's continental shelf subject to the requirement of due regard.[635] Although delineation of the course of pipelines on the continental shelf is subject to coastal State consent, this requirement does not apply to submarine cables laid on the continental shelf.[636]

8.   A coastal State 'may not impede the laying or maintenance of . . . cables' on the continental shelf unless the actions taken qualify as 'reasonable measures for the exploration of the continental shelf [or] the exploitation of its natural resources'.[637] Reasonableness in this context has not been defined, although the International Group of Experts agreed that a measure would be unreasonable if it rendered the laying of a submarine communication cables impossible or if it disproportionately

---

[630] Law of the Sea Convention, Art. 51(2).   [631] Law of the Sea Convention, Art. 51(2).
[632] Law of the Sea Convention, Arts. 58(1), 58(3).
[633] Law of the Sea Convention, Art. 56. The International Group of Experts noted, however, that while this may be the case in the law, a number of States subject such cable laying activities to consent requirements. See, e.g., People's Republic of China, Ministry of Commerce, Provisions Governing the Laying of Submarine Cables and Pipelines, Art. 4 (11 February 1989); India, Territorial Waters, Continental Shelf, Exclusive Economic Zone and other Maritime Zones Act, Art. 7, (25 August 1976).
[634] Law of the Sea Convention, Art. 76.   [635] Law of the Sea Convention, Art. 79(1).
[636] Law of the Sea Convention, Art. 79(3).   [637] Law of the Sea Convention, Art. 79(2).

increased the cost of laying them.[638] Similarly, a measure of a discriminatory character would generally be unreasonable. Finally, measures unrelated to the coastal State's sovereign right to explore and exploit natural resources and engage in related activities in the EEZ or on the continental shelf are unreasonable.

9.   The International Group of Experts could not achieve consensus on the balance of jurisdiction between the coastal State and the State laying the submarine communication cable on the coastal State's continental shelf or in its EEZ. In practice, deference is sometimes extended to the coastal State, even though the laying and maintenance of submarine communication cables qualifies as a high seas freedom.

10.   States enjoy the customary right to lay submarine communication cables in the high seas beyond the continental shelf.[639] This right is an integral facet of the customary freedom of the high seas, which is specifically provided for in the Law of the Sea Convention.[640]

11.   Land-locked States have the right of access to and from the sea for the purpose of exercising high seas freedoms.[641] The laying of submarine communication cables is one of the freedoms and, thus, land-locked States are entitled to lay submarine communication cables, in particular with a view to connecting their territories to the global cyber infrastructure. Transit of cables over the territory of neighbouring coastal States is subject to agreement between the landlocked State and the neighbouring States.[642]

12.   General agreement exists that the right to lay submarine communication cables includes all preparatory measures that are necessary to identify the appropriate route, as well as the right to maintain and repair a submarine communication cable. States that have laid or operate submarine communication cables also have the right to monitor and regularly inspect them.

13.   Over time existing cables will have to be replaced. Although replacement is expressly addressed in the Law of the Sea Convention

---

[638] For instance, offshore wind farms that effectively prevent a large area from being used for cable laying because manoeuvring a maintenance vessel among the pylons will be difficult or dangerous might arguably fall within this prohibition.

[639] Law of the Sea Convention, Art. 112(1).

[640] Law of the Sea Convention, Art. 87(1)(c).

[641] Law of the Sea Convention, Art. 125(1). A land-locked State is defined as 'a State which has no sea-coast'. Law of the Sea Convention, Art. 124(1)(a).

[642] Law of the Sea Convention, Art. 125(2–3).

only with respect to archipelagic waters,[643] the majority of the International Group of Experts agreed that States have the right to replace all existing cables (at least outside the limits of the territorial sea) that are outdated or have become inoperative. This finding is based on the fact that they are critical to the economy and security of all States. Limiting the right to repair, and not replacement, would require significant financial expenditures without necessarily extending the cables' lifespan. A minority of the Experts would limit replacement to archipelagic waters based on a view that had the drafters of the Law of the Sea Convention so intended, they would have extended the right of replacement to other areas. All of the Experts agreed that there is a right of repair *vis-à-vis* all cables.

14.   It is unsettled whether coastal States are entitled to establish cable protection zones that restrict certain activities, such as anchoring, bottom trawling, and sand mining, that pose threats to the integrity of submarine communication cables. Australia and New Zealand were among the first States to create cable corridors/protection zones that, within the territorial sea and EEZ, shield cables one mile on each side from vessel traffic and from other hazardous activities.[644] While international law provides a sufficient basis for cable protection zones within the territorial sea,[645] there is no equivalent clear norm with respect to either the EEZ or the continental shelf, and certainly not for the high seas.

15.   Without prejudice to the rules applicable during armed conflict (Part IV), the International Group of Experts agreed that the infliction of damage to cables by a State is prohibited as a matter of customary international law since doing so would run contrary to the object and purpose of the law governing submarine cables. The Experts based this conclusion on the fact that it would be incongruent to provide States a right to lay such cables without a corresponding obligation on the part of other States to respect them. Thus, for instance, the law of the sea does not provide a legal basis for a State to cut another State's submarine fibre optic cable in order to reduce trans-continental Internet traffic in times of tension.

---

[643] Law of the Sea Convention, Art. 51(2).
[644] Telecommunications and Other Legislation Amendment (Protection of Submarine Cables and Other Measures) Act (2005), No. 104, 2005 (Austl.); Submarine Cables and Pipeline Protection Act (1996), Public Act No. 22, 16 May 1996 (NZ).
[645] Law of the Sea Convention, Art. 21(1)(c).

16. Duly authorised vessels of States may take measures to identify vessels suspected of breaking a cable and to establish the relevant facts. They may require the master of a merchant vessel suspected of doing so to provide documentation regarding the vessel's nationality, which may be verified through investigation with the flag State and witness statements.[646]

17. As noted above, submarine communication cables can be physically tapped in order to collect data transmitted through them. The International Group of Experts agreed that doing so in the territorial or archipelagic waters of another State constitutes a violation of that State's sovereignty (Rule 4). In particular, employing a submarine or unmanned underwater vehicle to tap in territorial or archipelagic waters is inconsistent with the navigational regime of innocent passage as submarines are required to transit on the surface (Rule 48). The Experts noted, however, that a tapping operation in the territorial sea or archipelagic waters does not violate the sovereignty of other States, such as those that laid and operate the cable. They likewise agreed that tapping operations beyond waters subject to the sovereignty of the coastal or archipelagic State do not constitute a violation of sovereignty. These conclusions are without prejudice to the application of other international legal norms, such as a bilateral treaty governing the circumstances.

18. The Experts discussed the issue of causing unintentional damage while tapping a submarine communication cable. They were split as to whether the mere fact that the operation resulted in damage renders it a violation of the prohibition of causing damage to submarine cables. The majority of the Experts took the position that the existence of a special legal regime for submarine cables supports a conclusion that States engaging in tapping operations do so at their own risk. A few of the Experts were of the view that reasonable foreseeability is an element of the prohibition such that States will not be responsible for unintentional and unforeseeable consequences of their operations.

---

[646] 1884 Cable Convention, Art. 10. In 1959, the United States invoked Article 10 to board and investigate the Soviet trawler *Novorossiisk* for damaging five transatlantic cables. With the master's consent, a US warship inspected the vessel, and determined that there was a 'strong presumption' that the *Novorossiisk* violated the proscription in Article 2 of the Convention against intentional, wilful, or culpably negligent breaking or injuring a submarine cable. See *The Novorossiisk*, Dept. of State Bull. (20 April 1959), Vol. 40, No. 1034, at 555.

19.   States Parties to the Law of the Sea Convention must adopt laws that make the wilful or culpably negligent infliction of damage to a submarine communication cable beneath the high seas a punishable offence.[647] The requirement applies by extension to the EEZ.[648] In this regard, coastal States and States laying cables both have equal responsibility to prescribe rules against infliction of damage to submarine communication cables.

---

[647] Law of the Sea Convention, Art. 113.   [648] Law of the Sea Convention, Art. 58(2).

9

Air law

1. Modern aircraft are dependent upon computerised systems that are interconnected to multiple networks. This interconnectivity makes the aircraft increasingly vulnerable to cyber operations, such as interference with aircraft flight control systems, instruments, and on-board navigation and communications systems. Cyber means can also be used, for example, to cause ground- and space-based navigation and communication infrastructure to transmit spoofed signals or communications to civil and State aircraft. During an armed conflict, cyber operations could affect targeting and weapons delivery systems on military aircraft.

2. Whereas aircraft may be targeted by cyber means, they can also be used as platforms from which to mount cyber operations, including monitoring certain cyber communications. Additionally, many applications exist for airborne cyber infrastructure to carry out military and other State activities, such as command and control during an armed conflict or engaging in law enforcement operations.

3. Furthermore, advanced aviation technology is likely to enable the extension of computer networks by placing cyber infrastructure aboard aircraft, a prospect that is appealing to both State and commercial interests. Employing airborne infrastructure has the potential to provide broad area line-of-sight and persistent cyber services similar to those currently delivered by expensive space-based infrastructure. Indeed, private sector solar-powered unmanned aircraft designed to deliver Internet services are presently under development, while ultra-high altitude aircraft equipped with cyber capabilities will render it possible to loiter for extended periods of time and provide cyber services to remote locations.

4. Although it is generally considered that there is an altitude above the earth's surface where the application of air law ends and that of space law (Chapter 10) begins, the International Group of Experts acknowledged that no international agreement exists as to the precise delineation between air and space (see also chapeau for Chapter 10); the issue

remains unsettled as a matter of law. In most approaches, however, the altitude is roughly between 80 and 120 kilometres above sea level.

5.   The Chicago Convention has near universal application and the International Group of Experts considered most of its provisions, including those cited below, to reflect customary international law.

6.   For the purposes of this Manual, the International Group of Experts adopted the definition of 'aircraft' set forth in Annex 2 of the Chicago Convention: '[a]ny machine that can derive support in the atmosphere from the reactions of the air other than the reactions of the air against the earth's surface.'[649] A 'civil aircraft' is an aircraft that is not a State aircraft.[650] As used in this Manual, 'State aircraft' are those 'owned or used by a State serving exclusively non-commercial government functions',[651] including aircraft designated for military, customs, and police purposes.[652]

7.   'Military aircraft' are 'aircraft (i) operated by the armed forces of a State; (ii) bearing the military markings of that State; (iii) commanded by a member of the armed forces; and (iv) controlled, manned or preprogramed by a crew subject to regular armed forces discipline'.[653] The term 'aircraft' includes unmanned aircraft.[654] It must be cautioned that States did not agree to particular definitions of these types of aircraft when adopting the Chicago Convention and they may employ slightly different approaches to the precise application of rules with respect to State, civil, and military aircraft.

8.   With regard to the jurisdictional prerogatives of the State of registration, see also Rule 10.

9.   In addition to air law and space law, cyber activities undertaken from aboard aircraft may also be subject to general international law, the

---

[649]   Chicago Convention, Annex 2, 'Rules of the Air'. This definition includes both fixed and rotary wing aircraft but excludes machines such as hovercraft. *See also* AMW MANUAL, Rule. 1(d).

[650]   AMW MANUAL, Rule 1(h).

[651]   AMW MANUAL, Rule 1(cc). Chicago Convention, Art. 3(a).

[652]   AMW MANUAL, Rule 1(cc). *See also* Chicago Convention, Art. 3(b). Note that the Chicago Convention does not use the term 'exclusively non-commercial government functions'. Rather, it simply refers to aircraft used in military, customs, and police services. The International Group of Experts agreed that the reference to 'use' in the definition it adopted is intended to refer to aircraft that are serving governmental purposes at the time, even though they may not be a part of that State's air fleet.

[653]   AMW MANUAL, Rule 1(x). *See also* 1923 Hague Draft Rules for Aerial Warfare, Arts. 3, 14.

[654]   AMW MANUAL, Rule 1(d).

provisions of other applicable regimes of international law, such as international telecommunication law (Chapter 11) and the *jus ad bellum* (Chapter 14), and bi- or multi-lateral treaties. For instance, a State aircraft flying in international airspace (see definition in Rule 56) may engage in airborne cyber operations against another State that qualify as a prohibited intervention (Rule 66) or an unlawful use of force (Rule 68). By the same token, State cyber operations directed at an aircraft may sometimes violate international law irrespective of the aircraft's location, as when the operations are against an aircraft qualifying as a sovereign immune platform (Rule 5) or when the operations amount to an unlawful use of force against another State's civil or State aircraft.

10. If cyber operations in airspace also involve outer space, they are governed by both air law and space law (Chapter 10). For instance, if cyber operations initiated from an aircraft employ satellite technology, as in the case of transmitting publicly accessible broadcasts from an aircraft via a satellite to the satellite's terrestrial 'footprint', the operations of the satellite will be governed by space law, whereas the aircraft from which the cyber operations are being conducted is subject to air law. A cyber operation conducted from an aircraft against a satellite is also subject to both air law, as that is the location from which the operation is mounted, and space law, because its effects manifest in outer space.

11. The use of aircraft for cyber operations during an armed conflict is governed by the law of armed conflict (Part IV). In this regard, the Chicago Convention notes that it does not affect the 'freedom of action' of contracting States that are either party to an armed conflict or enjoy neutral status.[655]

Rule 55 – Control of aircraft conducting cyber operations in national airspace

A State may regulate the operation of aircraft, including those conducting cyber operations, in its national airspace.

1. This Rule is derived, in part, from Articles 1 and 2 of the Chicago Convention. The Experts agreed that customary international law also provides a basis for this Rule *vis-à-vis* State aircraft, in particular because territorial sovereignty extends to national airspace.

---

[655] Chicago Convention, Art. 89 (this principle also applies to declared national emergencies when the ICAO Council is notified).

2.   With respect to 'national airspace', Article 1 of the Chicago Convention recognises that every State has 'complete and exclusive sovereignty over the airspace above its territory'.[656] The Chicago Convention defines the territory of a State as its land area and territorial waters.[657] Thus, the airspace superjacent to a State's land territory and certain territorial waters is national airspace.

3.   In practice, there are certain disagreements among States as to the precise delineation of a particular State's national airspace. Wherever such differences exist, the potential for disputes over the right to regulate the operation of aircraft, including aircraft engaging in cyber operations, will also exist. For example, while there is universal agreement that a State may claim a territorial sea of up to twelve nautical miles from the baseline (Rule 48),[658] there are disagreements as to how to draw certain types of baselines under international law. Those advising on the operation of airborne cyber infrastructure near areas subject to territorial and maritime disputes must therefore be cognisant of the specific location of the aircraft concerned.

4.   As distinct from maritime transit through the territorial sea (Rule 48), there is no right of innocent passage for foreign aircraft through the airspace above a State's territorial sea.[659] Therefore, aircraft engaging in cyber operations while flying in that area are subject to the full application of this Rule.

5.   Pursuant to Article 5 of the Chicago Convention, States Parties have agreed to permit, on a non-discriminatory basis, all foreign civil aircraft not engaged in scheduled international air service the right to transit their airspace and make non-traffic stops without the necessity of obtaining prior permission. Thus, for example, the aircraft of a private security company in flight from a landlocked State that intends to conduct airborne cyber operations over international waters would be allowed to transit the territory of a State Party, subject to compliance

---

[656] Chicago Convention, Art. 1. *See also* Law of the Sea Convention, Art. 2 (specifically addressing the airspace above the territorial sea).

[657] Chicago Convention, Art. 2. Territorial waters include internal waters, archipelagic waters, and the territorial sea.

[658] Note that a coastal State claiming a territorial sea of less than 12 nautical miles may only claim a national airspace that is superjacent to the territorial sea and not up to 12 nautical miles.

[659] Law of the Sea Convention, Art. 17 (extending the right of innocent passage only to 'ships of all states') and Art. 19 (defining the launching, landing, or taking on board of any aircraft as disqualifying a ship's passage from innocent status).

with that State's national airspace regulations, and make stops in its territory for purposes like refuelling en route to its intended destination.

6. The aforementioned right only governs the right of transit. It does not regulate the cyber operations in which the aircraft might engage; such operations are subject to the laws and regulations of the subjacent State (see below), as well as other applicable international law norms, like respect for sovereignty (Rule 4). Moreover, States have reserved the right, for reasons of military necessity or public safety, to restrict or prohibit aircraft from flying over certain areas of their territory, and from flying over its entire territory during periods of emergency or in the interests of public safety (subject to certain conditions set forth in Article 9 of the Chicago Convention). Thus, for instance, it would be permissible for a State to prohibit civil aircraft from overflying militarily sensitive facilities or areas of civil strife in order to preclude the possibility of the aircraft conducting cyber operations, so long as the prohibition complies with Article 9 criteria, such as application without distinction to nationality.

7. During flight within a State's national airspace, civil aircraft are subject to the full jurisdiction (Rule 9) of that State. Accordingly, they can be ordered to land at a designated airport when an offence has been committed while in a State's national airspace that has an effect on its territory, legal order, or national security; that violates its air safety or aerial navigation regulations; or when the exercise of jurisdiction is necessary to ensure a State's compliance with an obligation arising under a bilateral or multilateral international instrument. For example, technology exists for airborne cyber infrastructure to be used to hack into Wi-Fi networks, eavesdrop on cell phone calls and text messages, and exfiltrate or otherwise interfere with data. If a civil aircraft of one State of registration operates such systems over another State without permission and contrary to the law of the subjacent State, the latter State has the right to order the aircraft to land to submit to its jurisdiction for violation of its criminal legislation. Doing so is an appropriate exercise of enforcement jurisdiction (Rules 8–9).

8. When an aircraft is in international airspace, generally only the State of registry may exercise enforcement jurisdiction (Rule 11) *vis-à-vis* cyber operations conducted from that aircraft. This does not preclude the exercise of extraterritorial prescriptive jurisdiction by any other State that is entitled to do so under international law (Rule 10).

9. Although civil aircraft not engaging in scheduled international air service enjoy the right to transit a State's airspace without prior permission, Article 5 of the Chicago Convention accords the States being overflown the right to require the aircraft to land or to terminate

their activity. A State might do so, for instance, when it has a basis for concluding that an aircraft's activities are inconsistent with the aims of the Convention, such as the safety of air navigation.[660] The International Group of Experts agreed that the authority to direct an aircraft to land would apply in the case of cyber operations undertaken by civil aircraft. In particular, it would encompass cyber operations directed at the State being overflown.

10.   In most situations, however, cyber operations are likely to be conducted by military aircraft, which, as noted, are State aircraft. States may not operate State aircraft over the territory of another State without authorisation from the latter.[661] The International Group of Experts agreed that if a State grants authorisation, it may, consistent with the exercise of its sovereign prerogatives in national airspace, set conditions on the overflight, such as prohibiting the conduct of cyber operations that are unrelated to the safety of the flight.[662]

11.   Consider a case in which a State aircraft enters another State's national airspace and conducts cyber operations therein, or there are reliable indications that it will do so. If it has penetrated the airspace without authorisation, violates any conditions of an authorisation (including conditions related to the conduct of cyber operations), or violates the territorial State's domestic laws and regulations by means of cyber operations, the territorial State may demand that the aircraft desist from the conduct and depart its airspace without delay.

12.   The International Group of Experts considered carefully the measures available to a State when a State aircraft of another State is within its airspace without its consent. The Experts agreed that if the State aircraft is conducting cyber operations rising to the level of an armed attack (Rule 71) against the subjacent State, or if that State has reasonable grounds to conclude that the aircraft is about to do so imminently (Rule 73), it is entitled to resort to necessary and proportionate (Rule 72) force in self-defence in order to expel the aircraft if it fails to desist and depart. The Experts likewise agreed that to the extent a State would be entitled to use force in a law enforcement situation, it analogously would be entitled to use force against an aircraft engaged in cyber operations that result in consequences justifying a law enforcement use of force.

[660] Chicago Convention, pmbl.
[661] Chicago Convention, Art. 3(c). The same requirement applies to aircraft engaged in scheduled international civil air service. *Id.* Art. 6.
[662] *See, e.g.,* DoD FOREIGN CLEARANCE GUIDE, para. C2.2.2.

13. The Experts were divided as to what activities constitute an armed attack. A minority of the Experts was of the view that the mere presence of a foreign military aircraft affecting the national security interests of the subjacent State, without the consent of that State, constitutes an armed attack *per se*.[663]

14. However, the majority of the International Group of Experts took the position that, although the presence of the military aircraft conducting cyber operations would be a clear violation of at least sovereignty (Rule 4), force may only be used by the subjacent State if the aircraft is in fact engaged in an armed attack, or if the subjacent State has reasonable grounds to conclude that an armed attack is imminent.

15. A number of the Experts were of the view that a further legal basis for forceful actions to expel a foreign State aircraft conducting cyber operations, separate from that of self-defence, is that the aircraft has violated the State's territorial integrity and that the State is therefore entitled to use force to expel the aircraft.

16. No unmanned aircraft, balloons, or other airborne objects, including those used to conduct cyber operations or to provide connectivity to the Internet, may be flown or otherwise placed in the airspace over another State's territory without authorisation from that State (except where international law would allow non-consensual entry into a State's territory, such as in the case of self-defence, Rule 71, or authorisation by the UN Security Council, Rule 76).[664]

Rule 56 – Cyber operations in international airspace

Subject to restrictions thereon contained in international law, a State may conduct cyber operations in international airspace.

1. This Rule reflects customary international law and is supported by provisions of the Chicago Convention and the Law of the Sea Convention.[665]

---

[663] They noted that the continued presence of military forces on the territory of another State in violation of a basing agreement constitutes aggression pursuant to the Definition of Aggression, Art. 3(e).

[664] Chicago Convention, Arts. 3(c), 8.

[665] Chicago Convention, Arts. 1, 2, 3(a), 12. While Article 12 of the Chicago Convention states that rules established under the Chicago Regime shall govern air operations over the high seas, Article 3(a) of the Chicago Convention specifically excludes 'State aircraft' (with the exception of Article 3(b–d)). Similarly, the 'Rules of the Air' regime does not govern the activities of State aircraft. Additionally, the Law of the Sea Convention recognises a

2. 'International airspace' is that which does not qualify as national airspace (Rule 55).[666] The International Group of Experts agreed that no State may claim sovereignty over international airspace. Accordingly, cyber operations in international airspace do not require the consent of any other State and States may freely conduct cyber operations in international airspace absent a prohibition set forth in international law, such as engaging in airborne cyber operations that violate another State's sovereignty (Rule 4), amount to unlawful intervention (Rule 66), or breach a State's neutrality during an international armed conflict (151).

3. Although some States claim a certain degree of authority to regulate aircraft operations beyond national airspace, for example through the establishment of Air Defence Identification Zones ('ADIZ', see discussion below), the Experts agreed that since the airspace in question is international in character, aircraft may conduct any cyber operations that would be lawful above the high seas.

4. All aircraft passing over an international strait must comply with the rules of aerial transit passage set forth in the Law of the Sea Convention,[667] whereas those transiting air routes above archipelagic waters must do so consistent with archipelagic sea lanes passage.[668] As with vessels, the aircraft must 'refrain from any activities other than those incident to their normal modes of continuous and expeditious transit unless rendered necessary by force majeure or by distress'.[669] For instance, they may not engage in cyber operations directed at the State(s) bordering the strait or the archipelagic State, respectively. The International Group of Experts agreed that cyber operations that constitute the 'normal mode' of operation of an aircraft, such as transmission of navigational and weather data, may be continued while in transit or archipelagic sea lanes passage (Rules 52 and 55, respectively).

5. A minority of the Experts was of the opinion that 'normal mode' for aircraft designed to conduct offensive cyber operations includes actually conducting such operations while engaged in continuous and

---

general freedom of overflight over the high seas. Law of the Sea Convention, Art. 87. The rules relating to a coastal State's rights in the contiguous zone and the exclusive economic zone have little impact on the conduct of overflight for the purpose of conducting cyber operations. Law of the Sea Convention, Parts II, V.

[666] *See, e.g.*, AMW Manual, Rule 1(a).   [667] Law of the Sea Convention, Art. 39.

[668] Law of the Sea Convention, Art. 53. Pursuant to Art. 51, an archipelagic State must respect existing agreements regarding archipelagic airspace.

[669] Law of the Sea Convention, Art. 39. *See also* Arts. 53(3), 54.

expeditious transit through an international strait or archipelagic air route, as long as the operations are not directed against the State(s) bordering the strait or the archipelagic State. The majority of the Experts did not agree that 'normal mode' for such aircraft includes offensive cyber operations. All the Experts concurred, however, that aircraft passing over an international strait or in an archipelagic air route may conduct those cyber operations that are necessary for force protection or self-defence.

6. While States may always impose higher standards for their State aircraft, State aircraft conducting cyber operations in international airspace must at least operate with due regard for the safety of navigation of civil aircraft (Rule 57) and for the rights of other States. For instance, a State aircraft conducting cyber operations must be attentive to whether said operations might endanger other aircraft in the area or unnecessarily impede the use of the airspace by other States.

7. A civil aircraft conducting cyber operations is generally free to fly anywhere in international airspace. However, its movements may be subject to the direction of an applicable air traffic control provider.[670] Most operations conducted by civil aircraft over international waters will occur within an International Civil Aviation Organization designated Flight Information Region (FIR). That organisation has designated a State to provide air traffic services inside each FIR, even in areas beyond the State's national airspace.[671] Thus, for instance, although a civil aircraft may want to loiter over a given area in international airspace within a FIR to facilitate cyber communications in that area, safety concerns may in certain cases necessitate instructions from the air traffic controller to deviate from the planned flight path.

8. Since they are not governed by the Chicago Convention regime, State aircraft, including military aircraft, are not subject to FIRs. Therefore, they may conduct cyber operations in international airspace without complying with air traffic control instructions while in a FIR. However, they are required to fly with due regard to the safety of other aircraft and the rights of other States and therefore often cooperate with air traffic control authorities.

---

[670] Article 12 of the Chicago Convention requires civil aircraft to comply with international rules of the air established under quasi-legislative authority of the ICAO. *See* Chicago Convention, Annex 2, 'Rules of the Air'.

[671] Such States may extend the applicability of their national air traffic regulations to civil aircraft operations within the FIR.

9.   Some States have established ADIZs, the authority for which flows from the State's sovereignty over its national airspace. Such zones extend into international airspace and are designed to ensure the security of the State concerned. Both civil and State aircraft that desire to enter a State's national airspace must comply with the conditions and procedures for entry set by that State.[672] A State could in theory prohibit the conduct of cyber operations, or particular types of cyber operations, within an ADIZ in international airspace, albeit only as a condition for entry into its national airspace. Such conditions must not negate the freedom of overflight of the high seas. In particular, a State may not impose any restrictions on aircraft that are merely transiting international airspace through an ADIZ.

Rule 57 – Cyber operations jeopardising the safety of international civil aviation

A State may not conduct cyber operations that jeopardise the safety of international civil aviation.

1.   Article 3(d) of the Chicago Convention requires States to exercise 'due regard' for the safety of navigation of international civil aviation when issuing regulations for the operation of their State aircraft. Additionally, Article 3 *bis* recognises that States must refrain from the use of 'weapons' against civil aircraft in flight. The International Group of Experts was of the view that Articles 3 and 3 *bis* restate customary international law, but are without prejudice to the provisions of the law of armed conflict, such as those governing qualification as a military objective (Rule 100).

2.   The Experts concurred that the term 'weapon' includes cyber weapons (Rule 103). Such weapons can have destructive effects on an aircraft in flight or injure those aboard it, as in the case of malware that affects aircraft control systems. They took particular notice of the fact that, at least for the majority of the International Group of Experts with respect to application of Rule 103, a cyber weapon need not be physically destructive, but rather may qualify as a weapon if its use can result in the loss of functionality of the object against which it is directed. This would include avionics and other systems on which the aircraft relies. Taken together, the aforementioned requirements mean that a State may not

---

[672] DoD Manual, para. 14.2.4.

engage in any cyber operations that endanger civil aircraft, except as specifically authorised under international law, for instance, in cases of self-defence (Rule 71).

3. Articles 3 *bis*(d) and 4 of the Chicago Convention prohibit States Parties from using civil aircraft for any purpose inconsistent with the Chicago Convention. The International Group of Experts concurred that this provision, which they considered reflective of customary international law, precludes a State from using civil aircraft to conduct cyber operations if such operations endanger civil aviation.

4. The International Group of Experts took note of Annex 17 to the Chicago Convention, which recommends that States Parties should 'ensure that measures are developed in order to protect critical information and communications technology systems used for civil aviation purposes from interference that may jeopardise the safety of civil aviation'. The Annex also 'encourage[s] entities involved with or responsible for the implementation of various aspects of the national civil aviation security programme to identify' such systems, 'including threats and vulnerabilities thereto, and develop protective measures to include, *inter alia*, security by design, supply chain security, network separation, and remote access control, as appropriate'.[673]

5. Although this Rule deals only with the activities of States that jeopardise the safety of international civil aviation, the International Group of Experts took notice of the Montreal Convention of 1971,[674] which requires States Parties to, *inter alia*, make a number of activities punishable under domestic law when conducted by any person.[675] The International Group of Experts agreed that these activities could also include cyber operations.

---

[673] Chicago Convention, Annex 17, Recommendations 4.9.1–4.9.2.
[674] The Montreal Convention of 1971 has 188 States Parties.
[675] Montreal Convention of 1971, Arts. 1, 3.

10

Space law

1.   The Rules in this Chapter address cyber activities in, from or through outer space. The International Group of Experts took note of the importance of outer space with regard to cyber activities ranging from civilian communications and navigation to military operations. In this regard, cyber operations could be directed against, or utilise, space-related cyber infrastructure (in particular satellites) for such purposes as retrieving or altering data, disrupting space-to-space communications, interfering with uplink or downlink communication signals, partially or completely destroying the software or hardware on a space system, and manipulating satellite controls. Particularly tempting may be cyber operations designed to acquire access to sensors aboard satellites in order to disrupt information collection or to obtain or distort the information they collect for military or economic purposes. Cyber operations could also be employed, for instance, to commandeer flight or payload control of a space object or to divert satellite downlink signals designated for particular servers and redirect them to others.

2.   Conceptually, when considering the relationship between cyber operations and outer space, it can be useful to distinguish between space-enabled cyber operations and cyber-enabled space operations. The former, such as satellite-to-earth and satellite-to-satellite cyber communications, have little to do with outer space beyond being enabled by cyber infrastructure based on space assets. Space law generally applies to these types of cyber operations in a limited fashion. As an example, space law *per se*, as distinguished from other regimes of international law that are applicable to space activities, plays only a small role in assessing the lawfulness of the transmission of malicious code via a satellite communications link. Rather, the bulk of legal analysis concerning such a cyber operation will depend on application of the other Chapters of this Manual.

3. In contrast, cyber-enabled space operations involve the actual operation of space assets or the conduct of space operations by cyber means. Examples include the employment of telemetry, tracking, and command systems for communications between ground stations and spacecraft and using cyber means to affect the functionality of a space asset or its payload. As an example, if cyber operations are used to take control of a satellite or its payload, the cyber operations are enabling an activity in outer space, whether they are fully or partially carried out therein.

4. The boundary of outer space has been discussed by governments, the UN, and the scientific and legal communities for decades, without resolution. A 1967 conclusion that 'no clear scientific or technical criteria could be found which would permit a precise and lasting definition of outer space and which would be acceptable to all States' remains accurate today.[676] Despite differences of opinion on this issue, most approaches locate the delineation between airspace and outer space at roughly between 80 and 120 kilometres above sea level (see also chapeau to Chapter 9). The International Group of Experts agreed that no State exercises sovereignty over outer space, the moon, or celestial bodies, nor may such sovereignty be claimed.[677]

5. For the purposes of this Manual, 'space object' refers to the 'component parts of a [man-made] space object as well as its launch vehicle and parts thereof'.[678] A 'launching state' is the State that 'launches or procures the launching of a space object; [or] from whose territory or facility a space object is launched'.[679] 'State of registry' denotes the State on whose registry the space object is listed.[680] In the event more than one

[676] Report of the Scientific and Technical Subcommittee on the Work of its Fifth Session, para. 36, UN Doc. A/AC.105/39 (6 September 1967).
[677] Outer Space Treaty, Art. II. See also Declaration on Friendly Relations, pmbl. (recalling 'the established principle that outer space, including the Moon and other celestial bodies, is not subject to national appropriation by claim of sovereignty, by means or use of occupation, or by any other means'). See also Resolution on International Cooperation in Outer Space, para. 1; Declaration on the Use of Outer Space, para. 3.
[678] Registration Convention, Art. I(b); Liability Convention, Art. I(d).
[679] Registration Convention, Art. I(a); Liability Convention, Art. I(c).
[680] Registration Convention, Art. I(c). Should a satellite not be carried on a register, the nationality of the owner of the satellite shall be deemed that of the satellite. On registration, see also Recommendations on Enhancing the Practice of States and International Intergovernmental Organizations in Registering Space Objects, GA Res. 62/101, UN Doc. A/RES/62/101 (10 January 2008). Note that States that are not Parties to the Registration Convention register in accordance with the Resolution on International Cooperation in Outer Space.

State is involved in the launching of a space object, the launching States must agree on which of them is to register the object.[681]

6.   In drafting this Chapter, the International Group of Experts relied extensively on various space law treaties. Although said treaties do not reflect customary international law in their entirety, the Experts agreed that the provisions of the instruments to which this Manual refers provide strong support for their conclusions that the Rules in this Chapter generally reflect customary law. The Experts were acutely aware, however, that with respect to customary international space law and its relation to cyber activities in or through space, State practice is often difficult to ascertain and there are only limited statements that would qualify as expressions of *opinio juris*.

7.   Space activities are to be carried out 'in accordance with international law, including the Charter of the United Nations'.[682] The legal regime of space law regulates space activities (as well as space objects), a concept that is generally understood to include the 'use', 'exploration', and 'scientific investigation' of outer space.[683] Most of the cyber activities involving outer space contemplated in this Manual fall within the ambit of 'use'. The International Group of Experts agreed that the term encompasses both economic and non-economic activities, whether public or private in nature, in outer space and on celestial bodies. Activities on the earth also qualify as space activities when they involve activities, or otherwise achieve effects, in outer space, such as the control of space objects. This is especially relevant with respect to cyber operations, as most cyber operations affecting or utilising space assets are initiated from the earth. To the extent space law applies to a particular circumstance involving cyber operations, it may, as *lex specialis*,[684] prevail over contrary rules found elsewhere in this Manual.[685]

---

[681] Registration Convention, Art. II(2).   [682] Outer Space Treaty, Art. III.

[683] Outer Space Treaty, Art. I.

[684] Discussions in the International Law Commission support the characterisation of space law as *lex specialis*. Analytical Study of the Study Group of the International Law Commission (finalised by Martti Koskenniemi) on Fragmentation of International Law: Difficulties Arising from the Diversification and Expansion of International Law, para. 129, UN Doc. A/CN.4/L.682 (13 April 2006).

[685] Caution must be exercised in this regard because, for instance, the UN Charter prevails, pursuant to Article 103 of that instrument, over space law and because other international agreements, such as the ITU Constitution or ITU Radio Regulations, may constitute the prevailing *lex specialis* regime instead.

8. Finally, the Experts took note of the importance of international telecommunication law with respect to certain space activities, since particular aspects of satellite communications and their protection are governed by that body of law (Chapter 11), as in the case of the prohibition of causing harmful interference (Rule 63).

Rule 58 – Peaceful purposes and uses of force

(a) **Cyber operations on the moon and other celestial bodies may be conducted only for peaceful purposes.**
(b) **Cyber operations in outer space are subject to international law limitations on the use of force.**

1. *Lit (a)* reflects Article IV of the Outer Space Treaty, which places specific restrictions on certain military activities in outer space. In particular, it provides that the earth's moon and other celestial bodies shall be used exclusively for peaceful purposes and forbids the establishment of military bases, installations and fortifications, the testing of any type of weapon, and the conduct of military manoeuvres on celestial bodies. The International Group of Experts agreed that Article IV applies fully to cyber related activities that fall within its scope, such as the installation of cyber infrastructure on the moon in order to conduct offensive military cyber operations against objects on the earth, in outer space, or on other celestial bodies.

2. According to Article IV, the use of military personnel on the moon and other celestial bodies for scientific research or other peaceful purposes is not prohibited, nor is the use of any equipment or facility necessary for their peaceful exploration.[686] Thus, cyber operations associated with activities such as establishing communications, research, or observation facilities on the moon or other celestial bodies (or testing such capabilities) are lawful. This is so even if they are conducted by military forces.

3. With respect to *lit.* (b), the International Group of Experts agreed that cyber activities in outer space may not involve the unlawful use of force (Rule 68). Article III of the Outer Space Treaty provides that 'activities in the exploration and use of outer space' shall be carried out 'in accordance with international law, including the Charter of the

---

[686] Outer Space Treaty, Art. IV.

United Nations, in the interest of maintaining international peace and security'. The reference to the UN Charter confirms that Article 2(4)'s prohibition of the threat or use of force applies fully to activities in outer space. Accordingly, any cyber operation that originates in, transits, or terminates in outer space and rises to the level of an unlawful threat or use of force is barred (Rule 68).

4.   Nevertheless, the International Group of Experts concurred that activities authorised by the UN Security Council under Chapter VII of the UN Charter in outer space, or having effects therein, are lawful (Rule 76). The Experts were also of the view that it is lawful to exercise the right of self-defence in outer space or to employ space-based assets to defend against armed attacks occurring on the earth (Rule 71). They based this conclusion on the incorporation by reference of existing international law, including the Charter of the United Nations, Outer Space Treaty,[687] and Moon Agreement.[688]

5.   To illustrate, it might be permissible to use cyber force in self-defence against a satellite that is being used to facilitate armed attacks (Rule 71) occurring on the earth. Similarly, it might be lawful to conduct cyber operations at the use of force level against a ground station in order to prevent another State from using a satellite for communications or navigational purposes in support of a terrestrial armed attack. Of course, each case has to be evaluated on its own merits. For instance, the defensive use of an anti-satellite weapon to physically destroy a satellite involved in a cyber armed attack would have to comply with, *inter alia*, the self-defence requirements of necessity and proportionality (Rule 72). In this regard, alternative courses of action, such as targeting ground control facilities, uplinks, or downlinks, dazzling or blinding the satellite, or moving or tipping the satellite would need to be considered. Special consideration would also have to be given to the amount of space debris that could be created by the operation, not only with respect to the law of self-defence, but, where applicable, other legal regimes, such as the law of armed conflict (Part IV) and the law of neutrality (Chapter 20). The Experts took note of the fact that space debris mitigation guidelines, although not legally binding, would likely factor into any decision regarding anti-satellite operations.[689]

---

[687] Outer Space Treaty, Art. III.   [688] Moon Agreement, Art. 2.

[689] IADC Space Debris Mitigation Guidelines; Space Debris Mitigation Guidelines of the UN Committee on the Peaceful Uses of Outer Space (UNCOPUOS), endorsed by GA Res. 62/217 (22 December 2007). Guideline 4 provides that '... the intentional

6. Although the Experts agreed that a cyber operation in or through outer space that crosses the use of force threshold violates international law (unless engaged in pursuant to the right of self-defence or in accordance with authorisation from the Security Council), they noted the existence of a controversy over whether certain cyber activities below that threshold are prohibited on the basis that they are not for 'peaceful purposes'. In this regard, the term 'peaceful purposes' not only appears in Article IV of the Outer Space Treaty, a provision reflected in *lit.* (a), but also in the instrument's preamble. The latter recognises the 'common interest ... in the ... progress of the exploration and use of outer space for peaceful purposes'. Other instruments likewise contain references to the peaceful use of outer space.[690]

7. In light of such provisions, the International Group of Experts discussed the concept of peaceful purposes in the context of the use of outer space generally. The Experts observed that from the beginning of the space age, outer space has been used for military purposes such as reconnaissance and surveillance. Moreover, a great deal of space technology has had a 'dual nature' in the sense that civilian space capabilities often stem from military space developments and many civilian space applications, such as commercial satellite imagery, are used for military purposes. Therefore, the Experts rejected the premise that any purported limitation on the use of outer space to peaceful purposes should be interpreted as 'non-military'.[691]

8. The International Group of Experts further observed that the reference to 'international law, including the Charter of the United Nations', in Article III of the Outer Space Treaty augurs against imposing any obligation to refrain from cyber activities in outer space that is broader than those already expressly set forth in international law. As an example of the application of other limitations, the Experts noted that a cyber operation not amounting to an unlawful use of force might nevertheless violate other Rules set forth in this Manual, such as those prohibiting interference with the peaceful space activities of other States (Rule 59) and harmful interference to wireless communications under

---

destruction of any on-orbit spacecraft ... or other harmful space activities that generate long-lived debris should be avoided'.

[690] *See, e.g.,* Moon Agreement, Arts. 2, 3(1); Liability Convention, pmbl.; Registration Convention, pmbl.; Declaration on the Use of Outer Space, pmbl., Annex, para. 1.

[691] The Experts further noted that Article IV of the Outer Space Treaty, by expressly referring to other celestial bodies, does not impose restrictions on military uses of outer space that are not expressly prohibited in the Article.

international telecommunication law (Rule 63). As a general matter, however, they concluded that *lit.* (b) does not extend to cyber activities in outer space that do not violate a specific primary rule of international law.

9. The International Group of Experts acknowledged the existence of a view that any cyber operation involving outer space that threatens international peace and security violates a purported general prohibition of activities in outer space that are not for peaceful purposes, even if said activities do not violate other rules of international law. This view is based on Article III of the Outer Space Treaty's requirement that States 'carry on activities in the exploration and use of outer space ... in the interest of maintaining international peace and security', as well as the use of the term 'peaceful purposes' in the instruments mentioned above.[692] For discussion of the term 'international peace and security', see also Rule 65.

10. Consider a case in which tensions exist between two States, but hostilities have not broken out. One of the States conducts cyber operations that result in blocking reconnaissance data from the other State's military satellites. Given the relations between the States, such an action exacerbates the situation in a manner that likely threatens continued peace between them.[693] The International Group of Experts was of the view that unless the cyber operation constitutes an integral element of a use of force (as in the case of preparation for an operation at that level), it does not breach this Rule. They noted, however, that it may constitute interference in violation of *lit.* (b) of Rule 59. By the alternative view that none of the Experts held, cyber operations blocking data would breach this Rule because they are not undertaken for peaceful purposes.

---

[692] Moon Agreement, Art. 3(1); Liability Convention, pmbl.; Agreement on the Rescue of Astronauts, the Return of Astronauts and the Return of Objects Launched into Outer Space, pmbl., 22 April 1968, 672 UNTS 119.

[693] Note, in this regard, that the US Department of Defense Space Policy highlights the risks of interfering with space systems, and states: 'Purposeful interference with US space systems, including their supporting infrastructure, will be considered an infringement of US rights. Such interference, or interference with other space systems upon which the United States relies, is irresponsible in peacetime and may be escalatory during a crisis.' Department of Defense Directive 3100.10, 18 October 2001. The National Space Policy of the United States of America contains a nearly identical statement: 'Purposeful interference with space systems, including supporting infrastructure, will be considered an infringement of a nation's rights'. National Space Policy of the United States of America, White House, 28 June 2010. Although an infringement of a State's rights will not always threaten international peace and security, it can sometimes do so.

11.   The International Group of Experts agreed that in the event hostilities, including those involving cyber operations, in, through, or from outer space, cross the threshold of armed conflict (Rules 82–83), the law of armed conflict will govern them. The fact that a State's cyber operation is conducted in self-defence (Rule 71) and therefore does not violate this Rule does not excuse violations of the law of armed conflict when the exchange between the States concerned qualifies as an armed conflict. For example, the law of armed conflict prohibition of conducting cyber attacks against civilian objects (Rule 99) would equally apply to cyber attacks against civilian space objects that are not being used for military purposes (and therefore do not qualify as military objectives). The Experts noted, in this context, the widespread phenomenon of dual-use satellites and other cyber infrastructure in outer space. Similarly, during an armed conflict the rule of proportionality (Rule 113) would come into play with respect to the creation of space debris that might harm civilian space objects. Moreover, the law of neutrality (Chapter 20) would apply with respect to space objects having neutral character.

Rule 59 – Respect for space activities

(a) A State must respect the right of States of registry to exercise jurisdiction and control over space objects appearing on their registries.

(b) A State must conduct its cyber operations involving outer space with due regard for the need to avoid interference with the peaceful space activities of other States.

1.   *Lit.* (a) applies the general requirement that a State must respect the jurisdictional prerogatives of other States with regard to their space objects. As set forth in Article VIII of the Outer Space Treaty, a space object is subject to the 'jurisdiction and control' of the State on whose national registry the object is carried. The State of registry has full authority over the space object, whether governmental, private, or commercial. In particular, that State enjoys prescriptive and enforcement jurisdiction (Rule 8) over it while in outer space or on a celestial body. For example, consider a communications satellite that is used by numerous States and private entities to conduct cyber activities. The State of registry is entitled to prescribe laws and regulations regarding such use and engage in enforcement and, when appropriate, adjudicatory actions with respect to their violation.

2.   Other States must respect the State of registry's jurisdictional prerogatives. A State that disregards regulations promulgated by the State of registry governing use of a space object, such as a communications satellite, may be in violation of *lit.* (a). Similarly, a State may not direct cyber operations against a space object registered in another State in order to enforce the former's domestic law. These conclusions are without prejudice to any authority under international law to take particular cyber measures, such as self-defence (Rule 71).

3.   Even though the State of registry enjoys jurisdiction and control over its space objects, it must be cautioned that other States may also have jurisdictional prerogatives over activities involving those objects or persons on-board them.[694] For example, other States may exercise prescriptive jurisdiction over cyber activities that involve a satellite registered by another State when those activities have harmful effects on their territory, as in the case of conducting economic espionage against its companies through the satellite's communications systems.

4.   *Lit.* (b) is based on Article IX of the Outer Space Treaty, which provides that States are to engage in their activities in outer space with 'due regard to the corresponding interests' of other Parties to the instrument.[695] The International Group of Experts agreed that this obligation is customary in nature. It is of particular relevance to cyber operations that might result in physical or optical interference or the creation of space debris that may be expected to affect the space activities of other States.

5.   Article IX further provides that if a State 'has reason to believe that an activity... planned by it or its nationals in outer space ... would cause potentially harmful interference' with other States' peaceful use of outer space, the former is to 'undertake appropriate international consultations before proceeding with any such activity'. However, the Experts noted that the obligation to consult has not been followed in State practice and therefore they could not conclude that it represents a customary international law requirement.

---

[694] Note that jurisdiction in outer space may be the subject of international agreements. For example, the International Space Station Agreement provides that each State Party will register its elements and 'shall retain jurisdiction and control over the elements it registers ... and over personnel in or on the Space Station who are its nationals.' ISS Agreement, Art. 5. Thus, there is no concurrent jurisdiction over persons aboard the International Space Station.

[695] Article IX also requires States to conduct studies of outer space in a fashion that avoids the harmful contamination of outer space or adverse changes to the earth's environment.

6. As used in this Rule, due regard, a standard of care that also appears in the law of the sea (Rule 45) and air law (Rule 57), is generally understood as requiring States to act in a manner that does not impede the exercise by other States of the rights they enjoy in outer space. To illustrate, consider a State's test of a cyber weapon designed to generate a power spike in one of its satellites intended for decommission that causes electrical equipment, compressed gases, or propellants to explode. Should the test create a debris field that endangers other States' satellites and spacecraft, it might violate a right the other State enjoys *vis-à-vis* its space activities.

7. Pursuant to the Outer Space Treaty and other space law instruments, astronauts are the 'envoys of mankind'.[696] States are required to render them all possible assistance in event of distress and to immediately inform other States of any phenomena in outer space that pose a threat to their life or health.[697] Indeed, astronauts are required to render assistance to astronauts of other States in conducting their space activities. The International Group of Experts agreed, therefore, that when cyber activities are conducted in or through outer space, States must consider the impact of their cyber activities on astronauts and, relatedly, the equipment on which astronauts depend for their survival.

8. The application of this Rule is without prejudice to Rule 63 regarding harmful interference in international telecommunication law. It must be cautioned that the term 'interference' in this Rule is not synonymous with that found in Rule 63, for the latter is limited to harmful interference with the wireless cyber communications or services of other States. This Rule, by contrast, encompasses all interference that impedes other States' lawful space activities irrespective of whether they involve wireless cyber communications or services. In some cases, a State's activity may implicate both Rules.

Rule 60 – Supervision, responsibility, and liability

(a) A State must authorise and supervise the cyber 'activities in outer space' of its non-governmental entities.

---

[696] Outer Space Treaty, Art. V; Convention on Registration of Objects Launched into Outer Space, Arts. 10, 12; Declaration on the Use of Outer Space, para. 9.

[697] In this regard, note that the ITU legal regime contains an obligation to prioritise safety of life communications (chapeau to Chapter 11).

(b) **Cyber operations involving space objects are subject to the responsibility and liability regime of space law.**

1.   *Lit.* (a) is drawn from Article VI of the Outer Space Treaty, which provides that States are responsible for assuring that their 'national activities in outer space', including those of non-governmental entities, 'are carried out in conformity with the provisions' of the Outer Space Treaty. It further provides, '[t]he activities of non-governmental entities in outer space . . . shall require authorisation and continuing supervision by the appropriate State Party to the Treaty.' If an international organisation registers a satellite it operates, it assumes the same obligations as States that do so.[698]

2.   As used in this Rule, a State's 'non-governmental entities' refers to those entities whose space object is carried on the registry of that State, as well as to natural and legal persons of that State's nationality who operate space objects. Accordingly, a State is generally responsible for, and must authorise and on a continuing basis supervise, the cyber activities in outer space (as discussed below) of its non-governmental entities even if the entities operate a space object carried on the registry of another State. It must be cautioned that authorisation and supervision obligations are borne by the 'appropriate' State. In determining which State is the appropriate one, factors such as nationality of the operator, registration status of the object, and location of the telemetry, tracking, and command systems are relevant considerations.

3.   The term 'activities in outer space' denotes activities that comprise more than the mere utilisation of outer space cyber infrastructure for cyber communications or other activities that solely transit outer space.[699] For example, an activity in outer space in the sense of this Rule occurs when a telecommunications company launches a communications satellite into outer space. The State in which the company is

---

[698] In 1979, the European Space Agency became a Party to the Convention on Registration of Objects Launched into Outer Space. *See* Space Object Registration by the European Space Agency: Current Policy and Practice, UN Doc. A/AC.105/C.2/2015/CRP.18 (13 April 2015). The European Organisation for the Exploitation of Meteorological Satellites (EUMETSAT) became a Party in 1997 and the European Telecommunications Satellite Organisation (EUTELSATIGO) in 2014.

[699] This is without prejudice to other applicable international law, such as international telecommunications law. For instance, the ITU Radio Regulations prohibit transmitting stations from being established or operated by private persons or entities without an appropriate licence issued by the government. ITU Radio Regulations, Art. 18.1.

registeréd and located must authorise and supervise on a continuing basis the operation of that satellite.

4. *Lit.* (b) acknowledges that space activities, including those involving cyber operations, are subject to the space law regime of responsibility and liability. The International Group of Experts agreed that to the extent that this regime fails to address a particular situation, the general rules of State responsibility set forth in Sections 1 to 3 in Chapter 4 apply.[700]

5. Illustrative of the space law responsibility and liability regime is Article VII of the Outer Space Treaty, which sets forth the general principle that launching States are internationally liable to other States, or their natural or juridical persons, for damage caused by their space objects. This principle is further developed by Article II of the Liability Convention for States Parties. That provision establishes an absolute liability regime according to which a launching State has to pay compensation for 'damage caused by its space object on the surface of the earth or to aircraft in flight', whether that object be governmental or non-governmental.[701] For instance, if cyber activities by a launching State, whether terrestrial or space-based, cause a satellite it has launched to crash on the earth, the launching State is liable for any physical damage irrespective of any lack of intent or negligence.

6. The International Group of Experts also considered the issue of absolute liability in cases where one State intentionally employs cyber operations against a launching State's space object that causes it to crash on the earth. The Experts distinguished two situations. The first occurs when the claimant State's gross negligence or intentional act wholly or partially causes the damage it has suffered. In such a case, Article VI of the Liability Convention bars claims against the launching State.

7. In the second situation, the negligent or intentional act is that of a third State. For example, assume State A is the sole launching State and is operating its satellite in accordance with all applicable international law. State B's cyber operation causes (either negligently or intentionally) the satellite to deorbit, thereby resulting in damage on the territory of State C. State C would be entitled to bring a claim against State A under the Liability Convention or the Outer Space Treaty (assuming State A is a Party to one or both) even if State C knows that State B's actions caused

---

[700] Articles on State Responsibility, Art. 55.

[701] Pursuant to Art. V(1) of the Liability Convention, in the case of multiple launching States, joint and several liability applies. The launching States may have concluded agreements amongst themselves as to which one will bear the brunt of liability.

the deorbit. Potentially, State A separately would have recourse against State B under Article VI of the Outer Space Treaty, as State B is responsible for its activities in outer space (assuming that directing the cyber capability against a satellite qualifies as an 'activity in outer space').

8.   A third key *lex specialis* rule appears in Article III of the Liability Convention. By the Article, the absolute liability regime does not apply to damage caused to one space object by another in outer space. It specifically provides that if damage is caused to a space object or to persons or property on board such a space object, liability only attaches 'if the damage is due to [the State's] fault or the fault of persons for whom it is responsible'.[702] Consider a case in which State A is conducting cyber operations against State B's communications satellite's control system's ground station. The operations alter the satellite's orbit and it collides with State C's satellite. State B is not liable because it was not at fault for the incident. By contrast, consider a situation in which a launching State executes an update of the on-board systems of one of its satellites. The State has failed to test the software adequately before installing it aboard the satellite. As a result, the system update causes the satellite to change orbital parameters and it collides with another State's space object. Assuming that failure can be established by the claimant State, the launching State bears liability for the damage caused because the failure to test the system update software fully before installing it likely constitutes negligence.

9.   Note that both Article II and III of the Liability Convention refer to 'damage'. Article I(a) of the Liability Convention defines damage as 'loss of life, personal injury or other impairment of health; or loss of or damage to property of States or of persons, natural or juridical, or property of international intergovernmental organisations'. The International Group of Experts agreed that the term 'damage', as used in the Convention, does not extend to deletion or alteration of data aboard a space object unless such deletion or alteration results in the aforementioned consequences (although the cyber operation in question may constitute interference, Rule 59). Nor does it extend to economic loss suffered as a result of loss of use of a space object. The Experts did concur that the concept of damage to property encompasses a space object's permanent loss of functionality.

---

[702] Liability Convention, Art. III.

10.   Consider the case of a satellite that is capable of rendezvous and proximity operations.[703] It connects with another satellite in orbit and transmits code that permanently disables or otherwise causes that satellite to permanently cease performing its intended function. Or consider the example of a cyber operation that causes the shutter of a photo reconnaissance satellite to close permanently. The Experts agreed that such consequences would qualify as 'damage' for the purpose of Article III.

---

[703] A space rendezvous and proximity operation is an orbital manoeuvre during which two spacecraft deliberately arrive at the same orbit and approach to a very close distance (e.g., within visual contact) for a specific purpose.

11

International telecommunication law

1. International telecommunication law is primarily concerned with the provision of international telecommunication services and the operation of telecommunication infrastructure. As such, it may be characterised as an enabling regime for international telecommunications, including those carried out by cyber means. It also addresses ancillary issues, such as the obligation of States to safeguard cyber infrastructure (Rule 61).

2. Although the International Group of Experts did not conclude that the Rules set forth in this Chapter necessarily reflect customary international law, it noted that nearly all States are Parties to the treaty regime of the International Telecommunication Union (ITU), the UN specialised agency charged with the regulation of international telecommunications. Therefore, the Experts agreed that it was useful to incorporate the following cyber-relevant treaty-based Rules in this Manual.

3. A 'telecommunication' is '[a]ny transmission, emission or reception of signs, signals, writing, images, and sounds or intelligence of any nature by wire, radio, optical or other electromagnetic systems'.[704] The International Group of Experts agreed that because the ITU legal regime is technology-neutral, emerging technological developments enabling the transfer of data by other media, such as over gamma rays, x-rays,[705] or physical conduits that are not currently in widespread use for telecommunications, are likely to fall within the scope of the term. Telecommunications by cyber means, that is, telecommunications that presently occur primarily over IP-based

[704] ITU Constitution, Annex, No. 1012. *See also* ITU Radio Regulations, Art. 1.3; ITU 1988 International Telecommunication Regulations, Art. 2(1); ITU 2012 International Telecommunication Regulations, Art. 2(1).
[705] The current range of the electromagnetic spectrum used for international telecommunication services is 3,000 GHz and below, excluding gamma rays and x-rays. ITU Radio Regulations, Art. 2.1.

networks, also qualify as telecommunications because they are transmitted over wire, the electromagnetic spectrum, or optical fibre. Sharing intelligence information via secure email, for instance, constitutes a telecommunication. However, if the same information is transmitted by use of a USB memory stick, it does not qualify as such.[706]

4. The law reflected in this Chapter is concerned with telecommunications that are 'international' in character. As used in this Manual, the term 'international telecommunications' encompasses those telecommunications that involve the transmission of data across State borders, as well as telecommunications that are transmitted from, to, or through extraterritorial regions like international waters, international airspace, and outer space (see discussion of the meaning of the term 'outer space' in the chapeau to Chapter 10).

5. An 'international telecommunication service' is the 'offering of a telecommunication capability between telecommunication offices or stations of any nature that are in or belong to different countries'.[707] In the cyber context, the principal international telecommunication service is the provision of connectivity to the Internet, whether by Internet service providers or other telecommunications companies, such as those that offer cellular data connectivity (e.g., 4G service). Additionally, for instance, the GPS or GLONASS satellite navigation systems qualify as international telecommunication services that are important in the cyber context. The term will also capture services currently under development, like access to the Internet from airplanes, dirigibles, or balloons. For the purposes of this Manual, international telecommunication services in the cyber context will be referred to as 'international cyber communication services'.

6. The treaty sources of international telecommunication law consist primarily of the ITU instruments − the Constitution, the Convention, and its two Administrative Regulations: the Radio Regulations and the International Telecommunication Regulations.[708] Under this regime, the ITU is the sole intergovernmental organisation that carries out: the global

---

[706] The Experts noted that even though data is nearly always in motion at the purely technical level even when it is stored, data processing within a CPU does not involve transmission in the sense of international telecommunication law and is therefore not considered a 'telecommunication'.

[707] ITU Constitution, Annex, No. 1011; ITU 1988 International Telecommunication Regulations, Art. 2(2); ITU 2012 International Telecommunication Regulations, Art. 2(2).

[708] ITU Constitution, Art. 4. The ITU Constitution and Convention were adopted at the 1992 Additional Plenipotentiary Conference in Geneva and amended at subsequent

allocation of frequency bands in the electromagnetic spectrum for various wireless telecommunication services, such as mobile telephony, GPS navigation, and satellite broadcasts; the coordination and recording of frequency assignments by States with respect to utilisation of these allocations (in this regard, see also Rule 63); and, as appropriate, the recording of orbital positions, whether used or intended to be used, of satellites.[709] The ITU also facilitates the international standardisation of telecommunications activities.[710]

7.   Additional rules that regulate certain international telecommunications by cyber means are found in the law of the sea. Of note are those addressing submarine communication cables (Rule 54) and unauthorised broadcasting on the high seas (Rule 46). Similarly, space law governs particular aspects of international telecommunications, as with the obligation to operate communications satellites with due regard for the activities of other States in outer space (*lit.* (b) of Rule 59); the requirement that States authorise and supervise the activities of non-governmental entities in outer space (*lit.* (a) of Rule 60), as in the case of a private company that launches and operates a communications satellite; and the determination of liability for damage caused by communications satellites (*lit.* (b) of Rule 60).

8.   States may agree to special arrangements for international telecommunication services, including international cyber communication services. The existence of special regimes, which is provided for in Articles 42 and 43 of the ITU Constitution, does not relieve Parties thereto of their obligations to other States under the ITU instruments, such as that to refrain from harmful interference with other States' telecommunication services (Rule 63).

---

plenipotentiary conferences (Kyoto in 1994, Minneapolis in 1998, Marrakesh in 2002, Antalya in 2006, Guadalajara in 2010, Busan in 2014). The ITU Radio Regulations were adopted in 1995 and subsequently revised and approved on numerous occasions, most recently in Geneva in 2015. The majority of the 2015 revisions entered into force as of 1 January 2017. There are currently two International Telecommunication Regulations in force, those of 1988 and 2012. States that are not Parties to the 2012 treaty remain bound by the ITU 1988 International Telecommunication Regulations, as are States that are Parties to the 2012 instrument with respect to non-Parties to that instrument.

[709] ITU Constitution, Art. 1(2)(a–b).

[710] The International Group of Experts noted that in addition to the ITU, other entities have an organisational and policy role with regard to international cyber communications issues. These include the Internet Assigned Numbers Authority (IANA) and the Internet Engineering Task Force (IETF).

9. The International Group of Experts took note of the fact that the ITU's legal regime affords priority to telecommunications concerning safety of life and government telecommunications.[711] The Experts decided not to address the prioritisation issue in a separate Rule in this Manual because it was agreed that, in the cyber context, such prioritisation has little practical relevance and is not broadly supported by State practice. As international cyber communication services are increasingly ubiquitous and higher bandwidth becomes available, the need to prioritise particular types of international cyber communications decreases. However, the Experts agreed that should situations arise in which the ability to engage in safety of life or government communications depends on their prioritisation, States must give these communications preference. Consider the case of a massive earthquake in a border area. In order to ensure the unhindered coordination of disaster relief among the States affected by the earthquake, the States could, to comply with the prioritisation requirement, require mobile operators and ISPs to limit certain high bandwidth-consuming traffic, such as file transfers and multimedia streaming.

10. The International Group of Experts took further note of Article 37 of the ITU Constitution, which deals with the secrecy of telecommunications. The Experts understood Article 37(1) as creating a presumption in favour of the secrecy of international correspondence conducted by cyber means. That said, Article 37(2) permits a State to provide such correspondence to national or international authorities, if so authorised under either domestic or international law. Because the Experts agreed that Article 37(2) provides States an extensive basis for abrogating the secrecy of international correspondence, they were unable to come to any definitive conclusion as to the extent to which Article 37 affects States' cyber operations. With regard to the secrecy of telecommunications, the Experts emphasised that States must, in particular, assess the lawfulness of their cyber operations *vis-à-vis* the international human right to privacy (Rule 35).

---

[711] ITU Constitution, Arts. 40 and 41, respectively. *See also* ITU 1988 International Telecommunication Regulations, Art. 5(1) and 5(2), respectively; ITU 2012 International Telecommunication Regulations, Art. 5(1) and 5(2), respectively.

Rule 61 – Duty to establish, maintain, and safeguard international telecommunication infrastructure

A State must take measures to ensure the establishment of international telecommunication infrastructure that is required for rapid and uninterrupted international telecommunications. If, in complying with this requirement, the State establishes cyber infrastructure for international telecommunications, it must maintain and safeguard that infrastructure.

1.   This Rule is based on Article 38 of the ITU Constitution. It is designed to foster the availability and quality of international telecommunication services. The Article provides, in relevant part, that:

(1) Member States shall take such steps as may be necessary to ensure the establishment, under the best technical conditions, of the channels and installations necessary to carry on the rapid and uninterrupted exchange of international telecommunications.
(2) So far as possible, these channels and installations must be operated by the methods and procedures which practical operating experience has shown to be the best. They must be maintained in proper operating condition and kept abreast of scientific and technical progress.
(3) Member States shall safeguard these channels and installations within their jurisdiction.
(4) [E]ach Member State shall take such steps as may be necessary to ensure maintenance of those sections of international telecommunication circuits within its control.[712]

2.   Accordingly, this Rule sets forth three distinct obligations for States: to ensure the establishment of infrastructure that facilitates rapid and uninterrupted international telecommunications; to safeguard that infrastructure; and to maintain it. The International Group of Experts agreed that a State's obligations to safeguard and maintain international telecommunication infrastructure do not attach *vis-à-vis* infrastructure that is no longer used to fulfil the State's duty with respect to the establishment of the infrastructure.

3.   The International Group of Experts agreed that the duties set forth in this Rule are obligations of conduct, not of result. Obligations of

---

[712] ITU Constitution, Art. 38.

conduct generally require States to undertake their 'best efforts' to comply by a means of their choice. Such obligations do not impose a duty on States to succeed in their efforts (see also discussion in Rule 7 on compliance with the due diligence principle). Thus, the Rule's obligations are subject to a condition of feasibility in the attendant circumstances; States shoulder no obligations that would be unreasonable for them to fulfil. In this regard, the financial wherewithal and technical capability of the State in question are especially relevant.

4.   Article 38(1) of the ITU Constitution imposes a general duty on States to ensure the establishment of 'channels and installations necessary to carry on the rapid and uninterrupted exchange of international tele-communications'. The International Group of Experts agreed that States may determine for themselves whether the 'channels and installations' should include particular international cyber communication infrastructure. Because this Rule reflects an obligation of conduct, should a State choose to comply with it by establishing, under the best technical conditions, cyber communication capacity, it need only do so insofar as those means are feasible and reasonable in the circumstances. For instance, if the cost of connecting a remote geographic area to a fibre optic cable for high-speed data transfer is prohibitively high for a particular State, the State can provide the best alternative that is feasible, such as a less expensive satellite connection. All of the Experts agreed, however, that this obligation does not pertain to the availability of end-user devices, such as computers and smartphones. As a practical matter, the Experts noted that ensuring the establishment of cyber infrastructure that provides connectivity to the global Internet is a highly effective way to enable rapid and uninterrupted exchange of international telecommunications.

5.   The International Group of Experts agreed that the Rule encompasses international telecommunication infrastructure operated by both States and private companies. Therefore, to discharge the duty to ensure the establishment of the infrastructure for 'rapid and uninterrupted' international telecommunications, a State can, for example, create a business environment that encourages investments by private companies in the laying of communication cables and the establishment of other cyber infrastructure that underlies the Internet. To the extent that private companies act in this field, the State is obliged to ensure the cyber infrastructure they operate is also maintained and safeguarded, as discussed below.

6.   The International Group of Experts agreed that the obligation to establish international telecommunication infrastructure is closely

related to Article 33 of the ITU Constitution, which sets forth the public's right to engage in international telecommunication services. In other words, if a State has established publicly available international telecommunication capability, the public may enjoy a right to use it for international telecommunications.

7.   Where international telecommunications are carried out by cyber means, Article 38(3) of the ITU Constitution obligates States to 'safeguard', and Article 38(2) and (4) to 'maintain', the underlying cyber infrastructure. The International Group of Experts noted that whereas the duty to safeguard relates to cyber infrastructure within a State's jurisdiction (Rule 8), the obligation to maintain is limited to that within its control. Although the notion of control is undefined in international telecommunication law, the Experts agreed that, as a minimum, it refers to cyber infrastructure that is under a State's exclusive governmental control, as in the case of infrastructure that is owned and operated by the State. By contrast, as a general matter, all cyber infrastructure within a State's territory is subject to its jurisdiction (Rule 9) such that a State can ensure, through the promulgation of domestic laws and regulations, that the cyber infrastructure owned and operated by the private sector is also safeguarded.

8.   The Experts agreed that the duties to safeguard and maintain include overall operational maintenance, as well as conformity to technical standards that ensure data can be transmitted reliably and efficiently. For instance, a State may set forth technical and operating conditions in the licences it issues to telecommunication service providers to make sure the objectives are achieved.[713]

9.   The International Group of Experts also discussed the lawfulness of a State supplying telecommunication services in another State where such

---

[713] See the EU Directive on privacy and electronic communications, which requires a provider of a publicly available electronic communications service to take appropriate technical and organisational measures to safeguard the security of its services. Directive 2002/58/EC of the European Parliament and of the Council Concerning the Processing of Personal Data and the Protection of Privacy in the Electronic Communications Sector (amended by Directive 2006/24/EC of the European Parliament and of the Council of 15 March 2006, and Directive 2009/136/EC of the European Parliament and of the Council of 25 November 2009), pmbl. pt. 20, 12 July 2002; Conditions which Apply to all Communications Networks and Service Providers: Consolidated Version of General Conditions Office of Communications (UK) ('Ofcom General Conditions') (May 2015), Art. 3(1)(a) (requiring a communications provider to take all necessary measures to maintain, to the greatest extent possible, the proper and effective functioning of the public communications network provided by it at all times).

services are non-existent, as in the case of providing access to the Internet via a communications satellite or from aboard an aircraft, without the latter State's consent. The Experts noted that each case must be assessed on its own merits. For instance, as discussed in Rule 55, if the aircraft is flying in another State's national airspace without authorisation from that State, the activity is unlawful by virtue of the aircraft's unconsented to presence in the State's airspace.

10.   With regard to the provision of telecommunication services *per se*, a minority of the Experts opined that the activity is lawful because no rule against such activity has crystallised into customary international law. However, the majority was of the view that a State supplying telecommunication services in another State without the latter's consent is impermissible on the ground that each State enjoys the sovereign prerogative to regulate its telecommunication sector, including who provides services and how they do so.[714] With respect to the restoration of international cyber communication services by one State that another State has suspended, see Rule 62.

11.   On the obligation of States to adopt domestic legislation regarding damage to submarine communication cables, see Rule 54.

Rule 62 – Suspension or stoppage of cyber communications

(a) **A State may suspend, either in part or in full, international cyber communication services within its territory. Immediate notice of such suspension must be provided to other States.**

(b) **A State may stop the transmission of a private cyber communication that appears contrary to its national laws, public order, or decency, or that is dangerous to its national security.**

1.   As noted in Rule 2, to the extent a State exercises control over cyber infrastructure and cyber activities within its territory, it does so on the basis of the principle of sovereignty. The sovereign right of States to regulate their telecommunications is also provided for in the preamble of the ITU Constitution. This Rule recognises that in the exercise of this sovereign prerogative, States may sometimes suspend international cyber communication services or stop the transmission of cyber communications. This right is without prejudice to any

---

[714] ITU Constitution, pmbl.

international law obligations the State concerned may shoulder prohibiting it from doing so in a particular case.

2.   *Lit.* (a) and (b) are based on Articles 35 and 34(2) of the ITU
Constitution, respectively, which specify the conditions for a State's
interruption of the flow of telecommunications as an exception to norms
that otherwise aim to ensure their continuity (see, for instance, Rule 61).

> ARTICLE 35 – Suspension of Services
>
> Each Member State reserves the right to suspend the international tele-
> communication service, either generally or only for certain relations and/
> or for certain kinds of correspondence, outgoing, incoming or in transit,
> provided that it immediately notifies such action to each of the other
> Member States through the Secretary-General.

and

> ARTICLE 34 – Stoppage of Telecommunications
>
> (2) Member States . . . reserve the right to cut off, in accordance with their
> national law, any . . . private telecommunications which may appear
> dangerous to the security of the State or contrary to its laws, to public
> order or to decency.

Based on these Articles, the International Group of Experts acknowledged two categories of situations in which suspension or stoppage is
lawful.

3.   *Lit.* (a) permits partial or full suspension of international telecommunication services, including the suspension of international cyber
communication services, such as communications over the Internet.
Suspension refers to the temporary interruption of services.[715] The
International Group of Experts agreed that the right encompasses suspension of incoming and outgoing communications, as well as those that
transit a State's territory. It likewise applies to communications that
occur on-board vessels or aircraft (Rule 10), or that transit satellites (*lit.*
(a) of Rule 59), over which the State exercises jurisdiction and control. If
a State suspends an international cyber communication service, it must
provide immediate notice of the suspension, as well as subsequent
restoration, to ITU Member States through the organisation's Secretary

---

[715] This is also reflected in the ITU 1988 International Telecommunication Regulations,
Art. 7(1), and ITU 2012 International Telecommunication Regulations, Art. 7(1), both
of which refer to 'suspension and . . . the subsequent return to normal conditions'.

General.[716] The Experts noted that States may be bound by treaty or customary law that limits or otherwise restricts their right under *lit.* (a).[717]

4. A State's authority to suspend an international cyber communication service was illustrated by the Egyptian government's blocking of international Internet and mobile telephony connections for several days in 2011 due to civil unrest. In the wake of popular protests that utilised Twitter, Facebook, and other social media sites, Egypt suspended such access throughout the country by government decision.[718] Although Egypt did not comply with the requirement to notify other States, the International Group of Experts agreed that the suspension was within its rights under international telecommunication law. This conclusion is without prejudice to the question of whether Egypt's action complied with other rules of international law, such as respect for the international human right to freedom of expression (Rule 35).

5. The Experts took notice of practical obstacles to a State's implementation of a decision to suspend international cyber communication services. In the Egyptian example, access was partially restored within hours of the governmental shutdown with the help of entities such as Google and Twitter that offered technological alternatives, like voice messaging and analogue connections. However, practical difficulties do not render the legal authority to suspend moot.

6. The International Group of Experts agreed that *lit.* (a) only addresses the authority of a State to suspend international cyber communication services. It was divided as to the question of the lawfulness of another State's activities to remotely restore telecommunication services in a State that has suspended service, for instance, by offering Internet access from a high altitude aircraft. A majority of the Experts was of the view that States must respect the sovereign prerogative of other States to regulate, including through suspension, their telecommunications and therefore activities designed to circumvent suspension would be unlawful as, for example, usurpation of an inherently governmental function (Rule 4).[719]

---

[716] ITU Constitution, Art. 35; ITU 1988 International Telecommunication Regulations, Art. 7; ITU 2012 International Telecommunication Regulations, Art. 7.

[717] For potential restrictions on such suspensions for States Parties, see the General Agreement on Trade in Services, Annex on Telecommunications, Art. 5, 15 April 1994, 1869 UNTS 183.

[718] Charles Arthur, *Egypt blocks social media websites in attempted clampdown on unrest*, THE GUARDIAN, 26 January 2011.

[719] ITU Constitution, pmbl.

The minority opined that since no rule exists under customary international law that prohibits the remote supply of international telecommunication capability to another State, the activity is lawful, unless other rules of international law are violated in the course of such conduct (such as Rule 55). With respect to providing telecommunication services to a State in which such services are non-existent, see Rule 61.

7.   According to *lit.* (b), a State may stop a private cyber communication, like an instant message, email, or Tweet, that is contrary to its national laws, public order, or decency, or that endangers the State's national security. As used in this Rule, the term 'private' means 'non-governmental'.[720] For example, a State may put mechanisms in place to block and report instant messages of private individuals sent on a social networking portal that include certain keywords indicating that a message involves child pornography or terrorist activity. No notification is required before or after stopping a particular private cyber communication pursuant to this Rule.

8.   The International Group of Experts emphasised that if a State exercises its right under *lit.* (a) or (b), its action is without prejudice to, *inter alia*, international human rights law (Chapter 6).

9.   The International Group of Experts agreed that pursuant to *lit.* (a), a receiving State may not suspend international cyber communication services upon which a diplomatic mission or consular post relies because according to Rule 42 it must permit the mission's or post's free electronic communications. Furthermore, *lit.* (b) does not allow a State to stop the official cyber communications of diplomatic missions or consular posts as they do not qualify as 'private'.

Rule 63 – Harmful interference

A State's use of radio stations may not harmfully interfere with other States' protected use of radio frequencies for wireless cyber communications or services.

1.   The prohibition of harmful interference by a State with the wireless cyber communications and services of another State is based on Article 45(1) of the ITU Constitution,[721] which provides that

---

[720] ITU Constitution, Annex no. 1014–1015.
[721] *See also* ITU Constitution, Art. 1(2)(b); ITU Radio Regulations, pmbl. pt. 0.4, Art. 15.1.

All stations, whatever their purpose, must be established and operated in such a manner as not to cause harmful interference to the radio services or communications of other Member States. . ..

2.   Wireless cyber communications and services take place over radio waves, that is, over a particular segment of the electromagnetic spectrum.[722] Wireless cyber services, for instance, include cellular data, Wi-Fi availability, GPS, and the provision of Internet connectivity via a communications satellite. With respect to the Rule's reference to 'radio stations', the International Group of Experts agreed that despite Article 45(1) of the ITU Constitution's mention of 'all stations', the Article is meant solely to address radio stations. The Experts based this conclusion on the fact that Article 45 appears in Chapter VII of the ITU Constitution, which is titled 'Special Provisions for Radio'.

3.   As set forth in Rule 64, the prohibition reflected in this Rule does not apply to military radio stations used for military purposes.

4.   The term 'stations' refers to any radio transmitting station, whether located on the earth or space-based, that emits radio frequency signals over the electromagnetic spectrum and is capable of causing harmful interference to the wireless services or communications of other States.[723] Cyber-relevant examples include satellite ground stations that transmit signals to communications satellites, communications satellites that transmit data to the earth, mobile phone transmission antennae, and towers of wireless Internet service providers (so-called 'WISPs').

5.   The ITU Constitution notes that 'radio frequencies and any associated orbits . . . are limited natural resources and that they must be used rationally, efficiently and economically . . . so that countries or groups of countries may have equitable access to those orbits and frequencies'.[724] As the utilisation of these limited resources by States has grown significantly, particularly with the advent and proliferation of wireless cyber activities, so too has the potential for unintentional harmful interference.

---

[722] Radio waves are 'electromagnetic waves of frequencies arbitrarily lower than 3 000 GHz, propagated in space without artificial guide'. ITU Radio Regulations, Art. 1.5.

[723] A [radio] station is defined in the ITU Radio Regulations as 'One or more transmitters or receivers or a combination of transmitters and receivers, including the accessory equipment, necessary at one location for carrying on a radio-communication service, or the radio astronomy service'. ITU Radio Regulations, Art. 1.61. In many instances, the ITU Radio Regulations specifically address 'transmitting stations'.

[724] ITU Constitution, Art. 44(2).

Therefore, the planning and coordination of their use on the international level is of crucial importance.

6.   The ITU serves a coordinating function for Member States in the administration of the electromagnetic spectrum as a common resource and of associated earth orbits.[725] In order for States to receive international recognition of the frequencies and associated earth orbits that they use, and to benefit from the resulting protection against harmful interference, their usage must conform to the ITU coordination and registration regime, or to any special arrangements made in accordance with Article 42 of the ITU Constitution.[726] The International Group of Experts concluded that the ITU regime governing use of the electromagnetic spectrum and associated earth orbits is well-established and applicable to their use for cyber activities.[727]

7.   'Harmful interference' is that which 'endangers the functioning of a radio navigation service . . . or seriously degrades, obstructs or repeatedly interrupts a radio communication service operating in accordance with the Radio Regulations'.[728] For the purposes of this Rule, harmful interference is understood as the serious degradation, obstruction, or interruption of cyber communications or services that rely upon the electromagnetic spectrum.

8.   The International Group of Experts agreed that this Rule applies exclusively to interference caused by one State with another's use of frequencies that enable cyber communications or services, wherever

---

[725] Spectrum administration began with the International Radiotelegraph Convention of 1927. International Radiotelegraph Convention, Washington, 25 November 1927. The ITU began to regulate orbital slots towards the end of the 1950s.

[726] ITU Radio Regulations, Arts. 8, 11. The ITU Radio Regulations establish the international framework for notification and recording of the use of electromagnetic frequencies and orbits. Pursuant to the Regulations, the use of electromagnetic frequencies and orbits is recorded in the Master International Frequency Register (MIFR) or in an agreed plan for frequency use. It should be noted that military uses of the spectrum and orbit resources are not transparently recorded with the MIFR, other than being generally designated as governmental uses or as 'not allocated' within a State's territory. This is consistent with Rule 64. For examples of the military's utilisation of the electromagnetic spectrum, see United States Department of Defense, JP 6-01, Joint Electromagnetic Spectrum Management Operations, 20 March 2012.

[727] Such technical coordination has been carried out on a consistent basis among States on bilateral, multilateral, and global levels since the mid-twentieth century.

[728] ITU Constitution, Annex, no. 1003; ITU Radio Regulations, Art. 1.169. From a technical perspective, harmful interference occurs when two or more electromagnetic waves of the same wavelength and amplitude, but different phases, overlap partially or fully, thereby degrading or cancelling each other.

those communications or services take place, including in outer space. The purpose of the Rule is to ensure the freedom of States from harmful interference by other States in their properly coordinated and MIFR-recorded use of electromagnetic spectrum radio frequencies. The interference in question can be intentional or unintentional. However, the protection from harmful interference is dependent upon the State having received international recognition for use of specific frequencies by having them duly recorded in accordance with the relevant provisions of the ITU Radio Regulations.

9.   Consider a case in which State A licenses a new wireless communications network to operate exclusively within its territory, utilising cyber infrastructure therein. State A has neither recorded the new frequencies used in the MIFR, nor fulfilled the requirement of coordinating the operator's use of frequencies with neighbouring States B and C. States B and C have already granted licences to operate a similar network pursuant to the ITU's requirements, according them rights of use and international recognition for the frequencies. State A's new operator activates its network, causing harmful interference to State B and C's operators. State A is in violation of this Rule.

10.   With regard to the deliberate causation of harmful interference, the International Group of Experts noted that States regularly engage in activities that are sometimes denoted as electronic warfare operations or simply 'jamming'. Jamming is carried out to block certain activities, including cyber activities, typically on the basis of their content.

11.   During peacetime, States have engaged in jamming operations to block radio, television, and satellite broadcasts on ideological or political grounds. Take, for example, the jamming by Iran of Eutelsat transmissions in 2012, including BBC Persian, the Voice of America Persian, and Radio Free Europe's Radio Farda,[729] or the jamming by Cuba of US broadcasting through Radio Marti. The International Group of Experts agreed that unless peacetime jamming is conducted by a military radio station (Rule 64) or takes place and has effects entirely within that State's territory, it generally constitutes a violation of this Rule. However, the Experts also agreed that extraterritorial jamming is lawful to prevent violation of *jus cogens* norms, as in the case of the radio broadcasts that incited the Rwandan genocide in

[729] Press Release, Eutelsat, Eutelsat Condemns Jamming of Broadcasts from Iran and Renews Appeals for Decisive Action to International Regulators (4 October 2012).

1994.[730] Finally, the Experts noted that jamming could be permissible in certain circumstances as a lawful countermeasure (Rule 20).

12. During an armed conflict, the permissibility of jamming is subject to the law of armed conflict (Part IV) as *lex specialis*. Take the case of deliberate jamming of enemy air defence radar systems or GPS navigational systems in order to support an airstrike on a military objective (Rule 100). If the jamming is likely to cause incidental loss of civilian lives or harm to civilian property, the loss or damage qualifies as collateral damage that must be considered in the proportionality analysis (Rule 113) and the precautions in attack requirements (Rules 114–120).

13. Intentional 'harmful interference' operations may constitute violations of other rules of international law. In particular, the provisions regarding restrictions on vessels in innocent passage (Rule 48) and aircraft and vessels in transit and archipelagic sea lanes passage (Rules 52 and 53, respectively) may be pertinent. Additionally, see the restrictions on aircraft overflying another State's national airspace (Rule 55).

Rule 64 – Exemption of military radio installations

A State retains its entire freedom under international telecommunication law with regard to military radio installations.

1. Article 48(1) of the ITU Constitution provides that 'Member States retain their entire freedom with regard to military radio installations', a provision that the International Group of Experts agreed reflects longstanding State practice with respect to the governance of international telecommunications. In this regard, they noted that an analogous exemption was included in the International Telegraph Union's (the predecessor of the International Telecommunication Union) International Telegraph Convention of 1906.[731] The exception was retained in subsequent versions of both Unions' Conventions.[732]

---

[730] *See The Prosecutor* v. *Ferdinand Nahimana, Jean-Bosco Barayagwiza, Hassan Ngeze*, Case No. ICTR-99-52-T, judgment and sentence, paras. 949–953, 970–974 (3 December 2003).

[731] International Radiotelegraph Convention, Berlin, 1906, Art. 21.

[732] *See, e.g.*, International Telecommunication Convention, Madrid, 1932, Art. 39; International Telecommunication Convention, Malaga–Torremolinos, 1973, Art. 38; ITU Constitution, Art. 48.

2. Although the ITU Convention does not define a 'radio installation', the International Group of Experts agreed that the term includes
devices that enable the wireless transmission of data over radio waves. To
the extent these or other radio installations are 'military', this Rule
applies.

3. With regard to the scope of the term 'military radio installations',
the International Group of Experts agreed that an installation operated
solely for military purposes, such as a military communications satellite,
qualifies. The Experts likewise concurred that the term applies to military
radio installations used by multinational forces, including peace forces.
Finally, certain non-military installations used solely for military purposes may also fall within the scope of this Rule, such as a reconnaissance
satellite operated by a civilian intelligence agency to gather military
intelligence. As a general matter, though, installations used for governmental purposes do not qualify as military radio installations.[733]

4. The Experts concurred that the Rule does not apply to non-
military radio installations that the military utilises together with non-
military users (so-called 'dual use' installations).[734] A prominent example
is the usage of the GPS navigation system, which is operated by the
United States Department of Defense, but serves both civilian and military purposes. The Experts also agreed that this Rule does not apply to a
State's military radio installation that provides services, such as wireless
Internet connectivity, solely to the public.

5. The exclusion of military installations from international telecommunication law is denoted as an 'entire freedom' in Article 48(1).
The International Group of Experts agreed that this means, for
example, that a State is not obliged to record a frequency assignment
for a military communications satellite in geostationary earth orbit
with the ITU,[735] as would otherwise be required by the ITU Radio

---

[733] Circular Letter from François Rancy, Director, Radiocommunication Bureau, to Admin-
istrations of Member States of the ITU, CR/389, 26 January 2016. ('Article 48 refers to
"military radio installations" and not to stations used for governmental purposes in
general . . .').
[734] ITU Constitution, Art. 48(3).
[735] A satellite earth orbit is the path of the satellite around the earth, influenced by
gravitational pull. The geostationary earth orbit, where most communications satellites
are placed, is at a distance of 35.786 km from the earth, situated directly above the
equator. Because a satellite that is positioned in the geostationary orbit circles at the
same speed and in the same direction as the earth rotates, it remains 'fixed' in relation to
an area on the earth.

Regulations.[736] Indeed, because a military communications satellite is likely to be utilised to transmit sensitive and classified information, making known the frequencies that such a satellite uses would facilitate the interception of this data by other States.

6. The Experts acknowledged that Article 48(2) obliges States to comply with the ITU's Administrative Regulations (that is, the Radio Regulations and the International Telecommunication Regulations) 'so far as possible'. Therefore, for instance, if a State operates a military communications satellite and has not recorded the frequencies the satellite uses, the State must, to the extent possible, avoid harmful interference with other States' coordinated and recorded use of the same frequencies.

7. Military radio installations that are operated from the territory of another State are subject to the receiving State's consent (Rule 2).

---

[736] *See, inter alia*, ITU Radio Regulations, Art. 8.

PART III

International peace and security and cyber activities

12

Peaceful settlement

Rule 65 – Peaceful settlement of disputes

(a) **States must attempt to settle their international disputes involving cyber activities that endanger international peace and security by peaceful means.**

(b) **If States attempt to settle international disputes involving cyber activities that do not endanger international peace and security, they must do so by peaceful means.**

1. The international law requirement that international disputes be settled by peaceful means has been reinforced in multilateral and bilateral treaties,[737] applied in the decisions of the International Court of Justice,[738] and affirmed in UN General Assembly resolutions.[739] It is well accepted that this obligation is customary in nature.[740]

2. *Lit.* (a) of this Rule is based on Articles 2(3) and 33(1) of the UN Charter, the latter of which provides that '[t]he parties to any dispute, the continuance of which is likely to endanger the maintenance of international peace and security, shall, first of all, seek a solution by negotiation, enquiry, mediation, conciliation, arbitration, judicial settlement, resort to regional agencies or arrangements, or other peaceful means of their own choice'. *Lit.* (b) derives from Article 2(3) of the UN Charter,

---

[737] *See, e.g.*, American Treaty on Pacific Settlement (Pact of Bogotá), 30 April 1948, 30 UNTS 55; European Convention for the Peaceful Settlement of Disputes, 29 April 1957, 320 UNTS 243; Simla Agreement on Bilateral Relations, India–Pak., 2 July 1972, 858 UNTS 71; Conference on Security and Co-Operation in Europe: Final Act, princ. V, 1 August 1975, 14 ILM 1292.

[738] *See, e.g.*, *Fisheries Jurisdiction (Spain v. Can.)* judgment, 1998 ICJ 432, para. 56 (4 December); *Aerial Incident* judgment, para. 53.

[739] *See, e.g.*, Declaration on Friendly Relations, princ. 2, which confirms '[t]he principle that States shall settle their international disputes by peaceful means in such a manner that international peace and security and justice are not endangered'.

[740] *Nicaragua* judgment, para. 290; UN GGE 2015 Report, paras. 26, 28(b).

which provides that '[a]ll Members shall settle their international disputes by peaceful means in such a manner that international peace and
security, and justice, are not endangered'. The difference between *lit.* (a)
and *lit.* (b) is that the obligation to attempt to settle international disputes
peacefully is, in the view of the International Group of Experts, only
obligatory when the dispute in question is likely to endanger international peace and security. Both are discussed in more detail below.

3.   As the term is used in this Rule, a 'dispute' is 'a disagreement on a
point of law or fact, a conflict of legal views or interests between
parties'.[741] An allegation by one State that another has hacked into its
cyber infrastructure in a manner that violates the principle of sovereignty
(Rule 4) is, for instance, a dispute between two States. So too is disagreement between them about the sufficiency of domestic implementation
legislation required by a bilateral agreement concerning prosecution of
cyber crimes. Furthermore, if one State exercises its adjudicatory criminal
jurisdiction (Rule 8) over another State's intelligence officers who are
accused of conducting cyber economic espionage from the latter's territory, and the latter State contests the facts or the legal basis upon which
the former's actions are taken, a dispute, as that term is used in this Rule,
exists. It must be cautioned that a dispute is not mere general tension
between States; rather, it comprises a specific claim by one State that is
rejected by another.[742]

4.   This Rule only applies to international disputes and not to purely
internal ones.[743] An international dispute is one that is between two or
more States. For instance, a domestic political dispute over a State's
investment in cyber infrastructure does not fall within the purview of
this Rule. However, a dispute between members of a military alliance
over their respective treaty obligations concerning joint cyber defence
qualifies. Sometimes an internal dispute may develop into an international one.[744] Consider a case in which a State is transmitting via the
Internet inflammatory and racist communications that denigrate an
internal ethnic population. Individuals of the same ethnicity in a neighbouring State are incited by the transmissions to engage in protests and

---

[741] *Mavrommatis Palestine Concessions (Greece v. UK)*, PCIJ (ser. A) No. 2, at 11 (30 August
1924). *See also Case Concerning Certain Property (Liech. v. Ger.)* judgment on preliminary objections, 2005 ICJ 6, para. 24 (10 February).

[742] THE CHARTER OF UNITED NATIONS: A COMMENTARY, at 192.

[743] THE CHARTER OF UNITED NATIONS: A COMMENTARY, at 193.

[744] OPPENHEIM'S INTERNATIONAL LAW, at 115; THE CHARTER OF UNITED NATIONS:
A COMMENTARY, at 193.

rallies against their government, even though that was not the purpose of the communications. The neighbouring State unsuccessfully demands that the former desist in its operations. This situation constitutes a dispute that is international in character and the Rule applies.

5. The Experts took notice of the fact that unlike Article 2(3) of the UN Charter, which specifically limits its application to 'international disputes', Article 33 refers to 'any dispute'. Nevertheless, the Experts agreed that *lit.* (a) is also only concerned with international disputes since, as discussed below, Article 33 particularises Article 2(3) in light of disputes that endanger international peace and security.

6. The Experts were divided as to whether a transnational dispute between a State and a non-State actor may qualify as an international dispute. For example, States may have disputes with groups that are located abroad, such as a hacker group that is conducting cyber operations against it. The majority rejected application of this Rule in such cases and took the position that it applies only to disputes between States. These Experts looked, for instance, to Article 2(4) of the UN Charter, which imposes no prohibition on States with respect to any use of force against non-State actors (Rule 68). In their view, it would be incongruent for Articles 2(3) and 33(1) to impose requirements regarding the peaceful settlement of disputes with non-State actors when Article 2(4) fails to prohibit the use of force by a State against them.

7. A few of the Experts argued that in light of the absence of explicit text indicating that Articles 2(3) and 33(1) do not apply *vis-à-vis* non-State actors, the Rule must be interpreted in the spirit of Article 1(1) of the UN Charter, which notes that one purpose of the United Nations is 'to bring about by peaceful means ... adjustment or settlement of international disputes or situations which might lead to a breach of the peace'. Accordingly, they suggested that a broad interpretation is merited. They also noted that the UN Security Council at times has called upon States to settle disputes with non-State actors by peaceful means[745] and that agreements between States and organised armed groups sometimes impose obligations during armed conflict.

8. The term 'international peace and security' stems from the preamble to the Covenant of the League of Nations[746] and has been replicated in, *inter alia*, the UN Charter provisions set forth above.

---

[745] *See, e.g.,* SC Res. 27, UN Doc. S/RES/459 (1 August 1947); SC Res. 322, UN Doc. S/RES/ 322 (22 November 1972); SC Res. 389, UN Doc S/RES/389 (22 April 1976).

[746] League of Nations Covenant, pmbl.

Although undefined in the UN Charter, it is generally accepted that the term refers to 'more than the absence of war' and extends to 'development of friendly relations' in a way that brings about the 'stabilization of international relations in order to curtail the likelihood of war'.[747] Although the International Group of Experts acknowledged that ascertaining when an international dispute endangers international peace and security is difficult due to the vagueness inherent in the notion, it agreed that situations involving cyber activities that risk leading to the outbreak of an international armed conflict (Rule 82), or even isolated uses of force (Rule 68), clearly qualify. So too do cyber activities that destabilise relations between States in a manner that creates an environment foreseeably susceptible to escalation to uses of force and armed conflict. Depending on the attendant circumstances, examples might include cyber operations: directed at critical infrastructure like transportation assets (e.g., air traffic control and railway control systems) or infrastructure that contains dangerous forces, such as dams and nuclear electrical generating stations; that are highly disruptive of key societal functions, such as the delivery of social services; and that have extremely severe consequences for the national economy. A few of the Experts were of the view that whenever a State's cyber operations amount to a prohibited intervention (Rule 66), international peace and security is endangered.

9.   In settling an international dispute involving cyber activities, a State may only resort to 'peaceful means' and must do so in 'a manner that international peace and security, and justice are not endangered'. With respect to the reference to means of dispute resolution that do not endanger 'justice', the International Group of Experts considered the matter and concluded that this aspect of Article 2(3) of the UN Charter has little cyber-specific relevance and therefore omitted it from the Rule. However, this in no way diminishes the general requirement set forth in Article 2(3) and rare cases implicating justice are conceivable. Consider a situation whereby one State is engaged in an international arbitration to resolve a major dispute with another State. The first State hacks into a governmental database of the other State and corrupts data that substantiates the latter's claims. In doing so, the first State has violated the requirement that international disputes be settled in a manner that does not endanger international justice.

---

[747] The Charter of United Nations: A Commentary, at 110.

10. Multiple options for solving an international dispute involving cyber activities by peaceful means exist. These include, but are not limited to, 'negotiation, enquiry, mediation, conciliation, arbitration, judicial settlement, [and] resort to regional agencies or arrangements'.[748] Fact-finding, good offices, and any other means appropriate to the dispute are also within the ambit of this Rule. The choice of means is a matter of decision for the States.

11. This Rule is without prejudice to internationally lawful unilateral action that a State takes when engaged in an international dispute, even though mutually agreed upon means of addressing an international dispute may often be preferred for political and other reasons. For instance, a State may impose trade sanctions involving the import of IT equipment from another State with which it has a dispute in order to influence that dispute's resolution in its favour. Similarly, the Rule does not prohibit the taking of lawful countermeasures (Rule 20). Consider the case of a dispute involving an internationally wrongful act committed by one State. The injured State responds by denying the responsible State access to critical governmental data that the latter stores, pursuant to a bilateral treaty between the two States, as a backup on servers located in the injured State. The countermeasure, to the extent it complies with the various requirements for countermeasures (Rules 22–23), is lawful. In the same vein, this Rule is without prejudice to uses of force pursuant to the law of self-defence when force is 'necessary', as the condition of necessity is understood in that law (Rule 72).

12. However, caution is merited when considering unilateral means of resolving a dispute. Consider a case in which a State blocks certain key cyber communications of another State that pass through communications cables in the former's territory in order to pressure the latter to settle a dispute. Even if the measure is not otherwise prohibited under international law, should the reasonably foreseeable consequence of the action be an outbreak of hostilities between the States, the measure would be proscribed by this Rule because it endangers international peace and security, as discussed above.

13. This Rule does not prohibit any action authorised or mandated by the UN Security Council (Rule 76), as such measures are *ipso facto* lawful.

---

[748] UN Charter, Art. 33(1).

14.   In attempting to settle an international dispute, States must act in good faith.[749] This means that a State may not obstruct the settlement of the dispute, for instance by employing delaying tactics, failing to respond to legitimate requests for evidence, or maltreating witnesses. In particular, a State is not acting in good faith if it takes measures that it claims are designed to settle the dispute, when in fact the State knows with certainty that the measures will not have that effect. Take the example of one State accusing another of using proxy actors to engage in hostile cyber operations against it on multiple occasions in the past. The foreign ministers of the States concerned agree to discuss the matter and attempt to resolve it at an international conference. The State accused of having used the proxies denies its involvement in any of the cyber operations in question, whereas in reality the proxy actors operated under that State's effective control (Rule 17). Lying about its activities is not acting in good faith.

15.   Pursuant to *lit.* (a), States that are parties to an international dispute that is likely to endanger international peace and security are under an obligation to seek a solution by peaceful means.[750] For instance, assume one State acquires cyber capabilities that another State perceives as threatening. The latter protests and it becomes probable that, if the dispute is not resolved, the situation will likely escalate to the point where international peace and security is threatened. In this case, the States involved are obligated to resort to a peaceful means to attempt to resolve the situation.

16.   The International Group of Experts agreed that Article 33 is essentially an application of Article 2(3) in the context of international disputes that endanger international peace and security. It was included in the Charter to emphasise that States must attempt to resolve a dispute before the UN General Assembly or Security Council become seized of the issue.[751]

---

[749]   Article 2(2) of the UN Charter requires that '[a]ll Members, in order to ensure to all of them the rights and benefits resulting from membership, shall fulfill in good faith the obligations assumed by them in accordance with the present Charter'. *See also Aerial Incident* judgment, para. 53; Declaration on Friendly Relations, princ. (g) in pmbl.; Draft Declaration of the Rights and Duties of States, Art. 13. With respect to treaties, *see also* the Vienna Convention on the Law of Treaties, Art. 26.

[750]   Article 33 has been applied in many decisions of the International Court of Justice. *See, e.g., North Sea Continental Shelf (FRG v. Den.; FRG v. Neth.),* judgment, 1969 ICJ 3, para. 86 (20 February); *Fisheries Jurisdiction (UK v. Ice.),* judgment, 1973 ICJ 26, para. 75 (2 February); *Nicaragua* judgment, para. 290.

[751]   THE CHARTER OF UNITED NATIONS: A COMMENTARY, at 1071.

17.   States have to make a good faith (as discussed above) attempt to resolve a dispute that endangers international peace and security; so long as an attempt is made, *lit.* (a) has not been breached even if said attempt proves unsuccessful. In other words, *lit.* (a) imposes an obligation of conduct, not of result. For example, assume that two States have executed a bilateral agreement setting forth a verification regime with respect to particular military cyber operations that have in the past endangered international peace and security because the States viewed them as threatening. Following conclusion of the agreement, one of the States alleges that the other is in violation thereof by concealing key data that it believes essential to the verification regime. The two States agree to third party oversight of compliance, but the dispute nevertheless persists. Since a good faith attempt to resolve the dispute was made, a violation of *lit.* (a) has not occurred.

18.   Neither does *lit.* (a) require that all peaceful means of dispute resolution be exhausted or that the efforts to resolve a dispute extend over a lengthy period of time. Rather, parties to a dispute have to seek to settle the dispute until the point at which successful resolution becomes unrealistic.[752] Should those attempts fail, the dispute must be referred to the Security Council.[753]

19.   Only actual disputes fall within the ambit of *lit.* (a). Those that are merely prospective in the sense of having not yet materialised are not encompassed in it. In other words, there is no obligation to attempt to prevent a dispute that could arise in the future, even though it might be foreseeable. To illustrate, assume that one State is engaged in cyber espionage operations (Rule 32) in a manner that might reasonably be characterised as violating the sovereignty (Rule 4) of the target State. The latter has voiced no objection. There is no dispute to resolve as understood in the context of this Rule.

20.   Although there are differing views as to whether the obligation set forth in *lit.* (a) is extinguished upon the outbreak of hostilities,[754] the International Group of Experts took the position that so long as settlement remains possible by peaceful means such as negotiation, the

---

[752] THE CHARTER OF UNITED NATIONS: A COMMENTARY, at 1150–1151.

[753] UN Charter, Art. 37(1). *See also* Manila Declaration on the Peaceful Settlement of International Disputes, Annex to GA Res. 37/10, Art. II, pt. 4(a), UN Doc. A/37/10 (15 November 1982).

[754] On the issue of the effect of armed conflict on treaty obligations, *see* International Law Commission, Draft Articles on the Effects of Armed Conflict on Treaties, with commentaries, UN Doc. A/66/10 (2011).

parties to the dispute must continue to seek resolution even though an international armed conflict (Rule 82) has broken out between them.[755] This obligation continues regardless of compliance or non-compliance with the *jus ad bellum* in the initiation of armed conflict.

21.   The Experts acknowledged a view, which none of them held, that the existence of an international armed conflict terminates the obligation set forth in *lit.* (a) on the basis that peace no longer exists between the parties to a dispute; in other words, there is no longer any peace to be endangered (at least as between States that are parties to the armed conflict). This view has its roots in the historical suspension of legal obligations between belligerents during an armed conflict. The Experts, however, took the position that while armed conflict may suspend certain obligations, it does not do so with respect to all legal obligations. They agreed that an obligation to continue to seek resolution of disputes during an armed conflict is consistent with the object and purpose of *lit.* (a).

22.   *Lit.* (b) reflects agreement within the International Group of Experts that Article 2(3) of the UN Charter does not impose an obligation to attempt to solve disputes that do not endanger international peace and security. However, if States seek to resolve such an international dispute, they must do so by peaceful means. Take the case of one State conducting cyber espionage against another. The latter finds out about the cyber espionage and summons the former's ambassador, who then denies any cyber espionage. The situation qualifies as a dispute, but there is no obligation to try and resolve the matter because it does not endanger international peace and security. However, if attempts to settle the dispute are made, the methods of dispute resolution must be peaceful and cannot endanger international peace and security.

23.   The Experts did take note of a viewpoint by which States are under an obligation to attempt to settle all international disputes. None of them considered it to be reflective of State practice and *opinio juris*.

24.   The International Group of Experts noted that States may agree by treaty to specific compulsory dispute resolution mechanisms. For instance, disputes over the interpretation or application of the Law of the Sea Convention must be submitted to one of the bodies set forth in Article 287 of the Convention when the dispute has proven insolvable by other peaceful means (subject to exceptions provided for in the Convention[756]). Similarly, disputes between States that are Parties to

---

[755] THE CHARTER OF UNITED NATIONS: A COMMENTARY, at 1074.
[756] Law of the Sea Convention, Arts. 297–298.

the Optional Protocol on the Compulsory Settlement of Disputes relating to the ITU instruments are under certain circumstances subject to compulsory arbitration,[757] and those between States Parties to the Optional Protocol to the Vienna Convention on Diplomatic Relations concerning the Compulsory Settlement of Disputes are sometimes subject to the compulsory jurisdiction of the International Court of Justice.[758] Since all means of compulsory dispute resolution qualify as 'peaceful', the Rule is without prejudice to such treaty law arrangements.

---

[757] Optional Protocol on the Compulsory Settlement of Disputes relating to the Constitution of the International Telecommunication Union, to the Convention of the International Telecommunication Union and to the Administrative Regulations Art. 1, 22 December 1992, 1825 UNTS 3.

[758] Optional Protocol to the Vienna Convention on Diplomatic Relations concerning the Compulsory Settlement of Disputes, Arts. I–III(1), 18 April 1961, 500 UNTS 241.

13

Prohibition of intervention

Rule 66 – Intervention by States

A State may not intervene, including by cyber means, in the internal or external affairs of another State.

1. Cyberspace presents States with opportunities for intervention in other States' internal or external affairs, in particular due to increasing global connectivity and the growing reliance of States on information technology. This Rule prohibits coercive intervention, including by cyber means, by one State into the internal or external affairs of another. It is based on the international law principle of sovereignty, specifically that aspect of the principle that provides for the sovereign equality of States (Rules 1–3).[759] The International Group of Experts agreed that the prohibition of intervention is a norm of customary international law.[760] Indeed, States regularly express or resort to the principle.[761] Moreover, the

---

[759] *Nicaragua* judgment, paras. 202, 205, 251. Lassa Oppenheim also states that the prohibition of intervention 'is the corollary of every state's right to sovereignty, territorial integrity and political independence.' OPPENHEIM'S INTERNATIONAL LAW, at 428.

[760] The International Group of Experts noted that although the UN Charter does not explicitly mention the principle of non-intervention, Article 2(1), (3), and (4) are nevertheless often looked to as a basis for the rule of international law regarding non-intervention. Note that the International Group of Experts did not significantly rely on the UN General Assembly's Declaration on the Inadmissibility of Intervention and Interference, as it agreed that the declaration did not represent customary international law in its entirety.

[761] *See, e.g.*, UN GGE 2015 Report, paras. 26, 28(b); Ministry of Foreign Affairs of China, The Central Conference on Work Relating to Foreign Affairs, Beijing (29 November 2014); Ministry of Foreign Affairs of Russia, Concept of the Foreign Policy of the Russian Federation, Art. 28 (12 February 2013); United States State Dept., Special Briefing, Secretary Clinton's Meeting with Colombian Foreign Minister Jaime Bermúdez (18 August 2009); Statement of Defense of the United States, Iran–United States Claims Tribunal, Claim No. A/30 44 n.33, 52–57 (1996); United States State Dept., Miami Plan of Action: First Summit of the Americas, para. 1 (11 December 1994); Remarks of the President of the United States, Gerald R. Ford, Remarks in Helsinki (1 August 1975); Final Communiqué of the Asian–African Conference of

International Court of Justice, international organisations, and the International Law Commission recognise the prohibition's customary status.[762]

2. This Rule addresses situations in which a State intervenes by cyber means in the 'internal or external affairs' (as discussed below) of another State, for example, by using cyber operations to remotely alter electronic ballots and thereby manipulate an election. It also encompasses situations in which a State intervenes by non-cyber means in cyber activities related to the internal or external affairs of another State. For instance, this Rule would prohibit the use by one State of non-cyber coercive means to compel another State to adopt particular domestic legislation related to Internet service provider liability or to refrain from becoming Party to a multilateral treaty dealing with cyber disarmament or human rights online (on human rights, see also Chapter 6).[763]

3. Inconsistent language is used to address the principle of non-intervention. In particular, States sometimes use the term 'interference' in lieu of 'intervention'. Instruments adopted by States and the UN, as well as judgments of the International Court of Justice, more commonly employ the term 'intervention'. For the purposes of this Rule, 'interference' refers to acts by States that intrude into affairs reserved to the sovereign prerogative of another State, but lack the requisite coerciveness (see discussion below) to rise to the level of intervention. The term intervention, the subject of this Rule, is limited to acts of interference with a sovereign prerogative of another State that have coercive effect, as described below.

4. The Rule only operates in relations between States.[764] For example, a private corporation conducting hostile cyber operations

---

Bandung (24 April 1955), para. G.4; Agreement between the Republic of India and the People's Republic of China on Trade and Intercourse between Tibet Region of China and India, princ. 3 of pmbl., 29 April 1954, 299 UNTS 57.

[762] *Armed Activities* judgment, paras. 161–165; *Nicaragua* judgment, para. 202; *Corfu Channel* judgment, at 35. *See also* Declaration on Friendly Relations, princ. 3; International Law Commission, Declaration on Rights and Duties of States, annexed to GA Res. 375 (IV) (6 December 1949), Art. 3. An early articulation of the non-intervention principle is found in the 1933 Montevideo Convention on the Rights and Duties of States, Art. 8 (26 December 1933), 49 Stat. 3097, TS 881.

[763] On the use of coercion with respect to the conclusion of a treaty, *see, e.g.*, Declaration on the Prohibition of Military, Political or Economic Coercion in the Conclusion of Treaties, Annex to Final Act of the United Nations Conference on the Law of Treaties, A/CONF.39/26 (26 March–24 May 1968; 9 April–22 May 1969).

[764] *See, e.g.*, United States Department of Justice, Office of Legal Counsel, Memorandum Opinion for the Attorney General, Intervention by States and Private Groups in the Internal Affairs of Another State (12 April 1961).

against a State's cyber infrastructure in a manner that would otherwise meet the criteria set forth below is not in violation of this Rule. However, if the firm's operations are attributable to a State pursuant to the law of State responsibility (Rules 15, 17), that State is in violation of the prohibition of intervention.

5.   The Experts noted that despite the frequency of breaches of the non-intervention principle in State practice, the International Court of Justice has observed: 'It is not to be expected that in the practice of States the application of the rules in question should have been perfect, in the sense that States should have refrained, with complete consistency, from ... intervention in each other's internal affairs.'[765] The Court also noted: 'Expressions of an *opinio juris* regarding the existence of the principle of non-intervention in customary international law are numerous and not difficult to find.'[766] Accordingly, the International Group of Experts agreed that the fact that the prohibition is often breached does not undermine the Rule as reflecting an extant principle of international law.

6.   That said, the precise contours and application of the prohibition of intervention are unclear in light of ever evolving and increasingly intertwined international relations. Nevertheless, the International Group of Experts agreed that a prohibited act of intervention consists of two elements. First, the act in question must relate to matters that involve the internal or external affairs of the target State. Second, it must be coercive in nature.

7.   The reference to 'internal or external affairs' specifies the scope of activities protected by the principle of non-intervention. The notion of 'internal affairs' derives from the concept of *domaine réservé*, which consists of matters 'not, in principle, regulated by international law'.[767] In other words, those matters on which international law does not speak or that international law leaves solely to the prerogative of States constitute *domaine réservé* and are therefore to be regarded as protected from intervention by other States. The International Group of Experts agreed that the full contours of a State's *domaine réservé* can only be discerned through a careful examination of State practice and *opinio juris* and that the scope of a State's *domaine réservé* evolves over time.

---

[765] *Nicaragua* judgment, para. 186.   [766] *Nicaragua* judgment, para. 202.
[767] *Nationality Decrees Issued in Tunis and Morocco*, advisory opinion, 1923 PCIJ (ser. B) No. 4, at 24 (7 February).

8. In the *Nicaragua* judgment, the International Court of Justice addressed the requirement that a prohibited intervention bear on a State's *domaine réservé* when it noted: 'A prohibited intervention must ... be one bearing on matters in which each State is permitted, by the principle of sovereignty, to decide freely.'[768] In particular, such matters include the 'choice of a political, economic, social, and cultural system, and the formulation of foreign policy'.[769] Thus, this Rule prohibits coercive cyber acts by a State that are intended to eliminate or limit another State's prerogatives on these matters. The International Group of Experts agreed that the range of protection offered by the Rule is broadly coextensive with the range of issues reserved to States by the international law principle of sovereignty (Rules 1–3).

9. Consider a situation in which one State has two official languages, those of the majority and minority ethnic groups. The government holds a referendum on the dual language policy that results in a decision that only the majority language will remain an official language. A neighbouring State, the population of which is predominantly of the same ethnic background as the minority in the first State, undertakes DoS operations against key governmental websites appearing solely in what is now the official language in an effort to coerce the government into reversing its decision and maintaining websites in both languages. Since a State's language policy in this situation is a matter of its internal affairs, the coercive cyber operations amount to a prohibited intervention.

10. The International Group of Experts agreed that the matter most clearly within a State's *domaine réservé* appears to be the choice of both the political system and its organisation, as these issues lie at the heart of sovereignty. Thus, cyber means that are coercive in nature may not be used to alter or suborn modification of another State's governmental or social structure. With regard to the element of coercion, see discussion below.

11. Intervention into the *domaine réservé* of a State need not be directed at State infrastructure or involve State activities. Rather, the key to satisfaction of this first element of intervention is that the act in question must be designed to undermine the State's authority over the *domaine réservé*. Take the case of a State that conducts disruptive cyber

---

[768] *Nicaragua* judgment, para. 205.
[769] *Nicaragua* judgment, para. 205. *See also* Declaration on Friendly Relations, princ. 3; Declaration on the Inadmissibility of Intervention and Interference, Art. I(b).

operations against another State's commercial banks in order to coerce that State to require the removal of online material the former deems offensive from private websites hosted in the latter's territory. The act qualifies as an intervention because the regulation of online content, without prejudice to international human rights law (Rule 35), falls within a State's *domaine réservé*.

12.   The Declaration on Friendly Relations is often cited as setting forth examples of prohibited intervention. Included among them are organising, instigating, assisting, financing, or participating in acts of civil strife or terrorism in another State or 'acquiescing in organised activities within its territory directed towards the commission of such acts'.[770] The International Court of Justice has recognised the substantive provisions of the Declaration as reflective of customary international law.[771] Accordingly, if, for instance, a State provides an insurgent group with a method for bypassing normal authentication to access otherwise restricted cyber infrastructure of the security services of the State against which the insurgents are operating, the act would amount to intervention because it facilitates the insurgent's anti-government activities.

13.   Note that the scope of *domaine réservé* may shrink as States commit issues related to cyberspace to international law regulation. Intra-State communications, for example, have traditionally been considered to fall entirely within the *domaine réservé* of the State concerned. However, international human rights law by which a State is bound (Chapter 6) may significantly narrow the premise that how a State controls, or otherwise takes measures that affect, the communications of individuals (for instance, by engaging in domestic electronic surveillance) on its own territory is solely an issue of domestic concern.

14.   A State may commit to the international legal system a matter previously regarded as within its *domaine réservé* by means of a treaty. It could become, for example, a Party to a multilateral treaty that standardises network maintenance and security. However, the fact that a State is Party to a bilateral or multilateral agreement does not in itself necessarily signal a surrender of the matter. Rather, it only does so when the State agrees to relinquish its control over the issue generally. If it relinquishes control only *vis-à-vis* Parties to the instrument, as in the case of a regional agreement regarding cyber activities, the issue can still remain within its *domaine réservé* as to non-Parties.

---

[770] Declaration on Friendly Relations, princ. 1. *See also* princ. 3.
[771] *Armed Activities* judgment, para. 162; *Nicaragua* judgment, para. 264.

15.   The International Court of Justice's reference in the *Nicaragua* judgment to 'decide freely' makes it clear that certain cyber operations intended to compel another State into compliance with its international legal obligations are excluded from the scope of applicability of this Rule. This is because the fact that one State owes an obligation to another State takes the matter out of the realm of *domaine réservé*, at least as to the latter State. Indeed, international law countenances various measures, such as acts of retorsion and countermeasures (Rule 20), designed to enable a State to induce another to honour its international legal obligations.

16.   The principle of non-intervention also protects the integrity of a State's external affairs to the extent such relations are the sole prerogative of the State.[772] Accordingly, matters protected by this Rule include the choice of extending diplomatic and consular relations, recognition of States or governments, membership in international organisations, and the formation or abrogation of treaties. It would violate the Rule, as an example, for State A to employ cyber means to alter electronic diplomatic communications between State B's Ministry of Foreign Affairs and State B's negotiators during the course of fragile talks involving State B and C in order to compel the abandonment of the talks (but see minority view on requirement of knowledge of coercion below).

17.   As confirmed by the International Court of Justice in the *Nicaragua* judgment, a constituent element of prohibited intervention is coercion. The Court observed: 'Intervention is wrongful when it uses methods of coercion . . .. The element of coercion . . . defines, and indeed forms the very essence of prohibited intervention. . ..'[773] Acts not involving coercion do not constitute intervention for purposes of this Rule.

18.   The term 'coercion' is not defined in international law. As used in this Manual, coercion is not limited to physical force, but rather refers to an affirmative act designed to deprive another State of its freedom of choice, that is, to force that State to act in an involuntary manner or involuntarily refrain from acting in a particular way.[774] Consider the case of a State that blocks the access of its citizens to another State's currency without violating any international law norms when doing so. The latter conducts cyber operations that severely hamper the former State's

---

[772] OPPENHEIM'S INTERNATIONAL LAW, at 430–431.   [773] *Nicaragua* judgment, para. 205.
[774] *See, e.g.,* Declaration on Friendly Relations, princ. 3 (stating that: 'No State may . . . coerce another State in order to obtain from it the subordination of the exercise of its sovereign rights and to secure from it advantages of any kind.').

electronic trading in an effort to compel that State to reopen access. Or take the case of a State that blocks the access of its citizens to certain foreign media and other websites abroad. A blocked State conducts cyber operations that severely hamper the first State's government media broadcasts in an effort to compel that State to desist in blocking access. In both cases, the first State's control over cyber activities on its territory is generally considered a matter of internal concern (unless implicating an applicable international human rights law norm to the contrary, Rule 35), and the second State has engaged in coercive cyber activities that intervene into the internal affairs of the first.

19.   The Experts agreed that mere coercion does not suffice to establish a breach of the prohibition of intervention. The majority of Experts was of the view that the coercive effort must be designed to influence outcomes in, or conduct with respect to, a matter reserved to a target State. For example, a State's malicious cyber campaign directed against cyber infrastructure owned by a particular ethnic group in a neighbouring State might violate the latter's sovereignty, but will not amount to prohibited intervention as it is not intended to influence any outcome in, or decision of, the target State. However, if the cyber campaign is designed to coerce the State to adopt a particular position in an ongoing internal ethnic controversy, it will so qualify. A few Experts took the position that to be coercive it is enough that an act has the effect of depriving the State of control over the matter in question. Thus, in the first example above there is, by this view, an intervention because the State is deprived by the cyber campaign of its sovereign right to control its inter-ethnic affairs without outside interference.

20.   The International Group of Experts agreed that to be coercive for the purposes of this Rule, the acts concerned need not be physical in nature. Consider the case of State A that launches targeted and highly disruptive DDoS operations against State B in an attempt to compel State B to withdraw recognition of State C. The fact that the cyber operations result in no physical consequences does not detract from their characterisation as a prohibited intervention. By way of contrast, a cyber operation that does not seek any change of conduct lacks the requisite coercive element.

21.   Furthermore, coercion must be distinguished from persuasion, criticism, public diplomacy, propaganda (see also discussion in Rule 4), retribution, mere maliciousness, and the like in the sense that, unlike coercion, such activities merely involve either influencing (as distinct from factually compelling) the voluntary actions of the target State, or

seek no action on the part of the target State at all. As an illustration, a State-sponsored public information campaign via the Internet designed to persuade another State of the logic of ratifying a particular treaty would not amount to a violation of the prohibition of intervention. Similarly, if a State's Ministry of Foreign Affairs publishes content on social media that is highly critical of another State's internal and external policies, the activity is not coercive in nature and therefore does not constitute prohibited intervention. The key is that the coercive act must have the potential for compelling the target State to engage in an action that it would otherwise not take (or refrain from taking an action it would otherwise take). A few Experts, however, argued that it is impossible to prejudge whether an act constitutes intervention without knowing its specific context and consequences. For them, the context and consequences of a particular act that would not normally qualify as coercive could raise it to that level.

22. The International Group of Experts acknowledged that the distinction between coercive and non-coercive cyber operations is not always clear. However, all of the Experts agreed that a cyber use of force (Rule 68) by one State against another is always coercive and therefore constitutes intervention. In this regard, they noted that the International Court of Justice in its *Nicaragua* judgment observed that acts amounting to force, such as military action or acts supporting military action, constitute 'particularly obvious' forms of intervention.[775] The Court further found that 'support given by the United States to the military and paramilitary activities of the *contras* in Nicaragua, including financial support, training, supply of weapons, intelligence and logistic support, constitute[d] a clear breach of the principle of non-intervention'.[776] This would apply equally to support of qualifying cyber activities, as well as support by cyber means of such non-cyber activities.

23. Coercion sufficient to support a finding of unlawful intervention may take either a direct or indirect form.[777] In its findings of fact, the International Court of Justice in the *Nicaragua* judgment determined that the United States had supplied assistance to rebels, including 'training, arming, equipping ... [rebel] military and paramilitary actions in and against Nicaragua'.[778] The Court held that the principle

---

[775] *Nicaragua* judgment, para. 205.   [776] *Nicaragua* judgment, para. 242.
[777] Declaration on Friendly Relations, princ. 3; Declaration on the Inadmissibility of Intervention and Interference, pmbl.
[778] *Nicaragua* judgment, para. 228.

of non-intervention 'forbids all States or groups of States to intervene directly or indirectly in internal or external affairs of other States'.[779] The same result would attach in the cyber context. If, for example, a State provides cyber weapons (Rule 103) to a non-State actor engaged in an insurgency against the government of another State, such assistance constitutes indirect prohibited intervention into the target State's internal affairs (as well as a use of force, Rule 68), even though the former will not be conducting the cyber operations itself.

24.   The Experts were divided, however, over the requisite causality of the coercive effect. The majority took the position that an act is coercive so long as there is a causal nexus to an infringement on the internal or external affairs of the target State (the effect); such causation of the requisite effect may be direct or indirect in nature. The minority would impose a requirement that the target State's action directly cause the effect. Consider the case of a State that gains unauthorised access into another State's governmental system to acquire sensitive domestic intelligence records. It then posts them on an open access hosting site. The goal is to generate a political crisis likely to skew an internal debate over the domestic monitoring of cyber activities. The first State hopes that the debate will lead to strict restrictions on domestic intelligence that will, in turn, facilitate the first State's industrial espionage in the second State. By the majority view, the act would constitute intervention because its purpose was to cause, albeit indirectly, the target State to take a decision it would otherwise not take with respect to domestic law enforcement. A few Experts were of the view that the act does not rise to the level of intervention because it does not directly compel the government to take any particular action.

25.   A related question is whether the target State must have knowledge of the cyber operation constituting the purported intervention. The majority concluded that such knowledge is not a precondition to a breach of this Rule. For them, a covert destructive cyber operation at the use of force level qualifies as an intervention even if the malware involved creates the impression that a mechanical malfunction caused the damage. The minority countered that the operation does not amount to an intervention because the target State is unaware of the coercive act; although the target State's action may be the result of the operation, its will has not been coerced. Or take the case of one State's use of covert

[779] *Nicaragua* judgment, para. 205.

cyber operations to alter electronic ballot results in another State such that a candidate who would not otherwise have been elected prevails. For the majority, the requirement of coercion is met because the target State is effectively forced, albeit unknowingly, into seating the candidate by virtue of the actions of the first State. By contrast, the minority took the position that coercion includes an element of pressure such that the target State must know that it is being compelled into a particular course of action, that is, the State is acting contrary to its will.

26. The previous situation must be distinguished from one in which a State is aware that it is being targeted with cyber operations, but does not know their originator's identity. The International Group of Experts agreed that the absence of certainty as to identity on the part of the target State does not preclude the operations from qualifying as intervention so long as they are, in fact, conducted by, or otherwise attributable to, a State (Rules 15–18), coercive in nature, and involve the target State's internal or external affairs. This is because the element of pressure is present such that the State is knowingly compelled to take or refrain from particular action irrespective of its ignorance as to who is conducting the cyber operations in question. Consider the example of Stuxnet, which would qualify as intervention if conducted by one or more States (absent a circumstance precluding wrongfulness, Rule 19). The fact that uncertainty remains as to the originator of the operation does not preclude its qualification as intervention, should it later be reliably established that it was conducted by a State.

27. Intent, the Experts concurred, is a further constitutive element of a violation of the prohibition of intervention. Situations in which cyber activities have a *de facto* coercive effect must be distinguished from those in which a State intends to coerce *de jure*. A State might, for example, engage in activities that would *de facto* assist insurgents in another State without harbouring the intention of doing so. For instance, a State might enhance the security of its national social media companies, thereby improving the security of social media used by foreign insurgent forces to communicate and making it more difficult for the State against which the insurgents are operating to access those communications. The State's actions would not constitute intervention because it did not intend to intervene in the internal affairs of the target State. Or consider on-going negotiations between two neighbouring States regarding poor cyber hygiene in one of them. As a result of that State's failure to properly maintain its systems, the other State's activities have been significantly

disrupted. Negotiations break down and in order to protect its systems, the latter blocks communications from the former. Since the former's cyber activities rely heavily on cyber infrastructure located in the latter, it is effectively forced to take the measures that were demanded during the negotiations. The underlying purpose of blocking the communications was only to protect, not to coerce. Therefore, the latter State has not violated this Rule.

28.   When coercion by a State is effected through other parties, the State need not share the other parties' objective; the sole requirement is that the State harbour the intent to coerce in a matter reserved to the target State. The classic case is *Nicaragua*, where the International Court of Justice concluded that it was unnecessary to determine whether the United States shared the intent of the insurgents to whom it was providing assistance to overthrow the government of Nicaragua. It sufficed that the United States intended, by the support, to coerce Nicaragua in matters regarding which Nicaragua was entitled to 'decide freely'.[780] Applying this finding by analogy in the cyber context, take the case of a State that provides cyber weapons (Rule 103) and training to insurgents in another State who seek to overthrow the latter's government. The first State need not intend its actions to result in the overthrow of the government. It may, for example, simply wish to create civil disorder. Its actions constitute an intervention irrespective of the insurgents' objectives so long as the two criteria for intervention are met *vis-à-vis* the first State.

29.   The International Group of Experts agreed that the fact that a coercive cyber operation fails to produce the desired outcome has no bearing on whether this Rule has been breached. As an example, a State may impose a ban on exports to another State. The latter launches highly disruptive cyber operations against the former's Ministry of Commerce in an effort to force that State to rescind the ban. Irrespective of whether rescission results, the cyber operations constitute prohibited intervention.

30.   The Experts were of the view that, in certain circumstances, a threat itself may violate this Rule. As with coercive acts, the threat must be coercive in nature and intrude into the internal or external affairs of another State. If, for instance, a State threatens to conduct a cyber operation that will undercut confidence in another State's stock exchange in order to compel that State to alter domestic fiscal policies, the threat

---

[780] *Nicaragua* judgment, para. 241.

constitutes a prohibited intervention. The threat need not be successful in compelling the target State into the desired conduct for it to amount to a violation of this Rule.

31. As discussed above, unlawful uses of force always qualify as acts of prohibited intervention. Threats of the unlawful use of force are also inherently interventions. Consequently, a wrongful threat of force violates both this Rule and Rule 68.

32. If a State consents to an act that would otherwise amount to a prohibited intervention, this Rule is not violated. As noted in Rule 19, consent precludes the international wrongfulness of an act. Recall that the most unambiguous case of intervention involves the use of force on another State's territory. If one State conducts cyber operations at the use of force level against insurgents in another State at the latter's request, there has been no unlawful intervention.

33. Cyber espionage *per se*, as distinct from the underlying acts that enable the espionage (see discussion in Rule 32), does not qualify as intervention because it lacks a coercive element. In the view of the International Group of Experts, this holds true even where intrusion into cyber infrastructure in order to conduct espionage requires the remote breaching of protective virtual barriers (e.g., the breaching of firewalls or the cracking of passwords). Similarly, accepted practices of diplomacy, such as a diplomatic protest regarding another State's intelligence gathering by cyber means, do not constitute intervention.

34. A majority of the International Group of Experts agreed that operations conducted by a State to protect its nationals who are in jeopardy abroad, or to facilitate efforts to do so, do not generally amount to a wrongful intervention, even if conducted without the consent of the territorial State, if the territorial State is not providing them adequate protection.[781] These Experts based their conclusion on the extensive State practice of engaging in these operations. As an example, for them, it would not constitute intervention for one State to use cyber measures to temporarily disable a State's defensive systems when necessary to evacuate the former's nationals during civil unrest in the latter. A few Experts took the position that the law on protection of nationals abroad has not sufficiently crystallised to the point where it can definitively be concluded that such activities do not constitute a prohibited intervention.

---

[781] R.J. VINCENT, NONINTERVENTION AND INTERNATIONAL ORDER 288 (1974) ('A right of states well established by their practice is that of intervention to protect the lives and property of their citizens.'); OPPENHEIM'S INTERNATIONAL LAW, at 439–447.

35. The International Group of Experts considered whether economic measures (so-called 'unilateral sanctions') by one State against another constitute intervention when they take place in the first State. Cyber-relevant examples include denying the latter State access to e-commerce websites located in the former or blocking or slowing access to servers in the former used by the latter to conduct economic transactions. In light of the extensive State practice of taking economic measures against other States in the non-cyber context, the Experts concurred that such measures generally do not amount to intervention, although it must be cautioned that they may violate applicable treaty obligations.[782] States remain free to choose their trading partners and may effectuate that choice by cyber means in their own State.[783] Despite this agreement, the Experts acknowledged a view by which cyber measures differ from classic economic action in the sense that they involve active technical measures, rather than simply desisting from trade and other economic activities, and that therefore economic measures taken by cyber means that are coercive in nature can qualify as intervention.

36. The International Group of Experts was divided over whether cyber operations in support of a humanitarian intervention that has neither been authorised by the UN Security Council (on actions authorised by the UN Security Council, see also Rule 76) nor consented to by the territorial State violate this Rule. An example on point is employing destructive cyber operations against cyber infrastructure being used to incite genocide. For the minority of the Experts who took the position that humanitarian intervention is an exception to the prohibition of the use of force, such operations would neither be an unlawful use of force (Rule 68) nor a prohibited intervention because the cyber operations would take on the legal character of the humanitarian intervention. For the majority, which took the position that there is no right of humanitarian intervention, the cyber operations would be prohibited by this Rule to the extent they otherwise qualified as prohibited intervention.

---

[782] As an example, for States Parties to the General Agreement on Tariffs and Trade, economic sanctions may violate an obligation owed a 'most favoured nation'. General Agreement on Tariffs and Trade, Art. I, 30 October, 1947, 55 UNTS 194.

[783] See, e.g., *Nicaragua* judgment, paras. 244–245; Defense of the United States, Iran–United States Claims Tribunal, Claim A/30, 57 (1996) ('Every state has the right to grant or deny foreign assistance, to permit or deny exports, to grant or deny loans or credits, and to grant or deny participation in national procurement or financial management, on such terms as it finds appropriate.') (citing *Iran* v. *United States*, AWD No. 382-B1-FT, 62, 19 Iran–US CTR 273 292 (31 August 1988)).

37. The prohibition of intervention applies to States irrespective of whether they are acting as Members of intergovernmental organisations. With respect to its application to the United Nations, see Rule 67. This Rule is without prejudice to any applicable provisions of the constitutive instruments of the intergovernmental organisation when that organisation is operating *inter se*.

38. The International Group of Experts cautioned that the failure of a cyber operation to qualify as intervention does not necessarily render it lawful, the paradigmatic example being a non-coercive violation of sovereignty by cyber means (Rule 4).

Rule 67 – Intervention by the United Nations

The United Nations may not intervene, including by cyber means, in matters that are essentially within the domestic jurisdiction of a State. This principle does not prejudice the taking of enforcement measures decided upon by the UN Security Council under Chapter VII of the United Nations Charter.

1. This Rule is based on Article 2(7) of the UN Charter, according to which the United Nations is not authorised to 'intervene in matters which are essentially within the domestic jurisdiction of any state'. It applies only to United Nations activities and is therefore distinct from Rule 66, which addresses activities conducted by or attributable to States. Although a few Experts argued that a customary Rule exists prohibiting all international organisations from so intervening,[784] the majority of the International Group of Experts was unwilling to go so far; therefore, the Rule is limited to UN activities.

2. The International Group of Experts agreed that the phrase 'matters which are essentially within the domestic jurisdiction of any state'[785] not only lacks clarity, but its understanding also evolves over time. However, it agreed that the phrase does not include issues encompassed in the purposes of the United Nations as set forth in Article 1 of the UN Charter. In particular, the phrase does not include matters involving 'international peace and security'.[786]

---

[784] They pointed to the common inclusion of non-intervention clauses in constitutive instruments of international organisations. *See, e.g.,* League of Nations Covenant, Art. 15(8); Charter of the Arab League, Art. 2, 22 March 1945; Charter Establishing the Commonwealth of Independent States, Art. 3, 22 January 1993, 1819 UNTS 31139.
[785] UN Charter, Art. 2(7). [786] UN Charter, Art. 1(1).

3. This is an especially important point with respect to cyber operations because the interconnected nature of cyber infrastructure and activities means that cyber related activities conducted in one State often affect those in another. This fact renders them particularly susceptible to being disruptive of international peace and security such that the United Nations may address them. Also significant is the exclusion of matters involving 'international problems of an economic, social, cultural, or humanitarian character and ... human rights'.[787] The centrality of cyber activities to international economic, social, cultural, and humanitarian matters affords the United Nations the opportunity to deal with them without violating this Rule. Likewise, the competency of the United Nations with respect to oversight of State compliance with international human rights obligations opens the door to significant United Nations involvement in situations that would otherwise be essentially domestic in character.

4. United Nations practice has increasingly limited the scope of Article 2(7) based on such purposes. Although the reach of Article 2(7) appears to be narrowing, States continue to rely on the Article as a shield against United Nations intervention in internal matters, especially when they pertain to national governmental systems and elections.[788] Adoption of numerous United Nations General Assembly resolutions have demonstrated State support for the premise that there remain matters lying exclusively within State domestic jurisdiction and therefore outside the reach of United Nations organs and activities.[789]

5. Unlike Rule 66 governing intervention by States, this Rule does not include a coercive element. Therefore, although the Rule is framed using the terminology of Article 2(7), the International Group of Experts agreed that a more appropriate characterisation of the prohibition is that the United Nations may not 'interfere' (as distinguished from the term 'intervene' as used in Rule 66) by cyber means with matters falling within a State's domestic jurisdiction. To illustrate, the United Nations may not require that a State adopt particular legislation with respect to cyber activities on its territory that exhibit a purely domestic character.

---

[787] UN Charter, Art. 1(3).
[788] THE CHARTER OF THE UNITED NATIONS: A COMMENTARY, at 280, 283, 294, 306.
[789] See, e.g., GA Res. 65/222, UN Doc. A/RES/65/222 (11 April 2011); GA Res. 65/203, UN Doc. A/RES/65/203 (16 March 2011).

6.   This Rule is without prejudice to the right of the Security Council to authorise or mandate cyber measures under Chapter VII of the UN Charter in order to maintain or restore international peace and security (in this regard, see also Rule 76).[790] When it does so, all States must accept and carry out its decisions.[791] For instance, it could adopt a binding resolution requiring States to deny access to the cyber communications of a particular State or authorise States to engage in cyber operations against a State. Compliance with such a resolution will not breach this Rule.

[790] UN Charter, Art. 39.   [791] UN Charter, Art. 25.

14

The use of force

1. The International Court of Justice has stated that Articles 2(4) (Rules 68–70) and 51 (Rule 71–5) of the United Nations Charter, regarding the prohibition of the use of force and self-defence respectively, apply to 'any use of force, regardless of the weapons employed'.[792] The International Group of Experts unanimously agreed that this statement is an accurate reflection of customary international law.[793] Therefore, the mere fact that a computer (rather than a more traditional weapon, weapon system, or platform) is used during an operation has no bearing on whether that operation amounts to a 'use of force' (or, for that matter, whether a State may use force in self-defence pursuant to Rule 71). In the cyber context, it is not the instrument used that determines whether the use of force threshold has been crossed, but rather, as described in Rule 69, the consequences of the operation and its surrounding circumstances. The Experts acknowledged a view by which any use of a method or means of warfare (Rule 103) by one State against another constitutes a use of force. However, they noted that a cyber method or means of warfare could be employed to cause consequences, such as minor disruption of cyber activities, that clearly do not amount to a use of force.

2. The Experts also rejected any suggestion that the nature of targeted cyber infrastructure is determinative of whether a cyber operation qualifies as a use of force. For instance, operations targeting other than critical cyber infrastructure may constitute uses of force when meeting the definition set forth in Rule 69, while those directed at critical infrastructure may not.

3. State practice is only beginning to clarify the application to cyber operations of the *jus ad bellum*, that aspect of international law governing a State's resort to force as an instrument of its national

---

[792] *Nuclear Weapons* advisory opinion, para. 39.
[793] *See, e.g.*, UN GGE 2013 Report, para. 19; UN GGE 2015 Report, paras. 25, 26, 28(c).

policy. In particular, the lack of agreed-upon definitions, criteria, and thresholds for application creates uncertainty when applying the *jus ad bellum* to the rapidly changing realities of cyber operations. The International Group of Experts acknowledged that as cyber threats and opportunities continue to emerge and evolve, State practice may alter contemporary interpretations of the *jus ad bellum* in the cyber context. The analysis set forth in this Chapter examines the norms resident in the *jus ad bellum* as they presently exist in the *lex lata*.

SECTION 1:   PROHIBITION OF THE USE OF FORCE

Rule 68 – Prohibition of threat or use of force

A cyber operation that constitutes a threat or use of force against the territorial integrity or political independence of any State, or that is in any other manner inconsistent with the purposes of the United Nations, is unlawful.

1.   Article 2(4) of the United Nations Charter provides that: 'All Members [of the United Nations] shall refrain in their international relations from the threat or use of force against the territorial integrity or political independence of any State, or in any other manner inconsistent with the Purposes of the United Nations.' The prohibition is undoubtedly a norm of customary international law.[794]

2.   In addition to the specific prohibition of threats or uses of force against the territorial integrity or political independence of any State, the United Nations Charter's *travaux préparatoires* suggest that the reference in Article 2(4) to threats or uses of force inconsistent with the 'purposes of the United Nations' (laid down in Article 1 of the Charter) was intended to create a presumption of illegality for any threat or use of force.[795] In other words, even acts that are not directed against either the territorial integrity or political independence of a State may violate the prohibition when inconsistent with the purposes of the United Nations. There are two widely acknowledged exceptions to the prohibition on the use of force – uses of force authorised by the Security Council under Chapter VII (Rule 76) and self-defence pursuant to Article 51 and

---

[794] *Nicaragua* judgment, paras. 188–190.
[795] *See* Doc. 1123, I/8, 6 UNCIO Docs. 65 (1945); Doc. 784, I/1/27, 6 UNCIO Docs. 336 (1945); Doc. 885, I/1/34, 6 UNCIO Docs. 387 (1945).

customary international law (Rule 71). The International Group of Experts did not address the lawfulness of other uses of force, such those incident to a humanitarian intervention, in the context of this Rule.

3.   The terms 'use of force' and 'threat of the use of force' are defined in Rules 69 and 70, respectively.

4.   An action qualifying as a 'use of force' need not necessarily be undertaken by a State's armed forces. For example, it is clear that a cyber operation that would qualify as a 'use of force' if conducted by the armed forces would equally be a 'use of force' if undertaken by a State's intelligence agencies or by a private contractor whose conduct is attributable to the State. With regard to those entities whose actions may be attributed to States, see Rules 15–18.

5.   Although, by its own express terms, Article 2(4) applies solely to Members of the United Nations, the prohibition also extends to non-Member States by virtue of customary international law. However, Article 2(4) and its customary international law counterpart do not apply to the acts of non-State actors, including individuals, organised groups, and terrorist organisations, unless they are attributable to a State pursuant to the law of State responsibility (Rule 17). In such a case, the State, not the non-State actor, would be deemed to be in violation. The actions of non-State actors may be unlawful under international and domestic law, but not as a violation of the prohibition of the use of force.

6.   The fact that a cyber operation fails to rise to the level of a use of force does not necessarily render it lawful under international law. In particular, a cyber operation may constitute a violation of sovereignty (Rule 4) or a breach of the prohibition of intervention (Rule 66).

Rule 69 – Definition of use of force

A cyber operation constitutes a use of force when its scale and effects are comparable to non-cyber operations rising to the level of a use of force.

1.   This Rule examines the term 'use of force' found in Rule 68. The United Nations Charter offers no criteria by which to determine when an act amounts to a use of force. In discussions regarding the appropriate threshold for a use of force, the International Group of Experts took notice of the *Nicaragua* judgment. In that case, the International Court of Justice stated that 'scale and effects' are to be considered when determining whether particular actions amount to an 'armed attack'

(Rule 71).[796] The Experts found the focus on scale and effects to be an equally useful approach when distinguishing acts that qualify as uses of force from those that do not. In other words, 'scale and effects' is a shorthand term that captures the quantitative and qualitative factors to be analysed in determining whether a cyber operation amounts to a use of force. The Experts agreed that there is no basis for excluding cyber operations from within the scope of actions that may constitute a use of force if the scale and effects of the operation in question are comparable to those of non-cyber operations that would qualify as such.[797]

2. There is no authoritative definition of, or criteria for, 'threat' or 'use of force'. However, certain categories of coercive operations are not uses of force. At the 1945 UN Charter drafting conference in San Francisco, States considered and rejected a proposal to include economic coercion as a use of force.[798] The issue arose again a quarter of a century later during the proceedings leading to the General Assembly's Declaration on Friendly Relations. The question of whether 'force' included 'all forms of pressure, including those of a political or economic character, which have the effect of threatening the territorial integrity or political independence of any State' was answered in the negative.[799]

3. As examples, neither non-destructive cyber psychological operations intended solely to undermine confidence in a government, nor a State's prohibition of e-commerce with another State designed to cause negative economic consequences, qualify as uses of force. Additionally, the International Court of Justice held in the *Nicaragua* case that merely funding guerrillas engaged in operations against another State did not reach the use of force threshold.[800] Thus, for instance, merely funding a hacktivist group conducting cyber operations as part of an insurgency would not be a use of force against the State involved in the armed conflict with the insurgents.

4. A use of force need not involve the employment of military or other armed forces by the State in question. In *Nicaragua*, the International

---

[796] *Nicaragua* judgment, para. 195.
[797] *See, e.g.*, the approach adopted in the DoD MANUAL, para. 16.3.1.
[798] 6 UNCIO Docs. 334, 609 (1945); Doc. 2, 617(e)(4), 3 UNCIO Docs. 251, 253–254 (1945).
[799] UN GAOR Special Comm. on Friendly Relations, UN Doc. A/AC.125/SR.110 to 114 (1970). *See also* Rep. of the Special Comm. on Friendly Relations and Cooperation Among States, 1969, UN GAOR, 24th Sess., Supp. No. 19, at 12, UN Doc. A/7619 (1969). The draft declaration contained text tracking that of UN Charter Art. 2(4).
[800] *Nicaragua* judgment, para. 228.

Court of Justice found that arming and training a guerrilla force that is engaged in hostilities against another State qualified as a use of force.[801] Therefore, a State that provides an organised armed group with malware and the training necessary to carry out cyber operations against another State has engaged in a use of force against the latter so long as that supply and training enable the group to conduct cyber operations that amount to a use of force. This situation must be distinguished from one in which the actions of a non-State group are attributable to a State pursuant to the law of State responsibility (Rules 15 and 17) or that of self-defence (Rule 71).

5.   This conclusion raises the question of whether affording sanctuary (safe haven) to those mounting cyber operations of the requisite severity amounts to a 'use of force' (or 'armed attack').[802] A minority of the Experts supported this view, whereas a majority of the International Group of Experts took the position that in most cases simply granting sanctuary does not qualify as a use of force by the State providing it. However, all of the Experts agreed that, in such circumstances, the State in question may be in violation of its due diligence obligation (Rules 6–7). For the majority, the provision of sanctuary coupled with other acts, such as substantial support or providing cyber defences for the non-State group, may, in certain circumstances, be a use of force.

6.   It is useful to consider the notion of 'use of force' in relation to that of 'armed attack', which is the threshold at which a State may lawfully use force in self-defence (Rule 71). In its *Nicaragua* judgment, the International Court of Justice distinguished the 'most grave' forms of the 'use of force' (those constituting an 'armed attack' for the purposes of the law of self-defence) from other less grave forms.[803] The International Group of Experts agreed, therefore, that any cyber operation that rises to the level of an 'armed attack' in terms of scale and effects pursuant to Rule 71, and that is conducted by or otherwise attributable to a State, qualifies as a 'use of force'.

7.   The International Group of Experts acknowledged a contrary view whereby the distinction between the two concepts is either so narrow as to be insignificant or non-existent. This position, articulated by the

---

[801] *Nicaragua* judgment, para. 228.

[802] *See* Declaration on Friendly Relations, princ. 1 (addressing the issue of State acquiescence to organised activities on its territory).

[803] *Nicaragua* judgment, para. 191. The Court pointed to the Declaration on Friendly Relations, noting that while certain of the actions referred to therein constituted armed attacks, others only qualified as uses of force.

United States after the *Nicaragua* judgment, asserts that any unlawful use of force qualifies as an armed attack triggering the right of self-defence; there is no gravity threshold distinguishing uses of force from armed attacks.[804] On this view, no gap exists between an unlawful use of force and an armed attack, although the principles of necessity and proportionality that apply to actions in self-defence may limit the responses available to a State that has been attacked.

8.   To summarise, some cyber actions are undeniably not uses of force, uses of force need not involve a State's direct use of armed force, and all armed attacks are uses of force. This leaves unresolved the question as to what actions short of an armed attack constitute a use of force. Acts that injure or kill persons or physically damage or destroy objects are uses of force (see Rule 71 expressing an analogous conclusion in the context of self-defence, but requiring the harm to be 'significant'). Since other cases are less clear, the International Group of Experts took notice of an approach that seeks to assess the likelihood that States will characterise a cyber operation as a use of force.[805] The method expounded operates on the premise that in the absence of a conclusive definitional threshold, States contemplating cyber operations, or that are the target thereof, must be highly sensitive to the international community's probable assessment of whether the operations violate the prohibition of the use of force.

9.   The approach focuses on both the level of harm inflicted and certain qualitative elements of a particular cyber operation. In great part, it is intended to identify cyber operations that are analogous to other non-kinetic or kinetic actions that the international community would describe as uses of force. To the extent such operations would be assessed as reaching the use of force threshold, so too would cyber operations of the same scale and effects. The approach suggests that States are likely to consider and place great weight on the following factors, *inter alia*, when deciding whether to characterise any operation, including a cyber operation, as a use of force. It must be emphasised that they are merely factors that influence States making use of force assessments; they are not formal legal criteria.

---

[804] *See, e.g.,* DoD MANUAL, para. 16.3.3.1. *See also* Abraham D. Sofaer, *International Law and the Use of Force*, 82 AMERICAN SOCIETY OF INTERNATIONAL LAW PROCEEDINGS 420, 422 (1988).

[805] This approach was originally proposed in Michael N. Schmitt, *Computer Network and the Use of Force in International Law: Thoughts on a Normative Framework*, 37 COLUM. J. TRANSNAT'L L. 885, 914 (1999).

(a) *Severity.* Subject to a *de minimis* rule, consequences involving physical harm to individuals or property will in and of themselves qualify a cyber operation as a use of force. Those generating mere inconvenience or irritation will never do so. Between the extremes, the more consequences impinge on critical national interests, the more they will contribute to the depiction of a cyber operation as a use of force. In this regard, the scope, duration, and intensity of the consequences will have great bearing on the appraisal of their severity. Severity is the most significant factor in the analysis.

(b) *Immediacy.* The sooner consequences manifest, the less opportunity States have to seek peaceful accommodation of a dispute or to otherwise forestall their harmful effects. Therefore, States harbour a greater concern about immediate consequences than those that are delayed or build slowly over time, and are more likely to characterise a cyber operation that produces immediate results as a use of force than one that takes weeks or months to achieve its intended effects.

(c) *Directness.* The greater the attenuation between the initial act and its consequences, the less likely States will be to deem the actor in violation of the prohibition of the use of force. Whereas the immediacy factor focuses on the temporal aspect of the consequences in question, directness examines the chain of causation. For instance, market forces, access to markets, and the like determine the eventual consequences of economic coercion (*e.g.*, economic downturn). The causal connection between the initial acts and their effects tends to be indirect – economic sanctions may take weeks or even months to have a significant effect. In armed actions, by contrast, cause and effect are closely related. An explosion, for example, directly harms people or objects. Cyber operations in which cause and effect are clearly linked are more likely to be characterised as uses of force than those in which they are highly attenuated.

(d) *Invasiveness.* Invasiveness refers to the degree to which cyber operations intrude into the target State or its cyber systems contrary to the interests of that State. As a rule, the more secure a targeted cyber system, the greater the concern as to its penetration. For example, intrusion into a military system that has been accredited at Evaluation Assurance Level 7 (EAL7) of the *Common Criteria* is more invasive than merely exploiting vulnerabilities of an openly accessible non-accredited system at a civilian university or small business.[806] Additionally, the more the intended effects of a cyber operation are limited to a particular State, the greater the perceived invasiveness of that operation.

Domain name is a highly visible indicator in cyberspace and for that reason may carry significance in assessing an operation's perceived invasiveness. Cyber operations that specifically target the domain name of a particular State (e.g., 'mil.ee') or of a particular State organ may, for this reason, be considered more invasive than those operations directed at non-State specific domain name extensions such as '.com'.

This factor must be cautiously applied in the cyber context. In particular, computer network exploitation is a pervasive tool of modern espionage. Though highly invasive, cyber espionage does not *per se* rise to the level of a use of force; indeed, there is no direct prohibition in international law on espionage (Rule 32). Thus, actions such as disabling cyber security mechanisms in order to monitor keystrokes would, despite their invasiveness, be unlikely to be seen as a use of force. Although international law does not prohibit espionage *per se*, this does not mean that acts undertaken in order to enable cyber espionage never qualify as a use of force. For example, using cyber means to create damage to cyber infrastructure that would appear to be the result of a technical malfunction in order to mask the fact that the infrastructure has been exploited could so qualify.

(e) *Measurability of effects.* This factor derives from the greater willingness of States to characterise actions as a use of force when consequences are apparent. Traditionally, the armed forces carried out operations that qualified as uses of force and the effects of the operations were generally measurable (as in the case of battle damage assessments). In the cyber realm, consequences may be less apparent. Therefore, the more quantifiable and identifiable a set of consequences, the easier it will be for a State to assess the situation when determining whether the cyber operation in question has reached the level of a use of force. Accordingly, a cyber operation that can be evaluated in very specific terms (e.g., amount of data corrupted, percentage of servers disabled, number of confidential files exfiltrated) is more likely

[806] Common Criteria for Information Technology Security Evaluation, International Standard ISO/IEC 15408, ver. 3.1 (July 2009).

to be characterised as a use of force than one with difficult to measure or subjective consequences.

(f) *Military character.* A nexus between the cyber operation in question and military operations heightens the likelihood of characterisation as a use of force. This contention is supported by the fact that the UN Charter is particularly concerned with military actions. Its preamble provides that 'armed force shall not be used, save in the common interest',[807] while Article 44 uses the term 'force' without the qualifier 'armed' in a situation that clearly refers to the use of military force. Further, the use of force has traditionally been understood to imply force employed by the military or other armed forces. Note that it has been suggested that the military character of the cyber infrastructure against which a cyber operation is directed is also a consideration that States will take into account.[808]

(g) *State involvement.* The extent of State involvement in a cyber operation lies along a continuum from operations conducted by a State itself (e.g., the activities of its armed forces or intelligence agencies) to those in which its involvement is peripheral. The clearer and closer a nexus between a State and cyber operations, the more likely it is that other States will characterise them as uses of force by that State.

(h) *Presumptive legality.* International law is generally prohibitive in nature.[809] Acts that are not forbidden are permitted; absent an express treaty or accepted customary law prohibition, an act is presumptively legal. For instance, international law does not prohibit propaganda, psychological operations, espionage, or mere economic pressure *per se*. Therefore, acts falling into these and other such categories are presumptively legal. This being so, they are less likely to be considered by States as uses of force.[810]

---

[807] UN Charter, pmbl.

[808] *See* DoD Manual, para. 16.3.1 ('[C]yber operations that cripple a military's logistics systems, and thus its ability to conduct and sustain military operations, might also be considered a use of force under *jus ad bellum*.').

[809] *Lotus* judgment, at 19.

[810] The criteria of the analysis may be evaluated in light of questions such as the following:

  (1) Severity: How many people were killed? How large an area was attacked? How much damage was done within this area?

  (2) Immediacy: How soon were the effects of the cyber operation felt? How quickly did its effects abate?

10.   The aforementioned factors are not exhaustive. Depending on the attendant circumstances, States may look to others, such as the prevailing political environment, whether the cyber operation portends the future use of military force, the identity of the attacker, any record of cyber operations by the attacker, and the nature of the target (such as critical infrastructure). Moreover, the factors operate in concert. As an example, a highly invasive operation that causes only inconvenience, such as temporary denial of service, is unlikely to be classified as a use of force. By contrast, some may categorise massive cyber operations that cripple an economy as a use of force, even though economic coercion is presumptively lawful.

11.   Finally, it must be understood that 'use of force' and 'armed attack' (Rule 71) are standards that serve different normative purposes. The 'use of force' standard is employed to determine whether a State has violated Article 2(4) of the UN Charter and its related customary international law prohibition. By contrast, the notion of 'armed attack' has to do with whether the target State may respond to an act with a use of force without itself violating the prohibition of using force. This distinction is critical in that the mere fact that a use of force has occurred does not alone justify a use of force in response.[811] States facing a use of force not amounting to an armed attack will, in the view of the International Group of Experts, have to resort to other measures if they wish to respond lawfully, such as countermeasures (Rule 20) or actions consistent with the plea of necessity (Rule 26).

(3) Directness: Was the action the proximate cause of the effects? Were there contributing causes giving rise to those effects?

(4) Invasiveness: Did the action involve penetrating a cyber network intended to be secure? Was the locus of the action within the target country?

(5) Measurability: How can the effects of the action be quantified? Are the effects of the action distinct from the results of parallel or competing actions? How certain is the calculation of the effects?

(6) Military character: Did the military conduct the cyber operation? Were the armed forces the target of the cyber operation?

(7) State involvement: Is the State directly or indirectly involved in the act in question? But for the acting State's sake, would the action have occurred?

(8) Presumptive legality: Has this category of action been generally characterised as a use of force, or characterised as one that is not? Are the means qualitatively similar to others presumed legitimate under international law?

[811] *But see* discussion of countermeasures rising to the level of use of force in Rule 22 (noting a minority view allowing countermeasures at this level).

Rule 70 – Definition of threat of force

A cyber operation, or threatened cyber operation, constitutes an unlawful threat of force when the threatened action, if carried out, would be an unlawful use of force.

1.   This Rule examines the term 'threat' as used in Rule 68.

2.   The phrase 'cyber operation, or threatened cyber operation' in this Rule applies to two situations. The first is a cyber operation that is used to communicate a threat to use force (whether kinetic or cyber). The second is a threat conveyed by any means (e.g., public pronouncements) to carry out cyber operations qualifying as a use of force.

3.   It is generally accepted that threats by States and officials in a position to make good those threats are lawful if the threatened action is itself lawful.[812] There are two recognised exceptions to the international law prohibition of the use of force: the exercise of the right of self-defence (Rule 71) and actions implementing a United Nations Security Council resolution under Chapter VII of the United Nations Charter (Rule 76). For instance, it would be lawful for a State to threaten that it will defend itself forcefully if subjected to a cyber armed attack. Threatening other actions that are not prohibited by international law would likewise be lawful.

4.   Although threats are usually intended to be coercive in effect, there is no requirement that a specific 'demand' accompany the threat. The essence of a threat is that it must be communicative in nature, that is, it must be intended to be conveyed to the target State. It can be made either explicitly or impliedly. Actions that simply endanger the security of the target State, but that are not communicative in nature, do not qualify. For example, consider a case in which tensions between two States are high. One State begins aggressively to develop the capability to conduct massive malicious cyber operations against the other. The mere acquisition of capabilities that can be used to conduct uses of force does not constitute a threat. However, if the leader of the State concerned announces, either on a conditional basis or otherwise, that the capabilities will be used for that purpose against the other State, the former will be in violation of this Rule.

---

[812]   By distinguishing lawful from unlawful threats, the International Court of Justice conceded the existence of the former: '[I]f it is to be lawful, the declared readiness of a State to use force must be a use of force that is in conformity with the Charter.' *Nuclear Weapons* advisory opinion, para. 47.

5.   The International Group of Experts was divided as to whether a State manifestly lacking any capability to make good its threat can violate this Rule. Despite the difference of opinion, it must be noted that cyber capability is not as dependent on a State's size, population, or economic and military capacity as is the capacity to use conventional force. This means that it may be more difficult for a State to evaluate the capacity of another State to make good on its threat to use force by cyber means. Therefore, this issue plays a diminished role in evaluating cyber threats.

6.   Similarly, no consensus could be achieved regarding a State that possesses the capability to carry out the threat but that clearly has no intention of doing so. An example would be that of a State that possesses an offensive cyber capability and whose leader utters threats against other States for purely domestic political reasons.

SECTION 2:   SELF-DEFENCE

Rule 71 – Self-defence against armed attack

A State that is the target of a cyber operation that rises to the level of an armed attack may exercise its inherent right of self-defence. Whether a cyber operation constitutes an armed attack depends on its scale and effects.

1.   According to Article 51 of the United Nations Charter, '[n]othing in the present Charter shall impair the inherent right of individual or collective self-defence if an armed attack occurs against a Member of the United Nations, until the Security Council has taken the measures necessary to maintain international peace and security'. This Article recognises and reflects the customary law right of self-defence.

2.   The International Group of Experts noted that the terms 'armed attack' and 'aggression' must be distinguished. This Rule deals with self-defence, for which the condition precedent is an armed attack. Aggression, by contrast, is one of the situations in which the UN Security Council may employ its powers under Chapter VII of the UN Charter (Rule 76). Although an act of aggression can constitute an armed attack, it may not always do so.[813]

---

[813]   *See, e.g.*, reference to Article 3(g) of the Definition of Aggression by the International Court of Justice in the *Nicaragua* judgment, para. 195.

3.   An armed attack must have a trans-border element. This criterion is always met when one State engages in a cyber operation otherwise qualifying as an armed attack against another State, or directs non-State actors, wherever they may be, to act on its behalf in doing so. The more difficult case involves cyber operations by non-State actors against a State that are launched from another State and that are not conducted on behalf of the latter. Although such operations have a trans-border element, whether non-State actors may initiate an armed attack as a matter of law is the subject of some controversy. This issue is dealt with below. With regard to cyber operations organised, conducted, and directed by non-State actors solely from within a State's own territory, States may respond with force in accordance with their domestic laws (informed by international law standards such as human rights law and, in situations of non-international armed conflict, the law of armed conflict).

4.   The right to employ force in self-defence extends beyond kinetic armed attacks to those that are perpetrated solely through cyber operations. The International Group of Experts unanimously concluded that some cyber operations may be sufficiently grave to warrant classifying them as an 'armed attack' within the meaning of the Charter. This conclusion is in accord with the International Court of Justice's insistence in its *Nuclear Weapons* advisory opinion that the choice of means of attack is immaterial to the issue of whether an operation qualifies as an armed attack.[814] Moreover, the position is consistent with State practice.[815] For example, it is universally accepted that chemical, biological, and radiological attacks of the requisite scale and effects to constitute armed attacks trigger the right of self-defence. This is so, despite their non-kinetic nature, because the ensuing consequences can include serious suffering or death. Identical reasoning would apply to cyber operations.

5.   The International Group of Experts discussed whether the notion of armed attack, because of the term 'armed', necessarily involves the employment of 'weapons' (Rule 103). The Experts took the position that it did not and that instead the critical factor was whether the effects of a cyber operation, as distinct from the means used to achieve the effects,

---

[814] *Nuclear Weapons* advisory opinion, para. 39.
[815] *See, e.g.*, NATO Wales Summit Declaration, para. 72; Government Response to the AIV/ CAVV Report, para. 4; The White House, International Strategy for Cyberspace: Prosperity, Security, and Openness in a Networked World (2011), at 10, 13; DoD MANUAL, para. 16.3.3.

were analogous to those that would result from an action otherwise qualifying as a kinetic armed attack. However, they acknowledged a view by which the term 'armed' applies solely to the use of weapons and that therefore unless the cyber operation involves the use of a cyber weapon (Rule 103), it does not qualify as an armed attack, irrespective of the consequences of the operation.

6. In the view of the International Group of Experts, the term 'armed attack' is not to be equated with the term 'use of force' appearing in Rule 69.[816] An armed attack presupposes at least a use of force in the sense of Article 2(4). However, as noted by the International Court of Justice, not every use of force rises to the level of an armed attack.[817] The scale and effects required for an act to be characterised as an armed attack necessarily exceed those qualifying the act as a use of force. Only in the event that the use of force reaches the threshold of an armed attack is a State entitled to respond using force in self-defence.

7. The phrase 'scale and effects' is drawn from the *Nicaragua* judgment.[818] In that case, the Court identified scale and effects as the criteria that distinguish actions qualifying as an armed attack from those that do not. It noted the need to 'distinguish the most grave forms of the use of force (those constituting an armed attack) from other less grave forms', but provided no further guidance in this regard.[819] Therefore, the parameters of the scale and effects criteria remain unsettled beyond the indication that they need to be grave.

8. That said, some cases are clear. For instance, acts of cyber intelligence gathering and cyber theft, as well as cyber operations that involve brief or periodic interruption of non-essential cyber services, do not qualify as armed attacks. By contrast, the International Group of Experts agreed that a cyber operation that seriously injures or kills a number of persons or that causes significant damage to, or destruction of, property would satisfy the scale and effects requirement.

9. The Experts noted that the law is unclear as to the precise point at which the effects of a cyber operation qualify that operation as an armed attack. In the *Nicaragua* judgment, the International Court of Justice distinguished between an armed attack and a 'mere frontier incident'.[820] This distinction has been criticised by numerous commentators who

---

[816] However, not all States accept this view. *See* discussion in Rule 69.
[817] *Nicaragua* judgment, para. 191.   [818] *Nicaragua* judgment, para. 195.
[819] *Nicaragua* judgment, para. 191.   [820] *Nicaragua* judgment, para. 195.

adopt the view that only inconsequential actions should be excluded.[821] In this regard, the International Court of Justice has subsequently indicated that an attack on a single military platform or installation might qualify as an armed attack.[822]

10.   A case illustrating the unsettled nature of the armed attack threshold is that of the 2010 Stuxnet operation. In light of the damage the operation caused to Iranian centrifuges, some members of the International Group of Experts were of the view that it reached the armed attack threshold (unless justifiable on the basis of anticipatory self-defence (Rule 73)). Other Experts took the contrary view, although, as discussed in Rule 68, all members considered it a use of force.

11.   An important issue is whether a State may exercise the right of self-defence in response to a series of cyber incidents that individually fall below the threshold of an armed attack. In other words, can they constitute an armed attack when aggregated? The International Group of Experts agreed that the determinative factor is whether the same originator (or originators acting in concert) has carried out smaller-scale incidents that are related and that taken together meet the requisite scale and effects. If there is convincing evidence that this is the case, there are grounds for treating the incidents as a composite armed attack.[823]

12.   The case of cyber operations that do not result in injury, death, damage, or destruction, but that otherwise have extensive negative effects, remains unsettled. Some of the Experts took the position that harm to persons or physical damage to property is a condition precedent to the characterisation of an incident as an armed attack. Others took the view that it is not the nature (injurious or destructive) of the consequences that matters, but rather the extent of the ensuing[824] effects. The classic

---

[821]   See, e.g., DINSTEIN, WAR, AGGRESSION AND SELF-DEFENCE, at 210–211; William H. Taft, Self Defense and the Oil Platforms Decision, 29 YALE J. INT'L L. 295, 300 (2004).

[822]   Oil Platforms judgment, paras. 57, 61.

[823]   This approach has been labelled the 'pin-prick' theory, the 'accumulation of effects' theory, and 'Nadelstichtaktik.'

[824]   See, e.g., Advisory Council on International Affairs, Cyber Warfare, No. 77, AIV / No 22, CAVV, at 21 (December 2011) (stating the implied approval by the Netherlands of the position that:

> 'if there are no actual or potential fatalities, casualties or physical damage', a cyber operation targeting 'essential functions of the state could conceivably be qualified as an "armed attack" ... if it could or did lead to serious disruption of the functioning of the state or serious and long-lasting consequences for the stability of the state.')

scenario illustrating this division of opinion is a cyber incident directed against a major international stock exchange that causes the market to crash. The International Group of Experts was divided over the characterisation of such an event. Some of the Experts were unprepared to label it as an armed attack because they were not satisfied that mere financial loss constitutes damage for the purpose of qualifying a cyber operation as an armed attack. Others emphasised the catastrophic effects such a crash would occasion and therefore regarded them as sufficient to characterise the operation as an armed attack. Likewise, some were of the view that a cyber operation directed against a State's critical infrastructure that causes severe, albeit not destructive, effects would qualify as an armed attack.

13.   A further challenging issue in the cyber context involves determining which effects to consider in assessing whether an action amounts to an armed attack. The International Group of Experts agreed that all reasonably foreseeable consequences of the cyber operation so qualify. Consider, for example, the case of a cyber operation targeting a water purification plant. Sickness and death caused by drinking contaminated water are foreseeable and should therefore be taken into account.

14.   The International Group of Experts was divided over the issue of whether the effects in question must have been intended. For instance, consider the example of cyber espionage by one State against another that unexpectedly results in significant damage to the latter's cyber infrastructure. Some of the Experts were unwilling to characterise the operation as an armed attack because the consequences are unintended, although they acknowledged that measures could be taken to counteract the negative effects of the operation (e.g., the plea of necessity discussed in Rule 26).[825] The majority of the International

---

This position was impliedly adopted in Government Response to AIV/CAVV Report, at 5 ('The findings of the AIV/CAVV with regard to the use of force and the right of self-defence are largely in line with the government's position.').

[825] *See, e.g.*, Harold Hongju Koh, Legal Adviser, Department of State, International Law in Cyberspace: Remarks as Prepared for Delivery to the USCYBERCOM Inter-Agency Legal Conference (18 September 2012), reprinted in 54 HARV. INT'L L. J. ONLINE, 4 (December 2012) ('In assessing whether an event constituted a use of force in or through cyberspace, we must evaluate factors including the context of the event, the actor perpetrating the action (recognising challenging issues of attribution in cyberspace), the target and location, effects and intent, among other possible issues.') *See also* the reference, albeit in the context of the use of force, to specific intent in the *Oil Platforms* judgment, para. 64, in support of their view, and UK Government Response to House of Commons Defence Committee's Sixth Report of Session 2012–13, para. 10 (22 March 2013).

Group of Experts was of the view that intention is irrelevant in qualifying an operation as an armed attack and that only the scale and effects matter. However, any response thereto would have to comport with the necessity and proportionality criteria (Rule 72); the former would prove a significant hurdle in this respect. All the Experts agreed that the lawfulness of the response would be determined by the reasonableness of the State's assessment as to whether an armed attack was underway against it.

15.   A cyber armed attack by one State (A) against another (B) may have bleed-over effects in a third State (C). The majority of the International Group of Experts supported the view that if those effects meet the scale and effects criteria for an armed attack, State C is also entitled to resort to the use of force in self-defence, so long as the defensive action complies with the necessity and proportionality criteria. Furthermore, for them, even if the cyber operations against State B had not qualified as an armed attack, this would not preclude the bleed-over effects from amounting to an armed attack against State C. The remaining Experts would not characterise the operation as an armed attack absent an intent to create such effects.

16.   It is also necessary to consider the issue of the 'originator' of a cyber operation in determining whether it qualifies as an armed attack. It is incontrovertible that a cyber operation by organs of a State may so qualify. It is equally indisputable that the actions of non-State actors may sometimes be attributed to a State for the purpose of finding an armed attack. In the *Nicaragua* judgment, the International Court of Justice stated that:

> An armed attack must be understood as including not merely action by regular forces across an international border, but also 'the sending by or on behalf of a State of armed bands, groups, irregulars or mercenaries, which carry out acts of armed force against another State of such gravity as to amount to' (*inter alia*) an actual armed attack conducted by regular forces, 'or its substantial involvement therein'.[826]

17.   For instance, if a group of private individuals undertakes cyber operations on behalf of one State directed against another State, and those actions reach the requisite scale and effects level, the first State will have committed an armed attack. This same conclusion would apply to cyber operations conducted by a single individual operating on behalf of a State.

---

[826] *Nicaragua* judgment, para. 195.

18.   The issue of whether acts of non-State actors can constitute an armed attack absent involvement by a State is controversial. Traditionally, Article 51 and the customary international law of self-defence were characterised as applicable solely to armed attacks undertaken by one State against another. Violent acts by non-State actors fell within the law enforcement paradigm. However, the international community characterised the 9/11 attacks by Al Qaeda on the United States as an armed attack triggering the inherent right of self-defence.[827] Such State practice appears to signal a willingness of States to apply the right of self-defence to attacks conducted by non-State actors. Moreover, while Article 2(4) addresses the actions of States, Article 51 contains no such limitation *vis-à-vis* armed attacks (although the text does make it clear that only States enjoy the right of self-defence). For its part, the International Court of Justice does not seem to have been prepared to adopt this approach, although it appears that there is a lack of unanimity on the Court in this regard.[828]

19.   A majority of the International Group of Experts concluded that State practice has established a right of self-defence in the face of cyber operations at the armed attack level by non-State actors acting without the involvement of a State, such as terrorist or rebel groups.[829] As an example, these Experts would consider a devastating cyber operation undertaken by a group of terrorists from within one State against critical infrastructure located in another as an armed attack by those cyber terrorists against the latter State. A minority of the Experts did not accept this premise, suggesting that the traditional approach by which only States, or non-State actors conducting operations on behalf of States, can mount an armed attack as a matter of law.

---

[827]   The Security Council adopted numerous resolutions recognising the applicability of the right of self-defence. *See, e.g.,* SC Res 1368, UN Doc. S/RES/1368 (12 September 2001); SC Res. 1373, UN Doc. S/RES/1373 (28 September 2001). International organisations such as NATO and many individual States took the same approach. *See, e.g.,* Press Release, NATO, Statement by the North Atlantic Council (12 September 2001); Terrorist Threat to the Americas, Res. 1, Twenty-Fourth Meeting of Consultation of Ministers of Foreign Affairs, Terrorist Threat to the Americas, OAS Doc. RC.24/RES.1/01 (21 September 2001); Brendan Pearson, *PM Commits to Mutual Defence,* AUSTL. FIN. REV., 15 September 2001, at 9.

[828]   *Wall* advisory opinion, para. 139; *Armed Activities* judgment, paras. 146–147.

[829]   For State positions in the cyber context, *see, e.g.,* DoD MANUAL, para. 16.3.3.4; Government Response to AIV/CAVV Report, at 5.

20.   The International Group of Experts acknowledged the significant uncertainty that exists within the international law community regarding such matters as the degree of requisite organisation a group must have (if any) to be capable of mounting an armed attack as a matter of law and any geographical limitations that may bear on this issue. Additionally, those Experts who took the position that a group unaffiliated with a State can conduct an armed attack as a matter of law were split over the issue of whether a single individual mounting an operation that meets the scale and effects threshold can do so.

21.   The object of a cyber operation meeting the trans-border and scale and effects requirements may also determine whether it qualifies as an armed attack. If it consists of property or persons within the affected State's territory, whether governmental or private, the action is an armed attack against that State. It must be noted that the International Group of Experts did not achieve consensus on whether further criteria must be satisfied in order to bring into operation the right of self-defence. While some took the position that attacks solely motivated by purely private interests would not trigger the right of self-defence, others were of the view that motives are irrelevant. This issue is likely to be resolved through State practice.

22.   It is sometimes unclear in international law whether a cyber operation can qualify as an armed attack if the object of the operation consists of property or citizens situated outside the State's territory. Attacks against non-commercial government facilities or equipment and government personnel certainly qualify as armed attacks so long as the above-mentioned criteria are met. For instance, the International Group of Experts agreed that a cyber operation undertaken by one State to kill another's head of State while abroad would amount to an armed attack. The determination of whether other operations are armed attacks depends on, but is not limited to, such factors as: the extent of damage caused by the operation; whether the property involved is governmental or private in character; the status of the individuals who have been targeted; and whether the operations were politically motivated, that is, conducted against the property or individuals because of their national-ity. No bright-line rule exists in such cases. Consider a cyber operation conducted by one State to kill the CEO of another State's State-owned corporation abroad. Opinions among the members of the International Group of Experts were divided as to whether the operation amounts to an armed attack.

23.   The exercise of the right of self-defence is subject to the requirements of necessity, proportionality, imminence, and immediacy (Rules 72–73). Of course, the right to engage in self-defence is also subject to the existence of a reasonable determination that an armed attack is about to occur or has occurred, as well as the identity of the attacker. These determinations are made *ex ante*, not *ex post facto*. Their reasonableness will be assessed based upon the information available at the time they were made, not in light of information that subsequently becomes available.

24.   Measures taken pursuant to the right of self-defence may in principle be conducted from, or directed against, entities on or in the territory of the originator or victim States, international waters, international airspace, or outer space, subject to the principles of necessity and proportionality that are related to self-defence (Rule 72). With respect to using of force in self-defence against the attacking State's diplomatic or consular premises in the target State, see Rule 39.

25.   When defensive cyber operations are initiated from, employ assets located in, or are launched into a State to which the attack cannot be attributed, the principle of sovereignty (Rule 4) must be carefully considered. It is indisputable that actions in self-defence may be taken on foreign territory with that State's consent without violating its sovereignty. Therefore, the key issue with regard to defensive action on another State's territory is how to characterise non-consensual actions. The International Group of Experts was divided. The majority concluded that self-defence against a cyber armed attack in these circumstances is permissible when it complies with the principle of necessity (Rule 72), is the only effective means of defence against the armed attack, and the territorial State is unable (e.g., because it lacks the expertise or technology) or unwilling to take effective actions to repress the relevant elements of the cyber armed attack. In particular, these Experts emphasised that States have a duty to ensure their territory is not used for acts contrary to international law (Rule 6). By contrast, a minority of the Group took the position that using force in self-defence on the territory of a State to which the armed attack is not attributable is, in the absence of either the consent of that State or an authorisation by the United Nations Security Council (Rule 76), impermissible, although other responses, such as an action based on the plea of necessity (Rule 26), might be lawful.

26.   Those Experts who accepted the lawfulness of cross-border defensive actions emphasised that the victim State must first demand

that the territorial State put an end to the activities comprising the armed attack. The victim State must also afford the territorial State an opportunity to address the situation. These requirements derive from an international law obligation to respect (to the greatest extent possible) the sovereignty of the State on which the defensive actions are to take place. Additionally, they are procedural safeguards against a mistaken (or premature) conclusion as to the unwillingness or inability of the territorial State to address the situation. There may be exceptional situations where there is no time to convey a demand to the latter or for the latter to resolve the situation. If immediate action to repel a cyber armed attack is required to defeat the attack or minimise its consequences, the targeted State may act immediately in self-defence. Thus, the requirements are context-specific.

27.   With respect to situations not falling within the parameters of this Rule, Rule 65 on the peaceful settlement of disputes, Rules 20–25 on countermeasures, and Rule 26 on the plea of necessity may be relevant.

Rule 72 – Necessity and proportionality

A use of force involving cyber operations undertaken by a State in the exercise of its right of self-defence must be necessary and proportionate.

1.   Actions in self-defence must meet two criteria – necessity and proportionality. The International Court of Justice acknowledged both in the *Nicaragua* judgment and later confirmed them in its *Oil Platforms* judgment.[830] The Nuremberg Tribunal also recognised the criteria.[831] As illustrated by these decisions, they undoubtedly reflect customary international law. It is important to note that the conditions of necessity and proportionality in the *jus ad bellum* are distinct from the concept of military necessity and the rule of proportionality in the *jus in bello*.

2.   Necessity requires that a use of force, including cyber operations that amount to a use of force (Rule 69), be needed to successfully repel an imminent armed attack or defeat one that is underway. This does not mean that force has to be the only available response to an armed attack. It merely requires that non-forceful measures be insufficient to

---

[830] *Nicaragua* judgment, paras. 176, 194; *Nuclear Weapons* advisory opinion, para. 41; *Oil Platforms* judgment, paras. 43, 73–74, 76.
[831] *Nuremburg Tribunal* judgment, at 435 (referring to the *Caroline* formula).

address the situation. Of course, the forceful actions may be combined with non-forceful measures such as diplomacy, economic sanctions, or law enforcement.

3.   The key to the necessity analysis in the cyber context is, therefore, the existence, or lack, of alternative courses of action that do not rise to the level of a use of force. Should passive (as distinct from active) cyber defences like firewalls be adequate to reliably and completely thwart a cyber armed attack, other measures, whether cyber or kinetic, at the level of a use of force are impermissible. Similarly, if active cyber operations not rising to the level of use of force suffice to deter or repel an armed attack (imminent or on-going), forceful cyber or kinetic alternatives will be barred by the necessity criterion. However, when measures falling short of a use of force cannot alone reasonably be expected to defeat an armed attack and prevent subsequent ones, cyber and kinetic operations that cross the use of force threshold are allowed under the law of self-defence.

4.   Necessity is judged from the perspective of the victim State. The determination of necessity must be reasonable in the attendant circumstances. For example, consider a case in which one State is conducting cyber armed attacks against another State's cyber infrastructure. The victim State responds with forceful cyber operations of its own to defend itself. Unbeknownst to that State, the attacking State had already decided to end its attacks. This fact would not render the victim State's defensive cyber operations unnecessary and, therefore, an unlawful use of cyber force in self-defence.

5.   Proportionality addresses the issue of how much force, including use of cyber force, is permissible once force is deemed necessary. The criterion limits the scale, scope, duration, and intensity of the defensive response to that required to end the situation that has given rise to the right to act in self-defence. It does not restrict the amount of force used to that employed in the armed attack since the level of force needed to successfully mount a defence is context-dependent; more force may be necessary, or less force may be sufficient, to defeat the armed attack or repel one that is imminent. In addition, there is no requirement that the defensive force be of the same nature as that constituting the armed attack. Therefore, a cyber use of force may be resorted to in response to a kinetic armed attack, and *vice versa*.[832]

---

[832] *See, e.g.*, DoD Manual, para. 16.3.3.2.

6. The proportionality requirement should not be construed as imposing a requirement to respond in kind. It may be that the originator of the cyber armed attack is relatively invulnerable to cyber operations. This would not preclude kinetic operations designed to compel the attacker to desist, although they must be scaled to that purpose.

Rule 73 – Imminence and immediacy

The right to use force in self-defence arises if a cyber armed attack occurs or is imminent. It is further subject to a requirement of immediacy.

1. Textually, Article 51 of the UN Charter refers to a situation in which 'an armed attack occurs'. Clearly, this covers incidents in which the effects of the armed attack have already materialised, that is, when the cyber armed attack has caused, or is in the process of causing, damage or injury. It also encompasses situations in which a cyber operation is the first step in the launch of a kinetic armed attack. The paradigmatic case involves cyber operations directed against another State's air defences to 'prepare the battlefield' for an air campaign.

2. The International Group of Experts took the position that even though Article 51 does not expressly provide for defensive action in anticipation of an armed attack, a State need not wait idly as the enemy prepares to attack. Instead, a State may defend itself once an armed attack is 'imminent'. Such action is labelled 'anticipatory self-defence' in international law.[833] This position is based on the standard of imminence articulated in the nineteenth century by US Secretary of State Webster following the *Caroline* incident. In correspondence with his British counterpart, Lord Ashburton, regarding a British incursion into American territory to attack Canadian rebels during the Mackenzie Rebellion, Webster opined that the right of self-defence applies only when the 'necessity of self-defence [is] instant, overwhelming, leaving no choice of means, and no moment for deliberation'.[834] Although the incident actually had nothing to do with actions taken in anticipation of

[833] For support regarding the notion, *see* Derek W. Bowett, SELF-DEFENCE IN INTERNATIONAL LAW 188–189 (1958). Bowett finds support for this in the *travaux* of the Charter's drafting committee. *Id.* at 182 (quoting Report of the Rapporteur of Committee I to Commission I, 6 UNCIO 459 (13 June 1945)).
[834] Letter from Daniel Webster to Lord Ashburton (6 August 1842), *reprinted in* 2 INT'L L. DIG. 412 (John Bassett Moore ed., 1906).

attack (the attacks in question were on-going), Webster's formulation has survived as the classic expression of the temporal threshold for anticipatory defensive actions; indeed, the Nuremberg Tribunal cited the *Caroline* correspondence with approval.[835]

3. The International Group of Experts acknowledged the view held by some commentators that acts in self-defence are permissible only once an attack has actually been launched; anticipatory self-defence is prohibited.[836] A nuanced version of this approach asserts that action in self-defence is permissible in the face of an incipient attack that has not reached its destination.[837] The speed of cyber operations would usually preclude them from falling into this category. None of the Experts shared these views.

4. There are variations among approaches to anticipatory self-defence.[838] One requires that the armed attack be about to be launched, thereby imposing a temporal limitation on anticipatory actions.[839] The majority of the International Group of Experts rejected this strict temporal analysis. It took particular note of the 'last feasible window of opportunity' standard.[840] By this standard, a State may act in anticipatory self-defence against an armed attack, whether cyber or kinetic, when the attacker is clearly committed to launching an armed attack and the victim State will lose its opportunity to effectively defend itself unless it acts. In other words, it may act anticipatorily only during the last window of opportunity to defend itself against an armed attack that is forthcoming. This window may present itself immediately before the attack in question, or, in some cases, long before it occurs. For these Experts, the critical question is not the temporal proximity of the anticipatory defensive action to the prospective armed attack, but whether a failure to act at that moment would reasonably be expected to result in the State being unable to defend itself effectively when that attack actually starts.

---

[835] *Nuremburg Tribunal* judgment, at 435.

[836] *See, e.g.*, Ian Brownlie, INTERNATIONAL LAW AND THE USE OF FORCE BETWEEN STATES 275–278 (1963).

[837] *See, e.g.*, DINSTEIN, WAR, AGGRESSION AND SELF-DEFENCE, at 203–204.

[838] *See* discussion of the variations in Terry D. Gill, *The Temporal Dimension of Self-Defence: Anticipation, Pre-emption, Prevention and Immediacy*, in INTERNATIONAL LAW AND ARMED CONFLICT: EXPLORING THE FAULTLINES 113 (Michael N. Schmitt and Jelena Pejic eds., 2007).

[839] *See, e.g.*, Derek W. Bowett, SELF-DEFENCE IN INTERNATIONAL LAW 187–192 (1958).

[840] *See, e.g.*, US Justice Dept. White Paper, Lawfulness of a Lethal Operation Directed Against a U.S. Citizen Who Is a Senior Operational Leader of Al–Qa'da or an Associated Force (n.d), at 7.

5.   Within the majority, a number of the Experts took the position that while the 'last feasible window of opportunity' standard was a correct statement of the law in principle, it did not translate into a licence to dispense altogether with the temporal element. In their view, the further removed the incipient attack is from being effectuated in temporal terms, the less likely it will be the only available option available.

6.   Consider a situation in which the intelligence service of a State receives incontrovertible information that another State is preparing to launch a cyber operation that will destroy the former's primary oil pipeline within the next two weeks. The operation involves causing microcontrollers along the pipeline to increase the pressure in it, resulting in a series of explosions. Since its intelligence service has no information on the specific vulnerability to be exploited, the first State cannot mount an effective cyber defence of the microcontrollers. However, the service does have information that those involved in conducting the operation will gather at a particular location and time. The target State would be justified in concluding that an armed attack is imminent, using force to defend itself is necessary (Rule 72), and strikes against those individuals would be lawful as proportionate (Rule 72) anticipatory self-defence.

7.   In assessing such cases, a distinction must be drawn between actions that constitute the initial phase of an armed attack and those that are merely preparatory. Take the case of the insertion of a logic bomb. The insertion qualifies as an imminent armed attack if the specified conditions for activation are likely to occur; the action is analogous to the laying of naval mines in shipping routes passing through the territorial sea of the target State. Such situations must be distinguished from the emplacement of remotely activated malware. If the initiator is merely acquiring the capability to initiate an armed attack in the future, the criterion of imminence is not satisfied.

8.   It should be cautioned with respect to the latter case that if the initiator has in fact decided to conduct an armed attack using the malware, the attack becomes imminent at the point that the victim State must act lest it lose the opportunity to defend itself effectively. Since it will often be difficult to make the distinction in practice, the lawfulness of any defensive response will be determined by the reasonableness of the victim State's assessment of the situation, as well as other requirements of self-defence, in particular necessity and proportionality (Rule 72).

9.   A few of the Experts were of the view that self-defence is a last resort measure that requires that the armed attack be about to be

launched, thereby imposing a temporal limitation on anticipatory actions. In their view, the last window of opportunity approach relies on a rather open standard that is subject to interpretation and therefore prone to abuse, arguably even more so with respect to anticipated cyber operations than with regard to traditional/kinetic attacks. For them, the standard is not *lex lata*.

10.   The International Group of Experts agreed that a preventive strike, that is, one against a prospective attacker who has not initiated any preparations or expressed either impliedly or explicitly an intention to carry out an armed attack, does not qualify as a lawful exercise of anticipatory self-defence. Accordingly, the fact that an overtly hostile State is capable of launching cyber armed attacks – even devastating ones – does not alone entitle a potential victim State to act defensively with force. The potential victim State must first reasonably conclude that the hostility has matured into an actual decision to attack.

11.   Until arriving at this conclusion, the victim State's response would be limited to actions short of the use of force, such as countermeasures (Rule 20) or referral of the matter to the Security Council (Rule 76). Of course, even if one State has the intent and opportunity to conduct a cyber armed attack against another, the right of the victim State to take forceful defensive measures does not mature until such time as failure to act would deprive the State of its ability to defend itself effectively against the attack. Because a State is acting in anticipation of, rather than during, an armed attack, the requirement that the decision to resort to action in self-defence be reasonable is especially demanding.[841]

12.   The requirement of immediacy (as distinct from the requirement of imminence discussed above) distinguishes an act of self-defence from mere retaliation. It refers to the period following the execution of an armed attack within which the victim State may reasonably respond in self-defence. Factors such as the temporal proximity between attack and response, the period necessary to identify the attacker, and the time required to prepare a response are relevant in this regard.

13.   A further issue is how to assess the period during which a self-defence situation continues following the completion of the particular incident providing the basis for the right of self-defence. For instance, a

---

[841] UK Government Response to House of Commons Defence Committee's Sixth Report of Session 2012–13, para. 10 (22 March 2013).

cyber armed attack may commence with a wave of cyber operations against the victim State. The self-defence situation does not necessarily conclude with the termination of those cyber operations. If it is reasonable to conclude that further cyber operations are likely to follow, the victim State may treat those operations as a 'cyber campaign' and continue to act in self-defence. However, if such a conclusion is not reasonable, any further use of force, whether kinetic or cyber, is liable to be characterised as mere retaliation. In the final analysis, the requirement of immediacy rests on a test of reasonableness in light of the circumstances prevailing at the time.

14.   In some cases, the fact that a cyber armed attack has occurred or is occurring may not be apparent for some time. This could be so because the cause of the damage or injury has not been identified. Similarly, the initiator of the attack may not be identified until well after the attack. The classic example of both situations is employment of a worm such as Stuxnet. In such cases, the criterion of immediacy is not met unless the conditions described above justify taking action.

Rule 74 – Collective self-defence

The right of self-defence may be exercised collectively. Collective self-defence against a cyber operation amounting to an armed attack may only be exercised at the request of the victim State and within the scope of the request.

1.   The right to collective self-defence authorises a State or multiple States to either conduct a joint defence against an attack launched against all of them or to come to the assistance of another State (or States) that is the victim of a cyber armed attack.[842] This right, explicitly set forth in Article 51 of the United Nations Charter, is recognised in customary international law.

2.   Before a State may come to the assistance of another State in collective self-defence, it must have received a request for such assistance from the victim of the armed attack.[843] Both the victim State and the

---

[842] For the different modalities of collective self-defence, *see* DINSTEIN, WAR, AGGRESSION AND SELF-DEFENCE, at 278–280.

[843] *Nicaragua* judgment, para. 199. In *Nicaragua*, the International Court of Justice articulated a requirement for a 'declaration' by the State that has been the victim of the armed attack. *Id.* paras. 232–234. The International Group of Experts concluded that this requirement is satisfied by the request for assistance.

State providing assistance must be satisfied that there is an imminent (Rule 73) or on-going cyber armed attack. There is no rule in customary international law permitting one State to engage in collective self-defence of another State solely on the basis of the former's own assessment of the situation.

3.   When a State exercises collective self-defence on behalf of another State, it must do so within the scope of the other's request and consent. In other words, the right to engage in collective self-defence is subject to the conditions and limitations set by the victim State. The latter State may, for instance, limit the assistance to non-kinetic measures or restrict the types of targets that may be made the object of cyber operations while operating in collective self-defence.

4.   Collective self-defence may be exercised either on the basis of a previously concluded collective defence treaty or an *ad hoc* arrangement. As an example, NATO Allies have agreed 'that an armed attack against one or more of them in Europe or North America shall be considered an attack against them all and consequently they agree that, if such an armed attack occurs, each of them, in exercise of the right of individual or collective self-defence recognised by Article 51 of the Charter of the United Nations, will assist the Party or Parties so attacked'.[844] There would be no bar to engaging in cyber operations pursuant to Article V of the North Atlantic Treaty. An example of an *ad hoc* arrangement is the assistance provided to Kuwait by a coalition of States in 1990–91 in response to the armed attack by Iraq. Again, cyber operations are permissible when employed by forces operating pursuant to such agreements.[845]

5.   The requirements of necessity, proportionality, imminence, and immediacy (Rules 72–73) apply to collective self-defence.

Rule 75 – Reporting measures of self-defence

Measures involving cyber operations undertaken by States in the exercise of the right of self-defence pursuant to Article 51 of the United Nations Charter shall be immediately reported to the United Nations Security Council.

---

[844] North Atlantic Treaty (Washington Treaty), Art. 5, 4 April 1949, 34 UNTS 243.

[845] The Article provides: 'In the event of a conflict between the obligations of the Members of the United Nations under the present Charter and their obligations under any other international agreement, their obligations under the present Charter shall prevail.'

1.   The requirement to report exercises of self-defence to the United Nations Security Council is found in Article 51 of the UN Charter. The failure of a Member of the United Nations to report actions that it takes in self-defence against a cyber armed attack to the Security Council is a violation of its obligations under Article 51.[846] However, the reporting requirement should not be interpreted as customary international law. In *Nicaragua*, the International Court of Justice specifically addressed this question. It held that 'it is clear that in customary international law it is not a condition of the lawfulness of the use of force in self-defence that a procedure so closely dependent on the content of a treaty commitment and of the institutions established by it should have been followed'.[847] Therefore, the failure does not divest the State in question of the right to act in self-defence.

2.   According to Article 51, the right to act in self-defence continues until the Security Council 'has taken measures necessary to maintain international peace and security'. The International Group of Experts agreed that the Council must expressly divest the State of its right of self-defence under Article 51 in such cases. The Experts further agreed that only the Security Council enjoys such authority, and that in the event the Security Council did in fact issue a stand down order, the measures the Council has taken, or is to take, would have to be effective to divest the victim State of its right to defend itself.

3.   The fact that a State is lawfully conducting actions in the exercise of its right of self-defence in the face of a cyber attack, or has elected not to do so, does not deprive the Security Council of its authority in relation to the maintenance of international peace and security under Chapter VII of the Charter.

---

[846] *Nicaragua* judgment, para. 235.   [847] *Nicaragua* judgment, para. 200.

15

Collective security

Rule 76 – United Nations Security Council

Should the United Nations Security Council determine that a cyber operation constitutes a threat to the peace, breach of the peace, or act of aggression, it may authorise non-forceful measures, including cyber operations, in response. If the Security Council considers such measures to be inadequate, it may decide upon forceful measures, including cyber measures.

1.   This Rule is based on Chapter VII of the United Nations Charter. Article 39 of the Charter empowers the Security Council to 'determine the existence of any threat to the peace, breach of the peace, or act of aggression and [to] make recommendations, or decide what measures shall be taken in accordance with Articles 41 and 42, to maintain or restore international peace and security'. To date, the Security Council has never determined that a cyber operation constitutes a threat to the peace, breach of the peace, or act of aggression. However, it is incontrovertible that the Security Council has the authority to do so.

2.   Although the Security Council typically exercises its authority under Article 39 with regard to specific incidents or situations, it has labelled two significant phenomena as threats to the peace – international terrorism[848] and the proliferation of weapons of mass destruction.[849] The Security Council could equally decide that particular types of cyber operations amount to a threat to the peace, breach of the peace, or act of aggression *in abstracto*, that is, without reference to particular acts that have occurred or are about to occur. For instance, it is within the authority of the Security Council to determine that cyber operations directed at national banking systems or critical national infrastructure qualify as such.

[848] *See, e.g.*, SC Res. 1373, UN Doc. S/RES/2001 (28 September 2001).
[849] *See, e.g.*, SC Res. 1540, UN Doc. S/RES/1540 (28 April 2004).

3.   Once it has made the Article 39 determination, the Security Council may consider taking measures pursuant to Article 41. That Article provides that the Council 'may decide what measures not involving the use of armed force are to be employed to give effect to its decisions, and it may call upon the Members of the United Nations to apply such measures. These may include complete or partial interruption of economic relations and of rail, sea, air, postal, telegraphic, radio, and other means of communication, and the severance of diplomatic relations'. Non-forceful measures are those that do not rise to the level of a use of force (Rule 68). The list of measures referred to in Article 41 of the Charter is not exhaustive.[850]

4.   The reference to 'complete or partial interruption of . . . postal, telegraphic, radio and other means of communication' in Article 41 is especially important in the cyber context. This provision, in light of the Council's wide margin of discretion, confirms that the Security Council may decide upon a complete or partial interruption of cyber communications with a State or non-State actor.[851]

5.   All United Nations Member States are obliged to implement Security Council decisions (as distinct from recommendations) under Chapter VII of the UN Charter.[852] Generally, Security Council resolutions leave it to States to decide upon the specific means by which they fulfil their obligation to implement the Council's decisions at the domestic level. In the case of sanctions involving cyber communications, domestic implementation would be indispensable. For instance, it may be necessary to require Internet service providers (government and private alike) to adopt restrictive measures such as domain name blacklisting or packet routing filtering in order to comply with a binding Security Council resolution. Accordingly, States might have to adopt domestic legislation or regulations that compel Internet service providers subject to their jurisdiction (Rule 8) to take the necessary action.

---

[850] *Tadić*, decision on the defence motion for interlocutory appeal, para. 35.

[851] For example, in 2001, the Monitoring Mechanism on Sanctions against UNITA raised the possibility of measures being taken to interrupt Internet connections with UNITA. Monitoring Mechanism on Sanctions against UNITA Report, appended to Letter from the Chairman of the Security Council Committee established pursuant to Resolution 864 to the President of the Security Council, paras. 64–69, UN Doc. S/2001/966 (12 October 2001).

[852] UN Charter, Art. 25.

6. The second sentence of this Rule is based on Article 42 of the Charter.[853] Once the Security Council determines that a threat to the peace, breach of the peace, or act of aggression exists and that non-forceful measures would be inadequate, or have proven to be inadequate, to maintain or restore international peace or security,[854] it may authorise the use of force (Rule 68), including by cyber means. Consider a situation in which a State is developing a nuclear weapons capability. That State has ignored demands by the Security Council to put an end to its activities and has weathered economic sanctions authorised pursuant to Article 41. The Security Council could authorise Member States to conduct cyber operations against that State designed to disrupt the weapons programme.

7. In the context of this Rule, the Security Council often provides that 'all necessary measures' (or similar language) may be taken to implement a resolution.[855] The phrase implies the authority to employ cyber operations at the use of force level against the State or entity that is the object of the resolution in question. It also encompasses taking kinetic action against the cyber capabilities of that State or entity. Of course, any measures taken must fall within the scope of the resolution's mandate or authorisation. On the distinction between mandates and authorisations, see Rule 77.

8. While Article 42 indicates that enforcement measures may be taken by 'air, sea or land forces of Members of the United Nations', the International Group of Experts agreed that any action undertaken on the basis of this Rule may be implemented by, or against, cyberspace capabilities.

---

[853] Art. 42 of the UN Charter provides: 'Should the Security Council consider that measures provided for in Article 41 would be inadequate or have proved to be inadequate, it may take such action by air, sea, or land forces as may be necessary to maintain or restore international peace and security. Such action may include demonstrations, blockade, and other operations by air, sea, or land forces of Members of the United Nations.'

[854] As the wording of this Rule makes clear, 'measures not involving the use of armed force' do not need to have been actually taken, i.e., the UN Security Council may immediately resort to the measures envisioned under the second sentence of this Rule.

[855] An example can be found in SC Res. 678, UN Doc. S/RES/678, para. 2 (29 November 1991), which provides: 'Authorizes Member States co-operating with the Government of Kuwait, unless Iraq on or before 15 January 1991 fully implements ... the above-mentioned resolutions, to use all necessary means to uphold and implement resolution 660 (1990) and all subsequent relevant resolutions and to restore international peace and security in the area.'

9. It is clear that, pursuant to Article 103 of the UN Charter, the Security Council need not take into consideration the legal obligations of Member States when acting under Chapter VII. In this context, it is important to note that a State's international law obligations are only overridden by operation of the Article for such period as is necessary to give effect to the Security Council resolution in question. It remains uncertain whether other rules of international law limit the authority of the Security Council to authorise or mandate action. For instance, conducting cyber attacks against civilian objects would generally violate the law of armed conflict (Rule 94), but it is unclear whether a Security Council authorisation to conduct such attacks would, as a matter of law, override the prohibition. Whatever the case, a Security Council decision to disregard rules of international law should not be taken lightly. The International Group of Experts agreed that under no circumstances may the Security Council deviate from rules of a *jus cogens* nature.

10. Peace operations are dealt with more fully in Rule 78.

Rule 77 – Regional organisations

International organisations, arrangements, or agencies of a regional character may conduct enforcement actions, involving or in response to cyber operations, pursuant to a mandate from, or authorisation by, the United Nations Security Council.

1. This Rule is based on Chapters VII and VIII of the UN Charter whereby the Security Council may turn to regional arrangements or agencies for enforcement action under its authority. While there is general agreement that a regional organisation has the power to undertake the type of non-forceful action referred to in Article 41 of the UN Charter without Security Council authorisation, it is a point of contention in international law as to whether the regional arrangement or agency may engage in the sort of enforcement actions encompassed in Article 42 absent express prior authorisation. On the application of Articles 41 and 42 in the cyber context, see Rule 76.

2. The term 'regional' is drawn from Article 52(1) of the UN Charter, according to which the arrangements or agencies addressed in Chapter VIII of the Charter are regional systems of collective security 'appropriate for regional action'. Qualification as a regional arrangement or agency is not clear-cut. For instance, NATO has always taken the position that it is not such an organisation because its purpose is primarily one of collective

defence as opposed to collective security. With respect to this Rule, technical qualification as a regional organisation is irrelevant because the Security Council may authorise the taking of enforcement measures by any grouping of States, whether established in advance or on an *ad hoc* basis, irrespective of any geographical or other limitations in the constitutive instrument of the organisation.

3. The phrase 'enforcement actions' in this Rule derives from Article 53(1) of the UN Charter.[856] It refers to the power conferred on the Security Council under Articles 41 and 42, that is, to authorise or mandate non-forceful or forceful measures in order to maintain or restore international peace and security. Enforcement action must be distinguished from action (including cyber operations) taken by regional arrangements or agencies on the basis of collective self-defence (Rule 74).

4. The text of the Rule makes clear that enforcement actions by regional arrangements or agencies may include cyber operations. It also recognises that enforcement actions may be taken in response to situations consisting in part or in whole of cyber activities.

5. The terms 'mandate' and 'authorisation' respectively distinguish situations in which the Security Council specifically designates a particular entity to conduct operations from those in which individual States or regional entities act pursuant to a broader authorisation by the Security Council that has not specifically designated them, such as an *ad hoc* coalition. (See also discussion in Rule 78).

Rule 78 – Peace operations

When conducting peace operations, States may engage in cyber operations in conformity with the peace operation's mandate or authorisation and applicable international law.

1. 'Peace operations', for the purposes of this Manual, comprise both peacekeeping and peace enforcement operations.[857] Peace operations can consist of both military and civilian components, while their forces can include military, law enforcement, and support personnel. Such

---

[856] This phrase or equivalent phrases were also used in UN Charter, Arts. 2(5) and (7), 5, 11(2), 45, 48–50. None of these provisions contains a definition.

[857] The term 'peace operations' also encompasses 'peace building' operations, that is, those operations intended to reduce the risk of lapsing into conflict. They involve strengthening national capacities for conflict management and laying the foundation for sustainable peace and development. *See* Capstone Doctrine, at 18.

operations may, under the circumstances described below, employ cyber operations to fulfil their mandate or authorisation.

2.   'Peacekeeping' operations may be conducted pursuant to a mandate issued, or authorisation granted, by an appropriate international organisation. Of particular note are those mandated or authorised by the UN Security Council under Chapter VI of the UN Charter. Peacekeeping operations may also be conducted by States acting on their own accord, either individually or in a coalition with other States.

3.   By contrast, a mandate or authorisation issued by the Security Council under Chapter VII of the UN Charter (Rule 76) is a fundamental precondition for 'peace enforcement' operations. Such operations may, when consistent with the mandate or authorisation or as necessary in self-defence, engage in cyber operations at the use of force level (Rule 68).

4.   Mandates or authorisations to conduct peace enforcement operations may also be granted in conformity with the constituent treaty of a regional organisation under Chapter VIII of the UN Charter. The approval of the Security Council is, pursuant to Article 53(1) of the UN Charter, necessary. On the specific case of regional organisations, see Rule 77.

5.   National self-defence operations under Article 51 of the UN Charter, whether exercised individually by a single State or collectively by a coalition of States or a military alliance, are addressed in Rules 71–75. They are not 'peace operations' in the sense of this Chapter.

6.   On the terms 'mandate' and 'authorisation', see Rule 77. Note that mandates may be granted to forces under UN command and control,[858] a regional organisation (Rule 77), an *ad hoc* coalition, or an individual State.

7.   Cyber operations undertaken during a peace operation must be conducted within the scope of the operation's mandate or authorisation. Mandates and authorisations typically set forth the tasks allocated to a peace force, as well as those measures that the peace force may take to perform the tasks, but are unlikely to expressly mention the use of cyber operations.

8.   In some cases, the use of cyber means may be the most effective means of carrying out specific tasks delineated in the mandate or authorisation, as when it is necessary to temporarily disable command and

---

[858] Note that States retain 'full command' over forces they contribute to an operation directed by the UN or a regional organisation. However, they are normally placed under the operational control of the UN or regional organisation conducting the operation.

control systems in order to fulfil it. Since a mandate or authorisation is unlikely to specifically address cyber operations, any assessment of the lawfulness of such operations will likely require its interpretation by the peace force.

9.   Consider a case in which the peace operation's mandate includes promoting a safe and secure environment and creating the conditions for a lasting political solution to a conflict by monitoring a ceasefire agreement. Such a mandate could be interpreted to permit the monitoring of the parties' cyber communications to ensure that they are not engaged in activities contrary to the agreement. Similarly, monitoring data traffic coming into and out of the peace operation's networks would generally be consistent with the need to maintain good network security and, therefore, to accomplish the peace operation's mission, as would passive monitoring of the electromagnetic spectrum.

10.   The International Group of Experts cautioned that cyber activities conducted pursuant to a mandate or authorisation must be consistent with not only its express terms, but also its object and purpose. To illustrate, if a peace operation is being conducted to monitor a ceasefire between parties, it would usually exceed the scope of the underlying mandate or authorisation to conduct cyber operations on behalf of one side to the conflict. As a general matter, peace operations typically have the aim of maintaining or restoring international peace and security (on the notion of international peace and security, see also Rule 65) and therefore cyber operations that only exacerbate a situation are impermissible.

11.   The operation's rules of engagement are also likely to govern the permissibility of engaging in cyber operations in furtherance of the peace operation's mandate or authorisation. Additionally, States contributing forces to a peace operation may make their agreement to contribute subject to national 'caveats' that restrict particular activities of their forces.

12.   It is essential to distinguish between peacekeeping and peace enforcement operations when assessing the lawfulness of a cyber operation conducted by a peace force. 'Peacekeeping' operations are governed by the principles of: (1) consent (of the territorial State); (2) impartiality; and (3) the use of force, including by cyber means, only in self-defence.[859]

---

[859] Report of the Special Committee on Peacekeeping, UN Doc. A/57/767, para. 46 (29 March 2003). It should be noted that peace operations must particularly comply with the principle of impartiality in situations involving two or more parties, as in monitoring a ceasefire.

13.   Of particular importance is the requirement of consent. Any cyber operations conducted by the peacekeeping force must fall within the scope of the host State's consent. For instance, a State that consents to the presence of a peacekeeping force may prohibit active cyber defence operations by that force. The host State's consent (Rule 19) must be in conformity with international law and will not override the international or domestic law obligations of a troop contributing State. The requirement of consent is without prejudice to the right of the peacekeeping force and its individual members to engage in self-defence.

14.   The aforementioned three traditional peacekeeping requirements do not apply to 'peace enforcement' operations mandated or authorised by the UN Security Council under Chapter VII of the UN Charter. On such mandates or authorisations, see Rule 76.

15.   The lawfulness of a cyber operations at the use of force level depends on the precise mandate or authorisation granted by the Security Council. If the Security Council has authorised forceful enforcement measures in general under Chapter VII, cyber operations that are necessary to support kinetic operations are lawful. For instance, if a peace enforcement operation has received a mandate or authorisation to conduct forceful measures, and aerial bombing is needed, the peace force may engage in those cyber operations necessary to pinpoint targets and bring down air defences. Sometimes, however, the Security Council resolution limits the peace enforcement operation, including any forceful activities, to the protection of certain objects and persons or to the performance of certain specific tasks.

16.   The Experts noted in this regard that irrespective of whether the mandate or authorisation permits cyber operations that qualify as a use of force, a peacekeeping or peace enforcement force may conduct those forceful operations that are necessary in individual or unit self-defence against an ongoing or imminent attack.

17.   UN-led peace operations may also employ force, whether kinetic or cyber in nature, as required to counter armed attempts to interfere with the execution of the mandate or authorisation ('defence of the mandate').[860] The forceful interference must be at a level that endangers the accomplishment of the peace operation's mission. For instance, if a forceful kinetic or cyber operation compromises the command and control systems of the peace operation, the peace force would be entitled

---

[860] Capstone Doctrine, at 34.

to use kinetic or cyber force to terminate the cyber operation. This conclusion is without prejudice to any international or domestic legal limitations that might otherwise apply in the situation at hand. The International Group of Experts cautioned that States take slightly different approaches to the parameters of permissible action in defence of the mandate or authorisation.

18.　　Many contemporary peace operations are mandated or authorised (in addition to those actions necessary to fulfil the core mission) to protect civilians within the capabilities of the mission and without prejudice to the primary responsibility of the host State to protect its inhabitants. Cyber activities, including those that cross the use of force threshold, that are instrumental to this task are lawful.

19.　　This raises the issue of whether a peace force may come to the assistance of others, such as a civilian population, by using cyber force when the use of force for this purpose is not expressly mandated or authorised. Consider a situation in which social media is being used to incite violence against a local ethnic group. The Experts concurred that it would be appropriate in these circumstances to target the offending social media accounts by cyber means, even if the cyber operation in question qualifies as a use of force.[861] Some of the Experts were of the view that the authority to defend the targeted ethnic group by cyber means is also to be found in the legal notion of 'coming to the defence of others' that appears in the domestic law of many States. They additionally pointed to the fact that most rules of engagement for peace operations presently allow for the resort to force in order to protect the civilian population, thereby denoting the general lawfulness of taking such measures.

20.　　In addition to compliance with the mandate or authorisation, peace operations and their related cyber operations must comport with other applicable international law. The two most pertinent legal regimes for peace operations are international human rights law (Chapter 6) and the law of armed conflict (Part IV). Certain aspects of international human rights law are particularly relevant in this context. The International Group of Experts agreed that cyber operations conducted by troops or police of contributing nations are generally subject to international human rights law norms *vis-à-vis* persons within their power or control (Rule 34). International human rights law will also be applicable

---

[861] Other legal regimes, such as the law of armed conflict, may apply in such situations.

if a peacekeeping or peace enforcement operation exercises effective control or administrative authority over territory, as in the case of United Nations transitional authority. Certain controversies surrounding the scope of applicability of international human rights law are discussed in Rule 34.

21.   As to peace operations undertaken by international organisations, the Experts agreed that international human rights law provisions in treaties are generally inapplicable to the organisations by virtue of the fact that they cannot become Parties to the instruments (although the forces of troop or police contributing nations will continue to be bound by treaties creating obligations for their State). Nevertheless, international organisations, as legal persons, may be bound by customary international human rights law (Chapter 6).[862] For instance, if an international organisation's peace force exercises the requisite control over particular territory and it is necessary to conduct cyber operations such as disrupting the use of social media that is being used for command and control purposes, the cyber operations must be carried out in compliance with the requirements of international human rights law. This is without prejudice to the applicability of the law of armed conflict when it has the character of *lex specialis* during an armed conflict.

22.   The International Group of Experts agreed that a peace operation's cyber operations have to comply with the law of armed conflict (Part IV) once its force becomes, and for such time as it remains, party to an international (Rule 82) or non-international armed conflict (Rule 83).[863] In such a situation, the peace force may conduct cyber operations consistent with the law of armed conflict, but it will not be protected from attack, whether through cyber means (Rule 92) or otherwise, by the law of armed conflict.

23.   The determination of whether, and for what time, a peace force becomes a 'party to an armed conflict' can involve complex issues of fact and law and is subject to a degree of controversy. It is clear that a peace

---

[862] *See, e.g.*, United Nations Safety Convention, Art. 20(a); Optional Protocol to the United Nations Safety Convention, Art. II(1); Decision No. 2005/24 of the Secretary-General's Policy Committee on Human Rights in Integrated Missions (2005); Capstone Doctrine, at 14–15, 27.

[863] The conclusion that the law of armed conflict binds a UN force when it is party to an armed conflict is supported by a number of instruments. *See, e.g.*, United Nations Safety Convention, Arts. 2(2), 20; UN Secretary General's Bulletin: Observance by United Nations Forces of International Humanitarian Law, ST/SGB/1999/13 (6 August 1999); Capstone Doctrine, at 15.

force qualifies as a party to an armed conflict when the force's kinetic or cyber operations reach the threshold of an international or non-international armed conflict in their own right (Rules 82 and 83, respectively).

24. The International Group of Experts agreed that a peace force may also sometimes become a party to an armed conflict even if its support to one or more of the parties to the conflict falls short of the actual use of force, as in the case of providing direct logistical support or tactical intelligence. Whether other forms of support that do not reach this level render the force a party to the conflict is unsettled in international law and should be assessed on a case-by-case basis. The Experts agreed, however, that mere deviation from a mandate or authorisation, or the fact that an activity exceeds the consent of the host State in a peacekeeping operation, does not alone render a peace force a party to an armed conflict.

25. The use of force (kinetic or cyber) in self-defence does not render a peace force a party to an armed conflict unless it reaches the threshold of armed conflict. Each case must be assessed on its merits. For instance, the International Group of Experts agreed that self-defence at the individual (personal) level does not result in a peace force becoming a party. However, if unit level self-defence or defence against forcible attempts to prevent the execution of the peace force's mandate or authorisation take place on a systematic and recurring basis, the peace force may become a party to an armed conflict. To illustrate, if a mandate provides for the disarmament of parties to an earlier armed conflict, and one of them forcibly resists being disarmed, the resulting violence between the resisting party and the peace force could reach the non-international armed conflict threshold. Once a peace force becomes a party, the rules of either international or non-international armed conflict will apply equally to all parties with respect to their cyber operations in the same manner as in any other armed conflict.

26. In determining the precise contours of the legal framework applicable to cyber operations deriving from the law of armed conflict, international human rights law, and other applicable legal regimes, it must be emphasised that the individual troop or police contributing States and the international organisation(s) involved may enjoy rights and bear obligations under international law that differ. Of particular note is the fact that during a peace enforcement operation in the context of armed conflict, different contributing nations conducting

cyber operations may be subject to differing provisions of the law of armed conflict, international human rights law, or other treaty law based on their respective Party or non-Party status, as well as to divergent obligations under domestic law. The forces involved may not escape the obligation to comply with treaty obligations binding their State based on their involvement in the operation, except when their actions are consistent with a Chapter VII mandate or authorisation. Although beyond the scope of this Manual, the nature of command and control arrangements is of particular relevance in this regard. On the issue of the responsibility of an international organisation, such as NATO, see Section 4 of Chapter 4.

27.   Cyber operations must respect the law of the State where the operation is being conducted, except when activities provided for are consistent with a Chapter VII mandate or authorisation under Chapter VII or otherwise provided for in an agreement with that State, as in a basing or status of forces agreement. This obligation arises because such operations may only be conducted with the consent of the State concerned. Peace forces contributed by a State must also comply with the domestic law of that State.

Rule 79 – Peace operations personnel, installations, materiel, units, and vehicles

(a) As long as they are entitled to the protection afforded civilians and civilian objects under the law of armed conflict, United Nations personnel, installations, materiel, units, and vehicles, including computers and computer networks that support United Nations operations, must be respected and protected and are not subject to cyber attack.

(b) Other personnel, installations, materiel, units, or vehicles, including computers and computer networks, involved in a humanitarian assistance or peacekeeping mission in accordance with the United Nations Charter are protected against cyber attack under the same conditions.

1.   This Rule is drawn from a number of sources. The obligation to respect and protect United Nations personnel, installations, materiel, units, or vehicles, and by extension their computers and computer networks, derives in great part from the United Nations Safety Convention. Article 7(1) specifies that United Nations personnel, units, vehicles,

equipment, and premises 'shall not be made the object of attack or of any action that prevents them from discharging their mandate' and that Contracting Parties have a duty to ensure the safety and security of United Nations personnel. The further extension of protection from attack to those involved in a humanitarian or peacekeeping operation finds support in Article 8(2)(b)(iii) and 8(2)(e)(iii) of the Rome Statute. This Rule is applicable in both international and non-international armed conflicts as customary law.[864]

2. The notion of 'respect' in *lit.* (a) of this Rule encompasses an obligation to refrain from interference with the fulfilment of the mandate. For instance, directing cyber operations against the implementing force's networks would be in violation of the Rule.[865] The obligation refers only to United Nations personnel as defined under international law[866] and to the installations, materiel, units, or vehicles, including computers and computer networks, that support United Nations operations. It does not apply to those persons and objects referred to in *lit.* (b).[867]

3. The obligation to 'respect' United Nations personnel also means that it is prohibited to attack, threaten, or harm them in any way,

---

[864] *See also* UK MANUAL, paras. 14.9, 14.15; AMW MANUAL, commentary accompanying Rule 98(b–c); NIAC MANUAL, para. 3.3; ICRC CUSTOMARY IHL STUDY, Rule 33.

[865] AMW MANUAL, commentary accompanying Rule 98(a); ICRC CUSTOMARY IHL STUDY, commentary accompanying Rule 33.

[866] United Nations Safety Convention, Art. 1(a). The Article defines 'United Nations personnel' as: '(i) Persons engaged or deployed by the Secretary-General of the United Nations as members of the military, police or civilian components of a United Nations operation; (ii) Other officials and experts on mission of the United Nations or its specialised agencies or the International Atomic Energy Agency who are present in an official capacity in the area where a United Nations operation is being conducted.'

[867] Art. 1(c) defines a 'United Nations operation' as: 'an operation established by the competent organ of the United Nations in accordance with the Charter of the United Nations and conducted under United Nations authority and control: (i) Where the operation is for the purpose of maintaining or restoring international peace and security; or (ii) Where the Security Council or the General Assembly has declared, for the purposes of this Convention, that there exists an exceptional risk to the safety of the personnel participating in the operation.'

In addition, Art. II of the Optional Protocol to the United Nations Safety Convention expands the term 'United Nations operation' to include: 'all other United Nations operations established by a competent organ of the United Nations in accordance with the Charter of the United Nations and conducted under United Nations authority and control for the purposes of: (a) Delivering humanitarian, political or development assistance in peace building, or (b) Delivering emergency humanitarian assistance.' Optional Protocol to the United Nations Safety Convention, Art. II.

including through cyber operations. The prohibition extends to persons or locations placed under United Nations protection within the context of the mandate.

4. The reference to 'protect' in *lit. (a)* refers to the duty to take those feasible steps necessary to ensure that others do not attack, threaten, harm, or interfere with them. The obligation means that States are under an obligation to take all appropriate and feasible measures to ensure the safety and security of such personnel.[868] In this regard, the International Group of Experts agreed that States must take necessary measures to ensure the safety and security of UN and associated personnel against cyber attacks[869] and to cooperate with the peace operation in preventing cyber attacks against them and their official premises, private accommodation, or means of transportation.[870] The obligation to cooperate entails, *inter alia*, the duty to take all practicable measures to prevent preparations in their respective territories for the commission of cyber attacks within or outside the territory of the State Party in question and the duty to exchange information and coordinate administrative and other measures to prevent the commission of such attacks.[871]

5. *Lit.* (b) applies to personnel who do not qualify as United Nations personnel. It also applies to operations that are not United Nations operations in the sense of Article 1(c) of the United Nations Safety Convention because they are not 'conducted under United Nations authority and control'.

6. Although not conducted under United Nations authority and control, the mission in question must be 'in accordance with the United Nations Charter' for *lit.* (b) to apply.[872] This will usually mean that the Security Council has authorised the mission. Additionally, the purpose of such a mission must either be to deliver humanitarian assistance or conduct peacekeeping (Rule 78). Humanitarian assistance and peacekeeping operations presuppose consent by the host nation and any States that are parties to the conflict.

7. During an armed conflict, members of a peace force enjoy the protections afforded by the law of armed conflict to civilians (Rule 94), including protection from cyber attacks (Rule 92), unless the force

---

[868] United Nations Safety Convention, Art. 7(2).
[869] United Nations Safety Convention, Art. 7(2).
[870] United Nations Safety Convention, Arts. 9, 11.
[871] United Nations Safety Convention, Art. 11.
[872] Rome Statute, Art. 8(2)(b)(iii), 8(2)(e)(iii).

becomes a party to the conflict (Rule 78).[873] This is so for members of forces under both *lit.* (a) and *lit* (b). Individual civilian or military members of a peace force nevertheless lose protection from attack even when the operation to which they are attached is not a party to an armed conflict if, and for such time as, they take a direct part in hostilities on an individual basis (Rule 97), whether by cyber or non-cyber means.

8.   This situation must be distinguished from that in which personnel of a peace operation use force solely in the exercise of their right to personal self-defence or to defend the unit from attack. The majority of the Experts was also of the view that the threshold of direct participation in the hostilities is not necessarily reached by the mere fact that peace force personnel resort to cyber or kinetic force in defence of the mandate or authorisation, provided that the resort to force is limited to such purpose and that the mandate or authorisation is not for activities that would themselves reach the armed conflict threshold.[874]

---

[873] Note that their protection may actually be greater than that of civilians pursuant to, when applicable, the United Nations Safety Convention, Art. 7. Moreover, both the ICRC CUSTOMARY IHL STUDY and the Rome Statute provide for a special status with regard to peace operations. ICRC CUSTOMARY IHL STUDY, Rule 33; Rome Statute, Art. 8 (2)(b)(iii), 8(2)(e)(iii).

[874] *Prosecutor* v. *Sesay Kallon and Gbao*, Trial Chamber judgment (Spec. Ct. for Sierra Leone, 2 March 2009), paras. 577–579.

PART IV

The law of cyber armed conflict

16

The law of armed conflict generally

Rule 80 – Applicability of the law of armed conflict

Cyber operations executed in the context of an armed conflict are subject to the law of armed conflict.

1. As with other operations, the law of armed conflict applies to cyber operations undertaken in the context of an armed conflict. Despite the novelty of cyber operations and the absence of specific rules within the law of armed conflict explicitly dealing with them, the International Group of Experts was unanimous in finding that the law of armed conflict applies to such activities during both international and non-international armed conflicts (Rules 82 and 83, respectively).[875]

2. A condition precedent to the application of the law of armed conflict is the existence of an armed conflict. The term 'armed conflict' was first used in a law of war codification in the 1949 Geneva Conventions,[876] but has never been authoritatively defined as a matter of treaty law. Yet, it has now replaced the term 'war' for most international law purposes. As used in this Manual, armed conflict refers to a situation involving hostilities, including those conducted using cyber means.[877] The term takes on different meanings when characterising hostilities as

---

[875] For instance, in 2015 the UN GGE cited the core principles of international humanitarian law. UN GGE 2015 Report, para. 28(d). *See also* The NATO Wales Summit Declaration, 2014, para. 72; Developments in the Field of Information and Telecommunications in the Context of International Security, Report of the Secretary General, at 2, UN Doc. A/69/112 (30 June 2014) (Australia); Developments in the Field of Information and Telecommunications in the Context of International Security, Report of the Secretary General, at 15, UN Doc. A/68/156 Add. 1 (9 September 2013) (Japan); European Union, Conclusions, General Affairs Council Meeting, Doc. 11357/13 (25 June 2013).

[876] Geneva Conventions I–IV, Art. 2. *See also* ICRC GENEVA CONVENTION I 2016 COMMENTARY, para. 209.

[877] Occupations that meet no armed resistance also qualify as armed conflicts despite the absence of hostilities. Geneva Conventions I–IV, Art. 2.

either international or non-international in character. Rules 82 and 83 discuss the extent of hostilities required to reach those thresholds.

3.   To illustrate, in 2007 Estonia was the target of persistent cyber operations. However, the law of armed conflict did not apply to those cyber operations because the situation did not rise to the level of an armed conflict. By contrast, the law of armed conflict applied to the cyber operations that occurred during the international armed conflict between Georgia and Russia in 2008, and applies to those that have taken place in the on-going conflict between Ukraine and Russia, because they were undertaken in furtherance of those conflicts. The latter cases illustrate that in a situation of on-going kinetic hostilities amounting to an armed conflict, the applicable law of international or non-international armed conflict will govern cyber operations undertaken in relation to that conflict. The precise aspects of the law of armed conflict that apply depend on whether the conflict is international or non-international in nature (Rules 82–83).

4.   The term 'cyber operations' includes, but is not limited to, 'cyber attacks' (Rule 92). As used in this Manual, cyber attacks is a term of art referring to a specific category of cyber operations. Certain cyber operations, such as those affecting the delivery of humanitarian assistance (Rule 145), are governed by the law of armed conflict even if they do not rise to the level of an 'attack'.

5.   The International Group of Experts adopted the phrase 'in the context of an armed conflict' as a compromise formula with respect to the scope of the law of armed conflict. All members of the International Group of Experts agreed that there must be a nexus between the cyber activity in question and the conflict for the law of armed conflict to apply to that activity. However, they differed as to the nature of that nexus.

6.   According to one view, the law of armed conflict governs any cyber activity conducted by a party to an armed conflict against its opponent (note, in this regard, the discussion on attributability in Rule 82). By a second view, the cyber activity must have been undertaken in furtherance of the hostilities, that is, in order to contribute to the originator's military effort. Consider a cyber operation conducted by State A's Ministry of Trade against a private corporation in enemy State B in order to acquire commercial secrets during an armed conflict. Pursuant to the first view, the law of armed conflict governs that operation because it is being conducted by a party to the armed conflict against a corporation of the enemy State. Those Experts adopting the second view concluded that the law of armed conflict would not apply because the link between the activity and the hostilities is insufficient.

7.   The International Group of Experts noted that the precise parameters of the phrase 'in the context of' are less clear in a non-international armed conflict. This is because a State retains certain law enforcement obligations and rights with respect to its territory, notwithstanding the armed conflict.[878] To the extent that it is involved in purely law enforcement activities that have no nexus to the conflict, domestic and human rights law, not the law of armed conflict, apply.

8.   The law of armed conflict does not embrace activities of private individuals or entities that are unrelated to the armed conflict. Take, for example, the case of a private corporation that is engaging in theft of intellectual property to achieve a market advantage over a competitor in the enemy State. In principle, the law of armed conflict does not govern such activity.

9.   The applicability of the law of armed conflict does not depend upon the qualification of the situation under the *jus ad bellum* (Chapter 14). Pursuant to the principle of equal application, even a resort to armed force that is unlawful from the perspective of *jus ad bellum* is subject to the law of armed conflict.[879]

10.   It should be noted that the application of the law of armed conflict to cyber operations can prove problematic. It is often difficult to identify the existence of a cyber operation, its originator, its intended object of attack, or its precise effects. Still, these questions of fact do not prejudice the application of the law of armed conflict.

11.   To the extent an express rule of the law of armed conflict does not regulate cyber activities, regard should be had to the Martens Clause, found in Hague Convention IV,[880] the 1949 Geneva Conventions,[881] and Additional Protocol I.[882] The text in Hague Convention IV provides that:

---

[878] Of course a State may also have law enforcement responsibilities during an international armed conflict. However, such responsibilities tend to be more pronounced during a non-international armed conflict.

[879] Paragraph 5 of the preamble to Additional Protocol I provides that its provisions, as well as those of the four 1949 Geneva Conventions, 'must be fully applied in all circumstances to all persons who are protected by those instruments, without any adverse distinction based on the nature or origin of the armed conflict or on the causes espoused by or attributed to the Parties to the conflict'. *See also* UK MANUAL, paras. 3.12, 3.12.1; CANADIAN MANUAL, para. 204; ICRC GENEVA CONVENTION I 2016 COMMENTARY, paras. 186, 215–216.

[880] Hague Convention IV, pmbl.

[881] Geneva Convention I, Art. 63; Geneva Convention II, Art. 62; Geneva Convention III, Art. 142; Geneva Convention IV, Art. 158.

[882] Additional Protocol I, Art. 1(2).

> Until a more complete code of the laws of war has been issued, the
> High Contracting Parties deem it expedient to declare that, in cases not
> included in the Regulations adopted by them, the inhabitants and the
> belligerents remain under the protection and the rule of the principles
> of the law of nations, as they result from the usages established among
> civilised peoples, from the laws of humanity, and the dictates of the
> public conscience.

12.   To the extent that cyber activities are conducted in the course of
an armed conflict, the Martens Clause, which reflects customary international law, functions to ensure that such activities are not conducted in
a legal vacuum. This point is without prejudice to the disputed question
of the applicability of human rights law during armed conflict.

Rule 81 – Geographical limitations

**Cyber operations are subject to geographical limitations imposed by
the relevant provisions of international law applicable during an
armed conflict.**

1.   The law of armed conflict, in conjunction with other fields of
international law (e.g., the law of the sea, air law, space law, and
general principles of State sovereignty applicable in armed conflict,[883]
as well as considerations arising from the *jus ad bellum* conditions of
proportionality and necessity), prescribes the geographic space in
which cyber operations may be conducted. Relevant legal issues
include the place from which operations are launched, the location
of any necessary instrumentalities, and the location of targeted cyber
systems. As a rule, cyber operations may be conducted from, on, or
with effects in the entire territory of the parties to the conflict,
international waters or airspace, and, subject to certain limitations,
outer space. Cyber operations are generally prohibited elsewhere. Of
particular importance in this regard is the law of neutrality because
cyber operations can transit neutral territory and may have unintended effects therein. Neutrality is discussed in Chapter 20.

2.   Restrictions based on geographical limitations may be particularly difficult to implement in the context of cyber warfare. For

---

[883] For instance, Art. 88 of the Law of the Sea Convention is inapplicable during armed
conflict.

instance, consider a cyber attack using cloud computing techniques. Data used to prosecute the attack from one State may be replicated across servers in a number of other States, including neutral States, but only observably reflected on the systems where the attack is initiated and completed. As discussed in Rule 151, there is no general prohibition of the mere transit of data through areas where the conduct of cyber operations is otherwise prohibited during an armed conflict.

3.   According to the traditional view of the law of armed conflict, military operations during a non-international armed conflict must be limited to the territory (including the territorial sea) and national airspace of the State in which the conflict is taking place. However, events over the past decade such as the conflict in Afghanistan and transnational counter-terrorist operations have caused this bright line to become somewhat blurred. Today, the exact geographical scope of non-international armed conflict raises a number of complex issues and is the subject to a degree of controversy. Some States and commentators now take the view that a non-international armed conflict may extend to areas beyond the borders of the State in question, arguing that it is the status of the actors, not geography, which is the determinative factor in classification of conflict (Rule 83).[884] Others maintain the traditional view, although they generally accept the notion of 'spill over' of that conflict into neighbouring States.[885]

Rule 82 – Characterisation as international armed conflict

An international armed conflict exists whenever there are hostilities, which may include or be limited to cyber operations, between two or more States.

1.   The generally accepted criteria for the existence of an international armed conflict, which reflect customary international law, are derived from Common Article 2 of the 1949 Geneva Conventions.[886] The Article provides:

---

[884] Harold Hongju Koh, The Obama Administration and International Law, Address at the Annual Meeting of the American Society of International Law (25 March 2010).

[885] ICRC Challenges Report, at 18–19; ICRC GENEVA CONVENTION I 2016 COMMENTARY, paras. 465–482.

[886] UK MANUAL, para. 3.2; DoD MANUAL, para. 3.3.1; CANADIAN MANUAL, at GL-9; GERMAN MANUAL, para. 202; AMW MANUAL, Rule 1(r).

> The present Convention shall apply to all cases of declared war or of any other armed conflict which may arise between two or more of the High Contracting Parties even if the state of war is not recognised by one of them. The Convention shall also apply to all cases of partial or total occupation of the territory of a High Contracting Party, even if the said occupation meets with no armed resistance.[887]

Reduced to basics, an armed conflict under this Rule requires both 'international' and 'armed' components.

2.   The International Group of Experts agreed that a conflict is international if two or more States are involved as parties on opposing sides. It also agreed that a conflict is international when an organised armed group that is under the 'overall control' of one State engages in hostilities against another State (see discussion below). As a practical matter, it may be difficult to ascertain whether a State is controlling a non-State actor's cyber activities.

3.   The question of whether the actions of a non-State organised armed group against one State may be attributed to another State such that a conflict is international was explicitly addressed in the International Criminal Tribunal for the Former Yugoslavia's *Tadić* Appeals Chamber judgment.[888] The Appeals Chamber articulated an 'overall control' test in determining that Bosnian Serb units were sufficiently directed by the Federal Republic of Yugoslavia to conclude that an international armed conflict existed.[889] As the Chamber explained,

> control by a State over subordinate armed forces or militias or para-military units may be of an overall character (and must comprise more than the mere provision of financial assistance or military equipment or training). This requirement, however, does not go so far as to include the issuing of specific orders by the State, or its direction of each individual operation. Under international law it is by no means necessary that the controlling authorities should plan all the operations of the units dependent on them, choose their targets, or give specific instructions concerning the conduct of military operations and any alleged violations of international humanitarian law. The control required by international law may be deemed to exist when a State (or, in the context of an armed conflict, the Party to the conflict) has a role in organising, coordinating or planning the military actions of the

---

[887] Geneva Conventions I–IV, Art. 2.
[888] *Tadić*, Appeals Chamber judgment, paras. 131–140, 145.
[889] *Tadić*, Appeals Chamber judgment, paras. 131, 145, 162.

ǀmilitary group, in addition to financing, training and equipping or ǀproviding operational support to that group.[890]

4.   The International Court of Justice has observed that the overall control test 'may well be ... applicable and suitable' for classification purposes;[891] the International Criminal Court has also adopted it.[892] Applying the test, if one State exercises overall control over an organised group of hackers that penetrates another State's cyber infrastructure and causes significant physical damage, the armed conflict qualifies as 'international' in nature. The first State need not have instructed the group to attack particular aspects of the infrastructure. Instead, it need only have exerted sufficient control over the group to direct it to mount a campaign against cyber targets.

5.   Mere support for a group of non-State actors involved in a non-international armed conflict does not 'internationalise' the conflict. In other words, support alone does not transform a non-international armed conflict into an international armed conflict between the supporting State and the State in whose territory the conflict is occurring. As noted above, the *Tadić* Appeals Chamber found that a State's financing, training, equipping, and provision of operational support to a non-State group was not, without more, sufficient to characterise the situation between the two States concerned as international.[893] If the State's support does not rise to the level of overall control of the group, it may nevertheless be unlawful as an intervention in the domestic affairs of the State concerned (Rule 66).[894]

6.   Despite the absence of a definitive bright-line test regarding support, the International Group of Experts did agree that the threshold for internationalisation is a high one. For example, merely taking measures to maintain rebel access to the national cyber infrastructure was not considered by the Experts to suffice. Similarly, the provision of cyber

---

[890] *Tadić*, Appeals Chamber judgment, para. 137.
[891] *Genocide* judgment, para. 404. Note that the Court also addressed the issue of the attribution of the genocide by Bosnian Serb armed forces at Srebrenica to the Federal Republic of Yugoslavia. It usefully distinguished between the degree of control necessary to classify a conflict as international and that required in order to hold a State internationally responsible for the acts of non-State actors. With regard to the latter situation, it adopted Art. 8 of the Articles on State Responsibility as an accurate reflection of customary international law. *Genocide* judgment, paras. 398–401, 413–414.
[892] *Lubanga* judgment, para. 541.   [893] *Tadić*, Appeals Chamber judgment, para. 137.
[894] UN Charter, Art. 2(1).

attack tools for rebel use would not reach the threshold. By contrast, providing specific intelligence on cyber vulnerabilities that renders particular rebel cyber attacks possible would, in their view, suffice.

7.   Some cases are more difficult to assess. Consider a cyber operation conducted by one State to assist rebels in another. The operation is designed to shut down the second State's cyber communications capabilities. It might be argued that the operation internationalises the conflict if the second State relies upon the system for military communications. Should it not so rely, it may be less easy to characterise the operation as sufficient to internationalise the conflict. Of course, if the first State actually participates in the conflict on behalf of the non-State group, and its actions reach the 'armed' level (see below), an international armed conflict between the two States would exist irrespective of the degree of control exercised over the group.

8.   The overall control test is inapplicable to the conduct of individuals, or insufficiently organised groups. According to the International Criminal Tribunal for the Former Yugoslavia, such individuals or groups must receive specific instructions (or subsequent public approval) from a State before their conduct can be attributed to that State for the purpose of determining the existence of an international armed conflict.[895] As an example, there is no definitive evidence that the hacktivists involved in the cyber operations against Estonia in 2007 operated pursuant to instructions from any State, nor did any State endorse and adopt the conduct. For these reasons (besides the issue of whether the conflict was 'armed'), the situation cannot be characterised as an international armed conflict.

9.   Some members of the International Group of Experts took the position that an international armed conflict can also exist between a State and a non-State organised armed group operating transnationally even if the group's conduct cannot be attributed to a State. They pointed out that such conflicts are not confined within the borders of a single State, and therefore have an international element.[896] The majority of the Experts rejected this view on the ground that such conflicts are non-international in character (Rule 83).

---

[895] *Tadić*, Appeals Chamber judgment, paras. 132, 137, 141, 145. Adoption or endorsement of conduct of a non-State group was first addressed in the *Tehran Hostages* judgment, para. 74.

[896] *See* discussion in HCJ 769/02, *The Public Committee against Torture in Israel* v. *The Government of Israel*, para. 18 [2006] (Isr.).

10.   For States Parties to <u>Additional Protocol I</u>, armed conflicts in which peoples are fighting against colonial domination, alien occupation, or racist regimes in the exercise of their right of self-determination are to be considered international armed conflicts.[897]

11.   In addition to being international, an international armed conflict must be 'armed'. The law of armed conflict does not directly address the meaning of the term 'armed conflict', but the notion clearly requires the existence of hostilities. Therefore, the International Group of Experts included the concept of hostilities in this Rule. Hostilities presuppose the collective application of means and methods of warfare (Rule 103). The constituent hostilities may involve any combination of kinetic and cyber operations, or cyber operations alone.[898]

12.   Although hostilities are undeniably a condition precedent to the armed component of international armed conflict, controversy exists as to the threshold of the requisite violence. According to the ICRC commentary to the 1949 Geneva Conventions: 'Any difference arising between two States and leading to the intervention of armed forces is an armed conflict ... It makes no difference how long the conflict lasts, or how much slaughter takes place.'[899] For example, a cyber operation that causes a fire to break out at a small military installation would suffice to initiate an international armed conflict.

13.   The competing view requires greater extent, duration, or intensity of hostilities, although proponents of this view have not agreed on any particular threshold.[900] Its advocates point out that State practice demonstrates that there have been a number of isolated incidents such as sporadic border clashes or naval incidents that were not treated as international armed conflicts. By analogy, a single cyber incident that causes only limited damage, destruction, injury, or death would not

---

[897]   Additional Protocol I, Art. 1(4).

[898]   ICRC Geneva Convention I 2016 Commentary, para. 255.

[899]   ICRC Geneva Convention I 2016 Commentary, para. 236; ICRC Geneva Convention I 1952 Commentary, at 32; ICRC Geneva Convention II 1960 Commentary, at 28; ICRC Geneva Convention III 1960 Commentary, at 23; ICRC Geneva Convention IV 1958 Commentary, at 20; *Tadić*, decision on the defence motion for interlocutory appeal, para. 70; DoD Manual, para. 3.4.2 ('any situation in which there is hostile action between the armed forces of two parties, regardless of the duration, intensity or scope of the fighting').

[900]   Christopher Greenwood, *Scope of Application of Humanitarian Law, in* The Handbook of International Humanitarian Law 45, 57 (Dieter Fleck ed., 2nd edn, 2008); Howard S. Levie, *The Status of Belligerent Personnel 'Splashed' and Rescued by a Neutral in the Persian Gulf Area*, 31 Va. J. Int'l L. 611, 613–614 (1991).

necessarily initiate an international armed conflict for these Experts. Notwithstanding this difference of opinion, it would be prudent to treat the threshold of international armed conflict as relatively low. In all likelihood, such incidents will be evaluated on a case-by-case basis in light of the attendant circumstances.

14.   To be 'armed', a conflict need not involve the employment of the armed forces. Nor is the involvement of the armed forces determinative. For example, should entities such as civilian intelligence agencies engage in cyber operations otherwise meeting the armed criterion as described above, an armed conflict may be triggered. Similarly, using the armed forces to conduct tasks that are normally the responsibility of non-military agencies does not alone initiate an armed conflict. Consider a situation in which units of the armed forces undertake cyber espionage directed at another State. The activity does not in itself result in an armed conflict, even if it is typically performed by civilian intelligence agencies, because the activity does not satisfy the armed criterion.

15.   The 2010 Stuxnet operation against SCADA systems in Iran, as a result of which centrifuges at a nuclear fuel processing plant were physically damaged, illustrates the difficulty of making the armed determination. The International Group of Experts was divided as to whether the damage sufficed to meet the armed criterion. Characterisation was further complicated by the fact that questions remain as to whether the Stuxnet operation was conducted by a State or by individuals whose conduct is attributable to a State for the purposes of finding an international armed conflict.

16.   As illustrated by the Stuxnet incident, significant legal and practical challenges stand in the way of definitively concluding that a cyber operation has initiated an international armed conflict. To date, no international armed conflict has been publicly characterised as having been solely precipitated in cyberspace. Nevertheless, the International Group of Experts agreed that cyber operations alone have the potential for crossing the threshold of international armed conflict.[901]

17.   So long as the armed and international criteria have been met, an international armed conflict exists. This is so even if a party does not recognise the conflict as such.[902] The determination is a factual one.

18.   In certain cases, the law of international armed conflict applies despite the absence of hostilities. In particular, a belligerent

[901] ICRC GENEVA CONVENTION I 2016 COMMENTARY, para. 255.
[902] Geneva Conventions I–IV, Art. 2.

occupation meeting with no armed resistance will, as a matter of law, trigger application of that body of law.[903] Additionally, an international armed conflict can come into existence merely by virtue of a declaration of war.[904] Finally, it is generally accepted that the establishment of a naval or aerial blockade initiates an international armed conflict.[905] However the international armed conflict arises, the law of armed conflict will govern all cyber operations conducted in the context of that conflict.

Rule 83 – Characterisation as non-international armed conflict

A non-international armed conflict exists whenever there is protracted armed violence, which may include or be limited to cyber operations, occurring between governmental armed forces and organised armed groups, or between such groups. The confrontation must reach a minimum level of intensity and the parties involved in the conflict must have a minimum degree of organisation.

1. This Rule is a general restatement of the customary international law of armed conflict regarding the threshold for the existence of a non-international armed conflict. The first sentence is based on Common Article 3 of the 1949 Geneva Conventions, which reflects customary international law.[906] That Article applies to 'armed conflicts not of an international character occurring in the territory of one of the High Contracting Parties', that is, to situations in which hostilities occur between governmental armed forces and non-governmental organised armed groups or between such groups.[907] The second sentence is based on case law development of the issues of intensity and organisation.

2. Application of the law of armed conflict does not depend on the type of military operation or on the specific means and methods of warfare employed. Therefore, cyber operations alone, in the absence of kinetic operations, can bring a non-international armed conflict into

---

[903] Geneva Conventions I–IV, Art. 2.   [904] Geneva Conventions I–IV, Art. 2.

[905] ICRC GENEVA CONVENTION I 2016 COMMENTARY, para. 223.

[906] Note that Art. 8(c) of the Rome Statute adopts the Common Article 3 threshold with regard to war crimes committed during a non-international armed conflict. *See also* UK MANUAL, para. 3.3; AMW MANUAL, commentary accompanying Rule 1(f); NIAC MANUAL, para. 1.1.1 (limiting the geographical scope of such conflicts).

[907] *Tadić*, decision on the defence motion for interlocutory appeal, paras. 67, 70; UK MANUAL, para. 3.5 (as amended). *See generally* DoD MANUAL, para. 3.3.1; CANADIAN MANUAL, at GL-13; GERMAN MANUAL, paras. 201–211.

existence. Given the threshold of violence and the degree of organisation of the armed groups that is required for a non-international armed conflict (discussed below), cyber operations in and of themselves will only in exceptional cases amount to a non-international armed conflict. Of course, if a conflict qualifies as a non-international armed conflict by virtue of on-going kinetic operations, the law of non-international armed conflict would govern any associated cyber operations.

3.   By Common Article 3, a non-international armed conflict occurs 'in the territory of one of the High Contracting Parties'. This text has generated a debate over the geographical scope of non-international armed conflict.[908] One school of thought holds that the word 'one' in the quoted phrase signifies that non-international armed conflicts are confined to those that take place within the territorial boundaries of a single State. By this interpretation, an armed conflict that crosses a border would generally qualify as an international armed conflict. A second school of thought, adopted by the majority of the International Group of Experts, holds that the 'one' is a reference to the territory of any of the Contracting Parties. Accordingly, the phrase imposes no territorial limitations so long as the relevant States are Parties to the 1949 Geneva Conventions.[909] Thus, if cyber attacks are undertaken during a non-international armed conflict from outside the territory of the State, that fact alone will not cause the conflict to be international in character.[910] It must also be borne in mind that the transit of data through cyber infrastructure located outside a State in which a non-international armed conflict is occurring does not render the conflict international.

4.   The law of armed conflict applies to all activities undertaken in pursuit of the armed conflict, and all associated effects (e.g., collateral damage), wherever they occur in the territory of a State involved in a non-international armed conflict. This means that in the State there is no 'zone of conflict' to which applicability of law of armed conflict is confined. Moreover, the International Group of Experts agreed that the law of armed conflict applies to activities conducted in the context of the conflict that occur outside the State in question. This is of particular importance because cyber activities in furtherance of a non-international armed conflict may well be launched remotely, far from the location of

---

[908] ICRC GENEVA CONVENTION I 2016 COMMENTARY, paras. 452–482.
[909] See, e.g., Hamdan v. Rumsfeld, 548 US 557, 630–631 (2006) (applying Common Article 3 to conflict occurring across multiple States' political boundaries).
[910] See, e.g., AMW MANUAL, commentary accompanying Rule 2(a).

the conventional hostilities. Some States have weak regulatory regimes governing cyber activities or are technically incapable of effectively policing cyber activities occurring on their territory. They offer an appealing base of operations for those engaged in cyber attacks against the government during a non-international armed conflict. The International Group of Experts acknowledged the existence of a narrower approach that accepts the possibility of a non-international armed conflict that crosses borders, but which imposes a requirement of geographical proximity to the State involved in the conflict.

5.   The term 'armed conflict' is not expressly defined in the law of armed conflict for the purposes of finding that a conflict is non-international in character. However, it is clear that 'situations of internal disturbances and tensions, such as riots, isolated and sporadic acts of violence, and other acts of a similar nature' are not included. This standard is set forth in Article 1(2) of Additional Protocol II and is today acknowledged as reflecting the customary international law distinction between non-international armed conflicts and hostilities not meeting the threshold for such conflicts.[911] Sporadic cyber incidents, including those that directly cause physical damage or injury, do not, therefore, constitute non-international armed conflict. Similarly, cyber operations that incite incidents such as civil unrest or domestic terrorism do not qualify. For instance, the calls that appeared on the Internet for riots by the Russian minority in Estonia in 2007 cannot be regarded as meeting that threshold.

6.   The threshold for non-international armed conflict has been further developed in case law. In *Tadić*, the International Criminal Tribunal for the Former Yugoslavia affirmed that a non-international armed conflict exists when there is protracted armed violence between organised armed groups within a State.[912] This holding is widely accepted as setting forth the two key criteria for qualification as a non-international armed conflict – intensity of the hostilities and the involvement of an organised armed group.[913] Subsequent judgments of the International Criminal Tribunal for the Former Yugoslavia have de-emphasised the importance

---

[911] Art. 8(f) of the Rome Statute excludes such situations from the ambit of 'armed conflicts not of an international character'. *See also* UK MANUAL, para. 15.2.1; CANADIAN MANUAL, para. 1709; AMW MANUAL, commentary accompanying Rule 2(a).

[912] *Tadić* decision on the defence motion for interlocutory appeal, para. 70.

[913] *See, e.g., Milošević* decision on motion, paras. 16–17; *Furundžija* judgment, para. 59; *Delalić* judgment, para. 183; UK MANUAL, para. 15.3.1.; ICRC GENEVA CONVENTION I 2016 COMMENTARY, para. 421.

THE LAW OF CYBER ARMED CONFLICT

of other factors, such as geographical scope and temporal duration, subordinating these concepts within the concept of intensity.[914]

7. Various indicative criteria have been suggested to facilitate the determination of whether a given situation has reached the requisite intensity threshold.[915] The International Criminal Tribunal for the Former Yugoslavia has looked to such factors as the gravity of attacks and their recurrence;[916] the temporal and territorial expansion of violence and the collective character of hostilities;[917] whether various parties are able to operate from a territory under their control;[918] an increase in the number of government forces;[919] the mobilisation of volunteers and the distribution and type of weapons among both parties to the conflict;[920] the fact that the conflict has led to a large displacement of people;[921] and whether the conflict is the subject of any relevant scrutiny or action by the Security Council.[922] In view of the intensity threshold, cyber operations alone can trigger a non-international armed conflict in only rare cases.

8. The development of further State practice notwithstanding, network intrusions, the deletion or destruction of data (even on a large scale), computer network exploitation, and data theft do not amount to a non-international armed conflict. The blocking of certain Internet functions and services would not, for example, suffice to trigger a non-international armed conflict, nor would defacing governmental or other official websites.

9. As noted in the *Tadić* Appeals Chamber judgment, the violence that qualifies an armed conflict as non-international must be 'protracted', although the term has not been quantified in the law.[923] It is clear,

---

[914] *Haradinaj* judgment, para. 49.

[915] *See, e.g., Haradinaj* judgment, paras. 40–49; *Lubanga* judgment, para. 538; ICRC GENEVA CONVENTION I 1952 COMMENTARY, at 49–50; ICRC GENEVA CONVENTION I 2016 COMMENTARY, paras. 414–437; ICRC GENEVA CONVENTION III 1960 COMMENTARY, at 35–36; ICRC GENEVA CONVENTION IV 1958 COMMENTARY, at 35–36.

[916] *Mrkšić* judgment, para. 419; *Hadžihasanović* judgment, para. 22; *Limaj* judgment, paras. 135–167.

[917] *Hadžihasanović* judgment, para. 22; *Milošević* decision on motion, paras. 28–29.

[918] *Milošević* decision on motion, para. 29; *Delalić* judgment, para. 187.

[919] *Limaj* judgment, paras. 146, 159, 164–165; *Milošević* decision on motion, para. 30.

[920] *Mrkšić* judgment, paras. 39–40, 407–408; *Milošević* decision on motion, para. 31.

[921] *Haradinaj* judgment, para. 49.   [922] *Mrkšić* judgment, paras. 420–421.

[923] *Tadić* decision on the defence motion for interlocutory appeal, para. 70. In *Abella*, the Inter-American Commission on Human Rights characterised a 30-hour clash between dissident armed forces and the Argentinian military as non-international armed conflict. *Abella* v. *Argentina*, Case 11.137, Inter-AmCtHR, Report No. 55/97, OEA\Ser.L\V\II.98, doc. 6 rev. (1998).

however, that the violence need not be continuous in nature.[924] Frequent, albeit not continuous, cyber attacks (Rule 92) occurring within a relatively well-defined period may be characterised as protracted.

10.   The International Group of Experts struggled with the question of whether non-destructive cyber operations conducted during civil disturbances or in connection with other acts of violence not qualifying as a non-international armed conflict can tip the scale and cause the hostilities to rise to the level of an armed conflict. For instance, assume an organised armed group has orchestrated civil disturbances. Although destruction of property is involved, such destruction is insufficiently severe to satisfy the intensity criterion for non-international armed conflict. The International Group of Experts achieved no consensus as to whether non-destructive but severe cyber operations may be considered in order to fulfil the intensity requirement.

11.   For a non-international armed conflict to exist, there must be at least one non-State organised armed group involved in the hostilities.[925] Such a group is 'armed' if it has the capacity of undertaking cyber attacks (Rule 92). It is 'organised' if it is under an established command structure and can conduct sustained military operations.[926] The extent of organisation does not have to reach the level of a conventional militarily disciplined unit.[927] However, cyber operations and computer attacks by private individuals do not suffice. Even small groups of hackers are unlikely to meet the requirement of organisation. Whether or not a given group is organised must be determined on a case-by-case basis.

12.   To assess organisation, the International Criminal Tribunal for the Former Yugoslavia has taken into account numerous factors. For instance, in *Limaj*, the Tribunal considered, *inter alia*: the organisation and structure of the Kosovo Liberation Army (KLA), which had a general staff and created eleven zones with a commander for each; the adoption of internal regulations; the nomination of a spokesperson; the issuance of orders, political statements, and communiqués; the existence of headquarters; the capacity to launch coordinated action involving multiple KLA units; the existence of a military police and issuance of

---

[924] In *Limaj*, the International Criminal Tribunal for the Former Yugoslavia concluded that the conflict in Kosovo in 1998 could be described as 'periodic armed clashes occurring virtually continuously at intervals averaging three to seven days over a widespread and expanding geographic area'. *Limaj* judgment, paras. 168, 171–173.

[925] AMW MANUAL, commentary accompanying Rule 2(a).

[926] *Limaj* judgment, para. 129.   [927] *Limaj* judgment, paras. 132–134.

disciplinary rules; the ability to recruit new members; the capacity to provide military training; the creation of weapons distribution channels; the use of uniforms and military equipment; and participation in political negotiations to resolve the Kosovo crisis.[928]

13.   This raises the question of a 'virtual' organisation, that is, one in which all activities that bear on the organisation criterion occur online. At one end of the spectrum are hackers who operate autonomously. The mere fact that many hackers are attacking a State, for example, would not render them organised. At the other is a distinct online group with a leadership structure that coordinates its activities by, for instance, allocating specified cyber targets amongst themselves, sharing attack tools, conducting cyber vulnerability assessments, and doing cyber damage assessment to determine whether 'reattack' is required. The group is operating 'cooperatively'. The majority of the International Group of Experts agreed that the failure of members of the group physically to meet does not alone preclude it from having the requisite degree of organisation.

14.   It has been asserted that the organisation must be of a nature to allow implementation of the law of armed conflict.[929] If so, the requirement would be difficult to comply with in the case of a virtual armed group since there would be no means to implement the law with regard to individuals with whom there is no physical contact. The International Group of Experts was divided as to whether such difficulty would bar qualification as an organised armed group.[930]

15.   The more difficult case is that of an informal grouping of individuals who operate not cooperatively, but rather 'collectively', that is simultaneously but without any coordination. Consider a situation in which an informal group, acting with a shared purpose, accesses a common website that contains tools and vulnerable targets, but does not organise their cyber attacks in any fashion. The majority of the International Group of Experts took the position that an informal grouping of individuals acting in a collective but otherwise uncoordinated fashion cannot comprise an organised armed group; there must be a distinct group with sufficient

---

[928] *Limaj* judgment, paras. 94–129. The International Criminal Tribunal for Rwanda uses the same test as the International Criminal Tribunal for Former Yugoslavia to evaluate both the intensity and organisation of the parties to the conflict for each of their cases. *Akayesu* judgment, paras. 619–621.

[929] ICRC ADDITIONAL PROTOCOLS 1987 COMMENTARY, para. 4470. This requirement is express with regard to Additional Protocol II conflicts (Art. 1(1)), but it is unclear whether it applies as well to Common Article 3 type conflicts.

[930] ICRC GENEVA CONVENTION I 2016 COMMENTARY, para. 437.

organisational structure that operates as a unit. Others suggested that whether an informal group meets the organisation criterion would depend upon a variety of context-specific factors, such as the existence of an informal leadership entity directing the group's activities in a general sense, identifying potential targets, and maintaining an inventory of effective hacker tools. All the Experts agreed that the mere fact that individuals are acting toward a collective goal does not satisfy the organisation criterion. For example, if a website makes available malware and a provides a list of potential cyber targets, those who independently use the site to conduct attacks would not constitute an organised armed group.

16. Although Common Article 3 specifically provides that its application does not affect the legal status of the parties to a conflict, States have often been reluctant to admit the existence of a non-international armed conflict. Whether a non-international armed conflict exists is a question of fact that depends on the level of violence taking place and the parties' degree of organisation. It is therefore an objective test that is unaffected by the subjective views of those engaged in the hostilities.[931]

17. Additional Protocol II governs certain non-international armed conflicts for Parties thereto. An Additional Protocol II conflict is one which takes place between the armed forces of a State and dissident armed forces or other organised armed groups that control sufficient territory so 'as to enable them to carry out sustained and concerted military operations'.[932] Unlike Common Article 3, Additional Protocol II does not apply to armed conflicts occurring only between non-State armed groups and requires physical control of territory. Control over cyber activities alone is insufficient to constitute control of territory for Additional Protocol II purposes (although control over cyber activities may be indicative of the degree of territorial control a group enjoys).

Rule 84 – Individual criminal responsibility for war crimes

Cyber operations may amount to war crimes and thus give rise to individual criminal responsibility under international law.

1. Serious violations of the law of armed conflict are war crimes that entail individual criminal responsibility under international law. It should be cautioned in this regard that not every violation of the law of

---

[931] *Akayesu* judgment, para. 603; ICRC GENEVA CONVENTION I 2016 COMMENTARY, paras. 861–869.

[932] Additional Protocol II, Art. 1(1).

armed conflict qualifies as a war crime. The International Group of Experts agreed that at least those violations characterised as grave breaches in Articles 50, 51, 130, and 147 of the Geneva Conventions I–IV, respectively, and Article 85 of Additional Protocol I, amount to war crimes as a matter of customary international law. Moreover, the Experts agreed that the offences set forth in Article 8 of the Rome Statute for both international and non-international armed conflict (Rules 82 and 83, respectively) likewise constitute war crimes under customary international law.[933]

2.   The International Group of Experts concluded that acts committed by cyber means may qualify as war crimes, for the law of armed conflict applies to new means and methods of warfare not contemplated at the time a customary law norm emerged.

3.   This Rule applies to both members of the armed forces and civilians engaging in cyber operations in the context of and associated with the armed conflict. It does not apply to individuals engaged in purely criminal cyber operations or malicious cyber activities unrelated to the on-going international or non-international armed conflict.

4.   Individuals may be held criminally responsible for cyber operations that constitute war crimes only when they possesses the necessary mental element (*mens rea*).[934] This will always be the case when the perpetrator had the intention to commit the crime (*dolus directus*). Some war crimes have a slightly less demanding *mens rea* requirement generally referred to as *dolus eventualis*, or recklessness.

5.   Individuals are criminally responsible for cyber operations they commit, or attempt to commit, that constitute war crimes. Three modes of perpetration give rise to individual criminal responsibility for war crimes by cyber means: (1) individual commission; (2) joint commission; and (3) commission through others. Individuals may also be individually responsible for attempted commission in all three forms of perpetration.

6.   Criminal responsibility attaches to an individual who commits, by means of a cyber operation, a prohibited act and does so with the

---

[933] ICRC CUSTOMARY IHL STUDY, Rule 156 and accompanying commentary; *Tadić* decision on the defence motion for Interlocutory Appeal, paras. 98–146. *See* Rome Statute, Arts. 2–3; ICTY Statute, Art. 7; Sierra Leone Statute, Art. 6. *See also* ICRC GENEVA CONVENTION I 2016 COMMENTARY, paras. 2950–3016.

[934] According to Article 30 of the Rome Statute, 'a person shall be criminally responsible and liable for punishment for a crime within the jurisdiction of the Court only if the material elements are committed with intent and knowledge'. However, it is important to stress that this is only the general rule, and that the specific subjective element is dependent on the individual war crime.

requisite *mens rea*. The term 'commit' refers to 'physically perpetrating a crime or engendering a culpable omission in violation of criminal law.'[935] As the International Criminal Tribunal for the Former Yugoslavia clarified in *Tadić* when referring to the term 'committed' in Article 7(1) of its Statute, it is to be understood as 'first and foremost the physical perpetration ... by the offender himself'.[936] Consider a case in which a member of the armed forces responsible for cyber operations accesses an industrial control system in the enemy State during an armed conflict. Using the access, the operator creates overpressure in the sole natural gas pipeline providing fuel to a town in the enemy's territory with the intent of depriving the population of the gas. The attack ruptures the pipeline and consequently the civilian population loses its only source of power, thereby foreseeably resulting in deaths due to harsh winter conditions. Neither the pipeline nor the town's population are valid military objectives. The operator has likely committed a war crime and may be held individually responsible for the offence.

7. International case law confirms that the individual criminal responsibility may also be based on omission where the underlying international rule contains a duty to act.[937] Of particular importance in this regard is superior or command responsibility (Rule 85) for failure to act to prevent a cyber operation that qualifies as a war crime.

8. War crimes by cyber means may also be committed by an individual acting jointly with another according to a common plan or purpose.[938] The jurisprudence of the International Criminal Tribunal for the former Yugoslavia has developed the concept of joint criminal enterprise in order to address these cases.[939] By contrast, the International Criminal Court establishes criminal responsibility on the basis of co-perpetration.[940]

---

[935] *Krstić* judgment, para. 601. *See also Tadić*, Appeals Chamber judgment, para. 188; *Prosecutor* v. *Kunarać*, Case No. IT-96-23-T& IT-96-23/1-T, Trial Chamber judgment, para. 390 (Int'l Crim. Trib. for the Former Yugoslavia 22 February 2001).

[936] *Tadić*, Appeals Chamber judgment, para. 188.

[937] *See, e.g., Krstić* judgment, para. 601.   [938] Rome Statute, Art. 25(3)(a).

[939] The *Tadić* Appeals Chamber first elaborated on 'common purpose', rather than 'joint criminal enterprise' in *Tadić*, Appeals Chamber judgment, paras. 190, 193–229. The Tribunal developed the concept of 'joint criminal enterprise' in a number of decisions. *Delalić* judgment, paras. 345–354; *Furundžija* judgment, para. 216.

[940] *Lubanga* judgment, para. 326.

9.   Despite the difference in approach, the International Group of Experts agreed that (1) the respective contributions of the individuals involved must be part of a common plan or an agreement, and (2) the individuals involved must make essential contributions in a coordinated manner that results in the fulfilment of the war crime's material elements.[941] The requisite contributions need not take place at the execution phase of the war crime in question, but may be confined to its planning and preparation.[942] Nor does the accused need to be present at the scene of the crime, so long as he exercised, jointly with others, control over it.[943] Criminal responsibility in such cases can be especially relevant in the cyber context since the interconnectivity of the cyber domain offers a nearly ideal environment for crimes committed jointly by different perpetrators.

10.   For instance, consider a case in which members of the technical branch of an intelligence service of one country develop malware designed to affect the control systems (and cause the crash) of commercial airliners of the enemy State. The malware is implanted during a close access operation by agents of the intelligence service's paramilitary branch. Individuals in both the technical and paramilitary branches will bear criminal responsibility based on co-perpetration.

11.   War crimes responsibility can arise in situations in which the perpetrator is acting 'through' another person, as when a superior orders a subordinate to engage in a cyber operation that amounts to a war crime. This is so 'regardless of whether that other person is criminally responsible'.[944] For instance, a subordinate may not realise that a cyber operation his superior has directed him to conduct will have consequences that qualify it as a war crime and, depending on the circumstances, therefore lack the requisite *mens rea*. So long as the superior has the requisite *mens rea*, and the operation otherwise constitutes a war crime, the superior will bear criminal responsibility for the operation.

---

[941] *The Prosecutor* v. *Jean-Pierre Bemba Gombo,* Case No. ICC-01/05-01/08, decision pursuant to Article 61(7)(a) and (b) of the Rome Statute on the charges of the prosecutor against Jean-Pierre Bemba Gombo, para. 350 (15 June 2009).

[942] *Lubanga* judgment, paras. 1003–1006.   [943] *Lubanga* judgment, para. 1005.

[944] Rome Statute, Art. 25(3)(a). *See also Prosecutor* v. *Germain Katanga and Mathieu Ngudjolo Chui,* Case No. ICC-01/04-01/07, decision on the confirmation of the charges, paras. 495–499 (30 September 2008) (explaining that an individual involved may not be criminally responsible when incapable of blame, for example, through youth or mental impairment).

12.   Article 25(3)(f) of the Rome Statute expressly recognises criminal liability for attempts to commit war crimes.[945] The International Group of Experts agreed that the notion of attempts to commit war crimes applies equally to cyber operations.[946] The Article defines an attempt to commit such a crime as 'taking action that commences its execution by means of a substantial step, but the crime does not occur because of circumstances independent of the person's intentions'. The Experts cautioned that international courts and tribunals have yet to fully develop the meaning of attempt in international criminal law.

13.   Individuals are criminally responsible for instigating, assisting in, facilitating, and aiding or abetting the commission, or attempted commission, of a war crime by cyber means. These forms of accessory or secondary responsibility for war crimes are reflected in Article 25(3)(b)–(d) of the Rome Statute. The International Group of Experts agreed that criminal liability will attach even if the offender is not perpetrating the war crime by cyber means directly, but participates in its commission.[947] In many legal systems, the responsibility of accomplices or accessories, or at least of some of them, is considered less grave than that of those who commit crimes. In cases requiring 'specific' intent, it may be sufficient for the participant to know about the principal perpetrator's 'specific' intent, without sharing it.

14.   Instigating refers to 'prompting another to commit an offence'.[948] To constitute instigation, there needs to be a causal relationship between the instigation and the commission of the crime.[949] As used in this Rule, instigation encompasses the notions of 'inducement' and 'solicitation' found in Article 25(3)(b) of the Rome Statute.[950] An example in the cyber context would be providing 'rewards' to individuals who conduct particular cyber operations, such as those causing deliberate deaths of civilians, that are war crimes.

15.   'Aiding' denotes assistance that is given in a material way.[951] For instance, an individual who provides the malware or information regarding vulnerabilities that was necessary to enable the war crime to be committed may be held responsible for that crime on the basis of

---

[945]   See also ICRC CUSTOMARY IHL STUDY, Rule 151.
[946]   ICRC CUSTOMARY IHL STUDY, Rule 151.
[947]   See, e.g., Tadić, Trial Chamber judgment, paras. 666, 669.
[948]   Krstić judgment, para. 601; Blaškić judgment, para. 280.
[949]   Prosecutor v. Bagilishema, Case No. ITCR-95-1A-T,Trial Chamber judgment, para. 30 (Int'l Crim. Trib. for Rwanda 7 June 2001); Blaškić judgment, para. 278.
[950]   See also Rome Statute, Art. 25(3)(c) and (d).
[951]   Furundžija judgment, paras. 190–249.

aiding it. 'Abetting' indicates some form of moral support or encouragement, or as expressed by the International Criminal Tribunal for the former Yugoslavia, 'facilitating the commission of a crime by being sympathetic thereto'.[952] As an example, posting online exhortations to continue the slaughter of civilians of a particular religious group during an armed conflict could amount to abetting if said exhortations were likely to be effective.

16.   Obeying a superior order to conduct cyber operations, part or all of which would amount to a war crime committed by cyber means, does not relieve a subordinate of criminal responsibility for the crime itself unless the subordinate was under a legal obligation to obey the order, the subordinate did not know that the act ordered was unlawful, and the act ordered was not manifestly unlawful.[953] The lack of a defence of superior orders unless these conditions are satisfied is of particular importance with respect to cyber operations. On the one hand, for instance, the absence of proximity to the targeted cyber infrastructure will often deprive those involved in a cyber operation of the ability to assess the current situation in the target area with respect to such matters as proportionality (Rule 113) and precautions in attack (Rules 114–120). On the other hand, an individual executing a commander's orders might have access to more and better information regarding, and an understanding of, the operation and its implications than the commander. In such a case, the subordinate may be the only individual who becomes, or should have become, aware of the illegality of the proposed operation.

17.   This Rule is without prejudice to the possibility that cyber operations may amount to a crime against humanity, genocide, or crime of aggression under international law.

Rule 85 – Criminal responsibility of commanders and superiors

(a) **Commanders and other superiors are criminally responsible for ordering cyber operations that constitute war crimes.**
(b) **Commanders are also criminally responsible if they knew or, owing to the circumstances at the time, should have known their subordinates were committing, were about to commit, or had**

---

[952] *Akayesu* judgment, para. 484.
[953] Rome Statute, Art. 33; ICTY Statute, Art. 7(4); ICTR Statute, Art. 6(4); Sierra Leone Statute, Art. 6(4), ICRC Customary IHL Study, Rule 155.

committed war crimes and failed to take all reasonable and available measures to prevent their commission or to punish those responsible.

1. This Rule emphasises that commanders and other superiors do not escape criminal responsibility by virtue of the fact that they did not personally commit an act that constitutes a war crime. It is found in treaty and case law.[954] Applicable in both international and non-international armed conflict, Rule 85 reflects customary international law.[955] No basis exists for excluding the application of the Rule to cyber operations that constitute war crimes.

2. Related Articles in Geneva Conventions I to IV set forth the principle expressed in *lit.* (a).[956] They stipulate that Parties to the instruments must enact domestic legislation that provides 'effective penal sanctions for persons committing, or ordering to be committed, any of the grave breaches' of the Conventions. The Articles further obligate Parties to search for persons alleged to have committed such offences and either bring them before their own courts or hand them over to another Party for prosecution when that Party has made out a *prima facie* case as to the matter in question.

3. In the context of cyber warfare, the Rule imposes criminal responsibility on any military commander or other superior (including civilians) who orders cyber operations amounting to a war crime.[957] A clear

---

[954] Geneva Convention I, Art. 49; Geneva Convention II, Art. 50; Geneva Convention III, Art. 129; Geneva Convention IV, Art. 146; Additional Protocol I, Arts. 86–87; Cultural Property Convention, Art. 28; Second Cultural Property Protocol, Art. 15(2); Rome Statute, Arts. 25(3)(b), 28.

[955] Rome Statute, Art. 25(3); ICTY Statute, Art. 7(1); ICTR Statute, Art. 6(1); Sierra Leone Statute, Art. 6(1); United Nations Transitional Administration in East Timor, Art. 14(3), UN Doc. UNTAET/REG/2000/15 (6 June 2000); DoD MANUAL, paras. 18.23.1, 18.23.3; UK MANUAL, paras. 16.36–16.36.6; CANADIAN MANUAL, para. 1504; ICRC CUSTOMARY IHL STUDY, Rules 152, 153. The jurisprudence of international tribunals illustrates the application of the principle of command responsibility. *See, e.g., The Prosecutor v. Tihomir Blaškić*, Case No. IT-95-14-T, Trial Chamber judgment, paras. 281–282 (Int'l Crim. Trib. for the Former Yugoslavia 3 March 2000); *Krstić* judgment, para. 605; *Kayishema* judgment, para. 223; *Akayesu* judgment, paras. 472–474, 483; *Delalić* judgment, paras. 333–334; *Martić*, Case No. IT-95-11-R61, review of indictment, paras. 20–1 (Int'l Crim. Trib. for the Former Yugoslavia 8 March 1996); *Prosecutor v. Rajić*, Case No. IT-95-12-R61, review of the indictment, paras. 1, 59, 71 (Int'l Crim. Trib. for the Former Yugoslavia 13 September 1996).

[956] Geneva Convention I, Art. 49; Geneva Convention II, Art. 50; Geneva Convention III, Art. 129; Geneva Convention IV, Art. 146.

[957] This extension is based on the Rome Statute, Art. 28(b).

example is ordering cyber attacks against civilians who are not directly participating in hostilities (Rules 94 and 97). Similarly, ordering indiscriminate cyber attacks (Rule 111) would result in the criminal responsibility of the person so ordering the attack, regardless of whether that individual took any personal part in the actual conduct of the operation.

4.   This Rule applies to crimes that occur or are attempted pursuant to the order.[958] It does not extend to orders to commit a war crime that remain unheeded.

5.   Responsibility extends down through the chain of command or control. For example, a subordinate commander who orders his or her troops to comply with an order from a superior to commit a particular war crime is equally responsible for ordering the war crime. Similarly, consider the case of a senior commander who orders cyber operations to be conducted to achieve a particular operational effect without specifying how those operations are to be conducted. A subordinate commander at any level who, in compliance with the order, directs those under his control to launch cyber attacks against protected persons or places would be individually responsible for the attacks.

6.   *Lit.* (b)'s requirement to take measures to prevent war crimes or punish those who have committed them is based on Articles 86 and 87 of Additional Protocol I. A commander or other superior who becomes aware that a cyber operation may have resulted in a war crime must accordingly take steps to ensure the matter is investigated as appropriate in the circumstances and reported to appropriate investigative and judicial authorities.[959]

7.   The concept of responsibility for acts that a commander or superior may not have ordered, but of which he or she should have known, was enunciated decades before adoption of Additional Protocol I in the case of General Yamashita. A US military commission following the Second World War held that Yamashita had failed to exercise 'effective control' over certain of his forces that had committed atrocities, and that the nature of the offences themselves provided *prima facie* evidence of his knowledge thereof.[960] In the decades since the decision, this finding has matured into the standard found in *lit.* (b).

---

[958] Rome Statute, Art. 25(3)(b).   [959] *See, e.g.,* Rome Statute, Art. 28(a)(ii), 28(b)(iii).

[960] Trial of General Tomoyuki Yamashita, 4 Law Reports Of Trials Of War Criminals 1, Sec. 12 (1948). It must be noted that the decision has sometimes been criticised on the basis that Yamashita was held responsible for acts committed in very remote areas.

8. Article 28(a) of the Rome Statute sets forth a contemporary articulation of the principle. It provides:

> A military commander or person effectively acting as a military commander shall be criminally responsible for crimes within the jurisdiction of the Court committed by forces under his or her effective command and control, or effective authority and control as the case may be, as a result of his or her failure to exercise control properly over such forces, where:
>
> (i) That military commander or person either knew or, owing to the circumstances at the time, should have known that the forces were committing or about to commit such crimes; and
> (ii) That military commander or person failed to take all necessary and reasonable measures within his or her power to prevent or repress their commission or to submit the matter to the competent authorities for investigation and prosecution.

As this extract illustrates, the key to the notion is the exercise of, or the ability to exercise, effective control over those who committed the actual offences.[961]

9. The extension of criminal responsibility to commanders who knew or should have known that an operation constituting a war crime has been, is being, or will be conducted is especially important in the context of cyber warfare.[962] In order to avoid criminal responsibility for the acts of their subordinates, commanders and other superiors must take appropriate steps to become aware of the operations being conducted by their units, understand those operations and their consequences, and exercise control over them.

10. The technical complexity of cyber operations complicates matters. Commanders or other superiors in the chain of command cannot be expected to have a deep knowledge of cyber operations; to

---

However, the legal principle of command responsibility enunciated in the case is uncontested.

[961] The principle also appears in the statutes of international criminal tribunals. ICTY Statute, Art. 7(3); ICTR Statute, Art. 6(3). *See also Prosecutor* v. *Blaškić,* Case No. IT-95-14-A, Appeals Chamber judgment, paras. 62, 91, 218, 417, 484, 632 (Int'l Crim. Trib. for the Former Yugoslavia 29 July 2004); *Prosecutor* v. *Halilović,* Case No. IT-01-48-T, Trial Chamber judgment, paras. 38–100, 747, 751–2 (Int'l Crim. Trib. for the Former Yugoslavia 16 November 2005); *Kordić and Čerkez,* Case No. IT-95-14/2-A, Appeals Chamber judgment, para. 827 (Int'l Crim. Trib. for the Former Yugoslavia 17 December 2004); *Kayishema* judgment, paras. 209–210, 216–218, 222–225, 228–229, 231. *See also* UK MANUAL, para. 16.36.5; CANADIAN MANUAL, para. 1621.

[962] Note that Art. 28 of the Rome Statute applies to all crimes within the jurisdiction of the International Criminal Court, not just war crimes.

some extent, they are entitled to rely on the knowledge and understanding of their subordinates. Nevertheless, the fact that cyber operations may be technically complicated does not alone relieve commanders or other superiors of the responsibility for exercising control over their subordinates. Wilful or negligent failure to acquire an understanding of such operations is never a justification for lack of knowledge. As a matter of law, commanders and other superiors are assumed to have the same degree of understanding as a 'reasonable' commander at a comparable level of command in a similar operational context. In all cases, the knowledge must be sufficient to allow them to fulfil their legal duty to act reasonably to identify, prevent, or stop the commission of cyber war crimes.

11.   Note that the individuals addressed by this Rule need not be a 'commander' or be acting as such. There is no requirement for military status. For example, Article 28(b) of the International Criminal Court Statute extends responsibility to 'superiors' who have 'effective responsibility and control' over their subordinates, although it appears to have set a slightly higher standard by using the phraseology knew or 'consciously disregarded information which clearly indicated' the commission of a war crime.[963] The Rule would encompass, for instance, civilian superiors in civilian intelligence or security agencies that conduct cyber operations during an armed conflict.

---

[963] Rome Statute, Art. 28(b). *See also Prosecutor* v. *Delalić,* Case No. IT-96-21-A, Appeals Chamber judgment, paras. 239, 254 (20 February 2001); UK MANUAL, para. 16.36.6; CANADIAN MANUAL, para. 1621.

17

Conduct of hostilities

SECTION 1: PARTICIPATION IN ARMED CONFLICT

Rule 86 – Participation generally

The law of armed conflict does not bar any category of person from participating in cyber operations. However, the legal consequences of participation differ, based on the nature of the armed conflict and the category to which an individual belongs.

1. The customary international law of armed conflict does not prohibit any individual from participating in an armed conflict, whether international or non-international. It should be noted that Article 43(2) of Additional Protocol I provides that 'members of the armed forces of a Party to a conflict (other than medical personnel and chaplains covered by Article 33 of Geneva Convention III) are combatants, that is to say they have the right to participate directly in hostilities'. This provision, applicable in international armed conflict, confirms that combatants enjoy immunity in respect of the acts undertaken as part of the hostilities. It does not prohibit others from engaging in those hostilities.

2. Although the law of armed conflict contains no prohibition on participation, it does set forth consequences that result from such participation. Three are of particular importance: combatant immunity, prisoner of war status, and targetability. The issue of targetability is dealt with in Rules 92–121 on attacks. Entitlement to combatant immunity and prisoner of war status depend on whether the individual concerned is a combatant in an international armed conflict. These issues are discussed in the following two Rules.

3. In accordance with Rule 97, a civilian who directly participates in hostilities loses certain protections attendant to civilian status for such time as he or she so participates.

Rule 87 – Members of the armed forces

In an international armed conflict, members of the armed forces of a party to the conflict who, in the course of cyber operations, fail to comply with the requirements of combatant status lose their entitlement to combatant immunity and prisoner of war status.

1.   The generally accepted understanding of combatancy derives from the Hague Regulations.[964] Geneva Convention III adopts the standard in Article 4A with regard to the entitlement to prisoner of war status.[965] Although Article 4A(1), (2), (3), and (6) is textually applicable only to prisoner of war status, it is universally understood as reflecting the customary international law criteria for combatancy. The notion of combatancy is limited to international armed conflict; there is no non-international armed conflict equivalent of either prisoner of war status or combatant immunity.

2.   According to the majority of the International Group of Experts, customary international law provides that individuals who are nationals of the capturing party are not entitled to combatant status.[966] A minority of the Experts argued that there is no basis in international law for this position.

3.   Combatants are entitled to treatment as prisoners of war in accordance with Geneva Convention III upon capture.[967] They are also entitled to combatant immunity, that is, they may not be prosecuted for having engaged in belligerent acts that are lawful under the law of armed conflict.[968] For instance, a combatant who conducts cyber operations that violate domestic criminal law may not be prosecuted for such actions so long as they are carried out in compliance with the law of armed conflict. Combatant immunity is a customary international law principle recognised in Article 43(2) of Additional Protocol I.

4.   There are two categories of combatant.[969] The first consists of 'members of the armed forces of a Party to the conflict as well as

---

[964] Hague Regulations, Art. 1.
[965] DoD Manual, para. 4.3.3; AMW Manual, Rule 10(b)(i) and accompanying commentary. *But see* ICRC Interpretive Guidance, at 22.
[966] *See, e.g., Prosecutor v. Koi* [1968] AC 829 (PC 1967). *See also* Dinstein, Conduct of Hostilities, at 55–56.
[967] Geneva Convention III, Art. 4A. Technically, they are entitled to this status as soon as they fall 'into the power of the enemy'. *Id.* Arts. 4A, 5.
[968] DoD Manual, para. 4.4.   [969] *See also* Rule 88 regarding *levées en masse*.

members of militias or volunteer corps forming part of such armed forces'.[970] This category primarily includes members of a State's armed forces.

5.   The second category comprises 'members of other militias and members of other volunteer corps, including those of organised resistance movements, belonging to a Party to the conflict'.[971] Such organised armed groups are assimilated to the armed forces and as a group must, pursuant to Article 4A(2) of Geneva Convention III and customary international law, fulfil four conditions:

(a) be commanded by a person responsible for his subordinates;
(b) wear a distinctive emblem or attire that is recognisable at a distance;
(c) carry arms openly; and
(d) conduct operations in accordance with the law of armed conflict.

Irregular forces that meet these conditions and belong to a party to the conflict qualify as combatants and are entitled to combatant immunity and prisoner of war status.[972]

6.   In Geneva Convention III, the four conditions are set forth with regard only to organised armed groups assimilated to the armed forces. The majority of the International Group of Experts took the position that the four requirements are implicit in the Convention for members of the armed forces and that, therefore, only members of the armed forces who meet the four requirements qualify for combatant status, and its attendant benefits. A minority of the Experts took the position that the requirements are limited to those groups assimilated to the armed forces. By this latter position, the sole condition for combatant status for members of the armed forces is their status as members.

7.   Every State organ meets the requirement of belonging to a party to the conflict. The issue of belonging only arises with respect to organised armed groups that are assimilated to the armed forces, that is, those groups addressed in Article 4A(2) of Geneva Convention III. The concept of 'belonging to' was examined during the meetings that resulted in

---

[970] Geneva Convention III, Art. 4A(1). *See also* Geneva Convention I, Art. 13(1); Geneva Convention II, Art. 13(1).

[971] Geneva Convention III, Art. 4A(2). *See also* Geneva Convention I, Art. 13(2); Geneva Convention II, Art. 13(2).

[972] DoD MANUAL, para. 4.4. *But see* ICRC INTERPRETIVE GUIDANCE, at 22 (noting that 'strictly speaking' the criteria apply only to status as a combatant with regard to prisoner of war entitlements).

the ICRC Interpretive Guidance.[973] The International Group of Experts agreed with the approach taken in the Guidance.

8.   By that approach, 'the concept of "belonging to" requires at least a *de facto* relationship between an organised group and a Party to the conflict'. Such a relationship need not be officially declared; it may be 'expressed through tacit agreement or conclusive behaviour that makes clear for which party the group is fighting'.[974] As an example, a State may turn to a group of private individuals to conduct cyber operations during an armed conflict because the group possesses capability or knowledge that State organs do not. The group belongs to that party to the conflict and, so long as it meets the other requirements of combatancy, its members will enjoy combatant status.

9.   If a person engaged in cyber operations during an armed conflict is a member of an organised armed group not belonging to a party to the conflict, it does not matter if the group and its members comply with the four criteria of combatancy. That person will not have combatant status and therefore not be entitled to combatant immunity or to be treated as a prisoner of war. Such a person would be an 'unprivileged belligerent', as discussed below.

10.   The condition of being commanded by a person responsible for subordinates is best understood as an aspect of the requirement that the group in question be 'organised'. The criterion of organisation was previously discussed in the context of non-international armed conflict (Rule 83). There, the unique nature of virtual organisations was highlighted. The same considerations apply in the present context. While not normally an issue in respect of regularly constituted State armed forces, or even well-established organised armed groups, a claim of combatant status could be significantly weakened if the individuals asserting that status are part of a loosely organised group or association. This could be the result, for example, of organising solely over the Internet. In a similar vein, members of such a group may have difficulty establishing that they are acting under a responsible commander. Even more problematic is the requirement that the group be subject to an internal disciplinary system capable of enforcing compliance with the law of armed conflict. Cumulatively, these requirements make it highly unlikely that a purely virtual organisation

---

[973] *See also* ICRC INTERPRETIVE GUIDANCE, at 23–24 (citing ICRC GENEVA CONVENTION II 1960 COMMENTARY).
[974] ICRC INTERPRETIVE GUIDANCE, at 23.

would qualify as an organised armed group for the purposes of determining combatant status.

11. Combatant status requires that the individual wear a 'fixed distinctive sign'.[975] The requirement is generally met through the wearing of uniforms. There is no basis for deviating from this general requirement for those engaged in cyber operations. Some members of the International Group of Experts suggested that individuals engaged in cyber operations, regardless of circumstances such as distance from the area of operations or clear separation from the civilian population, must always comply with this requirement to enjoy combatant status. They emphasised that the customary international law of armed conflict in relation to combatant immunity and prisoner of war status offers no exceptions to this rule. Although Article 44(3) of Additional Protocol I does provide for an exception,[976] it is not reflective of customary international law.[977]

12. Other Experts took the position that an exception to the requirement to wear a distinctive sign exists as a matter of customary international law. They argued that the requirement only applies in circumstances in which the failure to have a fixed distinctive sign might reasonably cause an attacker to be unable to distinguish between civilians and combatants, thus placing civilians at greater risk of mistaken attack. Consider a situation in which a Special Forces team is tasked to identify and attack a military cyber control facility located in a cluster of similar civilian facilities. A failure of the military personnel in the facility to wear uniforms would make it more difficult for the Special Forces team to distinguish the military from civilian facilities, thereby heightening the risk that the civilian facilities will mistakenly be made the object of attack.

13. Some of these Experts limited the exception in the previous paragraph to situations in which combatants engaged in cyber operations are located within a military objective for which there is a

---

[975] The ICRC CUSTOMARY IHL STUDY, Rule 106, provides that '[c]ombatants must distinguish themselves from the civilian population while they are engaged in an attack or in a military operation preparatory to an attack. If they fail to do so, they do not have the right to prisoner-of-war status.'

[976] Some States Parties to the Protocol limit its application to occupied territory and the situation referred in Art. 1(4) of the same treaty. *See, e.g.,* UK Additional Protocol Ratification Statement, para. (g). *See also* UK MANUAL, paras. 4.5–4.5.3.

[977] Michael J. Matheson, *Remarks in Session One: The United States Position on the Relation of Customary International Law to the Protocols Additional to the 1949 Geneva Conventions,* 2 AM. U. J. INT'L L. & POL'Y 419, 425 (1987).

separate requirement of marking, such as a warship or military aircraft. Since they are required to bear an external mark signifying nationality and military status, these Experts are of the view that that there is no requirement for military personnel on board to wear a distinctive sign indicating their status.[978]

14.   The issue of whether computers and software constitute weapons is discussed in Rule 103. However, even if they qualify as weapons, the requirement to carry arms openly has little application in the cyber context.

15.   The obligation to comply with the law of armed conflict attaches to the group as a whole. Individual members of a group that adopts the tactic of conducting cyber attacks (Rule 92) against civilian cyber infrastructure do not qualify for combatant status even if they individually comply with the law. By contrast, although a group may generally comply with the law, various individual members of the group may commit war crimes. Those who do retain their combatant status, but may be tried for the crimes.

16.   A party to a conflict may incorporate a paramilitary or armed law enforcement agency into its armed forces.[979] The majority of the International Group of Experts took the position that this provision of the law does not extend to intelligence or other government agencies that are not entrusted with law enforcement functions. However, a minority of the Experts argued that the issue fell within the classic domain of State sovereignty and that therefore a State is free to incorporate any entity it wishes into the armed forces.

17.   Although Article 43(3) of Additional Protocol I provides that the other parties to a conflict shall be notified of such incorporation, failure to so notify the enemy does not imply that the individuals concerned remain civilians.[980] Once such groups have been properly incorporated into the armed forces, their members enjoy the same privileges as members of the regular armed forces. The fact that they also continue to perform a law enforcement function has no bearing on this status. Absent incorporation, the cyber activities of the groups are governed by the rules pertaining to participation in hostilities (Rules 86 and 97).

---

[978] They will generally do so, however, in order to exhibit their status as members of the armed forces in the event that they become separated from the aircraft. AMW MANUAL, commentary accompanying Rule 117.

[979] Additional Protocol I, Art. 43(3).

[980] AMW MANUAL, commentary accompanying Rule 10.

18. Members of the armed forces or groups assimilated to the armed forces who do not qualify for combatant status (and civilians taking a direct part in hostilities, Rule 97) are unprivileged belligerents. An unprivileged belligerent, like any other individual, including a combatant, may be prosecuted for commission of a war crime.

19. All members of the International Group of Experts agreed that unprivileged belligerents enjoy no combatant immunity and are not entitled to prisoner of war status.[981] In particular, they are subject to prosecution under the domestic laws of the capturing State for conducting cyber operations that are unlawful under domestic law. This is so even if the acts are lawful under the law of armed conflict when committed by a combatant. The classic example is conducting cyber attacks (Rule 92) against military personnel or military objectives.

20. As noted above, a division of opinion exists with regard to the four conditions for combatant status that apply to groups assimilated to the armed forces. For those Experts who took the position that the conditions apply equally to the armed forces, a member of the armed forces captured while wearing no distinctive attire (or emblems) is not entitled to prisoner of war status. Those Experts taking the contrary position would conclude that the individual's membership in the armed forces suffices for entitlement to prisoner of war status, although, in certain specific circumstances, wearing civilian clothing might be perfidious (Rule 122) or subject the individual concerned to being treated as a spy (Rule 89).

21. The International Group of Experts agreed that unprivileged belligerency as such is not a war crime.[982] However, they acknowledged the existence of a contrary position.

22. In a non-international armed conflict, the notion of belligerent (combatant) immunity does not exist. Domestic law exclusively determines the question of any immunity from prosecution.[983] In this regard, it must be remembered that many cyber activities, like certain forms of hacking, have been criminalised in domestic law. For instance, if a

---

[981] DoD Manual, paras. 4.19.3, 4.19.4. Some members of the International Group of Experts took the position that civilians entitled to prisoner of war status pursuant to Art. 4A(4) and (5) of Geneva Convention III enjoy no immunity if they participate in hostilities, but would not lose prisoner of war status.

[982] AMW Manual, commentary accompanying Rule 111(b).

[983] UK Manual, paras. 15.6.1, 15.6.2. The statement is not absolute. For instance, consider the case of a foreign diplomat who has taken a direct part in hostilities in a manner that violates the law of the State to which she is accredited.

member of either the armed forces or the opposition forces hacks into the adversary's computer systems, domestic law will determine the legality of such actions. Note that domestic law often permits members of the armed forces and law enforcement agencies to conduct activities, such as the use of force, that would otherwise be unlawful.

23.   Any State or international tribunal with jurisdiction over the individual and the offence may prosecute someone, including a member of the State's security forces, who commits a war crime involving cyber activities during a non-international armed conflict.

Rule 88 – *Levée en masse*

In an international armed conflict, inhabitants of unoccupied territory who engage in cyber operations as part of a *levée en masse* enjoy combatant immunity and prisoner of war status.

1.   This Rule is based on Article 2 of the Hague Regulations and Article 4A(6) of Geneva Convention III. It reflects customary international law,[984] but does not apply to non-international armed conflict.

2.   A *levée en masse* consists of the inhabitants (but not an individual or a small group) of non-occupied territory 'who on the approach of the enemy spontaneously take up arms to resist invading forces, without having time to form themselves into regular armed units'.[985] *Levées en masse* need not be organised, and although their members must carry arms openly and respect the laws and customs of war, they need not wear a distinctive emblem or other identifying attire.[986] In light of the requirements for an invasion and for the territory to be unoccupied at the time the acts of resistance occur, the circumstances under which a *levée en masse* can exist are factually limited.[987]

3.   The ICRC Commentary to Geneva Convention III states that the notion of a *levée en masse* is 'applicable to populations which act in

---

[984] DoD Manual, para. 4.7; UK Manual, paras. 4.8, 11.12; Canadian Manual, para. 306; German Manual, paras. 310, 501; ICRC Customary IHL Study, commentary accompanying Rule 106.

[985] Geneva Convention III, Art. 4A(6). *See also* ICRC Customary IHL Study, commentary accompanying Rule 5, which explains that members of a *levée en masse* are an exception to the definition of civilians in that although they are not members of the armed forces, they qualify as combatants.

[986] ICRC Geneva Convention II 1960 Commentary, at 67.

[987] UK Manual, para. 4.8; German Manual, para. 310. *See also* ICRC Interpretive Guidance, at 25.

response to an order by their government given over the wireless'.[988] Extension to orders given by cyber means is appropriate.

4. As applied in the cyber context, application of the concept is somewhat problematic. Consider a case in which members of the population spontaneously begin to mount cyber operations in response to an invasion of their country without having had an opportunity to organise into regular armed units. If the operations involve a large segment of the population and if they target the invading force, those involved will arguably qualify as members of a *levée en masse*. However, the means and expertise necessary to engage effectively in cyber operations may be relatively limited in the population. It is unclear whether a *levée en masse* can be comprised solely of a significant portion of the cyber-capable members of the population, as distinct from the population more broadly.

5. Moreover, a *levée en masse* was historically understood as involving a general uprising of the population to repel an invasion by an approaching force. Since it did not contemplate military operations deep into enemy territory, it is questionable whether individuals launching cyber operations against enemy military objectives other than the invading forces can be considered members of a *levée en masse*.

6. The International Group of Experts was divided as to whether the privileges associated with the *levée en masse* concept apply to a civilian population countering a massive cyber attack, the effects of which are comparable to those of a physical invasion by enemy forces. According to a majority of the Experts, the concept of *levée en masse* is to be understood in a narrow sense as requiring the physical invasion of national territory.

Rule 89 – Spies

A member of the armed forces who has engaged in cyber espionage in enemy-controlled territory loses the right to be a prisoner of war and may be treated as a spy if captured before rejoining the armed forces to which he or she belongs.

1. This Rule applies only to cyber espionage conducted in the context of an armed conflict. With respect to cyber espionage during peacetime, see Rule 32.

---

[988] ICRC GENEVA CONVENTION II 1960 COMMENTARY, at 67.

2.   The formulation of this Rule is based on Articles 29 and 31 of the Hague Regulations, and Article 46 of Additional Protocol I, which the International Group of Experts agreed reflect customary international law.[989] It applies only in international armed conflict because the notions of combatant immunity and prisoner of war status have no application in non-international armed conflicts.

3.   This Rule is limited to cyber espionage conducted by members of the armed forces. It must be noted, however, that cyber espionage conducted by civilians may amount to 'direct participation in hostilities', thereby rendering them subject to attack (Rule 97) and may subject them to prosecution by the State that enjoys jurisdiction over the individual or the offence.[990]

4.   'Cyber espionage' is defined narrowly for the purposes of this Rule as any act undertaken clandestinely or under false pretences that uses cyber capabilities to gather (or attempt to gather) information with the intention of communicating it to the opposing party. 'Clandestinely' refers to activities undertaken secretly or secretively,[991] as with a cyber espionage operation designed to conceal the identity of the persons involved or the fact that it has occurred. An act of cyber information collection is 'under false pretences' when conducted so as to create the impression that the individual concerned is entitled to access the information in question.[992]

5.   Cyber espionage and other forms of information gathering do not *per se* violate the law of armed conflict. Thus, a member of the armed forces who engages in cyber espionage in enemy controlled territory while wearing the uniform of his armed forces is not a 'spy'. However, one who does so while wearing civilian attire or the uniform of the adversary is a spy.[993]

---

[989]   *See also* DoD Manual, para. 4.17; ICRC Customary IHL Study, Rule 107.

[990]   AMW Manual, Rule 119 and accompanying commentary.

[991]   AMW Manual, commentary accompanying Rule 118.

[992]   ICRC Additional Protocols 1987 Commentary, para. 1779.

[993]   DoD Manual, para. 4.17.2.1; UK Manual, para. 4.9.4; ICRC Customary IHL Study, commentary on Rule 107. Note that pursuant to Additional Protocol I, Art. 46(3): 'A member of the armed forces of a Party to the conflict who is a resident of territory occupied by an adverse Party and who, on behalf of the Party on which he depends, gathers or attempts to gather information of military value within that territory shall not be considered as engaging in espionage unless he does so through an act of false pretences or deliberately in a clandestine manner. Moreover, such a resident shall not lose his right to the status of prisoner of war and may not be treated as a spy unless he is captured while engaging in espionage.'

6. It is well accepted that spies who are captured in enemy-controlled territory do not enjoy combatant immunity or prisoner of war status. Therefore, they may be prosecuted under the domestic law of the target State and do not enjoy the protections afforded to captured members of the armed forces. However, 'a spy who, after rejoining the army to which he belongs, is subsequently captured by the enemy, is treated as a prisoner of war and incurs no responsibility for his previous acts of spying'.[994] This caveat applies to cyber espionage. Accordingly, if a member of the armed forces who has engaged in cyber espionage in enemy-controlled territory succeeds in rejoining his own forces, he is no longer liable to prosecution for those activities.

7. This Rule is limited to situations in which the individual concerned engages in cyber espionage while in 'enemy controlled territory'. As used in this Manual, the term encompasses both the 'zone of operations of a belligerent' referred to in Article 29 of the Hague Regulations and 'territory controlled by an adverse Party' in the sense of Article 46(2) of Additional Protocol I.[995] Thus, acts of cyber espionage also include those conducted by individuals at locations in an adverse party's territory in which enemy military forces are not presently operating, like areas far from the battlefield and those that are being contested by the opposing forces such that no force clearly 'controls' them.

8. Given the geographic limitation to enemy controlled territory, cyber spying will most likely occur as a close access cyber operation. Examples include using a flash drive to gain access to a computer system or intercepting signals while acting clandestinely. Cyber espionage that is performed from outside enemy controlled territory is not subject to this Rule. Thus, it does not encompass espionage conducted remotely by individuals from beyond enemy territory, even though the exfiltration may take place on enemy controlled territory.

9. Although there is no express prohibition of cyber espionage *per se* in the law of armed conflict, it is subject to all prohibitions and consequences set forth in that body of law. For instance, cyber espionage can in some circumstances violate the prohibition of perfidy (Rule 122).

10. The International Group of Experts agreed that the information in question must be gathered on behalf of a party to the conflict.

---

[994] Hague Regulations, Art. 31; Additional Protocol I, Art. 46(4); DoD MANUAL, para. 4.17.5.1; UK MANUAL, para. 4.9.4 (as amended); CANADIAN MANUAL, para. 320; AMW MANUAL, Rule 122.

[995] DoD MANUAL, para. 4.17.2; AMW MANUAL, Rule 118.

Cyber espionage conducted for a private corporation in order to surreptitiously gather information about the commercial activities of another private corporation, for example, is not encompassed in this Rule.

11.   The majority of the International Group of Experts took the position that the nature of the information gathered has no bearing on the characterisation of the activity as cyber espionage so long as it is gathered on behalf of a party to the conflict. By contrast, the minority agreed with the AMW Manual position that the information involved must be of some military value.[996]

12.   Certain acts of cyber espionage involve more than mere information-gathering activities and can cause damage to computer systems. For instance, a cyber espionage operation can be designed so as to cause damage to civilian cyber infrastructure to mask the fact of its exploitation from the enemy. In such a case, Rule 99 on attacks against civilian objects would apply.

Rule 90 – Mercenaries

Mercenaries involved in cyber operations do not enjoy combatant immunity or prisoner of war status.

1.   Article 47(1) of Additional Protocol I reflects the customary international law rule that mercenaries, including those engaged in cyber operations, are unprivileged belligerents.[997] As the notions of combatant status and belligerent immunity do not apply in non-international armed conflict, this Rule has no relevance to such conflicts.

2.   The most widely accepted definition of mercenary is found in Article 47(2) of Additional Protocol I. It sets forth six conditions that must be cumulatively fulfilled: special recruitment; direct participation in hostilities; desire for private gain as primary motivation; neither a national of a party to the conflict nor a resident of territory controlled by a party; not a member of the armed forces of a party to the conflict; and not sent by another State on official duty as a member of its armed forces. For example, consider a private company located in State A that is engaged by State B to conduct cyber operations on its behalf in its armed

---

[996]   AMW MANUAL, Rule 118 and accompanying commentary.
[997]   UK MANUAL, paras. 4.10–4.10.4 (as amended); CANADIAN MANUAL, para. 319; GERMAN MANUAL, para. 303; ICRC CUSTOMARY IHL STUDY, Rule 108.

conflict with State C. So long as the six criteria are fully met, its employees who conduct the cyber operations are mercenaries, and thus unprivileged belligerents. The same would be true with regard to a 'hacker for hire' who meets the criteria, even if operating alone and far from the battlefield.

3.   It is clear that no person qualifying as a mercenary enjoys combatant status. This is especially important in light of the criminalisation of mercenarism by many States.

Rule 91 – Civilians

Civilians are not prohibited from directly participating in cyber operations amounting to hostilities, but forfeit their protection from attacks for such time as they so participate.

1.   As noted in Rule 86, no rule of treaty or customary international law prohibits civilians from directly participating in hostilities during either international or non-international armed conflict. However, they lose their protection from attack (Rule 94) when doing so (Rule 97).[998]

2.   In accordance with customary international law, Article 50(1) of Additional Protocol I defines civilians in negative terms as being all persons who are members of neither the armed forces nor a *levée en masse*. This approach is implicit in Geneva Conventions III and IV. As a general matter, then, during an international armed conflict, civilians are persons who are not members of the armed forces or of groups assimilated to the armed forces (e.g., organised resistance groups belonging to a party to the conflict) (Rule 87) and who are not participants in a *levée en masse* (Rule 88).

3.   The majority of the International Group of Experts agreed that civilians retain civilian status even if they directly participate in cyber hostilities. For instance, consider an international armed conflict in which civilian patriotic hackers independently undertake offensive cyber operations against the enemy's forces. Such individuals may be lawfully targeted, and, unless they qualify as participants in a *levée en masse*, lack combatant immunity for their actions. A minority of the Group took the position that these individuals qualify as neither

---

[998] DoD Manual, para. 16.5.5; UK Manual, para. 5.3.2. (as amended); Canadian Manual, para. 318; NIAC Manual, paras. 1.1.2, 1.1.3, 2.1.1.2; AMW Manual, chapeau to sec. F.

combatants nor civilians, and therefore do not benefit from the protections of Geneva Conventions III or IV, respectively.

4.   The fact that there is no combatant status in respect of non-international armed conflict sometimes results in differing terminology. Neither Common Article 3 to the Geneva Conventions nor Additional Protocol II defines the term 'civilian'. For the purposes of this Manual, civilians in a non-international armed conflict are those individuals who are not members of the State's armed forces, dissident armed forces, or other organised armed groups.

5.   Although the law of armed conflict does not prohibit participation in a non-international armed conflict, all participants remain subject to its specific prohibitions, such as that on attacking individuals taking no active part in hostilities (Rule 94). Moreover, civilians are subject to prosecution under the domestic law of the State that captures them, which may include a prohibition on participation.

SECTION 2:   ATTACKS GENERALLY

1.   The law of armed conflict applies to the targeting of any person or object during armed conflict irrespective of the means or methods of warfare employed. Consequently, basic principles such as distinction and the prohibition of unnecessary suffering apply to cyber operations. The applicability of particular treaty rules is determined by such matters as whether a State is a Party to the treaty in question, its status as a party to the conflict, and the type of armed conflict (international or non-international, Rules 82 and 83, respectively).

2.   The principles and Rules governing attacks (Rules 92–120) apply equally to situations in which cyber means are used to take control of enemy weapons and weapon systems, as in the case of taking control of an unmanned combat aerial system (UCAS) and using it to conduct attacks.[999]

3.   Article 49(3) of Additional Protocol I limits the Protocol's provisions on the conduct of hostilities 'to any land, air or sea warfare which may affect the civilian population, individual civilians or civilian objects on land. They further apply to all attacks from the sea or from the air against objectives on land but do not otherwise affect the rules of

---

[999] *See, e.g.,* DoD MANUAL, para. 16.5.1.

international law applicable in armed conflict at sea or in the air'. The International Group of Experts agreed that despite this apparent limitation, State practice was such that the principles expressed in this Section, to the extent they reflect customary international law, generally apply to attacks to or from the land or outer space, at sea, or in the air.[1000]

Rule 92 – Definition of cyber attack

A cyber attack is a cyber operation, whether offensive or defensive, that is reasonably expected to cause injury or death to persons or damage or destruction to objects.

1.   For the purposes of the Manual, this definition applies equally in international and non-international armed conflict.[1001]

2.   The notion of 'attack' is a concept that serves as the basis for a number of specific limitations and prohibitions in the law of armed conflict. For instance, civilians and civilian objects may not be 'attacked' (Rules 92, 94, and 99). This Rule sets forth a definition of 'attack' that draws on that found in Article 49(1) of Additional Protocol I: 'attacks means acts of violence against the adversary, whether in offence or defence'. By this widely accepted definition, it is the use of violence against a target that distinguishes attacks from other military operations. Non-violent operations, such as psychological cyber operations and cyber espionage, do not qualify as attacks.[1002]

3.   'Acts of violence' should not be understood as limited to activities that release kinetic force, a point that is well settled in the law of armed conflict. In this regard, note that chemical, biological, or radiological attacks do not usually have a kinetic effect on their designated target, but it is universally agreed that they constitute attacks as a matter of law.[1003] The crux of the notion lies in the effects that are caused. Restated, the consequences of an operation, not its nature, are what generally determine the scope of the term 'attack'; 'violence' must be considered in the sense of violent consequences and is not limited to violent acts. For

---

[1000]   Experts involved in the AMW Manual process arrived at the same conclusion. AMW MANUAL, commentary accompanying Rule 30.

[1001]   NIAC MANUAL, para. 1.1.6; ICRC ADDITIONAL PROTOCOLS 1987 COMMENTARY, para. 4783 and n. 19.

[1002]   GERMAN MANUAL, para. 474.

[1003]   *Tadić*, decision on the defence motion for interlocutory appeal, paras. 120, 124 (regarding chemical weapons).

instance, a cyber operation that alters the running of a SCADA system controlling an electrical grid and results in a fire qualifies. Since the consequences are destructive, the operation is an attack.

4.   All members of the International Group of Experts agreed that the type of consequential harm set forth in this Rule qualifies an action as an attack, although, as discussed below, there are nuances to its application. The text of numerous Articles of Additional Protocol I, and the ICRC commentary thereto, supports this conclusion. For instance, Article 51(1) sets forth the general principle that the 'civilian population and individual civilians shall enjoy general protection against *dangers* arising from military operations'. Other Articles provide further support. The rules of proportionality speak of '*loss* of civilian life, *injury* to civilians, *damage* to civilian objects, or a combination thereof'.[1004] Those relating to protection of the environment refer to 'widespread, long-term, and severe *damage*',[1005] and the protection of dams, dykes, and nuclear electrical generating stations is framed in terms of 'severe *losses* among the civilian population'.[1006] The Experts agreed that *de minimis* damage or destruction does not meet the threshold of harm required by this Rule.

5.   The word 'cause' in this Rule is not limited to effects on the targeted cyber system. Rather, it encompasses any reasonably foreseeable consequential damage, destruction, injury, or death. Although cyber attacks seldom involve the release of direct physical force against the targeted cyber system, they can result in great harm to individuals or objects. For example, the release of dam waters by manipulating a SCADA system could cause extensive downstream destruction without damaging the system itself.

6.   The limitation in this Rule to operations against individuals or physical objects should not be understood as excluding cyber operations against data (which are non-physical entities) from the ambit of the term attack. Whenever an attack on data foreseeably results in the injury or death of individuals or damage or destruction of physical objects, those individuals or objects constitute the 'object of attack' and the operation therefore qualifies as an attack. Further, as discussed below, an operation against data upon which the functionality of physical objects relies can sometimes constitute an attack.

[1004] Additional Protocol I, Arts. 51(5)(b), 57(2)(a)(iii), 57(2)(b).
[1005] Additional Protocol I, Arts. 35(3), 55(1).   [1006] Additional Protocol I, Art. 56(1).

7. The phrase 'against the adversary' in Article 49(1) could cause confusion by suggesting that destructive operations must be directed at the enemy to qualify as attacks. The International Group of Experts agreed that such an interpretation would make little sense in light of, for instance, the prohibitions on attacking civilians and civilian objects.[1007] The Experts agreed that it is not the status of the cyber operation's target that qualifies it as an attack, but rather its consequences. Therefore, acts of violence, or those having violent effects, directed against civilians or civilian objects, or other protected persons or objects, are attacks.

8. While the notion of attack encompasses injury and death caused to individuals, the International Group of Experts agreed that it is, in light of the law of armed conflict's underlying humanitarian purposes, reasonable to extend the definition to serious illness and severe mental suffering that are tantamount to injury. In particular, note that Article 51 (2) of Additional Protocol I prohibits 'acts or threats of violence the primary purpose of which is to spread terror among the civilian population' (see also Rule 98). Since terror is a psychological condition resulting in mental suffering, inclusion of such suffering in this Rule is supportable through analogy.

9. With regard to digital cultural property, see Rule 142.

10. Within the International Group of Experts, there was extensive discussion about whether interference by cyber means with the functionality of an object constitutes damage or destruction for the purposes of this Rule. Although some of the Experts were of the opinion that it does not, a majority of them was of the view that interference with functionality qualifies as damage if restoration of functionality requires replacement of physical components. Consider a cyber operation that is directed against the computer-based control system of an electrical distribution grid. The operation causes the grid to cease operating. In order to restore distribution, either the control system or vital components thereof must be replaced. The cyber operation is an attack for the majority.

11. Some of the Experts in the majority further took the position that interference with functionality extends to situations in which reinstallation of the operating system or of particular data is required in order for the targeted cyber infrastructure to perform the function for which it was designed. They pointed in particular to purpose-built cyber

---

[1007] See also AMW MANUAL, commentary to Rule 1(e).

infrastructure designed to perform particular functions through manipulation of, or reliance upon, specific data. If, as a result of a cyber operation deleting or altering data, the infrastructure cannot perform its intended function, the operation in question, in the view of these Experts, amounts to an attack.

12.   Finally, a few Experts took the view that it is immaterial how an object is disabled; the loss of usability of cyber infrastructure constitutes damage that qualifies the cyber operation targeting it as an attack.[1008]

13.   The International Group of Experts discussed the characterisation of a cyber operation that does not cause the type of damage set forth above, but that results in large-scale adverse consequences, such as disrupting all email communications throughout the country (as distinct from damaging the system on which transmission relies). The majority of the Experts took the position that, although there might be logic in characterising the operation as an attack, the law of armed conflict does not presently extend this far. A minority took the position that should an armed conflict involving such cyber operations break out, the international community would generally regard them as attack. All Experts agreed, however, that relevant provisions of the law of armed conflict that address situations other than attack, such as the prohibition of collective punishment (Rule 144), apply to these operations.

14.   Notwithstanding disagreement over the precise definition of 'attack' in the cyber context, the International Group of Experts agreed that not all cyber operations qualify as attacks. For instance, it is clear that the term does not encompass cyber espionage *per se* unless the means or method by which it is conducted cause consequences that qualify as an attack (Rule 89). Moreover, it should not include cyber operations that would be akin to jamming because 'the jamming of radio communications or television broadcasts has not traditionally been considered an attack in the sense of [the law of armed conflict]'.[1009] In this regard, the Experts noted general agreement that cyber operations that merely cause inconvenience or irritation to the civilian population do not rise to the level of attack, although they cautioned that the scope of the term 'inconvenience' is unsettled.

15.   It should be noted that a cyber operation might not result in the requisite harm to the object of the operation, but cause foreseeable

---

[1008] ICRC Challenges Report, at 41.   [1009] ICRC Challenges Report, at 41–2.

collateral damage at the level set forth in this Rule. Such an operation amounts to an attack to which the relevant law of armed conflict applies, particularly that regarding proportionality (Rule 113).

16.   A cyber operation need not result in the intended destructive effect to qualify as an attack.[1010] During the negotiation of Additional Protocol I the issue of whether laying land mines constituted an attack arose. The 'general feeling' of the negotiators was that 'there is an attack whenever a person is directly endangered by a mine laid'.[1011] By analogy, the introduction of malware or production-level defects that are either time-delayed or activate on the occurrence of a particular event is an attack when the intended consequences meet the requisite threshold of harm. For the majority, this is so irrespective of whether they are activated. Some members, however, took the position that although there is no requirement that the cyber operation be successful, an attack only transpires once the malware is activated or the specified act occurs.

17.   An attack that is successfully intercepted and does not result in actual harm is still an attack under the law of armed conflict. Thus, a cyber operation that has been defeated by passive cyber defences such as firewalls, anti-virus software, and intrusion detection or prevention systems nevertheless qualifies as an attack if, absent such defences, it would have been likely to cause the requisite consequences.

18.   Cyber operations may be an integral part of an operation that constitutes an attack. As an example, a cyber operation may be used to disable defences of a target that is being kinetically attacked, as in the case of disabling the target's ability to employ electronic countermeasures that preclude a weapon from locking onto it. In such a case, the cyber operation is one component of an operation that qualifies as an attack, much as laser designation makes possible attacks using laser-guided bombs. The law of armed conflict on attacks applies fully to such cyber operations.

19.   If a cyber attack is conducted against civilians or civilian objects in the mistaken but reasonable belief that they constitute lawful targets, an attack has nonetheless occurred. However, if the attacker has fully complied with the requirement to verify the target (Rule 115), the attack will be lawful.

20.   It may be the case that the target of a cyber attack does not realise it has been attacked. For instance, a cyber attack directed

---

[1010] *See also* AMW MANUAL, commentary to Rule 1(e).
[1011] ICRC ADDITIONAL PROTOCOLS 1987 COMMENTARY, para. 1881.

against civilian infrastructure may be designed to appear as if the ensuing damage resulted from simple mechanical malfunction. The fact that a cyber attack is not recognised as such has no bearing on whether it qualifies as an attack and is subject to the law of armed conflict thereon.

21.   Care is required when identifying the originator of an attack. To illustrate, an individual may receive an email with an attachment containing malware. Execution of the malware, which occurs automatically upon opening, will cause the requisite level of harm. If that individual unwittingly forwards the email and it does cause such harm, he or she will not have conducted an attack; the email's originator will have done so. By contrast, if the intermediary forwards the email knowing it contains the malware, both individuals will have conducted the attack.

Rule 93 – Distinction

The principle of distinction applies to cyber attacks.

1.   The 1868 St Petersburg Declaration provides that 'the only legitimate object which States should endeavour to accomplish during war is to weaken the military forces of the enemy'. This general principle is the foundation upon which the principle of distinction is based. The principle of distinction is one of two 'cardinal' principles of the law of armed conflict recognised by the International Court of Justice in its advisory opinion on the *Legality of the Threat or Use of Nuclear Weapons*.[1012] The other is the prohibition of unnecessary suffering (Rule 104). According to the Court, these principles of customary international law are 'intransgressible'.[1013]

2.   Article 48 of Additional Protocol I codifies the customary international law principle: 'In order to ensure respect for and protection of the civilian population and civilian objects, the Parties to the conflict shall at all times distinguish between the civilian population and combatants and between civilian objects and military objectives and accordingly shall direct their operations only against military

---

[1012] *Nuclear Weapons* advisory opinion, para. 78. According to the Court, 'States must never make civilians the object of attack and must consequently never use weapons that are incapable of distinguishing between civilian and military targets.'

[1013] *Nuclear Weapons* advisory opinion, para. 79.

objectives.' The principle applies in both international and non-international armed conflict. It is included in virtually all military law of armed conflict manuals, is cited in unofficial compilations of the customary international law of armed conflict, and appears in the statutes of international tribunals.[1014]

3.   In non-international armed conflict, the principle of distinction obliges the parties to distinguish between civilians, on the one hand, and members of State armed forces and organised armed groups, including members of the regular or dissident armed forces, on the other.[1015] The International Group of Experts agreed that this obligation also requires the parties to distinguish between military objectives and civilian objects despite the fact that Article 13 of Additional Protocol II was originally not meant to extend to civilian objects.[1016]

4.   Articles 51 and 52 of Additional Protocol I reflect the principle of distinction by setting forth protections for the civilian population and civilian objects respectively (Rules 94–102). It also undergirds various Articles that extend special protection to particular protected persons and objects,[1017] and is the basis from which the rule of proportionality (Rule 113) and the requirement to take precautions in attack arise (Rules 114–120).

5.   Certain operations directed against the civilian population are lawful.[1018] For instance, psychological operations such as dropping leaflets or making propaganda broadcasts are not prohibited even if civilians are the intended audience.[1019] In the context of cyber warfare, transmitting email messages to the enemy population urging capitulation would

---

[1014] *See, e.g.,* DoD Manual, para. 2.5; UK Manual, para. 2.5–2.5.3 (as amended); Canadian Manual, para. 423; AMW Manual, Rule 10; NIAC Manual, para. 1.2.2; ICRC Customary IHL Study, Rules 1, 7; San Remo Manual, Rule 39; Rome Statute, Art. 8(2)(b)(i–ii), 8(2)(e)(i–ii).

[1015] NIAC Manual, para. 1.2.2. In *Tadić*, the International Criminal Tribunal for the Former Yugoslavia recognised distinction as applicable in non-international armed conflict. *Tadić*, decision on the defence motion for interlocutory appeal, paras. 122, 127.

[1016] ICRC Additional Protocols 1987 Commentary, para. 4759 (noting that Art. 13 of Protocol II provides no general protection for civilian objects). *But see* NIAC Manual, para. 1.2.2; ICRC Customary IHL Study, Rule 10 (identifying general protection for civilian objects in non-international armed conflict).

[1017] Additional Protocol I, Arts. 53–56.

[1018] ICRC Additional Protocols 1987 Commentary, para. 1875.

[1019] AMW Manual, commentary accompanying Rule 13(b). Of course, this is only so long as the actions do not violate the prohibition on terrorising the civilian population set forth in Rule 98.

likewise comport with the law of armed conflict.[1020] Only when a cyber operation against civilians or civilian objects (or other protected persons and objects) rises to the level of an attack is it prohibited by the principle of distinction and those rules of the law of armed conflict that derive from the principle. Whether a particular cyber operation qualifies as an 'attack' is the subject of Rule 92. Accordingly, and without prejudice to the requirement to take 'constant care' (Rule 114), the practical application of the principle of distinction in the cyber context is dependent in great part on the position one takes with regard to the definition of 'cyber attack' (Rule 92).[1021]

6.   Since the principle of distinction is intransgressible, any rationale or justification for an attack not permitted by the law of armed conflict is irrelevant in determining whether the principle has been violated.[1022] As an example, an attack against a civilian object would be unlawful even if it shortened the course of the conflict and thereby saved civilian lives. Similarly, cyber attacks against a civilian leader's private property designed to pressure him into capitulation would be unlawful if the property qualifies as a civilian object irrespective of whether the attacks would achieve their intended purpose.

7.   The principle of distinction, as used in this Rule, must not be confused with the obligation of combatants to distinguish themselves from the civilian population (Rule 87).

SECTION 3:   ATTACKS AGAINST PERSONS

Rule 94 – Prohibition of attacking civilians

The civilian population as such, as well as individual civilians, shall not be the object of cyber attack.

1.   This rule is based on the principle of distinction, set forth in Rule 93. It has been codified in Article 51(2) of Additional Protocol I and Article 13(2)

[1020] During the 2003 invasion of Iraq, '[t]housands of Iraqi military officers received e-mails on the Iraqi Defense Ministry e-mail system just before the war started'. They were told to place tanks and armoured vehicles in formation and abandon them, walk away, and go home. Richard A. Clarke and Robert K. Knake, CYBERWARFARE: THE NEXT THREAT TO NATIONAL SECURITY AND WHAT TO DO ABOUT IT (2010), at 9–10.

[1021] ICRC Challenges Report, at 41.

[1022] Of course, if a civilian is attacking a member of the armed forces for reasons unrelated to the conflict, the member of the armed forces may defend him or herself. This principle applies in the cyber context.

of Additional Protocol II and is undoubtedly reflective of customary international law in both international and non-international armed conflict.[1023]

2. As to the definition of 'civilian', see Rule 91. The 'civilian population' comprises all persons who are civilians. The presence within the civilian population of individuals who do not come within the definition of civilians does not deprive the population of its civilian character.[1024]

3. For a cyber operation to be prohibited by this Rule, it must qualify as an attack. The term 'attack' is defined in Rule 92.

4. Under this Rule, the 'object' of a cyber attack is the person against whom the cyber operation is directed. Although protected from being made the object of attack, civilians lose their protection for such time as they directly participate in hostilities (Rule 97).

5. To qualify as the object of an attack, the harm to the relevant person (or object) must meet the level set forth in Rule 92. For instance, consider the case of a cyber operation intended to harm a particular individual by manipulating her medical information stored in a hospital's database. She would be the object of attack, but the database would not be if the damage thereto does not rise to the level required for an attack. By contrast, consider the case of a cyber attack against the SCADA system of a chemical plant that is designed to cause an explosion. The explosion is planned to result in the release of toxic substances that will kill the surrounding population. The chemical plant and the population are both objects of attack because the requisite level of harm is reached as to each of them.

6. The fact that a cyber attack directed against a military objective (Rule 100) foreseeably causes incidental damage, destruction, injury, or death to civilians or civilian objects does not make those individuals and objects the 'objects of attack'. Consider a cyber operation designed to down military aircraft by attacking a military air traffic control system. The aircraft are lawful objects of attack. However, civilians on the ground who are injured or killed when the aircraft crash would not constitute objects of the attack. Instead, any protection such persons enjoy would derive from the rule of proportionality (Rule 113) and the requirement to take precautions in attack (Rules 114–120).

[1023] DoD Manual, paras. 5.3.2, 17.5; UK Manual, paras. 2.5.2 (as amended), 5.3; Canadian Manual, paras. 312, 423; German Manual, paras. 404, 502; AMW Manual, Rule 11 and accompanying commentary; NIAC Manual, para. 2.1.1.1; ICRC Customary IHL Study, Rule 1. *See also* Rome Statute, Art. 8(2)(b)(i–ii), 8(2)(e)(i–ii); *Martić* judgment, paras. 67–69; *Galić* Appeals Chamber judgment, paras. 190–192.
[1024] Additional Protocol I, Art. 50(2–3).

Rule 95 – Doubt as to status of persons

In case of doubt as to whether a person is a civilian, that person shall be considered to be a civilian.

1.   The International Group of Experts concluded that Rule 95 is reflective of customary international law and is applicable in international and non-international armed conflicts.[1025] The presumption of civilian status in cases of doubt is codified in Article 50(1) of Additional Protocol I. Some law of armed conflict manuals recognise this Rule.[1026]

2.   A number of Experts were unable to accept an interpretation of the Rule whereby the attacker alone bears the burden of disproving civilian status in cases of doubt. They noted that since a defender has an obligation to take passive precautions (Rule 121), such an outcome would be inappropriate. Subject to this interpretation, they accepted inclusion of Rule 95 in this Manual.

3.   The precise threshold at which the doubt is sufficient to bring this Rule into operation is unsettled. On ratification of Additional Protocol I, a number of States Parties made relevant statements concerning Article 50(1). The United Kingdom, for instance, observed that the Article applies only in cases of 'substantial doubt still remaining' after 'assessment of the information from all sources which is reasonably available to them at the relevant time'.[1027] In contrast to substantial doubt, the concept of 'reasonable doubt' has been used for the purposes of determining liability under international criminal law.[1028] Whatever the precise threshold of doubt necessary to bring the Rule into play, it is clear that the mere existence of some doubt is insufficient to establish a breach.

4.   The issue of doubt is especially important in the cyber context. In many countries, the use of computers and computer networks by civilians is pervasive, and the networks that civilians and the armed forces use may be conjoined. In such cases, computer use, or the use of a particular network, may not *per se* indicate military status. This predicament is compounded by the fact that the individuals are usually not physically visible while engaged in cyber activities.

[1025] *See, e.g.*, AMW Manual, commentary accompanying Rule 12(a); ICRC Customary IHL Study commentary accompanying Rule 6.

[1026] UK Manual, para. 5.3.1; Canadian Manual, para. 429.

[1027] UK Additional Protocol Ratification Statement, para. (h); UK Manual, para. 5.3.4 (as amended).

[1028] *Galić* Trial Chamber judgment, para. 55.

5.   The presumption as to civilian status is distinct from the issue of uncertainty as to direct participation in hostilities. In other words, the presumption set forth in this Rule applies when there is doubt as to whether the individual is a combatant or civilian. In the case of direct participation, the individual is by definition a civilian; thus, the matters about which doubt can exist relate to that individual's activities, not his or her status. On the presumption in the context of direct participation, see Rule 97.

6.   Although there is no directly equivalent rule in the law relating to non-international armed conflicts because the notion of combatancy does not exist in those conflicts (Rule 87), the customary principle of distinction applies. Consequently, during non-international armed conflicts, a presumption that an individual is a civilian protected against attack attaches whenever sufficient doubt on the matter exists.

Rule 96 – Persons as lawful objects of attack

The following persons may be made the object of cyber attacks:

(a) members of the armed forces;
(b) members of organised armed groups;
(c) civilians, if and for such time as they take a direct part in hostilities; and
(d) in an international armed conflict, participants in a *levée en masse*.

1.   This Rule applies in both international and non-international armed conflict, except as noted in *lit.* (d).[1029] Its precise formulation is derived by negative implication from other Rules set forth in this Manual. Rule 94 prohibits attacks against civilians, thereby suggesting that, subject to other restrictions in the law of armed conflict, those who are not civilians may be attacked. Rule 97 provides that despite being civilians, individuals who directly participate in hostilities lose their protection from attack. With regard to a *levée en masse*, the conclusion that its participants may be attacked is drawn by inference from the fact that they enjoy combatant status (Rule 88).

2.   Status or conduct may render an individual liable to attack. The targetability of the first two categories of persons is based on their

---

[1029] NIAC MANUAL, para. 2.1.1.

status, whereas the targetability of the latter two depends on the conduct in which they engage.

3.   The term 'members of the armed forces' is defined and discussed in Rule 87. In general, it refers to members of the regular armed forces and groups, such as certain volunteer groups or resistance movements, that are assimilated to the regular armed forces. However, members of the armed forces who are medical or religious personnel, or who are *hors de combat*, are not subject to attack.[1030] Individuals are *hors de combat* if they have been wounded or are sick and they are neither engaging in hostile acts nor attempting to escape, have been captured, or have surrendered. A member of the armed forces who, despite being sick or wounded, continues to engage in cyber operations directed against the enemy, or that enhance or preserve his or her own side's military capabilities, is not *hors de combat*.[1031]

4.   The International Group of Experts was divided over qualification as a member of an organised armed group (Rule 83) with respect to both international and non-international armed conflict. Some of the Experts took the position that mere membership in such a group suffices. In other words, once it is reliably established that an individual belongs to an organised armed group, that individual may be attacked on the same basis as a member of the armed forces. Other Experts adopted the position set forth in the ICRC Interpretive Guidance, which limits membership in organised armed groups to those individuals with a 'continuous combat function'.[1032] For these Experts, individuals who do not have such a function are to be treated as civilians who may only be attacked for such time as they directly participate in hostilities.

5.   All members of the International Group of Experts agreed that, with regard to a group that consists of both military and political or social wings, only the military wing qualifies as an organised armed group. As

---

[1030] Geneva Convention I, Arts. 24–25; Additional Protocol I, Art. 41; DoD MANUAL, para. 5.6.2; UK MANUAL, para. 5.6; CANADIAN MANUAL, para. 309; GERMAN MANUAL, para. 601; AMW MANUAL, Rule 15(b); NIAC MANUAL, paras. 2.3.2, 3.2; ICRC CUSTOMARY IHL STUDY, Rule 87.

[1031] *See, e.g.,* ICRC ADDITIONAL PROTOCOLS 1987 COMMENTARY, paras. 1621–1622 (characterising an attempt to communicate with one's own side as a 'hostile act').

[1032] ICRC INTERPRETIVE GUIDANCE, at 27. The notion involves an individual undertaking a 'continuous function for the group involving his or her direct participation in hostilities'. *Id.* at 33.

to civilians who are not members of an organised armed group but who directly participate in hostilities, see Rule 97.

6. The International Group of Experts was also divided over whether an organised armed group involved in an international armed conflict must 'belong to a party to the conflict' to be subject to this Rule. For instance, a particular group may be involved in cyber attacks for reasons other than providing support to one of the parties, such as religious or ethnic animosity towards their opponent or a desire to take advantage of the instability generated by the armed conflict to accumulate power. The notion of 'belonging to a party' is examined in Rule 87. Some Experts adopted the approach taken in the ICRC Interpretive Guidance by which members of a group that does not belong to a party to the conflict are to be treated as civilians for the purposes of that conflict.[1033] Accordingly, they can only be targeted for such time as they directly participate in hostilities. Other Experts took the position that for the purposes of this Rule, there is no requirement that a group belong to a party; all members of the group may be targeted based on their status as such.

7. An interesting question in this regard is the qualification of private contractors. The International Group of Experts agreed that individual contractors are civilians who may only be targeted based on their direct participation in the hostilities (Rule 97). The more difficult case involves a company that has been contracted by a party to the conflict to perform specific military operations such as cyber attacks against the enemy. The majority of Experts took the position that the company qualifies as an organised armed group belonging to a party.[1034] By contrast, the minority was of the view the contractual relationship would not be seen as a sufficient basis for regarding the company as belonging to a party (Rule 97). However, even according to the minority view, those members of the company directly participating in the hostilities may be attacked.

8. Civilian government employees, such as members of intelligence agencies, sometimes conduct cyber operations during an armed conflict.

[1033] The Guidance does note that the group may be a party to a separate non-international armed conflict with its opponent if the violence reaches the required threshold. ICRC INTERPRETIVE GUIDANCE, at 23–24.

[1034] See ICRC INTERPRETIVE GUIDANCE, at 38–39 (noting that contractors effectively incorporated into the armed forces of a party to the conflict by being given a continuous combat function would become members of an organised armed group and would no longer, for the purposes of the distinction principle, qualify as civilians). On qualification as an organised armed group, see Rule 83.

In the event a particular group of such individuals qualifies as an organised armed group, its members are subject to attack in accordance with this Rule. Other civilian government employees are civilians who are targetable only for such time as they directly participate in hostilities (Rule 97).

9.   Persons who are taking part in a *levée en masse* are targetable throughout the period of their participation therein. For targeting purposes, they are not treated as civilians directly participating in hostilities, that is, the 'for such time' criterion does not apply (Rule 97). The criteria for qualification as a *levée en masse* are discussed in Rule 88.

Rule 97 – Civilian direct participants in hostilities

Civilians enjoy protection against attack unless and for such time as they directly participate in hostilities.

1.   This Rule is drawn from Article 51(3) of Additional Protocol I and Article 13(3) of Additional Protocol II. It is customary international law in both international and non-international armed conflict.[1035]

2.   Rule 97 does not apply to members of the armed forces, organised armed groups, or participants in a *levée en masse*. For the purposes of this Rule, such individuals are not civilians.[1036] The Rule's application is limited to individuals who engage in hostilities without affiliation to any such group and to members of an *ad hoc* group that does not qualify as an 'organised armed group' (for instance, because it lacks the requisite degree of organisation). On the requirements for qualification as an organised armed group, especially with regard to 'continuous combat function', see Rule 96.

3.   An act of direct participation in hostilities by civilians renders them liable to be attacked by cyber or other lawful means. Additionally, harm to direct participants is not considered when assessing the proportionality of an attack (Rule 113) or determining the precautions

---

[1035] DoD Manual, paras. 5.9, 17.6; UK Manual, paras. 5.3.2 (as amended), 15.8; Canadian Manual, paras. 318, 1720; German Manual, para. 517; AMW Manual, chapeau to Sec. F; NIAC Manual, paras. 1.1.3, 2.1.1.2; ICRC Customary IHL Study, Rule 6.

[1036] The ICRC Interpretive Guidance limits its analysis of civilian status to situations involving the conduct of hostilities. ICRC Interpretive Guidance, at 11. That analysis, like that set forth in this Commentary, is without prejudice to the question of civilian status for other purposes, such as detention.

that must be taken to avoid harming civilians during military operations (Rules 114–120).

4.   In the cyber context, it is essential to emphasise that an 'act' is required by the individual concerned. For instance, an unwitting person whose computer has become a part of a botnet used for cyber attack is not, without more, a direct participant. However, in such a case, the computer itself may qualify as a military objective, provided it fulfils the definition of military objective under the circumstances ruling at the time (Rule 100).[1037]

5.   The International Group of Experts generally agreed with the three cumulative criteria for qualification of an act as direct participation that are set forth in the ICRC Interpretive Guidance. First, the act (or a closely related series of acts) must have the intended or actual effect of negatively affecting the adversary's military operations or capabilities, or inflicting death, physical harm, or material destruction on persons or objects protected against direct attack (threshold of harm).[1038] There is no requirement for physical damage to objects or harm to individuals. In other words, actions that do not qualify as a cyber attack will satisfy this criterion so long as they negatively affect the enemy militarily. An example of an operation satisfying the criterion is a cyber operation that disrupts the enemy's command and control network. Some members of the International Group of Experts took the position that acts that enhance one's own military capacity are included, as they necessarily weaken an adversary's relative position. An example is maintaining passive cyber defences of military cyber assets. Second, a direct causal link between the act in question and the harm intended or inflicted must exist (causal link).[1039] In the example where disruption is caused to the enemy's command and control centre, the disruption is directly caused by the cyber attack;

[1037] It must be cautioned that bots will often be located in at least some neutral States during an international armed conflict and therefore operations targeting them are subject to the restrictions and limitations found in Rule 150.

[1038] 'In order to reach the required threshold of harm, a specific act must be likely to adversely affect the military operations or military capacity of a party to an armed conflict or, alternatively, to inflict death, injury, or destruction on persons or objects protected against direct attack.' ICRC INTERPRETIVE GUIDANCE, at 47. See also AMW MANUAL, commentary accompanying Rule 29.

[1039] 'In order for the requirement of direct causation to be satisfied, there must be a direct causal link between a specific act and the harm likely to result either from that act, or from a coordinated military operation of which that act constitutes an integral part.' ICRC INTERPRETIVE GUIDANCE at 51. See also AMW MANUAL, commentary to Rule 29.

the criterion is met. Finally, the acts must be directly related to the hostilities (belligerent nexus).[1040] In the example, the fact that the system is used to direct enemy military operations fulfils the condition. It must be cautioned that although the majority agreed on these criteria, differences of opinion existed as to their precise application to particular actions.[1041]

6.   Clearly, conducting cyber attacks related to an armed conflict qualifies as an act of direct participation, as do any actions that make possible specific attacks, such as identifying vulnerabilities in a targeted system or designing malware in order to take advantage of particular vulnerabilities. Other unambiguous examples include gathering information on enemy operations by cyber means and passing it to one's own State's armed forces and conducting DDoS operations against enemy military external systems. On the other hand, designing malware and making it openly available online, even if it may be used by someone involved in the conflict to conduct an attack, does not constitute direct participation. Neither would be maintaining computer equipment generally, even if such equipment is subsequently used in the hostilities. A more difficult situation arises when malware is developed and provided to individuals in circumstances where it is clear that it will be used to conduct attacks, but where the precise intended target is unknown to the supplier. The International Group of Experts was divided as to whether the causal connection between the act of providing the malware and the subsequent attack is, in such a situation, sufficiently direct to qualify as direct participation.

7.   The criterion of belligerent nexus rules out acts of a purely criminal or private nature that occur during an armed conflict. For example, criminals who use cyber means to steal State funds belonging to a party to the conflict, but with a view to private gain, would not be direct participants in hostilities. Some members of the International Group of Experts, however, were of the view that if individuals use cyber means to steal funds, private or public, such theft would constitute direct

---

[1040] 'In order to meet the requirement of belligerent nexus, an act must be specifically designed to directly cause the required threshold of harm in support of a party to the conflict and to the detriment of another.' ICRC INTERPRETIVE GUIDANCE, at 58. See also AMW MANUAL, commentary accompanying Rule 29.

[1041] For instance, there is a well-known, on-going debate over whether assembly of improvised explosive devices or acting as a voluntary human shield qualifies as direct participation.

participation if, for example, the operation was conducted to finance particular military operations.

8.   Any act of direct participation in hostilities by a civilian renders that person targetable for such time as he or she is engaged in the qualifying act of direct participation.[1042] All of the Experts agreed that this would at least include actions immediately preceding or subsequent to the qualifying act.[1043] For instance, travelling to and from the location where a computer used to mount an operation is based would be encompassed in the notion. Some of the Experts took the position that the period of participation extended as far 'upstream' and 'downstream' as a causal link existed.[1044] In a cyber operation, this period might begin once an individual began probing the target system for vulnerabilities, extend throughout the duration of activities against that system, and include the period during which damage is assessed to determine whether 're-attack' is required.

9.   A particularly important issue in the cyber context is that of 'delayed effects'. An example is emplacement of a logic bomb designed to activate at some future point. Activation may occur upon lapse of a predetermined period, on command, or upon the performance of a particular action by the target system (e.g., activation of the fire control radar of a surface-to-air missile site). The majority of the International Group of Experts took the position that the duration of an individual's direct participation extends from the beginning of his involvement in mission planning to the point when he or she terminates an active role in the operation. In the example, the duration of the direct participation would run from the commencement of planning how to emplace the logic bomb through activation upon command by that individual. Note that the end of the period of direct participation may not necessarily correspond with the point at which the damage occurs. This would be so in the case of emplacement of the logic bomb by one individual and later activation by another. The key with regard to targetability is ascertaining when a particular individual's participation begins and ends.

10.   A minority of the International Group of Experts would characterise emplacement and activation by the same individual as separate acts of direct participation. By their view, the completion of emplacement would end the first period of direct participation and taking steps later to

---

[1042]   For further elaboration, see ICRC INTERPRETIVE GUIDANCE, at 70–73.
[1043]   ICRC INTERPRETIVE GUIDANCE, at 67–68.
[1044]   See DINSTEIN, CONDUCT OF HOSTILITIES, at 177.

activate the logic bomb would mark the commencement of a second period.

11.   A further issue regarding the period of direct participation, and thus susceptibility to attack, involves a situation in which an individual launches repeated cyber operations that qualify as direct participation. Such circumstances are highly likely to arise in the context of cyber operations, for an individual may mount numerous separate operations over time, either against the same cyber target or different ones. The International Group of Experts was split on the consequence of repeated actions with regard to the duration issue. Some of the Experts took the position, adopted in the ICRC Interpretive Guidance, that each act must be treated separately in terms of direct participation analysis.[1045] Other Experts argued that this position makes little operational sense. It would create a 'revolving door' of direct participation, and thus of targetability. For these Experts, direct participation begins with the first such cyber operation and continues throughout the period of intermittent activity.

12.   Consider the example of an individual hacktivist who has conducted, over the course of one month, seven cyber attacks against the enemy's command and control system. By the first view, the hacktivist was only targetable while conducting each individual attack. By the second, he was targetable for the entire month. Moreover, in the absence of a clear indication that the hacktivist would no longer engage in such attacks, he or she would have remained targetable beyond that period.

13.   The International Group of Experts was divided over the issue of whether a presumption against direct participation applies. Some Experts took the position that, in case of doubt as to whether a civilian is engaging in an act of direct participation (or as to whether a certain type of activity rises to the level of direct participation), a presumption against direct participation attaches.[1046] Other Experts objected to the analogy to Rule 95 (regarding the presumption in cases of doubt as to status). They were of the view that when doubt exists, the attacker must, as a matter of law, review all of the relevant information and act reasonably in the circumstances when deciding whether to conduct the attack. No presumption attaches.

[1045] ICRC INTERPRETIVE GUIDANCE, at 44–45, 70–71.
[1046] For the argument in favour of such a presumption, see ICRC INTERPRETIVE GUIDANCE, at 75–76.

Rule 98 – Terror attacks

Cyber attacks, or the threat thereof, the primary purpose of which is to spread terror among the civilian population, are prohibited.

1. Rule 98 is based upon Article 51(2) of Additional Protocol I and Article 13(2) of Additional Protocol II. It reflects customary international law and applies equally in non-international and international armed conflict.[1047]

2. To breach this Rule, a cyber operation must amount to a 'cyber attack', or threat thereof, as that term is applied and interpreted in Rule 92. The limitation to cyber attacks is supported by the ICRC Additional Protocols 1987 Commentary, which notes with respect to Article 51(2) that: 'This provision is intended to prohibit acts of violence the primary purpose of which is to spread terror among the civilian population without offering substantial military advantage.'[1048] As an example of the Rule's application, a cyber attack against a mass transit system that causes death or injury violates the Rule if the primary purpose of the attack is to terrorise the civilian population. It should be noted that such an operation would also constitute an unlawful attack against civilians and civilian objects (Rules 94 and 99).

3. The prohibition in this Rule extends to threats of cyber attacks, whether conveyed by cyber or non-cyber means. For instance, a threat to use a cyber attack to disable a city's water distribution system to contaminate drinking water and cause death or illness would violate the Rule if made with the primary purpose of spreading terror among the civilian population. On the other hand, consider the example of a false tweet (Twitter message) sent out in order to cause panic, falsely indicating that a highly contagious and deadly disease is spreading rapidly throughout the population. Because the tweet is neither an attack (Rule 92) nor a threat thereof, it does not violate this Rule.

4. It must be emphasised that the essence of the prohibition is its focus on the purpose of the cyber attack, specifically the spreading of terror among a civilian population. While a lawful cyber attack against a military objective, including combatants, might cause terror, this is not the type of attack addressed in this Rule. As noted in the ICRC

[1047] *Galić* Appeals Chamber judgment, paras. 86–98, 101–104; DoD MANUAL, paras. 5.3.2, 17.5; UK MANUAL, paras. 5.21, 5.21.1; CANADIAN MANUAL, paras. 617, 1720; GERMAN MANUAL, para. 507; NIAC MANUAL, para. 2.3.9; ICRC CUSTOMARY IHL STUDY, Rule 2; AMW MANUAL, Rule 18 and accompanying commentary.

[1048] ICRC ADDITIONAL PROTOCOLS 1987 COMMENTARY, para. 1940 (emphasis added).

Additional Protocols 1987 Commentary to Article 51(2), 'there is no doubt that acts of violence related to a state of war almost always give rise to some degree of terror among the population'.[1049]

5.   A violation of Rule 98 requires an intent to spread terror amongst the population. The International Group of Experts agreed that terrifying one or only a few individuals, even if that is the primary purpose of the act or threat, does not suffice, although engaging in an act of violence against one person in order to terrorise a significant segment of the population would violate this Rule.[1050] Consensus also existed that this Rule does not prohibit conducting attacks against enemy combatants in order to terrorise them.

6.   The text of Rule 98 only extends to conducting or threatening cyber terror attacks. However, employing cyber means to communicate a threat of kinetic attack with the primary purpose of terrorising the civilian population is likewise prohibited by the law of armed conflict.

7.   It should be noted that Article 33 of Geneva Convention IV prohibits 'measures of intimidation or of terrorism'. Unlike the norm set forth in Article 51(2) of Additional Protocol I, which is reflected in this Rule, the Article 33 prohibition is not limited to attacks that have a primary purpose of terrorising those individuals. However, it extends only to protected persons as defined in Article 4 of that treaty. A minority of the International Group of Experts took the position that the confluence of Article 33, Article 51(2), and State practice has resulted in a customary norm prohibiting any operations, including cyber operations, intended (whether the primary purpose or not) to terrorise the civilian population.

SECTION 4:   ATTACKS AGAINST OBJECTS

Rule 99 – Prohibition of attacking civilian objects

Civilian objects shall not be made the object of cyber attacks. Cyber infrastructure may only be made the object of attack if it qualifies as a military objective.

1.   The prohibition of attacking civilian objects derives historically from the 1868 St Petersburg Declaration, which provided that 'the only

---

[1049] ICRC ADDITIONAL PROTOCOLS 1987 COMMENTARY, para. 1940. *See also* UK MANUAL, para. 5.21.1; ICRC ADDITIONAL PROTOCOLS 1987 COMMENTARY, para. 4786.
[1050] *Galić* Trial Chamber judgment, para. 133.

legitimate object which States should endeavour to accomplish during war is to weaken the military forces of the enemy'.[1051] This norm has since been codified in Article 52(1) of Additional Protocol I and applies in international and non-international armed conflict as customary international law.[1052]

2. For the definition of 'cyber infrastructure' see the Glossary.

3. To be prohibited by this Rule, a cyber operation must qualify as an 'attack'. The term attack is defined in Rule 92.

4. Civilian objects are those objects that do not qualify as military objectives. Civilian objects and military objectives are defined in Rule 100. The International Group of Experts agreed that the determination of whether an object is a civilian object protected from attack, and not a military objective, must be made on a case-by-case basis.

5. The mere fact that a cyber attack is directed against a civilian object is sufficient to violate this Rule; it does not matter whether the attack is unsuccessful.

6. It is important to distinguish this Rule, which prohibits directing cyber attacks at civilian objects, from that which prohibits indiscriminate cyber attacks (Rule 111). The present Rule prohibits attacks that make a protected object the 'object of attack'. In other words, the attacker is 'aiming' at the civilian object in question. Indiscriminate attacks, by contrast, are unlawful because they are not directed at any particular object (or person), irrespective of whether some of the targets struck qualify as military objectives. This Rule must also be distinguished from Rule 105, which prohibits the use of indiscriminate methods or means of warfare.

Rule 100 – Civilian objects and military objectives

Civilian objects are all objects that are not military objectives. Military objectives are those objects which by their nature, location, purpose, or use, make an effective contribution to military action and whose total or partial destruction, capture or neutralisation, in the

---

[1051] St Petersburg Declaration, pmbl. *See also* Hague Regulations, Art. 25 (noting 'attack or bombardment . . . of towns, villages, dwellings, or buildings which are undefended is prohibited').

[1052] DoD MANUAL, paras. 5.6.2, 17.5; UK MANUAL, para. 5.24; CANADIAN MANUAL, para. 423; GERMAN MANUAL, para. 451; AMW MANUAL, Rule 11 and accompanying commentary; NIAC MANUAL, para. 2.1.1.1; ICRC CUSTOMARY IHL STUDY, Rules 7, 9, 10. *See also* Rome Statute, Art. 8(2)(b)(ii), 8(2)(e)(iii, xii).

circumstances ruling at the time, offers a definite military advantage. Cyber infrastructure may qualify as a military objectives.

1.   Article 52(1) of Additional Protocol I defines civilian objects in the negative as 'all objects which are not military objectives'. The term 'military objective' was first defined in the 1923 Hague Draft Rules of Air Warfare as 'an objective whereof the total or partial destruction would constitute an obvious military advantage for the belligerent'.[1053] It has since been codified in Article 52(2) of Additional Protocol I, which defines military objectives as 'those objects which by their nature, location, purpose or use make an effective contribution to military action and whose total or partial destruction, capture or neutralisation, in the circumstances ruling at the time, offers a definite military advantage'. This definition has been adopted by many States in their military manuals and is considered reflective of customary international law in both non-international and international armed conflict.[1054] It also appears in numerous other treaty instruments.[1055]

2.   For the definition of 'cyber infrastructure', see the Glossary.

3.   As used in this Manual, the term 'military objectives' refers only to those objects meeting the definition set forth in this Rule. The International Group of Experts took this approach on the basis that the lawful targetability of individuals is dependent on either status (Rule 96) or conduct (Rule 97), and therefore requires a different analysis from that set forth in Article 52(2) of Additional Protocol I.

4.   The term 'military objective' is being used in this Rule, and throughout the Manual, in its legal sense. It is a term of art in the law of armed conflict. This legal term is not to be confused with the meaning of the military objective in operational usage, that is, the goal of a military operation. For example, an operation may be designed to neutralise particular electronic communications. The messages are military objectives in the operational sense, but they do not constitute a military objective in the legal sense for the reasons set forth below. However, the hardware necessary to transmit and receive the messages would amount to a military objective in the legal sense.

[1053]   Hague Air Warfare Rules, Art. 24(1).

[1054]   DoD Manual, para. 5.7.1.1; UK Manual, para. 5.4.1; Canadian Manual, para. 406; German Manual, para. 442; AMW Manual, Rule 1(y); NIAC Manual, para. 1.1.4; ICRC Customary IHL Study, Rule 8; San Remo Manual, Rule 40.

[1055]   Mines Protocol, Art. 2(4); Protocol on Prohibitions and Restrictions on the Use of Incendiary Weapons, Art. 1(3), 10 October 1980, 1342 UNTS 137.

5. The meaning of the term 'object' is essential to understanding this and other Rules found in the Manual. An 'object' is characterised in the ICRC Additional Protocols 1987 Commentary as something 'visible and tangible'.[1056] This usage is not to be confused with the meaning ascribed to the term in the field of computer science, which connotes entities that can be manipulated by the commands of a programming language. For the purpose of this Manual, computers, computer networks, and other tangible components of cyber infrastructure constitute objects.

6. The majority of the International Group of Experts agreed that the law of armed conflict notion of 'object' is not to be interpreted as including data, at least in the current state of the law. In the view of these Experts, data is intangible and therefore neither falls within the 'ordinary meaning' of the term object,[1057] nor comports with the explanation of it offered in the ICRC Additional Protocols 1987 Commentary. Therefore, an attack on data *per se* does not qualify as an attack. They agreed, however, that, as noted in Rule 92, a cyber operation targeting data may sometimes qualify as an attack when the operation affects the functionality of cyber infrastructure or results in other consequences that would qualify the cyber operation in question as an attack.

7. A minority of the Experts was of the opinion that, for the purposes of targeting, certain data should be regarded as an object. In their view, the majority position is under inclusive in the sense that failure to include cyber operations targeting data *per se* in the scope of the term 'attack' would mean that even the deletion of essential civilian datasets such as social security data, tax records, and bank accounts would potentially escape the regulatory reach of the law of armed conflict, thereby running counter to the principle (reflected in Article 48 of Additional Protocol I) that the civilian population enjoys general protection from the effects of hostilities. For these Experts, the key factor, based on the underlying object and purpose of Article 52 of Additional Protocol I, is one of the severity of the operation's consequences, not the nature of harm. Thus, they were of the view that, at a minimum, civilian data that is 'essential' to the well-being of the civilian population is encompassed in the notion of civilian objects and protected as such.[1058]

[1056] ICRC Additional Protocols 1987 Commentary, paras. 2007–2008.
[1057] Vienna Convention on the Law of Treaties, Art. 31(1).
[1058] ICRC Challenges Report, at 41–42.

8.   Objects may qualify as military objectives based on any of the four criteria set forth in the Rule (nature, location, purpose, or use).[1059] 'Nature' involves the inherent character of an object, and typically refers to those objects that are fundamentally military and designed to contribute to military action.[1060] Military computers and other military cyber infrastructure are paradigmatic examples of objects that satisfy the nature criterion. Of particular importance in the cyber context are military command, control, communications, computer, intelligence, surveillance, and reconnaissance ('C4ISR') systems. For instance, military cyber systems, wherever located, and the facilities in which they are permanently housed, qualify as military objectives. The fact that civilians (whether government employees or contractors) may be operating these systems is irrelevant to the question of whether they qualify as military objectives.

9.   Objects may also qualify as military objectives by their 'location'. Location normally refers to a geographical area of particular military importance;[1061] therefore, for instance, an IP address (or a range of IP addresses) is not a location (although it is associated with cyber infrastructure that may qualify as a military objective). It is not the actual use of an area but the fact that by its location it makes an effective contribution to enemy military action that renders it a military objective. For instance, a cyber operation against a reservoir's SCADA system might be employed to release waters into an area in which enemy military operations are expected, thereby denying its use to the enemy (subject to Rule 143). In this case, the area of land is a military objective by location because of its military utility to the enemy. This characterisation justifies using cyber means to release the reservoir's waters.

10.   When a civilian object or facility is used for military ends, it becomes a military objective through the 'use' criterion.[1062] For instance, if a party to the conflict uses a certain civilian computer network for military purposes, that network loses its civilian character and becomes a military objective. This is so even if the network also continues to be used

---

[1059] *See* AMW MANUAL, Rule 22 and accompanying commentary: DoD MANUAL, para.5.7.6; UK MANUAL, paras. 5.4.4(c–e).

[1060] ICRC ADDITIONAL PROTOCOLS 1987 COMMENTARY, para. 2020 (stating 'this category comprises all objects directly used by the armed forces').

[1061] ICRC ADDITIONAL PROTOCOLS 1987 COMMENTARY, para. 2021.

[1062] Hague Regulations, Art. 27 (noting that civilian objects enjoy protected status unless 'used at the time for military purposes'). *See also* ICRC ADDITIONAL PROTOCOLS 1987 COMMENTARY, para. 2022.

for civilian purposes (with regard to attacking such 'dual-use' entities, see Rule 101). Further examples of civilian objects that may become military objectives by use, and which would therefore be liable to cyber attack, include civilian rail networks being used by the military, civilian television or radio stations that regularly broadcast military information, and civilian airfields used to launch and recover military aircraft. Care must be taken in applying this criterion. For example, an entire computer network does not necessarily qualify as a military objective based on the mere fact that an individual router so qualifies.

11. The issue of civilian factories drew particular attention from the International Group of Experts. All of the Experts agreed that a factory that produces computer hardware or software under contract to the enemy's armed forces is a military objective by use, even if it also produces items for other than military purposes. They further agreed that a factory producing items that the military only occasionally acquires is not a military objective. The difficult case involves a factory that produces items that are not specifically intended for the military, but which are frequently put to military use. Although the Experts agreed that the issue of whether such a factory qualifies as a military objective by use depends on the scale, scope, and importance of the military acquisitions, they were unable to arrive at any definitive conclusions as to precise thresholds.

12. Civilian objects that have become military objectives by use can revert to civilian status if military use is discontinued. Once that occurs, they regain their protection from attack. However, if the discontinuance is only temporary, and the civilian object will be used for military purposes in the future, the object remains a military objective through the 'purpose' criterion. It must be cautioned that the mere fact that a civilian object was once used for military purposes does not alone suffice to establish that it will be so used in the future.

13. The 'purpose' criterion refers to the intended future use of an object, that is, the object is not presently being used for military purposes, but is expected to be so used in the future.[1063] It acquires the status of a military objective as soon as such a purpose becomes clear; an attacker need not await its conversion to a military objective through use if the purpose has already crystallised to a sufficient degree. For instance, if reliable information becomes available that a party to the conflict is about

---

[1063] ICRC ADDITIONAL PROTOCOLS 1987 COMMENTARY, para. 2022.

to purchase particular computer hardware or software for military purposes, those items immediately become military objectives. Similarly, a party that makes known its intention to appropriate civilian transponders on a communications satellite for military use renders those transponders military objectives.

14.   Difficulty often arises in determining the enemy's intentions. The law of armed conflict provides no particular standard of likelihood for concluding that a civilian object will be converted to military use, nor does it set forth the requisite degree of reliability with respect to the information on which such a determination is made. Instead, the law generally requires the attacker to act as a reasonable party would in the same or similar circumstances. In other words, the legal question to be asked is whether a reasonable attacker in the circumstances would determine that the reasonably available information is reliable enough to conclude that the civilian object is going to be converted to military use.

15.   To qualify as a military objective, the object in question must, through one of the four criteria, make 'an effective contribution to military action'. This limiting clause requires that a prospective target contribute to the execution of the enemy's operations or otherwise directly support the military activities of the enemy.[1064] For instance, if a factory makes computer hardware that is used by the military, the contribution qualifies. Similarly, a website passing coded messages to resistance forces behind enemy lines is making an effective contribution to military action, thereby rendering the cyber infrastructure supporting the website a military objective. One merely inspiring patriotic sentiment among the population, by contrast, is not making such a contribution, and therefore, as a civilian object, is not subject to cyber attack.

16.   The majority of the International Group of Experts was of the opinion that objects that satisfy the nature criterion are always targetable, subject to other applicable rules of the law of armed conflict. For these Experts, the requirements that a military objective be an object that makes an effective contribution to military action and that attacking it will yield a definite military advantage are inherently met for objects that are military in nature. Under this view, a military computer network necessarily makes an effective contribution and its destruction, damage,

---

[1064] Hague Regulations, Art. 23(g) (prohibiting destruction not 'imperatively demanded by the necessities of war').

or neutralisation always provide an attacker with a definite military advantage.

17.   A minority of the Experts held the view that the definition of military advantage limits attacks on objects that might qualify by their nature to situations in which a resulting definite military advantage can be identified. In the network attack example, these Experts took the position that even though the network is military in nature, a determination must still be made as to whether a military advantage accrues to the attacker through the network's destruction, damage, or neutralisation before it qualifies as a military objective.[1065]

18.   A major issue in the law of armed conflict is whether 'war-sustaining' objects qualify as military objectives. The US Department of Defense Law of War Manual gives an affirmative answer to this question. The Manual states that '[a]lthough terms such as "war-fighting," "war-supporting," and "war-sustaining" are not explicitly reflected in the treaty definitions of military objective, the United States has interpreted the military objective definition to include these concepts'.[1066] It goes on to offer the example of 'economic objects associated … with war-supporting or war-sustaining industries'.[1067] Advocates of this approach would, as an illustration, argue that it is lawful to launch cyber attacks against the enemy State's oil export industry if the war effort depends on revenue from oil sales.

19.   A majority of the International Group of Experts rejected this approach on the ground that the connection between war-sustaining activities and military action is too remote. These Experts would limit the notion of military objective to those objects that are war-fighting (used in combat) or war-supporting (making an effective contribution to military action, as with factories producing hardware or software for use by the military) and that otherwise fulfil the criteria of a military objective as defined above.

[1065] This opinion is based on the wording of Art. 52(2) of Additional Protocol I, which sets forth a two-pronged test: (1) the object 'make[s] an effective contribution to military action' and (2) its 'total or particular destruction, capture or neutralisation, in the circumstances ruling at the time, offers a definite military advantage'. The majority agreed with the two-prong test, but took the position that the second prong is always met with regard to military objectives by nature.

[1066] DoD MANUAL, para. 5.7.6.2.

[1067] DoD MANUAL, para. 5.7.8. *See also* AMW MANUAL, commentary accompanying Rule 24.

20. 'Military advantage' refers to that advantage accruing from an attack. Such advantage must be assessed by reference to the attack considered as a whole and not only from isolated or particular parts of an attack.[1068] For instance, cyber attacks may be conducted against a military objective far from where a major operation is about to be mounted in order to deceive the enemy as to the actual location of the pending operation. In itself, the military value of the cyber attack is insignificant since the operations are planned to occur elsewhere. However, the success of the ruse may determine the success of the overall operation. In this case, the military advantage is that anticipated from the operation as a whole, of which the ruse is a part. This point is also crucial with regard to the application of the rule of proportionality (Rule 113) and the requirement to take precautions in attack (Rules 114–120). It must be cautioned that the notion of 'attack considered as a whole' refers to a specific operation or series of related operations, not the entire war.

21. The term 'military advantage' is meant to exclude advantage that is not military in nature. In particular, it would exclude advantage that is exclusively economic, political, or psychological. Thus, for instance, a cyber attack on a civilian business sector, while yielding an advantage to the attacker in the sense that it would generally weaken the enemy State, would not usually result in military advantage in the sense of affecting on-going or prospective military operations in a relatively direct fashion. The sector would also fail to qualify as a military objective on the basis that it does not make an effective contribution to military action.

22. To qualify as a military objective, the military advantage likely to result must be 'definite'. The ICRC Additional Protocols 1987 Commentary provides:

> It is not legitimate to launch an attack which only offers potential or indeterminate advantages. Those ordering or executing the attack must have sufficient information available to take this requirement into account; in case of doubt, the safety of the civilian population, which is the aim of the Protocol, must be taken into consideration.[1069]

[1068] UK MANUAL, para. 5.4.4(j); UK Additional Protocol Ratification Statement, para. (i); GERMAN MANUAL, para. 444; ICRC CUSTOMARY IHL STUDY, commentary accompanying Rule 14.
[1069] ICRC ADDITIONAL PROTOCOLS 1987 COMMENTARY, para. 2024.

23. The term 'definite' does not imply any particular quantum of advantage. A cyber attack is lawful when the attacker reasonably concludes that the 'total or partial destruction, capture, or neutralisation' of the nominated target will yield an actual military advantage. Cyber attacks expected to produce only a speculative advantage are prohibited.[1070]

24. The assessment of advantage is made with regard to the 'circumstances ruling at the time'. For example, a civilian air traffic control system used for military purposes while a damaged military system is being repaired qualifies as a military objective and may be subjected to cyber attack. However, once the military system is restored and the civilian system is returned to exclusive civilian use, it no longer qualifies as a military objective (absent apparently reliable information that allows the attacker to reasonably conclude that the enemy will use it again for military purposes). It would neither qualify on the basis of any of the four criteria, nor would an attack thereon yield any definite military advantage.

25. The military advantage need not result from the destruction or damage of the military objective itself. The reference to capture and neutralisation is especially important in this regard. Consider a cyber attack on a server through which the transmissions of an enemy command and control facility pass. No damage is done to the command and control facility, but that facility has been neutralised in a manner that results in definite military advantage for the attacker.

26. Cyber operations create opportunities to influence civilian morale. Possibilities range from denial of service operations to cyber-facilitated psychological warfare. An effect on civilian morale may not be considered when determining whether an object of attack qualifies as a military objective because a decline in civilian morale is not a 'military advantage' as that term is used in this Rule. Of course, an attack carried out against an object that otherwise qualifies as a military objective can have an incidental negative impact on civilian morale. This fact has no bearing on the target's qualification as a military objective. It is important to note that a decline in civilian morale does not constitute collateral damage in the context of either the rule of proportionality (Rule 113) or the requirement to take precautions in attack (Rules 114–120).

[1070] UK MANUAL, para. 5.4.4(i).

27.   When assessing whether a nominated target is a military objective in the cyber context, it must be borne in mind that military personnel
may use the Internet and other cyber infrastructure for reasons unrelated
(or only indirectly related) to the hostilities. For instance, military personnel in the field often use civilian phone or email services to communicate with families and friends, pay bills, etc. The International Group of
Experts was divided over whether such use renders that civilian cyber
infrastructure subject to attack as a military objective through use.

28.   The majority took the position that the cyber infrastructure upon
which the services depend does not so qualify because the services do not
make an effective contribution to the enemy's military action and, by
extension, their denial would not yield a definite military advantage to an
attacker. The minority suggested that since the use of the cyber infrastructure contributes to the morale of the enemy forces, conducting an
attack against it would confer a military advantage. They cautioned that
this sort of conclusion should not be crafted so broadly as to suggest that
any object qualifies as a military objective if damage to it hurts enemy
morale. For the Experts taking this position, the deciding factor in this
particular case is the actual use by military forces deployed to the area of
operations. Moreover, they emphasised that the issues of proportionality
and precautions in attack would have to be considered by an attacker. All
of the Experts concurred that if civilian email services are being used to
transmit militarily useful information, the infrastructure used to transmit
it qualifies as a military objective.

29.   Another interesting case discussed by the International Group of
Experts involved media reports. If such reports effectively contribute to the
enemy's operational picture, depriving the enemy of them might offer a
definite military advantage (Rule 139). Some members of the International
Group of Experts took the position that cyber infrastructure supporting
their transmission qualifies as a military objective, although they cautioned
that the infrastructure could only be attacked subject to the Rules set forth in
this Chapter, especially those on proportionality (Rule 113) and precautions
in attack (Rules 114–120). In particular, they noted that the latter requirement would usually result in an obligation to only mount cyber operations
designed to block the broadcasts in question. Other Experts argued that the
nexus between the cyber infrastructure and military action is too remote to
qualify the infrastructure as a military objective. The International Group of
Experts agreed that all such assessments are necessarily contextual.

30.   An attacker's assessment that an object is a military objective is
made *ex ante,* that is, in light of the facts as reasonably assessed by the

attacker at the time of the decision to attack. For example, if a cyber attack subsequently proves unsuccessful because effective enemy cyber defences prevented it and the attack yielded no military advantage, the lack of success does not deprive the object of its character as a military objective.

Rule 101 – Objects used for civilian and military purposes

Cyber infrastructure used for both civilian and military purposes is a military objective.

1. The object and purpose of this Rule is to clarify the issue of 'dual-use' objects, since it is often the case that civilian and military users share computers, computer networks, and other cyber infrastructure. By this Rule, any use or intended future use effectively contributing to military action renders an object a military objective so long as its destruction, capture, or neutralisation offers a definite military advantage in the circumstances ruling at the time (Rule 100). As a matter of law, status as a civilian object and military objective cannot coexist; an object is either one or the other. This principle confirms that all dual-use objects and facilities are military objectives, without qualification.[1071]

2. For the definition of 'cyber infrastructure', see the Glossary.

3. An attack (Rule 92) on a military objective that is also used in part for civilian purposes is subject to the rule of proportionality (Rule 113) and the requirement to take precautions in attack (Rules 114–120). Accordingly, an attacker is required to consider any expected harm to protected civilians or civilian objects, or to clearly distinguishable civilian components of the military objective, when determining whether an attack would be lawful. Take the case of a pending attack against a server farm that contains servers used by the military. Civilian companies are using a number of servers in the farm exclusively for civilian purposes. The planned cyber attack will be conducted against the facility's heating, ventilation, and air conditioning system in order to cause the facility to overheat, and thereby damage the servers it contains. Expected damage to the civilian servers must be factored into the proportionality calculation and be considered when assessing feasible precautions in attack.

[1071] DoD Manual, para. 5.7.1.2; AMW Manual, commentary accompanying Rule 22(d); ICRC Customary IHL Study, commentary accompanying Rule 8 (noting that status depends on application of the definition of military objective).

4.   Cyber operations pose unique challenges in this regard. Consider a network that is being used for both military and civilian purposes. It may be impossible to know over which part of the network military transmissions will pass. In such cases, the entire network (or at least those aspects in which transmission is reasonably likely) qualifies as a military objective. The analogy is a road network used by both military and civilian vehicles. Although an attacker may not know with certainty which roads will be travelled by enemy military forces (or which road will be taken if another is blocked), so long as it is reasonably likely that a road in the network may be used, the network is a military objective subject to attack. There is no reason to treat computer networks differently.

5.   Recent conflicts have highlighted the use of social media for military purposes. For example, Facebook has been used for the organisation of armed resistance operations and Twitter for the transmission of information of military value. Three cautionary notes are necessary with respect to application of this Rule in such cases. First, it must be remembered that the Rule is without prejudice to the rule of proportionality (Rule 113) and the requirement to take precautions in attack (Rules 114–120). Second, the legality of cyber operations against social media sites depends in part on whether the operations rise to the level of an attack (Rule 92). If they do not, the issue of qualification as a military objective is moot. Third, their military use does not mean that Facebook or Twitter as such may be targeted; only those components thereof used for military purposes may be attacked.

6.   In theory, strict application of the definition of military objective could lead to the conclusion that the entire Internet can become a military objective if used for military purposes. However, the International Group of Experts unanimously agreed that the circumstances under which the Internet in its entirety would become subject to attack are so highly unlikely as to render the possibility purely theoretical at the present time. Instead, the International Group of Experts agreed that, as a legal and practical matter, virtually any attack against the Internet would have to be limited to discrete segments thereof. In this regard, particular attention must be paid to the requirement to conduct operations in a manner designed to minimise harm to the civilian population and civilian objects (Rule 114), as well as the limitations on treating multiple military objectives as a single target (Rule 112).

7.   An attack on the Internet itself, or large portions thereof, might equally run afoul of the rule of proportionality (Rule 113). The Internet is used for civilian emergency response, civil defence, disaster relief, and

law enforcement activities. It is also employed for medical diagnosis, access to medical records, ordering medicine, and so forth. Any damage, destruction, injury, or death resulting from disruption of such services would have to be considered in determining whether a prospective attack on the Internet comports with the rule of proportionality.

8. A complicated case involves a system that generates imagery or location data for civilian use but that is also useful to the military during an armed conflict. For instance, the system may provide precise real-time information regarding ship, including warship, location. Similarly, such a system may generate high-resolution imagery of land-based objects and locations, including military objectives. If the enemy uses the imagery, the system becomes a military objective by the use or purpose criteria. Since it also serves civilian purposes, the rule of proportionality (Rule 113) and the requirement to take precautions in attack (Rules 114–120) would, depending on the effects caused, apply to any attack on it. In particular, if it is feasible to degrade, deny, disrupt, or alter the signals in question using cyber means not amounting to an attack (or otherwise avoiding the causation of collateral damage), instead of conducting an operation that rises to the level of an attack and that causes collateral damage, doing so would be required by operation of Rule 116. If the contemplated operation does not rise to the level of an attack, very few law of armed conflict issues would remain. For instance, it would be lawful to alter the position data of vessels, although the requirement of 'due regard' would apply *vis-à-vis* merchant vessels and neutral warships. In the event infrastructure associated with the system is located in neutral territory, or is of neutral character and is located outside belligerent territory, account must also be taken of the limitations set forth in Rules 150–153.

9. The notion of dual-use targeting must be distinguished from the question of whether civilian objects may be requisitioned, or otherwise used, for military purposes. Consider the case of military forces requiring more network bandwidth to conduct military operations. To acquire the required bandwidth, a party to the conflict may, subject to the Rules in this Manual, engage in network throttling of civilian (or governmental) systems or block network access by civilians in its own or enemy territory. This situation is analogous to taking control of public roadways for exclusive use by the military. However, the party may not acquire network bandwidth, whether governmental or private, through actions on neutral territory or involving neutral platforms outside belligerent territory (Rules 150–151).

Rule 102 – Doubt as to status of objects

In case of doubt as to whether an object and associated cyber infrastructure that is normally dedicated to civilian purposes is being used to make an effective contribution to military action, a determination that it is so being used may only be made following a careful assessment.

1.   This Rule applies in international and non-international armed conflict.[1072]

2.   For the definition of 'cyber infrastructure', see the Glossary.

3.   Rule 102 addresses the topic of doubt as to the conversion of an object, including the cyber infrastructure upon which it relies, to a military objective through use. In treaty law, the issue of doubt is regulated in Article 52(3) of Additional Protocol I for Parties to that instrument. The Article provides: 'in case of doubt whether an object which is normally dedicated to civilian purposes ... is being used to make an effective contribution to military action, it shall be presumed not to be so used'. It establishes, in the event of doubt, a rebuttable presumption that objects ordinarily devoted exclusively to civilian use are not used for military purposes. In other words, doubt is legally resolved in favour of civilian status. Article 3(8)(a) of the Amended Mines Protocol contains identical language.

4.   Note that the scope of the Rule is limited to the criterion of use in relation to qualification of an object and its associated cyber infrastructure as a military objective. Further, the Rule only applies as to the issue of whether or not the object in question is 'making an effective contribution to military action'.[1073] It does not bear on the issue of whether or not destruction, damage, capture, or neutralisation will yield a definite military advantage. The sole issue addressed by this Rule is the standard for assessing whether a civilian object and its associated cyber infrastructure has been converted to military use. All other questions with regard to qualification as a military objective are addressed through application of the requirement to do everything feasible to verify the target (Rule 115).

5.   The International Group of Experts could not achieve agreement on whether Article 52(3) of Additional Protocol I reflects customary

---

[1072] UK MANUAL, paras. 5.24.3, 5.4.2 (both as amended); CANADIAN MANUAL, para. 429; GERMAN MANUAL, para. 446; AMW MANUAL, Rule 12(b); ICRC CUSTOMARY IHL STUDY, commentary accompanying Rule 10.

[1073] Additional Protocol I, Art. 52(2).

international law. The majority of the Experts took the position that it does. The ICRC Customary IHL Study acknowledges a lack of clarity regarding the issue; nevertheless, the Study seems to support the position that Article 52(3), especially in light of its reaffirmation in Article 8(3)(a) of the Amended Mines Protocol, is customary international law.[1074] Other Experts denied the existence of a presumption of civilian use and argued that the Article improperly shifted the burden of proof with regard to the precise use of an object from the defender to the attacker.[1075] The Experts who objected to the presumption's customary status took the position that such presumptions apply only to doubt as to the status of individuals (Rule 95). Since the text of the Rules required consensus, this disagreement resulted in adoption of the phrase 'may only be made following a careful assessment', instead of the more definitive 'shall be considered' language of Rule 95.

6. This Rule binds all who plan, approve, or execute an attack. They must do everything feasible to verify that the objectives to be attacked are neither civilian objects nor subject to special protection (Rule 115). When in doubt, the individuals involved in the operation should request additional information.[1076]

7. Rule 102 applies in the case of objects 'normally dedicated to civilian purposes' and any cyber infrastructure upon which they rely.[1077] Non-exhaustive examples include: civilian Internet services, civilian social media sites, civilian residences, commercial businesses, factories, libraries, and educational facilities.[1078] The term 'normally dedicated' denotes that the object has not been used for military purposes in any regular or substantial way. Infrequent or insignificant use by the military does not permanently deprive an object of civilian status.

8. In cases where a particular nominated target is normally employed for civilian purposes but an attacker suspects that it may have been converted, at least in part, to military use, the target may only be attacked following a careful assessment of the situation. The assessment must be sufficient to establish that there are reasonable grounds to conclude that the conversion has occurred. In arriving at this conclusion, an attacker

---

[1074] ICRC CUSTOMARY IHL STUDY, commentary accompanying Rule 10.

[1075] United States Department of Defense, CONDUCT OF THE PERSIAN GULF WAR: FINAL REPORT TO CONGRESS 616 (April 1992).

[1076] ICRC ADDITIONAL PROTOCOLS 1987 COMMENTARY, para. 2195.

[1077] Additional Protocol I, Art. 52(3). See also AMW MANUAL, commentary accompanying Rule 12(b).

[1078] UK MANUAL, para. 5.4.2.

must take into account all the information reasonably available at the time. One important criterion in establishing the reasonableness of the conclusion is the apparent reliability of the information, including the credibility of the source or sensor, the timeliness of the information, the likelihood of deception, and the possibility of misinterpretation of data.

9.   Absolute certainty that an object has been so converted is not necessary. Doubt is often present in armed conflict and any such requirement would clearly run contrary to State practice. What is required is sufficiently reliable information that would lead a reasonable commander to conclude the enemy is using the potential target for military purposes, that is, to make an effective contribution to military action. In other words, a reasonable attacker would not hesitate before conducting the strike despite the doubt.[1079]

10.   Issues of doubt must be assessed in light of the information reasonably available to the attacker at the time of attack and not that revealed after the fact; the analysis is *ex ante*.[1080] An attacker who has taken all feasible steps to discern the use of an object and reasonably concludes the enemy is using the target for military purposes has complied with the requirements under this Rule. The reasonableness of the conclusion must be assessed based on the information gathering capabilities available to the attacker and not on information and intelligence capabilities that may be possessed by other armed forces or nations. Of course, in some circumstances, an attacker may lack the means to gather information reasonably to conclude the object is being so used; the absence of such means cannot be used to justify an attack.

11.   It must be recalled that formerly civilian objects that have become military objectives through use will revert to civilian status as

---

[1079] AMW MANUAL, commentary accompanying Rule 12(b).

[1080] The UK Additional Protocols Ratification Statement, para. (c), states: 'Military commanders and others responsible for planning, deciding upon, or executing attacks necessarily have to reach decisions on the basis of their assessment of the information from all sources which is reasonably available to them at the relevant time'. Similarly, Canada made the following Statement of Understanding on ratification of Additional Protocol I: 'It is the understanding of the Government of Canada that, in relation to Articles 48, 51 to 60 inclusive, 62 and 67, military commanders and others responsible for planning, deciding upon or executing attacks have to reach decisions on the basis of their assessment of the information reasonably available to them at the relevant time and that such decisions cannot be judged on the basis of information which has subsequently come to light.' Canada Additional Protocol Ratification Statement, *reprinted in* DOCUMENTS ON THE LAWS OF WAR 502 (Adam Roberts and Richard Guelff eds., 3rd edn, 2000).

soon as the military use ceases. For instance, where the military temporarily (perhaps even momentarily) uses an information system normally dedicated to civilian use, particular attention must be paid to the possibility of any reconversion to civilian use. Consider a case in which a human intelligence source reports that a university computer system in enemy territory is being used for military purposes. A cyber operational planning team is charged with assessing the accuracy of this report, but is unable to confirm that the system is presently being put to military use. In this circumstance, it may not be attacked; only measures short of attack would be permissible. One must be cautious in this regard. If the cyber infrastructure might have been converted back to purely civilian use but will be used for military purposes in the future, it qualifies as a military objective by virtue of the purpose criterion (Rule 100).

12.   Defenders must facilitate an attacker's efforts to resolve the status of 'objects dedicated to religion, art, science or charitable purposes, historic monuments, hospitals, and places where the sick and wounded are collected' by means of distinctive markings or by notifying the attacker beforehand.[1081]

SECTION 5: MEANS AND METHODS OF WARFARE

1.   Cyber operations are not explicitly referred to in existing law of armed conflict treaties. However, in the *Nuclear Weapons* advisory opinion, the International Court of Justice affirmed that 'the established principles and rules of humanitarian law... appl[y] to all forms of warfare, and to all kinds of weapons, those of the past, those of the present and those of the future'.[1082] The International Group of Experts adopted the same approach by concluding that the general rules that determine the legality of weapons will also determine the lawfulness of cyber methods and means of warfare.

2.   The Rules set out in this Section apply in relation to methods and means of warfare that a State develops or procures for use by its own armed forces. Moreover, they apply to any means of warfare over which a State acquires control. A State that acquires control by cyber means over enemy weapons is subject to the law of armed conflict applicable to those weapons. Consider the case of an Unmanned Combat Aerial System

---

[1081] Hague Regulations, Art. 27.   [1082] *Nuclear Weapons* advisory opinion, para. 86.

(UCAS) armed with cluster munitions. If a State that acquires control over this system by employing a cyber operation is a Party to the Cluster Munitions Convention,[1083] it would be prohibited from using the UCAS to deliver such weapons. The notion of acquiring control implies that the Party using cyber means exercises sufficient control over the system to employ it as if it were its own. This situation must be distinguished from one in which cyber means are used to attack, neutralise, or otherwise interfere with enemy systems, as in the case of taking control of an enemy UCAS in order to cause it to crash.

Rule 103 – Definitions of means and methods of warfare

For the purposes of this Manual:

(a) **'means of cyber warfare' are cyber weapons and their associated cyber systems; and**
(b) **'methods of cyber warfare' are the cyber tactics, techniques, and procedures by which hostilities are conducted.**

1.   The terms 'means' and 'methods' of warfare are legal terms of art used in the law of armed conflict. They should not be confused with the broader, non-legal term 'cyber operation' used throughout this Manual. Cyber operation simply denotes a particular cyber activity. The definitions set forth in this Rule are applicable in both international and non-international armed conflict.

2.   For the purposes of this Manual, cyber weapons are cyber means of warfare that are used, designed, or intended to be used to cause injury to, or death of, persons or damage to, or destruction of, objects, that is, that result in the consequences required for qualification of a cyber operation as an attack (Rule 92).[1084] The term 'means of cyber warfare' encompasses both cyber weapons and cyber weapon systems. A weapon is generally understood as that aspect of the system used to cause damage or destruction to objects or injury or death to persons. Cyber means of warfare

---

[1083] Convention on Cluster Munitions, 3 December 2008, 48 ILM 357 (2009).
[1084] *See* AMW MANUAL, commentary accompanying Rule 1(t). *See also* International Committee of the Red Cross, *A Guide to the Legal Review of New Weapons, Means, and Methods of Warfare: Measures to Implement Article 36 of Additional Protocol I of 1977*, 88 INTERNATIONAL REVIEW OF THE RED CROSS, 931, 937 n. 17 (2006) (referring to a proposed definition of weapons put forward by the US DoD Working Group as 'All arms, munitions, materiel, instruments, mechanisms or devices that have an intended effect of injuring, damaging, destroying or disabling personnel or property.').

therefore include any cyber device, materiel, instrument, mechanism, equipment, or software used, designed, or intended to be used to conduct a cyber attack (Rule 92).

3. A distinction must be drawn between the computer system, which qualifies as a means of warfare, and the cyber infrastructure (e.g., the Internet) that connects the computer system to the target that the system is used to attack. The cyber infrastructure is not a means of warfare because an object must be in the control of an attacking party to comprise a means of warfare.

4. The term 'methods of warfare' refers to how cyber operations are mounted, as distinct from the instruments used to conduct them.[1085] Consider use of a botnet to conduct a destructive distributed denial of service attack. In this example, the botnet is the means of cyber warfare while the distributed denial of service attack is the method of cyber warfare.

5. The phrase 'cyber tactics, techniques, and procedures whereby hostilities are conducted'[1086] does not include cyber activities that, for instance, involve communications between friendly forces. On the other hand, it is intended to denote more than those operations that rise to the level of an 'attack' (Rule 92). For example, a particular type of cyber operation designed to interfere with the enemy's capability to communicate may not qualify as an attack (as that term is used in this Manual), but would constitute a method of warfare.

Rule 104 – Superfluous injury or unnecessary suffering

It is prohibited to employ means or methods of cyber warfare that are of a nature to cause superfluous injury or unnecessary suffering.

1. Article 23(e) of the Hague Regulations and Article 35(2) of Additional Protocol I provide the basis for the Rule.[1087] It reflects customary

---

[1085] See AMW MANUAL, Rule 1(v) and accompanying commentary.

[1086] As to the meaning of tactics, techniques, and procedures, see US DEPARTMENT OF THE ARMY, FIELD MANUAL 3.0 (change 1), OPERATIONS, paras. D-5 to D-6 (27 February 2008).

[1087] These notions find their origin in the Preamble to the 1868 St Petersburg Declaration. See also Rome Statute, Art. 8(2)(b)(xx); Conventional Weapons Convention, pmbl; Convention on the Prohibition on the Use, Stockpiling, Production and Transfer of Anti-Personnel Mines and on their Destruction, pmbl., 3 December 1997, 2056 UNTS 211.

international law and is applicable in both international and non-international armed conflict.[1088]

2.   This Rule applies only to injury or suffering caused to combatants, members of organised armed groups, and civilians directly participating in hostilities. Other individuals are immune from attack in the first place. Any incidental harm to them caused during an attack would be governed by the rule of proportionality (Rule 113) and the requirement to take precautions in attack (Rules 114–120). In other words, superfluous injury and unnecessary suffering are not to be equated with the notion of incidental injury to civilians.

3.   The term 'superfluous injury or unnecessary suffering' refers to a situation in which a weapon or a particular use of a weapon aggravates suffering without providing any further military advantage to an attacker.[1089] As noted by the International Court of Justice, weapons may not 'cause a harm greater than that unavoidable to achieve legitimate military objectives'.[1090]

4.   The use of the word 'nature' confirms that a cyber means or method of warfare violates this Rule if it will cause unnecessary suffering or superfluous injury, regardless of whether it was intended to do so. Means or methods of cyber warfare also violate the prohibition if designed to needlessly aggravate injuries or suffering.[1091]

5.   Only the normal use of a means or method of cyber warfare is considered when assessing compliance with the Rule; its purpose is to judge its lawfulness *per se*. The assessment is made by reference to the envisioned use of the means or method of cyber warfare under normal circumstances and when directed at its intended category of target. The

---

[1088]   *See* DoD Manual, para. 19.6; UK Manual, para. 6.1; Canadian Manual, paras. 502, 506, 508; German Manual, paras. 401, 402; AMW Manual, Rule 5(b); NIAC Manual, paras. 1.2.3, 2.2.1.3; ICRC Customary IHL Study, Rule 70.

[1089]   Although there is historical significance to the use of the two terms, 'unnecessary suffering' and 'superfluous injury', for the purposes of this Manual the International Group of Experts treated them as a unitary concept. Doing so is consistent with the original authentic French text '*maux superflus*' in the 1899 and 1907 Hague Regulations. *See* AMW Manual, commentary accompanying Rule 5(b); ICRC Additional Protocols 1987 Commentary, para. 1426. Use of both terms emphasises that the concept extends to both physical and severe mental harm.

[1090]   *Nuclear Weapons* advisory opinion, para. 78.

[1091]   The International Group of Experts took the same position in this regard as their counterparts who drafted the AMW Manual. AMW Manual, commentary accompanying Rule 5(b).

prohibition extends to the use of otherwise lawful means of warfare that have been altered in order to exacerbate suffering or injury.

6. Means and methods of cyber warfare will only in rare cases violate this Rule. It is, however, conceivable that means or methods of warfare that are lawful in the abstract could bring about suffering that is unnecessary in relation to the military advantage sought. For example, consider an enemy combatant who has an Internet-addressable pacemaker device with a built-in defibrillator. It would be lawful to take control of the pacemaker to kill that individual or render him *hors de combat,* for example by using the defibrillation function to stop the heart. However, it would be unlawful to conduct the operation in a manner that is intended to cause additional pain and suffering for their own sake, that is, unrelated or patently excessive to the lawful military purpose of the operation.[1092] Examples of such unlawful actions would include stopping the target's heart and then reviving him multiple times before finally killing him. Doing so would occasion suffering that serves no military purpose.

Rule 105 – Indiscriminate means or methods

It is prohibited to employ means or methods of cyber warfare that are indiscriminate by nature. Means or methods of cyber warfare are indiscriminate by nature when they cannot be:

(a) directed at a specific military objective, or
(b) limited in their effects as required by the law of armed conflict

and consequently are of a nature to strike military objectives and civilians or civilian objects without distinction.

1. Rule 105 is based on Article 51(4)(b) and (c) of Additional Protocol I and represents customary international law in both international and non-international armed conflict.[1093] It derives from the

---

[1092] Such conduct would amount to cruel, inhuman, or degrading treatment or, under certain circumstances, even torture. For the definition of torture, see Convention against Torture and Other Forms of Cruel, Inhuman or Degrading Treatment or Punishment, Art. 1, 10 December 1984, 1465 UNTS 85. Regarding cruel, inhuman, or degrading treatment, see *Delalić* judgment, para. 543.

[1093] DoD Manual, para. 6.7; UK Manual, para. 6.4; Canadian Manual, para. 509; German Manual, paras. 401, 454–456; AMW Manual, Rule 5(a); NIAC Manual, para. 2.2.1.1; ICRC Customary IHL Study, Rules 12, 71. *See also* Rome Statute, Art. 8 (2)(b)(xx); Amended Mines Protocol, Art. 3(8)(b) (prohibiting booby traps that 'cannot be directed at a specific military objective').

customary principle of distinction, which is codified in Article 48 of Additional Protocol I and set forth in Rule 93.

2.   This Rule deals only with the lawfulness of means or methods of cyber warfare *per se,* as distinct from the lawfulness of their use in particular circumstances (with regard to the indiscriminate use of weapons, see Rule 111). In other words, the issue with which this Rule is concerned is whether the contemplated cyber weapon is inherently indiscriminate.

3.   *Lit.* (a) prohibits the use of any means or method of warfare that cannot be directed against a specific lawful target. The Rule does not prohibit imprecise means or methods of warfare. Instead, the prohibition extends only to those means or methods that are essentially 'shots in the dark'. Restated, an indiscriminate cyber means or method under *lit.* (a) is one for which it is impossible to predict with any reasonable certainty whether it will strike a specific military objective rather than cyber infrastructure protected by the law of armed conflict. The understandings as to when a weapon is incapable of being directed at a specific military objective may evolve over time towards heightened requirements with improvements in the accuracy of weapons due to technological developments and the wider availability of systems with increased precision.[1094]

4.   *Lit.* (b) addresses cyber means or methods that are capable of being directed against a specific target in compliance with *lit.* (a), but are of a nature to have effects that cannot be limited in any circumstances.[1095] The crux of *lit.* (b) is a prohibition of weapons that by their nature generate effects that are incapable of being controlled and therefore can spread uncontrollably into civilian and other protected cyber infrastructure and cause the requisite degree of harm. In particular, *lit.* (b) encompasses cyber weapons that create an uncontrollable chain of events.[1096] To illustrate, assume that malware employed by a State is capable of targeting specific military computer networks. However, once introduced into such a network, it will inevitably, and harmfully, spread into civilian networks in a manner beyond the control of the attacker. Such malware would violate *lit.* (b) of this Rule. To the extent the effects of the means or method of warfare can be limited in particular circumstances, it does not violate *lit.* (b).

[1094] AMW MANUAL, commentary accompanying Rule 5(a).
[1095] ICRC ADDITIONAL PROTOCOLS 1987 COMMENTARY, para. 1963.
[1096] AMW MANUAL, commentary accompanying Rule 5(a).

5.   The harmful effects that are likely to be uncontrollably spread by virtue of the cyber means or method in question must rise to the level of harm that would amount to collateral damage (Rule 113). In particular, the uncontrollable spread of harmless effects or those that are merely inconvenient or annoying is irrelevant when assessing the legality of a means or method of cyber warfare under *lit.* (b). Consider the employment of Stuxnet-like malware that spreads widely into civilian systems, but only damages specific enemy technical equipment. The malware does not violate *lit.* (b).

6.   Use of means of warfare that have indiscriminate effects in a particular attack due to unforeseeable system malfunction or reconfiguration does not violate this Rule. Of course, the weapon must only be fielded after it has been assessed as lawful, pursuant to a proper and thorough legal review (Rule 110).

7.   The International Group of Experts struggled to identify means and methods of cyber warfare that might violate this Rule. For instance, even though a cyber means of warfare may be unable to distinguish one target from another, it could lawfully be introduced into a closed military network. In such a case, there would be little risk of it striking protected systems or having uncontrollable effects on such systems. Nevertheless, in light of the rapidly advancing state of technology in this field, the International Group of Experts agreed that the inclusion of the Rule was useful.

Rule 106 – Cyber booby traps

It is forbidden to employ cyber booby traps associated with certain objects specified in the law of armed conflict.

1.   This Rule is derived from the Mines Protocol and Amended Mines Protocol. It reflects customary international law in both international and non-international armed conflict.[1097] Both Protocols define a booby trap as 'any device or material which is designed, constructed or adapted to

---

[1097]   DoD Manual, para. 6.12.4.8; UK Manual, para. 6.7; Canadian Manual, para. 522; German Manual, para. 415; NIAC Manual, para. 2.2.3.1; ICRC Customary IHL Study, Rule 80. Note that the scope of Amended Protocol II extends to non-international armed conflict for Parties thereto. Amended Mines Protocol, Art. 1(2). Note also that the Convention on Conventional Weapons extends to non-international armed conflict for Parties thereto that have ratified the extension in scope. Conventional Weapons Convention, Art. 1(2), as amended 21 December 2001, 2260 UNTS 82.

kill or injure, and which functions unexpectedly when a person disturbs or approaches an apparently harmless object or performs an apparently safe act'.[1098] Definitional factors significantly limit the scope of the prohibition.

2.   The International Group of Experts struggled with the question of whether a cyber booby trap qualifies as a device. The Experts agreed that the appropriate way to interpret the term in the cyber context is to focus on the function of the entity in question. In other words, there is no reason as a matter of law to differentiate between a physical object that serves as a booby trap and cyber means of achieving an equivalent objective. The alternative view is that only tangible equipment may constitute a device for the purposes of this Rule.

3.   A number of other definitional factors affect the application of this Rule. First, a cyber booby trap must be deliberately configured to operate unexpectedly. Codes that inadvertently or incidentally function in an unforeseen manner are not booby traps in the legal sense because they are not designed to operate as such. Second, to qualify as cyber booby traps, codes or malware must be 'designed, constructed, or adapted to kill or injure'.[1099] In the cyber context the operation of the cyber means of warfare must eventually and intentionally result in such consequences. Cyber weapons that only harm objects are outside the scope of the definition. Third, to qualify as a cyber booby trap, a cyber weapon must appear innocuous or harmless to a reasonable observer, or the observer must be performing an apparently safe act. In other words, the person setting the cyber booby trap must intend the act that will trigger it to appear harmless.[1100] Finally, the cyber weapon must in some way be associated with certain specified objects.[1101] Several are of particular

---

[1098] Amended Mines Protocol, Art. 2(4); Mines Protocol, Art. 2(2).
[1099] Amended Mines Protocol, Art. 2(4); Mines Protocol, Art. 2(2).
[1100] Consider the example of a device fitted to a door, referred to in the UK MANUAL, para. 6.7.1.
[1101] Amended Mines Protocol, Art. 7; Mines Protocol, Art. 6(1). The prohibition extends to 'any booby-trap in the form of an apparently harmless portable object which is specifically designed and constructed to contain explosive material and to detonate when it is disturbed or approached' and to those attached to: (i) internationally recognised protective emblems, signs, or signals; (ii) sick, wounded, or dead persons; (iii) burial or cremation sites or graves; (iv) medical facilities, medical equipment, medical supplies, or medical transportation; (v) children's toys or other portable objects or products specially designed for the feeding, health, hygiene, clothing, or education of children; (vi) food or drink; (vii) kitchen utensils or appliances except in military establishments, military locations, or military supply depots; (viii) objects clearly of a

relevance in the cyber context. These include objects associated with medical functions; the care or education of children; religious functions; and cultural, historic, or spiritual functions.

4. As an illustration of this Rule, consider an email with an attachment containing malware, such as an embedded kill-switch, sent to an employee of a water treatment plant, purportedly from his physician. When opened, the malware is designed to cause the purification process at the plant, which serves both military and civilian users, to be suspended, thus allowing untreated water into the water supply on which the soldiers rely. Illness is the intended purpose. The malware is an unlawful cyber booby trap because the recipient reasonably believes that the act of opening an email from his physician is safe to himself and others, and because it appears to be related to medical activities. This is so regardless of whether the operation complies with the rule of proportionality (Rule 113).

5. Treaty provisions confirm that this Rule operates without prejudice to other aspects of the law of armed conflict. Thus, a cyber booby trap that does not violate this Rule may nonetheless violate the Rule against perfidy (Rule 122) or other rules of the law of armed conflict. Moreover, note that the Mines Protocol and Amended Mines Protocol impose specific requirements regarding use of booby traps, including provisions as to precautions and removal.[1102]

Rule 107 – Starvation

Starvation of civilians as a method of cyber warfare is prohibited.

1. This Rule is based on Article 54(1) of Additional Protocol I and Article 14 of Additional Protocol II. It reflects customary international law in both international and non-international armed conflicts.[1103]

2. For the purposes of this Manual, the term 'starvation' means deliberately depriving a civilian population of nourishment (including

---

religious nature; (ix) historic monuments, works of art or places of worship which constitute the cultural or spiritual heritage of peoples; (x) animals or their carcasses. Mines Protocol, Art. 6(1).

[1102] Amended Mines Protocol, Arts. 9, 10; Mines Protocol, Art. 7.

[1103] UK MANUAL, paras. 5.27, 15.19; CANADIAN MANUAL, paras. 618, 708, 1721; AMW MANUAL, Rule 97(a); NIAC MANUAL, para. 2.3.10; ICRC CUSTOMARY IHL STUDY, Rule 53. See also Rome Statute, Art. 8(2)(b)(xxv).

water) with a view to weakening or killing it.[1104] The civilian population need not comprise the enemy's entire population.

3.   Reference to 'as a method of cyber warfare' excludes from the Rule the incidental starvation of the civilian population as a result of the armed conflict. For the Rule to be breached, starvation must be a tactic deliberately employed by one of the parties to the conflict against the civilian population.

4.   Cyber operations will only violate this Rule in exceptional cases. Such a violation could, however, arise during an armed conflict in which a party to the conflict seeks to annihilate the enemy civilian population through starvation. Consider a case in which a party launches cyber operations for the exclusive purpose of disrupting transportation of food to civilian population centres and targets food processing and storage facilities in order to cause civilian food stocks to spoil. It is the civilian hunger that these operations are designed to cause that qualifies them as prohibited starvation of the population (see also Rule 141 regarding protection of objects indispensable to the civilian population). Denying foodstuffs to enemy armed forces or organised armed enemy groups does not violate this Rule, even if the incidental effect affects civilians.[1105] Such incidental starvation would instead be assessed pursuant to the rules of proportionality (Rule 113) and precautions (Rules 114–120).

Rule 108 – Belligerent reprisals

Belligerent reprisals by way of cyber operations against:

(a) **prisoners of war;**
(b) **interned civilians, civilians in occupied territory or otherwise in the hands of an adverse party to the conflict, and their property;**
(c) **those *hors de combat*; and**
(d) **medical and religious personnel, facilities, vehicles, and equipment are prohibited. Where not prohibited by international law, belligerent reprisals are subject to stringent conditions.**

[1104] ICRC ADDITIONAL PROTOCOLS 1987 COMMENTARY, para. 2089. The AMW Manual, in the commentary accompanying Rule 97(a), refers to 'annihilating or weakening the civilian population by deliberately depriving it of its sources of food, drinking water or of other essential supplies, thereby causing it to suffer hunger or otherwise affecting its subsistence'.

[1105] UK MANUAL, para. 5.27.1; AMW MANUAL, commentary accompanying Rule 97(a).

1. This Rule is based on the various prohibitions on belligerent reprisal set forth in the Geneva Conventions, the relevant provisions of which are discussed below. The concept of belligerent reprisal is limited to international armed conflict.[1106]

2. Belligerent reprisals in the context of this Manual are cyber operations that would be in violation of the law of armed conflict were they not being undertaken in response to violations by the enemy. Cyber reprisals may only be undertaken in order to induce or compel compliance with the law by the enemy. Their sole motivating purpose of securing future compliance by the adverse party is what distinguishes them from revenge, punishment, and retaliation.[1107]

3. As dealt with in this Manual, belligerent cyber reprisals are distinct from cyber countermeasures (Rule 20). Unlike countermeasures, belligerent reprisals occur only during an armed conflict, are undertaken only in response to violations of the law of armed conflict, and allow for the use of armed force.

4. International consensus as to the legality of some forms of belligerent reprisal is lacking. Nevertheless, the International Group of Experts agreed that it is incontrovertible that reprisals using cyber means are prohibited if undertaken against the wounded, sick, shipwrecked; medical personnel, medical units, medical establishments, or medical transports; chaplains;[1108] prisoners of war;[1109] or interned civilians and civilians in the hands of an adverse party to the conflict who are protected by Geneva Convention IV, or their property.[1110] The near-universal ratification of the Geneva Conventions and consistent subsequent State practice confirm that these prohibitions are now accepted as customary international law that binds all States.

[1106] *See* ICRC Customary IHL Study, Rule 148; ICRC Geneva Convention I 2016 Commentary, paras. 904–905.

[1107] *Naulilaa* arbitral award, at 1025; DoD Manual, para. 18.18.1; ICRC Geneva Convention I 2016 Commentary, para. 2731; Frits Kalshoven, Belligerent Reprisals 33 (2nd edn, 2005).

[1108] Geneva Convention I, Art. 46; Geneva Convention II, Art. 47. *See also* DoD Manual, para. 7.2.3; UK Manual, para. 16.18.a; German Manual, paras. 476–479.

[1109] Geneva Convention III, Art. 13. *See also* DoD Manual, para. 9.5.4; UK Manual, para. 16.18.b; Canadian Manual, para. 1019; German Manual, para. 479.

[1110] Mines Protocol, Art. 3 (prohibiting the use of booby traps as a means of reprisal against the civilian population); Geneva Convention IV, Art. 33. *See also* DoD Manual, para. 10.5.4; UK Manual, para. 16.18.c; Canadian Manual, para. 1121; German Manual, para. 479; ICRC Customary IHL Study, Rule 146.

5. With regard to belligerent reprisals other than against the persons and objects enumerated in this Rule, the ICRC Customary IHL Study concludes that to be lawful, reprisals: (1) may only be taken in reaction to a prior serious violation of the law of armed conflict and only for the purpose of inducing the adversary to comply with the law; (2) may only be carried out as a measure of last resort when no other lawful measures to induce the adversary to respect the law exist; (3) must be proportionate to the original violation; (4) must be approved by the highest level of government; and (5) must cease as soon as the adversary complies with the law.[1111] States generally accept these conditions.[1112]

6. There is no requirement that reprisals be in kind. Cyber operations may be used to conduct belligerent reprisals in response to kinetic violations of the law of armed conflict, and *vice versa*.

7. Consider a situation in which the armed forces of one State are bombing military medical facilities in another State, which is not a Party to Additional Protocol I.[1113] In response and after repeated demands to desist, the latter's Prime Minister approves a cyber attack against a power generation facility used exclusively to provide power to the civilian population. The cyber attack is intended solely to compel the first State to refrain from continuing to attack medical facilities, and the Prime Minister has issued strict orders to cease reprisal operations as soon as the State does so. The second State's belligerent reprisals would comply with this Rule (although the same result will not hold for a Party to Additional Protocol I for which Article 52(1) prohibits reprisals against civilian objects). By contrast, a

---

[1111] ICRC CUSTOMARY IHL STUDY, Rule 145 and accompanying commentary. It must be noted that the Study suggests that it is difficult to 'assert that a right to resort to such reprisals continues to exist on the strength of the practice of only a limited number of States, some of which is ambiguous. Hence, there appears, at a minimum, to exist a trend in favour of prohibiting such reprisals.' *Id.*, commentary accompanying Rule 146. Anticipatory reprisals are not permitted, nor can they be in response to a violation of another type of law. The duty to make a prior demand for cessation of unlawful conduct before undertaking a belligerent reprisal and the obligation to make the purpose of a reprisal public are generally included as sub-conditions of the requirement that the taking of reprisals is a measure of last resort, or as separate conditions.

[1112] *See generally* DoD MANUAL, para. 18.18.2.3; UK MANUAL, paras. 16.19.1, 16.19.2; CANADIAN MANUAL, para. 1507; GERMAN MANUAL, para. 478.

[1113] That is, which is not subject to Additional Protocol I, Art. 52(1) (prohibiting reprisals against civilian property).

decision to conduct cyber attacks against the bombing State's military medical facilities would be unlawful as a prohibited reprisal since, as noted, they are protected from attack in reprisal.

8. Some members of the International Group of Experts were of the opinion that reprisals against cultural property are prohibited as a matter of customary international law.[1114] Other members of the Group were not convinced that such a prohibition had crystallised into a rule of customary international law, but acknowledged that States Parties to the 1954 Hague Cultural Property Convention would be prohibited by Article 4(4) from conducting such operations.

Rule 109 – Reprisals under Additional Protocol I

Additional Protocol I prohibits States Parties from making the civilian population, individual civilians, civilian objects, cultural objects and places of worship, objects indispensable to the survival of the civilian population, the natural environment, and dams, dykes, and nuclear electrical generating stations the object of a cyber attack by way of reprisal.

1. Articles 20, 51(6), 52(1), 53(c), 54(4), 55(2), and 56(4) of Additional Protocol I provide the basis for this Rule, which applies in international armed conflicts.[1115] Upon ratification of Additional Protocol I, certain States adopted understandings with regard to reprisals against civilians that have the effect of making the prohibition conditional. Noteworthy in this regard are the United Kingdom[1116] and

---

[1114] ICRC CUSTOMARY LAW STUDY, Rule 147.

[1115] *See also* Amended Mines Protocol, Art. 3(7); Mines Protocol, Art. 3(2).

[1116] The United Kingdom noted that: 'The obligations of Articles 51 and 55 are accepted on the basis that any adverse party against which the UK might be engaged will itself scrupulously observe those obligations. If an adverse party makes serious and deliberate attacks, in violation of Article 51 or Article 52 against the civilian population or civilians or against civilian objects, or, in violation of Articles 53, 54 and 55, on objects or items protected by those Articles, the UK will regard itself as entitled to take measures otherwise prohibited by the Articles in question to the extent that it considers such measures necessary for the sole purpose of compelling the adverse party to cease committing violations under those Articles, but only after formal warning to the adverse party requiring cessation of the violations has been disregarded and then only after a decision taken at the highest level of government.' UK Additional Protocol Ratification Statement, para. (m).

France.[1117] Therefore, in application of this Rule, States must determine their position *vis-à-vis* Article 51(6) of Additional Protocol I and whether that instrument is applicable in the conflict in question.[1118]

2.   The International Criminal Tribunal for the Former Yugoslavia has held that reprisals against civilians violate customary international law.[1119] However, commentators and States contest the Tribunal's holding with respect to the assertion of customary status.[1120] Additionally, in its Customary IHL Study, the International Committee of the Red Cross concluded that, because of contrary practice, a customary rule prohibiting reprisal attacks on civilians had yet to crystallise.[1121] Application of this Rule is accordingly limited to those States that are Parties to Additional Protocol I and have not reserved on the issue.

3.   The concept of belligerent reprisal does not exist in non-international armed conflict. Therefore, a rule setting forth a prohibition of conducting attacks against already protected persons and objects would be superfluous.

Rule 110 – Weapons review

(a) **All States are required to ensure that the cyber means of warfare that they acquire or use comply with the rules of the law of armed conflict that bind them.**

(b) **States that are Parties to Additional Protocol I are required in the study, development, acquisition, or adoption of a new means or method of cyber warfare to determine whether its employment would, in some or all circumstances, be prohibited by that Protocol or by any other rule of international law applicable to them.**

1.   The terms 'means' and 'method' of cyber warfare are defined in Rule 103.

[1117] In ratifying Additional Protocol I, France did not reserve in relation to Art. 51(6). It did, however, make a statement in relation to Art. 51(8) that appears to be intended to retain the possibility of reprisals against civilians. French Additional Protocol Ratification Statement, para. 11, www.icrc.org/ihl.nsf/NORM/D8041036B40EBC44C1256A34004897B2?OpenDocument.

[1118] The UK position is set out in UK MANUAL, paras. 16.19.1, 16.19.2.

[1119] *Prosecutor v. Kupreškić*, Case No. IT-95-16-T, Trial Chamber judgment, paras. 527–533 (Int'l Crim. Trib. for the Former Yugoslavia 14 January 2000).

[1120] *See* DoD MANUAL, para. 18.18.3.4; DINSTEIN, CONDUCT OF HOSTILITIES, at 294–295.

[1121] ICRC CUSTOMARY IHL STUDY, commentary accompanying Rule 146.

2. *Lit.* (a) of this Rule derives from the general duty of compliance with the law of armed conflict as reflected in Article 1 of the 1907 Hague Convention IV and Common Article 1 of the 1949 Geneva Conventions. The International Group of Experts agreed that in the case of means of warfare, this limited obligation has crystallised through State practice into customary international law.[1122] *Lit.* (b) is based on Article 36 of Additional Protocol I. The International Group of Experts was divided as to whether it represents customary international law and therefore it is set forth as an obligation applicable only to States Parties to that treaty.

3. This Rule extends to any cyber weapon acquired or used by a State. It encompasses, *inter alia*, cyber weapons designed as such that are procured by States, cyber weapons developed by the armed forces in order to exploit vulnerabilities, and malicious software not originally developed for military purposes that is subsequently acquired by States for use in armed conflict.

4. As regards *lit.* (a), the International Group of Experts was divided as to whether there is an affirmative duty to conduct a formal legal review of means of warfare prior to their use. The majority took the position that this obligation is satisfied so long as a State has taken steps to ensure that its means of warfare comply with the law of armed conflict. For instance, the advice of a legal advisor at the relevant level of command was deemed by these Experts to suffice in lieu of a formal legal review.

5. *Lit.* (a) only requires States to take those steps necessary to ensure means of cyber warfare they acquire or use comply with the law of armed conflict. The International Group of Experts was split over whether the obligation extends to methods of warfare. Some argued that it does, whereas others suggested that, although methods of warfare must comply with the law of armed conflict generally, there is no affirmative duty to take the specific step of conducting a formal legal review to ensure such compliance.

6. The obligations set forth in *lit.* (b) are broader, encompassing the study, development, acquisition, and adoption of new means and methods of cyber warfare. Further, the paragraph requires the review to address whether employment of the means or method will comply with international law generally, not only the law of armed conflict. For

---

[1122] DoD Manual, para. 16.6; UK Manual, paras. 6.20–6.20.1; Canadian Manual, para. 530; German Manual, para. 405; AMW Manual, Rule 9. *See also* US Air Force, Legal Review of Weapons and Cyber Capabilities, Air Force Instruction 51-402 (27 July 2011).

instance, the review would necessarily include assessment of any applicable arms control regime.

7.   Article 36 prescribes no particular methodology for conducting the reviews required by *lit.* (b), nor is there any obligation for a State to disclose the review.[1123]

8.   With regard to both *lit.* (a) and *lit.* (b), the fact that a supplying State has already reviewed a method or means of cyber warfare does not relieve an acquiring State of its obligation to consider the means by reference to its own international law obligations. In complying with this obligation, the acquiring State may consider a legal assessment conducted by the supplying State, but retains the obligation to satisfy itself as to compliance with the legal rules by which it is bound. A determination by any State that the employment of a weapon is prohibited or permitted does not bind other States.[1124]

9.   The determination of the legality of a means or method of cyber warfare must be made by reference to its normal expected use at the time the evaluation is conducted.[1125] If a means or method of cyber warfare is being developed for immediate operational use, the lawyer who advises the commander planning to use it will be responsible for advising whether the cyber weapon or the intended method of its use accord with the State's international law obligations. Any significant changes to means or methods necessitate a new legal review. A State is not required to foresee or analyse possible misuses of a cyber weapon, for almost any weapon can be misused in ways that would be prohibited.

10.   For example, consider a cyber capability to degrade an adversary's land-based radar system. The software that causes the degradation of the radar signal is the weapon and requires a legal review, as would any significant changes to it. Minor changes that do not affect their operational effects, such as testing or debugging to eliminate unwanted functionality, would not trigger the requirement for a subsequent review.

11.   Legal reviews of a means or method of cyber warfare should consider such matters as whether: (1) it is, in its normal or intended circumstances of use, of a nature to cause superfluous injury or unnecessary suffering (Rule 104); (2) it is by nature indiscriminate (Rule 105); (3) its use is intended, or may be expected to, breach law

---

[1123]   *See* ICRC ADDITIONAL PROTOCOLS 1987 COMMENTARY, para. 1470 (discussing disclosure).
[1124]   ICRC ADDITIONAL PROTOCOLS 1987 COMMENTARY, para. 1469.
[1125]   ICRC ADDITIONAL PROTOCOLS 1987 COMMENTARY, para. 1466.

of armed conflict rules pertaining to the environment by which the State is bound;[1126] and (4) there is any particular provision of treaty or customary international law that directly addresses it.

12. Information that might support a legal review includes a technical description of the cyber means or method, the nature of the generic targets it is to engage, its intended effect on the target, how it will achieve this effect, its precision and ability to distinguish the target system from any civilian systems with which it is networked, and the scope of intended effects. Such information can come from sources like test results, reports as to past operational use, computer modelling, operational analysis, concepts of use documents, and general information regarding its employment.

13. The Experts recognised that there may be significant difficulties in accumulating sufficient and reliable information on which to base the legal review. For instance, replicating in advance the environment in which a new cyber weapon is intended to be used can be problematic, thereby frustrating such activities as advance testing and computer modelling. Nevertheless, they agreed such difficulties do not relieve States of the obligation to review the lawfulness of new cyber weapons.

SECTION 6: CONDUCT OF ATTACKS

Rule 111 – Indiscriminate attacks

Cyber attacks that are not directed at a lawful target, and consequently are of a nature to strike lawful targets and civilians or civilian objects without distinction, are prohibited.

1. This Rule is based on Article 51(4)(a) to (c) of Additional Protocol I and is considered customary international law.[1127] It applies in both international and non-international armed conflict.[1128]

[1126] These rules are found in Environmental Modification Convention, Art. I(1), and Additional Protocol I, Arts. 35(3) and 55, for Parties thereto. The customary status of rules specifically protecting the environment is unsettled.

[1127] UK MANUAL, paras. 5.23–5.23.2; CANADIAN MANUAL, paras. 416, 613; GERMAN MANUAL, para. 4034; AMW MANUAL, Rule 13; ICRC CUSTOMARY IHL STUDY, Rules 11–12; SAN REMO MANUAL, Rule 42(b).

[1128] Amended Mines Protocol, Art. 3(8); ICRC CUSTOMARY IHL STUDY, commentary accompanying Rule 11; NIAC MANUAL, para. 2.1.1.3; AMW MANUAL, commentary accompanying Rule 13.

2.   Rule 111 prohibits cyber attacks (Rule 92) that are not directed at a member of the armed forces, a member of an organised armed group, a civilian directly participating in hostilities, or a military objective, that is, a 'lawful target'. The cyber weapon in question is capable of being directed at a lawful target (and is therefore not prohibited by Rule 105), but the attacker fails so to direct it. For example, consider a cyber attack in which a malicious script is embedded in a document file posted on a public website. When a vulnerable computer's browser downloads and processes that file, the script runs and the computer is damaged. The attacker knows that both military and civilian users access the web server. The placement of the malware is indiscriminate because opening the document will infect the computer of anyone accessing the website who has a computing device running software that is vulnerable to that attack vector. A discriminate means of warfare has been employed indiscriminately.

3.   Note that Rule 105 provides that attacks employing means or methods of warfare that cannot be directed, and those having uncontrollable effects, are indiscriminate as such and therefore prohibited. However, this Rule encompasses situations in which the cyber means and methods in question, albeit not indiscriminate on this basis in every circumstance, cannot be directed in the particular attendant circumstances. The International Group of Experts unanimously agreed that cyber attacks employing means or methods of warfare that in the circumstances cannot be directed at a specific military objective, or which in the circumstances produce effects that cannot be limited as required by the law of armed conflict, are prohibited.[1129] This conclusion is based on Article 51(4)(b) and (c), which the Experts agreed reflects customary international law. Thus, they acknowledged that weapons that are otherwise discriminate might be incapable of being employed discriminately in certain circumstances.

4.   For example, consider malware designed to disable a certain type of SCADA system upon installation (and thereby damage systems reliant upon it) with a flash drive. Use on a military base where its effects will be limited to the targeted system is discriminate. However, delivering malware via flash drives left at various cyber conferences in the hope they

---

[1129] UK MANUAL, para. 5.23.3; ICRC ADDITIONAL PROTOCOLS 1987 COMMENTARY, para. 1962; AMW MANUAL, para. 2 of commentary accompanying Rule 13(a) and paras. 5–8 of commentary accompanying Rule 13(b).

will eventually be used at a military base (but that also would be likely to disable civilian systems) would violate this Rule.

5. Indiscriminate attacks must be distinguished from attacks intentionally directed against civilians and civilian objects (Rules 94 and 99). Whether an attack is indiscriminate should be assessed on a case-by-case basis. Factors to consider include: the nature of the system into which the malware is introduced or which is placed at risk; the nature of the method or means of cyber warfare employed; the extent and quality of planning; and any evidence of indifference on the part of the cyber operator planning, approving, or conducting the attack.[1130]

6. Indiscriminate attacks, like direct attacks against civilians and civilian objects, need not be successful to be unlawful. For instance, an indiscriminate cyber attack launched into a network serving both civilian and military users without regard for whom it will affect may be blocked by the network's firewall. The fact that the attack was launched suffices to violate this Rule.

7. Rule 111 must be distinguished from Rule 112. Whereas the former prohibits attacks that are indiscriminate because they are not aimed, the latter prohibits another form of indiscriminate attacks, those that are aimed at cyber infrastructure that contains both military objectives and civilian cyber assets in situations in which the military objectives alone could have been targeted.

Rule 112 – Clearly separated and distinct military objectives

A cyber attack that treats as a single target a number of clearly discrete cyber military objectives in cyber infrastructure primarily used for civilian purposes is prohibited if to do so would harm protected persons or objects.

1. This Rule is based on Article 51(5)(a) of Additional Protocol I. It reflects customary international law in both international and non-international armed conflict.[1131]

[1130] *See, e.g., Martić* judgment, paras. 462–463 (reviewing the specific circumstance of an attack with cluster munitions into a densely populated area and finding that an indiscriminate attack occurred); UK MANUAL, para. 5.23.3; AMW MANUAL, commentary accompanying Rule 13(b).

[1131] Amended Mines Protocol, Art. 3(9); UK MANUAL, para. 5.23.2; CANADIAN MANUAL, para. 416; GERMAN MANUAL, para. 456; AMW MANUAL, commentary accompanying

2. The attacks proscribed by the Rule violate the law of armed conflict because they are indiscriminate. In traditional armed conflict, this principle precludes targeting an area in which civilian objects and military objectives are comingled when it is feasible to individually attack the military targets therein. With regard to cyber operations, the prohibition should not be conceived of in the physical sense, and thus territorially. As an example, military computers may be connected to a network that predominantly hosts civilian computers. Assume that the military computers can be attacked individually (for instance, if their IP addresses are known). However, the attacker chooses a method of cyber attack that will neutralise the military computers, but also damage the civilian ones. This method of cyber attack would violate Rule 112 because the attacker treats the military computers as a single target and by doing so harms the civilian computers when it is not necessary to do so. Similarly, consider two military servers located in a server farm that is part of a large data centre primarily hosting servers for civilian use. An attack that shuts down the entire server farm's cooling system in order to overheat and damage the servers it contains would violate this Rule if it is technically feasible to use cyber means to just shut down the cooling subsystems of the server clusters containing the two military servers.

3. The International Group of Experts took the position that this Rule applies even when an attack is proportionate (Rule 113). In other words, a cyber attack against a dual-use system will be unlawful whenever the individual military components thereof could have been attacked separately. In much the same way that area bombing is impermissible in an air attack when attacking individual targets located in a concentration of civilians, cyber attacks must be directed, if feasible, against individual military parts of a cyber infrastructure consisting of military and civilian components.

Rule 113 – Proportionality

A cyber attack that may be expected to cause incidental loss of civilian life, injury to civilians, damage to civilian objects, or a combination thereof, which would be excessive in relation to the concrete and direct military advantage anticipated is prohibited.

Rule 13(c); NIAC MANUAL, commentary accompanying 2.1.1.3; ICRC CUSTOMARY IHL STUDY, Rule 13.

1. This Rule is based on Articles 51(5)(b) and 57(2)(iii) of Additional Protocol I.[1132] It is often referred to as the rule of proportionality, although as a technical legal matter the issue is one of excessiveness, not proportionality. This principle is generally accepted as customary international law applicable in international and non-international armed conflicts.[1133]

2. As stated in Rules 94 and 99, it is unlawful to make civilians or civilian objects the object of cyber attack. By contrast, this Rule deals with situations in which civilians or civilian objects are incidentally harmed, that is, they are not the intended objects of attack. Incidental death of, or injury to, civilians, or damage to, or destruction of civilian objects, is often termed 'collateral damage'. As this Rule makes clear, the fact that civilians or civilian objects suffer harm during a cyber attack on a lawful military objective does not necessarily render said attack unlawful *per se*. Rather, the lawfulness of an attack in which collateral damage results depends on the relationship between the harm an attacker reasonably expects to incidentally cause to civilians and civilian objects and the military advantage that the attacker anticipates gaining as a result of the attack.

3. This Rule envisages a situation where a cyber attack on a military objective will result in harm to civilian objects, including computers, networks, or other cyber infrastructure, or to civilians, that could not be avoided pursuant to Rules 114–120. It should be noted in this regard that cyber attacks on military objectives are sometimes launched via civilian communications cables, satellites, or other infrastructure. When this is the case, the attacks might harm that infrastructure. In other words, a cyber attack can cause collateral damage both during transit and because of the cyber attack itself. Both forms of collateral damage are to be considered in application of this Rule.

4. As an example of the Rule's operation, consider the case of a cyber attack on the Global Positioning System. The system is dual-use and thus a lawful target. However, depriving the civilian users of key information such as navigational data is likely to cause damage to, for instance, merchant vessels and civil aircraft relying on Global

---

[1132] *See also* Second Cultural Property Protocol, Art. 7; Amended Mines Protocol, Art. 3(8); Mines Protocol, Art. 3(3).

[1133] DoD MANUAL, paras. 5.12, 16.5.1.1; UK MANUAL, paras. 5.23.2, 15.15.1; CANADIAN MANUAL, at GL-5; AMW MANUAL, Rule 14 and accompanying commentary; NIAC MANUAL, para. 2.1.1.4; ICRC CUSTOMARY IHL STUDY, Rule 14; ICRC ADDITIONAL PROTOCOLS 1987 COMMENTARY, para. 4772; ICRC Challenges Report, at 42–43.

Positioning System guidance. If this expected harm is excessive in relation to the anticipated military advantage of the operation, the operation would be forbidden.[1134]

5. Cyber operations may cause inconvenience, irritation, stress, or fear. These consequences do not qualify as collateral damage because they do not amount to 'incidental loss of civilian life, injury to civilians, damage to civilian objects'[1135] and are not to be considered when applying this Rule. The International Group of Experts agreed that the notion of 'damage to civilian objects' might, in certain circumstances, include deprivation of functionality (Rule 92). When this is the case, it is to be factored into the proportionality evaluation.

6. Collateral damage can consist of both direct and indirect effects. Direct effects are 'the immediate, first order consequences [of a cyber attack], unaltered by intervening events or mechanisms'. By contrast, indirect effects of a cyber attack comprise 'the delayed and/or displaced second-, third-, and higher-order consequences of action, created through intermediate events or mechanisms'.[1136] The collateral damage considered in the proportionality calculation includes any indirect effects that should be expected by those individuals planning, approving, or executing a cyber attack. As noted in the United States submission to the United Nations Group of Governmental Experts: 'In addition to the potential physical damage that a cyber activity may cause, such as death or injury that may result from effects on critical infrastructure, parties must assess the potential effects of a cyber attack on civilian objects that are not military objectives, such as private, civilian computers that hold no military significance but may be networked to military objectives.'[1137]

7. For example, if Global Positioning Satellite data is blocked or otherwise disrupted, accidents involving transportation systems relying on the data can be expected in the short term, at least until adoption of other navigational aids and techniques. Similarly, an attacker may decide to insert malware into a specific military computer system that will not only disable that system, but also likely spread to a limited number of civilian computer systems, thereby causing the type of

---

[1134] Rome Statute, Art. 8(2)(b)(iv).
[1135] DoD Manual, 16. 5.1.1; AMW Manual, commentary accompanying Rule 14.
[1136] Joint Chiefs of Staff, Joint Publication 3–60: Joint Targeting I-10 (2007).
[1137] United States Submission to the United Nations Group of Government Experts on Developments in the Field of Information and Telecommunications in the Context of International Security, in Digest of United States Practice in International Law 2014, at 737. See also DoD Manual, para. 16.5.1.1.

damage qualifying as collateral damage for the purposes of this Manual. These effects, if they are or should have been expected, must be considered in the proportionality analysis.[1138] By contrast, if the malware is unexpectedly or unforeseeably transferred via, for instance, a portable storage device into civilian systems, the ensuing consequences will not be considered when assessing compliance with this Rule.

8. Only collateral damage that is excessive to the anticipated concrete and direct military advantage is prohibited. The term 'excessive' is not defined in international law. However, as stated in the AMW Manual, excessiveness 'is not a matter of counting civilian casualties and comparing them to the number of enemy combatants that have been put out of action'.[1139] The amount of harm done to civilians and their property in the abstract is not the primary issue. Instead, the question is whether the harm that may be expected is excessive relative to the anticipated military advantage given the circumstances prevailing at the time. Despite an assertion to the contrary in the ICRC Additional Protocols 1987 Commentary,[1140] the majority of the International Group of Experts took the position that extensive collateral damage may be legal if the anticipated concrete and direct military advantage is sufficiently great. Conversely, even slight damage may be unlawful if the military advantage expected is negligible.

9. The term 'concrete and direct' removes mere speculation from the equation of military advantage. While the advantage from a military action is seldom precisely predictable, requiring the anticipated advantage to be concrete and direct obliges decision-makers to anticipate a real and quantifiable benefit.[1141] The commentary to

---

[1138] *See, e.g.,* United States Submission to the United Nations Group of Government Experts on Developments in the Field of Information and Telecommunications in the Context of International Security, in Digest of United States Practice in International Law 2014, at 737: 'Given the interconnectivity of ICTs, there is a serious risk that any given cyber activity might cause unintended or cascading effects on civilians and civilian objects. When undertaking a proportionality evaluation, parties to an armed conflict should consider the risk of unintended or cascading effects on civilians and civilian objects in launching a particular cyber attack, as well as the harm to civilian uses of dual-use infrastructure that may be the target of an attack.'

[1139] AMW MANUAL, commentary accompanying Rule 14.

[1140] ICRC ADDITIONAL PROTOCOLS 1987 COMMENTARY, para. 1980.

[1141] UK MANUAL, para. 5.33.3 (as amended); CANADIAN MANUAL, para. 415. The AMW Manual observes that the 'term "concrete and direct" refers to military advantage that is clearly identifiable and, in many cases, quantifiable'. AMW MANUAL, commentary accompanying Rule 14.

Article 51 of Additional Protocol I states that 'the expression "concrete and direct" was intended to show that the advantage concerned should be substantial and relatively close, and that advantages which are hardly perceptible and those which would only appear in the long term should be disregarded'.[1142]

10.   When determining the concrete and direct military advantage anticipated, it is generally accepted as customary international law that the 'military advantage anticipated from an attack is intended to refer to the advantage anticipated from the attack considered as a whole and not only from isolated or particular parts of the attack'.[1143] For instance, a cyber operation could occur in conjunction with another form of military action, such as a cyber attack on an installation's air defence radar during conventional strikes on that installation. In this case, the concrete and direct military advantage to be considered with regard to the cyber attack would be that anticipated from the entire attack, not just the effect on the air defences. Similarly, a single cyber attack might be planned to convince the enemy that a particular target set is going to be the focus of forth-coming attacks, thereby causing the enemy to misdirect its defensive measures. The actual focus of the main attack lies elsewhere. Any expected collateral damage from the first cyber attack must be assessed in light of the anticipated military advantage the operation contributed to the main attack.

11.   It is important to note that the standard for this Rule is prospect-ive. The use of the words 'expected' and 'anticipated' indicates that its application requires an assessment of the reasonableness of the determin-ation at the time the attack in question was planned, approved, or executed.[1144] In making such determinations, all apparently reliable

---

[1142] ICRC ADDITIONAL PROTOCOLS 1987 COMMENTARY, para. 2209.

[1143] The text is drawn from the UK Additional Protocols Ratification Statement, para. (i). Australia, Germany, Italy, and the Netherlands have issued similar Understandings, www.icrc.org/ihl.nsf/WebSign?ReadForm&id=740&ps=P. See also UK MANUAL, para. 5.33.5; CANADIAN MANUAL, para. 415; GERMAN MANUAL, para. 444; ICRC CUS-TOMARY IHL STUDY, commentary accompanying Rule 14; NIAC MANUAL, commentary accompanying para. 2.1.1.4. For the purposes of international criminal law, the Rome Statute employs the term 'overall' in referring to military advantage. Rome Statute, Art. 8 (2)(b)(iv). Footnote 36 of Art. 8(2)(b)(iv) of the Rome Statute Elements of the Crimes states: 'The expression "concrete and direct overall military advantage" refers to a military advantage that is foreseeable by the perpetrator at the relevant time.'

[1144] See Galić Trial Chamber judgment, paras. 58–60; Trial of Wilhelm List and Others (The Hostages Trial), Case No. 47, VIII LAW REPORTS OF TRIALS OF WAR CRIMINALS 34, 69

information that is reasonably available must be considered.[1145] The Rule is not to be applied with the benefit of hindsight.

12. Expectation and anticipation do not require absolute certainty of occurrence. By the same token, the mere possibility of occurrence does not suffice to attribute expectation or anticipation to those planning, approving, or executing a cyber attack. The terms 'expected' and 'anticipated' allow for a 'fairly broad margin of judgment'.[1146]

13. There was a discussion among the International Group of Experts over whether and to what extent uncertainty as to collateral damage affects application of the Rule. The issue is of particular relevance in the context of cyber attacks in that it is sometimes quite difficult to reliably determine likely collateral damage in advance. A minority of the Experts took the position that the lower the probability of collateral damage, the less the military advantage needed to justify the operation through application of the rule of proportionality. The majority of Experts rejected this approach on the basis that once collateral damage is expected, it must be calculated into the proportionality analysis as such; it is not appropriate to consider the degree of certainty as to possible collateral damage. The attacker either reasonably expects it or the possibility of collateral damage is merely speculative, in which case it would not be considered in assessing proportionality.

14. The International Criminal Tribunal for the Former Yugoslavia addressed the question of the reasonableness of the ultimate proportionality decision in the *Galić* judgment. The Trial Chamber held that: 'In determining whether an attack was proportionate, it is necessary to examine whether a reasonably well-informed person in the circumstances of the actual perpetrator, making reasonable use of the information available to him or her, could have expected excessive civilian casualties to result from the attack.'[1147]

(UN War Crimes Commission 1948) (setting forth 'Rendulic Rule'); AMW Manual, commentary accompanying Rule 14.

[1145] UK Manual, para. 5.20.4 (as amended); Canadian Manual, para. 418; NIAC Manual, commentary accompanying para. 2.1.1.4. *See also* UK Additional Protocols Ratification Statement, para. (c): 'Military commanders and others responsible for planning, deciding upon, or executing attacks necessarily have to reach decisions on the basis of their assessment of the information from all sources which is reasonably available to them at the relevant time.' Austria, Belgium, Canada, Italy, the Netherlands, New Zealand, and Spain made similar statements, www.icrc.org/ihl.nsf/WebSign?Read Form&id=740&ps=P.

[1146] ICRC Additional Protocols 1987 Commentary, para. 2210.

[1147] *Galić* Trial Chamber judgment, para. 58.

15.   Sparing one's own forces or capabilities was considered by a minority of the International Group of Experts to be a factor when performing a proportionality calculation. Consider a situation in which an attacker decides not to map the 'cyber battle space' for fear that doing so might reveal information that could enhance an enemy counterattack. The majority of the International Group of Experts rejected the premise that the maintenance of one's own forces and capabilities in this situation is appropriate for inclusion in the calculation of military advantage. Instead, they took the position that such considerations are only appropriate when evaluating feasibility in the precautions in attack context (Rules 114–120).

16.   This Rule must be clearly distinguished from the requirement to take precautions in attack (Rules 114–120), which requires an attacker to take steps to minimise civilian harm regardless of whether expected collateral damage is excessive in relation to the military advantage anticipated.

17.   On the rule of proportionality, see also Rules 117 and 119.

SECTION 7:   PRECAUTIONS

Rule 114 – Constant care

During hostilities involving cyber operations, constant care shall be taken to spare the civilian population, individual civilians, and civilian objects.

1.   The Rule is based on Article 57(1) of Additional Protocol I and is considered customary in both international armed conflict and non-international armed conflict.[1148]

2.   The notion of hostilities is defined in Rule 82. It is not limited to cyber attacks (Rule 92).[1149]

[1148] Second Cultural Property Protocol, Art. 7(b); Amended Mines Protocol, Art. 3(10); Mines Protocol, Art. 3(4); DoD MANUAL, paras. 5.3.3.4, 16.5.1.1, 16.5.3, 17.7; UK MANUAL, paras. 5.32 (as amended), 15.15, 15.15.1; GERMAN MANUAL, para. 447; AMW MANUAL, Rules 30, 34, chapeau to Sec. G; NIAC MANUAL, para. 2.1.2; ICRC CUSTOMARY IHL STUDY, Rule 15.
[1149] UK MANUAL, para. 5.32; ICRC ADDITIONAL PROTOCOLS 1987 COMMENTARY, para. 2191. See also ICRC ADDITIONAL PROTOCOLS 1987 COMMENTARY, para. 1875 (offering an explanation of the term 'operations').

3. As used in this Rule, the term 'spare' refers to the broad general duty to 'respect' the civilian population, that is, to consider deleterious effects of military operations on civilians.[1150] It supplements the obligation to distinguish between combatants and civilians and between military objectives and civilian objects (Rule 93) and the rule of proportionality (Rule 113).

4. The law of armed conflict does not define the term 'constant care'. The International Group of Experts agreed that in cyber operations, the duty of care requires commanders and all others involved in the operations to be continuously sensitive to the effects of their activities on the civilian population and civilian objects, and to seek to avoid any unnecessary effects thereon.[1151]

5. Use of the word 'constant' denotes that the duty to take care to protect civilians and civilian objects is of a continuing nature throughout cyber operations; all those involved in the operation must discharge the duty. The law admits of no situation in which, or time when, individuals involved in the planning and execution process may ignore the effects of their operations on civilians or civilian objects.[1152] In the cyber context, this requires situational awareness at all times, not merely during the preparatory stage of an operation.

6. Given the complexity of cyber operations, the high probability of affecting civilian systems, and the sometimes limited understanding of their nature and effects on the part of those charged with approving cyber operations, mission planners should, where feasible, have technical experts available to assist them in determining whether appropriate precautionary measures have been taken.

7. In light of the duty to respect the civilian population, it is self-evidently unlawful to use the presence of civilians to shield a lawful target from cyber attack or to otherwise shield, favour, or impede military operations. For instance, placing civilians at an electrical generating facility qualifying as a military objective in order to shield it from cyber attack would violate this Rule. This prohibition, set forth in Article 51(7) of the Additional Protocol, reflects customary law.[1153] Although the

---

[1150] ICRC ADDITIONAL PROTOCOLS 1987 COMMENTARY, para. 2191.

[1151] UK MANUAL, para. 5.32.1.

[1152] AMW MANUAL, commentary accompanying Rule 30.

[1153] DoD MANUAL, para. 5.16; AMW MANUAL, Rule 45; ICRC CUSTOMARY IHL STUDY, Rule 97. *See also* Rome Statute, Art. 8(2)(b)(xxiii). Specific prohibitions on using prisoners of war and civilians protected under Geneva Convention IV exist. Geneva Convention III, Art. 23; Geneva Convention IV, Art. 28.

prohibition does not extend to civilian objects in general (as distinct from civilians), it is expressly prohibited to use medical facilities for the purposes of shielding.[1154] Extension of the prohibition to the use of medical cyber infrastructure as a shield is reasonable.

Rule 115 – Verification of targets

Those who plan or decide upon a cyber attack shall do everything feasible to verify that the objectives to be attacked are neither civilians nor civilian objects and are not subject to special protection.

1.   This Rule is based on Article 57(2)(a)(i) of Additional Protocol I and is accepted as customary international law in both international and non-international armed conflicts.[1155] It applies to cyber operations that qualify as an 'attack'. The term 'attack' is defined in Rule 92.

2.   An important feature of Rule 115 is its focus on planners and decision-makers. Those who execute cyber attacks may sometimes also be the ones who approve them. In the case of certain attacks, the individual actually executing the attack has the capability to determine the nature of the target and to cancel the operation. That individual is thus in a position to decide whether the attack is to be undertaken and therefore is obligated to exercise his or her capability to verify that the person or object to be attacked is a lawful target. On other occasions, the person executing the attack may not be privy to information as to its character or even the identity of the target. He or she may simply be carrying out instructions to deliver the cyber weapon against a predetermined part of the cyber infrastructure. Under these circumstances, the duty of the individual carrying out the cyber attack to verify would be limited to those measures that are feasible in the circumstances.[1156]

3.   The limitation of this Rule to those who plan or decide upon cyber attacks should not be interpreted as relieving others of the obligation to take appropriate steps should information come to their attention that suggests an intended target of a cyber attack is a protected person or

[1154] Additional Protocol I, Art. 12(4).
[1155] *Galić* Trial Chamber judgment, para. 58; UK MANUAL, para. 5.32.2 (as amended); CANADIAN MANUAL, para. 417; GERMAN MANUAL, para. 457; AMW MANUAL, Rule 32 (a) and chapeau to Sec. G; NIAC MANUAL, commentary accompanying para. 2.1.2; ICRC CUSTOMARY IHL STUDY, Rule 16.
[1156] AMW MANUAL, commentary accompanying Rule 35.

object, or that the attack would otherwise be prohibited. For example, assume that a cyber attack is planned and all preparations are completed, including mapping the network and determining the nature of the target system. The attackers are awaiting authorisation by the approving authority. Assume further that an operator is continuously monitoring the network. Any material changes in the cyber environment of the proposed target must be relayed to the commander and other relevant personnel as soon as possible.

4. The obligation to do 'everything feasible' is to be interpreted identically to the obligation to take 'all feasible precautions' in Rule 116. 'Feasible' has been widely interpreted as that which is 'practicable or practically possible, taking into account all circumstances ruling at the time, including humanitarian and military considerations'.[1157] In the context of cyber attacks, feasible precautions might include gathering intelligence on the network through mapping or other processes in order to allow those responsible reasonably to determine the attack's likely effects, particularly on the civilian population or civilian objects. There is no obligation to take measures that are not feasible. It may, for example, not be feasible to map the target because doing so will disclose, and thus enable defences against, the intended operation.

5. When gathering sufficient information to verify the target is not practicable or practically possible, the decision-maker may have to refrain from conducting an attack, or otherwise modify the concept of operations. For instance, if an attacker is unable to gather reliable information as to the nature of a proposed cyber target system, the decision-maker would be obligated to limit the scope of the attack to only those components or capabilities of the system with regard to which there is sufficient information to verify their status as lawful targets.

Rule 116 – Choice of means or methods

Those who plan or decide upon a cyber attack shall take all feasible precautions in the choice of means or methods of warfare employed in such an attack, with a view to avoiding, and in any event to

---

[1157] Amended Mines Protocol, Art. 3(10); UK Additional Protocols Ratification Statement, para. (b). *See also* DoD MANUAL, para. 5.3.3; UK MANUAL, para. 5.32 (as amended); CANADIAN MANUAL, at A-4; AMW MANUAL, Rule 1(q); ICRC CUSTOMARY IHL STUDY, commentary accompanying Rule 15.

minimising, incidental injury to civilians, loss of civilian life, and damage to or destruction of civilian objects.

1. This Rule is based upon Article 57(2)(a)(ii) of Additional Protocol I. It reflects customary international law and is applicable in international and non-international armed conflicts.[1158]

2. Even if the harm to civilians and civilian objects expected to result during an attack is not excessive relative to the anticipated military advantage, and is therefore in compliance with Rule 113, feasible precautions must be taken to minimise collateral damage. Rule 116 specifically addresses the obligation to consider alternative weapons or tactics to minimise collateral damage to civilians or civilian property. It should be noted that the Rule requires consideration of both cyber and kinetic options for achieving the desired military effect while minimising collateral damage.

3. The term 'all feasible precautions' in this Rule has the same meaning as 'everything feasible' in Rule 115 and the commentary to that Rule applies equally here. In particular, an attacker need not select alternative weapons or tactics that will yield less military advantage to the attacker.

4. 'Means' and 'methods' are defined in Rule 103.[1159] With regard to the application of this Rule to those who execute attacks, see Rule 115.

5. The issue of indirect effects is central to cyber operations because of the interconnectivity of cyber infrastructure, particularly between military and civilian systems. The International Group of Experts agreed that a person who is planning or using a cyber means or method must take all feasible precautions to avoid, or at least minimise, indirect as well as direct collateral damage. This obligation affects not only the choice of the cyber means used, but also how it is employed.

6. To illustrate operation of this Rule, consider the case of an attacker who seeks to insert malware into a closed military network. One method of doing so would involve placing the malware on a thumb drive used by someone working on that closed network. The attacker would have to

---

[1158] DoD Manual, para. 5.11.3; UK Manual, paras. 5.32, 5.32.4 (both as amended); Canadian Manual, para. 417; German Manual, paras. 457, 510; AMW Manual, Rule 32(b), chapeau to Sec. G; NIAC Manual, para. 2.1.2.b; ICRC Customary IHL Study, Rule 17.

[1159] See, e.g., UK Manual, para. 5.32.4. Further, para. 5.32.5 provides a list of factors to be considered when considering the appropriate means or method of attack.

assess the possibility that the thumb drive might also be used on computers connected to civilian networks and thereby cause collateral damage. In such a case, it might be possible to design different malware (means) that will minimise the likelihood of collateral damage.

Rule 117 – Precautions as to proportionality

Those who plan or decide upon attacks shall refrain from deciding to launch any cyber attack that may be expected to cause incidental loss of civilian life, injury to civilians, damage to civilian objects, or a combination thereof, which would be excessive in relation to the concrete and direct military advantage anticipated.

1.   Rule 117 is based on Article 57(2)(a)(iii) of Additional Protocol I. It reflects customary international law and is applicable in international and non-international armed conflicts.[1160]

2.   This Rule is to be distinguished from Rule 113. Rule 113 sets forth the general rule on proportionality and is rooted in Article 51(5)(b) of Additional Protocol I. Rule 117 merely emphasises that individuals who plan or decide upon cyber attacks have a continuing personal obligation to assess proportionality. As noted in Rule 115, in many situations an individual executing a cyber attack will be in a position to 'decide upon' it. This is particularly important in the context of Rule 117. For instance, if a cyber operator becomes aware that an attack being executed will unexpectedly result in excessive collateral damage, he or she must terminate the attack. Rule 119 addresses the duty to cancel or suspend attacks when new information becomes available that indicates the attack will violate the rule of proportionality.

3.   Rule 117 applies in the same fashion as Rule 113. The commentary to that Rule applies equally here.

Rule 118 – Choice of targets

For States Parties to Additional Protocol I, when a choice is possible between several military objectives for obtaining a similar military advantage, the objective to be selected for cyber attack shall be that the attack on which may be expected to cause the least danger to civilian lives and to civilian objects.

[1160] CANADIAN MANUAL, para. 417; GERMAN MANUAL, para. 457; AMW MANUAL, Rule 32 (c) and chapeau to Sec. G; ICRC CUSTOMARY IHL STUDY, Rule 18.

1. This Rule is based on Article 57(3) of Additional Protocol I. A substantial majority of the International Group of Experts agreed that this Rule reflects customary international law and is applicable in international and non-international armed conflicts.[1161] However, a minority of the Experts took the position that Article 57(3) had not matured into customary international law and therefore this Rule is not binding on States that are not Parties to that instrument.

2. Rule 118 applies to cyber operations that qualify as an 'attack'. The term 'attack' is defined in Rule 92.

3. In contrast to the other sub-paragraphs of Article 57, Article 57(3) does not specify to whom it is directed. Therefore, Rule 118 has been drafted to apply to all persons who are involved in target selection, approval, and execution of the attack.

4. Based upon the text of Article 57(3), the International Group of Experts understood the consequences of the danger referred to in this Rule as limited to injury, death, damage, or destruction by the direct or indirect effects of a cyber attack. Damage would, for the majority of the International Group of Experts, include, in certain circumstances, deprivation of functionality (Rule 92).

5. Whether a choice is possible is a question of fact to be determined in the circumstances ruling at the time. For the Rule to apply the options must be more than mere possibilities; they must be reasonable with regard to such factors as practicality, military viability, and technological prospect of success.

6. It must be borne in mind that the Rule only applies in the case of targets the attack upon which will yield similar military advantage. The military advantage does not have to be identical qualitatively or quantitatively. Instead, the issue is whether an attack on the alternative target would achieve comparable military effects.[1162]

7. The military advantage is to be determined in light of the operation as a whole and not based solely on that accruing from an individual attack. Thus, even if the alternative attack is likely to occasion less collateral damage, there will be no obligation to undertake it if it would not achieve the military purpose for which the original attack is designed.

[1161] UK MANUAL, para. 5.32 (as amended); CANADIAN MANUAL, para. 716; GERMAN MANUAL, para. 457; AMW MANUAL, Rule 33, chapeau to Sec. G; NIAC MANUAL, para. 2.1.2d; ICRC CUSTOMARY IHL STUDY, Rule 21.

[1162] AMW MANUAL, commentary accompanying Rule 33.

8. For instance, consider a situation in which an attacker seeks to disrupt enemy command and control. One option is to conduct cyber attacks against elements of the dual-use electrical grid on which the enemy's communication system relies. However, such attacks are likely to result in significant, albeit proportional, collateral damage. A second militarily feasible option is to conduct cyber attacks directly against the enemy's command and control network. If the latter would be expected to achieve the desired effect on enemy command and control (the same military advantage), while resulting in less collateral damage, this option must be selected.

Rule 119 – Cancellation or suspension of attack

Those who plan, approve, or execute a cyber attack shall cancel or suspend the attack if it becomes apparent that:

(a) **the objective is not a military one or is subject to special protection; or**
(b) **the attack may be expected to cause, directly or indirectly, incidental loss of civilian life, injury to civilians, damage to civilian objects, or a combination thereof that would be excessive in relation to the concrete and direct military advantage anticipated.**

1. Rule 119 reflects Article 57(2)(b) of Additional Protocol I. It is customary in character and applies in both international armed conflict and non-international armed conflict.[1163]

2. This Rule applies to cyber operations that qualify as an 'attack'. The term 'attack' is defined in Rule 92.

3. *Lit.* (a) reflects the fact that the requirement to ensure that protected persons and objects are not attacked applies beyond the planning phase into the operation's execution. It is a corollary to Rule 115, which sets forth a requirement to take feasible measures to verify the status of the target.

4. *Lit.* (b) is a corollary to Rule 113, which sets forth the general rule of proportionality, and Rule 117, which applies to those who plan or approve attacks. It applies to situations in which, although all necessary precautions have been taken, new information makes it clear that a cyber

---

[1163] NIAC MANUAL, para. 2.1.2(c); ICRC CUSTOMARY IHL STUDY, Rule 19.

attack that has been previously decided upon will cause excessive collateral damage. The interpretation of the terms used in this Rule is identical to that set forth in Rule 113.

5.   The practicality of suspending or cancelling a cyber attack is case-specific. For instance, in some cases, such as the placement of a logic bomb as part of a rootkit, there may be many opportunities to cancel or suspend. Duration of the cyber attack itself, which can range from seconds to months, can also determine the attacker's ability to suspend or cancel.

6.   The requirement of 'constant care' in Rule 114 implies a duty to take 'all feasible measures' to determine whether an attack should be cancelled or suspended. An example is monitoring the operation.

7.   The notion of facts 'becoming apparent' is not entirely passive. Rather, an attacker who initiates a cyber attack has a duty to monitor the attack as long as it is feasible to do so. Some cyber attacks may be difficult to continuously monitor, thus making it practically difficult to know whether to cancel or suspend them. This would heighten the degree of scrutiny that is merited during the planning and decision phases of the attack.

8.   Consider a case in which, before the initiation of hostilities, one State distributes rootkits in a segment of the military communication network of another State. After hostilities have commenced, a cyber operation to activate the logic bombs on board these rootkits is approved. In the course of this operation, the rootkits' network sniffer detects that the target State has recently connected its emergency services communication system to its military communication network, thereby raising the issue of proportionality. The acting State must suspend its cyber attack until it can satisfy itself that the attack would be proportionate, for example by conducting further reconnaissance to ascertain the likely harm to the civilian population that will be caused by the disabling of the emergency services communication system.

Rule 120 – Warnings

Effective advance warning shall be given of cyber attacks that may affect the civilian population unless circumstances do not permit.

1.   This Rule derives from Article 57(2)(c) of Additional Protocol I and Article 26 of the Hague Regulations. The International Group of

Experts agreed that it reflects of customary international law applicable in international armed conflicts.[1164]

2. The Experts also agreed that this Rule extends to non-international armed conflicts as a matter of customary international law, although they acknowledged arguments that its application is limited during such conflicts to certain treaty obligations.[1165]

3. Rule 120 applies only to cyber attacks as defined in Rule 92; it does not apply to cyber operations falling short of that level. Additionally, it does not apply to situations in which civilian objects will be damaged or destroyed without the civilian population being placed at risk. This point is especially important in the cyber context since cyber attacks will often damage civilian cyber infrastructure without risking harm to persons.

4. The law of armed conflict does not define the term 'affect' as used in Article 57(2)(c) of Additional Protocol I. In light of the limitation of the Article's application to attacks and the reference to 'loss of civilian life [and] injury to civilians' in other aspects of the requirement to take precautions in attack (Rules 116–119), the majority of the International Group of Experts concluded that the Rule applies only in cases where civilians are at risk of injury or death. The minority took a broader approach by noting the requirement to take precautions to 'spare' the civilian population in Rule 114. All the Experts agreed that effects consisting of mere inconvenience, irritation, stress, or fear to civilians would not meet the threshold of this Rule.[1166]

5. For the purposes of the Rule, 'effective' means that the intended recipient is likely to receive the warning and understand it in sufficient time to be able to act.[1167] Cyber means may be an effective way of delivering a warning of both cyber and kinetic attacks. Other warning techniques may also be effective in giving warning of a cyber attack. The

---

[1164] UK Manual, para. 5.32.8; Canadian Manual, para. 420; German Manual, paras. 447, 453, 457; AMW Manual, Rule 37 and accompanying commentary; ICRC Customary IHL Study, Rule 20.

[1165] For States Parties, Art. 3(11) of the Amended Mines Protocol sets forth a warning requirement in non-international armed conflict with respect to, *inter alia*, booby traps (Rule 106). Similarly, warning requirements exist with regard to cultural property (Rule 142) for States Parties to the Second Cultural Property Protocol, Arts. 6(d), 13(2)(c)(ii). *See also* AMW Manual, Rule 96.

[1166] AMW Manual, commentary accompanying Rule 37.

[1167] *See* UK Manual, para. 5.32.8.

determination of whether a warning is likely to be effective depends on the attendant circumstances.

6.   Warnings may be conveyed through the enemy if it is reasonable to conclude in the circumstances that the enemy will warn its population. For instance, if dual-use cyber infrastructure is to be attacked, the attacking force may elect to warn the enemy of the impending attack on the assumption that the enemy will warn the civilian population to take steps to minimise any expected collateral damage. However, if it is unreasonable to conclude the enemy will do so (perhaps because the enemy wants to use affected civilians and civilian objects as shields), such a warning will not suffice. Instead, the attacker would need to directly warn the civilian population itself, subject to the conditions set forth in this commentary.

7.   The means of warning need only be effective; there is no requirement that the means chosen be the most effective available. For instance, a party to the conflict may intend to attack a service provider that serves both military and civilian users. The attacker may elect to provide notice of the impending attack via national news media rather than by sending text messages to each civilian user. Even though the technique might be a more effective means of warning, notification through the media would be sufficiently effective to meet the requirements of this Rule.

8.   The phrase 'unless circumstances do not permit' reflects the fact that warnings can prejudice an attack.[1168] When cyber attacks require surprise, warnings do not have to be given. For example, surprise may be necessary to ensure that the enemy does not mount effective cyber defences against an attack. Similarly, surprise may be necessary to ensure the enemy does not pre-empt an attack by striking first at the attacker's cyber assets. Consider, for example, a cyber operation involving placement of a kill-switch into the target computer's control system, to be activated on the occurrence of some future event or after the passage of a specified period. A warning that would give the enemy an opportunity to locate and neutralise the device need not be given (or may be general). Surprise might also be necessary for force protection. As an example, a warning could allow the enemy to monitor the cyber attack such that it will be able to strike back. Equally, the cyber

---

[1168] UK MANUAL para. 5.32.8; CANADIAN MANUAL, para. 420; AMW MANUAL, commentary accompanying Rule 37; ICRC ADDITIONAL PROTOCOLS 1987 COMMENTARY, para. 2223.

attack may form part of a broader military operation and advance warning may expose the troops involved to greater risk. Given the current state of technology, the likelihood of warnings being feasible in the cyber context is low.

9. Warnings of cyber attacks, or cyber warnings of kinetic attacks, may have a general character. An example would be a warning that cyber attacks are to be conducted against dual-use electrical generation facilities throughout enemy territory without specifying precise targets.

10. A party to the conflict may issue a warning as a ruse, that is, in order to mislead the enemy (Rule 123). For instance, a false announcement of a cyber attack affecting dual-use systems might prove militarily useful in causing the enemy to take its military assets off-line. However, even though ruses of war are not prohibited in this regard, they are unlawful if they have the effect of influencing the population to disregard future valid warnings of attack.

Rule 121 – Precautions against the effects of cyber attacks

The parties to an armed conflict shall, to the maximum extent feasible, take necessary precautions to protect the civilian population, individual civilians, and civilian objects under their control against the dangers resulting from cyber attacks.

1. This Rule is based on Article 58(c) of Additional Protocol I. It reflects customary international law applicable in international armed conflicts.[1169]

2. The majority of the International Group of Experts took the position that the Rule's application was limited to international armed conflict. These Experts doubted that international law would impose a general obligation on a State to take actions to protect its own population from attacks during a non-international armed conflict; any decision to do so would be, as a general matter, within its sovereign discretion. A minority of the Experts would extend application of the Rule to non-international armed conflicts.[1170]

[1169] DoD Manual, para. 5.14; UK Manual, paras. 5.36–5.36.2; Canadian Manual, para. 421; German Manual, para. 513; AMW Manual, Rules 42–45; ICRC Customary IHL Study, Rule 22.

[1170] ICRC Customary IHL Study, Rule 22. See also the obligation to take passive precautions with respect to cultural property. Second Cultural Property Protocol, Art. 8;

3.   The obligation to take precautions under this Rule differs from that under Rules 114–120 insofar as this Rule relates to precautions against the effects of cyber attacks, that is, to 'passive precautions' that must be taken by the parties to the conflict in anticipation of the possibility of cyber attacks. In other words, whereas Rules 114–120 set forth an attacker's obligations as to precautions, Rule 121 addresses those of a defender. Examples of passive precautions include segregating military from civilian cyber infrastructure; segregating computer systems on which critical civilian infrastructure depends from the Internet; backing up important civilian data; making advance arrangements to ensure the timely repair of important computer systems; digitally recording important cultural or spiritual objects to facilitate reconstruction in the event of their destruction; and using anti-virus measures to protect civilian systems that might suffer damage or destruction during an attack on military cyber infrastructure.

4.   Not all sub-paragraphs of Article 58 of Additional Protocol I have been incorporated into this Rule since Article 58(c), which this Rule reflects, captures the totality of the requirement to take passive precautions; it is a 'catch-all' provision that encompasses the requirements set forth in the other sub-paragraphs. The omission of the remaining sub-paragraphs of Article 58 should therefore not be interpreted as implying that the obligation to take passive precautions is in any way diminished in the case of cyber attacks.

5.   Note that Article 58(c) refers to protection against the 'dangers resulting from military operations', while Rule 121 limits applicability to 'attacks'. All members of the International Group of Experts agreed that precautions against cyber attacks were encompassed in the Rule. A majority of them, however, was unwilling to extend its application to all cyber operations on two grounds. First, these Experts maintained that Article 58 applies only to attacks, as indicated by the title of the Article in Additional Protocol I. Second, even if Article 58 is meant to apply to all operations, they took the position that no equivalent customary law exists. The minority took the contrary position on the basis that Article 58(c) refers to 'operations' and that therefore the norm should be understood in its broader sense.

6.   Passive precautionary obligations are subject to the caveat 'to the maximum extent feasible'. The term 'maximum extent' emphasises the

AMW Manual, chapeau to Sec. H; NIAC Manual, para. 2.3.7 (placement of military objectives).

importance of taking the requisite measures. It does not imply, however, the existence of an obligation to take measures that, though theoretically possible, are not practically possible.[1171] Indeed, the ICRC commentary to Article 58 notes 'it is clear that precautions should not go beyond the point where the life of the population would become difficult or even impossible'.[1172] As to the meaning of the word 'feasible' for the purposes of this Manual, see Rule 115.

7. It may not always be feasible for parties to a conflict to segregate potential military objectives from civilian objects. For example, a power generation plant or an air traffic control centre may serve both military and civilian purposes. Civilians and civilian objects might be present at these lawful targets and it may not be feasible to segregate them in accordance with this Rule. Similarly, it might be impossible to segregate the civilian and military functions of the infrastructure. When segregation cannot be accomplished, a party to the conflict remains obliged, to the maximum extent feasible, to take other measures to protect civilians and civilian objects under its control from the dangers attendant to cyber attacks.

8. The concept of 'control' was thought of in territorial terms during the negotiations of Additional Protocol I.[1173] The International Group of Experts was divided over the meaning to be attributed to the term in the cyber context. A majority of the Experts concluded that all civilian cyber infrastructure and activities located in territory under the control of a party to the conflict are subject to this Rule. This would include the party's unoccupied territory and occupied enemy territory. Those in the minority took a more nuanced approach, asserting that the prohibition should not necessarily be conceived of territorially. For them, not every computer system within territory controlled by a party is within its control for the purpose of the Rule. As an example, military communications may travel through civilian computer systems, servers, and routers over which a party has no *de facto* control. For these Experts, the obligation in this Rule would not apply in such cases. In view of the 'maximum extent feasible' caveat, this division of opinion results in only minor differences in application of the Rule. All the Experts agreed that if the party can dictate the operations of a civilian computer system, it is under the control of that party.

9. The International Group of Experts agreed that the term 'dangers' does not refer to the risk of inconvenience or irritation. For example, the Rule does not require a party to the conflict to protect civilians from

---

[1171] *See* Rule 115.   [1172] ICRC ADDITIONAL PROTOCOLS 1987 COMMENTARY, para. 2245.
[1173] ICRC ADDITIONAL PROTOCOLS 1987 COMMENTARY, para. 2239.

cyber operations that cause temporary inability to access a website. Similarly, the party is not obliged to protect against the mere defacement of websites. The Rule is designed to protect against death or injury to civilians or damage to civilian property, that is, collateral damage. A minority of the International Group of Experts would include negative effects falling short of this threshold, such as major disruption of day-to-day life (as distinct from mere inconvenience or irritation).

10. Although paragraphs (a) and (b) of Article 58 of Additional Protocol I are not restated in this Rule, they provide useful guidance. Article 58(a) imposes a requirement to remove civilians and civilian objects from the vicinity of military objectives.[1174] Two scenarios in the cyber context illustrate the danger contemplated. First, a military objective may be attacked by cyber means in a way that harms nearby civilians or civilian objects. In such a case, the physical removal of the civilians and civilian objects would be required to the extent feasible. Second, cyber attacks may have indirect effects on civilian computers, computer networks, or other cyber infrastructure. Appropriate precautions in such situations may include separating, compartmentalising, or otherwise shielding civilian cyber systems.

11. The obligation in Article 58(b) of Additional Protocol I to 'avoid locating military objectives within or near densely populated areas', which is implicit in this Rule, addresses the situation in which civilian objects are not (yet) located in the vicinity of military objectives; it is preventive in character.[1175] In the cyber context, there is no direct equivalent to 'densely populated areas'. For instance, although mostly civilians use social media, the media cannot be equated with densely populated areas because the notion involves physical presence. However, the requirement does apply with respect to physically locating cyber infrastructure liable to attack in densely populated areas.

12. The ICRC commentary to Article 58 offers several further examples of passive precautions. These include well-trained civil defence forces, systems for warnings of impending attacks, and responsive fire and emergency services.[1176] Cyber equivalents might include distributing protective software products, monitoring networks and systems,

---

[1174] AMW Manual, Rule 43; ICRC Customary IHL Study, Rule 24.
[1175] AMW Manual, Rule 42; ICRC Customary IHL Study, Rule 23.
[1176] ICRC Additional Protocols 1987 Commentary, paras. 2257–2258. *See also* ICRC Customary IHL Study, commentary accompanying Rule 22.

maintaining a strategic cyber reserve of bandwidth and cyber capability, and developing response capabilities that prevent bleed over into the civilian system.

13.   Rule 121 does not bear on the 'dual-use' issue (Rule 101). State practice clearly establishes the legality of using cyber infrastructure for both military and civilian purposes. Instead, the Rule addresses the issue of proximity (whether real or virtual) of civilians and civilian objects to cyber infrastructure that qualifies as a military objective, including dual-use targets.

14.   State practice also demonstrates that the failure of a defender to take passive precautions does not, in itself, preclude the other side from conducting a cyber attack.[1177] Nevertheless, the International Group of Experts agreed that even when the enemy does not take passive precautions, an attacker remains bound by the Rules governing attacks, especially proportionality (Rule 113) and the requirement to take active precautions (Rules 114–120).[1178] Some of the Experts took the position that the failure of a party to take passive precautions is an appropriate consideration when determining whether an attacker has complied with its obligations to take active precautions.

SECTION 8:   PERFIDY AND IMPROPER USE

Rule 122 – Perfidy

In the conduct of hostilities involving cyber operations, it is prohibited to kill or injure an adversary by resort to perfidy. Acts that invite the confidence of an adversary to believe that he or she is entitled to, or is obliged to accord, protection under the law of armed conflict, with intent to betray that confidence, constitute perfidy.

1.   Perfidy, also referred to as 'treachery', is defined in Article 37(1) of Additional Protocol I as '[a]cts inviting the confidence of an adversary to lead him to believe that he is entitled to, or is obliged to accord, protection under the rules of international law applicable in armed conflict, with the intent to betray that confidence'. The prohibition against killing

---

[1177]   ICRC Customary IHL Study, commentary accompanying Rule 22.
[1178]   See Additional Protocol I, Art. 51(8); AMW Manual, Rule 46; ICRC Customary IHL Study, commentary accompanying Rule 22.

or wounding by perfidy also appears in Article 23(b) of the Hague Regulations. This Rule applies in both international and non-international armed conflict and is considered customary international law.[1179]

2.   Whereas Article 37(1) of Additional Protocol I includes acts that result in the capture of an adversary, the majority of the International Group of Experts concluded that customary international law prohibits only those perfidious acts intended to result in death or injury.[1180] This position is based in part on the fact that capture is not referred to in the Hague Regulations or the Rome Statute.[1181] The remaining Experts took the position that, as a matter of customary international law, the prohibition also extends to capture.[1182] Of course, the prohibition of perfidious acts leading to capture extends to States Parties to Additional Protocol I during conflicts in which that instrument applies.

3.   The prohibition has four elements: (1) an act inviting particular confidence of the adversary; (2) an intent to betray that confidence; (3) a specific protection provided for in international law; and (4) death or injury of the adversary.[1183]

4.   The notion of 'adversary' is sufficiently broad to encompass the situation in which the deceived person is not necessarily the person whose death or injury results from the deception, provided the individual killed or injured was an intended target of the cyber attack.

5.   In order to breach the prohibition against perfidy, the perfidious act must be the proximate cause of the death or injury.[1184] Consider the case of a perfidious email inviting the enemy to a meeting with a representative of the International Committee of the Red Cross, but which is actually intended to lead enemy forces into an ambush. The enemy is deceived, and, while travelling to the purported meeting, its vehicle strikes a landmine (which was not foreseen by the senders of the

---

[1179] Hague Regulations, Art. 23(f); DoD MANUAL, para. 5.22; UK MANUAL, paras. 5.9, 15.12; CANADIAN MANUAL, paras. 603, 706, 857; GERMAN MANUAL, para. 472; AMW MANUAL, commentary accompanying Rule 111(a); NIAC MANUAL, para. 2.3.6; ICRC CUSTOMARY IHL STUDY, Rule 65. See also Rome Statute, Art. 8(2)(b)(xi), 8(2)(e)(ix).

[1180] See AMW MANUAL, commentary accompanying Rule 111(a) (discussing whether the prohibition against perfidy extends to acts resulting in capture).

[1181] Hague Regulations, Art. 23(b). See also Rome Statute, Art. 8(2)(b)(xi).

[1182] ICRC CUSTOMARY IHL STUDY, Rule 65.

[1183] ICRC ADDITIONAL PROTOCOLS 1987 COMMENTARY, para. 1500; Rome Statute Elements of the Crimes, Arts. 8(2)(b)(xi), 8(2)(e)(ix).

[1184] BOTHE, ET AL., NEW RULES, at 204.

email). Any resulting deaths were not proximately caused by the perfidious email because they were not foreseeable; therefore, the prohibition set forth in this Rule has not been breached.

6. Proximate cause should not be confused with temporal proximity. In the cyber context, it is possible that a perfidious act inviting the adversary's confidence will occur at a point in time that is remote from the act that causes the death or injury. An example is an email sent by a military unit to the adversary indicating an intention to surrender some days later at a specific location. At the appointed time and location, the adversary is ambushed and some of its troops are killed. Rule 122 has been violated, even though substantial time has passed since the initiating perfidious act.

7. The International Group of Experts was split as to whether the perfidious act must actually result in the injury or death of the adversary. The ICRC commentary to Article 37 indicates that the issue was problematic, but that 'it seems evident that the attempted or unsuccessful act also falls under the scope of this prohibition'.[1185] On this basis, some Experts took the position that the perfidious act need not be successful. Others were of the view that this position does not accurately reflect customary law, as evidenced in part by the plain text of Article 23(b) of the Hague Regulations and Article 37 of Additional Protocol I.

8. The reference to inviting confidence refers to creating a situation in which the enemy has confidence that the person or object involved is either protected by the law of armed conflict or is obliged to accord such protection to the party that is the subject of the deception. Examples include feigning the status of civilians (Rule 91), civilian objects (Rule 100), medical personnel or entities (Rules 131–132), United Nations personnel or objects (Rule 79), or persons who are *hors de combat* (Rule 96).

9. The International Group of Experts was divided as to whether the confidence referred to in this Rule encompasses that of a cyber system. Some Experts were of the view that it does. An example would be a situation in which the enemy commander is known to have a pacemaker that can be adjusted and monitored remotely. Malware programmed to falsely authenticate itself as being generated by a legitimate medical source is introduced into the medical personnel network. The attacker uses it to disrupt the pacemaker of the

---

[1185] ICRC ADDITIONAL PROTOCOLS 1987 COMMENTARY, para. 1493.

commander, causing a heart attack. In this example, the confidence of the adverse party's computer system has been betrayed and, according to the majority of the Experts, the Rule has been violated. Other Experts took the position that the notion of confidence presupposes human involvement, such that influencing a machine's processes without consequently affecting human perception falls outside the Rule.

10.   The perfidy Rule does not extend to perfidious acts that result in damage or destruction of property.[1186] Such perfidious conduct might, however, be prohibited by another rule of the law of international armed conflict. For example, the feigning of United Nations observer status to gain access to an adversary's military headquarters to enable a close access operation against its secure computer network would not breach the perfidy rule, but would nonetheless be prohibited (Rule 125).

11.   Perfidy must be distinguished from espionage (Rule 89). However, a cyber operation with the primary purpose of espionage that fulfils the perfidy criteria and results in the death or injury of an adversary violates this Rule.

12.   In an armed conflict, simply failing to identify oneself as a combatant is not perfidy, although it may result in a loss of entitlement to claim combatant immunity or prisoner of war status (Rule 87).[1187] Similarly, in the cyber context there is no obligation specifically to mark websites, IP addresses, or other information technology facilities that are used for military purposes in order to distinguish them from civilian objects. However, it may be perfidious to make such websites (or other cyber entities) appear to have civilian status with a view to deceiving the enemy in order to kill or injure.

13.   There is a distinction between feigning protected status and masking the originator of the attack. A cyber attack in which the originator is concealed does not equate to feigning protected status. It is therefore not perfidious to conduct cyber operations that do not disclose the originator of the operation. The situation is analogous to a sniper attack in which the location of the attacker or identity of the sniper may never be known. However, an operation that is masked in a manner that invites an adversary to conclude that the originator is a civilian or other protected person is prohibited if the result of the operation is death or injury of the enemy.

[1186] AMW MANUAL, commentary accompanying Rule 111(a).

[1187] See Rules 86 and 93 for further discussion of the requirement for combatants to distinguish themselves from the civilian population.

14. The integrated nature of cyber infrastructure makes it likely that civilian cyber infrastructure will be involved in cyber attacks. The fact that cyber attacks causing death or injury are conducted over civilian cyber infrastructure does not in itself make them perfidious. In this respect, cyber infrastructure is no different from civilian infrastructure used to launch a kinetic attack. Examples include roads used by military convoys or civilian airports used by military aircraft. The exception to this general rule is infrastructure that enjoys specially protected status, such as a medical computer network. This issue is further discussed below at Rule 132.

15. Perfidy by cyber means must be distinguished from cyber ruses, which are lawful. Ruses are acts designed to mislead, confuse, or induce an adversary to act recklessly, but that do not violate the law of armed conflict (Rule 123).

Rule 123 – Ruses

Cyber operations that qualify as ruses of war are permitted.

1. This Rule is drawn from Article 37(2) of Additional Protocol I. Ruses are permitted in both international and non-international armed conflict.[1188]

2. 'Ruses of war' are acts intended to mislead the enemy or to induce enemy forces to act recklessly, but that do not violate the law of armed conflict. They are not perfidious because they do not invite the confidence of the enemy with respect to protected status. The following are examples of permissible ruses:[1189]

(1) creation of a 'dummy' computer system simulating non-existent forces;
(2) transmission of false information causing an opponent erroneously to believe operations are about to occur or are underway;
(3) use of false computer identifiers, computer networks (e.g., honeynets or honeypots), or computer transmissions;
(4) feigned cyber attacks that do not violate Rule 98;

[1188] DoD Manual, para. 5.21; UK Manual, paras. 5.17, 15.12; German Manual, para. 471; AMW Manual, commentary accompanying Rule 113; NIAC Manual, commentary accompanying para. 2.3.6; ICRC Customary IHL Study, Rule 57.

[1189] For examples of ruses, see Department of the Army, Field Manual 27-10, The Law of Land Warfare para. 51 (1956). See also UK Manual, para. 5.17.2; Canadian Manual, para. 856; AMW Manual, Rule 116.

(5) bogus orders purporting to have been issued by the enemy commander;
(6) psychological warfare activities;
(7) transmitting false intelligence information intended for interception; and
(8) use of enemy codes, signals, and passwords.

3. A common element of ruses of war is the presentation to the enemy of a 'false appearance of what is actually going on, thereby lawfully gaining a military advantage'.[1190] Consider, for example, the use of a software decoy to deceive the enemy. In response to a rogue software agent that is tasked with modifying XML tags, the software decoy deflects the enemy's cyber operators by redirecting their attention to a honeypot that contains false XML tags that appear to have greater military value than those under attack. The action is a lawful ruse.

4. It is permissible to camouflage persons and objects to blend in with (i.e., to be visually indistinct from) surroundings, including civilian surroundings, so long as doing so does not amount to perfidy (Rule 122).[1191] The International Group of Experts was split, however, as to whether it would be lawful to camouflage a computer or computer network to blend in with a civilian system in a manner that did not constitute perfidy. For instance, a military computer system might be hosted on a public cloud virtual private server in order to appear to be commercial in nature to make it harder to detect. The majority of the Experts took the position that doing so would be unlawful if the operation undermined the principle of distinction (Rule 93) by placing civilians and civilian objects at increased risk.[1192] The minority suggested that only the rule of perfidy applies to such cases.

Rule 124 – Improper use of the protective indicators

It is prohibited to make improper use of the protective emblems, signs, or signals that are set forth in the law of armed conflict.

1. This Rule of customary and treaty law applies during both international and non-international armed conflict.[1193]

[1190] AMW MANUAL, commentary accompanying Rule 116(a).
[1191] AMW MANUAL, Rule 116(e) and accompanying commentary.
[1192] AMW MANUAL, commentary accompanying Rule 116(e).
[1193] Hague Regulations, Art. 23(f); Additional Protocol I, Art. 38(1); Additional Protocol II, Art. 12; Additional Protocol III, Art. 6(1); DoD MANUAL, paras. 7.15, 16.5.4; UK MANUAL, para. 5.10 (as amended); CANADIAN MANUAL, paras. 604–605; GERMAN

2. The Red Cross and the Red Crescent (as well as the Red Lion and Sun, now in disuse[1194]) have long been recognised as distinctive protective emblems.[1195] Additional Protocol III to the 1949 Geneva Conventions establishes the Red Crystal as an additional distinctive emblem with equal status.[1196] This Rule also encompasses improper use of the distinctive sign for civil defence,[1197] the distinctive emblem for cultural property,[1198] the flag of truce,[1199] and electronic protective markings such as those set forth in Annex I of Additional Protocol I.[1200] Improper use of these distinctive indicators jeopardises identification of the protected persons and objects entitled to display them, undermines the future credibility of the indicators, and places persons and objects entitled to their protection at greater risk.

3. Unlike the Rule relating to perfidy, this Rule's prohibitions are absolute.[1201] They are not limited to actions resulting (or intending to result) in the death, injury, or, in the case of a State Party to Additional Protocol I, capture of an adversary.

4. The term 'improper use' generally refers to 'any use other than that for which the emblems were intended', namely identification of the objects, locations, and personnel serving a protected function.[1202] The mere display of a protective emblem, even when a reasonable person would realise its false nature, violates the Rule. Improper use does not

---

MANUAL, paras. 641, 932; AMW MANUAL, Rule 112(a) and (b). NIAC MANUAL, para. 2.3.4; ICRC CUSTOMARY IHL STUDY, Rules 58, 59, 61. See also Rome Statute, Art. 8(2)(b)(vii). It is important to note that the latter provision is of more limited scope, applying only when 'resulting in death or serious personal injury'. Moreover, the Rome Statute contains no equivalent rule in relation to non-international armed conflict.

[1194] The Red Lion and Sun has not been used since 1980. In that year, the government of the Islamic Republic of Iran declared that it would use the Red Crescent. See AMW MANUAL, n. 404.

[1195] Geneva Convention I, Arts. 38–44; Geneva Convention II, Arts. 41–45.

[1196] Additional Protocol III, Art. 2(1).

[1197] Additional Protocol I, Art. 66; UK MANUAL, para. 5.10, n. 41.

[1198] Cultural Property Convention, Arts. 16–17; DoD MANUAL, para. 5.18.7.2; AMW MANUAL, commentary accompanying Rule 112(a).

[1199] Hague Regulations, Art. 23(f); Additional Protocol I, Art. 38(1); DoD MANUAL, para. 12.4; AMW MANUAL, commentary accompanying Rule 112; ICRC CUSTOMARY IHL STUDY, Rule 58.

[1200] Additional Protocol I, Annex I, Art. 9, as amended 30 November 1993.

[1201] ICRC ADDITIONAL PROTOCOLS 1987 COMMENTARY, para. 1532.

[1202] ICRC CUSTOMARY IHL STUDY, commentary accompanying Rule 61.

encompass feigning protected status when protective indicators are not being displayed or used. As an example, consider an email from a Hotmail account to enemy forces that includes a bare assertion that the sender is a delegate of the International Committee of the Red Cross. The action does not breach the Rule because it does not misuse the organisation's emblem.

5.   The International Group of Experts struggled with the issue of whether the prohibitions set forth in this Rule applied beyond the recognised and specified indicators. For instance, they discussed whether the use of an email employing the International Committee of the Red Cross domain name for purposes related to the conflict violate this Rule. The Experts took two different approaches.

6.   By the first approach, based upon strict textual interpretation of the underlying treaty law, this Rule bears only on protective indicators, as distinct from the protected persons or objects they identify. For proponents of this approach, only cyber operations that employ electronic reproductions of the relevant graphic emblems, or which display the other protective indicators set forth in the law of armed conflict, are prohibited. Consider, for example, the use of an email message spoofed to originate from the 'icrc.org' domain in order to bypass the enemy's network data filters and deliver a piece of malware to the military network. As this operation does not specifically misuse the Red Cross symbol, the Experts taking this position concluded that the action would not violate this Rule.

7.   By the second approach, based upon a teleological interpretation of the underlying treaty law, the key factor in analysing such situations is use of an indicator upon which others would reasonably rely in extending protection provided for under the law of armed conflict. For these Experts, the previous example would violate this Rule because the domain name 'icrc.org' invites confidence as to the affiliation of the originator.[1203]

8.   This Rule is without prejudice to the adoption of an agreement between parties to the conflict as to cyber or other indicators of specially protected status.[1204]

[1203] An argument in favour of this view would be to treat Art. 44 of Geneva Convention I as extending not only to the words 'Red Cross' or 'Geneva Cross' but also to 'ICRC'.

[1204] Geneva Conventions I–III, Art. 6; Geneva Convention IV, Art. 7; ICRC ADDITIONAL PROTOCOLS 1987 COMMENTARY, para. 1557.

Rule 125 – Improper use of United Nations emblem

It is prohibited to make use of the distinctive emblem of the United Nations in cyber operations, except as authorised by that organisation.

1.   Both treaty and customary international law recognise that unauthorised use of the distinctive emblem of the United Nations is prohibited in international and non-international armed conflict.[1205]

2.   Any use of its emblem not authorised by the organisation constitutes a violation of this Rule, subject to the exception set forth in the following paragraph. For instance, sending an email masquerading as a United Nations communication and containing the United Nations emblem is prohibited. The prohibition applies irrespective of whether United Nations personnel are deployed to the area of armed conflict.

3.   In circumstances where the United Nations is a party to an armed conflict or militarily intervenes in an on-going one, the emblem loses its protective function since United Nations military personnel and equipment are lawful targets. Of course, United Nations personnel performing non-military functions, and their material and equipment, remain protected under the law of armed conflict as civilians and civilian objects respectively.

4.   As in the case of the protective indicators addressed in Rule 124, the International Group of Experts was split on the issue of whether the emblem has to be used in order to violate this Rule. Whereas some took the position that it does, others maintained that any unauthorised use of an apparently authoritative indication of United Nations status suffices. For a discussion of this matter, see Rule 124.

Rule 126 – Improper use of enemy indicators

It is prohibited to make use of the flags, military emblems, insignia, or uniforms of the enemy while visible to the enemy during an attack, including a cyber attack.

1.   This Rule is based on Article 23(f) of the Hague Regulations and Article 39(2) of Additional Protocol I. It applies in both

---

[1205] Additional Protocol I, Art. 38(2); UK MANUAL, para. 5.10.c; CANADIAN MANUAL, para. 605(c); AMW MANUAL, Rule 112(e); NIAC MANUAL, commentary accompanying para. 2.3.4; ICRC CUSTOMARY IHL STUDY, Rule 60. *See also* Rome Statute, Art. 8(2)(b)(vii).

international and non-international armed conflict and reflects customary international law.[1206]

2.   There was consensus among the International Group of Experts that the use of enemy uniforms, insignia, and emblems is prohibited when engaging in an attack during both international and non-international armed conflict.[1207] Article 39(2) of Additional Protocol I extends the prohibition beyond use during attacks to actions intended to shield, favour, protect, or impede military operations.[1208] The extension is not generally considered to form part of customary international law.[1209]

3.   This Rule originates from a historical requirement for visual distinction between opposing forces and their equipment on the battlefield. As such, the terms "'emblem, insignia, or uniforms" refer only to concrete visual objects, including national symbols marked on military vehicles and aircraft'.[1210] It is unlikely that improper use of enemy uniforms and other indicators will occur during a remote access cyber attack, as the cyber operators would not be in visual contact with the adversary. However, the use of them during a close access cyber attack is prohibited.

4.   The reference to 'while visible to the enemy' has been included in this Rule because the International Group of Experts split over the issue of whether customary law prohibits use during any attack, irrespective of the attendant circumstances. The majority of the International Group of Experts took the position that such a broad interpretation would serve no purpose since it is only when the attacker's use is apparent to the enemy that the act benefits the attacker or places its opponent at a disadvantage. In their estimation, the prohibition therefore only applies when the individual conducting the cyber attack is physically visible to his or her adversary. The other Experts were of the view that no such limitation should be placed on the prohibition since it appears in neither Article 39

[1206] DoD MANUAL, para. 5.23.1; UK MANUAL, para. 5.11; CANADIAN MANUAL, para. 607; GERMAN MANUAL, para. 473; AMW MANUAL, Rule 112(c); NIAC MANUAL, para. 2.3.5; ICRC CUSTOMARY IHL STUDY, Rule 62. *See also* Rome Statute, Art. 8(2)(b)(vii).

[1207] Combatants captured while wearing enemy uniforms do not enjoy belligerent immunity and are not entitled to prisoner of war status. *See* Rules 86–87.

[1208] Canada has made a reservation to its application of Art. 39(2) to the effect that it would apply the prohibition only while engaging in attacks and not in order to shield, favour, protect, or impede military operations. CANADIAN MANUAL, para. 607.

[1209] There are divergent views as to what constitutes improper use. *See* AMW MANUAL, commentary accompanying Rule 112(c); NIAC MANUAL, commentary accompanying para. 2.3.5; ICRC CUSTOMARY IHL Study, commentary accompanying Rule 62.

[1210] BOTHE, *ET AL.*, NEW RULES, at 214.

(2) of Additional Protocol I, nor the ICRC Customary IHL Study's discussion of that Article. However, Experts agreed that the conduct cited in this Rule violated customary international law.

5. Unlike misuse of protective indicators (Rule 124), the Rule does not extend to use of the enemy's emblem or other indicators of enemy status in the cyber communications themselves. In other words, it is permissible to feign enemy authorship of a cyber communication. This distinction is supported by State practice regarding lawful ruses. For instance, the UK Manual cites the following examples of ruses, each of which is adaptable to cyber operations: 'transmitting bogus signal messages and sending bogus despatches and newspapers with a view to their being intercepted by the enemy; making use of the enemy's signals, passwords, radio code signs, and words of command; conducting a false military exercise on the radio while substantial troop movements are taking place on the ground; pretending to communicate with troops or reinforcements which do not exist; . . . [and] giving false ground signals to enable airborne personnel or supplies to be dropped in a hostile area, or to induce aircraft to land in a hostile area'.[1211]

6. The application of this Rule is somewhat problematic in the cyber context because of the possibility of remotely acquiring control of enemy systems without having physical possession of them. Military computer hardware is regularly marked. However, such markings are seldom used to distinguish it from enemy computer hardware. For this reason, the International Group of Experts agreed that the Rule has no application with regard to enemy marked computer hardware over which control has been remotely acquired and that is used for conducting attacks against the enemy.

7. Situations involving cyber operation employed to gain control of other enemy military equipment are more complicated. For instance, it might be possible to acquire control of an enemy surface-to-air missile site that has been marked with the enemy emblem. In such a case, it would be impossible to remove the enemy's emblem before using the site to attack enemy aircraft. The ICRC commentary to Article 39(2) addresses the analogous situation of capturing an enemy tank on the battlefield and using it against the enemy. The commentary asserts that enemy markings would first have to be removed. As justification for applying such a strict rule, the commentary cites the persistent abuse of

---

[1211] UK MANUAL, para. 5.17.2. *See also* DoD MANUAL, para. 5.23.1.5; CANADIAN MANUAL, para. 856; GERMAN MANUAL, para. 471; AMW MANUAL, commentary accompanying Rule 116(c).

enemy uniforms and emblems following the Second World War.[1212] The majority of the International Group of Experts took the position that military equipment, the control of which is taken by cyber means, may not be used for an attack while bearing enemy markings. A minority of the Experts noted that the commentary both labelled the issue 'a delicate question' and observed that the equipment could be withdrawn to the rear in order to be re-marked.[1213] These Experts took the position that the tank scenario should be resolved by assessing the feasibility of removing or obscuring the enemy markings. In the surface-to-air missile site scenario, they concluded that the site might be used to conduct attacks since it is not feasible to remove or obscure the enemy markings prior to doing so. They argued that the Rule is not absolute; it is context-dependent, particularly with regard to feasibility.

8.   An exception to Article 39(2) of Additional Protocol I exists for armed conflict at sea. The exception allows a warship to fly enemy (or neutral) flags as long as it displays its true colours immediately before an armed engagement.[1214] Therefore, warships flying the enemy or neutral flag may conduct cyber operations until an engagement commences. The International Group of Experts agreed that the law is unsettled as to whether a cyber attack (as distinct from a cyber operation) would be prohibited as an engagement from a warship displaying enemy or neutral flags.

9.   The International Group of Experts noted the existence of separate requirements beyond the scope of this Rule to mark warships and military aircraft. For instance, in air warfare only properly marked military aircraft may exercise belligerent rights.[1215] Such issues arise in the case of acquiring control of enemy warships or military aircraft to conduct belligerent activities other than attack. Consider a cyber operation to assume control of an enemy's unmanned aerial vehicle (UAV) while in flight. The question is whether it must be marked with the capturing party's military marks before undertaking, for example, reconnaissance missions. Some Experts took the view that most States would not interpret this requirement as absolute in character. In their view, the captured UAV would not have to first land immediately and be marked with the acquiring State's markings. Cyber operations, in their

---

[1212] ICRC ADDITIONAL PROTOCOLS 1987 COMMENTARY, para. 1576.
[1213] ICRC ADDITIONAL PROTOCOLS 1987 COMMENTARY, para. 1576.
[1214] DoD MANUAL, para. 13.13.1; SAN REMO MANUAL, Rule 110.
[1215] AMW MANUAL, Rules 1(x), 17; Hague Air Warfare Rules, Arts. 3, 13.

estimation, undercut the basis for asserting the absolute character of the Rule. Other Experts, however, considered that there is an absolute prohibition of employing the captured UAV for military purposes until the relevant military and national markings have been applied.

Rule 127 – Improper use of neutral indicators

In cyber operations, it is prohibited to make use of flags, military emblems, insignia, or uniforms of neutral or other States not parties to the conflict.

1. This Rule is based on Article 39(1) of Additional Protocol I. It applies to international armed conflict and is considered part of customary international law.[1216] An exception to the Rule exists in relation to naval warfare.[1217]

2. It is unsettled whether this Rule applies to non-international armed conflict. The ICRC Customary IHL Study argues that there is a 'legitimate expectation that the parties to a non-international armed conflict abide by this rule'.[1218] A contrary view is that the Rule does not apply in non-international armed conflict because the law of neutrality is limited to international armed conflicts (see also chapeau to Chapter 20).[1219] See Rules 150–154 for a discussion of neutrality.

3. The phrase 'other States not parties to the conflict' is drawn from the text of Article 39(1). It was included in order to cover States that have adopted a narrow interpretation of neutrality.

4. The International Group of Experts agreed that wearing the uniform of a neutral State's armed forces to conduct a close access cyber attack would be prohibited under this Rule. However, as in the case of protective indicators (Rule 124) and United Nations emblems (Rule 125), the Group was divided over whether employment of other indicators of

---

[1216] DoD Manual, para. 5.24.1; UK Manual, para. 5.11; Canadian Manual, para. 606; German Manual, para. 473; AMW Manual, Rule 112(d); ICRC Customary IHL Study, Rule 63.

[1217] Additional Protocol I, Art. 39(3) (stating that it does not affect 'the existing generally recognised rules of international law applicable to espionage or to the use of flags in the conduct of armed conflict at sea'); DoD Manual, para. 5.24.1; San Remo Manual, Rule 110.

[1218] ICRC Customary IHL Study, commentary accompanying Rule 63. See also NIAC Manual, para. 2.3.4.

[1219] AMW Manual, commentary accompanying Rule 112(d). The AMW Manual notes that the conduct would nevertheless 'be regarded as improper'.

neutral status is prohibited. For example, there was a lack of consensus as to use of a neutral State's government domain name. For a discussion of the two positions, see Rule 124.

SECTION 9:   BLOCKADES AND ZONES

A. Blockades

1.   The question of whether and to what extent the law of blockade applies in the cyber context proved to be a particularly challenging issue for the International Group of Experts. Blockade is a method of warfare consisting of belligerent operations to prevent all vessels and aircraft (enemy and neutral; on the latter, see Chapter 20) from entering or exiting specified ports, airports, or coastal areas belonging to, occupied by, or under the control of an enemy belligerent State.[1220] A blockade may be established as part of military operations directed against military forces or as an economic operation with the strategic goal of weakening an enemy's military power through the degradation of its economy.[1221]

2.   While the law of blockade originally evolved in the context of maritime operations, the advent of aviation made blockade law relevant to aircraft as well. Not only are aircraft used to enforce a naval blockade, but it has also been recognised that a blockade to prevent aircraft from entering or exiting specified airfields or coastal areas belonging to, occupied by, or under the control of the enemy, constitutes a lawful method of aerial warfare.[1222]

3.   The common elements of a blockade are: it must be declared and notified; the commencement, duration, location, and extent of the blockade must be specified in the declaration; the blockade must be effective; the forces maintaining the blockade may be stationed at a distance from the coast determined by military requirements; a combination of lawful methods and means of warfare may enforce the blockade; access to neutral ports, coasts, and airfields may not be blocked; cessation, lifting, extension, re-establishment, or other alteration of a blockade must be

---

[1220] DoD MANUAL, para. 13.10. For a definition of aerial blockade, *see* AMW MANUAL, chapeau to Sec. V.

[1221] *See* GERMAN MANUAL, paras. 1014, 1051–1053.

[1222] AMW MANUAL, chapeau to Sec. V.

declared and notified; and the blockading party must apply the blockade impartially to the aircraft and vessels of every State.[1223]

4. Given the increasing use of computers and computer systems in the operation of vessels and aircraft, cyber means can be used to facilitate the establishment and enforcement of a naval or aerial blockade. Rule 128 reflects this practice. A more difficult question is whether the use of cyber means to block neutral and enemy cyber communications to or from enemy territory or areas under enemy control – a so-called 'cyber blockade' – is subject to the law of blockade.[1224]

5. The issue prompted significant debate within the International Group of Experts. It centred on the applicability of the criteria for blockade in the cyber context, the technical feasibility of a cyber blockade and, thus, characterisation of the rules governing cyber blockade as *lex lata* or *lex ferenda*.

6. A minority of the Experts considered such cyber operations to be mere electronic jamming, that is, akin to electronic warfare. The majority took notice of the fact that naval or aerial blockades were often designed to create a particular effect that could be achieved by cyber means. For example, a legitimate goal of blockade has always been to affect negatively the enemy's economy. Since economic activity is conducted through communications via the Internet, the majority of the International Group of Experts concluded that it is reasonable to apply the law of blockade to operations designed to block cyber communications into and out of territory under enemy control. For them, these operations are qualitatively distinct from jamming communications.

7. The establishment of a blockade traditionally required the specification of a particular geographical line that aircraft or vessels might not cross. This raises the question of whether a line of blockade can be articulated in a declaration of cyber blockade and whether it is feasible

---

[1223] DoD Manual, paras. 13.10.2; UK Manual, paras. 13.65–13.73; Canadian Manual, para. 848; German Manual, para. 1052; AMW Manual, Sec. V; San Remo Manual, Rules 93–95, 97, 99–101.

[1224] This question was prompted by the statement made by the Estonian Minister of Defence, who declared that the 2007 DDoS attacks against his nation 'can effectively be compared to when your ports are shut to the sea'. While the Defence Minister did not explicitly use the term 'blockade', it is obvious that he drew a parallel between the closure of ports and DDoS attacks that blocked Estonia's important websites. Johnny Ryan, '*iWar*': *A New Threat, its Convenience – and our Increasing Vulnerability*, NATO Review (Winter 2007), www.nato.int/docu/review/2007/issue4/english/analysis2.html.

to block all cyber communications crossing it. The Technical Experts advised that it is possible to do both.

8.   A further conceptual difficulty is that blockade law, as presently understood, is geographically restricted. Naval and air blockades involve preventing access to or from 'specified ports, airfields, or coastal areas'.[1225] In light of the relative freedom of navigation of neutral vessels and aircraft in international waters and airspace, the concept only has relevance when blockade operations are mounted in these areas, thereby interfering with neutral rights. The minority of the International Group of Experts strictly applied this paradigm in the cyber context, with the result that it would be conceptually impossible to establish a cyber blockade of landlocked territory. The majority concluded that a cyber blockade is a meaningful notion in these circumstances because it may be effectively enforced solely from belligerent territory without breaching the neutrality of adjacent States.

9.   The International Group of Experts struggled with the meaning of the effectiveness criterion in its application to cyber blockades. A minority of the Experts took the position that sufficient effectiveness was unattainable because the communications in question could be achieved by other means, such as radio and telephone. The majority drew support for their position by reference to air and sea movements. They pointed to the fact that the carriage of materials by air, which could not be shipped by sea due to a naval blockade, did not make a naval blockade ineffective, and *vice versa*.

10.   A cyber blockade may be rendered effective by other than cyber means. For example, a party to the conflict could enforce a cyber blockade with a combination of cyber (e.g., denying access to Internet Exchange route servers by modifying the routing tables), electronic warfare (e.g., employing directed energy weapons to interfere with radio frequency communication), and kinetic means (e.g., severing Internet trunk lines and destroying network centres in enemy territory by airstrikes).

11.   Cyber blockades may not bar, or otherwise seriously affect, the use of neutral cyber infrastructure for communications between the neutral State and other neutral States.[1226]

[1225] DoD MANUAL, para. 13.10; AMW MANUAL, chapeau to Sec. V.
[1226] DoD MANUAL, para. 13.10.2.5; UK MANUAL, para. 13.71; CANADIAN MANUAL, para. 848; AMW MANUAL, Rule 150; SAN REMO MANUAL, Rule 99.

12.   The law of blockade applies in international armed conflicts. In a non-international armed conflict, a State that is a party to the conflict may impose restrictions on the entry into and exit from areas that were formerly under its control and that are subject to its territorial sovereignty. So long as the State limits its operations to its own territory, waters, and airspace, they do not amount to a blockade in a legal sense. It is a matter of dispute whether a State involved in a non-international armed conflict may establish and enforce a blockade in international waters or airspace. Non-State actors are not entitled to establish and enforce a naval, aerial, or, *a fortiori*, cyber blockade.[1227]

13.   To summarise, some members of the International Group of Experts completely rejected the notion of a cyber blockade as a matter of existing law. Others accepted it conceptually, but pointed to practical difficulties in meeting the legal criteria (or took divergent approaches to their application in the cyber context). Still others asserted that cyber blockades are lawful, capable of meeting traditional criteria, and practically and technically feasible. Since the International Group of Experts could not achieve consensus on Rules regarding the existence, establishment, and enforcement of a cyber blockade, the following Rules only address how cyber means may be used as a component of a traditional naval or air blockade.

B. Zones

1.   The concept of zones is grounded in operational doctrine and not international law. Operational zones include, *inter alia*, exclusion zones, no-fly zones, warning zones, and the immediate vicinity of naval or aerial operations.[1228] They are not 'free fire zones' or 'areas of unrestricted warfare'. During an armed conflict, belligerents remain fully subject to the law of armed conflict within zones.[1229] Neutral, civilian, and other protected objects or persons retain their protection under that law when

---

[1227]   AMW Manual, chapeau to Sec. V.

[1228]   *See generally* DoD Manual, para. 13.9; UK Manual, paras. 12.58–58.2, 13.77–13.80; Canadian Manual, para. 852; German Manual, paras. 448, 1048–1050; AMW Manual, Sec. P; San Remo Manual, paras. 105–108.

[1229]   DoD Manual, para. 13.9.2; UK Manual, paras. 13.77, 13.78; Canadian Manual, para. 852; German Manual, para. 1050; AMW Manual, chapeau to Sec. P, Rules 105 (a), 107(a). During peacetime, international law regarding self-defence (Rules 71–75) and force protection applies fully within such zones.

they enter such zones, even if they have ignored the instructions issued by the party that established them.

2.   Penetration of a zone may be considered when assessing whether the object or person concerned qualifies as a lawful target.[1230] Consider the penetration of a closed and sensitive military network (i.e., the equivalent of a zone) during an armed conflict. The system provides a clear warning that intrusion will subject the intruder to automatic 'hack-back' or other measures. Despite having been placed on sufficient notice and afforded the opportunity to withdraw or desist, the intruder persists. In this case, it would generally be reasonable to conclude that the intrusion is hostile. As such, those individuals authorising or executing the intrusion and the hardware and software they employ may reasonably be considered lawful targets (Rules 96–97, 99–100).

3.   Cyber exclusion zone issues arise in two contexts – use of cyber means or methods in the enforcement of naval and aerial zones and the creation of unique cyber exclusion zones. The former is dealt with in the Rules that follow. With respect to the latter, the Technical Experts emphasised the difficulty of defining zones in cyberspace. Moreover, compliance with the terms of a defined zone might be technically challenging since in many cases the communications concerned may rely upon cyber infrastructure over which the sender has no control.

4.   In light of the facts that zones are operational concepts, that those who establish them are not relieved of their legal obligations, and that maintenance is technically difficult, the International Group of Experts agreed that the articulation of Rules governing cyber zones was inappropriate. Consequently, the sole zones issue addressed in this Manual is the use of cyber operations in support of aerial and naval zones (Rule 130).

Rule 128 – Maintenance and enforcement of blockades

Cyber methods and means of warfare may be used to maintain and enforce a naval or aerial blockade provided that they do not, alone or

---

[1230] The *jus ad bellum* significance of penetrating a zone is that the act may be a relevant consideration when assessing whether an armed attack has occurred or is imminent. AMW MANUAL, commentary accompanying Rule 105(a). In certain narrowly defined circumstances, the mere fact that a zone has been penetrated can be sufficiently determinative that an armed attack (Rule 71) is underway.

in combination with other methods, result in acts inconsistent with the law of international armed conflict.

1. Conducted appropriately, cyber operations can prove valuable to a military commander in maintaining and enforcing a naval or aerial blockade. Remote access cyber operations against propulsion and navigation systems are examples of the sort of cyber operations that can support blockades. Any use of cyber operations to enforce or maintain a blockade is subject to the same restrictions as kinetic means and methods of warfare. In particular, a blockade is unlawful when the harm to the civilian population is, or may be expected to be, excessive in relation to the concrete and direct military advantage anticipated from the blockade.[1231]

Rule 129 – Effect of blockades on neutral activities

The use of cyber operations to enforce a naval or aerial blockade must not have the effect of barring, or otherwise seriously affecting, access to neutral territory.

1. According to well-established principles of the international law applicable to armed conflict, belligerent measures must be applied with due regard to, and must not violate, the rights of neutral States. For instance, Article 1 of Hague Convention V provides that 'the territory of neutral Powers is inviolable'.[1232] In the context of aerial and naval blockades, both the AMW Manual and the San Remo Manual provide that a blockade may not bar access to the airspace, ports, and coasts of neutral States.[1233] The same position has been adopted for the purposes of the present Manual.

2. The term 'access' in this Rule denotes physical access by aircraft or vessels. Cyber operations can have the effect of barring access in many situations. For instance, a cyber operation that interferes with the propulsion or navigation systems of neutral aircraft or vessels can

---

[1231] CANADIAN MANUAL, para. 850; AMW MANUAL, Rule 157(b); SAN REMO MANUAL, para. 102(b).

[1232] *See also* Hague Convention XIII, Art. 1 (stating 'Belligerents are bound to respect the sovereign rights of neutral Powers and to abstain, in neutral territory or in neutral waters, from any act which would, if knowingly permitted by any Power, constitute a violation of neutrality.').

[1233] AMW MANUAL, Rule 150; SAN REMO MANUAL, Rule 99. *See also* DoD MANUAL, para. 13.10.2.5; UK MANUAL, para. 13.71; CANADIAN MANUAL, para. 848.

effectively prevent them from operating in neutral airspace or sea areas. Similarly, a cyber operation that interferes with port or airfield operations can effectively keep vessels or aircraft from using those facilities and, thus, from accessing neutral territory. If they physically bar access, cyber operations in support of a blockade are prohibited. A majority of the Experts agreed that the law of naval or aerial blockade does not prohibit cyber operations used to enforce a blockade that have the effect of interfering with access to neutral cyber infrastructure or with cyber communications between neutral States.

3.   Those Experts who accepted the concept of cyber blockade (see chapeau to Section 9 of this Chapter) agreed that such a blockade, as distinct from cyber measures taken to enforce a naval or aerial blockade, would be subject to a prohibition of cyber operations that impede access to neutral cyber infrastructure or interfere with cyber communications between neutral States. In particular, they noted that the cyber infrastructure physically situated in the territory of a neutral State is already protected by that State's territorial sovereignty (Rules 1–3) unless the protection is lost pursuant to international law (Rules 76 and 151). These Experts would limit operation of the prohibition to cyber communications between neutral States. Article 54 of the Hague Regulations provides that submarine cables connecting an occupied territory with neutral territory may be seized or destroyed 'in case of absolute necessity', subject to restoration and compensation after the end of war.

Rule 130 – Zones

To the extent that States establish zones, whether in peacetime or during armed conflict, lawful cyber operations may be used to exercise their rights in such zones.

1.   As discussed in the chapeau to this Section, various types of zones may be established during an armed conflict. The existence of such zones has no bearing on the legal rights and obligations of States, whether belligerent or neutral, within and beyond sovereign territory. For instance, States enjoy the rights of self-defence (Rule 71), of freedom of navigation, and to conduct hostilities in international waters and airspace (subject to the due regard principle). However, the existence of a zone may affect the exercise of such rights. As an example, a warship may take penetration of a warning zone into account when assessing whether an aircraft is about to attack it.

2. Cyber operations may be used to declare and notify the establishment of a zone, and subsequently to maintain it. For example, cyber means may serve to communicate restrictions regarding passage through a zone or to warn aircraft or vessels that are approaching it. Similarly, where activity within a zone leaves a vessel or aircraft open to attack as a military objective, cyber operations may be used to assist in, or carry out, the attack, as long as the cyber attack complies with the law of armed conflict.

18

Certain persons, objects, and activities

1.   In addition to the general protection afforded to civilians and civilian objects, the law of armed conflict provides protection to specific classes of persons, objects, and activities. The Rules set forth in this chapter apply these provisions in the cyber context.

2.   These Rules are without prejudice to the right of the parties to a conflict to enter into special agreements. They may agree at any time to protect persons or objects not otherwise covered by the law of armed conflict, as well as to implement additional provisions for protected persons or objects beyond those required by that law. As a rule, special agreements may only be concluded with a view to enhancing protection.[1234] For example, the parties to a conflict may conclude a special agreement providing greater protection for cyber infrastructure supporting the operation of works and installations containing dangerous forces than that set forth in Rule 140 by agreeing to an absolute prohibition of attacks against them, whether by cyber or kinetic means.[1235] Similarly, a special agreement could be concluded to protect cyber infrastructure supporting sensitive facilities not addressed by the Rule, such as oil production installations, oil drilling platforms, petroleum storage facilities, oil refineries, or chemical production facilities.[1236] The unique nature of cyberspace and the activities that occur therein may render such agreements particularly relevant and useful. An impartial humanitarian organisation, such as the International Committee of the Red Cross, may facilitate the conclusion and implementation of special agreements.[1237]

[1234] See Geneva Conventions I–IV, Art. 3; Geneva Conventions I–III, Art. 6; Geneva Convention IV, Art. 7. *See also* AMW MANUAL, Rule 99 and accompanying commentary.

[1235] AMW MANUAL, commentary accompanying Rule 99.

[1236] AMW MANUAL, commentary accompanying Rule 99.

[1237] AMW MANUAL, commentary accompanying Rule 99.

3. The fact that certain persons, objects, and activities that enjoy specific protection under the law of armed conflict are not addressed in this chapter's Rules must not be interpreted as implying that they lack such protection in the cyber context. Where the application of a particular law of armed conflict protective norm did not appear to raise issues peculiar to cyber warfare, the International Group of Experts concluded that it was not necessary to reflect this in the present Manual. Therefore, it is essential to bear in mind that, to the extent persons, objects, and activities benefit from the protection of the law of armed conflict generally, they will equally enjoy such protection with regard to cyber operations and attacks.

SECTION 1:   MEDICAL AND RELIGIOUS PERSONNEL AND MEDICAL UNITS, TRANSPORTS, AND MATERIAL

Rule 131 – Medical and religious personnel, medical units and transports

Medical and religious personnel, medical units, and medical transports must be respected and protected and, in particular, may not be made the object of cyber attack.

1. The general obligations to respect and protect medical units, medical means of transport, and medical personnel are set forth in Articles 19, 24, 25, 35, and 36 of Geneva Convention I; Articles 22, 24, 25, 27, 36 to 39 of Geneva Convention II; Articles 18 to 22 of Geneva Convention IV; Articles 12, 15, 21 to 24, and 26 of Additional Protocol I; and Article 9 of Additional Protocol II. Religious personnel are protected pursuant to Article 24 of Geneva Convention I; Chapter 4 of Geneva Convention II; Article 33 of Geneva Convention III; Article 15 of Additional Protocol I; and Article 9 of Additional Protocol II. Medical and religious personnel, medical units, and medical transports may lose their protected status pursuant to Rule 134.

2. The Rule applies in both international and non-international armed conflict as customary international law.[1238]

3. The term 'religious personnel' does not refer to every member of a religious society. Rather, it denotes those individuals defined in

---

[1238] DoD Manual, paras. 7.10, 7.11, 17.15.2; UK Manual, paras. 7.10–7.22, 7.30, 15.45–15.47 (as amended); Canadian Manual, Chapter 9, Sec. 3; German Manual, paras. 610, 612, 624, 816; AMW Manual, Secs. K, L; NIAC Manual, paras. 3.2, 4.2.1; ICRC Customary IHL Study, Rules 25, 27–30. *See also* Rome Statute, Art. 8(2)(b)(xxiv), 8(2)(e)(ii); ICRC Geneva Convention I 2016 Commentary, paras. 1799, 1804.

Article 8(d) of Additional Protocol I. In particular, it encompasses chaplains attached to the armed forces. The International Group of Experts agreed that the term applies in the same sense in non-international armed conflict.[1239]

4.   Although not addressed in this Rule, it must also be borne in mind that places of worship are specifically protected, albeit not absolutely, from attack or any other hostile act in accordance with Article 27 of the Hague Regulations and Article 53 of Additional Protocol I, which in the opinion of the International Group of Experts reflect customary international law.[1240]

5.   The requirement to 'respect and protect' involves separate obligations. The duty to respect is breached by actions that impede or prevent medical or religious personnel, medical units, or medical transports from performing their medical or religious functions, or that otherwise adversely affect the humanitarian functions of medical or religious personnel, units, or transports.[1241] It includes, but is not limited to, the prohibition on attacks. For instance, this Rule would prohibit altering data in the Global Positioning System of a medical helicopter in order to misdirect it, even though the operation would not qualify as an attack on a medical transport (Rule 92). Similarly, blocking the online broadcast of a religious service for combat troops would be prohibited. It must be cautioned that the Rule does not extend to situations that occur only incidentally, as in the case of the overall blocking of enemy communications.

6.   By contrast, the duty to protect implies the taking of positive measures to ensure respect by others (e.g., non-State actors) for medical and religious personnel, medical units, and medical transports.[1242] For instance, the obligation would require a military force with the capability to do so to defend a hospital in an area under its control against cyber attacks by hacktivists, when and to the extent feasible.[1243]

[1239] ICRC Customary IHL Study, commentary accompanying Rule 27.
[1240] DoD Manual, para. 5.6.2; UK Manual, paras. 5.25, 15.18; Canadian Manual, paras. 443, 1723; AMW Manual, Rules 1(o), 95(a).
[1241] AMW Manual, commentary accompanying Rule 71.
[1242] AMW Manual, commentary accompanying Rule 71; ICRC Geneva Convention I 2016 Commentary, para.1805.
[1243] See Hague Regulations, Art. 27 (concerning 'hospitals and places where the sick and wounded are collected'); ICRC Geneva Convention I 2016 Commentary, para. 1875.

Rule 132 – Medical computers, computer networks, and data

Computers, computer networks, and data that form an integral part of the operations or administration of medical units and transports must be respected and protected, and in particular may not be made the object of attack.

1.   The protection set forth in this Rule derives from the broader protection to which medical personnel, units, and transports are entitled (Rule 131). It applies in both international and non-international armed conflict as customary international law.[1244]

2.   The concepts of 'respect' and 'protect' are explained in Rule 131. It does not violate this Rule to conduct non-damaging cyber reconnaissance to determine whether the medical facility or transports (or associated computers, computer networks, and data) in question are being misused for militarily harmful acts (Rule 134).

3.   The 'data' referred to in this Rule are those that are essential for the operation of medical units and transports. Examples include data necessary for the proper use of medical equipment and for tracking the inventory of medical supplies. Personal medical data required for the treatment of patients is likewise protected from alteration, deletion, or any other act by cyber means that would negatively affect their care, regardless of whether the act amounts to a cyber attack.[1245]

4.   If the objects referred to in this Rule are also being used to commit, outside their humanitarian functions, acts harmful to the enemy, they lose their protection against attack, subject to Rule 134. This situation is particularly relevant in the cyber context because medical data can be stored in the same data centre, server, or computer as military data.

Rule 133 – Identification

All feasible measures shall be taken to ensure that computers, computer networks, and data that form an integral part of the operations

---

[1244] DoD MANUAL, paras. 7.10, 7.11, 17.15.2; UK MANUAL, paras. 7.10–7.22 (as amended), 15.45–15.47; CANADIAN MANUAL, paras. 447, 448, 918; AMW MANUAL, commentary accompanying Sec. K; NIAC MANUAL, para. 4.2.1; ICRC CUSTOMARY IHL STUDY, Rules 25, 28–30.

[1245] ICRC Challenges Report, at 43 (stating that 'the obligation to respect and protect medical facilities must be understood as extending to medical data belonging to those facilities').

**or administration of medical units and transports are clearly identi-
fied through appropriate means, including electronic markings. Failure to so identify them does not deprive them of their protected status.**

1.   This Rule applies the law of armed conflict provisions as to the
marking of medical units and medical transports with a distinctive
emblem to computers, computer networks, and data that form an integral part of their operations. It applies in both international and non-
international armed conflict as customary international law.[1246]

2.   For the meaning of the term 'data' in this context, see Rule 132.

3.   Electronic markings are provided for under Articles 8(m) and 18
(5) of Additional Protocol I as additional means to facilitate the identification of medical units and transports. These markings may be used to
supplement the distinctive emblems. Use of appropriate electronic markings by States that are not Parties to Additional Protocol I is also
encouraged.

4.   It is the contribution to the medical function that computers,
computer networks, and data that form an integral part of the operations
or administration of medical units and transports make that determines
their protected status.[1247] Distinctive emblems and other means of identification only facilitate identification and do not, of themselves, confer
protected status. This principle is codified in Article 1 of Annex I of
Additional Protocol I (as amended in 1993) and in paragraph 4 of the
Preamble to Additional Protocol III. Since protected status is not derived
from the distinctive emblem or other means of identification *per se*, such
computers, computer networks, and data are protected regardless of
whether they bear the distinctive emblem or other means of identification.[1248] The phrase 'all feasible measures' is included in this Rule to
emphasise the fact that military, humanitarian, technical, or other considerations might make marking impractical in certain circumstances.

[1246] Additional Protocol I, Art. 18; Additional Protocol II, Art. 12; Geneva Convention I,
Art. 42; Geneva Convention II, Arts. 43, 44; Geneva Convention IV, Arts. 18, 20–22;
DoD MANUAL, paras. 7.15, 17.16; UK MANUAL paras. 7.23–7.23.3 (as amended), 15.48;
CANADIAN MANUAL, paras. 915, 916, 917; GERMAN MANUAL paras. 635, 638; AMW
MANUAL, Rule 72(a), chapeau to Sec. K; NIAC MANUAL, commentary accompanying
para. 3.2.

[1247] *See* AMW MANUAL, commentary accompanying Rule 72(c).

[1248] *See* DoD MANUAL, para. 7.15.3.2; GERMAN MANUAL, para. 612; AMW MANUAL, Rule 72
(d) and accompanying commentary; ICRC CUSTOMARY IHL STUDY, commentary
accompanying Rule 30.

5.   In the cyber context, marking could be achieved by adding identifiers to the data or by notifying, directly or indirectly, the other party to the conflict of unique identifiers related to the relevant computers, computer networks, or data.[1249] Consider the storage of military medical data in a cloud computing data centre. The party storing the data notifies the enemy that the files containing its military medical data have the unique name extension '.mil.med.B' and that this naming convention will not be used on any file that is not exclusively medical. The enemy verifies the nature of these files through intelligence analysis and incorporates special protections for this data into its cyber operational planning process. Both parties have complied with this Rule.

Rule 134 – Loss of protection and warnings

The protection to which medical units and transports, including computers, computer networks, and data that form an integral part of their operations or administration, are entitled by virtue of this Section does not cease unless they are used to commit, outside their humanitarian function, acts harmful to the enemy. In such situations protection may cease only after a warning setting a reasonable time limit for compliance, when appropriate, remains unheeded.

1.   This Rule applies in international and in non-international armed conflicts and reflects customary international law.[1250] With respect to international armed conflicts, the Rule is based on Article 27 of the Hague Regulations, Articles 21 and 22 of Geneva Convention I, Articles 34 and 35 of Geneva Convention II, Article 19 of Geneva Convention IV, and Article 13 of Additional Protocol I. In the case of non-international armed conflicts, it is based on Article 11(2) of Additional Protocol II.

2.   The term 'acts harmful' in this Rule has the same meaning as 'hostile acts' in Article 11(2) of Additional Protocol II.[1251] The notion of 'acts harmful to the enemy' encompasses acts the purpose or effect of

---

[1249]   Additional Protocol I, Annex I, Art. 1(4), as amended 30 November 1993 (providing, 'The High Contracting Parties and in particular the Parties to the conflict are invited at all times to agree upon additional or other signals, means or systems which enhance the possibility of identification and take full advantage of technological developments in this field').

[1250]   DoD Manual, paras. 7.17.1.2, 17.15.2; UK Manual, para. 7.13.1; Canadian Manual, paras. 447, 918; German Manual, paras. 613, 618–619; AMW Manual, Rule 74(a–b); NIAC Manual, para. 4.2.1; Customary IHL Study, Rules 25, 28–29.

[1251]   ICRC Additional Protocols 1987 Commentary, para. 4720.

which is to harm the enemy by impeding their military operations, or enhancing one's own.[1252] It not only includes acts inflicting harm on the enemy by direct attack, but also those adversely affecting enemy military operations, as with collecting intelligence and transmitting military communications.[1253]

3.   Acts that are not considered harmful to the enemy include:

(a) that the personnel of a medical unit are equipped with light individual weapons for their own defence or for that of the wounded, sick, or shipwrecked in their charge;
(b) that a medical unit is guarded by sentries or an escort;
(c) that portable arms and ammunition taken from the wounded and sick, and not yet handed over to the proper service, are found in the medical unit; or
(d) that members of the armed forces or other combatants are in the medical unit for medical or other authorised reasons, consistent with the mission of the medical unit.[1254]

4.   The fact that a medical computer system is equipped with software that, although not intended to be used for acts harmful to the enemy, is capable of being so used, does not *per se* deprive it of protected status. Consider a software application or software agent resident on a medical computer system that is capable of being used to participate in a DDoS attack. The system as a whole retains its protection, although the agent or application becomes a lawful military objective if used or going to be used for military purposes (provided all other requirements for qualification as a military

---

[1252] ICRC ADDITIONAL PROTOCOLS 1987 COMMENTARY, para. 550. *See also* AMW MANUAL, commentary accompanying Rule 74(a); ICRC GENEVA CONVENTION I 1952 COMMENTARY, at 200–201; ICRC GENEVA CONVENTION I 2016 COMMENTARY, paras. 1839–1845, 1995–2010, 2389–2391, 2457–2460.

[1253] AMW MANUAL, commentary accompanying Rule 74(a); ICRC GENEVA CONVENTION I 2016 COMMENTARY, para. 1851.

[1254] Additional Protocol I, Art. 13; Geneva Convention I, Art. 22; Geneva Convention IV, Art. 19. *See also* AMW MANUAL, commentary accompanying Rule 74(c); ICRC GENEVA CONVENTION I 2016 COMMENTARY, paras. 1860–1883. Note that the reference to 'light individual weapons' appears in Art. 13(2)(a) of Additional Protocol I, which applies only to civilian medical facilities. A similar though slightly different reference is contained in Article 22 of Geneva Convention I with regard to military medical facilities: 'The following conditions shall not be considered as depriving a medical unit or establishment of the protection guaranteed by Article 19: 1. That the personnel of the unit or establishment are armed, and that they use the arms in their own defence, or in that of the wounded and sick in their charge . . .'.

objective have been met). Similarly, the installation of intrusion detection software designed to prevent an attack on a medical computer system will not deprive it of its protected status.

5.   Even if there is a valid reason for discontinuing the specific protection of medical units or transports (including medical computers, computer networks, and data), due warning must be issued setting, where appropriate, a reasonable time limit for compliance before an attack may be conducted.[1255] The warning may take various forms, such as an email to the hospital, a radio message, or a press release. In many instances, it may simply consist of an order to cease the harmful act within a specified period.[1256] The relevant legal question is whether the means selected are such that the warning is sufficiently likely to reach the enemy.

6.   As noted in this Rule, the requirement to set a reasonable time limit for compliance only arises 'whenever appropriate', that is, when it is feasible to do so.[1257] For instance, if the misuse of the medical computers in question is causing immediate serious harm, it will typically not be feasible to afford an opportunity for compliance before responding, or it may be necessary substantially to reduce the time limit for compliance.

SECTION 2:   DETAINED PERSONS

1.   This Section addresses certain cyber-relevant provisions of the law of armed conflict governing the treatment of prisoners of war, interned protected persons, and others who are detained, including security detainees, detained civilians who have taken a direct part in hostilities, and those detained on criminal charges with a nexus to the armed conflict. It must be understood that there is an extensive body of law governing the treatment of detained persons. The following Rules deal

---

[1255] Additional Protocol I, Art. 13(1); Additional Protocol II, Art. 11(2); Geneva Convention I, Art. 21; Geneva Convention II, Art. 34; Geneva Convention IV, Art. 19. *See also* DoD MANUAL, paras. 7.17.1.2, 17.15.2; UK MANUAL, para. 7.13.1; CANADIAN MANUAL, para. 918; GERMAN MANUAL, para. 618; AMW MANUAL, commentary accompanying Rule 74(b).

[1256] AMW MANUAL, commentary accompanying Rule 74(b).

[1257] *See* Additional Protocol I, Art. 13(1); Additional Protocol II, Art. 11(2); Geneva Convention I, Art. 21; Geneva Convention II, Art. 34; Geneva Convention IV, Art. 19; AMW MANUAL, Rule 74(b).

only with those few aspects of that law that raise issues relating to cyber operations and activities.

2.   The legal regime governing detention of the various categories of detained persons differs based on the characterisation of the conflict (Rules 82–83). In particular, and with the exception of Common Article 3, the protections set forth in Geneva Conventions III and IV apply only in international armed conflict, although certain analogous customary provisions may apply to non-international armed conflict.

Rule 135 – Protection of detained persons

Prisoners of war, interned protected persons, and other detained persons must be protected from the harmful effects of cyber operations.

1.   The categories of prisoner of war under Geneva Convention III[1258] and interned civilians under Geneva Convention IV relate only to international armed conflicts. Those instruments and Article 75 of Additional Protocol I, which the Experts considered to reflect customary international law, govern their treatment. The treatment of detained persons in the context of a non-international armed conflict is governed by Common Article 3 of the 1949 Geneva Conventions, customary international law, and, when applicable for Parties thereto, the relevant provisions of Additional Protocol II.[1259]

2.   Detaining parties[1260] are responsible for the security and well-being of prisoners of war, interned protected persons, and other detainees.[1261] Precautions must be taken to protect them from the harmful effects of cyber operations.[1262] All detained persons are also protected

---

[1258]   This would include civilian cyber specialists who have been authorised to accompany the armed forces. See DoD MANUAL, para. 16.5.5 reflecting Geneva Convention III, Art. 4A(4).

[1259]   Additional Protocol II, Arts. 4, 5 (as well as other applicable law, such as, in certain circumstances, human rights law).

[1260]   In an international armed conflict, the correct term is 'detaining power'. However, because this Rule encompasses norms applicable in international and non-international armed conflict, the generic term 'detaining party' has been adopted in this Manual.

[1261]   See generally Geneva Convention III, Art. 12; Geneva Convention IV, Art. 29; Hague Regulations, Arts. 4, 7; DoD MANUAL, para. 8.2.1; UK MANUAL, paras. 8.26, 9.37–9.118; CANADIAN MANUAL, paras. 1014, 1129; GERMAN MANUAL, paras. 592–595, 702, 704, 714–726.

[1262]   Additional Protocol II, Art. 5(2)(c); Geneva Convention III, Art. 23; Geneva Convention IV, Art. 83; UK MANUAL, paras. 8.35, 8.39, 9.39; GERMAN MANUAL, paras. 543, 710, 714.

from cyber activities that contribute to or result in outrages on personal dignity; torture; or cruel, inhuman, humiliating, or degrading treatment.[1263]

3.   It is prohibited to employ cyber means to prevent or frustrate a detaining party's efforts to honour its obligations, such as recording personal details, with respect to prisoners of war, interned protected persons, and other detainees.[1264]

4.   Feasible measures must be taken to protect personal data relating to prisoners of war and interned protected persons from the effects of cyber operations, for example by being stored separately from data or objects that constitute a military objective. Such data must be respected and may not be modified or publicly exposed.[1265] This applies to data in the possession of the detaining party, any Protecting Power, and the International Committee of the Red Cross.

5.   Detaining parties must ensure their networks and computers are not employed to violate the honour or respect owed to prisoners of war and interned protected persons.[1266] Protection extends beyond the physical person.[1267] Prohibited cyber actions include posting defamatory information that reveals embarrassing or derogatory information or their emotional state.[1268] This would embrace, for example, posting information or images on the Internet that could be demeaning or that could subject prisoners of war or interned protected persons to public ridicule or public curiosity.

6.   Treaties governing the treatment of prisoners of war and interned protected persons generally guarantee a detention regime of privacy and protection from public abuse and curiosity.[1269] Detaining parties must

---

[1263] Additional Protocol I, Art. 75(2)(b), 85(4)(c); Additional Protocol II, Art. 4(2)(e); Geneva Conventions I–IV Art. 3; Geneva Convention III, Art. 14; Geneva Convention IV, Art. 27; UK MANUAL, paras. 8.29(d), 9.21; GERMAN MANUAL, paras. 595, 704.

[1264] Additional Protocol II, Art. 5(2)(b); Geneva Convention III, Arts. 70, 71 (stating provisions accounting for prisoners writing to family members); Geneva Convention IV, Arts. 106, 107.

[1265] Geneva Convention III, Art. 13; Geneva Convention IV, Art. 27.

[1266] Geneva Convention III, Arts. 13, 14; Geneva Convention IV, Art. 27.

[1267] ICRC GENEVA CONVENTION III 1960 COMMENTARY, at 144; ICRC GENEVA CONVENTION IV 1958 COMMENTARY, at 201–202.

[1268] ICRC GENEVA CONVENTION III 1960 COMMENTARY, at 145 (discussing protection against 'libel, slander, insult and any violation of secrets of a personal nature'); ICRC GENEVA CONVENTION IV COMMENTARY, at 202. See also CANADIAN MANUAL, para. 1016; GERMAN MANUAL, paras. 595, 704.

[1269] Geneva Convention III, Art. 13; Geneva Convention IV, Art. 27. See also UK MANUAL, paras. 8.28, 8.29(d), 9.21.

guard against intrusion by public and private actors into the communications, financial assets, or electronic records of prisoners of war or interned protected persons.[1270]

Rule 136 – Correspondence of detained persons

The right of prisoners of war, interned protected persons, and other detained persons to certain correspondence must not be interfered with by cyber operations.

1. In an international armed conflict, detaining parties must permit prisoners of war and interned protected persons to maintain relations with the exterior[1271] and to notify families of their detention within one week of arrival at a place of detention or internment.[1272] The obligations reflect customary international law.[1273]

2. Individuals detained for security reasons in non-international armed conflict are entitled under customary international law to correspond with their families, subject to reasonable conditions.[1274] In particular, persons who are detained in the context of a non-international armed conflict to which Additional Protocol II applies are specifically permitted to maintain correspondence with family members.[1275]

3. The correspondence addressed in this Rule denotes communication with family or other private persons of a strictly personal, non-military, non-political nature. Traditionally, the term 'correspondence' referred to letters or other handwritten communications. It is unclear whether, as a matter of law, correspondence includes electronic communications such as email. This is because the law is clear that a right of correspondence exists, but is not prescriptive as to its form.

4. The detaining party may take into consideration such factors as the difficulty of achieving an acceptable level of assurance that electronic communications are not being misused when determining

---

[1270] UK Manual, para. 8.29(d); ICRC Customary IHL Study, commentary accompanying Rule 122.

[1271] Geneva Convention III, Arts. 69–77; Geneva Convention IV, Arts. 105–116; UK Manual, paras. 8.62, 8.63, 9.61, 9.62; German Manual, paras. 595, 721.

[1272] Geneva Convention III, Art. 70; Geneva Convention IV, Art. 106; UK Manual, paras. 8.42, 9.45.

[1273] ICRC Customary IHL Study, Rule 125.

[1274] ICRC Customary IHL Study, Rule 125.

[1275] Additional Protocol II, Art. 5(2)(b). See also UK Manual, para. 15.41.b; NIAC Manual, para. 3.6 (regarding notification of status and location).

which mode of communication to allow. Although this Rule is meant to apply to the detaining party and not to interference by others, the detaining party will, if it permits electronic correspondence, be obliged to take basic reasonable and feasible security measures to ensure the message is delivered intact to the recipient.

5.   The customary right of detained persons to correspond with their families is subject to reasonable conditions relating, *inter alia*, to frequency and to the need for censorship by the authorities.[1276] If the detaining party decides to permit electronic communications, the setting of conditions will be particularly important because of factors like the difficulty of verifying the identity of the recipient of outgoing communications and the risk of malware being spread through incoming messages. Such conditions do not constitute interference with correspondence for the purpose of this Rule.[1277]

6.   The term 'interference' denotes activities by the detaining party that deny or impede the detainees' right to correspond or that take advantage of that right for the detaining party's own purposes. For instance, manipulating such correspondence to include malicious computer codes in order to engage in espionage, conduct a cyber attack, or mount a psychological operation is prohibited by the terms of this Rule.

Rule 137 – Compelled participation in military activities

Prisoners of war and interned protected persons shall not be compelled to participate in or support cyber operations directed against their own country.

1.   This Rule is based on Article 23(h) of the Hague Regulations; Articles 50 and 130 of Geneva Convention III; and Articles 40, 51, and 147 of Geneva Convention IV. It reflects customary international law in international armed conflict.[1278] Indeed, the law of armed

---

[1276] Geneva Convention III, Art. 76; Geneva Convention IV, Art. 112; UK MANUAL, paras. 9.59, 9.66.

[1277] So long as they do not violate Geneva Convention III, Art. 76, or Geneva Convention IV, Art. 112.

[1278] *See also* Rome Statute, Art. 8(2)(a)(v); CANADIAN MANUAL, paras. 1030, 1124; UNITED STATES ARMY, ARMY REGULATION 190–8: ENEMY PRISONERS OF WAR, RETAINED PERSONNEL, CIVILIAN INTERNEES AND OTHER DETAINEES, paras. 4-4, 4-5 (1997); GERMAN MANUAL, paras. 596, 720.

conflict extends the prohibition beyond those encompassed by this Rule. For example, nationals of a State who find themselves in enemy territory and protected persons in occupied territory enjoy the same protection.[1279] The Rule is not applicable in non-international armed conflict.

2. The prohibition is particularly relevant in the cyber context. Prisoners of war, by virtue of their former duties with enemy armed forces, may possess knowledge as to enemy computer systems or networks. Such knowledge would be of great value to a detaining party planning a cyber operation. Certain civilian detainees might likewise possess expertise or knowledge of operationally or strategically important information systems. Notwithstanding the obvious advantage of compelling these individuals to engage in cyber operations harmful to their country, doing so is prohibited.

SECTION 3: CHILDREN

Rule 138 – Protection of children

It is prohibited to conscript or enlist children into the armed forces or to allow them to take part in cyber hostilities.

1. This Rule applies in international and non-international armed conflict and reflects customary international law.[1280] More specific treaty law obligations are to be found in Article 38 of the Convention on the Rights of the Child; Articles 1, 2, and 4 of the Optional Protocol to the Convention on the Rights of the Child on the Involvement of Children in Armed Conflict; Article 77(2) of Additional Protocol I; and Article 4(3) (c) of Additional Protocol II. It should be noted that Article 4 of the Optional Protocol applies to organised armed groups, as distinct from the armed forces of a State. These rules are consistent with the general protection afforded to children under the law of armed conflict.[1281]

[1279] Geneva Convention IV, Arts. 40, 51; UK MANUAL, paras. 9.30, 9.77.
[1280] *Lubanga* judgment, paras. 600–628; GERMAN MANUAL, paras. 306, 505; NIAC MANUAL, para. 3.5; ICRC CUSTOMARY IHL STUDY, Rules 136–137. *See also* Rome Statute, Art. 8(2)(b)(xxvi), 8(2)(e)(vii); Sierra Leone Statute, Art. 4(c).
[1281] *See* CRC Optional Protocol, pmbl. (stating: 'Considering therefore that to strengthen further the implementation of rights recognised in the Convention on the Rights of the Child there is a need to increase the protection of children from involvement in armed conflict.') *See also* Convention concerning the Prohibition and Immediate Action for

2.   For the purposes of this Rule, the term 'children' refers to persons under the age of fifteen years.[1282] Provisions of the Optional Protocol apply the prohibition to persons under the age of eighteen years and bind States Parties to that instrument.[1283] The International Group of Experts did not achieve consensus on whether customary international law had evolved to this standard or remained at fifteen years. Accordingly, this Rule adopts the position that children under the age of fifteen may never be used in the conduct of cyber hostilities.[1284]

3.   Rule 138 prohibits the conscription or enlistment of children into the armed forces or any other organised armed group under any circumstances. The prohibition extends to the conscription and enlistment of children who are not subsequently used to participate in hostilities.

4.   States must, therefore, take all feasible measures to ensure that children do not participate in hostilities (Rule 97).[1285] The State's obligation in this regard applies regardless of whether the children are to be used by the armed forces or organised armed groups or operate on their own.[1286] There is no reason to exclude engaging in cyber activities from the ambit of participation.

5.   The term 'take part' was adopted from Rule 137 of the ICRC Customary IHL Study. Various instruments dealing with the use of children in armed conflicts employ different criteria regarding the activities in question. For instance, Additional Protocol I uses the phrase 'direct part in hostilities',[1287] while Additional Protocol II refers to 'take part'.[1288] The Rome Statute uses the phrase 'participate actively in hostilities'.[1289] Interpretations of these criteria vary. Some commentators and

the Elimination of the Worst Forms of Child Labour, Art. 3(a), 17 June 1999, ILO Convention No. 182. The International Criminal Court has observed: 'These provisions recognise the fact that "children are particularly vulnerable [and] require privileged treatment in comparison with the rest of the civilian population". The principal objective underlying these prohibitions historically is to protect children under the age of 15 from the risks that are associated with armed conflict, and first and foremost they are directed at securing their physical and psychological well-being.' *Lubanga* judgment, para. 605.

[1282]   Rome Statute, Art. 8(2)(b)(xxvi); CRC, Art. 38(2–3); UK MANUAL, paras. 4.11, 15.7–15.7.1; CANADIAN MANUAL, para. 1714; GERMAN MANUAL, paras. 306, 505; ICRC CUSTOMARY IHL STUDY, commentary accompanying Rule 136.

[1283]   CRC Optional Protocol Arts. 1, 2, 4(1).   [1284]   *Lubanga* judgment, paras. 620–628.

[1285]   CRC Optional Protocol, Arts. 1, 4(2); Rome Statute, Art. 8(2)(b)(xxvi), 8(2)(e)(vii); CRC, Art. 38(2).

[1286]   CRC Optional Protocol, Arts. 1, 4(2).   [1287]   Additional Protocol I, Art. 77(2).

[1288]   Additional Protocol II, Art. 4(3)(c).

[1289]   Rome Statute, Art. 8(2)(b)(xxvi), 8(2)(e)(vii).

tribunals treat 'active' and 'direct' participation as synonymous, while others take the position that they are distinct.[1290] In light of the prohibition's object and purpose, the International Group of Experts agreed that the term 'take part' was appropriate for inclusion in this Rule.

SECTION 4:   JOURNALISTS

Rule 139 – Protection of journalists

Civilian journalists engaged in dangerous professional missions in areas of armed conflict are civilians and shall be respected as such, in particular with regard to cyber attacks, as long as they are not taking a direct part in hostilities.

1.   This Rule, based on Article 79 of Additional Protocol I, reflects customary international law applicable in international and non-international armed conflict.[1291] It is especially relevant in the cyber context because of the heavy reliance of contemporary journalists on computers and communication systems and networks.

2.   Some Experts took the position that Rule 34 of the ICRC Customary IHL Study accurately reflects customary international law. According to that rule, 'civilian journalists engaged in professional missions in areas of armed conflict must be respected and protected, as long as they are not taking a direct part in hostilities'. The accompanying commentary asserts 'there is also practice which indicates that journalists exercising their professional activities in relation to an armed conflict must be protected'.

3.   However, the majority of the International Group of Experts took the view that the only customary obligation is to 'respect' journalists, rather than 'protect' them. Parties to the conflict must not harm journalists, but are not obliged to protect them from being harmed by others, for

---

[1290] Compare *Akayesu* judgment, para. 629, and ICRC INTERPRETIVE GUIDANCE, fn. 84, with *Lubanga* judgment, para. 627.

[1291] UK MANUAL, para. 8.18; CANADIAN MANUAL, paras. 313, 441; GERMAN MANUAL, para. 515; NIAC MANUAL, para. 3.10; ICRC CUSTOMARY IHL STUDY, RULE 34; US Department of Defense, *Memorandum on 1977 Protocols Additional to the Geneva Conventions: Customary International Law Implications* (9 May 1986) *reprinted in* UNITED STATES ARMY JUDGE ADVOCATE GENERAL'S SCHOOL, LAW OF WAR DOCUMENTARY SUPPLEMENT 234 (2011) (citing with approval Additional Protocol I, Art. 79, 'as supportable for inclusion in customary law through state practice').

instance, by cyber means. A majority of the Experts also took the position that this Rule applies only to the obligation to respect the journalists themselves and not to their journalistic activities or products, such as content posted on a website. This is particularly relevant in the cyber context given the dependency of many journalistic activities on systems and equipment that are vulnerable to cyber operations. Of course, as explained below, such systems and equipment are protected as civilian objects unless they become military objectives pursuant to Rule 100.

4. For purposes of this Rule, 'journalists' includes reporters, cameramen, photographers, and sound technicians.[1292] The ICRC commentary to Article 79 of Additional Protocol I limits the term to persons 'working for the press and other media'.[1293] The International Group of Experts agreed that the term 'journalist' extends to those affiliated with established, exclusively online, media organisations. No consensus was reached as to whether it includes private individuals who produce web blogs unaffiliated with the established media.

5. The law of armed conflict distinguishes 'war correspondents' from 'journalists engaged in dangerous professional missions'.[1294] War correspondents are formally accredited by the armed forces they accompany. Although they are civilians, unlike journalists they have prisoner of war status if captured.[1295] Members of the armed forces conducting journalism as part of their duties are not journalists as a matter of the law of armed conflict, but rather combatants.[1296]

6. The law of armed conflict does not prohibit the censorship of journalists or war correspondents by cyber or other means.[1297] The lack of such a prohibition has practical significance in military operations. Consider the case of imminent or on-going offensive operations.

[1292] This definition accords generally with the United Nations Convention on the Protection of Journalists Engaged in Dangerous Missions in Areas of Armed Conflict, Annex I, Art. 2(a), UN Doc. A/10147 (1 August 1975) (identifying as 'journalists' any 'correspondent, reporter, photographer, and their technical film, radio and television assistants who are ordinarily engaged in any of these activities as their principal occupation').

[1293] ICRC ADDITIONAL PROTOCOLS 1987 COMMENTARY, para. 3260.

[1294] *Compare* Geneva Convention III, Art. 4A(4), *with* Additional Protocol I, Art. 79(1–2). *See also* CANADIAN MANUAL, paras. 313–314; ICRC CUSTOMARY IHL STUDY, commentary accompanying Rule 34.

[1295] Geneva Convention III, Art. 4A(4); DoD MANUAL, para. 4.24.2.1; 11.5; UK MANUAL, para. 8.18; CANADIAN MANUAL, para. 314; GERMAN MANUAL, para. 515.

[1296] ICRC ADDITIONAL PROTOCOLS 1987 COMMENTARY, para. 3262.

[1297] To the extent censorship rules exist, they are in the domain of municipal or domestic law.

A potential implication of the speed and pervasiveness of modern journalistic communications is that a report could jeopardise the success of the operations or place those involved at increased risk. It would not be a violation of the law of armed conflict to prevent or restrict reports on such operations.

7.   Journalistic equipment does not enjoy special status. Equipment belonging to or used by journalists in their professional activities is protected as a civilian object unless it qualifies as a military objective pursuant to Rule 100. Thus, computers, data, networks, communications, and connections used for journalism enjoy no protection beyond their status as civilian objects. In some circumstances, the systems and equipment may be requisitioned or confiscated in accordance with Rule 149.

8.   As civilians, journalists are subject to the Rule regarding direct participation in hostilities. Although journalistic activities such as investigating, conducting interviews, taking notes, and making recordings using cyber facilities and materials are not regarded as acts of direct participation *per se*, such actions, if undertaken in direct support of military operations, could rise to that level.

9.   The issue of whether the use of electronic or other media to spread propaganda qualifies as direct participation in hostilities (and the associated question of whether the objects used qualify as military objectives) is unsettled. The majority of the International Group of Experts took the position that spreading propaganda does not *per se* constitute direct participation in hostilities (Rule 97),[1298] while the minority suggested that the use of networks or computers to spread propaganda might convert journalistic equipment into a military objective such that they are subject to cyber attacks.[1299]

10.   However, a majority of the International Group of Experts also took the position that broadcasts used to incite war crimes, genocide, or crimes against humanity render a journalist a direct participant and qualify the equipment used as a military objective liable to attack, including by cyber means.[1300] A few of the Experts disagreed. In any case, these situations are highly fact-specific.

[1298] ICRC INTERPRETIVE GUIDANCE, at 51.

[1299] *But see* Final Report to the Prosecutor by the Committee Established to Review the NATO Bombing Campaign Against the Federal Republic of Yugoslavia, 39 ILM 1257, para. 76 (13 June 2000).

[1300] The direct participation constituent elements of 'threshold of harm' and 'direct causation' can be met by harm to protected persons or objects. ICRC INTERPRETIVE GUIDANCE, at 47–57. On incitement to genocide, see *Ferdinand Nahimana* et al. v.

SECTION 5: INSTALLATIONS CONTAINING DANGEROUS FORCES

Rule 140 – Duty of care during attacks on dams, dykes, and nuclear electrical generating stations

In order to avoid the release of dangerous forces and consequent severe losses among the civilian population, particular care must be taken during cyber attacks against works and installations containing dangerous forces, namely dams, dykes, and nuclear electrical generating stations, as well as installations located in their vicinity.

1. Article 56 of Additional Protocol I and Article 15 of Additional Protocol II provide that, subject to certain exceptions, the works and installations referred to in this Rule cannot be attacked, even when they are military objectives, if such attack may cause the release of dangerous forces and result in severe losses among the civilian population. There is general agreement that the two Articles do not constitute customary international law.[1301] This Rule, which is drawn from Rule 42 of the ICRC Customary IHL Study, reflects a more limited prohibition than those in the Additional Protocols. The International Group of Experts agreed that it is customary in nature.[1302] It follows that Parties to the two instruments are bound by a higher level of protection than that set forth in this Rule.[1303]

2. Rule 140 is a special precautionary Rule regarding the degree of care to be taken when undertaking a cyber attack on an installation qualifying as a military objective (Rule 100) that contains dangerous forces.[1304] Even States not Parties to Additional Protocols I or II acknowledge that the civilian population enjoys protection against excessive collateral damage that is to be expected from attacks on dams, dykes, and nuclear electrical generating

---

Prosecutor, paras. 677–715, Case No. ICTR 99-52-A, Appeals Chamber judgment (Int'l Crim. Trib. for Rwanda 28 November 2007).

[1301] ICRC CUSTOMARY IHL STUDY, commentary accompanying Rule 42.

[1302] *See also* AMW MANUAL, Rule 36; NIAC MANUAL, para. 4.2.3.

[1303] UK MANUAL, paras. 5.30 (as amended)–5.30.10, 15.51–15.51.1; CANADIAN MANUAL, para. 444; GERMAN MANUAL, paras. 464–470; AMW MANUAL, commentary accompanying Rule 36. Some States Parties have qualified their obligations under Art. 56 of Additional Protocol I for purposes of reprisal. For instance, the United Kingdom made a statement on ratification reserving the right for high levels of command to authorise attack of installations that contribute to the enemy's war effort. UK Additional Protocols Ratification Statement, para. (n).

[1304] ICRC ADDITIONAL PROTOCOLS 1987 COMMENTARY, para. 4817.

stations pursuant to the rule of proportionality (Rule 113).[1305] In that the risk of collateral damage is especially acute when attacking such objects, particular care must be taken to avoid the release of dangerous forces likely to cause severe losses among the civilian population.

3.   The majority of the International Group of Experts took the position that the term 'particular care' means that in determining which precautions are practically possible, account must be taken of the particular dangers posed by the forces referred to in the Rule. Consider malware intended to reduce enemy electrical supply by targeting a hydro power facility. Paying insufficient attention when planning the attack to the effects on the facility's associated gates, and thereby risking destructive downstream consequences, would violate this Rule.

4.   A minority of the Experts was of the view that the word 'particular' should not appear in the Rule because the requirement to take precautions in attack (Rules 114–120) already requires doing everything feasible to avoid collateral damage. In their view, the notion of particular care adds nothing to the requirement to take all feasible precautions. For instance, in the example above, the precautions requirement would likewise have necessitated consideration of the possibility of water control system damage. However, because they believed that 'particular care' does not add an obligation of substance to the Rule, they decided not to block consensus on the Rule.

5.   The term 'severe losses' is drawn from Article 56(1) of Additional Protocol I. The determination as to whether the release of dangerous forces will cause severe losses among the civilian population must be judged in good faith on the basis of objective elements, such as the existence of densely populated areas of civilians that could be affected by the release of dangerous forces.[1306]

6.   This Rule is confined to dams, dykes, nuclear electrical generating stations, and military objectives located in their vicinity,[1307] as well as to computers and computer networks that form an integral part, and support the operations, of such works or installations. It does not apply to any other works or installations containing dangerous forces or

---

[1305] DoD MANUAL, para. 5.13. The Manual states: 'Attack of facilities, works, or installations containing dangerous forces, such as dams, nuclear power plants, or facilities producing weapons of mass destruction, is permissible so long as it is conducted in accordance with other applicable rules, including the rules of discrimination and proportionality.'
[1306] ICRC ADDITIONAL PROTOCOLS 1987 COMMENTARY, paras. 2154, 4821.
[1307] ICRC ADDITIONAL PROTOCOLS 1987 COMMENTARY, paras. 2147–2153.

substances, such as chemical plants and petroleum refineries.[1308] Rules 99–101 and 113–120 govern attacks on these facilities.

7. The requirement to take particular care when attacking the installations and supporting cyber infrastructure referred to in this Rule does not apply when they are used regularly in direct support of military operations and attack is the only feasible way to terminate the use.[1309] Such support must be a departure from the installation's ordinary function. For example, occasional military use of electricity generated by a nuclear power station does not bar the application of the Rule. If the protection ceases and any of the computers and computer networks that support the dams, dykes, and nuclear electrical generating stations are the object of a cyber attack, all feasible precautions must be taken to avoid the release of the dangerous forces in accordance with the general requirement to take precautions in attack (Rules 114–120).[1310] Of course, the rule of proportionality also applies (Rule 113).

8. Article 56(6) of Additional Protocol I provides for the optional identification of works and installations containing dangerous forces. As a matter of good practice, and when feasible, works and installations containing dangerous forces should also be identified with agreed-upon electronic markings, which would be particularly useful with regard to cyber operations.[1311] Electronic markings can be used to supplement the special sign that indicates dams, dykes, and nuclear electrical generating stations. The absence of electronic or physical markings does not deprive them of their protected status.

SECTION 6: OBJECTS INDISPENSABLE TO THE SURVIVAL OF THE CIVILIAN POPULATION

Rule 141 – Protection of objects indispensable to survival

Attacking, destroying, removing, or rendering useless objects indispensable to the survival of the civilian population by means of cyber operations is prohibited.

[1308] AMW MANUAL, commentary accompanying Rule 36.

[1309] Additional Protocol I, Art. 56(2). *See also* UK MANUAL, paras. 5.30.5, fn. 124; CANADIAN MANUAL, para. 444; GERMAN MANUAL, para. 465.

[1310] Additional Protocol I, Art. 56(3).

[1311] Additional Protocol I, Art. 56(6). Art. 56(7) sets forth a physical means of marking installations containing dangerous forces. *See also* UK MANUAL, para. 5.30.9.

1.   This Rule is based on Article 54(2) of Additional Protocol I for international armed conflict and reflects customary international law. It supplements the protection of civilians against direct attack (Rule 94). While it is a distinct and independent rule, it should also be considered together with the Rule prohibiting starvation of civilians as a method of warfare (Rule 107).

2.   The majority of the International Group of Experts took the position that the Rule applies in non-international armed conflict as a matter of customary international law.[1312] A minority of the Experts noted that Article 14 of Additional Protocol II prohibits the stated activities only when undertaken for the purpose of starvation of civilians as a method of combat. Accordingly, they were of the view that customary law applicable in non-international armed conflict is only violated when the specified activities are undertaken in order to starve the civilian population.

3.   Application of the Rule, as with Article 54(2), is limited to situations in which the objects are attacked, destroyed, removed, or rendered useless for the 'specific purpose of denying them for their sustenance value to the civilian population or to the adverse Party'. The motive underlying this intent is irrelevant so long as the purpose is to deny the civilian population their sustenance value. Operations with other purposes having this effect are not prohibited by this Rule.[1313] Thus, for example, objects incidentally destroyed during a cyber attack on a military objective (collateral damage) do not come within its scope of application.[1314] Similarly, if any of these objects qualify in the circumstances ruling at the time as a military objective, an attack against them does not violate the Rule.

4.   The cited provisions of Additional Protocols I and II offer the following examples of objects indispensable to the survival of the

[1312] See Partial Award, Western Front, Aerial Bombardment and Related Claims 1, 3, 5, 9–13, 14, 21, 25 and 26 (Eri. v. Eth.) 26 RIAA paras. 98–105 (Eritrea–Ethiopia Claims Commission 2005); UK MANUAL, para. 5.27; CANADIAN MANUAL, para. 445; GERMAN MANUAL, para. 463; AMW MANUAL, Rule 97(b); NIAC MANUAL, commentary accompanying para. 2.3.10; ICRC CUSTOMARY IHL STUDY, Rule 54. See also Rome Statute, Art. 8(2)(b)(xxv).
[1313] Additional Protocol I, Art. 54(2). See, e.g., UK Additional Protocols Ratification Statement, para. (l) (stating this provision 'has no application to attacks that are carried out for a specific purpose other than denying sustenance to the civilian population or the adverse Party'); DoD MANUAL, para. 5.20.4; AMW MANUAL, commentary accompanying Rule 97(b).
[1314] UK MANUAL, para. 5.27.2.

civilian population: foodstuffs, agricultural areas for the production of foodstuffs, crops, livestock, drinking water installations and supplies, and irrigation works. Food and medical supplies are also generally accepted as essential to the survival of the civilian population, and Additional Protocol I mentions clothing, bedding, and means of shelter.[1315] Although these lists are not exhaustive, the objects to which the Rule applies must be 'indispensable to survival'.[1316] This is a very narrow category; objects not required for survival (e.g., those that merely enhance civilian well-being or quality of life) fall outside the scope of application of this Rule, although they are protected by the general rules on the protection of civilian objects (Rules 99–101).

5. The Internet (or other communications networks) does not, in and of itself, qualify as an object indispensable to the survival of the civilian population. In the context of cyber operations, however, cyber infrastructure indispensable to the functioning of electrical generators, irrigation works and installations, drinking water installations, and food production facilities could, depending on the circumstances, qualify.

6. As is clear from its text, the Rule extends beyond a prohibition of cyber attack (Rule 92). It proscribes any act designed to deny sustenance to the civilian population or to the adverse party.

7. In international armed conflicts,[1317] the prohibition does not apply if the objects in question are used by the enemy solely for the sustenance of their forces or in direct support of military action.[1318] The majority of the International Group of Experts concluded that, despite these two exceptions, cyber operations may not be conducted against the objects if those operations can be expected to so deprive the civilian population of food or water that it starves or is forced to move.[1319] A minority suggested that insufficient State practice existed to support the proposition.

[1315] Additional Protocol I, Art. 69(1) (governing occupied territory); Additional Protocol II, Art. 18(2); Geneva Convention IV, Art. 55 (limited to Art. 4 protected persons); UK MANUAL, para. 5.27; CANADIAN MANUAL, para. 445; GERMAN MANUAL, para. 463; AMW MANUAL, Rule 97(b); NIAC MANUAL, commentary accompanying para. 2.3.10.

[1316] ICRC ADDITIONAL PROTOCOLS 1987 COMMENTARY, para. 2103.

[1317] ICRC CUSTOMARY IHL STUDY, commentary accompanying Rule 54 (asserting that this exception does not apply to non-international armed conflicts 'because Article 14 of Additional Protocol II does not provide for it and there is no practice supporting it').

[1318] Additional Protocol I, Art. 54(3).

[1319] See, e.g., UK MANUAL, para. 5.19; CANADIAN MANUAL, para. 445; ICRC CUSTOMARY IHL STUDY, commentary accompanying Rule 54.

SECTION 7:   CULTURAL PROPERTY

Rule 142 – Respect for and protection of cultural property

The parties to an armed conflict must respect and protect cultural property that may be affected by cyber operations or that is located in cyberspace. In particular, they are prohibited from using digital cultural property for military purposes.

1.   This Rule reflects the general theme contained in the 1954 Hague Cultural Property Convention and its Protocols of 1954 and 1999, as well as Additional Protocols I and II. It applies in both international and non-international armed conflict and is customary international law.[1320]

2.   Cultural property comprises 'moveable or immoveable property of great importance to the cultural heritage of every people'.[1321] Under the 1999 Second Protocol to the 1954 Hague Cultural Property Convention, cultural property that is the 'cultural heritage of the greatest importance for humanity' enjoys enhanced protection.[1322] This Manual adopts the former definition because it reflects customary international law;[1323] the latter definition is relevant only for States Parties to the Second Protocol.

3.   The reference to 'respect and protect' in this Rule is drawn from Articles 2 and 4 of the 1954 Hague Cultural Property Convention. In addition to a prohibition of attacking cultural property,[1324] 'respect' refers, in particular, to the obligation to take all feasible measures to avoid harming cultural property during the conduct of military

---

[1320] Additional Protocol I, Art. 53; Additional Protocol II, Art. 16; Cultural Property Convention, Arts. 18–19. Apart from the 1954 Convention, other relevant international treaty law supports the proposition generally. Hague Regulations, Art. 27; Convention (IX) concerning Bombardment by Naval Forces in Time of War, Art. 5, 18 October 1907, 1 Bevans 681; Treaty on the Protection of Artistic and Scientific Institutions and Historic Monuments (Roerich Pact), 15 April 1935, 167 LNTS 279; DoD MANUAL, paras. 5.18, 17.11; UK MANUAL, paras. 5.25–5.26.8 (as amended), 15.18–15.18.3, 15.52; CANADIAN MANUAL, paras. 111, 443; NIAC MANUAL, para. 4.2.2; ICRC CUSTOMARY IHL STUDY, Rules 38–39. *See also* Rome Statute, Art. 8(2)(b)(ix), 8(2)(e)(iv).

[1321] Cultural Property Convention, Art. 1(a) (providing examples of the categories of property); AMW MANUAL, Rule 1(o).

[1322] Second Cultural Property Protocol, Art. 10(a) (requiring also that objects enjoy domestic legal protection and not be used for military purposes).

[1323] UK MANUAL, paras. 5.25, 5.25.2; AMW MANUAL, Rule 1(o).

[1324] UK MANUAL, para. 5.25.1; GERMAN MANUAL, para. 903; AMW MANUAL, Rules 95–96.

operations.[1325] The International Group of Experts agreed that this obligation extends to cyber operations. 'Protect', by contrast, denotes the obligation to take feasible protective measures to safeguard cultural property against harm caused by others during military operations.[1326] For States Parties to the 1954 Hague Cultural Property Convention and its 1999 Second Protocol, additional protective measures are required.

4.   The International Group of Experts considered whether intangible items could qualify as 'property' for law of armed conflict purposes. Recall that in the context of civilian objects, as that term is used in Article 52 of Additional Protocol I, the Group generally rejected characterisation of intangible items such as data as an 'object' (Rule 100). Problematic in this regard is the fact that Article 53 of the same instrument refers to 'cultural objects'. For some members of the Group, this led to the conclusion that cultural property must be tangible in nature and that intangible items like data do not qualify.

5.   Other Experts emphasised that the term 'property' is not always limited to tangible objects. An example of a notion of intangible property that is well accepted in international law and that appears in most domestic legal systems is intellectual property. For these Experts, the critical question is whether the intangible property is cultural in nature. Examples include objects that are created and stored on a computing device and therefore only exist in digital form, such as musical scores, digital films, documents pertaining to e-government, and scientific data. Certain copies of objects of which a physical manifestation exists (or has existed) that can be used to create replicas also qualify as cultural property.[1327]

6.   No member of the International Group of Experts taking this position asserted that all digital manifestations of cultural property are entitled to the protection of this Rule. Protection only applies to digital copies or versions where the original is either inaccessible or has been destroyed, and where the number of digital copies that can be made is limited. Consider the example of a single extremely high-resolution image of Leonardo da Vinci's *Mona Lisa* comprising a terabyte of information. Such a digital copy might, and in the event of the destruction of the original *Mona Lisa* would, qualify as cultural

---

[1325] UK MANUAL, para. 5.25.3; GERMAN MANUAL, para. 903; AMW MANUAL, Rule 95(c) and commentary accompanying Rule 96.

[1326] AMW MANUAL, Rule 94.

[1327] An important historical example of objects used for the purpose of building replicas are the historical maps, photographs, building plans, etc., which facilitated the rebuilding of Warsaw's Old Town after World War II.

property. However, due to the high speed and low cost of digital reproduction, once such a digital image has been replicated and widely downloaded, no single digital copy of the artwork would be protected by this Rule. This is because protection of cultural property is afforded based on the value and irreplaceability of the original work of art, and on the difficulty, time, and expense involved in reproducing faithful copies of that original. The logic underlying this Rule does not apply in cases where large numbers of high-quality reproductions can be made.

7.   In the digital cultural property context, the term 'respect and protect' prohibits any alteration, damage, deletion, or destruction of the data, as well as its exploitation for military purposes. For instance, the use of digitised historical archives regarding a population to determine the ethnic origin of individuals with a view to facilitating genocide, crimes against humanity, or war crimes is clearly unlawful. Merely temporarily denying or degrading access, for example by affecting the functioning of electronic devices used for such access, is beyond the ambit of the protection of cultural property.

8.   Like its physical counterpart, digital cultural property may not be used for military purposes. As an example, steganographically modified pieces of digital art lose any protection as cultural property in light of their use for military ends.

9.   Article 16 of the Cultural Property Convention establishes a distinctive emblem for marking cultural property. It is appropriate to use such markings on qualifying digital cultural property. Additionally, use of a digital marking equivalent that places attackers on notice that the digital items qualify as protected cultural property is appropriate. Whilst no such marking has been formally established, multiple technological solutions are possible, including file-naming conventions, the use of tagging-data with machine-interpretable encoding schemes, published lists of IP addresses of digital cultural property, or generic top-level domain names.

10.   Although cultural property may be attacked if it qualifies as a military objective, a decision to conduct such an attack must be taken at an appropriately high level. Parties to the conflict must give due consideration to the fact that the target is cultural property. Moreover, an attacker is required to provide an effective advance warning when feasible and may only conduct an attack once the warning remains unheeded after a reasonable period for compliance.[1328]

[1328] Second Cultural Property Protocol, Arts. 6(d), 13(2)(c)(ii); AMW Manual, Rule 96.

SECTION 8:   THE NATURAL ENVIRONMENT

Rule 143 – Protection of the natural environment

(a) **The natural environment is a civilian object and as such enjoys general protection from cyber attacks and their effects.**

(b) **States Parties to Additional Protocol I are prohibited from employing cyber methods or means of warfare which are intended, or may be expected, to cause widespread, long-term, and severe damage to the natural environment.**

1.   *Lit.* (a) is based on the principle of distinction (Rule 93) as well as the prohibition of attacking civilian objects (Rule 99). The International Group of Experts agreed that it accurately reflects customary international law in international armed conflict.[1329] The majority of the International Group of Experts took the position that *lit.* (a) also applies to non-international armed conflicts.[1330]

2.   *Lit.* (b) is based on Articles 35(3) and 55 of Additional Protocol I. Since the International Group of Experts was divided over whether *lit.* (b) reflects customary international law,[1331] it has been drafted to apply only to States that are Parties to the Protocol. Although Additional Protocol I does not apply to non-international armed conflict, some Experts took the position that its provisions on the environment apply as a matter of customary law in such conflicts.

3.   There is no generally accepted definition of the 'natural environment'.[1332] For the purposes of this Manual, the International Group of Experts adopted, with the exception of outer space, the definition set forth in Article II of the 1977 Environmental Modification Convention: 'the dynamics, composition or structure of the earth, including its biota, lithosphere, hydrosphere and atmosphere'.[1333] The Experts were divided over whether the term should encompass outer space. Those Experts opposing inclusion based their view on the lack of conclusive State practice and *opinio juris.*

[1329]   DoD Manual, para. 6.10.3.1; Canadian Manual, paras. 446, 620, 709; German Manual, para. 401; AMW Manual, chapeau to Sec. M; ICRC Customary IHL study, Rule 43.

[1330]   UK Manual, para. 15.20; AMW Manual, commentary accompanying Rules 88–89; NIAC Manual, para. 4.2.4; ICRC Customary IHL Study, commentary accompanying Rule 43.

[1331]   ICRC Customary IHL Study, Rule 45.   [1332]   AMW Manual, chapeau to Sec. M.

[1333]   Environmental Modification Convention, Art. II.

4. All members of the International Group of Experts concluded that the environment is a civilian object that, as such, is protected from direct cyber attacks unless and until it becomes a military objective (Rules 99–101). Therefore, those who plan, approve, or conduct a cyber attack must apply the rule of proportionality (Rule 113) and the requirement to take precautions in attack (Rules 114–120) with respect to expected collateral damage to the natural environment.[1334] For example, when planning a cyber attack against a military petroleum storage facility, the expected damage to the natural environment through any spillage of petroleum must be considered.

5. Furthermore, the destruction of the natural environment carried out wantonly is prohibited.[1335] 'Wanton' means that the destruction is the consequence of a deliberate action taken maliciously, that is, the action cannot be justified as militarily necessary.[1336] For instance, it would be unlawful to use cyber means to trigger a release of oil into a waterway simply to cause environmental damage.

6. States Parties to Additional Protocol I are prohibited from conducting cyber attacks that are intended or may be expected to cause 'widespread, long-term, and severe' damage to the natural environment.[1337] As to the expression, the ICRC commentary to Additional Protocol I notes that during negotiations at the Diplomatic Conference,

> The time or duration required (i.e., long-term) was considered by some to be measured in decades. Some representatives referred to twenty or thirty years as being a minimum period. Others referred to battlefield destruction in France in the First World War as being outside the scope of the prohibition ... It appeared to be a widely shared assumption that battlefield damage incidental to conventional warfare would not normally be proscribed by this provision. What the article is primarily directed to is thus such damage as would be likely to prejudice, over a long-term, the continued survival of the civilian population or would risk causing it major health problems.[1338]

[1334] DoD MANUAL, para. 6.10.3.1; AMW MANUAL, commentary accompanying Rule 88. *See also* Rome Statute, Art. 8(2)(b)(iv).

[1335] Hague Regulations, Art. 23(g); AMW MANUAL, Rule 88; ICRC CUSTOMARY IHL STUDY, commentary accompanying Rule 43. *See also* Rome Statute, Art. 8(2)(a)(iv).

[1336] Geneva Convention IV, Art. 147; AMW MANUAL, commentary accompanying Rule 88. *See also* Rome Statute, Art. 8(2)(a)(iv), 8(2)(e)(xii).

[1337] Additional Protocol I, Arts. 35(3), 55. *See also* UK MANUAL, para. 5.29; CANADIAN MANUAL, para. 446; GERMAN MANUAL, para. 403.

[1338] ICRC ADDITIONAL PROTOCOLS 1987 COMMENTARY, para. 1454.

7.   The conjunctive nature of the phrase 'widespread, long-term, and severe' makes it clear that the Rule is only breached when the environmental damage is exceptionally serious.[1339]

SECTION 9:   COLLECTIVE PUNISHMENT

Rule 144 – Collective punishment

Collective punishment by cyber means is prohibited.

1.   This Rule is based on Article 50 of the Hague Regulations, Article 87 of Geneva Convention III, Article 33 of Geneva Convention IV, Article 75(2)(d) of Additional Protocol I, and Article 4(2)(b) of Additional Protocol II. It is recognised as customary international law applicable in international and non-international armed conflict.[1340]

2.   The Rule prohibits the use of cyber means to impose retaliatory sanctions on persons or groups for acts in which they were not involved. The majority of the International Group of Experts agreed that, as noted in the ICRC commentary to Geneva Convention IV, the notion of prohibited collective punishment should be understood liberally. It 'does not refer to punishments inflicted under penal law ... [but rather to] penalties of any kind inflicted on persons or entire groups of persons ... for acts those persons have not committed'.[1341] The ICRC Additional Protocols 1987 Commentary similarly notes that 'the concept of collective punishment must be understood in the broadest sense; it covers not only legal sentences but sanctions and harassment of any sort, administrative, by police action or otherwise'.[1342] As an example, the majority of the Experts agreed that shutting off all Internet access in an area with the primary purpose of punishing its inhabitants for acts committed by some individuals is collective punishment. A minority of the Experts disagreed,

---

[1339]   Under the Environmental Modification Convention, the corresponding criteria are disjunctive. Environmental Modification Convention, Art. II.

[1340]   DoD MANUAL, paras. 8.16.2.1, 17.6.7; UK MANUAL, paras. 8.121.a, 9.4.d, 9.24.d, 15.38. b; CANADIAN MANUAL, paras. 1039, 1135, 1713; GERMAN MANUAL, paras. 507, 536; NIAC MANUAL, para. 1.2.4; ICRC CUSTOMARY IHL STUDY, Rule 103. See also ICTR Statute, Art. 4(b); Sierra Leone statute, Art. 3(b).

[1341]   ICRC GENEVA CONVENTION IV COMMENTARY, at 225.

[1342]   ICRC ADDITIONAL PROTOCOLS 1987 COMMENTARY, para. 3055.

taking the position that the term 'punishment' does not encompass the imposition of mere inconvenience or annoyance. However, all of the Experts concurred that, for instance, confiscation of all the personal computers in a village in retaliation for cyber attacks conducted by a small cell of insurgents would violate the prohibition of collective punishment.

3. Collective punishment is to be contrasted with measures taken by an Occupying Power in accordance with Rules 146–149 to ensure its own security or to promote public order and the security of the population. It is also to be distinguished from actions justifiable under those Rules that are directed at individuals, but that may have unintended or undesired effects on others.

4. Although Article 50 of the Hague Regulations applies only in occupied territory, Article 33 of Geneva Convention IV applies to persons protected by that instrument in both occupied territory and a party's own territory.[1343] Additionally, Article 75(2)(d) of Additional Protocol I and Article 4(2)(b) of Additional Protocol II apply 'at any time and in any place whatsoever'. The International Group of Experts therefore agreed that this Rule is not limited in application to occupied territories.

SECTION 10: HUMANITARIAN ASSISTANCE

Rule 145 – Humanitarian assistance

Cyber operations shall not be designed or conducted to interfere unduly with impartial efforts to provide humanitarian assistance.

1. This Rule is based on Articles 23 and 59 of Geneva Convention IV and Articles 69 and 70 of Additional Protocol I. The Rule applies in international armed conflict and is customary in nature.[1344]

2. The International Group of Experts did not achieve consensus on this Rule's application in non-international armed conflict. Some Experts argued it is inapplicable to such conflicts, except as treaty law for States Parties to Additional Protocol II. Others took the position

---

[1343] For the definition of 'protected persons', *see* Geneva Convention IV, Art. 4.

[1344] AMW MANUAL, Rule 102(a–b) and accompanying commentary. *See also* Rome Statute, Art. 8(2)(b)(iii).

that the Rule is not only encompassed in Article 18(2) of Additional Protocol II, but also reflects customary international law for States that are not Parties to that instrument.[1345] A number of the Experts adopting the latter view emphasised, however, that delivery of humanitarian assistance requires the receiving State's consent.[1346] With regard to consent, these Experts were split. Some took the position that such consent may not be withheld unreasonably,[1347] while others argued that that the provision of humanitarian assistance is entirely at the discretion of the receiving State.[1348]

3. Although the ICRC Customary IHL Study provides that 'Objects used for humanitarian relief operations must be respected and protected',[1349] this Rule is oriented toward State action regarding the tolerance of, and support for, humanitarian assistance efforts. The International Group of Experts considered the present formulation better adapted to the cyber context.

4. The prohibition set forth in this Rule applies to all territory. Article 23 of Geneva Convention IV guarantees 'free passage' to a broad range of relief consignments 'intended only for civilians of another High Contracting Party, even if the latter is its adversary'.[1350] Combined with the provisions on ensuring that the population of occupied territory or territory otherwise under a party's control is properly provided with humanitarian assistance, the obligation to refrain from interference with humanitarian assistance knows no geographical limit.

5. The term 'humanitarian assistance' is employed here as a term of art. Not all efforts to provide materiel or support to a civilian population constitute humanitarian assistance for the purposes of the Rule. Rather, humanitarian assistance is to be understood as analogous to the term 'relief actions' found in Article 70 of Additional Protocol I. Efforts to

---

[1345] Rome Statute, Art. 8.2(e)(iii); AMW Manual, commentary accompanying Rule 102(a–b); ICRC Customary IHL Study, Rules 31–32. See also UK Manual, para. 15.54; NIAC Manual, para. 5.1.

[1346] Additional Protocol II, Art. 18(2). See also UK Manual , para. 15.54.

[1347] UK Manual, at 409, n. 129; AMW Manual, commentary accompanying Rule 100(a).

[1348] This position can only be taken by States that are not Parties to Additional Protocol II or by Parties thereto during a non-international armed conflict to which the treaty does not apply. ICRC Additional Protocols 1987 Commentary, para. 4885, explains that Art. 18(2) is not subject to unbridled discretion.

[1349] ICRC Customary IHL Study, Rule 32.

[1350] Art. 13 of Geneva Convention IV extends the Part (which contains Art. 23) to 'the whole of the populations of the countries in conflict'.

deliver essential supplies and support that relieve suffering qualify. Examples of items that have a humanitarian character include 'food and medical supplies ... clothing, bedding, means of shelter or other supplies essential to ... survival'.[1351]

6. The provision of humanitarian assistance is subject to the agreement of the parties to the conflict and therefore reasonable conditions may be imposed.[1352] However, the conditions may not 'interfere unduly' with relief efforts. For the purposes of this Rule, the term means to conduct cyber operations to frustrate or prevent legitimate and impartial relief efforts or in a manner unsupported by valid military considerations.[1353]

7. Consider an example in which one State is engaged in an international armed conflict with another State on the latter's territory. Several non-governmental organisations have established an infrastructure for humanitarian relief operations to assist the internally displaced population of the latter State. In its cyber operations against that State, the first State is obligated to avoid undue interference with the communications and other cyber activities of the non-governmental organisations offering humanitarian assistance.

[1351] Additional Protocol I, Art. 69(1).
[1352] Additional Protocol I, Art. 70(1–3); UK MANUAL, para. 9.12.2; CANADIAN MANUAL, para. 1113; GERMAN MANUAL, para. 503.
[1353] See also AMW MANUAL, commentary accompanying Rule 101.

19

Occupation

1. The concept of occupation does not extend to non-international armed conflicts.[1354]

2. All members of the International Group of Experts agreed that territory is 'occupied' once it is actually placed under the authority of the hostile army. This occurs when the Occupying Power substitutes its own authority for that of the occupied territory's government, which must have been rendered incapable of performing public functions.[1355] The occupation extends to the territory where such authority has been established and can be exercised. While some of the Experts were of the view that occupation includes situations in which a party to the conflict is in a position to substitute its authority,[1356] others took the position that actual exercise of authority is a condition precedent to occupation.[1357] Occupation ends as soon as the exercise of military authority over foreign territory ends or has otherwise become ineffective.[1358]

3. The International Group of Experts agreed that there is no legal notion of occupation of cyberspace. Furthermore, cyber operations cannot alone suffice to establish or maintain the degree of authority over territory necessary to constitute an occupation. However, cyber

---

[1354] Geneva Conventions I–IV, Art. 2. In that occupation is the exercise of authority of a State over another State's territory, it logically does not apply to non-international armed conflicts. See also DoD MANUAL, para. 11.1.3.3; AMW MANUAL, commentary accompanying Rule 100(a).

[1355] Hague Regulations, Art. 43.

[1356] ICRC GENEVA CONVENTION I 2016 COMMENTARY, paras. 301–304; INTERNATIONAL COMMITTEE OF THE RED CROSS, OCCUPATION AND OTHER FORMS OF ADMINISTRATION OF FOREIGN TERRITORY 19 (Tristan Ferraro ed., 2012).

[1357] These Experts relied on *Armed Activities* judgment, para. 173.

[1358] Hague Regulations, Art. 42; *Armed Activities* judgment, para. 172; *Wall* advisory opinion, paras. 78, 89. For those who are of the view that occupation begins when a State is in position to exercise its authority, occupation would end when it is no longer in such a position.

operations can be employed to help establish or maintain the requisite authority, for example, by enabling the issuance of certain notices required by the law of occupation to the population. Conversely, cyber operations are capable of disrupting or degrading computer systems used by an Occupying Power to maintain authority.

4.   For the purposes of this chapter, the term 'protected persons' refers to the civilians who 'find themselves … in the hands' of an Occupying Power of which they are not nationals.[1359] This includes civilians in occupied territory.[1360]

5.   None of the Rules below relieve the Occupying Power of any obligations it would otherwise bear pursuant to the law of belligerent occupation. For example, the seizure of a government computer by occupation forces would be governed by the general rule regarding seizure of any government property set forth in Article 53 of the Hague Regulations. Similarly, the rules regarding compelled labour set forth in Article 51 of Geneva Convention IV and Article 23 of the Hague Regulations apply equally in relation to cyber activities.

6.   Protected persons may under no circumstances renounce any of their rights under the law of occupation.[1361]

7.   The Rules of this chapter are based solely on the extant law of occupation, principally that set forth in the Hague Regulations and Geneva Convention IV, both of which reflect customary international law. It must be understood that United Nations Security Council resolutions may sometimes modify the application of these traditional rules.

Rule 146 – Respect for protected persons in occupied territory

Protected persons in occupied territory must be respected and protected from the harmful effects of cyber operations.

1.   This Rule is based on Article 27 of Geneva Convention IV.[1362] The International Group of Experts agreed that it reflects customary international law.

[1359] Geneva Convention IV, Art. 4. Note, however, that, according to Art. 4, protection is not accorded if they are nationals of a neutral or co-belligerent State that has normal diplomatic representation in the State.

[1360] Hague Regulations, Art. 42. The end of occupation must not be confused with the end of an armed conflict. Additional Protocol I, Art. 3(b).

[1361] Geneva Convention IV, Art. 8.

[1362] See also Hague Regulations, Art. 46 (concerning respect for family honour and rights of persons in occupied territory).

2. Subject to special provisions related to health, age, and gender,[1363] the Occupying Power must treat all protected persons with the same consideration, without any adverse distinction based, in particular, on race, religion, or political opinion.[1364] Accordingly, blocking Internet access of an element of the civilian population defined by reference to race, religion, or political affiliation would be prohibited by this Rule. However, the Occupying Power may take such measures of control and security with respect to protected persons as may be necessitated by the conflict (Rules 147 and 149).

3. Protected persons in occupied territory must be allowed to transmit news of a strictly personal nature to members of their families, wherever they may be, and to receive news from them without undue delay.[1365] Although the Occupying Power may allow such correspondence to consist of email correspondence or social media entries, it may impose restrictions on their transmission.[1366] Similarly, it may limit Internet access to certain times of the day, prevent attachments from being forwarded, reduce connection speed, or restrict the use of media streaming or peer-to-peer services. A means must remain, however, that enables family news to be transmitted on a periodic basis. For example, the occupation authorities may curb Internet traffic for security reasons, but allow family correspondence through the postal system.

4. The reference to 'respect' in this Rule denotes the obligation of the Occupying Power to avoid harming the civilian population as a result of any cyber operations it may conduct, subject to Rules 147–149. By contrast, 'protected' refers to the obligation of the Occupying Power to take feasible measures to ensure the security and well-being of the civilian population with regard to cyber operations conducted by others, such as insurgents or criminals. The obligation to respect and protect necessarily involves compliance with the other Rules in this chapter.

5. Pursuant to Article 51 of Geneva Convention IV, only protected persons over eighteen years of age may be compelled to work under

---

[1363] Geneva Convention IV, Arts. 16, 24, 27.
[1364] Geneva Convention IV, Arts. 13, 27; UK MANUAL, para. 9.21.
[1365] Geneva Convention IV, Art. 25; UK MANUAL, paras. 9.10, 9.10.1; GERMAN MANUAL, para. 538. Arts. 25 and 140 of Geneva Convention IV discuss the roles of neutral intermediaries and the Central Information Agency if it becomes difficult to exchange family correspondence through the ordinary post. In such circumstances, the use of email and texting is likely to provide a satisfactory solution, if available, and, in the case of occupation, if permitted by the Occupying Power.
[1366] Geneva Convention IV, Art. 25.

certain conditions.[1367] It is forbidden to require children to undertake any cyber-related work, regardless of its purpose (Rule 138).

6.   Article 23(h) of the Hague Regulations prohibits a party to the conflict from compelling enemy nationals to take part in military operations. Thus, although protected persons may have language skills, cultural understanding, knowledge as to computer systems operated in their own country, or other information that would enable the Occupying Power to undertake effective cyber military operations, such compulsory involvement is prohibited. The Group agreed that this prohibition extended to cyber activities that are preparatory to military operations, precautionary cyber measures to protect the Occupying Power's own computer networks, and general maintenance of the Occupying Power's computer networks that are used for military operations. Additionally, pursuant to Article 51 of Geneva Convention IV, the Occupying Power may not compel protected persons to serve in its armed or auxiliary forces.[1368]

7.   The Occupying Power shall, to the extent feasible in the circumstances and without any adverse distinction, ensure the continuance of computer operations that are essential to the survival of the civilian population of the occupied territory.[1369] Examples may include, depending on the circumstances, the operation of SCADA systems necessary for the functioning of utilities such as power grids, water purification plants, and sewage processing facilities.

Rule 147 – Public order and safety in occupied territory

The Occupying Power shall take all the measures in its power to restore and ensure, as far as possible, public order and safety, while respecting, unless absolutely prevented, the laws in force in the country, including the laws applicable to cyber activities.

[1367] According to Art. 51 of Geneva Convention IV, the Occupying Power may compel protected persons over eighteen years of age to do 'work which is necessary either for the needs of the army of occupation, or for the public utility services, or for the feeding, sheltering, clothing, transportation or health of the population of the occupied country'. See also DoD MANUAL, para. 11.20.2.1; UK MANUAL, para. 11.52; GERMAN MANUAL, para. 564.

[1368] Geneva Convention IV, Art. 147. See also DoD MANUAL, para. 11.20.1.1.; UK MANUAL, para. 11.53.a.

[1369] See Additional Protocol I, Art. 69(1), which the International Group of Experts agreed reflects customary international law. See also Rule 141.

1. This Rule is based on Article 43 of the Hague Regulations and Articles 27 and 64 of Geneva Convention IV. It reflects customary international law.

2. The Occupying Power has an obligation to restore and ensure public order and safety, including administration of the territory for the population's benefit and maintenance of its critical infrastructure. This entails an obligation to restore and maintain cyber infrastructure essential for the functioning of the occupied territory. Examples might include the transport and electricity systems and the water supply network. Similarly, if the Occupying Power learns, for example, of websites or social media that are inciting sectarian violence or contributing to cyber crime, it has the obligation to do what it can to block or otherwise prevent such activities.

3. According to Article 43 of the Hague Regulations, the Occupying Power must, unless absolutely prevented, maintain the laws applicable in the occupied territory. The reference in Article 64 of Geneva Convention IV to 'penal laws' is widely accepted as extending to all the laws in force;[1370] hence, domestic laws that regulate cyber activities retain their validity. Examples are penal laws on cyber crime and the interception of telecommunications, statutes that deal with Internet service providers, and laws that govern freedom of speech or intrusions into privacy.

4. This Rule encompasses laws that do not directly address cyber activities, but are relevant thereto. An example of such a law is one providing for freedom of religious expression. Absent a valid justification under the law of occupation, this Rule would preclude the Occupying Power from banning the exercise of religious freedom by cyber means.

5. The Occupying Power is entitled to curb the freedom of expression in cyberspace, despite laws to the contrary, as necessary for its security.[1371] This might be done, for example, by imposing censorship to counter resistance attempts to organise or regroup using social media. The Occupying Power may also take measures inconsistent with existing

---

[1370] ICRC GENEVA CONVENTION IV 1958 COMMENTARY, at 335; DoD MANUAL, para. 11.9.1; GERMAN MANUAL, para. 547.
[1371] See, e.g., UK MANUAL, para. 11.34. The UK Manual states: 'For legitimate reasons of security only, censorship may be imposed on the press, films, radio, television, theatres, and public entertainment, or to limit or prohibit telegram, postal, or telecommunications. To the same extent, existing press laws need not be respected, the publication of newspapers may be prohibited or subjected to restrictions, and the distribution of newspapers to unoccupied parts of the country or neutral countries may be stopped.' See also DoD MANUAL, para. 11.7.2.

law if its computer networks outside occupied territory fall victim to cyber attacks launched from occupied territory.

6.   The Occupying Power is entitled to repeal or suspend laws in force that prejudice its cyber operations or military communications in cases where they constitute a threat to its security. It may also repeal legislation that is inconsistent with its Geneva Convention IV obligations, or with other rules of international law.[1372] For instance, the Occupying Power may enact legislation replacing discriminatory domestic legislation that, if retained, would exclude certain groups of people, based on their race, religion, or political affiliation, from expressing their opinions and beliefs. The Occupying Power may use cyber means to disseminate such new laws, and, consistent with international legal norms, to ensure compliance with them.

7.   An Occupying Power may enact new laws when required to enable it to ensure public order and safety, to fulfil its obligations under the law of occupation, or to maintain the orderly administration of the territory.[1373] For example, the Occupying Power may adopt regulations aimed at countering cyber crime that is significantly harming the financial stability of the occupied territory.

Rule 148 – Security of the Occupying Power

The Occupying Power may take measures necessary to ensure its general security, including the integrity and reliability of its own cyber systems.

1.   This Rule is based on Articles 27 and 64 of Geneva Convention IV. It reflects customary international law.[1374] It envisages taking cyber measures with regard to the security of the Occupying Power in general. The concluding clause of the Rule emphasises that its scope extends to the protection of the Occupying Power's cyber systems.

2.   Examples of measures that might be taken in accordance with this Rule include steps to: shut down communications systems used to transmit information about the Occupying Power to insurgent forces; prohibit email references to military movements, posture, weapons, capabilities, or activities; implement militarily necessary restrictions on

---

[1372] DoD MANUAL, para. 11.9.2; UK MANUAL, para. 11.25.
[1373] Geneva Convention IV, Art. 64; Hague Regulations, Art. 43.
[1374] UK MANUAL, paras. 11.15, 11.34–11.38; CANADIAN MANUAL, para. 1207.

the use of certain servers; impose time restrictions on use of the Internet when military authorities need bandwidth; or place restrictions on use of the Internet by individuals that pose a security threat. Consider the example of an Occupying Power with reason to believe steganography is being used to pass bomb-making instructions to members of a resistance movement. If there is no effective way to determine which files contain the coded messages, the Occupying Power may prevent or restrict cyber communications by those it reasonably believes are involved in such activities. In limited circumstances, it may, to the extent necessary, restrict communications generally until the situation is resolved satisfactorily.

3. The restrictions imposed on protected persons shall not exceed those that are necessary to address the legitimate security concerns of the Occupying Power.[1375] The determination of necessity must be based on all attendant circumstances, such as the availability of other forms of communication.

Rule 149 – Confiscation and requisition of property

To the extent the law of occupation permits the confiscation or requisition of property, taking control of cyber infrastructure or systems is likewise permitted.

1. This Rule is based on Articles 46, 52, 53, 55, and 56 of the Hague Regulations and Article 55 of Geneva Convention IV.[1376] It reflects customary international law.[1377]

2. A distinction must be made between use of the terms 'confiscation' and 'requisition' in this Rule. The Occupying Power may 'confiscate' State movable property, including cyber property such as computers, computer systems, and other computing and memory devices, for use in military operations. Private property may not be confiscated. 'Requisition' by the Occupying Power is the taking of private goods or services with compensation.[1378] Such taking is only

---

[1375] 'What is essential is that the measures of constraint they adopt should not affect the fundamental rights of the persons concerned.' ICRC GENEVA CONVENTION IV 1958 COMMENTARY, at 207.

[1376] On the temporary requisition of hospitals, see Geneva Convention IV, Art. 57.

[1377] *See also* Additional Protocol I, Art. 14; Geneva Convention IV, Art. 57; DoD MANUAL, para. 11.18; GERMAN MANUAL, paras. 552–561; ICRC CUSTOMARY IHL STUDY, Rule 51.

[1378] On the requisition of labour, see Geneva Convention IV, Art. 51.

permissible for the administration of occupied territory or for the needs of the occupying forces, and then only if the requirements of the civilian population have been taken into account.

3.   For the purposes of this Rule, the majority of the International Group of Experts agreed that, *sensu stricto*, data does not qualify as property. However, this fact does not preclude the Occupying Power from making use of State data for its military operations. A minority of the Experts was of the view that data can qualify as property.

4.   The Occupying Power is obliged to safeguard the capital value of immovable State property (as distinct from movable property) and administer it with appropriate respect.[1379] Such property includes the buildings in which cyber infrastructure is located. Whether that cyber infrastructure qualifies as immovable State property depends on whether it can be removed without substantially damaging the building. If it cannot be so removed, it is immovable property entitled to the protection of immovable State property. Accordingly, the Occupying Power would be prohibited from taking any actions that would reduce its capital value. Cyber infrastructure that can be removed without occasioning significant damage to the structure of the building is movable property subject to the rules set forth in the preceding paragraphs.

5.   Based on Articles 46 and 52 of the Hague Regulations, private cyber property (or cyber services) must in principle be respected and may not be confiscated. It may only be requisitioned for the needs of the army of occupation and the administration of occupied territory. For example, it would be appropriate to requisition a privately owned server in order to facilitate administration of the territory or to demand access to the Internet from a private Internet service provider when needed by the occupation force. Requisitions of goods and services must be in proportion to the occupied State's resources and may not oblige inhabitants to take part in military operations against their own country.[1380]

6.   It may be difficult to distinguish cyber property belonging to the State from private cyber property. Cyber infrastructure can be owned jointly in public–private partnerships or government cyber infrastructure can be established and maintained by private companies based on public

---

[1379] Hague Regulations, Art. 55; DoD Manual, para. 11.18.5.2; UK Manual, para. 11.86.

[1380] If they involve the requisition of foodstuffs or medicine, the requisitions are only permissible 'if the requirements of the civilian population have been taken into account'. Geneva Convention IV, Art. 55. *See also* UK Manual, para. 11.76.

concessions. When doubts arise about the private or public character of cyber assets, some States maintain a general presumption that it is public unless and until its private nature becomes evident.[1381] Where both State and private interests in computers, computer networks, or other cyber property coexist, the property may be seized, but private interests therein must be compensated.[1382]

7. Cyber property (including State cyber property) of municipalities and of institutions dedicated to religion, charity, education, and the arts and sciences shall be treated as private property.[1383] As such, it may be requisitioned (and not confiscated) provided the preconditions mentioned above are fulfilled.

8. Based on Article 53 of the Hague Regulations, equipment adapted for the transmission of news may be seized even if it is private property. It must be returned to the owner and compensation paid when it is no longer needed. Today, every cell phone or computer connected to the Internet is capable of transmitting news. The Experts agreed that extending the application of this Rule to all such items would be contrary to the object and purpose of the underlying treaty provision from which the Rule derives. Therefore, 'equipment adapted for the transmission of news' should be understood as equipment that 'journalists' (Rule 139) use and that is operated by the organisations to which they belong.

9. The term 'taking control' refers to physical confiscation or requisition of property. The question in the cyber context is whether it extends to 'virtual' confiscation or requisition. The majority of the International Group of Experts agreed that it does to the extent that (1) the Occupying Power can employ the property for its own purposes, and (2) the owner is denied its use. The minority considered that physical possession of the property is an essential ingredient of this Rule.

10. Submarine cables (including those components on land) connecting occupied with neutral territory are subject to a special regime set forth in Article 54 of the Hague Regulations. They may not be seized or destroyed except in the case of absolute necessity and compensation must

---

[1381] DoD Manual, para. 11.18.4.3; UK Manual, para. 11.90.

[1382] DoD Manual, para. 11.18.4.2; UK Manual, para. 11.90; Canadian Manual, para. 1235.

[1383] Hague Regulations, Art. 56; DoD Manual, para. 11.18.6.4; UK Manual, para. 11.76.1; German Manual, para. 559.

subsequently be paid. Since submarine communication cables facilitate cyber communications, this point has particular relevance in the cyber context. The International Group of Experts came to no conclusion as to whether this customary norm applies more broadly to other objects necessary for cyber communications (e.g., satellite uplink and downlink stations) between occupied territories and neutral States.[1384]

[1384] *See* DoD MANUAL, para. 11.18.2.4.

20

Neutrality

1. The law of neutrality applies only during international armed conflict. It is based on Hague Conventions V and XIII and customary international law.[1385] The International Group of Experts unanimously agreed that the law of neutrality applies to cyber operations.

2. 'Neutral State' denotes a State that is not a party to the international armed conflict in question.[1386] For the purposes of this Manual, 'neutral cyber infrastructure' means public or private cyber infrastructure that is located within neutral territory (including civilian cyber infrastructure owned by a party to the conflict or nationals of that party) or that has the nationality of a neutral State (and is located outside belligerent territory). 'Neutral territory' comprises the land territory of neutral States, as well as waters subject to their territorial sovereignty (internal waters, territorial sea, and, where applicable, archipelagic waters) and the airspace above those areas.[1387]

3. The law of neutrality regulates the relationship between the parties to an international armed conflict on the one hand and States that are not party to the conflict on the other. Its key purposes are to (1) protect neutral States and their citizens against the conflict's harmful effects; (2) safeguard neutral rights, such as engaging in commerce on

---

[1385] DoD Manual, para. 16.4 and Chapter 15; German Manual, paras. 1101–1155; AMW Manual, Sec. X. The UK Manual and the San Remo Manual recognise the continuing relevance of the law of neutrality throughout the documents, while the Canadian Manual devotes Chapter 13 to the topic. Note that neutrals are obligated to comply with the law of armed conflict in certain cases despite their non-belligerent status. Additional Protocol I, Art. 19; Geneva Convention I, Art. 4; Geneva Convention II, Art. 5.

[1386] DoD Manual, para. 15.1.2.2; UK Manual, para. 12.11; Canadian Manual, para. 1302; German Manual, para. 1101; AMW Manual, Rule 1(aa); San Remo Manual, para. 13 (d); ICRC 2016 Geneva Convention I 1952 Commentary, para. 916.

[1387] See German Manual, paras. 1108, 1118; AMW Manual, commentary accompanying Rule 166; San Remo Manual, para. 14.

the high seas; and (3) protect parties to the conflict against action or inaction on the part of neutral States that benefits their enemy. The global distribution of cyber assets and activities, as well as global dependency on cyber infrastructure, means that cyber operations of the parties to a conflict can easily affect private or public neutral cyber infrastructure. Accordingly, neutrality is particularly relevant in modern armed conflict.

4. The International Group of Experts was mindful of the fact that the law of neutrality developed based on situations in which entrance into or exit from a neutral State's territory is a physical act. The fact that cyberspace involves worldwide connectivity irrespective of geopolitical borders challenges certain assumptions upon which the law of neutrality is based. For instance, a single email message sent from belligerent territory may automatically be routed through neutral cyber infrastructure before reaching its intended destination; the sender or the owner of the neutral cyber infrastructure cannot necessarily control the route it takes. The Rules set forth in this chapter have considered this reality. Given the difficulty of controlling cyber infrastructure and routes, any conclusions about violations of a State's neutrality or whether a neutral State has violated its obligations under the law of neutrality should only be arrived at after careful consideration.

5. Cyber infrastructure located within the territory of a neutral State is not only subject to that State's jurisdiction, but also is protected by that State's territorial sovereignty. It is considered neutral in character irrespective of public or private ownership or of the nationality of the owners (provided that it is not used for the exercise of belligerent rights, Rule 153).

6. The term 'exercise of belligerent rights' is synonymous with the terms 'hostile act' in Hague Convention V and 'act of hostility' under Hague Convention XIII.[1388] The International Group of Experts decided to use 'belligerent rights' in this chapter to avoid confusion with the term 'hostile act', which is an operational term of art. Exercise of belligerent rights is accordingly to be understood in the broadest sense as actions that a party to the conflict is entitled to take in connection with the conflict, including cyber operations. Belligerent

---

[1388] Hague V, Art. 10; Hague Convention XIII, Art. 2. *See also* SAN REMO MANUAL, paras. 15–16.

rights are not limited to 'attacks' as defined in Rule 92, but it should be noted that the term does not extend to espionage conducted against the neutral State.

7. On the misuse of neutral indicators, see Rule 127.

Rule 150 – Protection of neutral cyber infrastructure

The exercise of belligerent rights by cyber means directed against neutral cyber infrastructure is prohibited.

1. It is a well-established principle of the law of neutrality that parties to a conflict are prohibited from conducting hostilities within neutral territory. The inviolability of neutral territory is laid down in Article 1 of Hague Convention V and Article 1 of Hague Convention XIII. The norm is customary in character.[1389]

2. Neutral cyber infrastructure physically located in international airspace, high seas areas, or outer space is protected by virtue of the State of nationality's sovereignty.

3. The term 'directed against' refers to an operation intended to detrimentally affect neutral cyber infrastructure. As to operations passing through such infrastructure or employing it for operations against the enemy, see Rule 151.

4. The International Group of Experts struggled with the situation in which a cyber attack against a military objective in belligerent territory has spill-over effects in neutral territory. For example, a cyber attack on a server in belligerent territory could significantly affect services in neutral territory. The Experts concurred that if such effects are not foreseeable, the attack does not violate the law of neutrality. As to effects that are foreseeable, the International Group of Experts noted that the law of neutrality seeks to balance the right of belligerents to effectively conduct military operations with the right of neutral States to remain generally unaffected by the conflict. Each case must be assessed on its own merits by balancing these competing rights. The Experts agreed that the effects on the neutral State to be considered in making this assessment are not limited to physical effects. They also agreed that, in practice, States would be unlikely to regard *de minimis* effects as precluding the prosecution of an otherwise legitimate attack.

[1389] DoD MANUAL, para. 15.3.1.1; UK MANUAL, para. 1.43; GERMAN MANUAL, paras. 1108, 1118, 1149; SAN REMO MANUAL, para. 15; Hague Air Warfare Rules, Arts. 39–40.

5. It is important to note that neutral cyber infrastructure located in neutral territory may lose its protection under Rule 153. Moreover, neutral cyber infrastructure located outside neutral territory, such as undersea cables, may be attacked if it constitutes a lawful military objective. Such infrastructure may also be subject to capture.

Rule 151 – Cyber operations in neutral territory

The exercise of belligerent rights by cyber means in neutral territory is prohibited.

1. This Rule is based on Articles 2 and 3 of Hague Convention V and Articles 2 and 5 of Hague Convention XIII. It reflects customary international law.[1390] Whereas Rule 150 addresses operations against neutral cyber infrastructure, this Rule deals with the use of such infrastructure on neutral territory by a belligerent. It prohibits the armed forces of a party to the conflict from conducting cyber operations from neutral territory. In addition to conducting cyber operations from within neutral territory, it encompasses remotely taking control of neutral cyber infrastructure and using it for said purposes.

2. The Rule does not apply to private individuals (including civilians directly participating in hostilities, as discussed in Rule 97), entities, or groups unless their conduct is attributable (Rules 15 and 17) to a party to an international armed conflict.

3. Although the Rule only addresses the exercise of belligerent rights in neutral territory, it would also constitute a breach of neutrality to use neutral non-commercial government cyber infrastructure that is located outside neutral territory (but not within belligerent territory) for belligerent purposes. For instance, it is prohibited to route military communications through cyber systems aboard a neutral State's government ships or State aircraft because those platforms enjoy sovereign immunity (Rule 5).

4. Using a public, internationally and openly accessible network such as the Internet for military purposes does not violate the law of neutrality. This is so even if it, or components thereof, is located in neutral territory. Although there is no express treaty law directly on point, the majority of

---

[1390] DoD MANUAL, para. 15.3.1.2; UK MANUAL, para. 1.43.b; CANADIAN MANUAL, para. 1304; GERMAN MANUAL, paras. 1108, 1120, 1150; AMW MANUAL, Rule 167(a) and accompanying commentary; SAN REMO MANUAL, para. 15.

the International Group of Experts agreed that Article 8 of Hague Convention V, which provides that a neutral Power need not 'forbid or restrict the use on behalf of the belligerents of telegraph or telephone cables or of wireless telegraphy apparatus belonging to it or to companies or private individuals', can be applied to cyber communications systems. They further agreed that the Article reflects customary international law.[1391] A minority of the Experts would limit the application of Article 8 to the items referred to therein and prohibit the use of other means of cyber communication through neutral territory.

5.   The International Group of Experts considered the issue of transportation of cyber weapons (Rule 103) across neutral territory. The Experts agreed that physically transporting cyber weapons is prohibited by Article 2 of Hague Convention V, which prohibits movement of munitions of war or supplies across the territory of a neutral Power.

6.   A majority of the International Group of Experts took the position that transmission of cyber weapons across cyber infrastructure located in the neutral State is also prohibited based on that Article. They noted that malware may be broken into packets when transmitted, but saw no reason to differentiate between the transmission of a complete cyber weapon or a cyber weapon in packets on the basis that the transmission of individual components of a traditional weapon would violate neutrality. They cautioned, however, that the obligation of the neutral Power to take action to prevent such transmission only attaches when that State has knowledge of the transmission and can take measures to terminate it (Rule 152).

7.   A minority of the Experts pointed to Article 8 of Hague Convention V as providing an express exception to the general rule.[1392] These Experts rejected an analogous application of Article 2 to the transmission of data even if it qualified as a cyber weapon on the basis that the object and purpose of that provision is only to prevent the physical transport of weapons, as illustrated by the inclusion of Article 8 in the Convention.

8.   The International Group of Experts agreed that a neutral State may restrict or prohibit the use of its cyber infrastructure by belligerents. When it does so, the measures in question must be impartially applied to all belligerents.[1393]

[1391] See DoD MANUAL, para. 16.4.1; AMW MANUAL, Rule 167(b).

[1392] This was the position adopted in the AMW Manual. AMW MANUAL, commentary accompanying Rule 167(b). This is the view adopted in the DoD MANUAL, para. 16.4.1.

[1393] Hague Convention V, Art. 9(1). See also DoD MANUAL, para. 16.4.1.

10.   On the transit of belligerent warships through a neutral State's territorial sea, see Rule 49 on 'mere passage'.

Rule 152 – Neutral obligations

A neutral State may not knowingly allow the exercise of belligerent rights by the parties to the conflict from cyber infrastructure located in its territory or under its exclusive control.

1.   This Rule, which reflects customary international law,[1394] is derived from Article 5 of Hague Convention V, according to which '[a] neutral Power must not allow any of the acts referred to in Articles 2 to 4 to occur on its territory'. In the context of cyber operations, it is of importance to note that according to Article 3 of Hague Convention V,

> belligerents are . . . forbidden to:
>
> (a) Erect on the territory of a neutral Power a wireless telegraphy station or other apparatus for the purpose of communicating with belligerent forces on land or sea;
> (b) Use any installation of this kind established by them before the war on the territory of a neutral Power for purely military purposes, and which has not been opened for the service of public messages.

2.   Adapting the object and purpose of Hague Convention V to cyber operations, a neutral State may not allow a party to the conflict to use its pre-existing cyber infrastructure on neutral territory for military purposes or to establish any new cyber infrastructure for those purposes.

3.   The obligation set forth in this Rule extends not only to a party's cyber infrastructure on neutral territory, but also to the exercise of belligerent rights employing other cyber infrastructure located there. An exception applies to public, internationally and openly accessible networks, such as the Internet, which may be used for military communications (Rule 151). To the extent that a neutral State does place restrictions on the use of such networks, the restrictions must be impartially applied to all parties to the conflict.[1395] As noted with regard to Rule 151,

---

[1394] DoD Manual, para. 15.3.2; UK Manual, para. 1.43.a; German Manual, para. 1111; AMW Manual, Rule 168(a); San Remo Manual, para. 22. *See also* this Rule's peacetime counterpart, Rule 6 of this Manual.
[1395] Hague Convention V, Art. 9.

the International Group of Experts was divided as to whether the transmission of cyber weapons across neutral territory using such a network is
prohibited. It was similarly divided as to whether a neutral State is
obligated to prevent such transmission.

4. The phrase 'under its exclusive control' is employed here to refer
to non-commercial government cyber infrastructure (see also discussion
of 'governmental control' in Rule 6). With regard to such infrastructure,
this Rule applies regardless of the infrastructure's location because the
obligation derives from its government character.

5. Rule 152 presupposes knowledge, whether actual or constructive, by the neutral State. A neutral State has actual knowledge if its
organs have detected a cyber operation conducted by a party to the
conflict originating from its territory or if the aggrieved party to the
conflict has credibly informed the neutral State that a cyber operation
has been initiated from its territory. Constructive knowledge exists in
situations in which a State should reasonably have known in the
attendant circumstances of the activity. The International Group of
Experts was split as to whether the extension to constructive knowledge implies a duty on behalf of the neutral State actively to monitor,
to the extent feasible, the use of cyber infrastructure on its territory.
Whereas some members took the position that it does, and that
therefore a neutral State must diligently monitor for belligerent activity,[1396] the majority suggested that no such duty exists.

6. The phrase 'may not knowingly allow' implies a duty on the
part of neutral States to take all feasible measures to terminate any
exercise of belligerent rights employing cyber infrastructure falling
within the scope of this Rule.[1397] However, as with constructive
knowledge, the International Group of Experts could achieve no
consensus as to whether the neutral State has a duty to take measures to prevent the exercise of belligerent rights, in particular by
monitoring cyber activities.

7. A few Experts took the position that this obligation is implied
in the duty to 'not knowingly allow'.[1398] These Experts suggested that
to the extent preventive measures such as monitoring are feasible they

---

[1396] AMW MANUAL, Rule 170(b).
[1397] DoD MANUAL, para. 15.3.2.2; GERMAN MANUAL, paras. 1109, 1125, 1151; AMW
MANUAL, commentary accompanying Rule 168(a); SAN REMO MANUAL, paras. 15, 18,
22. See also Hague Air Warfare Rules, Arts. 42, 47.
[1398] Hague XIII, Art. 8; AMW MANUAL, Rule 170(b).

are required. Feasibility is, of course, dependent on the attendant circumstances, such as the technological capacity of the State concerned. A majority of the Experts rejected this position, arguing that the sole duty of the neutral State is to terminate use, as distinct from preventing it. These Experts pointed, in particular, to the practical difficulties inherent in complying with any duty to determine the belligerent character of a packet traversing its networks.

8.   Measures taken by a neutral that are in compliance with this Rule do not constitute a hostile act and, *a fortiori*, do not constitute an armed attack (Rule 71) against the party to the conflict violating its neutrality.[1399] As to activities on neutral territory that do not have belligerent nexus, see Rule 6.

Rule 153 – Response by parties to the conflict to violations

If a neutral State fails to terminate the exercise of belligerent rights on its territory, the aggrieved party to the conflict may take such steps, including by cyber operations, as are necessary to counter that conduct.

1.   This Rule is generally accepted as customary international law. A form of 'self-help', it provides an aggrieved party to the conflict with a remedy for the enemy's unlawful activities on neutral territory, including belligerent use of neutral cyber infrastructure that remains unaddressed by the neutral State.[1400]

2.   The Rule does not apply to every violation of neutrality, but rather only to those that negatively affect the opposing party. Any other violations are exclusively the concern of the neutral State. For instance, a denial of service operation by one party against neutral cyber infrastructure does not necessarily result in a military advantage *vis-à-vis* its enemy. In such cases, the enemy is not entitled to terminate the denial of service operation under this Rule. Any response would be reserved exclusively to the neutral State.

3.   The operation of this Rule depends upon two criteria. First, the violation of the neutral State's territory must be 'serious'. Minor

[1399] Hague Convention V, Art. 10; SAN REMO MANUAL, Rule 22 and accompanying commentary.
[1400] DoD MANUAL, para. 15.4.2; UK MANUAL, para. 1.43(a); CANADIAN MANUAL, para. 1304 (3); AMW MANUAL, Rule 168(b); SAN REMO MANUAL, Rule 22.

violations do not trigger the application of this Rule.[1401] In other words, the party violating the neutral status must, by that violation, gain a meaningful military advantage over the adversary. Seriousness cannot be determined *in abstracto*, but rather depends upon the circumstances ruling at the time. It may be based on either the pervasiveness of the violation or on the advantage that accrues to the violator because of that violation. For example, the International Group of Experts agreed that establishing the capability to hack into personal email accounts of low-level members of the enemy armed forces does not trigger this Rule. By contrast, assume that one of the parties to the conflict has diminished cyber capability because of the hostilities. Use by that party of neutral cyber infrastructure in order to undertake cyber operations against the enemy would qualify as serious.

4. Second, the exercise of belligerent rights on neutral territory by a party to the conflict must represent an immediate threat to the security of the aggrieved party and there must be no feasible and timely alternative to taking action on neutral territory.[1402] Therefore, the Rule only applies if the neutral State is either unwilling or unable to comply with its obligations under Rule 152. When this is the case, the aggrieved party is entitled to terminate a violation of neutrality by its adversary once the neutral State has exhausted all measures at its disposal to do so, but nevertheless has been unsuccessful. Obviously, the aggrieved party may also act when the neutral State does nothing to terminate the violation.

5. Measures of self-help are subject to a requirement of prior notification that allows a reasonable time for the neutral State to address the violation. Only if the violation immediately threatens the security of the aggrieved party may that party, in the absence of any feasible and timely alternative, use such immediate force as is necessary to terminate the violation.

6. Consider the example of a belligerent that is routing cyber operations against its enemy through a server in a neutral State. The enemy State notifies the neutral State and demands that it prevent the use of its cyber infrastructure. If the neutral State fails to terminate the operations in a timely manner, the aggrieved belligerent may lawfully launch a cyber operation to destroy the server's functionality.

[1401] SAN REMO MANUAL, Rule 22.   [1402] SAN REMO MANUAL, Rule 22.

Rule 154 – Neutrality and Security Council actions

A State may not rely upon the law of neutrality to justify conduct, including cyber operations, that would be incompatible with preventive or enforcement measures decided upon by the Security Council under Chapter VII of the Charter of the United Nations.

1. This Rule is based on Article 25 of the UN Charter, which requires Member States to comply with Security Council decisions set forth in its resolutions. It also derives from Article 103 of the Charter, which makes treaty obligations such as those arising from Hague Conventions V and XIII inapplicable in the face of Security Council action under Chapter VII.[1403] Subject to a prohibition of measures that violate *jus cogens* norms, the same holds true for obligations under customary international law that are incompatible with Security Council decisions.

2. Rule 154 applies both when the Security Council responds to a breach of the peace, or an act of aggression (by deciding upon an enforcement measure) and when it takes measures in the face of a threat to the peace.[1404] It operates in three situations. First, if a Security Council resolution requires States to take a particular action, they may not rely on the law of neutrality to avoid doing so. Second, a Security Council resolution may prohibit the taking of a certain action by States. The law of neutrality offers no justification for engaging in such conduct. Third, States are prohibited by this Rule from engaging in any activities that might interfere with actions taken by other States pursuant to a Security Council resolution.

3. Consider a situation in which the Security Council has determined that a particular State has engaged in a breach of the peace. The situation now qualifies as an international armed conflict. Among other acts, the State is conducting highly destructive cyber attacks against the enemy's civilian cyber infrastructure. In response, the Security Council passes a resolution authorising all Member States to employ their cyber assets and capabilities to terminate the attacks. States acting in compliance with this resolution would not be in breach of their obligations under the law of neutrality, even though they are neutral in the conflict.

[1403] *See also* GERMAN MANUAL, para. 1103; AMW MANUAL, Rule 165; SAN REMO MANUAL, paras. 7–9.

[1404] UN Charter, Art. 39 (setting forth these situations).

GLOSSARY

Active Cyber Defence: The taking of proactive defensive measures outside the defended cyber infrastructure. A 'hack-back' (see below) is a type of active cyber defence.

Bandwidth: The capacity of a communication channel to pass data through the channel in a given amount of time, usually expressed in bits per second.

Botnet: A network of compromised computers, so-called 'bots', remotely controlled by an intruder, 'the botherder', used to conduct coordinated cyber operations, such as 'distributed denial of service' operations (see below). There is no practical limit on the number of bots that can be assimilated into a botnet.

Close Access Operation: A 'cyber operation' (see below) requiring the actor's physical proximity to the targeted system.

Cloud Computing: A model for enabling ubiquitous, convenient, on-demand network access to a shared pool of configurable computing resources (such as networks, servers, applications, and services) that can be rapidly provisioned and released with minimal management effort or service provider interaction. Cloud computing allows for efficient pooling of computer resources and the ability to scale resource to demand.[1405]

Common Criteria: International standard for evaluating the security properties of IT products.

Computer Emergency Response Team (CERT): A team that provides initial emergency response aid and triage services to the victims or potential victims of 'cyber operations' (see below) or cyber crimes, usually in a manner that involves coordination between private sector and government entities. These teams also maintain situational awareness about malicious cyber activities and new developments in the design and use of 'malware' (see below), providing defenders of computer networks with advice on how to address security threats and vulnerabilities associated with those activities and malware.

[1405] Drawn from The National Institute of Standards in Technology, US Department of Commerce, definition of Cloud Computing, Special Publication 800-145, September 2011.

Computer Network: An infrastructure of interconnected devices or nodes that enables the exchange of data. The data exchange medium may be wired (e.g., Ethernet over twisted pair, fibre-optic, etc.), wireless (e.g., Wi-Fi, Bluetooth), or a combination of the two.

Computer System: One or more interconnected computers with associated software and peripheral devices. It can include sensors and/or (programmable logic) controllers, connected over a computer network. Computer systems can be general purpose (e.g. a laptop) or specialised (e.g. the 'blue force tracking system').

Critical Infrastructure: Physical or virtual systems and assets of a State that are so vital that their incapacitation or destruction may debilitate a State's security, economy, public health or safety, or the environment.

Cyber: Connotes a relationship with information technology.

Cyber Activity: Any activity that involves the use of cyber infrastructure or employs cyber means to affect the operation of such infrastructure. Such activities include, but are not limited to, cyber operations.

Cyber Attack: See Rule 92.

Cyber Espionage: See Rule 32.

Cyber Infrastructure: The communications, storage, and computing devices upon which information systems are built and operate.

Cyber Operation: The employment of cyber capabilities to achieve objectives in or through cyberspace. In this Manual, the term is generally used in an operational context (see also 'cyber activity').

Cyber Reconnaissance: The use of cyber capabilities to obtain information about activities, information resources, or system capabilities.

Cyber System: See 'computer system'.

Cyberspace: The environment formed by physical and non-physical components to store, modify, and exchange data using computer networks.

Data: The basic element that can be processed or produced by a computer to convey information. The fundamental digital data measurement is a byte.

Data Centre: A physical facility used for the storage and processing of large volumes of data. A data centre can be used solely by users belonging to a single enterprise or shared among multiple enterprises, as in 'cloud computing' (see above) data centres. A data centre can be stationary or mobile (e.g., housed in a cargo container transported via ship, truck, or aircraft).

Database: A collection of interrelated data stored together in one or more computerised files.[1406]

Denial of Service (DoS): The non-availability of computer system resources to their users. A denial of service can result from a 'cyber operation' (see above).

[1406] Glossary of Software Engineering Technology, Institute of Electrical and Electronics Engineers (IEEE) Std 610.12 (28 September 1990).

Distributed Denial of Service (DDoS): A technique that employs multiple computing devices (e.g., computers or smartphones), such as the bots of a 'botnet' (see above), to cause a 'denial of service' (see above) to a single or multiple targets.

Domain Name: A unique, alphanumeric, human-readable name for a computer. All computers that are addressable via the Internet have a unique globally routable Internet protocol (IP) address. IP addresses can be registered with a Domain Name System (DNS) service provider. A DNS server uses a structured zone file to translate domain names into IP addresses and *vice versa*. The Internet Assigned Numbers Authority (IANA) is the central authority for assigning top-level domain (TLD) names and IP addresses. The term 'top-level domain name' refers to the highest level in the hierarchy of the Internet domain name system. Examples of such TLDs, also sometimes referred to as domain name extensions, include: '.org', '.int', and '.mil'.

Electronic Warfare: The use of electromagnetic (EM) or directed energy to exploit the electromagnetic spectrum. It may include interception or identification of EM emissions (e.g., SIGINT), employment of EM energy, prevention of hostile use of the EM spectrum by an adversary, and actions to ensure efficient employment of that spectrum by the user-State. An example of electronic warfare is radio frequency jamming.

Firmware: Low level programming that acts as an interface between hardware and software.

Hack back: A type of 'active cyber defence' (see above), the main purpose of which is to take action against an identified source of a malicious cyber operation. Typically, a hack back is designed to mitigate the effects of, or stop, the malicious activity, or to gather technical evidence that can be used for attribution purposes.

Hacktivist: A private citizen who on his or her own initiative engages in hacking for, *inter alia*, ideological, political, religious, or patriotic reasons.

Hardware: See 'cyber infrastructure'.

Honeynet: A virtual environment consisting of multiple honeypots, designed to deceive an intruder into assuming that he or she has located a network of computing devices of targeting value.

Honeypot: A deception technique in which a person seeking to defend computer systems against malicious cyber operations uses a physical or virtual environment designed to lure the attention of intruders with the aim of: deceiving the intruders about the nature of the environment; having the intruders waste resources on the decoy environment; and gathering counter-intelligence about the intruder's intent, identity, and means and methods of cyber operation. Typically, the honeypot is co-resident with the actual systems the intruder wishes to target.

Internet: A global system of interconnected computer networks that use the Internet Protocol suite and a clearly defined routing policy.

Internet Protocol (IP): A protocol for addressing hosts and routing datagrams (i.e., packets) from a source host to the destination host across one or more IP networks.

Internet Protocol (IP) Address: A unique identifier for a device on an IP network, including the Internet.[1407]

Internet Service Provider (ISP): An organisation that provides the network connectivity that enables computer network users to access the Internet.

Jamming: See 'electronic warfare'.

Logic Bomb: 'Malware' (see below) that is designed to initiate a malicious sequence of actions if specified conditions are met.

Malware: 'Software' (see below) that may be stored and executed in other software, firmware, or hardware that is designed adversely to affect the performance of a computer system. Examples of malware include Trojan horses, 'rootkits', 'viruses' and 'worms' (see below).

Metadata: Data that provides information about other data, such as its time of creation and origin. Metadata is essential when categorising, searching, storing, and understanding information.

Network Sniffer: 'Software' (see below) used to observe and record network traffic.

Network Throttling: A technique to limit the availability of bandwidth to users of communications networks, also known as 'bandwidth throttling' and 'network bandwidth throttling'.

Passive Cyber Defence: The taking of measures for detecting and mitigating cyber intrusions and the effects of cyber operations that does not involve launching a preventive, pre-emptive, or counter-operation against the source. Examples of passive cyber defence measures are firewalls, patches, anti-virus software, and digital forensics tools.[1408]

Phishing: A type of social engineering attack most commonly executed by the use of email, social networks, or instant messaging. The perpetrator attempts to lure unsuspecting victims into visiting a malicious website, opening an infected document, or executing actions on behalf of the attacker. The purpose of a phishing operation is generally to acquire sensitive information, such as user credentials, personal data, or credit card details.

Rootkit: 'Malware' (see above) installed on a compromised computer that allows a perpetrator to maintain privileged access to that computer and to conceal his or her activities therein from the operating system and the legitimate users of that computer.

[1407] Internet Assigned Numbers Authority, Glossary of terms *available at*: www.iana.org/glossary.

[1408] This term should be distinguished from the legal term of art 'passive precautions' (Rule 121).

Server: A physical or virtual computer dedicated to running one or more computing services. Examples include network and database servers.

Server Farm: A form of cluster computing in which a large number of servers are collocated in a 'data centre' (see above).

Software: The non-physical components of a computer system and cyber infrastructure. These components encompass programs, including operating systems, applications, and related configuration and run-time data.

Software Agent: A computer process, managed by a computer operating system, which performs one or more tasks on behalf of a human user. It is possible for software agents to operate autonomously or to communicate and coordinate their actions with other software agents in a distributed computing environment. For instance, software agents are used for executing queries across distributed repositories of information available via the World Wide Web (WWW).

Spear-phishing: A 'phishing' (see above) operation that targets particular individuals and involves a higher level of sophistication and tailored content. Many malicious cyber operations begin with a spear-phishing campaign.

Spoofing: Impersonating a legitimate resource or user to gain unauthorised entry into an information system or to make it appear that some other organisation or individual has initiated or undertaken certain cyber activity.

Steganography: The technique of hiding content within other content. For example, there are computer-based steganographic techniques and tools for embedding the contents of a computer file containing engineering diagrams and text into an image file (e.g., a JPG document) such that the existence of the engineering data in the image file is difficult for the observer to detect.

Stuxnet: A computer worm that was designed to target 'Supervisory Control and Data Acquisition (SCADA)' (see below) systems developed by Siemens Corporation. The payload of the Stuxnet 'malware' (see above) included a programmable logic controller 'rootkit' (see above). Stuxnet was used to target centrifuges involved in the enrichment of uranium in Iran.

Supervisory Control and Data Acquisition (SCADA): Computer systems and instrumentation that provide for monitoring and controlling industrial, infrastructure, and facility-based processes, such as the operation of power plants, water treatment facilities, electrical distribution systems, oil and gas pipelines, airports, and factories.

Virus: A type of 'malware' (see above) with self-replicating capability that attaches itself to an application program or other executable system component and leaves no obvious signs of its presence.[1409]

Very Small Aperture Terminal (VSAT): A portable satellite ground station used for two-way communications. VSATs are commonly used for broadband

---

[1409] NIA GLOSSARY.

satellite communications at remote locations, for instance by emergency rescue teams and vessels at sea.

Website: A set of related web pages containing information. A website is hosted on one or more web servers. The World Wide Web (WWW) is comprised of all of the publicly accessible websites.

Whaling: Also known as whale phishing, is a type of 'spear-phishing' (see above) attack that specifically targets an organisation's senior management, executives, and other high profile individuals.

Wi-Fi: A type of high-speed wireless networking.

Worm: A type of 'malware' (see above) that is able to self-replicate and autonomously spread across 'computer networks' (see above), unlike a virus that relies on embedding in another application in order to propagate to other computer systems.

XML Tag: A markup construct that is part of the open standard known as the Extensible Markup Language (XML). The tag is both human- and machine-readable and used to encode the syntactic parts of the content of a document. For example, in the electronic version of this Manual, a string of text containing a legal term of art could be delimited by the opening and closing tags <legal-term> and </legal term>, for example <legal-term> necessity </legal term>.

INDEX